Inside Today's Home

THIRD EDITION

Inside Today's Home

RAY FAULKNER Stanford University   **SARAH FAULKNER**

HOLT, RINEHART AND WINSTON, INC. NEW YORK · CHICAGO

SAN FRANCISCO · ATLANTA · DALLAS · MONTREAL · TORONTO · LONDON

Preface to the Third Edition

INSIDE TODAY'S HOME is a book about people in relation to the environment they create for their home life. Its theme and informing principle are shelter as a place where individuals can live in emotional and physical security, at ease with their surroundings and stimulated by them. Contemporary human needs and contemporary ways of responding to environmental needs are the focus of its concern. The approach sought in INSIDE TODAY'S HOME is that which emerges functionally from fresh solutions to problems intelligently analyzed—problems of expressing in the design, construction, furnishing, and setting of houses and apartments the perceptions and activities of their occupants —not from the ephemera and restive demands of current fashion.

The changes in ways of living brought about by an expanding, mobile, and increasingly aware society, together with the development of new materials and technologies and of improvements in older means, have challenged architects and designers to experiment with original and more relevant solutions. In this new, third edition, INSIDE TODAY'S HOME is revised both in content and organization and in the quantity and character of its illustrations to emphasize the experimental nature of much of today's work. In all, there are now well over 700 black-and-white illustrations—plans and sections as well as photographs— selected to represent the widest possible range of ideas, costs, materials, and processes. A number of illustrations from the old edition have been retained to demonstrate the timelessness that good design can achieve. Altogether new to this edition is the series of color plates, reproduced on 32 pages of coated stock and distributed throughout the book. Another feature fresh to the third edition of INSIDE TODAY'S HOME is the section, at the end of the book, of five chapters on historical homes and furnishings. These chapters are a reflection of the somewhat paradoxical revival of interest in the history of domestic design that has accompanied the keen sense of experimentation characteristic of our time.

INSIDE TODAY'S HOME is organized in six major divisions whose sequence indicates *one* way in which the problem of home planning can be approached. These individual sections, however, can be taken in any order that may suit individual requirements.

Part I, *Our Activities, Space, and Equipment,* focuses on the understanding of certain basic human needs that are primary to the achievement of a successful home. These include shelter from the elements, some degree of privacy from the community, and space and furnishings that are appropriate for diverse activities. The most gratifying environment nurtures individuality and allows one time and space to enjoy the company of others or to be alone in order to follow personal inclinations and to use one's abilities fully. This is most readily achieved by a thorough analysis of typical home activities, such as group living, private living, and housekeeping, and it is on such patterns of behavior that this section concentrates.

Specific ideas of beauty vary from period to period, from nation to nation, and from person to person. In spite of this multiplicity, there are a few guides or principles that are valuable in the creation and appreciation of design. Part II, *Design and Color,* explores the relationship between function and form, the countless ways in which variety and unity can be combined, and the interplay of balance, rhythm, and emphasis. Space and form, line, texture, and ornament, and light and color are discussed as bases for the understanding of design.

Each material has its individual characteristics, and when these distinctive qualities are understood and respected, the result is more likely to be pleasing, individual, useful, and economical than when they are ignored. Part III, *Materials,* deals with the nature of materials old and new, and with the many ways in which they can be used—from the traditional methods of construction with stone and wood to the latest designs in plastic furniture.

Part IV, *Major Elements,* deals with the basic units of which a house is composed: walls and fireplaces; windows and doors; floors and ceilings; lighting, heating, and acoustical apparatuses; and the joy of many households, enrichment. Focusing attention on these elements one at a time leads to an expanded understanding of their specific requirements and contributions. A satisfying home, however, is much more than the sum of its parts, and the ideal is strongly realized when all aspects of the home seem coherent with one another.

Part V, *The Whole House,* recapitulates and brings together the earlier chapters in its concentration on planning from the "inside out"—from the way in which the plan of the house influences the family living pattern to the expression of that pattern on the design and materials of the exterior and the landscape. It concludes with a discussion of costs and budgets.

Part VI, *Our Historical Heritage,* comprises five chapters on the historic styles in architecture, furnishings, and landscape that have most strongly affected our culture. This heritage of styles offers a source for a wider range of solutions to the problems of developing a home and gives a broader basis for developing critical judgment. A recognition of the forces and ideals expressed in historic work can lead to an enhanced appreciation of what the past accomplished and a more acute awareness of the relationship of the past to today's work. This section concentrates on the mainstream of our historical legacy, beginning with the Renaissance in Western Europe. Influences from earlier ages and from many parts of the world converged in Europe from the fifteenth to the nineteenth centuries, and, in turn, influenced traditions in the United States. Today we take for granted that ideas and objects from any era and any part of the earth can be valid and beautiful as sources of inspiration or pure aesthetic pleasure.

A great many architects, designers, publications, museums, and manufacturers have contributed ideas, illustrative materials, and encouragement to this book. Teachers and students have shaped much of our thinking through their perceptive questions and comments. We wish especially to acknowledge the help given us by Professors Maxine L. Miller of California State College at Los Angeles, Maie Nygren of Oklahoma State University, and Mary Jo Weale of Florida State University in their full and generous critiques of the entire manuscript and its illustrations for the third edition. James Parker of the Metropolitan Museum of Art in New York City and Marvin D. Schwartz of the Brooklyn Museum were good enough to examine the five historical chapters and help us make them an accurate reflection of the period styles they review. Our publishers, by their enthusiasm and progressive approach, have greatly facilitated the revision and helped to make it topical and colorful. And our four boys have continued to remind us that planning and keeping a home for family living is far more important than striving for decorative effects. To all, we extend our gratitude.

Stanford, California   R. F.
February 1968   S. F.

Contents

Opposite. For his own family in Cedar Rapids, Iowa, architect Ray Crites designed a visually exciting space for group living (1964). According to mood and weather, it offers a variety of environments. At the far end is a high-ceilinged outer living room, with sliding doors that lead onto a balcony projecting into the woods. A step up is an alcove with a dropped ceiling and a freestanding fireplace on a brick hearth. Sliding glass doors open to decks on either side. The ceiling rises suddenly again over an inner living room in the center of the house, with high windows and an overhanging balcony. A dining room (out of sight in this photograph and partially shielded by a bookcase-buffet) completes the 42-foot sweep of space. (See Chap. 17 and Color Fig. 21 for the plan and an exterior view.) (*Photograph by Julius Shulman*)

Part I · OUR ACTIVITIES, SPACE, AND EQUIPMENT

A sheltered entrance is a welcoming introduction to a house. Loch Crane, architect. (*Photograph by Maynard L. Parker Modern Photography*)

1 · A Beginning

Shelter is a basic human need that can be satisfied in various ways. Single-family dwellings, row houses, small or large apartment complexes, mobile homes, and even houseboats are some of the possibilities, and these can be in towns or cities, in suburbs or in the country. To a considerable degree the environment shapes man; but man *can* choose and shape his environment to suit his needs to a considerable degree, particularly in the United States, today. Fortunately there are many experts ready to share their experience, and there are many publications on the subject. *But* if a home is to be really one's own, one's active participation in its development is necessary. Among the first questions to be answered are: How do I want to live? What activities give greatest satisfaction? Which forms, colors, and materials give me most pleasure? What will all of this cost in time, energy, and money?

In planning a living room, for example, it is logical first to analyze the activities for which the room is intended and then to consider the size, shape, character, and cost of the needed space and equipment. Except in one-room apartments, though, a living room is seldom an isolated unit. How it relates to other areas in the dwelling, to the sun and wind, to the outlook and to the outdoor-living space must be considered, for piecemeal planning is seldom successful.

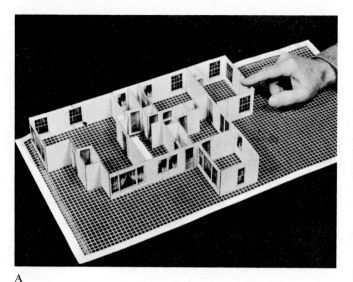

A

There is no better investment than thoughtful planning. (*Leslie Creations*)

B

Developing an appropriate home environment is not a matter of following a style, historic or contemporary. It is accomplished by analyzing and solving today's problems directly. There are, of course, trends that change as does the life from which they develop. In this century alone there have been a number of overlapping phases. As the new century began, the last vestiges of the heavily ornamented, bulky Victorian style were dying away; there was a renewed interest in copying historic work; and, most importantly, a reappraisal of the role of the machine in architecture and the allied arts was starting. The Arts and Crafts movement of William Morris in the late nineteenth century had denied the machine and insisted on handcrafting as the only true way to beauty. Art Nouveau in the early twentieth century was an attempt to get away from both machine ugliness and imitation of the past by studying (not copying) nature and producing organic forms. At the same time, some individuals and groups championed the machine and insisted that its control would lead to a new aesthetic.

During the 1920s the work of the Bauhaus, a school at Weimar, Germany, that recognized the need for collaboration between artists and workmen, became influential. Its most notable contribution was the beginnings of the International style in architecture, with its emphasis on space rather than on mass, on the beauty of unornamented materials and structure, and on simplicity and clarity. A more short-lived outgrowth was the clumsy "modernistic" phase of skyscraper bookcases, angular tables and lamps, and stuccoed buildings with occasional rounded corners and the ubiquitous glass brick.

"Machine style," a more considered result of the Bauhaus philosophy, came to prominence in the 1930s and still flourishes, as exemplified by the chair in Figure 9B and by the furnishings in Figure 12.* Many of the results are truly beautiful: sensitively proportioned forms, handsome materials, and pure precision. At the same time, the Scandinavians were exploring very similar concepts of beauty but in more sensuous, organic forms and expressed them in their traditional handcrafted (or partially so) technique.

World War II produced phenomenal technological advances that were assimilated during the following decades. *Naturalism,* an age-old philosophy reinvigorated by Frank Lloyd Wright, however, describes the essence of the trend that came into its own in the 1940s, and it is still a leading one today. It begins with recognition of man's nature and extends to a sympathetic understanding of the nature that surrounds us. The distinctive qualities of materials— wood, stone, stainless steel, and vinyl—are respected and revealed. Structures are related to their sites, and furnishings to architecture. Naturalism is an approach in which well-founded individualism can flourish.

The 1960s brought even greater freedom—to combine old and new, handmade with machine-made—and more courageous use of materials, ornament, texture, and especially color. Our desire for continuity and personal expression is recognized and encouraged. Old furniture and accessories, family heirlooms, and personal memorabilia are unhesitatingly combined with the newest furniture from all over the world in an eighteenth-century Colonial house or in a skyscraper apartment. The latest industrial techniques and materials are used in the building of houses whose warmth and solidity make them seem ageless. In return for this freedom, more demands are put on judgment, because there are no rigid rules. We need to know who we are; to have clear concepts of what we want to achieve, how to go about getting what we want, and how to evaluate the result. The house shown in Figures 6A through 7B is an example of the application of these concepts.

A THREE-BEDROOM HOUSE

A few years ago Jane Chapman guided seventy-five students in an adult-education program through the planning of a house. The majority decided that they wanted:

- 1500 to 2000 square feet of enclosed space
- An open plan that provided both spaciousness and privacy, and that could be expanded
- Three bedrooms and two baths, with the master bedroom separate from the others and merging with the living room
- A family workshop near the kitchen and carport that could be completely closed off with doors
- A separate dining room
- A total cost of $20,000–$30,000

They were much more concerned with convenience, the pleasantness of interiors, and the relationship of the inside to outdoor-living space than with matters of style.

*Figure numbers for the illustrations in this book are the same as the page numbers on which they appear.

A house in San Diego planned for convenient and stimulating living. Loch Crane, architect. (*Photographs by Maynard L. Parker Modern Photography*)

Above. The exterior evolved from a natural, informal concept of home living. It is unpretentiously charming. The covered walk and carport, the garden fence, and the pergola at the right join the structure with its site.

Right. The plan provides 2030 square feet of adroitly subdivided interior space for diverse activities. The living room can be joined with or separated from the adjacent dining room and master bedroom. Kitchen, utility room, and shop, conveniently near the carport, form a central core between the living room and the family workshop. Children's bedrooms and bath are grouped at the front of the house.

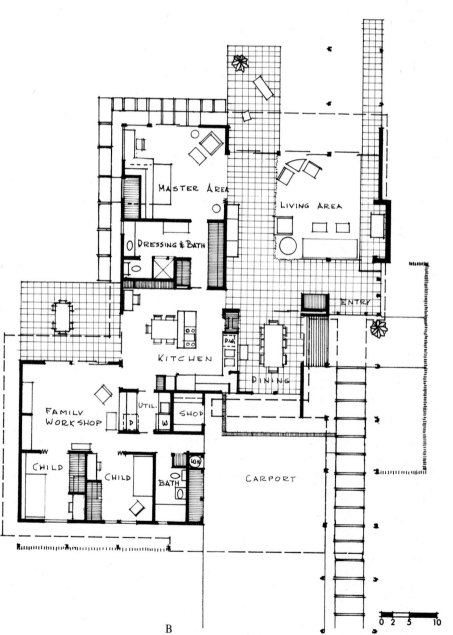

A

Above. Spacious and flexible, the living room could be furnished in many ways. Here the seating area with comfortable chairs and sofa is defined by a softly textured rug, while the traffic lanes are marked by durable quarry tile. Under a low ceiling, the fireplace and room-wide hearth seem like a sheltering alcove. Storage cabinets opposite the fireplace comprise an entertainment center containing television, hi-fi radio and record player, equipment for projecting movies or slides, and games.

Below. Casually furnished, the family workshop is an open, free space that could be used for children's play, dancing, or hobbies. The only fixed elements are a sewing center and a storage cabinet. With the doors to the children's bedrooms opened, the space is greatly extended, and sliding glass doors on the opposite wall give a view of the garden and access to a sheltered terrace for relaxation or dining.

B

In the design developed by architect Loch Crane from these criteria, every foot of space was ingeniously planned for livability, economy of time and energy, visual pleasure, and the possibilities for individualization. As can be seen in Fig. 6B, the plan is a dynamically ordered complex of interlocking rectangles. Large windows and broad openings between rooms give spacious views through the house into the garden, but each room can be completely closed off with swinging, sliding, or folding doors. Thoughtful zoning brings together—or separates—the diverse aspects of home living.

The **entrance zone** includes the carport, the covered walk, and the entry area, and gives protected access to two entrances. The main, or guest, entrance leads into the living-dining area and then to the master bedroom. The family entrance at the left of the carport gives easy access to the children's bedrooms, the family workshop, and the kitchen. In the past these would have been called the "front" and "back" doors, but both are on the front at a conveniently short distance from the street and sidewalk.

The **group-living zone** has been divided into two separated spaces to minimize conflicts. The more formal living-dining area, which merges with the master bedroom, is for comparatively quiet entertainment and relaxation. Doubling as a play space for children, the family workshop is a casual, multipurpose room convenient to the children's bedrooms, the kitchen, and the carport shop.

Private living is provided for in two areas at opposite ends of the house. The ample master bedroom, with a bed that becomes a sofa during the day, is furnished in a similar manner to the living room and is adjacent to a well-planned dressing room and compartmentalized bathroom.

The **housekeeping zone** consists of a central kitchen, from which all but one of the rooms can be seen, plus the utility room with laundry equipment, the family workshop with its sewing center, and the toolshop.

Circulation is efficiently handled with minimum space allotted to hallways. The architect has so related areas to one another, and the doors to each, that even though the rooms are used for circulation, the paths stay clear of busy areas. Also, there are alternative routes that can be used. For example, the working portion of the kitchen is convenient but easily by-passed.

The house has been made attractive and spaciously open in many ways. A great sense of continuity and distance is established as one approaches the main entrance under a covered walk that leads into a low-ceilinged entry screened from the living room by panels of translucent, embroidered textile. It is possible, however, to see the long hearth and to notice that the low ceiling continues through this side of the room and out into the garden as a covered pergola. Then, to open up the center of the house, the architect has raised the ceiling with a double-pitched roof that has high windows at the end. For utility and visual interest, wood and plaster cover the walls and ceilings. The exposed ceiling beams and planks give a strong directional movement. Well proportioned and comfortable, the furniture is in character with the architecture.

As in all worthy architecture, the exterior is an outgrowth of the plan and of interior space. Wood and glass, the major exterior materials, contrast happily with the large masonry chimney. The gently pitched roof, lightened with openings and with projecting beams, seems homelike. Covered walks, garden fences, and paved areas with built-in benches extend the structure into the landscape. (For other views of this home see Fig. 3 and Chaps. 2, 3, and 4.)

TWO CONTEMPORARY CHAIRS

Although not so fundamental as safe, convenient shelter, comfortable seating is important, and we now turn to an analysis of two chairs (Figs. 9A and B). The steel and cane chair at the right is surprisingly comfortable, despite its size and weight, for short-term, casual sitting. Both the height and the angles of the seat and back are suited to average persons, and the upholstery is somewhat resilient. Its cost is moderate, and its upkeep minimal. Light in weight, it is easily moved, and its slender, open form takes almost no visual space. The deliberately exposed frame has an elegant, frankly machine-made, precise beauty, but its graceful lines and cane (or leather) upholstery keep it from seeming coldly mechanistic. It exemplifies clean-cut but humanized industrial design, and it would seem at home, indoors or out, wherever these qualities are appropriate.

Deep relaxation over long periods is promised by the lounge chair with tall back and supportive arms. It is a chair dimensioned for a man, although its deep cushioning resiliently takes bodies of many sizes and shapes. Its price is moderately high, and the amount of upkeep needed would depend primarily on the fabric with which it is covered. All of its complex inner construction is hidden, so that only its well-proportioned forms and the pecan-wood base are seen. This is a substantial piece of furniture and gives a comforting sense of permanence. It is large, heavy, and opaque, but it is neither bulky nor awkward. Somewhat formal in character, the chair could be individualized with different upholstery fabrics. As you read on in this book, you might decide to which homes each of these chairs would be most completely suited.

FOUR GOALS OF HOME PLANNING AND FURNISHING

From the previous discussion, we can define *home design* as the organization of space and equipment for satisfying living. But what makes a piece of furniture, a room, a whole house "good"? A chair, for example, is good if it:

Two of the many contemporary trends in furniture are illustrated by two chairs that differ markedly from each other.

Left. Luxurious comfort is provided by a modern lounge chair with reminiscences of historic approaches. (*Tomlinson*)

Below. Designed by Poul Kjaerholm, a chromed-steel chair with seat and back of cane (or leather) is a recent Scandinavian development. (*Lunning Design Unit, Georg Jensen Inc.*)

A

B

- Gives comfortable support, thereby fulfilling its requirements of use
- Is worth the original cost, plus the time, energy, and money required to keep it clean and in good repair; in short, if it is economical
- Gives pleasure when seen or touched; in short, if it is beautiful
- Has a character of its own and also suits the family so well that it "belongs" in their home; in short, if it has individuality

Home planning and furnishing, then, have four goals: **use, economy, beauty,** and **individuality.** Underlying all of these is appropriateness.

Use is a central concept in creating today's homes. We want homes that serve their purposes, that "work" effectively—space that is planned for all family activities; chairs that earn the space they take; storage that is convenient and accessible; lighting, heating, and plumbing that do their jobs. Overemphasis on the utilitarian can, of course, lead to a laboratory-like coldness, but such excesses in no way diminish the primary importance of having our homes serve us well.

Economy refers to the management of human, material, and monetary resources. Human resources consist of abilities plus time and energy. Each person's productivity is in part determined by the environment he has for work and relaxation. It is sound economy to give college students space and furnishings well planned for study, sleeping, and dressing (Figs. 11A and B). Those who garden for a hobby are happier and accomplish more if they have a pleasant, convenient work center, and housewives deserve suitable kitchens (see Chap. 4). Time and energy for life-enhancing avocations have been increased by laborsaving devices. More fundamental, though, is having every part of the home organized for maximum efficiency. In building, buying, or renting space as well as in furnishing it, think of the time you will have to spend on housekeeping and how much time you want for other activities.

Material resources are all the things that have been purchased or received as gifts. It is regrettably easy to overlook some of them and to rush unthinkingly to buy a new object when something already owned would, with a little repair or adaptation, do as well.

The economy of monetary resources is considered in detail in Chapter 20, but it might be worthwhile to read it quickly now. A system of using your money is well worth the little time it takes to plan and follow. Each purchase should contribute its full share to the total plan. It should be worth what you pay for it and not cost more than you can reasonably afford. Remember, too, that cost is both original and continuing. A long-wearing, easily maintained carpet with a relatively high price tag may, in the long run, be a better investment than a less expensive one that is not durable or easily kept.

One kind of economy is the remodeling of an old house, an example of which is shown in Figure 11C. This well-located old house was built in Illinois some years ago, but the single window in the back wall of the living room did little to light the room or to open it to the pleasant landscape. The owners took out the entire wall and replaced it with insulating glass. A small window near the corner was converted into a door that makes the terrace and lawn easily accessible. At comparatively little expense, the room was transformed from an interior that was dark and confining into a living space that is well lighted, cheerful, and airy.

A double room in a Vassar College living unit is economically compact but pleasant and efficiently organized. Marcel Breuer, architect. (*Photograph by Joseph W. Molitor*)

A

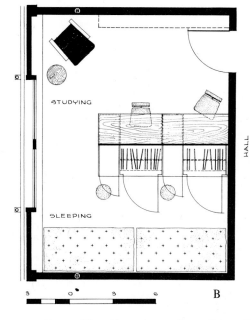

B

Above. The plan shows how the study and sleeping areas are separated by a wall of closets.

Above. The study area with its two desks, easy chair, wall storage shelves, and refreshing view seems spacious and conducive to work.

That remodeling can be worthwhile is illustrated in an Illinois living room made light and spacious by a new window wall and simplified fireplace, a decisive color scheme, and a few new furnishings. Milton Schwartz, architect. (*Photograph by Bill Hedrich, Hedrich-Blessing. Reprinted from* Better Homes & Gardens)

C

In Houston, Texas, the Gerald S. Gordons' living room is a humanized expression of machine-age trends. A sense of space and a refinement of detail in both structure and furniture build up to a climax in the soaring windows. Bolton and Barnstone, architects. (*Photograph by Fred Winchell*)

Beauty is that quality which pleases the senses and lifts the spirit. Although beauty submits to no rigid laws or inviolable principles, there are guiding aims and principles (discussed in Chap. 5) that are helpful in achieving it. The elements of visual beauty—space and form, line, texture, and light and color—can be organized in myriad ways to create whatever effect is most desired (see Chaps. 6 and 7). Of considerable consequence is the way in which materials are selected and worked, because this also contributes to beauty, as well as to use, economy, and individuality. Each material has its own potentialities and limitations, which are examined in Chapters 8, 9, and 10.

Two divergent kinds of beauty—each appropriate to the people who live with it and to the geographical setting—are shown in Figure 12 and Color Figure 1. In the Gordons' Texas living room, the lofty serene space, which continues through the window wall, is the dominant element. Its rectangularity is precisely defined by an uninterrupted pinkish-red brick wall opposite a wall of wood storage cabinets. A white plaster ceiling and an off-white hard-surface floor give a cool spaciousness, desirable in this climate. The window wall and the furniture group are each almost symmetrically balanced. The gently curving forms of the chairs contrast effectively with the predominant linear, angular rhythms of the architecture. Large areas of smooth textures are enlivened by the surface qualities of the brick wall and the fur rug. The well-chosen materials have been precisely machined into clean-cut, rigorously disciplined shapes characteristic of the International style in architecture and the Machine style in furniture. In general character, the room is urbane, dignified, elegant. The owners' comments on it are illuminating: "We feel that we are living in a piece of sculpture, unique in that it is spacious, comfortable, and above all—beautiful."

Carrying forward the historic tradition of Spanish-American architecture, Cliff May joined old and new ideas in an indoor-outdoor ranch house in which each room opens onto an appropriate outdoor space. It is a low, rambling structure superbly fitted to its rugged canyon site and to informal country living. The basic materials—stone quarried on the site and California redwood—were allowed to retain much of their natural character. Red quarry tiles make a handsome, easily maintained floor. The sweep of space is rhythmically articulated and unified by emphatic posts and beams and by a skylight that runs the length

More ingenuity than money was used to furnish one room of their apartment as an office by a husband-wife team of architect and interior designer. Simple shelving, built around the perimeter of the room, provides support on one side for the drawing board desks; the desks are supported on the other side by columns of cardboard mailing tubes glued together, which provide convenient files for architectural drawings. The tack boards are of Homosote wallboard covered with tan vinyl suede. Inexpensive enrichment comes from the fabric that covers one wall, the oversized cane wastebasket, and the handcrafted rag rug. (See Chaps. 5 and 16 for two other views of this apartment.) David K. Specter and Aivi Gallen-Kallela, designers. (*Photograph by Gene Maggio, New York Times Studio*)

A BEGINNING · 13

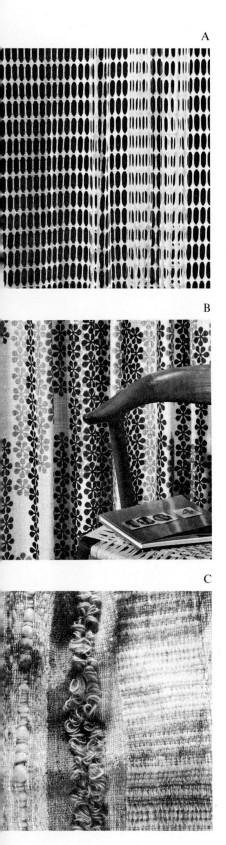

A

B

C

of the house. The gently double-pitched ceiling, covered with roughly split boards, rises from a massive, recessed stone fireplace on one side and from a smooth wood wall on the opposite side. Focused on the fireplace is an off-center furniture group in which simple contemporary and ornate antique Spanish furniture are brought together. It is a "natural" house and is planned and furnished with distinctive individuality.

Each of the houses that have been discussed is beautiful in its own way. They differ from each other because their owners did not want the same kind of home environment. One wanted tranquil, highly ordered spaciousness, smooth surfaces, and a minimum of pattern. The other sought a more rugged sense of enclosure for a less formal pattern of living.

Individuality—the quality that differentiates your home from those of your friends and makes you and them feel that it is really yours—is important. No one wants his home to have the generalized character of a hotel lobby or bedroom, which, necessarily, aims at the common denominator of many diverse personalities. Usually, however, if a home is the natural outgrowth of a family's interests and preferences, individuality will develop as naturally as the personalities of those who have made it. Individuality at its best is a development, not something superimposed from outside; and it grows most convincingly out of fundamentals, not accessories. In a mass-production age, the quest for individuality is often overdramatized: the result is a shallow, self-conscious desire to be different—often in a different way every few years—and it may lead to nothing more than a house full of impersonal, but fashionable, decorator's touches. It is far better to be just yourself, making the most of your strengths and weaknesses, and to let your home shape itself easily and naturally.

Use, beauty, economy, and **individuality** are as closely related as the warp and woof of a textile. None can be completely dissociated from the others and retain full significance. On the other hand, you cannot consider all these factors simultaneously. In selecting draperies for a window wall (Figs. 14A, B, and C) for example, you might first focus attention on utility—how well the material controls the transmission of light and extreme outdoor temperatures, the privacy it affords, and its sound-absorbing qualities. Then you might look at the price tag while thinking about ease of upkeep and life expectancy. Color, texture, and pattern are highly important considerations. Finally, there are your own preferences, as well as the character of the room in which it will hang. Each factor must be balanced against the others so that your choice will be wise, not whimsical, and your satisfaction lasting.

Three textiles that could be used for window treatment differ from each other in fiber, design, character, and cost.

Top. "Oval," a 118-inch open-weave casement net of polyester fiber imported from West Germany, is washable, dimensionally stable, and long-lasting. Over the years the cost would be low. (*Knoll Associates Inc.*)

Center. Printed in three colors on Beta, a Fiberglas yarn, "Flower Fence" has a vigorous, staggered pattern. The original cost is moderate, it does not require ironing, and it is fireproof. (*Ben Rose, Designer and Printer*)

Bottom. "Swazilace," of mohair and linen, handspun and handwoven in West Africa, is intricately textured, highly individualized, and expensive. (*Jack Lenor Larsen, Inc.*)

The living room in architect Juan Sordo Madaleno's own house in Mexico City is notable for its large scale and its broadly treated forms. The angular simplicity of the architecture and furniture is emphasized by vivid colors in fabrics and by areas of concentrated enrichment. (*Reprinted from Verna Cook Shipway and Warren Shipway, Mexican Homes of Today. Copyright © 1964, Architectural Book Publishing Co., Inc.*)

APPROACHING THE PROBLEM

No two individuals face the problem of home planning and furnishing in identical ways. The following six steps indicate one approach—but by no means the only possible one—that you might take when planning your home.

Inventory your present possessions; then list expected additions. Listing in an orderly way all that you now own is an easy but strategic first step. Such a list is a surprising index of both personality and resources.

Equipment for eating is a good example. A critical look at dishes, glassware, silverware, and table linens tells quickly what type of meals can be well served. Informal buffet suppers are feasible only if suitable trays, plates, and tumblers are on the shelves. Accumulated glass stemware, seldom used, may represent a big investment in money and storage. Those who do not yet have households can start thinking about what they want. Perhaps some of the desired things are remote probabilities. Distinguishing between these and the more likely possibilities will save time and future disappointment.

Table settings, of course, are only a fraction of home furnishings. Furniture, lamps, rugs, and draperies are more basic. Then comes the miscellany related to a family's interests—books and magazines, musical instruments, sports gear, or paintings and sculpture. Making a careful inventory, perhaps at three- or five-year intervals, alerts you to what and how much you possess, where and how often each object is used, how deeply it is enjoyed, and where it is stored. Possessions help make home life more satisfying. They should be used and cherished but not allowed to mold an artificial way of living.

List favored activities. Individuals differ markedly in the hobbies or work they enjoy, and good homes reflect this diversity. Some activities, such as conversation or reading, require no special equipment other than comfortable seats, appropriate illumination, and protection from disconcerting noise. Other activities, like weaving and furniture making, make more demands. Listing your possessions and activities is the groundwork for the next stages of planning.

Decide on the general character of your home. Each room, chair, and textile illustrated in this chapter has a definite personality. Each not only expresses, but leads toward, a way of living. Beyond these are an almost infinite number of personalities, basic ideas, or themes around which a home can grow.

It is a provocative exercise to think about the varied ways of providing for possessions and activities so that the family's individuality will be evident. Beware, though, of some of the major pitfalls. Choosing a theme merely because it is the fashionable trend may be simply playing into the hands of those whose job is to make people dissatisfied with what they had last year. Also, trying to copy what friends have achieved seldom leads to long-term satisfaction. Another path to almost certain failure is to decide on a theme and then force all family life to conform to it—space for children's play, for example, may well differ in character from that planned for adult group living. Finally, it is risky to decide too quickly on your home's character before all the factors that can make home life pleasant are understood.

Learn the ways and means of achieving the desired character. You can start by simply looking, listening, and touching. Then ask questions and make comparisons to help develop a vocabulary, a reservoir of ideas, and some guiding principles. Sources of inspiration and enlightenment are legion: stores, museums, motion pictures, and television; your own home, those of friends, and exhibition houses; and books, magazines, and newspapers.

A good beginning is to investigate a single aspect of the total problem with some thoroughness. It matters not a bit with what you start; but it is more fun to begin with something of special interest. Seating equipment is a good illustration. One of the first steps is to learn what kinds of chairs, stools, sofas, and benches are available. The variety is amazing, for seating can be for one person or for two or for more; fixed or movable; hard or soft, high or low, with or without backs or arms; of wood, cane, metal, plastic, or stone. It can be cheap or costly, easy or difficult to maintain, sturdy or fragile in construction. Its shape can be rectangular, curved, even triangular, and it can be ornamented or plain. Size, actual and apparent, ranges from small to big, while weight goes from heavy to light. Character ranges from formal to informal, relaxing to activating, and unusual to commonplace. This list might be continued for several pages if materials are considered. Wood, for example, can be hard or soft, fine- or coarse-grained, light or dark, red or brown, yellow or black. Upholstery can be of wool, cotton, silk, leather, fur, or plastic, and each of these materials can be had in many colors and textures.

You might prefer to begin this study with tables or chests, textiles or floor coverings, dishes or glassware, house plans or landscape design. Whatever the field, though, keep asking these questions: How well does this object meet the human needs for which it was produced? What would it cost in money, time, and energy? What degree and kind of beauty does it have? Does it have desirable individuality?

Consider finances. Costs, original and continuing, are factors never to be ignored. How much is available for spending? Over what period of time? What expenditures will give greatest satisfaction?

The financial resources of the young and unmarried, the about-to-be-married, or the just-married are usually modest, and every penny must count. Furthermore, there is likelihood of one or more moves before permanent settling. Family life often begins in small, rented, possibly furnished quarters. Then, as family and finances increase, there is usually a move to a larger, unfurnished, rented space or to a home of one's own. Thus, planning and spending for an only partially predictable future is in order.

Although there is no single way to solve the problem of wise initial spending, the following suggestions have merit:

- Get a few good basic objects, such as a bed, a comfortable sofa, and storage chests that are durable, pleasing in character, and that can be used flexibly. Concentrate spending on these.
- Fill in with frankly inexpensive, perhaps-temporary things, such as Chinese split-cane chairs, small rugs, and colorful accessories.
- Tend to avoid the moderately expensive things that are not quite what is wanted—not really excellent in design, structure, or material—but that cost too much to be discarded easily later.

In short, hit high and low in the beginning, fill in the scale as you go along. As tastes mature and needs become more definite, the general character of a home often changes. While avoiding commonplace furnishings, also think twice about those pieces so aggressively individualistic that they will fit in only one environment.

Continually remember the desired goal. It is surprisingly hard to keep in mind what you set out to achieve, surprisingly easy to alter your course without realizing it. Irresistible bargains, impulse buying of any kind, or simply failing to remind yourself what is wanted can lead you over the years far from the intended route and into an uncongenial environment.

To be sure, it may be necessary to change ideas. One may move from California to Maine, from city to country. Economic conditions may change, and the family may increase or decrease. Tastes may evolve in new directions. When such changes occur, make intelligent, considered modifications, but do not let the accidental or the incidental shift the course.

Achieving a good home is far more than deciding on a color scheme and selecting and arranging furniture. The roots of a good home are in the family's needs and wishes, and its major expression is the plan and the architectural shell that shape space for living. Its full development takes us out into the landscape and to the community beyond. For several decades technologists and homemakers have given more concentrated attention to home design than ever before. Time-motion studies and technical advances at first took center stage. Although these important studies are being continued, attention is also being given to spiritual factors. Concern with the effects on human happiness of new ways of heating and lighting, of shaping and coloring homes is catching up with technical advances. With an unparalleled array of potentialities at our command, we can create homes that are, in the words of architect Richard Neutra, "soul anchorages." In the next three chapters we will consider the problem of how living with others, private living, and housekeeping can be pleasant as well as efficient.

In the Gene Bavingers' inventive, uniquely personal home in Oklahoma, the architect's chief concern was that of total involvement. Work, play, and sleep take place in free space rather than in separate boxes. Open stairs curve up from a lower-level kitchen-dining area past a studio, a conversation pit covered with soft carpeting, and hanging saucers for sleeping that are protected by netting and that can be secluded by curtains for privacy. In such an environment, the occupants are aware of the whole space and of the interrelation of all home activities. Bruce Goff, architect. (*Photograph by Julius Shulman*)

18 - OUR ACTIVITIES, SPACE, AND EQUIPMENT

The English great hall was one of the many ancestors of contemporary multipurpose space. At Penshurst Place, built in 1388, it is a large room—64 by 39 feet—with a vaulted wood ceiling 48 feet high. In the center of the room the fire was built in a pit, and at the far end is the minstrels' gallery. Although it was used for dining and sometimes for sleeping, its major function was to provide space in which all members of the household could congregate to enjoy vigorous, highly diversified recreation. (*Reprinted from John Nash,* The Mansions of England in the Olden Time)

2 · Living with Others

Living with one's family and entertaining friends are enterprises as rewarding as they are diversified. Some of the activities—conversation, games, making music, eating, and small children's play—are as old as man himself. In medieval England and seventeenth-century America these activities were accommodated in the main hall of the house (Figs. 19 and 36B), where everyone gathered for warmth, recreation, and companionship. Comparatively recently, reading, watching television, listening to hi-fi music, and pursuing home hobbies have become important in family life and have made new and quite different demands on the group-living space. Architectural design is only beginning to catch up with what families actually do in homes today.

The emphasis given to each group activity varies from individual to individual and from family to family. Furthermore, changes are inevitable for individuals and families as the years pass. Because none but the very wealthy can provide equally well for all, most of us must decide carefully which group activities give greatest satisfaction, then plan accordingly. A logical first step is to consider specific group activities, the environment and equipment desirable for each, and then to find suggestions and principles helpful in solving specific and general problems.

19

A

Mrs. Arthur Berger's warm, welcoming living room in Dallas, Texas, discriminatingly combines the old and the new. O'Neil Ford, architect. (*Photographs by Ulric Meisel. Reprinted from* Interiors. *Copyright* © *1956, Whitney Publications, Inc.*)

Above. A simple but sensitively proportioned fireplace and a light-colored area rug stabilize the major furniture group, which has been set away from the walls to give a feeling of airy spaciousness.

Below. A window wall, thinly curtained and protected by the overhanging roof, together with glass doors to the left and a window at the back of the fireplace give well-balanced natural lighting without glare or exposure. Brick walls on both sides of the room continue beyond the window wall and visually extend the room into the landscape.

B

GROUP ENTERTAINMENT AND LEISURE

Conversation

Conversation is the major group activity, pervading all parts of the home but reaching greatest intensity in the living and dining spaces. Basic needs are:

- *Space* sufficient for the normal number of persons. Each person in an easy chair, for example, needs a space 3 feet wide by $2\frac{1}{3}$ feet deep, but with legs stretched out he may need a space 5 feet deep.
- *Comfortable* seats for each participant; a minimum of one good seat for each permanent member of the family and additional ones to accommodate guests.
- *Arrangement* of seats and tables in a generally circular or elliptical pattern so that each person can look at others easily and talk without shouting; arrangement should be ready for group conversation without moving furniture. A diameter of 8 to 10 feet is desirable.
- *Light* of moderate intensity with highlights at strategic points.
- *Surfaces* (tables, shelves, and so on) on which to put things.

Conversation thrives in a warm, friendly room if the architecture, furnishings, and accessories are spirited but not overpowering, distractions are minimized, and sounds are softened. This kind of environment has been created in the Arthur Bergers' home (Figs. 20A and B). Handsome old and new furniture pieces are sensitively brought together and reveal their character against a background of mellow brick and wood. A light-colored rug, contrasting with the deep-brown concrete floor, defines the conversation area, in which sofa, chairs, and tables are arranged for a friendly interchange of ideas and sentiments. Although strictly rectangular, this living-dining space is far from boxy. As the plan (Fig. 21) shows, the entrance to the house is an ample gallery with glass walls on the long sides. A broad opening leads to the L-shaped space with a dining area at the kitchen end. Firmly anchored by the substantial fireplace, window walls in the dining and living space open on two sides to sheltered terraces. A wood ceiling with exposed beams warms the room visually and tempers sound. Finally, the room is enhanced by a few distinctive Oriental objects, while several large plants add a decorative quality as well as relate the enclosed space to the garden.

Group conversation is also the normal accompaniment of meals because the furniture and its arrangements afford ideal conditions for an hour or so (Figs. 31A and C). Terraces and patios become natural conversation centers when they offer good seating and some shelter, as illustrated in Figure 25.

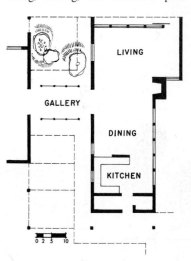

Mrs. Berger's group-living space is simple but interesting in shape. A glass-walled gallery and two open courts clearly separate the private bedroom area to the left from the living, dining, and kitchen space.

Reading

Members of a literate culture enjoy reading if the reading material is stimulating and the reading conditions are good. Minimum essentials are:

- *Seating* that gives adequate support to the back (to the neck, arms, and back for maximum comfort); resilient but not soporific
- *Light* coming over one shoulder; moderately strong daylight or artificial light that illumines the room and concentrates fairly intense but diffused light on the reading material
- *Security* from distracting sights, sounds, and household traffic

Desirable additions are a chairside table, accessible shelves to hold books and magazines, and enough space to stretch the eyes occasionally. Such conditions, good for more or less casual reading, can be easily achieved in typical living rooms. If, however, one or more members of the family do concentrated reading, greater seclusion is needed, and bedrooms or a study should be appropriately planned.

Music

In many American families, music is limited to radio, record player, and television, but more and more fortunate families enjoy creating their own music. This usually centers around a piano placed flat against a wall that is large enough for the instrument and with space for the participants. More serious musicians may want a "music center," preferably in a corner or alcove that keeps all needed paraphernalia together and out of the way of other activities. An intermediate step is to place the piano at a right angle to the wall, thereby demarcating a partially segregated area.

Good conditions for listening to music are similar to those for group conversation—a workable arrangement of seats and tables, moderate illumination, and a minimum of distractions—except for the more serious concern about the quality of the sound. Although the quality of musical sounds is primarily determined by the instruments and performers, the room's materials and shape are critical. Acoustically, materials are classified as sound-reflecting, or "live," if they bounce the sound, as does plaster or glass; and as sound-absorbing, or "dead," if they soak up sound, as do heavy draperies, rugs, books, cork, or other acoustical materials. An excess of live materials gives strident amplification and reverberation; having too many dead surfaces robs music of its brilliance. It has also been found that live surfaces should be opposite dead surfaces. Then, too, experts have long known that musical sounds are best in those rooms in which opposite surfaces are not parallel to each other or in which the space is broken up in some way.

Planning architecture and furnishings for conversation, reading, recorded music, and television is a challenging design problem, as seen below and opposite.

A symmetrical conversation center is well planned for a man who enjoys friends, books, and music. A radio-phonograph is accessibly but unobtrusively housed in the cabinet at the left, the speakers are built into the walls. The room's shape and sloping ceiling, the books, upholstered furniture, and brick and matting on the floor improve acoustics. Both natural and artificial light are diffused by the ceiling panels of translucent glass. Harwell Hamilton Harris, architect. (*Photograph by Maynard L. Parker. Blue Ridge Glass Corporation*)

Happily, many devices that improve acoustics are favored for other reasons. The varied materials used in many contemporary rooms to add color and texture interest range from "live" to "dead." If properly balanced and located, they temper music pleasantly. The L-shaped beamed ceiling of the Bergers' living room (Figs. 20A, 20B, and 21), and the sloping ceiling and the books in the Havens' room (Fig. 22), give visual, as well as aural, satisfaction. Freestanding cabinets and fireplaces (Figs. 30A and 35A), or almost any deviations from an unrelieved boxed-in feeling, create stimulating spatial patterns.

High-fidelity stereo speakers perform best when they are mounted in or placed against a live wall facing a dead one. The exact placement of the speakers to achieve a well-balanced quality of sound will depend on the size of the room and the positions of the listeners. For convenience, the tuner and record player should be separated from the speakers so that the operator can get the desired balance, a feat next to impossible if his ear is too near them. Placing the tuner and player where they can be easily reached is better than having them in a hard-to-get-at corner (Fig. 23).

The entertainment center of a house in Copenhagen has components built into a unit along one wall. Easily accessible, it is also out of the way. The lightweight but comfortable lounge chair invites relaxed listening or looking; the stools are low enough to be helpful in tuning the radio or choosing a record from the files. (*Reprinted from* High Fidelity Magazine, *April 1967*)

Television, Movies, and Slides

Bringing the theater, cinema, concert hall, sports field, and even the classroom into the home has altered patterns of home leisure markedly. Television especially, but also movies and slides, have become potent forces in getting the family together for inexpensive home entertainment. Major considerations for these activities are good seating, control of light and sound, and protection for those who do not care to watch:

- *Seating* requirements are much like those for conversation, except that the seating should be arranged within a 60-degree angle to avoid distortion. Easily moved or folding chairs give welcome flexibility; backrests or cushions on the floor increase a room's seating capacity.
- *Height of screen* should be as near eye level as possible.

- *Some lighting* is necessary, but it is best when it is of low intensity and shines neither on the screen nor in the viewers' eyes.
- *Acoustical control* is similar to that for music.

Although still cumbersome, especially in depth, television receivers can be put in many places. Living rooms and family rooms are typical locations. If mounted in walls, television receivers can be treated as part of the wall design, and they can be located to face more than one room. They can also be mounted on portable stands and pushed from place to place. Ideally, screens for movies or slides are permanently mounted and when not in use should disappear behind a valance.

Quiet Indoor Games

Cards, checkers, and chess require concentrated effort. They are most relaxing when played on a well-illuminated table about $2\frac{1}{4}$ feet high while the players sit on moderately high, straight chairs in a spot free from distractions. Folding card tables or the new lower dining tables, and dining chairs set up in the living, dining, or family space, suffice for most families. Serious gamesters, however, may want table and chairs permanently and suitably placed.

Active Indoor Entertainment

Dancing, Ping-Pong, pool, and other active games require plenty of space, a durable floor, and furniture easily pushed out of the way. Experience has shown that family rooms, discussed on pages 36–37, are a good solution.

Outdoor Games

Croquet, badminton, and Ping-Pong as well as the less rigidly ruled outdoor sports should not be forgotten. They will not give much satisfaction, though, unless sufficient space for the game, and convenient storage for the necessary gear, is provided. The frequency with which outdoor space is enjoyed depends

Planned outdoor-living space can add an important physical and emotional dimension to home life, as shown in the figures below and on page 25.

An extensive paved terrace, sheltered by the wings of a ranch house, offers sun or shade, has space for children and adults, and requires minimum maintenance. Douglas Baylis, landscape architect. Cliff May, architect. (*Photograph by Julius Shulman*)

In hilly country in West Los Angeles, California, an indoor-outdoor house takes advantage of both contemporary technology and traditional materials. The rough masonry fireplace wall, the split-pine ceiling, the rough-sawn posts and beams, and the tile floor are reminiscent of early southwestern ranch houses, but the glass window wall, the skylight, and the generous and comfortable seating are in the modern idiom. White and earth colors contribute to the atmosphere of cool spaciousness. Cliff May, designer. (*Photograph by Julius Shulman*)

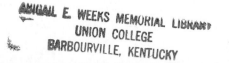

2

The living room of a concrete house on the Cape Cod waterfront contrasts a warm analogous color scheme (red, red-orange, and orange) with the blue sky and ocean, the green foliage, and the sandy beaches seen through glass walls on three sides. The bright cranberry red of the rug is picked up by the two upholstered chairs near the freestanding fireplace. Cushions on the white chairs (lower right) are Chinese vermilion. The sofa and the panel in the terrace wall are burnt orange; the opaque door on the left, dark rust. The imperturbable background of white and gray planes banded in black acts as a foil for the intensity of the color and light. Robert Damora, architect; Melanie Kahane, A.I.D., interior decorator. (*Photograph by Robert Damora*)

on the durability and dryness of the underfoot surfaces, the protection from wind and the privacy given by fences or hedges, and the comfort with which one can rest while others expend their energies. The ample paved terrace curving around the lawn shown in Figure 24 is admirably conceived for many outdoor activities.

In the year-round moderate climate of Cuernavaca, Mexico, a loggia, open to the south and to a pool but protected by the house, two walls of glass, and a heavily beamed ceiling, is a center for casual living. Its usefulness is extended into the evening hours by the many lighting fixtures and the outdoor fireplace. Rodolfo Ayala, architect. (*Reprinted from Verna Cook Shipway and Warren Shipway,* Mexican Homes of Today. *Copyright © 1964, Architectural Book Publishing Co., Inc.*)

Small Children's Activities

The needs of small children range from active noisy play to quiet moments, from eagerness to be with others of their own age to desire to be alone, from wanting to be with the family to carefully avoiding it. Needed is space adequate for the discharge of abundant energy and convenient to a toilet and to the outdoors as well as to the kitchen for easy supervision. Walls, floors, and furniture should take punishment gracefully and lend themselves to change. Light, warmth, and fresh air are requisites. Ideally, all this is segregated from what, it is hoped, will be the quieter portions of the house.

Clearly the living room is unsuitable and the dining space only slightly better. The kitchen has the needed durability, but even without children's play it is usually the most intensively used room in the house; it also has the household's greatest assembly of potential hazards. The fast-disappearing basements and attics had the requisite space and ease of maintenance but were often cold, dark, and damp and far from Mother's supervising eye. Garages and carports have obvious disadvantages. This leaves us with the children's bedrooms, because these already are, or should be, planned for children to make their own. A widened bedroom hallway can be both economical and efficient (Fig. 33E); children's bedrooms can open into a multipurpose room (Fig. 33D) or combine with each other (Fig. 64C) to make a space large enough to serve as playroom, library, museum, and hobby center as well as study and retreat.

These factors, together with adult needs for informal space, have led to the "family room." Because this space its often used for eating, we will withhold discussion of it until we have considered the diverse ways in which families eat today.

EATING WITH FAMILY AND FRIENDS

Eating is a lively part of group living, for meals are one of the few daily events that brings an entire family together with a single purpose. Here, too, there have been marked changes in the last few decades. During the thirties and forties, family and house size shrank, and household help became scarce. Few families were able and willing to reserve a completely separate space for eating that would be used for only about three hours a day. Recently, however, as incomes have increased, and as disillusion with completely open group living has set in, a trend toward dining rooms per se has been gaining ground. When planning dining situations, the requirements for meals in general should first be considered, then specific requirements for meals of different types. In general there is need for:

- *Surfaces* on which to put food and utensils, usually 27–30 inches high but variable in size, shape, and type—tables that seat all or serve only one, counters, arms of chairs, and the like
- *Seats* giving comfortable, upright support, such as chairs, stools, built-in or movable benches
- *Light,* natural and artificial, that illumines food and table without glare
- *Ventilation* without drafts

To these essentials we quickly add that *convenience to kitchen and dish storage* saves energy, *freedom from excessive noise* saves nerves and helps digestion, and

The Herbert Monts' home (seen in the next four figures) in New York State capitalizes on an exposed steel, structural frame to give high-ceilinged, unusually flexible spaciousness. Zones for boys and parents at opposite ends of the house are separated by a "common ground." Stanley Salzman of Edelman and Salzman, architect. (*Photographs* © *Maris, Ezra Stoller Associates*)

A

Above. An ample playroom, adjacent to the boys' bedrooms and near the play yard, is a free-for-all, multi-purpose area. Here it is set up as a gymnasium.

Below. The living room can be joined with the common area and playroom to give an uninterrupted space 61 feet long when two sets of folding doors are pushed back.

B

A

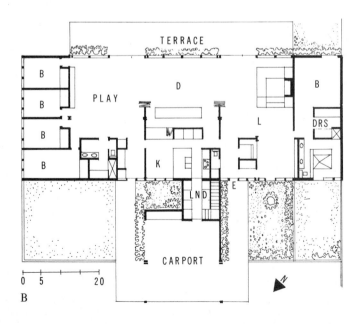

B

TERRACE

B
B
B
B

PLAY

D

L

B

DRS

K

LND

E

CARPORT

0 5   20

N

A sunken conversation area around the fireplace is a companionable retreat for quiet social interchange. Bright pillows contrast vividly with the black upholstered pads, the fireplace, and the tile hearth.

The plan, an exceptional example of shaping space for both communal and private use, shows the three zones, each of which is related to appropriate outdoor space. From the entrance-carport area, protected and enhanced by fences and planting, doors give direct access to the living room, laundry and carport, and playroom. The center zone is composed of the kitchen and dining space. The adults' zone includes the living room, parents' bedroom, dressing and bath room, and a private outdoor court. (*Reprinted from* Architectural Record, Record Houses of 1964. *Copyright © 1964 by McGraw-Hill, Inc., with all rights reserved*)

pleasant surroundings and table settings raise spirits. A few of the many ways of planning dining space are shown in Figures 30A through 31C. Chapter 4 includes illustrations of well-planned facilities for eating in the kitchen, and Chapter 14 takes up selection and arrangement of furniture.

Family sit-down meals deserve first attention. For these there ought to be one adequately large, relatively permanent space planned so that the table can be prepared, the seating arranged, the meal served and eaten, and the table cleared with minimum interference to and from other activities.

Holiday celebrations are important family events but occur so seldom that the necessary space can rarely be reserved for them alone. This suggests a dining area with at least one end opening into the living or activity space, thereby permitting the celebration area to extend as the number of participants increases. Figures 6B and 28B are excellent examples.

Formal meals at home raise special problems because of the cost in space, equipment, and time. Well-segregated dining space (Figs. 30A through D) is almost a necessity in order to set the table in advance, to give the guests a pleasant surprise with the table setting and allow them to enjoy a meal uninterrupted by other activities, and then to screen the table when the meal is over.

Buffet meals, like self-service grocery stores and cafeterias, permit one to see what he is getting and distribute the labor of serving food. Also, they make it possible to use all the group-living space for eating and usually lead to a lively informality. If such meals are to be handled often and successfully, you might emulate cafeterias, where good carrying trays and not-too-precious dishes and glassware are provided, food is served from counters near the kitchen, traffic is directed so that tray-laden people do not collide, and a place is provided to rest body and food when dinner is in hand. The serving bars and furnishings in Figures 28B and 35B are thoughtfully designed for buffet meals.

Hurry-up meals in which speed and economy of effort are primary goals have a few advantages. Those who wish to eat this way might look at lunch counters, where a counter with stools on one side and a food-preparation center on the other function with a dispiriting efficiency.

Outdoor meals can punctuate eating routines with a refreshing change of surroundings, a different type of food, another eating pattern. In all parts of the country outdoor eating could be much more frequent if it were planned for with the same attention given to indoor meals. At its best, outdoor eating takes place in an appropriately furnished space near the kitchen or barbecue. Firm paving, a protecting roof, solid enclosure on two or three sides and garden fences or hedges on the others are well worth their cost. But, of course, even without all this, picnics and barbecues can be happy family or guest affairs in which all can participate, actively or as spectators, in what can be the fun of cooking, serving, eating, and even after-meal cleanup.

Small children's meals are a vital part of home life and an aspect of the educational process often poorly handled. We might as well acknowledge that eating is both an adventure and a problem for small children. They will play, experiment, and make mistakes. Common sense suggests providing a place—preferably in the kitchen, play space, or family room—where children can spill or scatter food on durable, easy-to-clean surfaces. But at an early age children want to eat with adults and quite rightly object to conditions midway between those for adults and those for household pets. Here, again, the plan of the house, the way it is finished and furnished, strongly affects the manner of family living.

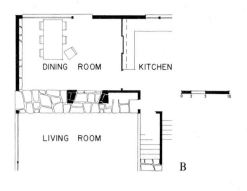

B

The manner in which the dining space is related to the general group-living area is important.

A

Left and above. A change of level and a two-way fireplace clearly differentiate a living room from a dining room without loss of visual spaciousness. If desired, the two spaces could be completely separated with a screen or folding doors. The bedroom balcony above creates additional vistas but can be closed for privacy. Contrasting materials, each used in large, simple areas, enrich and diversify the rigorously geometric design. Breuer and Noyes, architects. (*Photograph by Ben Schnall*)

D

Right and below. An L-shaped space for living and dining, related to a patio for large informal gatherings, has sliding doors on three sides to create a segregated dining room for more-formal meals. Such flexibility is a welcome dividend, especially in smaller houses. Thornton Abell, architect. (*Photograph by Julius Shulman*)

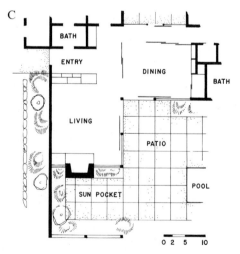

Left and above. A corner of the living room in a small town house with a built-in, cushioned bench and an angled table avoids the "dining room" look. Although efficient for eating, it takes little space and can be used for games, homework, and the like. Gordon Drake, architect. (*Photograph by Morley Baer*)

Below. A separate dining room in Loch Crane's San Diego house can be joined with the living room when sliding doors are pushed back. The panels in the right wall can be opened to make a pass-through to the kitchen. Other views of this house and the plan are shown on pages 3, 6, 7, 45, and 61. (*Photograph by Maynard L. Parker Modern Photography*)

A

C

PLANNING FOR GROUP LIVING

After considering the character and demands of specific group activities, we can formulate several generalizations useful in planning:

- Each group activity occurs in more than one part of the house and yard. Eating takes place in dining or living spaces, kitchens, family rooms, or patios. Conversation is enjoyed everywhere, and music, willy-nilly, often pervades the remotest corners of the home. Thus, planning today is more a matter of organizing space for activities than of arranging "rooms."
- In terms of noise and movement, group pursuits are notably diverse but they fall into three general categories. The full development of each type is best realized when homes are appropriately zoned.

  Quiet, sedentary activities, such as reading and quiet games, involve little physical movement. They produce minimum noise but suffer greatly from distractions, which suggests grouping them in a quiet zone of the dwelling.

  Noisy, sedentary activities, which include eating and music, deserve an acoustically controlled part of the group-living space more or less separated from those areas where quietness is desirable.

  Noisy, active activities take as much space as can be found. They interfere with other home pursuits and give furnishings, floors, and walls considerable drubbing. Play or family space and the outdoors are logical centers.

- Planning for group living demands the concerted endeavor of the whole family. Each member has a right to express his desires and to realize them in so far as feasible. The six steps suggested in Chapter 1 for **Approaching the Problem** (pp. 15–17) are directly applicable.

Although planning is discussed more fully in Chapter 17, a few basic points are worth introducing here:

Group-living areas can be one large space divided for different activities in many ways.

A

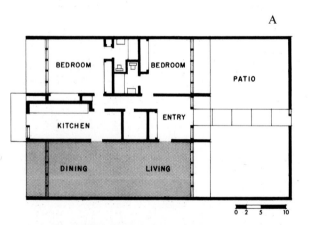

B

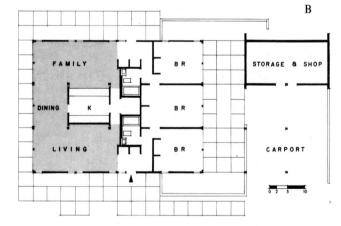

A simple rectangle relies on furniture arrangement that can be changed easily as the need arises. Although the great flexibility is an asset, it is not easy to get two distinct areas unless freestanding cabinets or screens are used. Curtis and Davis, architects.

The shape of the space can establish a sense of separateness without loss of visual extension. Locating the kitchen so that it divides the space and is convenient to three possible dining areas is commendable. Charles M. Goodman, architect.

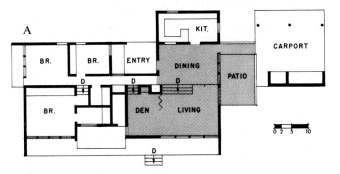

A

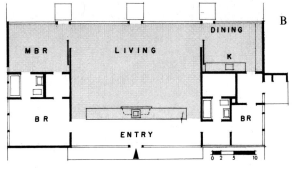

B

Different levels of floors, or ceilings, is one of the devices sometimes used. Placing the patio near the kitchen simplifies the serving of outdoor meals. A folding door secludes the den from the living room. John Portman, architect.

Movable walls and sliding or folding doors open or close off space as desired. Edward L. Barnes, architect.

The space for living together can be divided into separate rooms, sometimes on more than one floor. In addition to the living and dining room, there can be a family room, a seclusion room, or a study.

C

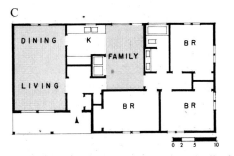

D

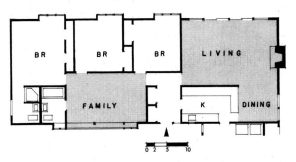

Using the entrance and kitchen as a buffer between the quiet living-dining room and the more noisy family room reduces conflicts. As in Fig. 32B, the placement of the kitchen facilitates serving food in either the dining or family space, or the terrace. Auburn Construction Company.

A family room adjoining children's bedrooms makes good play space. Completely separating it from the kitchen makes supervision of children's activities and serving food in this room difficult, but kitchen work does not get entangled with other pursuits. Anshen and Allen, architects.

E

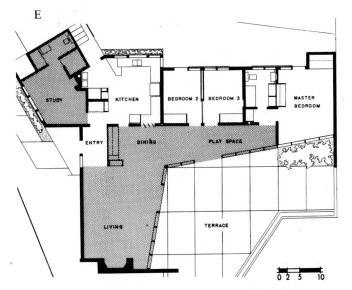

F

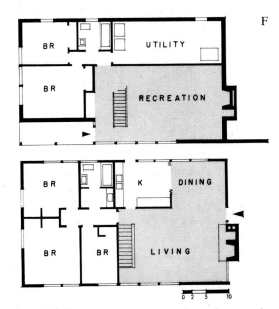

A study, or seclusion room, in one wing of a house is a welcome retreat from the openness of the living, dining, and play space, which, however, functions well for family living and for social events. Spencer and Ambrose, architects.

Putting a family room on a separate floor gives nearly maximum isolation, for better or for worse. Keys, Satterlee, and Lethbridge, architects.

- There is no "best" shape for group-living space, for each type has its merits and demerits determined in good part by specific conditions.
- Locating group-living space near the main entrance, outdoor-living space, and kitchen has advantages.
- Orientation is determined by several factors, chief of which are sun and wind, protected view, and public streets.

Open Plans

Before the 1929 depression, many houses had four or five areas of ample size for group living: an entrance hall, a living room, a dining room, a usable front porch, and possibly a den or library. As families grew smaller and entertainment less home-centered, and as building and maintenance costs soared and maids were hard to find, group-living space shrank. Parlors, dining rooms, and dens became rarities. Entrance halls contracted to vestibules, while attics and basements practically disappeared. In order to make the remaining interior areas at least seem spacious, the open plan evolved. Today, homes are getting larger again and include more separate rooms, but the possibilities of open planning are still being explored, vertically as well as horizontally, exteriorly as well as interiorly.

Homes with a minimum of fixed, opaque, floor-to-ceiling partitions and a maximum of flexible group-living space have many virtues. Instead of tightly enclosed, boxlike rooms, space is organized as a continuous entity flowing from indoors to outdoors, from one level to another, designed for diverse purposes. A simple example, shown in Figures 35A and B, combines maximum flexibility with

A

In contemporary open planning, entrance areas and passageways often merge with one another and with the space for group living. In this Los Angeles example the only separation between the entrance and the living room is a built-in sofa and a cabinet that shields the sofa but allows a view through the living room into the garden. A heavy-duty brick floor and a dropped ceiling visually define the circulation area without enclosing it. The freestanding fireplace, open on three sides, both separates and joins the living room and the dining room beyond it. Carl Maston, architect. (*Photograph by Julius Shulman*)

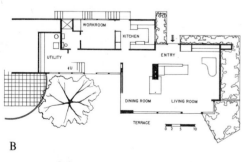

B

34

A

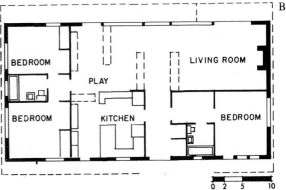

B

In a small, rectangular house, more than one third of the total area is an open space that can be partitioned for differing needs by moving caster-mounted cabinets wherever they are wanted. George Rockrise, architect. (*Photograph by Ernest Braun*)

BEDROOM

BEDROOM

PLAY

KITCHEN

LIVING ROOM

BEDROOM

0 2 5 10

economy. In this home a group-living area measuring 13½ by 40 feet can be quickly rearranged with movable, freestanding cabinets. Another example of open planning on a much larger scale is shown in Figures 27A through 28B.

The advantages of open plans include a sense of spaciousness beyond actual dimensions, diversified use of this space, and recognition of the fact that family activities are not isolated events. But open plans have disadvantages: noisy activities interfere with those requiring quiet; and the retiring soul finds minimum refuge when he wants to be alone. Also, if not sensitively planned, the space may seem barnlike. These disadvantages can be overcome in several ways. First is shaping the space with walls and furniture so that different functions are segregated. L-shaped rooms, furniture at right angles to walls, and flexible screens or movable walls, as illustrated in this and other chapters, are some of the major design possibilities. Second is planning for noise control with surfaces that absorb noise. Third is the provision of some segregated areas—family rooms for active pursuits, seclusion rooms for quiet study or relaxation.

Below. The Cleo Hovels of Hopkins, Minnesota, transformed a dreary, little-used basement into a cheerful multipurpose room. Through sensible planning and wise selection of furniture, it now accommodates a variety of family pursuits and reduces pressure on other parts of the home. Notice that the heater room, the workshop, the closet, and the lavatory are completely separated. The kitchen is partially enclosed, while the studio area is open but sequestered in a corner. (*Reprinted from* Better Homes & Gardens)

A

Family Rooms

Often called the newest room in the house, a family room is in fact the oldest, with a continuous history wherever man has lived. To mention but a few instances, cave dwellers and lake dwellers had family rooms; Pompeian atria and medieval great halls sheltered multifarious activities, and Early Colonial (Fig. 36B) and farm kitchens have often been the center of family life. Contemporary examples show great variety. The converted basement in Minnesota (Fig. 36A) incorporates a kitchen and eating area, space for children's play and television, plus a studio. In Figure 1, the living room is in reality a family room where a large space has been discreetly divided into areas for different kinds of activities by changes in furnishings, ceiling heights, and degrees of openness or enclosure. The Monts' home (Figs. 27A–28B) also shows a continuous space, with one end primarily for adults, the opposite end for children, and an area for eating logically located between the two.

Typical family rooms include eating space for children, grownups, and guests; comfortable furniture for sitting or lying down; space for small children's

Below. New England homes often consisted of one multipurpose room in which the household spent most of its time indoors. It served as kitchen, dining room, living room, and sometimes even bedroom. The hall of a house built about 1684 at Essex, Massachusetts, has a low, heavily rafted ceiling, a broad brick fireplace for heating and cooking flanked by two carved side chairs, a painted chest of drawers from the Connecticut River Valley to hold clothing and linen, and a stretcher-base table and pine bench for eating. The very broad plank floor is covered only by a deerskin. The eating utensils are of wood. The pewter dish is attributed to John Dolbeare of Boston. (*Henry Francis du Pont Winterthur Museum*)

B

activities and possibly for adult hobbies. They are ideal locations for television, radios, and record players as well as for homemade music. They help keep living rooms quiet and most of the family together in an informal, durably furnished, easily maintained area. Although family rooms can have varied locations, they are usually most successful when directly adjoining the kitchen. Easy access to livable outdoor areas is almost as imperative.

Seclusion Rooms

Seclusion rooms are as important for some individuals as are family rooms. They are much like the older studies or dens except that they belong to no one person. In contrast to family rooms, those designed for seclusion are typically small. The degree of insulation from distractions is a matter of preference. Figure 37A is an aerie with an expansive view of the landscape and is several degrees removed from group activities. At the other extreme, seclusion rooms can be completely private, in which case they can also serve as guest rooms, as in Figure 37B.

Getting away from some group activities is as important as being part of them, and it can be achieved by diverse means.

A

Left. The chief reason for this balcony, hung halfway between floor and roof, is simply delight. It is a place in which to loaf and dream, to read, to listen to soft music, or to exchange confidences. The angled ceiling and large areas of glass make it seem like a vacation spot. Kolbeck and Petersen, architects. (*Photograph by Ernest Braun*)

B

Left. A seclusion room can be small but restful and appropriate for homework or an overnight guest if the furnishings are suitable and compactly related to the walls. (*Photograph by Robert C. Cleveland*)

37

Most persons want as much space for group living as is possible, but such space is seldom wisely achieved by reducing bedrooms, kitchens, baths, and storage to cramped cubbyholes. In small houses, group-living space may range from a meager minimum of 300 square feet to a more ample 500 square feet or better. In larger houses, the space is limited only by needs and resources. The decision depends on how much space is wanted and can be afforded, but apparent size can be greatly increased by the ways and means detailed in Chapters 5, 6, and 7. The illusion of space, however, is only a palliative for space-hungry families.

The many details discussed in the preceding sections are important, but they should not obscure major goals. The social quarters of any home should give every person a sense of security in the family group and encourage each to play his best role in the family pattern. Each individual deserves opportunity to express his own feelings and to do at least some things the way he wants. In short, group-living space ought to promote the security, self-realization, and socialization of each member of the family.

Dining is a social occasion involving both practical and aesthetic considerations for maximum enjoyment. Designer Wendell Castle fulfills utilitarian needs in his furniture, but his chief concern is with the aesthetic effect. His monumental, sculptured dining table of white oak is suspended from the ceiling, incorporates a lighting fixture, and is visually supported by the surrounding sculptured chairs. The result is an object of such notable artistic merit that it needs no other justification, but it also serves as dining furniture that will incorporate people as part of the total composition. (*Photograph by Charles A. Arnold, Jr.*)

A twelfth-century chamber in a French Romanesque castle, as reconstructed by the French architect Viollet-le-Duc, is a spacious retreat for the lord and his lady. Characteristic of the period are the heavily beamed ceiling and the hooded fireplace. The narrow windows have draperies on swinging rods. The bed with its protecting curtains and the built-in seat with cushions offered a degree of comfort rare in the Middle Ages.

3 · Private Living

Individuals need varying degrees of privacy for sleeping, napping, or just stretching out to relax, for dressing and undressing as well as for keeping clean. Other facets of private living are introduced when overnight guests are entertained or when hobbies or tasks that demand seclusion are done at home. Finally, members of the family need not only time but space in which to collect their thoughts or pursue their dreams, to get to know themselves as individuals again.

SLEEPING AND DRESSING

Primitive man slept on the ground, on rock ledges, in caves, or in trees, seeking only protection from the elements and his enemies. As civilization advanced and man began to build sheltering structures, he usually reserved in them a place for sleeping, although this was not usually separated from other areas. Historically, man was late in isolating sleeping space, and then he did not do so continuously. From the decline of the Roman Empire until the Renaissance, for example, it was fairly common practice for most persons to sleep on pallets, often on the floor, in rooms used for different daytime activities. Medieval great halls (Fig. 19) often served in this way, while a privileged few enjoyed spacious private quarters (Fig. 39). Today we assume that seldom will more than two persons sleep in one room and that care will be taken to make their sleep effective.

39

Some research has indicated that sleeping time can be reduced by about two hours in a windowless cubicle in which air, light, and sound are precisely and automatically controlled. Such conditions are efficient, but human beings are not quite this single-minded. Sometimes it is pleasant to go to bed early and read, occasionally glancing up at a picture or a textile. It is fun to wake up in a room, not a cubicle, and to lie in bed looking through a window or listening to the call of a bird or to the burbling of a baby. It is relaxing to curl up or stretch out on your bed in the afternoon. Often bedrooms offer the best conditions in the home for concentrated reading or study. For these reasons, sleeping, for the past few centuries, has taken place in a moderately sized, multipurpose, segregated space.

The requisites for **sleeping** and **napping** are:

- A *bed* or *beds* long and wide enough for one or two persons.
- A *bedside table* or built-in storage headboard for what is needed near the bed.
- A *light source* over the bed for reading or emergencies.
- *Control of natural light* by draperies or blinds. If the room is moderately dark in color, reducing the intensity of natural light is easier to achieve.
- *Ventilation,* best with windows or ventilators in opposite walls, next best in adjacent walls, least good when confined to one. Being able to let hot air out through windows at ceiling height greatly reduces summer heat.
- *Quietness,* achieved by locating bedrooms away from, or insulating them against, noisy areas and by using sound-absorbing materials.

Dressing and **undressing,** involving varied movements, require conditions quite different from those best for sleeping:

- *Space* sufficient to stand in, stretch, turn around, and bend over and to see oneself full-length in a mirror
- *Mirror,* full length if possible
- *Seating* for dealing with hosiery and shoes
- *Storage* for all type of clothes within the reach of an arm or the step of a foot; a minimum of 5 feet of hanging space per person
- *Dressing table* with a well-lighted mirror and storage space
- *Lighting,* artificial or natural, so that you can find what is wanted and see how you look in it

Ideally, all of this takes place in a separate dressing area between the sleeping space and bath, as has been done in Figures 6B and 42A, but too often it is sandwiched into whatever space the bed and other furniture leave in the bedroom. Under these conditions, it becomes less frustrating if a "dressing area" is planned for each occupant of the room. Certainly, each person deserves his own closet, including or near his chest of drawers (Figs. 41A and B). Adding a mirror, good lighting, and a chair makes such dressing centers adequate.

DESIGNING BEDROOMS

Bedrooms vary in terms of the number of persons sharing them, the accommodations they offer, and the relative emphasis placed on each activity carried out in the room. At one extreme is the sleeping cubicle found in inexpensive hotels, summer camps, trains, or ships. Then come those with adequate space

A

An ingenious system of modular units that can be compactly arranged in various ways brings together all that is needed for sleeping, dressing, and study. Although planned for dormitories, it would function equally well in children's rooms or for house guests. Charles Eames, designer. (*Herman Miller Inc.*)

Above. The study unit has an ample desk, shelves for books, and good illumination. Shelves and lightweight wire baskets (instead of drawers) are adjustable to suit individual needs for spacesaving convenience. The backs of the closet doors have racks for ties and towels, a mirror, and a receptacle for soiled clothes. When not in use, the bed can be folded into the wall, and the closet doors conceal the miscellany stored behind them.

Right. In this plan the units for two persons have been placed against two opposite walls for minimum interference and conflict. The center of the room is free and open.

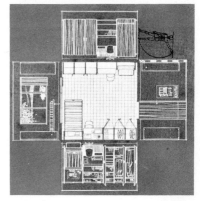

B

for the bed, chest of drawers, and a chair, plus just enough room in which to dress. Better are those somewhat larger rooms that are planned and furnished for reading or relaxation in a comfortable chair and for writing or working at a desk or sewing table. At the very other end of the scale are the one-room apartments in which all the amenities for comfortable living must be provided (Color Fig. 3).

The number of sleeping areas in a house is conditioned by the family's size and economic status. Since two-bedroom houses are adequate for only a few families, three bedrooms have become standard. Surveys, though, indicate that almost one third of those seeking homes want four bedrooms. A room for each child is desirable but often not feasible for large families.

The location of bedrooms is influenced by the emphasis a family gives to the opposing needs of supervision and seclusion. Young children need to be near their parents at night, unless an intercommunication system is installed to pick up distress signals. Placing children's bedrooms near the kitchen makes daytime control easier; convenient access to outdoor play areas saves housekeeping effort. With older children, the amount of surveillance they still need must be balanced against the degrees of quiet and independence that separated areas for private living will give to the different age levels.

Location and arrangement of bedrooms and bathrooms are the first steps toward comfortable private living.

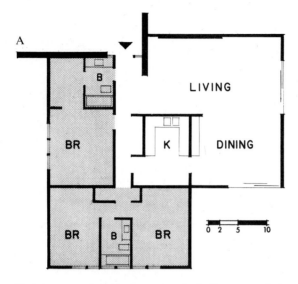

A

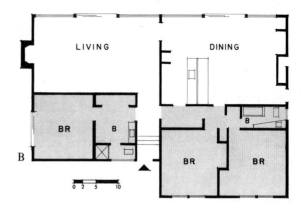

B

Both parents and children may find greater peace if their bedrooms and baths are separated. Dreyfuss and Blackford, architects.

Bedrooms and bathrooms are typically grouped together in the quietest part of the house. In this plan, three bedrooms and two bathrooms can be reached from a central hall. The bathroom near the entrance is convenient for guests and for the occupants of the master bedroom. Palmer and Kreisel, architects.

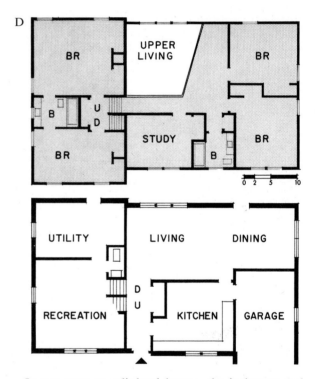

D

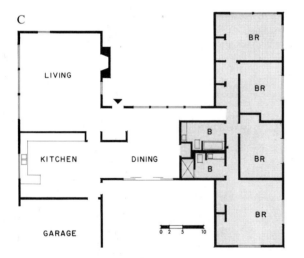

C

In more complex plan shapes, bedrooms and baths can be in a segregated wing remote from household noises. Richard Pollman, architect.

In two-story or split-level houses, the bedrooms and baths are usually upstairs, as in this house designed by James G. Durham. On some sites, however, it may be preferable to have them on the lower level, or they can be divided between the two levels, as illustrated in Chapter 17.

Four ways in which bedrooms and baths can be fitted into house plans are shown on this page. Ideally, each person should be able to go directly from a convenient outside entrance to his bedroom without going through other rooms. This means either a bedroom hall leading off the entrance area or outside doors to each room.

Location of doors and windows is at least as critical in bedrooms as in any part of the house. The doors, if there is more than one, should be as close together as is compatible with other requirements. Because the most frequently used traffic path is between the door leading into the room and the closet and chest of drawers, it is sensible to keep this path short and direct. If the door is not directly in line with the bed or dressing area, some privacy is afforded even when the door is open. Grouping the windows, as in Figures 41B, 42A, and 45A, makes rooms seem larger and gives more usable wall space, although the need for ventilation suggests windows in two or more walls.

The need for convenient storage in bedrooms is exceeded only by the same need in kitchens. Basic principles are designing the storage space for what it is to hold, keeping all space for each person's clothes together, and having this space near the door. The storage in a boy's bedroom (Fig. 43B) has been combined in a convenient built-in unit along one wall by the door.

Boys' bedrooms often differ markedly in character from those for girls.

A

B

Above. A girl's bedroom appropriately feminine and delicate. Light-blue wallpaper with a floral pattern sets off the old brass bedstead; the other walls are painted white. The rug, on a brown cork floor, repeats the color of the wallpaper. Morgan Stedman, architect. (*Photograph by Maynard L. Parker Modern Photography*)

Right. A boy's bedroom designed for rugged use. Concrete floor, wood walls and ceiling, plastic-surfaced desk and counter, and pegboard for displays are all durable and easily maintained. Anshen and Allen, architects. (*Photograph by Maynard L. Parker Modern Photography*)

Bedrooms are one of the most appropriate places in the home in which to indulge your individuality. Perhaps bright, light colors are not quieting, but if you yearn for them and the rest of the family does not, your bedroom is a good place to satisfy this urge. Photographs with sentimental appeal or cherished collections differentiate your bedroom from those belonging to others. Even in small rooms, there is usually adequate cubic footage for such memorabilia if bookcases, shelves, and cupboards are integrated with walls that will not be harmed by hooks and thumbtacks.

Boys enjoy rough-and-ready rooms with as much free floor space as possible, surfaces on which treasures can be displayed, and drawers in which they can be kept—all of which can be seen in Figure 43B. Girls typically like soft colors and floral patterns, as illustrated in Figure 43A. Movable partitions in or between children's bedrooms permit the freedom of large open spaces or quiet seclusion at will (Fig. 44).

Folding walls between two small bedrooms and a play area can be pushed back to make one large space or closed for the privacy needed for sleeping or study. Fehr and Granger, architects. (*Photograph by William Howland*)

A

The master bedroom in Loch Crane's San Diego house is a retreat for the parents. (*Photographs by Maynard L. Parker Modern Photography*)

Above. A strong architectural quality is established by the decisive treatment of ceiling, walls and windows, and built-in furniture.

B

Left. The bedroom seems like a restful alcove off the living room when the broad folding door is open. Unity is attained by the similarity of character and furnishings. Note the way in which the carpeting ties the rooms together.

When husband and wife share a bedroom, a different situation arises: it should suit and express both. Figures 45A and B show a bedroom, briefly discussed in Chapter 1, that is also a secluded sitting room for two persons. Built-in furniture concentrated against one wall brings together the bed, storage cupboards, shelves, and a desk, thereby leaving a sizable part of the room free and open. A comfortable chair, an ottoman, and a table in one corner suggest reading or relaxation. The walls contrast medium-dark textured wood with smooth white plaster. On one side, a curtained window wall opens the room to a terrace and to an extensive vista, while windows over the desk balance the illumination and improve ventilation. Wall-to-wall carpeting and a beamed wood ceiling increase the visual delight, as do the bright pillows, the accessories, the lamps, and the plant. Dressing space and bath are concentrated in a separate room, conveniently placed between bedroom and housekeeping areas (Fig. 6B).

No one would mistake this for a hotel bedroom because the owners have expressed themselves in a spirited way. The contrasts are strong and unexpected, the harmony richly complex. One wall, planned for clothes storage, is unified and enlivened with shutters on closets and cupboards and for controlling light from the windows. Burton Schutt, architect. (*Photograph by Julius Shulman*)

HYGIENE

For several decades, bathrooms were the home's most standardized room, and until recently we took for granted the three unrelated white fixtures conspicuously standing out from the walls of the smallest room in the house. Walls were invariably of plaster or tiles, timidly pastel in color. Windows were small and frequently hard to reach. Such bathrooms promised little beyond a dispiriting efficiency and often failed to live up to even that minimum essential.

Nowadays people want more, larger, and more colorful bathrooms with big basins and counter tops. Bigger medicine chests as well as extra shelf and clothes-hamper space are invariably mentioned. People ask for lots of light, rapid and effective ventilation, quick heat, and sound-absorbing materials. Color and texture are not overlooked by these homemakers, who have found that cheerful bathrooms help get everyone's day off to a good start.

In a small but uncrowded bathroom in architect Winston Elting's home (Fig. 47A), redwood walls and cabinets harmonize with the treatment of the other rooms in the house. High windows combine privacy with good light and ventilation. Sliding, mirrored doors, more efficient than the usual swinging type, cover the medicine chest. In a larger bathroom (Fig. 47B) a wall with a folding door divides the space into two units. One has a washbasin and toilet, which can be made private by closing another folding door, and the other has a washbasin and tub. This makes it possible for two or more persons to use the room simultaneously.

A

Right. In a warm, individualized bathroom, the walls, cabinets, and ceiling are of specially treated wood. Efficiency is increased by placing two washbasins in a commodious cabinet with an ample medicine chest above. A wide wooden rim around the tub and the tier of towel rods are unusual but workable details. Schweikher and Elting, architects. (*Photograph by Bill Hedrich, Hedrich-Blessing*)

B

Left. A bathroom divided into compartments is a timesaving solution. All surfaces are durable and easily cleaned. Large washbasins with adequate counter space are set in storage cabinets, the lower drawer of which can be used as a pull-out step for children. Windows, skylights, and appropriate lighting fixtures give excellent illumination. An outside door lessens traffic through the house, especially by children. (*Armstrong Cork Company*)

Designing Bathrooms

Location of bathrooms is primarily a matter of convenience, privacy, and cost (Figs. 48A to E). In a one-bathroom house, you should be able to reach this important room from the bedrooms without going through or getting in sight of group-living space, but the bathroom should also be as near the kitchen and living space as feasible. This tough assignment is well handled in the plan shown in Figure 48B. The desire to multiply bathrooms is checked only by their cost. Ideally, a home for three or more persons should have at least two bathrooms, as should one with sleeping quarters on two floors. As the family increases so should the plumbing. The ideal number can be decreased, however, if the tub or shower and the toilet are in separate compartments or if washbasins are put in bedrooms.

Location and arrangement of bathrooms determine their use and cost.

Right. Powder rooms near the guest entrance, or wash-up rooms near the family entrance and play space, keep either guests or dirt out of the other bathrooms. In two-story houses, their usefulness far outweighs their minimum cost.

Far right. Family bathrooms that must serve everyone should be large and centrally located but out of sight of the group-living space. Plumbing costs are highest when fixtures are scattered.

Middle right. Semiprivate bathrooms, planned for two or three members of the family, are located near bedrooms but are entered from the bedroom hall. Plumbing costs are lower when fixtures are on two walls.

Bottom right. Private bathrooms for one or two persons are entered only through the bedroom or dressing room. Plumbing costs are lowest when all fixtures are on one wall.

Bottom far right. Service cores concentrate all plumbing, including that of kitchen and laundry. This reduces construction costs but takes very careful planning to achieve satisfactory zoning and a conveniently livable arrangement of rooms.

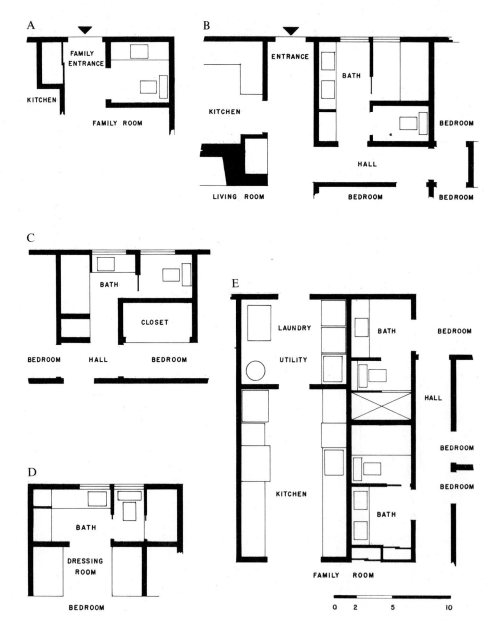

Size, location of doors and windows, the arrangement of fixtures, provision for storage, and finishes for walls, floors, and ceilings are important considerations in planning bathrooms:

- Minimum size is about 5½ by 6 feet, but these dimensions preclude use by more than one person at a time (often a necessary inconvenience), seriously limit storage space, and give the occupant claustrophobia. A few more square feet are usually well worth their cost.
- The door is best located so that when opened it will not hit a person using any of the fixtures, will shield the toilet, and can be left partially open for ventilation without giving full view of the room (from anyplace where people are likely to be).
- Critical factors in window design are light, ventilation, easy operation, and privacy. Ordinarily this suggests high windows not directly over any fixtures, but new devices facilitate opening and closing windows even when they are above washbasins (Fig. 47A).
- Typical arrangements of fixtures are illustrated on page 48. Usability is much increased at relatively small expense by divided bathrooms.
- Storage at point of first use is a cardinal principle in getting the miscellany of things associated with hygiene conveniently and accessibly housed. Medicine cabinets plus spacious cupboards are needed.
- Finishes for walls and floors permit great freedom. In addition to painted plaster and tile, the repertory includes brick and properly finished wood; laminated plastics, such as Formica, and plastic-impregnated cork; and waterproof wallpaper, textiles, or wallboard.
- Bathroom fixtures, unlike most furniture, are built in, and their size and shape are critical factors in planning. Typical dimensions are listed below:

Standard Bathroom Fixture Sizes and Clearances

Fixture	Small DEPTH WIDTH		Large DEPTH WIDTH
Bathtub	2′6″ x 4′	to	3′ x 5′
Washbasin	1′3″ x 1′6″	to	2′ x 2′
Toilet	2′ x 1′10″	to	2′6″ x 2′
Shower	2′6″ x 2′6″	to	3′6″ x 3′6″
Bathinette	1′9″ x 2′11″	to	2′ x 3′

Clearances

Space between front of tub and opposite wall	2′6″ to 3′6″
Space in front of toilet	1′6″ to 2′
Space at sides of toilet	1′ to 1′6″
Space between fronts of fixtures	2′ to 3′

Thus, no longer do bathrooms have to look like laboratories. The materials mentioned above come in a tremendous range of colors and textures. Improved natural and artificial light make possible the use of colors once regarded as too dark, and a new respect for individuality leads to color combinations formerly considered unsuitable. Bright towels, even paintings and sculpture, lift bathrooms out of the category of commonplace little cubicles.

A
Hans Wegner has designed a sofa bed that is trim and easy to adjust. (*Frederick Lunning*)
B

Above left. Typical of contemporary Danish furniture are the natural materials skillfully shaped into slender, vital forms. Cane panels on the back contrast happily with the teak frame and with the resilient cushion mattress covered with woolen fabric.

Above right. The cane panels raise easily to enlarge the sleeping area and disclose pillows and extra blankets.

HOUSE GUESTS

The pleasure afforded overnight guests and their hosts is almost directly proportional to the manner in which the guests are accommodated. They have the same basic private-life needs as members of the family: a secluded place to sleep and dress, storage for clothes, bathroom facilities, and the possibility of getting outside the family circle from time to time. From the ideal down to the minimum, these accommodations are offered by:

- A guestroom that is a bedroom-sitting room with private bath, separated from family areas and always in readiness because it is used for no other purpose
- A secluded room or study that doubles as a guestroom, a sensible solution because a room well planned for seclusion has most of the qualities of a good guestroom (Fig. 51A)
- A quiet alcove off the group-living space that can readily be made private by folding or sliding doors, curtains, or screens
- An extra bed in one or more of the bedrooms—perhaps a bunk, as shown in the boy's room (Fig. 43B), or a studio couch, as shown in the girl's room (Fig. 43A)
- A living room sofa bed, one type of which is seen in Figures 50A and B

Few can afford a spare guestroom, but if a family expects to have house guests with any frequency, it should direct its efforts toward making their visits as pleasant as possible.

INDIVIDUAL WORK AND HOBBIES

With today's emphasis on individuality, personal expression, and self-realization, space and equipment for satisfying such urges are becoming increasingly important—and at a time when both space and equipment are very expensive. Solving this problem is possible but not easy, now that spare rooms, basements, attics, and backyard sheds have become scarce.

Writing necessitates a desk, in or around which the needed paraphernalia can be conveniently kept. A desk in the living space, especially if in a secluded corner (Fig. 51B), can provide for the needs of a small family. In larger families it is far more satisfactory to have a desk for the housewife in the kitchen or master bedroom, one for each child in his bedroom, and to give some thought to where the man of the house can readily put pen to paper.

Knitting and crocheting can be done wherever one can read, but mending and sewing, whether as work or a hobby, are not so easily disposed of. The collection of needles, scissors, and "findings" seems to invite disorder and the fingers of small children, to which they are a definite hazard. Adding a sewing machine and space for a cutting table brings further complications. In order of desirability are a special sewing room, which is nowadays a luxury; space in the master bedroom; or a spot in the already overcrowded kitchen or laundry. Wherever sewing is fitted in—and regrettably that is often just the way it is handled—well-planned storage is a requisite.

A

Designed as a "studio-library" in which to do serious reading and some art work, this room with its two studio couches could also be used as a multipurpose bedroom or for house guests. Keck and Keck, architects. (*Photograph by Bill Hedrich, Hedrich-Blessing*)

B

Built-in bookshelves and a desk at right angles to the wall make a compact, pleasant study or writing corner, separated but not isolated from the rest of the room. Harwell Hamilton Harris, architect. (*Photograph by Julius Shulman*)

51

A

B

Right. A really comfortable chair placed in a well-lighted bedroom corner invites relaxation. Inexpensive India prints and hemp rugs add color and texture to an ordinary, old room. (*Reprinted from* Living for Young Homemakers)

Right and below. Space for solitude or quiet companionship is provided by a bedroom patio, enclosed by walls of adobe brick. The grilled opening into the children's play yard may be closed with shutters for greater privacy. Cliff May, architect. (*Photograph by Julius Shulman*)

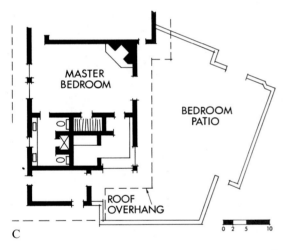

C

Such pursuits as weaving, woodworking, designing, or painting, whether done as a hobby or on a more professional level, deserve appropriate space and equipment. Important as these may be to individuals, such enterprises can quickly endanger the composure of the rest of the family unless they are somewhat isolated in a family room or completely segregated in a separate room (Fig. 13).

SOLITUDE

For parents raising families—as well as for the children being raised—occasional solitude is a rare and precious gift. Comments on what people want and do not have in contemporary houses indicate that for many persons, especially housewives, this need is acute. Too often the bathroom is the only haven—and this leads to many complications. Much importance is given to the two-

week vacation when one "gets away from it all." Good as this is, it is no substitute for the half-hour vacations most individuals need every day. This brings
us back to the real need for planning multipurpose bedrooms (Figs. 45B and
52A) and to the desirability of private space indoors and out (Figs. 52B and C
and Color Fig. 4.).

In art history instructor William Woody's home his creative philosophy of total involvement has resulted in a unique expression. Reclaimed old furniture, pieces of billboard
posters taped on the walls, and a ceiling pulsating with fluorescent paint are incorporated so completely that the barriers between art and its setting dissolve into what he
calls "one huge three-dimensional object." (*Photograph by Phil Larose*)

Colorful, even whimsical, utensils and accessories delight the eyes and hands of those who see or use them. (*Hammacher Schlemmer*)

4 · Housekeeping

Women have had much to say on the subject of making homes easier to manage. Among their suggestions are garages that are convenient to kitchens for carrying groceries from the car to the place where they are stored and then used (Figs. 64C and D), and space for eating in or adjacent to the kitchen (Figs. 55C and 64B). They want more appliances than ever in kitchens plus well-planned laundries and "decontamination rooms," where children can clean up before infiltrating the rest of the house (Fig. 6B). If necessary, they would give up gadgets for more space, especially storage space throughout the house. Quite rightly, though, they do not want these efficiencies at the sacrifice of beauty and individuality.

The greatest laborsaving possibility at our command is sensible planning of the whole house and yard. Under the general concept of **use** would come:

- Planning rooms and outdoor areas that are appropriate in size, shape, and location to their intended uses
- Keeping related areas together, such as dining space, kitchen, garage, and service yard
- Finding furnishings and equipment that are genuinely useful
- Storing objects conveniently near where they are used

Economy suggests:

- Selecting durable and easily maintained materials and forms
- Having no more furniture and accessories than are used or enjoyed
- Having appliances that really minimize labor and save time

54

Beauty and **individuality,** important in themselves, also lift the worker's spirit and make housework seem easier and less time-consuming.

Although most home work is concentrated in the kitchen, laundry, and garage or shop, some of it must be done throughout every part of the house and yard. "Straightening up" and cleaning, sewing, miscellaneous repairs, and garden maintenance (discussed in Chap. 19) are examples.

Before getting into the necessary detailed analyses of kitchen planning, let us look at a kitchen-dining space that goes courageously off the beaten path (Figs. 55A, B, and C). Although efficiency was duly considered, the goal was a

A

The Morgan Evanses' family room and kitchen is efficient for their family, but warmth and congeniality are emphasized. Frederick Barienbrock, architect. (*Photographs by Julius Shulman*)

Left. The cooking island of knotty pine with red tilework surface separates and hides the clutter of meal preparations from the more social dining and lounging area, but it does not isolate the cook from social interchange.

Below left. On the family-room side, the angled island makes an inviting recess for built-in seating and for a table whose shape was suggested by the space.

B

C

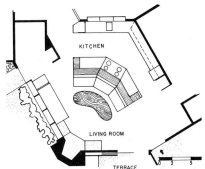

Above. The refreshingly different but workable shape of an irregular hexagon individualizes the whole space. A fireplace with a broad hearth and an adjacent built-in couch invites people to linger and enjoy this family center.

common space to keep the family happily together. The space-dividing island, 4 feet high, obscures most of the kitchen clutter yet allows the housewife to participate in group activities while preparing meals. The food-preparation zone has a range in the island, while the opposite wall not only integrates the sink, refrigerator, and mixing counters but offers a view of the outdoor play yard. The family-room side of the island has a built-in bench to provide comfortable seats for several persons. One end of the island contains family-room storage; the other end holds dishes. The bench faces a raised fireplace nicely related to a seating ledge and bookshelves at the left and to a sofa, desk, and music-storage area at the right. Interest in the utilitarian should certainly not cause one to overlook the liberating shape of the room and the divider, the intimately lowered ceiling over the relaxation area, the welcome surprise of light from high windows, and the congenial combination of knotty wood and brick. This is not only an island kitchen but an open kitchen, frankly acknowledging that preparing meals is good fun in a family setting.

PREPARING AND SERVING MEALS

Few areas of the home have received such intensive study as the kitchen. Manufacturers yearly produce new equipment designed to make kitchens more efficient and more attractive. Home economists have studied every phase of meal preparation and have given us facts, figures, and formulas that are of great help in evaluating the work areas of the home. They found that the housewife's physical limitations vary with her height and that energy is conserved if normal work curves are considered in designing kitchens (Fig. 56). Their studies of kitchen

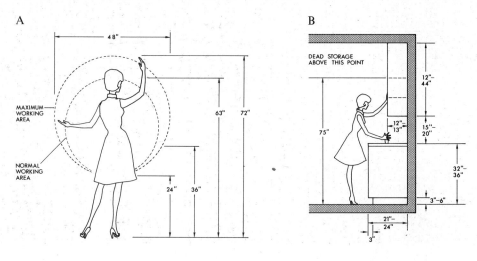

Kitchen dimensions should be based on the height and reach of the persons using that room. The dimensions here are for average women.

3

A studio apartment in a high-rise building overlooking San Francisco Bay has been given individuality by the choice of furnishings, color, and accessories. The size, solidity, and comfort of the furniture, the intensity of the reds, greens, and bronzes, suggest its masculine tenant. A pair of eighteenth-century Japanese screens, one on each side wall, and a wall-to-wall carpet of bronze green, visually widen the room and give textural interest. A chest used as a coffee table, three Tansu chests lining the unseen wall on the right, and the Mandarin-red ceramic bases on the lamps further the Oriental theme, which has been allied with clean, contemporary lines in the furniture. F. D. Stout, A.I.D., designer.

4

An unusually generous terrace provides a sheltered transition between the enclosed portions of the house and the landscape in a Connecticut home. It is protected by the truncated hood of the roof and, on two sides, by the L-shaped wings of the house. The other two sides are defined by low walls that serve as seats. The oranges, browns, yellows, and beige of wood and concrete block merge into the natural colors in the landscape but contrast with the blue seats and black backs of the chairs, and with the cool colors of the adjoining bedroom. Ulrich Franzen & Associates, architects. (*Photograph © Ezra Stoller*)

procedures indicated that there should be five work centers: the *refrigerator, sink, mixing, cooking,* and *serving centers,* each with its special requirements. These findings are basic but generalized, covering how kitchens can be planned for efficiency, not how they should look.* Coupled with the chart of standard appliance sizes, they can be used as a foundation for planning the work areas of the kitchen.

Standard Kitchen Appliance and Cabinet Sizes

Appliance	*Small*		*Large*	
	DEPTH WIDTH		DEPTH WIDTH	
Range	1'9" x 1'8"	to	2'2" x 3'4"	
Refrigerator	2'1" x 2'	to	2'6" x 3'	
Sink	1'8" x 2'	to	2'1" x 5'6"	
Automatic washer	2'1" x 2'1"	to	2'7" x 3'8"	
Automatic dryer	2'1" x 2'1"	to	2'7" x 3'8"	
Ironing board	3'8" x 11"	to	4'6" x 1'3"	
Ironer	1'3" x 2'2"	to	1'5" x 2'11"	
Cabinets, base	2'1" deep; 15", 18", 21", 24", 30" wide; 2'6"–3' high			
Cabinets, wall	6"–13" deep; 15", 18", 21", 24", 30" wide; 12", 18", 30" high			
Attachment or ventilation for some washers, dryers, stoves, and so on	3"–5" (at back)			

The Work Centers

The design of the five work centers and the sequence in which they are placed determines how easy a kitchen is to work in and how much energy is expended in everyday tasks. Each work center should have adjacent counter and cabinet space of at least the sizes indicated to provide convenient working space and plenty of storage.

The **refrigerator center** is usually placed either first or last in the work sequence: near the outside entrance and the sink, for easy storage of food requiring refrigeration, or near the serving center and dining area, for ease in serving refrigerated foods. In addition to the **refrigerator,** it should have:

A **counter** at least 1½ feet wide and usually 3 feet high, on the latch side of the refrigerator door, on which to place supplies. This can often be integrated with the counter space of adjacent centers.

Wall cabinets to store serving dishes for cold food and storage dishes for foods going into the refrigerator. File space for trays often fits well here.

A **base cabinet** with drawers for bottle openers, refrigerator and freezer supplies, and bottle storage.

The refrigerator center often incorporates a **freezer;** but a larger freezer may be placed in a storage area outside the kitchen.

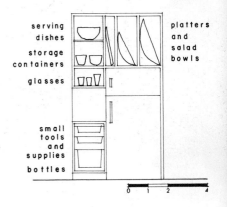

*Research conducted over the last twenty years by Professor Helen E. McCullough and her colleagues and reported in *Architectural Forum,* February and March 1946, and in the 16th Annual Short Course in Residential Construction, January 18–19, 1961, Small Homes Council-Building Research Council, University of Illinois.

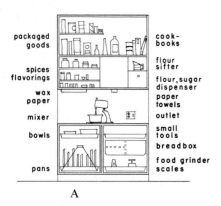

packaged goods
spices flavorings
wax paper
mixer
bowls
pans

cook-books
flour sifter
flour, sugar dispenser
paper towels
outlet
small tools
breadbox
food grinder scales

A

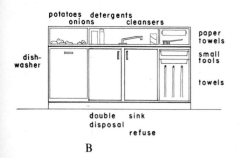

potatoes detergents
onions   cleansers

dish-washer

paper towels
small tools
towels

double   sink
disposal
        refuse

B

C

ventilating fan
serving dishes
uncooked cereals

surface units
pans small tools
large pans

trays
platters
seasonings
oven

lids
griddle

The **mixing center** is for all kinds of mixing—breads and pastries, salads and casseroles. It can be located between the refrigerator, in which many mix-first items are stored, and the sink, or next to the stove. It should have:

A **counter** at least $3\frac{1}{2}$ feet wide and not more than $2\frac{1}{2}$–$2\frac{2}{3}$ feet high, in contrast to the standard 3-foot height, to lessen fatigue. Because much time is spent here, knee space and a stool could be included.

Wall cabinets to store condiments, packaged foods, and cookbooks.

Base cabinets with drawers for small tools and drawers or sliding shelves for bowls, pans, and heavy items used in mixing.

Specially designed storage spaces for flour, sugar, and bread are often incorporated into wall or base cabinets in this center.

The **sink center** is indeed multipurpose, serving for the washing of fruits and vegetables, dishes, and children's hands, and providing water for mixing, cooking, freezing, and drinking. It may also be used for storage of tableware, although the serving center is often a better place for this. Because it is desirable to have the sink center near both the cooking and the mixing centers, it is often located between them. The sink center needs:

Counters on both sides—$2\frac{1}{2}$ feet wide on the left, 3 feet wide on the right, usually 3 feet high—and with at least one of them a waterproof drainboard.

Double sinks are convenient for hand dishwashing, although they are sometimes too small for large cooking pans. A **single large sink** is usually adequate with a dishwasher. **Two separated sinks** are especially convenient when more than one person is using the kitchen.

A **dishwasher,** if incorporated, is most convenient to use when on the left of the sink, but the location of dish storage is a factor. The 2-foot counter width on top of a front-opening dishwasher is adequate for stacking dishes.

Cabinet space for those items that are usually used at the sink, such as utensils for cleaning, cutting, and straining food; dish cloths and towels; and soaps. It is convenient to store foods that need peeling or water or both at or near this center, a miscellany ranging from potatoes and onions to coffee and dried fruits.

Provision for trash and garbage.

A **stool** and **knee space,** which ease the labor of cleaning vegetables and dishes.

The **cooking center** becomes the busiest area for half an hour or so prior to eating. Near the sink and mixing centers, and convenient to the eating space, is the most desirable location for this center. It should consist of:

Gas or electric **surface units** incorporated into a range or installed in a heat-resistant counter.

A **heat-resistant counter,** 2 feet wide and usually 3 feet high, on at least one side of the surface units *and* built-in wall ovens.

An **oven** or ovens, either beneath the surface units (which requires stooping) or over the units (where it is a hazard to head and eyes and requires considerable agility to remove hot pans safely). **Built-in wall ovens** can be placed at a more convenient waist-high level, but should not interrupt the flow of counter space.

Wall cabinets nearby for small cooking utensils and seasonings.

Base cabinets for larger, heavier items.

Ventilation by a quiet exhaust fan over the cooking surface.

The **serving center** is used for storing those items that go directly from storage to table—tableware, linens and accessories, toasters, and such foods as sugar and catsup. Often integrated with either the cooking or the refrigerator center, it should be close to the eating table and should have:

A **durable counter,** at least 2 feet wide, 2½–3 feet high, with or without a pass-through to facilitate serving.

Ample cabinet space designed for the items to be stored. If between kitchen and dining area, this can be accessible from either side. It usually needs to be supplemented by cupboard space in the dining area or by a pantry.

Besides these centers, a **storage wall** is often advisable to accommodate extra supplies and is especially necessary if wall-cabinet space over counters is lost to windows and ovens. Cleaning equipment and supplies need a well-planned closet either in the kitchen or in the laundry.

Storage Space in the Work Centers

The **amount** of storage space in the work centers is a critical factor in their design. The research done in this field indicates that the size of the counter space given for each of the five work centers will ensure enough storage space for the average kitchen if wall and base cabinets are placed above and below the counter. Where windows, range, or corners cut into these figures, compensating space should be provided elsewhere. When the centers are placed alongside one another, all counters between appliances may be eliminated *except the largest counter, which should then be made 1 foot wider.* If these formulas are followed, the counter space provided by the work centers comes to at least 10 lineal feet, ample for kitchen supplies but leaving space for dinnerware for only four persons. An extra 5 feet of wall-cabinet space is needed for each set of dinnerware for twelve.

The **quality** of the storage space is equally important and deserves careful thinking about objects in relation to their use and to those who use them:

- *Convenience.* Time and energy are conserved if items are stored where they are first used rather than putting all similar things—pots and pans or sharp knives, for example—in one place. Drawers in base cabinets are more convenient than fixed shelves. Pull-out shelves are intermediate.
- *Visibility.* Storing items (except for such identical articles as tumblers) only one row deep facilitates finding them.
- *Accessibility.* Logic indicates putting the most frequently used items at the most convenient height, heavy objects below, and those seldom used above.
- *Flexibility.* Adjustable shelves and drawers with removable dividers adapt to changes in needs of families and to the design of kitchen tools.
- *Maintenance.* Open shelves are efficient for items used daily, but enclosed storage for those used less often reduces cleaning.

Placement of Work Centers

The cardinal principle of work-center organization is appropriateness to the individual using the kitchen most intensively. For most situations, however, the following generalizations hold:

- **Traffic** in and around the work centers should be limited to that connected with getting meals. Miscellaneous traffic should be diverted elsewhere.
- **Distances** between counters and appliances that face each other should be 5 feet, and between counter and breakfast table at least 3½ feet. Distances between work centers should be short and the routes as direct as possible while still allowing for the necessary counters and storage.
- **Sequence** of work centers should be from right to left, for a right-handed person, to reduce work motion, starting with the refrigerator center and proceeding with sink, mixing, cooking, and serving centers.
- **Standard arrangements** of work centers fall into four categories: one-wall, L-shaped, corridor, and U-shaped, as illustrated in Figures 60A to D. At times an island is used to shield the work space from view or to supplement it.

Although most kitchens are basically related to one of these four types, those designed to solve special problems or to meet individual needs may differ markedly from standard practice.

Top near right. **One-wall** kitchens can be fitted into alcoves and concealed with folding doors when not in use. They are available in complete prefabricated units and economically concentrate plumbing and wiring. They are, however, suitable only for "kitchenettes," because if equipment and storage are normal size, many steps are wasted.

Top far right. **L-shaped** plans have somewhat less distance between centers, leave room for eating and laundry, and divert miscellaneous traffic a little. They are not, however, very efficient.

Bottom near right. **U-shaped** kitchens are the most compact and efficient and have the further grace of almost eliminating bothersome intrusion.

Bottom far right. **Corridor** arrangements also decrease distances between work centers but invite unwelcome traffic if there are often-used doors at both ends.

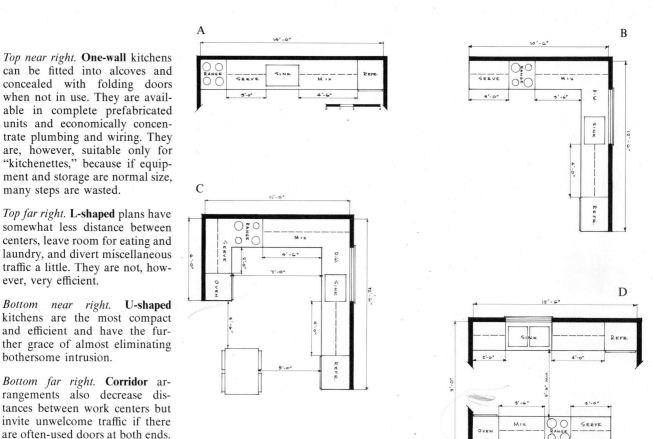

None of the gracelessness characteristic of many kitchens that flaunt their utility in laboratory terms is found in this enjoyable cooking-eating space. The colors of natural wood serve as a foil for the floor and for counter tops, which can be any color the owner prefers. Loch Crane, architect. (*Photograph by Maynard L. Parker Modern Photography*)

DESIGNING THE KITCHEN

The San Diego house discussed and illustrated in Chapters 1, 2, and 3 has a noteworthy kitchen (Fig. 61). Many of the research findings reported earlier, plus those from a study of energy-saving kitchens, form the basis for a design that correlates efficiency and pleasantness. The latter study (developed by the Agricultural Research Service, U.S. Department of Agriculture) had as its goal the reduction of walking, stooping, lifting, and reaching in meal preparation and in other kitchen activities. Study of the house plan (Fig. 6B) reveals that this ample, almost square area is divided by an island into two zones, one for food preparation and the other for eating, planning, and storage.

The food-preparation zone is a "broken-U" shape. The five work centers are placed in a viable sequence, with the refrigerator, sink, mixing, and cooking centers in a step-saving triangle, and with the serving center at the end, next to the range, for ease in serving up hot foods and for convenience to all dining areas. Each center has been planned not only for storage at point of use, but also for conservation of energy.

The **refrigerator center,** for example, is only a step from the mixing center and a few steps from the family dining table.

The **mixing center** has accordion doors that fold back to reveal most of the supplies and utensils needed for baking. It also has knee space under the counter so that the cook can sit while mixing.

The **sink center** has shallow cabinets ranged along the back of its counter for detergents and cleaning tools, and for foods needing water, such as potatoes, coffee, and canned soup. The dishwasher is at the left of the sink for ease in loading and for unloading directly into the adjoining closet, which is also accessible from the dining room. The accordion door on the closet opens up the whole space in one motion. Over the sink is a pass-through to the dining room that is high enough above the counter to hide kitchen clutter and that can be closed off entirely by sliding doors.

The **cooking center** is divided into two sections. The most-used top burners are incorporated into the serving center in an island backed by a higher storage cupboard that has space for things that will be used at the family dining table—toaster, silverware, and linens. There is ample counter space for both cooking and serving needs, and drawers and cupboards underneath for pots and pans. The less-used oven, with cupboards above and below, has been placed to the right of the refrigerator, where its convenient waist-high level fits in well. The island counter suffices as a not-too-convenient surface on which to place pans coming out of the oven.

Storage for cleaning supplies and brooms is provided in a tall cabinet beside the oven, and a long storage wall beside the desk can be used as a very accessible pantry.

Maintenance is lessened and **illumination** improved by light-colored, laminated plastic counter tops, cabinets of light birch, a plastic tile floor of a spot-concealing pattern, and a lowered panel of lighting above the sink. Natural light comes in through the sliding doors that open onto the terrace, and is counterbalanced by that coming from the formal dining room by way of the pass-through. The plan is open enough to be pleasant and unconfining, closed enough so that the work areas do not need to be kept in strict order all the time.

The **location of the kitchen in the total plan** is one of the principal reasons that it is successful. Figuratively and literally the hub of the house, it serves as the connecting link between adults' and children's wings, and is only a few steps from both indoor eating in the formal dining room and outdoor eating on the terrace off the family workshop. It is convenient to the carport and also to the front entry, which can be monitored through the pass-through above the sink and through the windows of the dining room. The working part of the kitchen is off to one side, out of the way of through traffic but easily accessible, while the circulation paths meet at the family dining table on the other side of the island. The utility or laundry room, with washer, dryer, laundry tub, and cupboards, is quite close but can be closed off from view and for sound control.

All of the principles, details, and suggestions that are available in books and magazines do not mean that kitchen design is a matter of formulas and of stereotypes, nor that there is one "ideal" plan suitable for all. Both the Evanses' and the San Diego kitchens (Figs. 55 and 61) are personalized ways of integrating food preparation with other aspects of family life.

Figures 63A and B reveal kitchens that feature indoor-outdoor relationships. The conditions conducive to comfortable outdoor eating are ease in getting food from the kitchen to the terrace and an attractive place in which to

Kitchens in many climates can be pleasant and well lighted with large areas of glass.

A

Above. In Minnesota, the Petersons' opposite-wall type of kitchen is efficient because it is not a passageway. It is also cheerful because of the pleasant views of the porch and enclosed, tree-shaded terrace beyond. Carl Graffunder, architect. (*Photograph by Warren Reynolds, Infinity Inc. Reprinted from* Better Homes & Gardens)

Left. In California, a U-shaped kitchen gains light and spaciousness from the dramatic high windows and the sloping ceiling. Open shelves above the sink allow the cook to see the dining area and the view beyond. Henry Hill, architect. (*Photograph by Morley Baer*)

B

Kitchens can be placed in almost any part of the house, but steps will be saved if they are the shortest feasible distance from indoor- and outdoor-eating spaces and from the garage and service area. Further, they should be convenient to the main entrance and not far from a lavatory. As long as these requirements are considered, they can be in the suggested locations on this and the facing page.

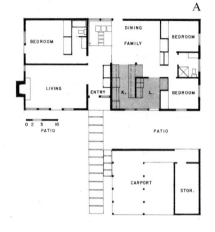

A

B

C

enjoy the meal. In Minnesota, the Petersons' kitchen opens onto a protected porch and walled garden through a glass wall that stretches from the floor to the pitched ceiling. In the high-ceilinged California home a compact cooking area allows the housewife to enjoy views through open shelves and above the cabinets. The breakfast area is flooded with light from many windows; a door leads onto the terrace for open-air dining.

Some kitchens are planned with children foremost in mind, others for two-cook families or for families that do almost no cooking. There are also kitchens for families in which servants do the work. Kitchens are successful only when they satisfy their users, because as with every part of the home, a food-preparation space takes on full meaning only when it is gratifying to use.

We have approached kitchen design from the inside out—from personal needs through cooking activities and the necessary equipment to the character of the space as a unit in the family life. Generalizing about design is imprudent in view of individual urges and preferences, but we shall discuss some further basic considerations.

Size, for example, is determined not only by the number of persons using the kitchen and the amount of food prepared for family or guests, but also by the kind and number of other activities that take place in the kitchen areas. The space needed in small homes for food preparation alone may vary from around 60 to 130 square feet, but in larger homes more space may be needed. The addition of laundries or eating space, hobby and relaxation centers may raise the total to 300 square feet or more. As mentioned earlier, a majority of families want ample kitchens, but efficiency and pleasantness are determined by shape, doors and windows, and location in the house plan as well as by size.

Shape has no ready-made rules. Although typically rectangular, other shapes are possible (Fig. 55C). It is generally agreed, though, that a small food-preparation area requires fewer steps if its shape falls between that of a square and a rectangle with proportions of about 2 : 3.

Doors in kitchens are necessary evils—necessary as entrances and exits, evils because they take space, determine location of work centers, and invite traffic. Efficiency is increased when the number of doors is kept to a minimum, when doors are as close to one another as is feasible, and when no major work center comes between them. This has been accomplished in Figures 64C and D, but elsewhere other factors may render this impossible. In the Petersons' home (Fig. 63A), for example, the lot and the house plan necessitated a long, narrow kitchen and utility room with doors at each end, but the architect avoided making it a thoroughfare.

Top left. At the *front,* as in this Idaho house designed by architects Grider and La Marche.

Center left. At the *back,* a solution illustrated by Robert Engelbrecht's plan for a home in New York State.

Bottom left. At the *side,* as shown in a California home planned by Paderewski, Mitchell, and Dean.

Right. On the *first floor* of a two-story house, a typical solution well handled by Louis F. Bodkin III for a home in Oregon.

D

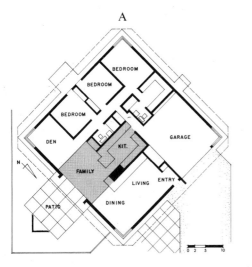

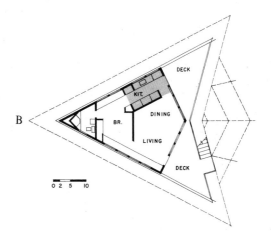

In the *center,* as in R. Duane Conner's compact plan for a home in Oklahoma City.

On the *second floor* of a two-story house when, as in this Florida plan by George Ely and Glenn Johnson, the view and the climate make the upper floor more desirable.

Windows make kitchens light and pleasant and provide ventilation, but they take space. Minimum window area should equal at least 10 percent of the floor area, but 15–20 percent is better. If possible, at least one counter should have ample daylight and afford an outlook. Contemporary architects have developed many ingenious ways of daylighting kitchens without sacrificing wall space. In the Petersons' kitchen a skylight and small windows between counters and wall cabinets maximize use of walls. High windows in the California kitchen (Fig. 63B) flood the food-preparation area with daylight and let the housewife enjoy an expansive view without taking an inch of usable space.

Location of kitchens is a matter of critical importance, but there are many good solutions, as shown on pages 64–65.

Kitchens require the most maintenance of any room in the house. They are noisy—and the center of the housewife's work. These factors suggest selecting shapes and materials for floors, counters, cupboards, walls, and ceilings for *wear-resistance, ease in cleaning, sound control,* and *pleasantness* to sight and touch.

New ways of living, new concepts of planning, and technological advances have produced kitchens that are handsome and efficient. In a later section of this chapter ways of reducing housework in the kitchen and elsewhere will be discussed. Chapters 5, 6, and 7 deal with design and color, while Chapters 8, 9, and 10 analyze the qualities of materials. In these chapters are many facts and ideas applicable to all phases of kitchen design.

LAUNDRY

Every week many millions of pounds of clothing and household linens are washed in American homes. But two factors have changed the way in which this is done: the development of automatic washers and dryers, and the trend toward getting laundry equipment out of dark, inconvenient basements. Provisions for home laundering range from using the sink or washbasin for rinsing out little things to having a fully equipped, separate laundry. The size and age distribution of the family, the size of the house, and the attitude toward sending laundry out are factors in laundry planning.

Laundry activities fall into four categories:

- **Receiving, sorting,** and **preparing,** which require a counter, a cart, or simply the top of the washer
- **Washing,** which necessitates laundry trays or a washer or both, plus storage for supplies
- **Drying,** in an automatic dryer or a convenient drying yard
- **Finishing** and **ironing,** for which an ironing board or ironer is needed plus space to put finished laundry and, ideally, space and equipment for mending

A sensibly planned laundry is shown in Figure 66.

In small houses, laundry space is often reduced to a minimum and compacted into the utility room, the kitchen, the basement, or the garage. Utility rooms segregate the clutter and noise of laundry work. Rooms with laundry trays or deep sinks and that serve as family entrances are also good places to

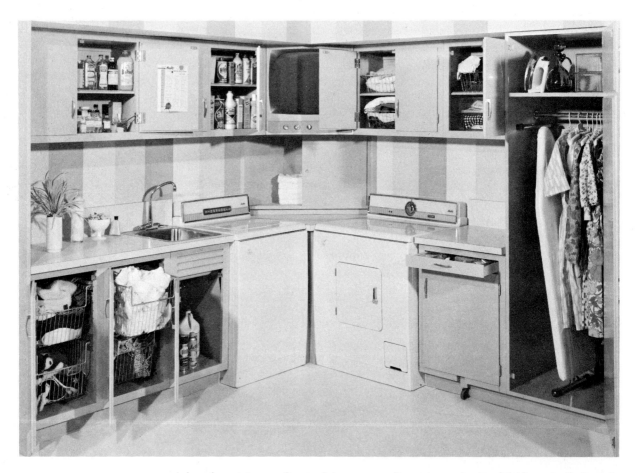

A laundry center can be good to see as well as to use. At the right is a small closet in which to hang clothes and store an ironing board. The washer, dryer, and counter tops form a convenient work area, with storage cupboards above. The small sink is equally useful for hand-washing and for washing hands. Well-ventilated, lightweight sliding baskets simplify sorting. (*The Maytag Company*)

clean up after play or work. Figure 64A shows such a laundry convenient to, but separated from, the food-preparation area. Although space may be saved by having a laundry in the kitchen, the inevitable clutter and noise are bothersome.

Basements and garages, having little in their favor, are to be avoided if possible. One other location, however, has been successfully tried in some houses, and that is the bedroom wing, usually in some space adjoining the bathroom. Since most laundry originates in and returns to bedrooms, and laundering is seldom done at night, this location deserves consideration. Washing and ironing, wherever they are done, are more pleasant in a well-lighted place made cheerful with color or even pictures on the walls.

KEEPING THE HOME ORDERLY AND CLEAN

Families, but chiefly housewives, spend many hours a week in housekeeping, but there are numerous ways to reduce this work. One is careful attention to the design, arrangement, and materials of every part of the home.

Maintaining order can be facilitated in several ways:

- Plan conveniently located centers for each major activity with every needed item near at hand. If this planning is applied to reading and hobbies quite as much as to laundry work, things are more likely to be put away immediately after use and to be found easily when needed.
- Have a well-considered location for each object: chairs, tables, and lamps placed so that they seldom need to be moved and convenient storage for everything not in continuous use—in short, a workable furniture arrangement plus adequate storage.
- Have a maximum of fixed objects. Built-in seating, tables, and lighting fixtures stay where they belong despite the whims of children and adults. Alternatives to built-in furniture are units (Fig. 69) designed to look and act almost as though they were integral parts of the house—they fit tightly together and against the wall to save space—and lighting fixtures that can be fastened to walls.
- Select movable objects with mobility in mind. They should be lightweight, easy to grasp, and resistant to the wear that moving brings. For example, pull-up and dining chairs ought to be sturdy yet easy to lift (Fig. 67A), not the kind that demand a floor-scraping shove.
- Store or discard everything not often used or enjoyed. Households have a tendency to become cluttered with objects no longer important to the family. The time and space they require can be used for more satisfying purposes.

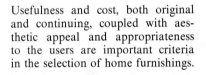

Usefulness and cost, both original and continuing, coupled with aesthetic appeal and appropriateness to the users are important criteria in the selection of home furnishings.

A

Above. Carrying forward the tradition of bentwood furniture, the "Prague" armchair is exceptionally durable but light in weight and has a rare, dateless beauty. (*Stendig, Inc.*)

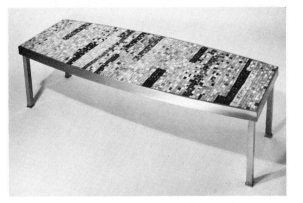

Left. Glass mosaic and mat-polished brass form a sturdy, individualized coffee table. Moderately high in original cost, it is almost maintenance-free. Margot Stewart, designer. (*Helga Photo Studio, Inc.*)

B

Cleaning, too, can be much less of a chore if forms, colors, and materials are chosen with maintenance in mind and if there is good storage for cleaning supplies.

Dust and dirt are unhygienic, unpleasant to see and touch, and tend to shorten the life of anything on which they remain. They are most harmful and difficult to dislodge if they become embedded in the material. Although intricate forms, clear, bright colors, and lustrous surfaces are visually stimulating, ease of maintenance suggests a predominance of:

- Forms that are broad and simple with a minimum of separate parts, moldings, or crevices into which dust and dirt settle and from which they are hard to remove.
- Furnishings that either come to the floor or are supported on a minimum number of legs high enough to make it easy to clean under them.
- Surfaces that are smooth and impenetrable, such as well-sealed wood or concrete, ceramic or plastic tile. Almost everyone, to be sure, also wants the richness and warmth of textured fabrics. These are hard to keep really clean but compensate by not showing obvious dirt. Fibers that do not absorb dirt and textiles treated to resist soil and stain, however, are easily maintained.
- Colors that are grayed and neither extremely light nor dark. These are the colors in which nature abounds. They are also the colors on which a little dust or dirt passes unnoticed.
- Surfaces that are patterned rather than plain. Color-varied surfaces are easier to maintain than those of solid colors, but those easiest to keep looking well have small, complex patterns, as in Figures 67B and 68B and C.
- Surfaces that are dull rather than glossy. Mirrors and shiny metals bring brilliance and accents but they show fingerprints, water spots, and dust. Mat surfaces, with their lack of luster and gloss, take such inevitables in their stride.

That this drive for efficiency need not lead to dullness is well exemplified by the mosaic coffee table (Fig. 67B), which not only meets the requisites listed above but is liquid-proof, durable, and handsome. All this applies equally well to the textile (Fig. 68A) that refuses to absorb stains or dirt.

Spilled and *spattered liquids* constantly threaten the housekeeper. Water is the most common but the least serious, while other liquids, from beverages to ink, may stain or bleach porous, noncolorfast materials. To economize on work and possible replacement use:

- Waterproof materials wherever feasible. Especially needed in kitchens, laundries, and bathrooms, they also merit consideration where food is served, especially to children, and in family rooms. Glass, metal, and glazed ceramics are history's chief waterproof surfaces, to which have been added a host of new materials that are opening the way to easier housekeeping.
- Materials that do not show water marks. In general, plain shiny surfaces, whether glass, metal, plastic, or painted wood, show water spots, removable only by polishing. On surfaces that are dull or patterned, such as the mosaic table and plastic flooring, they are scarcely noticeable.
- Colorfast materials. Here science has made many and mighty contributions, of which the fiberglass textile is one example.

Easy-to-keep and long-lasting curtain, upholstery, and flooring materials are widely available at comparatively low cost.

Top. A scrolled motif translated from a seventeenth-century brocatelle makes a Fiberglas textile richly decorative. Dan Cooper, designer. (*Owens-Corning Fiberglas Corporation*)

Center. Tightly woven wool and silk are combined in many colors to create a spirited, long-lasting upholstery material. (*Isabel Scott Fabrics Corporation*)

Bottom. This vinyl and asbestos floor covering with a pebbled pattern takes little care and wears for many years. (*Azrock Floor Products*)

A

B

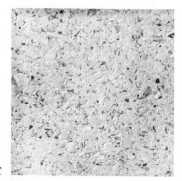

C

Spacesaving modular furniture units can be selected and arranged to meet individual needs. Oriental in inspiration, these units are skillfully crafted of hardwood that is rich in color and grain pattern. They might well be regarded as a lifetime investment. (*Baker Furniture Company*)

Even in the most careful households, *surfaces* get *scratched* and *dented*. Here, again, knowledge of materials in terms of use is valuable:

- Resilient materials, such as vinyl or cork, take blows or scratches with scarcely a record of the event.
- Rigid materials, such as masonry, metal, and some plastics, are seldom affected by moderate abuse, but will crack, break, or dent under heavy blows. If and when this happens, repair is difficult, sometimes impossible.
- Wood, especially the harder types, ages gracefully if finished to reveal its color and grain. Like sterling silverware, it grows richer with use. It seems to make minor scratches and blemishes part of itself. Dents can be sanded or filled. If split, wood can be glued back together.
- Glossy finishes almost always resist scratching and abrasion better than those that are dull. *But* the blemishes are more conspicuous.
- Patterns, especially those that are small and indistinct, conceal blemishes quite as much as they camouflage dust, water marks, and stains.

If carried to an extreme, the above suggestions could lead to a home monotonously gray with a profusion of little texture patterns everywhere and no plain, bright, dark, or light colors, no sparkling surfaces. This, of course, is not intended. But for easy housekeeping, the suggestions can be applied to most of the large surfaces of walls, floors, and furniture.

The urge to travel has led to notable advances in the design of mobile homes.

Right. The compact cooking area has a four-burner stove, a double sink, a refrigerator, and convenient storage. The gaucho bed and dinette are a cheerful living-dining center but can be converted into extra sleeping space. Ample wardrobes are near the double bed. (*Ford Motor Company*)

Above right. A friendly, homelike character in no way detracts from maximum efficiency in a restricted space. (*Photograph by Maynard L. Parker Modern Photography. Reprinted by permission from* House Beautiful Magazine)

A MOBILE HOME

Housekeeping in a mobile home presents a great challenge to designers. Because of its small size, every inch of space must be efficiently planned. Because it is always on view it must be easily maintained. Because it is mass-produced it needs a few distinctive touches to keep it from being anonymous. The owners of the Ford Condor Coach shown in Figures 70A and B started with the standard model, which has clean-lined, built-in furniture that fits compactly together to simplify cleaning and make the best use of space. The sleeping area has bedding storage underneath and in the built-in headboard. The dinette table and benches convert into a double bed, as does the gaucho bed opposite. The two seats up front swivel around to become lounge chairs.

The materials used are all very durable, slow to soil, readily cleaned, economical of time and effort, but attractive in themselves and easily kept that way. Walnut plywood on walls, ceiling, and furniture brings its own beauty and warmth. The counter top is a light-colored Formica, reflecting light and brightening the work area; the range and its hood are of softly gleaming dark metal. The bedspreads and upholstery are of nonmussing, dirt-concealing tweed, and the drapery material that repeats the linear pattern of the plywood provides privacy while carrying the eye around the small interior, helping to expand the restricted space.

The owners have limited but emphasized their contributions. The wool carpeting that completely covers the floor has a decided impact. Used instead of the standard light-colored vinyl flooring, it has warmth and luxury that is unexpected but quite sensible. It is easily cleaned with a vacuum cleaner, and the shaggy effect of the long loops hides minor spots and dirt. The leather-and-wood stool again is a surprise, but in keeping with the natural appearance that has been emphasized; also, it is easy to move and store. Housekeeping has been made simple and pleasant because designer and owner used care, imagination, and restrained boldness in their planning.

A
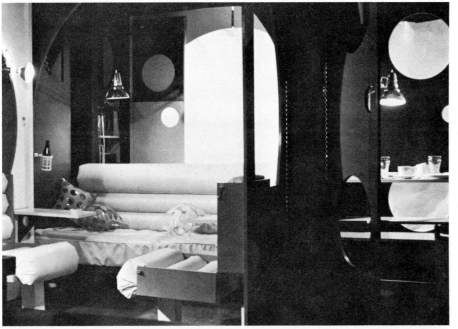

The Super Cube, designed by Les Walker, is an imaginative experiment in prefabricated living, a mobile home that could be folded up and transported in one piece. It comes as a box approximately seven feet square. When the plywood wall panels are opened, they create separated spaces with built-in furnishings for relaxation, dining, sleeping, and office work. Although the shell is standardized, the furnishings can be varied to meet individual needs. Red, white, and blue predominate in the prototype model, but any colors could be used. (*Photograph by Les Walker*)

B

Opposite. A detail of a Chinese "green dragon" porcelain vase, Ch'ing dynasty (1662–1795), shows an unusually spirited rhythmic pattern, which is a major device for unifying diverse forms. (*National Gallery of Art, Washington, D.C., Widener Collection*)

Part II · DESIGN AND COLOR

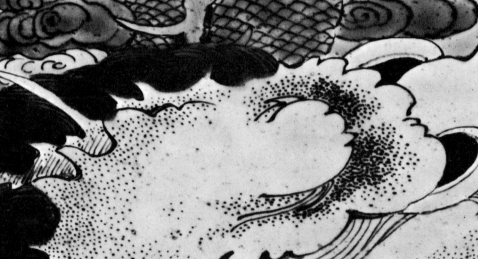

Sensitively shaped china, covered with a smooth white glaze, shows how form alone can give gratifying variety in unity. Designed by Tapio Wirkkala of Finland. (*Rosenthal China Corporation*)

5 · Design: Aims and Principles

The word *design* has several meanings: purpose, aim, or organization; plan or scheme; selection and organization. When these are put together, they describe the total design procedure of deciding on one's aims, of developing a plan or approach, and of selecting and organizing the forms and materials best suited to the purposes.

In home planning and furnishing, however, design is often limited to the creation, or selection and organization, of form, space, color, and texture to achieve beauty and individuality. In this and the two following chapters the focus of attention will be on design in this limited sense, but it will not be forgotten that utility and economy are equally important goals.

Design for beauty has no laws, recipes, or rigid standards to trouble or comfort us, because beauty and creative individuality are close partners. Design is a freehanded, not a fixed, process. Although much design is the result of deliberate analysis and synthesis, we have become highly receptive to "lucky accidents," and are awakened by the unexpected. At its best, each object and each epoch seeks and finds its own appropriate organization. There are, however, useful observations and guides that will be introduced by analyzing two exceptionally beautiful American living rooms. The Port Royal parlor (Color Fig. 5) is a consummate example of eighteenth-century design that is equaled by the twentieth-century living space created by Frank Lloyd Wright in his own house "Taliesin" in Spring Green, Wisconsin (Fig. 76).

Although different in every detail, these two rooms have many basic characteristics in common. Both were planned and furnished for group use. Their space is adequate in size and appropriate in shape. Comfortable sofas and chairs, tables, and ledges are arranged for family leisure and entertaining. Both rooms, however, go well beyond merely satisfying physiological requirements. Materials have been chosen, shaped, or ornamented to please the senses and to extend a hospitable welcome with no sacrifice of utility. Notice, too, that in each room, paintings, china or vases, patterned textiles, flowers, and plants are used either for aesthetic satisfaction or sentimental attachment. In short, these rooms express and fulfill their utilitarian and aesthetic purposes.

Each room seems all of a piece—that is, holds together cohesively because architecture and furnishings have a dominant character. One is formal and

The living room in Frank Lloyd Wright's Wisconsin home (1911–1925) is ruggedly informal. Furnishings and structure are dynamically united in bold, richly varied interpenetrating planes. (*Photograph by Maynard L. Parker Modern Photography*)

refined, the other informal and vigorous. Interest is held in each by two seemingly paradoxical qualities, namely, forceful unity and stimulating diversity. The Port Royal parlor is a contrapuntal union of the strictly rectangular architectural background and the curvilinear forms in the furnishings. Shunning monotony, these curves range from the strong, sculptural legs of the chair in the left foreground to the intricate tracery in the Oriental rug. Wright's room has relatively few curves but an ingeniously diversified organization of horizontals, verticals, and diagonals. As basic materials he chose wood and stone, both of which have an organic variety of color, grain, and texture.

The different ways in which these rooms are balanced is a vital factor in determining their character. Typical of eighteenth-century design, the dominant, symmetrical placement of fireplace, furniture, and accessories brings unquestioned equipoise to the Port Royal parlor; but the lively forms activate what might have been an inert arrangement. The asymmetrical placement of the fireplace, the painting, and the furniture in the Taliesin room is a sensitive balancing of visual weights without exact repetition.

An all-pervading beat, or pulse, brings to every part of these rooms a rhythmic expectedness. But here the similarity ends. Crisp and delicate, the rhythms in the Port Royal parlor are reminiscent of Mozart, whereas the vigorous, almost martial beat favored by Wright recalls the powerful energy of Beethoven or Brahms. Although graceful and flowing, the eighteenth-century rhythmic pattern has a classic quality of self-containment quite different from the expanding, interpenetrating planes that open Wright's alcove to the space beyond.

A constant human need is to have our attention held by intricate, contrasting, large, or centrally located forms, then released by simple, quiet ones. Although not large, the Port Royal fireplace is made important by its central position and marble facing, the carved pilasters and moldings, the painting, and the crystal chandeliers and china on the mantle. It is further strengthened by the almost symmetrical furniture arrangement around an intricately patterned Oriental rug. The Taliesin fireplace, also prominently placed, holds attention with its bold stonework, furniture arrangement, plants, flowers, and a painting. In both rooms the adjacent surfaces are comparatively unobtrusive, giving further emphasis to the fireplaces.

In the following, more comprehensive, discussion of five major aims and principles of design—**form follows function, variety in unity, balance, rhythm,** and **emphasis**—we will see how basic these concepts are to all aspects of home planning and furnishing and how they open paths to individualized expressions.

TWO AIMS OF DESIGN

Form follows function and **variety in unity,** constant aims and concepts in historic and contemporary art, apply directly to home design.

Form Follows Function

That the design of anything should grow out of its intended purposes seems obvious, but countless inefficient kitchens, poorly illuminated bathrooms, depressing living rooms, and dining tables with leg-entangling supports prove that design is too often illogical or arbitrary. Nearly everything in the home has its utilitarian aspects, and these ought to be basic considerations in its design.

Utility, though, is not the only factor in design, for all objects represent expenditures of money, time, and energy, and they are possible sources of aesthetic pleasure and individual expression. A spoon or a sofa is *completely* functional only when it is useful, economical, and beautiful to an individual. This lifts the design and selection of silverware or seating, for example, well above the mere supplying of equipment that fits its user's anatomy. Then there are those objects intended only for the spirit—paintings, sculpture, and accessories, whose claim on us is their beauty. These are at the opposite end of the scale from the primarily utilitarian furnace and garden hose, but they are of great significance to the whole man living a full life.

Designing or selecting for all functions is complex. Detailed analysis of specific and general requirements is essential. Factor must be weighed against factor, and usually compromises have to be made. Suppose, for example, that you are looking for a coffee table to put in a contemporary living space where adults relax and children want to play. It is easy to find many that are suitable in size, shape, and height; it is not easy to locate a coffee table that is also moderately priced and easy to maintain, that has some storage space and no dangerously sharp corners, and that is pleasing in itself and appropriate to the home. The major difficulty centers around the fact that several of the criteria are contradictory. When this happens, it is sensible to give up the qualities of lesser importance and to buy or make a table having those deemed most important.

There are many ways to shape materials into door hardware that integrates usefulness and aesthetic satisfaction.

Form follows function is often misinterpreted as meaning "utility dictates shape." That this is not the case should be clear from the discussion of the Port Royal parlor and Wright's living area. These rooms and their furnishings show

A   B

Above left. Handcrafted knobs of multicolored Venetian glass are rewarding to see and to use. Paolo Venini, designer. (*Yale and Towne*)

Above right. A contemporary Spanish door handle of brass is easy to operate and aesthetically eventful. (*Clavos, Inc.*)

that utility is only *one* of several functions basic to design and that there is more than one way to solve any design problem. Far from being restricting, a study of the functions of any object can inspire quite different solutions, as is illustrated by the door handles in Figures 78A and B.

Variety in Unity

All nature and all art show variety in unity. Our own bodies with their unified diversity are the examples best known to us. Our hands, for example, are amazing units in which each part differs from the others yet is coherent with the whole. The Port Royal parlor demonstrates a happy union of American furniture, Oriental rugs, French draperies, and English cut glass. Each has its own distinctive flavor, but they have in common such qualities as refinement and elegance.

Unity may be defined as oneness, or as being formed of parts that constitute a whole. It is most successfully achieved out of the strength and clarity of a motivating idea. In home design, this is the general character discussed in Chapter 1. Why should a home be unified? Because a unified home satisfies the desire for wholeness and brings a welcome peace and security not found in a furniture store or in a home that resembles one.

Unity may be achieved by several specific means:

- Sameness or repetition is the surest, most obvious, and least interesting means. Having all walls the same color and texture forcefully establishes a unified background. Uniformity of furniture design also leads to integration, as in Figure 80, but must be skillfully handled to avoid monotony.
- Similarity and harmony are but one step removed from repetition and lead directly toward unity while introducing some variety. The walls in a home might be of one hue, but some could be lighter or darker, warmer or cooler, stronger or weaker, or different in texture.
- Congruence of forms that are *actively* related without being identical produces a particularly powerful unity. For example, a button and a buttonhole are more strongly united than are two buttons. A floor plan in which rooms are integrally related to one another seems more of an entity than does one in which a series of boxes open off a hall.
- Emphasizing those parts that most forcefully express the basic character strengthens unity. Much can be done with miscellaneous furniture by putting in prominent positions pieces that have the desired qualities, relegating to secondary positions the pieces that contribute less to the unity of the home.
- Enclosures help unify parts of a home by separating them from their surroundings. Hedges or fences around gardens, and frames around pictures, are examples.

Variety may be defined as diversity or multiformity. It arouses and holds interest as well as brings vitality through friendly differences. Diversity introduces welcome surprises and heightens the total effect (Fig. 81). If carried too far, it destroys unity, because variety can lead to anarchy just as unity can lead to monotony.

Diversity of materials, forms, colors, or textures, and contrasts of all sorts, are some of the major ways and means of attaining variety. Variety can be as subtle as a scarcely noticeable difference in the textures of two pillows on a sofa or as clamorous as a polished copper hood on a rough stone fireplace. Because variety draws and fixes attention, it should be used full strength only where you want people to look hard and long, in dilution where you want simply to relieve monotony in subordinate places.

Variety has been discussed separately from unity for the sake of clarity. In practice, though, the two are inseparable partners, but the exact relationship between the two is a matter of opinion. Some experts find it advisable to begin with variety and work toward unity. Others, including the authors, believe that variety should grow out of unity as a development of basic ideas, much as an oak tree develops from an acorn. It seems more effective to start with an idea or a purpose from which unity and variety grow together than with a series of ideas that have to be "pulled together."

Rarely do homes have too much unity, and for those few that do the simple remedy of introducing some marked variety suffices to give them life. For example, in the room setting in Figure 80, the use of similar forms in the sofa and chairs gives a strong unity that is relieved and yet heightened by the provocative

Unity and variety can be pushed to extremes and still be reconciled, as shown in the figures on this and the opposite page.

Repetition of form is relieved by the excitement of op-art patterns in this room setting. Alexander Girard, designer. (*Herman Miller, Inc.*)

A profusion of pattern is unified by a decisive and pervading black-and-white color scheme. David Eugene Bell, interior designer. (*Bloomingdale's, New York*)

patterns based on optical illusions in the cushions, one tabletop, the rug, and the wall hanging. The pervading geometrical rhythms are softened by the grouping of potted, flowering plants and a sizable animal sculpture lying unexpectedly near the coffee table. At the other extreme, some homes sacrifice unity for variety; here, too, the solution is simple—establish a dominant theme, reinforced by one or more subordinate ones. In Figure 81, an almost overwhelming profusion of pattern is unified by limiting the colors to black and white, underscored by a dark charcoal-gray rug. Extending the floral print wallpaper onto the window wall and repeating it on the chair cushions helps to stabilize the design as do the sizable areas of either stark white or black in sofa, chair, and game table.

The Port Royal parlor can also be used to illustrate the way dominance and subordination can be handled to achieve variety in unity. The basic theme, *rectangularity,* is forcefully expressed in the larger elements—the shape of the room and the rugs, the design of the windows and fireplace. In strong contrast is the second theme, many kinds of *curves,* seen in the shapes of the furniture and the patterns of rugs and other textiles, draperies, chandeliers, plates, bowls, and flowers. Unity is not synonymous with sameness; variety can be disciplined.

PRINCIPLES OF DESIGN

In the search for ways to create beauty, man has evolved principles based on observation of nature and study of worthy art. **Balance, rhythm,** and **emphasis** are a simple but inclusive trio of principles useful in achieving the basic aims of **form follows function** and **variety in unity.**

Balance

Defined as equilibrium, balance is a major principle in all phases of living —from furniture arrangements to bank accounts. Through balance we get a sense of equipoise, but this may range from static permanence through repose and from suspended animation to actual motion. It is achieved when interplaying forces, attractions, or weights tend toward resolution.

There are many examples of divergent kinds of balance in nature. The Rock of Gibraltar typifies static permanence, with changes too slight to be noticed. Sand dunes, in contrast, are continuously shifting, but without loss of equilibrium. Trees, too are always in a changing equilibrium, because their shape changes as they grow and because winds and the seasons affect them. Thus balance can be an ever-changing resolution of forces as well as an equalization of deadweights. It is also evident that balance exists in four dimensions—time as well as length, breadth, and width.

In balancing an interior, we deal with the "visual weights" of architecture and furnishings. The visual weight of anything is determined by the psychological impact it makes on us. Objects of large size or of such physically heavy material as stone command respect. Bright colors or strong contrasts of all sorts are quickly noticed and vividly remembered. Elaborate detail arouses interest, while anything unusual or unexpected has an importance beyond its size. At the other pole, the small, the somber, the harmonious, or the typical usually settles into the background. Everything in the home is a psychological factor in design, but the forcefulness of each item varies markedly. For example, a small spot of bright color can balance a large grayed area; visually, a significant painting may be as "heavy" as many square feet of plain wall. Well-balanced interiors hold this interplay of forces in poise.

The balance in a home is as ever-changing as is nature's equilibrium, but in different ways. People are the first factor, for a room is never complete except when being used. As people move about, they not only see a home from different angles but actually change the equilibrium by the areas to which they go and by the clothes they wear. The second factor is light. Natural illumination is altering every minute of the day and changes markedly with sky conditions and the seasons. Only within small limits can its effects be controlled, yet it affects our homes drastically. For example, subtle nuances of color and very fine detail can be readily appreciated in moderately bright light, but they are all but obscured in very strong sunlight or at dusk. Artificial light can be precisely controlled but has to be flexible to meet a number of needs, and flexibility brings variance. The third factor is the composite of all the little things that happen in the course of a day (the reading material and other portable paraphernalia brought in and left) as well as the modifications that come with the months and years (the scarcely noticed fading of textiles and mellowing of wood, to say nothing of the replacement of outworn or unwanted objects). What does all this mean? Simply that in view of these inevitable changes, many of them beyond our strict control, the fundamental pattern of equilibrium should be strong enough to take these on-slaughts in stride; to gain from, rather than be destroyed by, them.

It is customary to differentiate three types of balance: **symmetrical, asymmetrical,** and **radial.**

Symmetrical balance (Fig. 84A), also known as formal or passive balance, is achieved when one side of the object is the exact reverse (or mirror image) of the other half. Our clothes, furniture, and household equipment are nearly all symmetrical to fit our symmetrical bodies. Classic architecture, including American eighteenth-century work, is also based on symmetry because of the implied stateliness and reserve that are qualities admired by classicists. It is easy to appreciate because we can see quickly that, since one side is the reversed replica of the other, the two must be in equilibrium. The effect is typically quiet and reposed, perhaps because it demands little effort from the observer. Its overtones of stateliness and dignity are not easy to explain, but certainly people stand or sit as symmetrically as they comfortably can when they wish to appear dignified. Symmetrical balance tends to stress the center, creating a logical focal point for something one wishes to emphasize. But the resultant division into two equal parts usually reduces apparent size.

A

Although the above observations are generally true of symmetrical balance as typically used in homes, it is important to note that totally different effects are possible. Violent rhythms or swirling curves, regardless of symmetrical arrangement, will not seem quiet or reposed (Fig. 83B). Shapes or colors that lead the eyes away from the middle weaken the focal point at the center.

Basically, symmetrical balance is as simple as *A B A*, the pattern from which it is derived, and this simplicity contributes to its popularity. Although very easy to handle at an elementary level, it can be as imaginative, subtle, and complex as in the Port Royal parlor. Although few entire homes or even single rooms are completely symmetrical—utility and the need for variety rule

B

A late Italian Baroque console table (eighteenth century) balances swirling asymmetrical curves within a strongly symmetrical framework. The result is an energetic formality appropriate to the exuberant luxury of the period. [*Nelson Gallery-Atkins Museum (Nelson Fund), Kansas City, Missouri*]

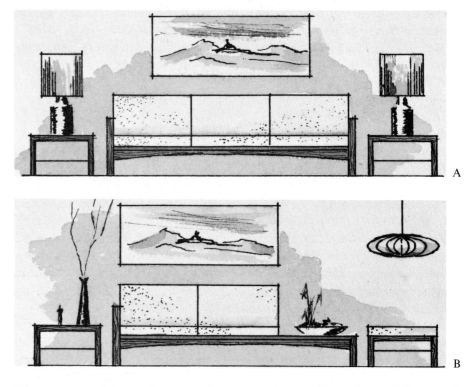

Symmetrical balance usually seems formal and static. (*George McLean*)

A

Asymmetrical balance suggests informality and movement. (*George McLean*)

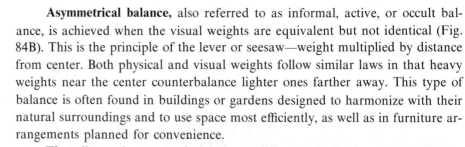

B

this out—many have such symmetrical parts as centered fireplaces (Color Fig. 5) or a sofa with identical tables and lamps at both ends (Fig. 84A). Often, however, symmetry is arbitrarily imposed or comes out of habit or laziness when it is not appropriate. Then it can lead to inconvenience or dullness. For example, doors in centers of walls are seldom logical because they leave two equal areas that may be difficult to furnish unless the room is very large, and they bring traffic into the room's center.

Symmetry is indicated *but not dictated* when:
- Formal or reposed effects are wanted
- Focusing attention on something important is desirable
- Use suggests symmetry
- Contrast with natural surroundings is sought

Symmetry is a good way to achieve unmistakable order. Use it when it comes naturally, but do not force it because of the false assumption that symmetry is "correct."

C

Asymmetrical balance, also referred to as informal, active, or occult balance, is achieved when the visual weights are equivalent but not identical (Fig. 84B). This is the principle of the lever or seesaw—weight multiplied by distance from center. Both physical and visual weights follow similar laws in that heavy weights near the center counterbalance lighter ones farther away. This type of balance is often found in buildings or gardens designed to harmonize with their natural surroundings and to use space most efficiently, as well as in furniture arrangements planned for convenience.

The effects of asymmetrical balance differ markedly from those of symmetry. Asymmetry stirs us more quickly and vigorously, and it suggests movement, spontaneity, and informality. Because it is less obvious than formal balance, it arouses our curiosity to see how equilibrium was found. Subject to no formula, asymmetry allows full freedom and flexibility in arrangements for utility as well as for beauty and individuality.

Asymmetrical balance is indicated when:

- Informality and flexibility are desired
- An effect of spaciousness is sought
- Use suggests asymmetry
- Harmony with nature is a goal

Contemporary trends toward informal, relaxed living find apt expression in homes planned asymmetrically, just as those of the eighteenth century favored symmetry as an environment for the formality of their occupants.

Radial balance results when all parts are balanced and repeated around the center, as in the spokes of a wheel or the petals of a daisy. Its chief characteristic is a circular movement out from, toward, or around a center. In homes it is found chiefly in such circular objects as plates and bowls, lighting fixtures, flower arrangements, and textile patterns. Although of lesser importance than the two preceding types, radial balance makes its own distinctive contribution in many small objects.

A

Earlier in this section we stated that balance applies to all aspects of living. Figure 85B demonstrates that house plans, quite as much as living rooms or abstract paintings, can be sensitively equilibrated. In this plan, two wings of different size and shape are asymmetrically disposed and joined by a somewhat off-center hall and two paved terraces. Interior partitions subdivide the wings into spaces counterbalanced in size and shape, not only for use but for aesthetic satisfaction. This aspect of design is seldom noticed until you walk through or live in a house. Then it may become even more important than the composure of a painting on a wall, for it consciously or subconsciously affects us all of the time. A well-balanced house plan gives a continuing sense of assurance and order, a feeling that things are as they ought to be.

B

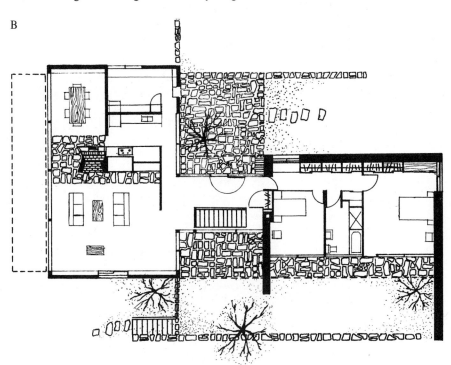

A sensitive, functional example of asymmetrical balance in the plan of a contemporary Connecticut house. The central unit consists of an entrance terrace, a hallway, and another small, protected terrace. The larger size of the group-living wing (*left*) is counterbalanced by the weightiness of the thick stone projecting walls of the bedroom wing (*right*). Marcel Breuer, architect.

85

A ▦ ▦ ▦ ▦ ▦ ▦ ▦

B ▦ ● ▦ ● ▦ ● ▦

C ▦ ▦ ▦ ▦ ▦ ▦

Top. Identical squares aligned at regular intervals establish a strong, easily predictable rhythm through *repetition. Center.* Putting black circles between pairs of gray squares develops a pulsating rhythm through *alternation* of two contrasting shapes and visual weights. *Bottom.* A simple *progression* from a square to successively longer rectangles produces a more complex, evolving rhythm. (*Robert Goudy*)

Below. Simple and composed in shape, a contemporary stoneware bowl has been enhanced with a rhythmic pattern that emphasizes its rounded form through repetition and contrast. Repeated black squares, arranged in easy diagonal rows that can be read from left to right or vice versa, alternate with diagonal lines that follow the curvature of the bowl. Marguerite Wildenhain, ceramist. (*M. H. de Young Memorial Museum, San Francisco*)

Rhythm

Defined as continuity, recurrence, or organized movement, rhythm is a second major design principle and one through which an underlying unity and evolving variety can be gained. It is exemplified in time by the repetition of our heartbeats, the alternation of day and night, and the progression of one season into another. In form and space it is seen in the more or less repetitive character of the leaves on a tree, the alternating light and dark stripes of a zebra, and the sequences and transitions of curves in a river.

Rhythm contributes to the beauty of homes in several ways. Unity and harmony are consequences of rhythmic repetition and progression. Character and individuality are in part determined by the fundamental rhythms—gay and light in the Port Royal parlor, dynamic and rugged in Wright's living room, and precise and serene in the Gordons' home (Fig. 12). Lastly, homes gain a quality of "aliveness" through the implied movement and direction that rhythm induces. This, however, is fully achieved only when a congruent pattern of rhythms prevails.

Repetition and **progression** are the two primary ways of developing rhythm. **Repetition** is as simple as repeated rectangles or curves, colors or textures; but it can be given more intriguing complexity by **alternating** shapes, colors, or textures. Even the most commonplace home is full of repetition—evidence of its universal appeal and also of the fact that simply repeating anything anywhere is not very stimulating. Some useful guides are:

- Repeat strongly and consistently the forms or colors that underline the basic character.
- Avoid repeating that which is ordinary or commonplace.
- Too much repetition, unrelieved by contrast of some sort, leads to monotony.
- Too little repetition leads to confusion.

The fundamentals of rhythm are simple. Their inspired application is another matter, as is shown in two pieces of ceramics.

D

E

Right. A Chinese porcelain vase from the Sung Dynasty (A.D. 960–1279) has an exuberant interplay of lines in progressive sequence of size, shape, direction, and thickness. Our eyes are invited to explore many complex paths that make us more vividly aware of the jar's spheroid form. (*Los Angeles County Museum*)

Sequential progressions, whether combined with repetition or used alone, can vitalize three-dimensional forms and space or two-dimensional surfaces.

The space in an Arizona living room is shaped by walls that have a pronounced progression from large to small in size, from horizontal to vertical in shape, and in their angular placement. The uniform concrete blocks generate a steady, quiet repetition. Blaine Drake, architect. (*Photograph by Julius Shulman*)

A

Progression is a sequence or transition produced by increasing or decreasing one or more qualities. It is ordered, systematic change. Because progression suggests onward motion by successive changes toward a goal, it can be more dynamic than simple reiteration.

Progressions of size, shape, and direction are handsomely dealt with in the dominant portion of the living room in Figure 87A. Above the fireplace is a horizontal rectangle that is the largest expanse of uninterrupted wall. Next comes the wall to which the vine clings, smaller in size and moderately vertical in feeling. This progression is brought to a conclusion by the smallest unit, the definitely vertical pier behind the built-in end table. Accompanying these size and shape changes is a change of direction, for these walls show an angular progression of location. Notice, too, how the lowered ceiling seems to originate

B

A contemporary Danish version of the Windsor chair brings new life to the complex curvilinear and angular rhythmic sequences that have endowed this design with continued visual appeal for generations. The equal spacing of the spindles in the back and the repetition of shape in the legs and stretchers stabilize the design. Within this framework of regular recurrence are many kinds of progressions that vitalize the forms—the varied curves in the back, the changing direction and tapering of the spindles, and the increasing heights of the spindles above the armrest—to produce a notable variety in unity. Morgens Lassen, designer. (*Pacific Overseas Inc.*)

Progressions do not have to follow a regular, repeated pattern, as is shown in Angelo Testa's design for a printed fabric called "Stirs." Progressions from long to short, from thick to thin, and from black to medium gray are playfully organized as variations on a theme.

in the fireplace wall, just touches the middle wall, and appears to carry through the vertical pier to the wall beyond. Also observe that the ledge and seat begin by paralleling the center wall, then angle out into the room to add one more step to the angular sequence of position of the walls behind. The repeated grid pattern of the concrete blocks emphasizes each change much more than would walls of smooth plaster. Unlike the regular, expected sequences in the Chinese jar and the Arizona living room (Figs. 86E and 87A), the progressions in the textile design (Fig. 88) are more freely handled. Fifteen similar shapes, none duplicating any other, progress with imperfect consistency, from large near the center to small toward the edges. There is also transition, again not monotonously regular, from dark to lighter values. This pattern demonstrates equally well some of the possibilities of variations on a theme, a kind of diversity in oneness, and a lively asymmetrical balance.

Emphasis

The third design principle, emphasis, is often referred to as **dominance** and **subordination.** Emphasis is concerned with giving proper significance to each part and to the whole, calling more attention to the important parts than to those of lesser consequence and introducing variety that will not become either frittery or chaotic. It has to do with focal points, "rest areas," and progressive degrees of interest in between. Without emphasis, homes would be as monotonous as the ticking of a clock, and without subordination as clamorous and competitive as a traffic jam.

Many homes suffer from a lack of appropriate dominance and subordination. Such homes may have rooms in which almost everything has about the same dead level of nonimportance or, at the opposite extreme, rooms in which too many assertive elements compete for simultaneous attention. Neither is satisfying. Much more livable are those rooms in which attention is directed toward a few important elements—a substantial fireplace, a distinguished piece of furniture or a painting, or a window with an outlook—shown to advantage by quieter areas. Rooms of this kind result in neither boredom nor overstimulation. Attention is held and relaxed at many levels.

Two steps are involved in creating a pattern of emphasis: deciding how important each unit is or should be and then giving it the appropriate degree of visual importance. This is not so simple as the superficial concept of "centers of interest and backgrounds," because here we are dealing with a scale of degrees of significance, not with two categories. A start can be made by thinking in terms of four levels of emphasis, such as emphatic, dominant, subdominant, and subordinate (although this, too, is an oversimplification because there can be innumerable levels). In planning a room, it can be worthwhile to list everything under one of these headings.

Emphatic	Dominant	Subdominant	Subordinate
Fireplace	View of garden	Wall treatment	Floor
	Major furniture group: sofa, chairs, end and coffee tables, lamps, large picture	Desk and smaller pictures	Ceiling
		Plants and flower arrangements	Draperies
			Radio-phonograph

If this were the list, the next step might be consideration of such ways of making the fireplace emphatic as size, position, design, and materials. A large, unobtrusively curtained window could key up the view of an attractive garden. The major furniture group might be arranged to direct attention toward the fireplace but also permit one to see the garden. Its size would automatically make it important, but this could be built up or lessened by the design of the furnishings together with the color and pattern of the upholstery. Walls of wood or of plaster painted a subdued but not lifeless color are possibilities. Placed in an out-of-the-way location, the desk might be allied with small pictures. Plants and flowers could be disposed where needed. Presumably the floor would have little pattern, if any, and be a neutral color, while painted plaster would be a natural choice for the ceiling. The radio-phonograph could be subordinated by building it into the wall or incorporating it with bookshelves or an end table.

Other conditions and desires would lead to different solutions. An extensive view might become the room's emphatic feature. Fine antique furniture might justify concentration on it, or distinctive Oriental rugs might become the center of attention.

Many people, however, do not have an impressive fireplace, an extensive view, or a distinctive collection of furniture, paintings, or rugs. Fortunately, there are many ways of creating interest in a dull room. One approach is to concentrate spending on one important piece of furniture, to locate it prominently, and key it up with accessories, a painting, or a mirror. Funds permitting, one or two other distinctive pieces, less emphatic than the major unit, might be secured and made the centers of secondary groups. A strongly patterned wallpaper or a large map on one wall would also be effective. Very low in cost is an out-of-the-ordinary color scheme achieved by painting walls, ceiling, furniture, and perhaps even the floor so that the color harmonies and contrasts become noteworthy. Other possibilities are shown in Figures 89 through 91.

The treatment of walls and windows can transform a commonplace room into gratifying living space, as shown in the figures on this and the top of the next page.

In a Chicago apartment, a large wall map lifts a simple furniture group to significance without overshadowing it. Built-in bookcases and an antique barometer visually enliven end wall and make it useful. (*Photograph by Carl Ullrich, Inc. Marshall Field & Company*)

Two ill-proportioned windows chopped the end wall of an apartment living room into a series of visually distracting rectangles. A well-designed framework of wood, decisively patterned draperies, and a few decorative accessories made it into a coherent focus of attention. (*Celanese Fibers Company*)

A

Shelves and cupboards on walls, together with varied decorative accessories, can produce individualized centers of attention, as in the next two figures.

An unusual corner arrangement of modular units combines storage cabinets and bookshelves with a place to display paintings and sculpture. The carved chair, bench, and headboard contrast pleasantly with the unadorned wall units. (*Royal Systems*)

B

A New York apartment that seems open and airy yet rich in interest combines Finnish and American ideas and objects. From this angle the roughly textured, flame-colored Finnish rug used as a wall hanging is dominant, and the antique Finnish clock is a secondary accent. From other parts of the room the shelves, with their collection, or the old spinning wheel near the steel ribbon space-divider take precedence. Aivi Gallen-Kallela and David Kenneth Specter, designers. (*Photograph by Gene Maggio, New York Times Studio*)

In thinking about dominance in a home:

- Decide on the levels of importance of different parts of the home. Play up each according to its significance.
- Limit the number of interesting centers. One dominant and two or three subdominant areas are about as much as a typical room can take.
- Arrange the parts in proportion to their import. Central positions, for example, are conspicuous. Also, an object gains if "built up" with others less important, a practice widely followed (for beauty as well as use) in relating tables, chairs, lamps, and pictures to a sofa.
- Use the attraction of visual weights thoughtfully. Large forms, intense colors, bright lights, contrast or opposition, and anything unusual compel attention.
- Elimination of the superfluous, of that which obscures or confuses, is often one of the best and least expensive ways to emphasize basic character.

OTHER PRINCIPLES

Harmony, proportion, and scale are important concepts but not quite so comprehensive as the three major principles discussed earlier.

Harmony, defined as consonance, concord, or agreement among the parts, is one facet of unity. It springs from the same sources, such as emphasizing a single motivating idea and making good use of repetition and similarity. Relationships of forms, one to another, can range from the repetitive harmony of identical shapes to the challenging dissonance of a square allied with a jagged "free form."

A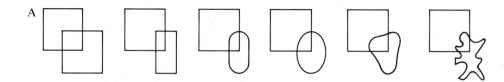

Proportion is a term with many meanings, but all of them are concerned with relationships of magnitude, quantity, or degree. In art and architecture, it can be defined as the relation of one part to another part or to the whole, or of one object to another. It refers to ratios, relative sizes and arrangements, and involves shape relationships. If, for example, the ratios of height to breadth in rectangles are changed, the shapes are altered (Fig. 92B).

The proportion of a shape affects its expressive quality. *Left.* A square divided into two equal parts seems logical but not very interesting. *Center.* Markedly unequal division produces contrast and emphasis. *Right.* Some persons find proportions approximating those of the "golden section" especially satisfying. (*George McLean*)

B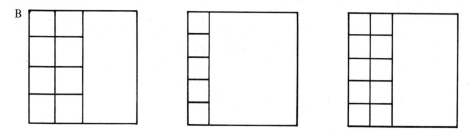

In spite of enormous expenditure of time and energy, no foolproof system of proportioning that holds good in all cases has been devised. The so-called golden section, which often gives safe, pleasing results comes nearest. It consists of dividing a line or form so that the smaller portion has the same ratio to the larger as the larger has to the whole. The progression 1, 2, 3, 5, 8, 13, 21 · · ·, in which each term is the sum of the two preceding ones, approximates this relationship. For those in need of formulas this is as good as any, but its applications are limited.

All efforts to define "perfect proportions" demonstrate their true insignificance when one deals with real problems involving use, economy, individuality, and materials. Few persons complain that a fork or a floor-lamp stand is poorly proportioned because it is long and thin, that a soup bowl or a sofa is ugly because it is low and broad: they are shaped that way for very good reasons. Should we then discard the whole concept of proportion because some writers have ossified it? No, the concept is valid because it is inescapable; it is only rigid formulas that are suspect.

Scale refers primarily to the *relative* size or character of an object or to its parts compared to other objects either in whole or in part. Forks are small and sofas large, but either can be small or large in scale depending on its shape and ornamentation.

The cupboard and the highboy in Figures 93A and B illustrate the differences between proportion and scale. Although both pieces take about the same amount of space, the overall proportions (or shapes) are dissimilar. The oak cupboard is lower and broader, and these proportions are accentuated by the two

Two handsome pieces of American furniture show how drastically the handling of proportion and scale changed in one century.

Above. A cupboard of sturdy oak (1660–1680), comparatively low and substantial, was strongly influenced by sixteenth-century Elizabethan furniture. (*The Metropolitan Museum of Art, New York*)

Left. A mahogany chest (c. 1765) from Philadelphia shows the stately proportions and fanciful, intricate ornamentation favored at that time. (*The Metropolitan Museum of Art, New York, Kennedy Fund, 1918*)

horizontal units, which are quite unlike in character but similar in size and shape. The mahogany highboy is higher and thinner, and these proportions are emphasized by the slightly accented distinction between the lower and upper sections. In scale, the cupboard is large, robust, and bold, in contrast to the small scale and delicate refinement of the highboy. Compare the scale of the moldings of the two pieces, or of the substantial columnar supports of the cupboard with the graceful legs of the highboy. Notice that the character of each piece is determined at least as much by the proportions and scale as by the ornamentation.

A vital consideration in homes is "human scale." Physically, typical persons are between 5 and 6 feet tall and weigh between 100 and 200 pounds. These figures act as a yardstick for sizes of rooms, furniture, and equipment. Suitably scaled homes make us look and feel like normal human beings, not like midgets or giants.

We can, though, adapt ourselves to a wide range of different scales if *all major elements are congruent.* The two rooms for contemporary Americans in Figures 94A and B could hardly be less similar, yet each is excellent in its own way for its intended purpose. The difference in scale is pronounced. One fireplace, small in size and recessed in the wall, is made small in scale by the delicately detailed tile border, the charming little fire screen, and the refined wood panels

C

Left. Even when the overall dimensions of two objects are identical, the way in which they are proportioned and scaled can make their character and apparent size markedly dissimilar. The chair at the left looks large, heavy, and bulky; the one at the right looks higher, lighter, and smaller. (*George McLean*)

Above. An intimate California sitting room is consistent in its small scale and elaboration of detail, both of which are accentuated by the boldly patterned fabric wall covering. (*Gump's*)

A

Below. An exceptionally vigorous living room is congruent with its rocky, mountainous site near Taxco, Mexico, and with its owner's wishes. Almost everything is large in scale, boldly formed, open and uncluttered. Anshen and Allen, architects.

B

and moldings. The other is a massive block boldly jutting out into the room. Large, textured concrete blocks and vigorously rough stonework stand for what they are without any distracting detail. Almost every component of each room is consistent, even the bouquet of tulips in one and the coarse-leaved banana plant seen through the glass wall of the other. Imagine, if possible, the lamps or coffee table from the first room placed in the second. Without some contrast, however, the effect of any kind of scale is weakened. In the first room, the large-patterned textile used for walls and draperies alerts us to the smallness of everything else but remains consistent through the intricacy within the pattern. The normal-sized pillows, books, and pottery in the second emphasize the boldness of other elements.

Scale, however, is only one of the factors that so sharply differentiate these two rooms. Some of the others are tabulated below:

	Sitting Room	*Living Space*
Form Follows Function	Small, intimate, secluded, formal room for a few persons.	Large, free, open, informal space for groups.
	Forms are delicate, refined, richly detailed.	Forms are large, vigorous, rough, and without ornament.
Variety in Unity	Unity through consistent, small-scale, curvilinear refinement.	Unity through large areas of a few materials treated naturally; straight lines predominate.
	Pronounced variety of size, shape, material, and ornament; decided contrast of scenic wall pattern.	Limited diversity—but strong and compelling; strong contrast of solidity and openness.
Balance	Symmetrical.	Asymmetrical.
Rhythm	Easy, graceful, and flowing but self-contained.	Strong and direct, angular, continuing from one object to another and beyond.
Emphasis	Many emphatic areas and small spots.	Emphasis is on whole or large units; almost no concentration in small areas.
Harmony	Consistency of all parts.	Consistency of all parts.
Proportion	Slender.	Blocky.
Scale	Small.	Large.

Design is a matter of relationships, and the aims and principles discussed are all concerned with the relationships among all the parts and the whole of the house. *Form follows function* describes the relation between total design and purpose; *variety in unity* deals with diversity as related to oneness; *balance, rhythm,* and *emphasis* refer to the ways in which various components are selected and related as means to equilibrium, continuity, and dominance and subordination. Considered together, they help us achieve beauty, and since they are guides rather than rules, offer ample opportunities to express individuality. At one time beauty was regarded as being closely akin to uselessness; individuality was associated with freakishness. Utility and economy, substantial practical partners, were on the other side of the fence. Such thinking was unsound: no one of our goals is at odds with the others; the design of our homes can relate utility, economy, beauty, and individuality—if the problem is grasped and solved realistically. But in this chapter the conscious concentration was on design for beauty.

A chest of drawers curves up from a capacious drawer at the bottom to progressively smaller ones at the top, with each drawer pull a sculptured fantasy. The designers, Fabio De Sanctis and Ugo Sterpini, have interpreted the traditional aims and principles in a fresh and imaginative manner. (*Photograph by Ferdinand Boesch. The Museum of Contemporary Crafts*)

An aerial view of the Château du Champs and its gardens, an eighteenth-century estate near Paris, shows a decisive, formal handling of space and form, line, texture, and enrichment. Bullet de Chamberlain, architect. (*Photograph by Aéro-Photo Paris*)

6 · Space and Form

Writers use words, mathematicians use numbers, and musicians use sounds to express their verbal, mathematical, and musical ideas. In home design the vocabulary is called the plastic elements. These include *space* and *form, line* and *texture,* which will be emphasized in this chapter. *Light* and *color* will be treated in Chapter 7. Much as such chemical elements as oxygen and carbon form the compounds of the physical world, the plastic elements comprise our visual environment. And they are the means through which designers, in accord with the aims and principles of design, create expressive beauty.

When architect Willis Mills designed his own home in New Canaan, Connecticut (Figs. 98A, B and 99A, B), he chose what many would call an unbuildable site, because there is a 45-foot drop between relatively level areas at the top and bottom. No ordinary house could have been built on this rocky hillside, which challenged him to design an exceptional house on three levels. Topography dictated that garage and entrance hall be on the top floor, which also seemed a logical level for a secluded two-bedroom-and-study unit high among the treetops. The living-dining area, the kitchen, and another bedroom were placed on the middle level, with good indoor-outdoor relationship provided by a large

97

A

B

A

Strict rectangularity of space and form unifies architect Willis Mills' own home in New Canaan, Connecticut. (*Photographs by Joseph W. Molitor*)

Above opposite. On level ground at the top of a steep site, the horizontal garage and bedroom unit is firmly anchored to the ground. Along the left side, a walk and a wood deck lead to the entrance.

Below opposite. Precise detailing of the structure heightens the drama of two-story windows, boldly cantilevered deck and terrace, and the plunging slope beyond.

Above. In the living room, the excitement of the hillside has been exploited by making its two-story height apparent from the entrance balcony, from which this photograph was taken, and by the tall, narrow corner window.

Right. The uncomplicated rectangles of the plan are orderly but functionally varied in size and shape. The diagonal balconies and terrace are welcome contrasts.

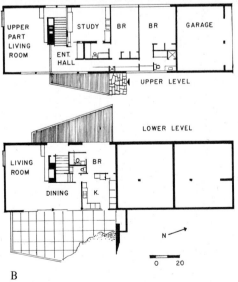

B

terrace toward the southeast and a small deck on the northwest. A gameroom and a heater room are in the "basement" that emerges above the ground toward the south.

Space, as far as the eye can see, is the chief element in the design, and it is fully exploited in the relationship of architecture to environment. As approached from the road, the house is seen as an unpretentious, one-story block. That this "block" is not a solid mass but a series of planes enclosing space is quietly stated: the side walls and roof project beyond the end wall, and the recessed end wall is painted in a contrasting color. This calm horizontality heightens the effect of what happens as one goes along a flagstone walk to a narrowing deck. In contrast to the security of stone set in the ground, this light wooden deck boldly projects into space as a series of planes. It becomes a movement into space inviting exploration. From it one's eyes can freely roam through the trees, up to the sky or down to the terrace and rocky hillside. Continued through a transparent plane of glass at a right angle, the deck becomes an entrance hall, which offers a momentary glimpse down into the two-story living room. Then comes a securely enclosed stairway. Near the bottom one can pause on a landing opening to the southwest deck, then turn and go down two steps to receive the full impact of the lofty living area. From here the spatial drama of the site is heightened by a two-story window wall facing the southeast terrace and by an unexpectedly tall window offering a close-up study of the trees to the south. The one-story dining alcove, recessed under the entrance hall, emphasizes through contrast the living room's height. Thus anyone coming into this home experiences a carefully planned sequence of spaces contrasting in size, shape, and direction, enclosed by opaque walls and expanded through glass to terraces and the landscape.

With the exception of the three diagonal decks and terrace, the space and form of this home are precisely rectangular. This rectangularity accentuates the irregularities of the site and carries forward a New England tradition of building on the square. The hillside suggests predominantly vertical forms, but these are counterbalanced by the horizontal decks and terraces. Although no detail imitates historical work, the forms are as simple and forthright as vernacular architecture in this region. No jogs or ornaments break the quiet unity of the flat enclosing surfaces. Here, though, similarity ends, for the disposition of forms is calculated to make space a free-flowing continuity rather than a series of rooms separated from one another and the site.

Line plays an active part in that it accentuates the dominant directions of the planes with which it is integral. One might first notice the pronounced vertical grooves in the natural redwood exterior, the linear thinness of wood and metal between planes of glass, which echo the slender vertical trunks of the surrounding trees. Strips of wood dividing the concrete terrace into squares perform numerous aesthetic functions: they relieve the monotony and humanize the scale of a large plane of concrete; they echo the rectangularity of the house; and they throw into relief the free curve of the flower bed, the natural shapes of rocks and plants.

Textures are sensitively employed. Basically, they show a limited range of varying degrees of smoothness—sanded redwood and white-wood trim, glass in sliding aluminum sashes on exterior, evenly surfaced plaster walls and wood floors inside. There are, however, contrasts. The smooth, precise restraint of the exterior is a foil for rocks and trees. Inside, textured rugs and upholstery

A screen, a desk, and a low table have been economically joined in one unit. Intersecting and projecting planes, clearly defined so that each one maintains its identity, let space flow through and around what might have been a bulky mass. (*Photograph by William Howland*)

plus shelves filled with books are sufficient punctuation in view of the landscape textures integrated with the interior by means of large areas of glass.

That refreshing organizations of space are not limited to new houses on acreage sites is illustrated in Figure 101. The problem faced by the occupants of this one-room apartment was that of segregating sleeping from living space without making confining cubicles. Their solution was a freestanding screen of perforated Masonite. On the bedroom side, a stock door veneered with Philippine mahogany makes an ample desk, while on the other side a similar door, at a lower height, forms a coffee table. In addition to its multiple usefulness, this piece of furniture activates a monotonous room. It is, in fact, almost a diagram of the visual and emotional impact possible to achieve with intersecting hovering planes, undisguised materials, and structure.

SPACE

Defined as the distance, void, or interval between things, space is the most vital plastic element in home design. Geoffrey Scott has described its importance in these words (from *The Architecture of Humanism*, Doubleday & Co., 1954, pp. 168–169):

. . . Architecture alone of the Arts can give space its full value. It can surround us with a void of three dimensions; and whatever delight may be derived from that is the gift of architecture alone. Painting can depict space; poetry, like Shelley's, can recall its image; music can give us its analogy; but architecture deals with space directly; it uses space as a material and sets us in the midst. . . .

But though we may overlook it, space affects us and can control our spirit; and a large part of the pleasure we obtain from architecture—pleasure which seems unaccountable or for which we do not trouble to account—springs in reality from space. Even from a utilitarian point of view, space is logically our end. To enclose a space is the object of building; when we build we do but detach a convenient quantity of space, seclude it and protect it, and all architecture springs from that necessity. But aesthetically space is even more supreme. . . . [The architect] designs his space as a work of art; that is, he attempts through its means to excite a certain mood in those who enter it.

Space suggests the possibility of change, freedom to move bodily, visually, or psychologically until we collide with or are averted by a barrier. For this reason, space, the least tangible plastic element, is nonetheless preeminent. We live *with* and move *around* form, but we live and move *in* space. As we move through such sensitively designed space as in the Millses' house, we participate in its expansion and contraction as naturally as we breathe. As we look at or walk around such furnishings as the space-divider, our eyes or maybe our hands and feet explore what is open and what is closed. Anyone who has ridden in a crowded car to a beach knows the sense of release afforded by getting out into expanses of sand, water, and sky. And no one can forget the deep breath and bodily stretch evoked by a larger segment of space after a long telephone conversation in a crowded booth. We adapt ourselves as well as we can to the space that envelops and includes us. In doing so, we share in its triumphs or its failures.

Some of the contemporary ways of enclosing space so that it liberates our spirits, is useful, and is economical are illustrated in an inexpensive tract house (Figs. 103A and B) that seems much more extensive than its actual dimensions.

First, large surfaces have been ordered into an unmistakable unity, strong and clear enough to be appreciated at once, yet with enough surprises to keep it interesting. Neither rigid nor static, this order emphasizes spatial continuity by encouraging one's eyes to roam freely in many directions—through the south window wall or the high and low glass to the west, up to the sloping ceiling, through and under the furniture.

Second, enclosing forms have been treated as planes, not solid masses, except for the sturdy brick fireplace. These planes preserve their independence through differing size, shape, direction, and material. From wall to wall, the floor is covered with a soft-textured carpet that is in friendly opposition to the surface qualities of glass, plaster, wood, and brick. It maintains its position as a stabilizing element. The ceiling, in contrast, expresses movement gently in its two sloping planes, dynamically in the ridge beam that accentuates the room's longer dimension. These rhythmic continuities are emphasized by the lively interplay of glass and wood in the west wall. The design of the west wall deserves special attention because it shows one of the most effective devices for opening interior space and relating indoors to outdoors. It is a screen of wood and glass against weather and visual intrusion rather than a wall in the conventional sense. Instead of tightly enclosing the wall toward the street from top to

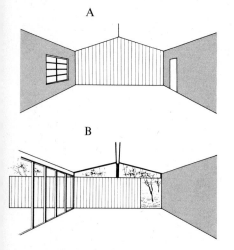

A

B

Top. A room seems small and confining when the openings are small and isolated and the corners tightly enclosed.
Above. The same room seems much larger if space is borrowed from outdoors. (*Walter Zowajski*)

A

Many devices make this small house in Wichita, Kansas, seem spacious beyond its actual dimensions. Harold Himes, architect.

Above. In the living-dining room, glass at the right and above the redwood screen wall balances the daylight and extends sight lines. The group-living space is visually and usably doubled by continuing the wall as a fence sheltering an outdoor terrace. (*Photograph by Julius Shulman*)

B

The efficiently zoned plan joins two protected outdoor-living areas to their enclosed counterparts.

bottom and from corner to corner, it stops short of the right corner and the ceiling and seems to interpenetrate the south window wall and continue as a protecting garden wall for the terrace. Its independence from the other enclosing planes is heightened by the use of a different material—redwood stained like driftwood and with pronounced vertical grooves. The carefully calculated yet unexpected high and low glass gives surprise and contrast of dark and light, and of up, across, and down movements. The difference from conventional planning is illustrated in the diagram at the bottom of page 102. Not only is space borrowed from outdoors, but the planes become active aesthetic forces rather than merely enclosing backgrounds.

Third, furniture selection and arrangement contribute handsomely to the whole effect. Furniture has been limited to a minimum to avoid an overcrowded feeling. Moderately small in size and in scale, chairs, tables, and the bench are simple but spirited in form. The coffee table is as steady and severely rectangular as the floor. The bench against the window wall is lighter and more active, as befits its location. The top is of spaced slats in keeping with the alternating solids and voids of the window wall, while the angles of the supports are similar to those in the ceilings. Showing their sculptural structure frankly, the chairs combine straight, angled, and curved forms. They were specifically designed to stand free in a room and, consequently, to be good looking from any

A

The Robie house, Chicago, is a magnificent example of masonry construction integrating space and form. It stands as a pioneer statement of concepts that are still being explored. Frank Lloyd Wright, architect. (*Photograph by Bill Engdahl, Hedrich-Blessing*)

Above. Seeming to hover above their flat, commonplace site, the horizontal planes extend out into space but are solidly anchored by the substantial central masses.

Below left. The major group-living space is on the second floor in order to gain light and views without loss of privacy. The way in which the living and dining areas, the billiard and children's rooms below, flow around the central fireplace-stairway core and out to terraces and gardens exemplifies Mr. Wright's mastery of unconstrained, fluent, continuingly varying space-form relationships.

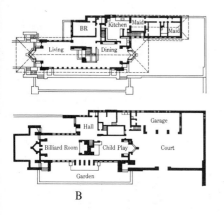

B

angle. All the furniture mentioned so far stands well off the floor on slender supports to allow unimpeded vision underneath. Only the sofa is bulky and enclosing. Appropriately placed against a solid wall, it contrasts with the airy furniture, as the fireplace does with the areas of glass.

Unprecedented in its imaginative boldness and still unsurpassed in its beauty, the Robie house (Figs. 104A and B), designed by Frank Lloyd Wright and built in Chicago in 1909, remains one of the greatest of contemporary homes. Although suffering the early ridicule that is the fate of most important advances in the arts, it has inspired and influenced domestic architecture in many .ways. Long before most architects and home builders had awakened to the fact that they were living in the twentieth century, Wright demonstrated a full realization of ways to create space-form relationships beautiful in themselves, expressive of modern technology, and, most important, of the life of the people who live in them.

Wright's conquest of space, as vital as any conquest in the sciences, resulted from an analysis and dissection of the stereotype house, a sorting-out and evaluating of its many components, and then a reorganization of them with expansive vitality. The open plan allows the space, intersected and shaped by vertical planes, to flow through the interior and out to the terraces and the garden. Windows in continuous bands become transparent planes for light and for outlook rather than isolated holes punched through walls. Cantilevered roofs projecting boldly beyond supporting walls temper the light, shelter the terraces, and stretch the house out into its surroundings. A spirited sequence of movement pervades every part of this composition because Wright handled the plan, the interior, the exterior, and the landscape as an organic entity.

FORM AND LINE

Defined as three-dimensional shape or structure, or as intrinsic character, **form** is the counterpart of space. Except for purposes of analysis and clarification, the two are inseparable, because form gives space whatever shape it has and space reveals, even determines, form. Usually, however, form seems more constant and permanent, whereas space implies the possibility of change. Two other terms associated with form deserve definition. *Area* refers to the two-dimensional extent of a shape, such as the floor area of a house or the wall area of a room. *Plane* is a two-dimensional shape, which in contemporary usage has come to imply a spatial form that is an active force, as the roof planes of the Robie house.

Line theoretically has but one dimension, although lines can actually be thick or thin. In interior design, line is frequently used to describe the outlines of a form or space, or the dominant direction, as when the "lines" of furniture or of houses are said to be pleasing, or horizontal. But line also can be used to ornament a form or to accentuate it. In fabrics (Fig. 110), wallpapers, or ceramics the ornamentation can be predominantly linear. In Figure 98B, the mass of the house is horizontal, but the grooves in the siding, the folds of the drapery, and the thin lines of the window mullions suggest vertical movement, reinforcing the dramatic height of the two-story window wall.

That forms and lines can be causative forces affecting our feelings is demonstrated in the living room corner shown in Figure 105. The horizontal

A corner of a living room designed by Bertha Shaefer in which diversified forms, each suited to its purpose, are sympathetically combined. (*M. Singer & Sons*)

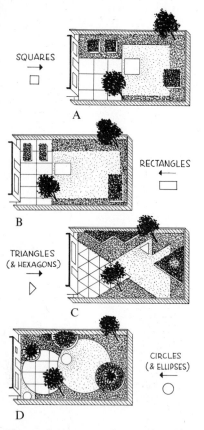

SQUARES →
□

A

RECTANGLES ←
▭

B

TRIANGLES
(& HEXAGONS) →
▷

C

CIRCLES
(& ELLIPSES) ←
○

D

The predominance of one geometric form unifies and gives decisive character to each of four garden plans. Diversified planting would satisfy the need for variety. (*Reprinted from* Sunset Ideas for Landscaping Your Home)

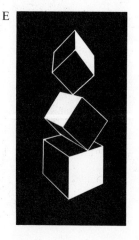

E

sofa and tables establish a dominant, easy repose. A markedly different kind of eye movement and feeling is induced when one looks at the counterbalancing, subordinate verticals. The folds of the draperies stand straight and tall, as does the sculpture in the corner. Less emphatically, the slender legs of sofa and nested tables, and the flowers in the vase, express an upright, stabilized resistance to gravity. A few diagonals and curves introduce needed diversity with their special expressive qualities. The most conspicuous diagonal is in the sofa, which is strengthened by the table behind it. Less immediately noticeable are the triangular, diagonally mounted legs of the coffee table, the outline of the lamp, the slight tilt of the sofa's end, and the casual placement of the book, magazine, and pillows. In varying degrees, these diagonals bring a greater feeling of activity than do either horizontals or verticals. The circular coffee table, with its rounded accessories, and the lamp bring the poised, unified fluidity inherent in circles and spheres. More active are the canoe-shaped braces supporting the glass tabletop. One has only to imagine this room with all possible forms horizontal or vertical, diagonal or curved to begin appreciating what each type of shape can contribute.

EXPRESSIVENESS OF FORM AND LINE

Forms, planes, and lines shape the space in which we live by defining its physical limits. Over and above their fundamental work in making our environment livable, these plastic elements have qualities that add to or detract from the beauty and individuality of homes. From these qualities, all parts of our homes derive much of their character, their emotional impact or mood. We shall look first at the expressive powers of shape, then of size and direction, and finally at a few of the effects produced by different relationships.

Shape

Stripped to essentials, space and form may be described as rectilinear, angled, or curved shapes. Although each of these categories has its own identity, there are no limits to the ways in which they can be varied (Fig. 107A–C) and combined for specific desired effects. They are fundamental in the "language of vision," as consequential in home design as they are in painting or sculpture.

In spite of its definiteness, **rectangularity** can encompass great diversity. *Cubes* can vary in size, color, or texture, and they can rest stably on one side, insecurely on one edge, or precariously on one corner (Fig. 106E). Each of these positions calls forth a different emotional response. Rectangular forms can do all this and also range in shape from linear thinness—as in the window frames of the Millses' house—to the almost cubical fullness typical of television receivers. If passive stability is wanted, cubes resting firmly on one side are a possibility; for a feeling of movement directed along one line, a slender rectangle may be the solution, as it was in the ceiling beam of the Kansas tract house.

That rectangularity is typical of the larger spaces and forms in homes today is evident in all but an outstanding few of the illustrations in this and preceding chapters. So general is this boxlike shape that we can only wonder why there is no single term to describe it, unless the word *room* has come to take on this meaning. It is prevalent not only in entire houses and rooms but in such furniture as beds, tables, storage units, and television sets, as well as

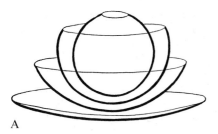
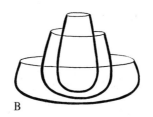

A   B   C

Curvilinear forms in glass or any other material can range from a globe to a disk, can taper toward a point or can spread outward. Each has its special expressive qualities. (*Steuben Glass*)

in many sofas, chairs, and benches. Among the reasons for this widespread acceptance, we might note that rectangles:

- Are easily handled on designers' drafting boards, by carpenters and masons on the site, and by machines in factories
- Fig snugly together—an important factor when multitudinous parts of buildings coming from many sources are assembled on the job and when space is becoming increasingly expensive
- Have a sturdy secure relationship of exactly 90 degrees, which gives a sense of definiteness and certainty
- Establish an incipient unity and rhythm when repeated

D

The qualities of clarity, stability, and certainty that combine to make rectangular forms favored also can give a harsh, boxlike monotony that many persons want to alleviate with other shapes and that some wish to avoid as much as possible. The right angle, though, has a pure, strong, absolute character—its own quality of beauty.

Triangular forms and pyramids differ from rectangles in their pointed, dynamic character (Fig. 107D), as do hexagons and octagons to a lesser degree. This difference can be readily seen in the garden plans or by comparing the Millses' and Reifs' living rooms (Figs. 99A and 119). Although from a structural point of view triangles are one of the most stable forms known (their shape cannot be altered without breaking or bending one or more sides), they express greater flexibility than rectangles because the angles can be varied to suit the need.

E

Used with discretion and in a large size, as in the ceiling of a living room (Fig. 103A) or the gable end of a pitched-roof house (Fig. 120A), triangles are secure yet dynamic. Small repeated triangles or diamond shapes in textiles, tiles, or wallpaper add briskness to interiors, while a three-sided table between two chairs sets up a congenial relationship. *Diagonals,* which are related to triangles, generally increase apparent size (Fig. 106C). Because these angular shapes imply motion and are relatively uncommon, they usually attract and hold attention beyond what their dimensions suggest.

Curved forms bring together the lively combination of continuity and constant change. They remind us sympathetically of flowers, trees, clouds, and our own bodies. Until recently large curvilinear elements, such as circular rooms, domed or vaulted ceilings, and curved stairways, have been rare in contemporary houses, but there is increasing interest in their possibilities. Notable exceptions are the Swiss living room (Fig. 108) and the houses designed by Frank Lloyd Wright, John Johansen, and Bruce Goff shown in Chapter 8. In gardens, however, curves are widely used (Figs. 97, 109, and 115).

Circles and *spheres* have a unique complex of qualities:

- They are man's and nature's most conservative and economical forms, since they not only enclose the greatest area or volume with the least amount of surface but strongly resist breakage and other damage.
- They are as rigidly defined geometrically as squares or cubes, but they do not seem so static, probably because we cannot forget that balls and wheels roll easily.
- They have an unequaled unity because every point on the edge or surface is equidistant from the center, which is a natural focal point, especially when accented.

Inside our homes, circles and spheres are usually most noticeable in plates, bowls and vases, lampshades and pillows, and in a few tables and stools (Fig. 105). They are also the basic motif in some textiles, wallpapers, and floor coverings.

Cones and *cylinders* indicate a definite, directional movement not found in circles, spheres, or cubes. Although cones and cylinders resemble each other, there is an important difference. Cones, like pyramids, reach toward a climactic, terminal peak, whereas cylinders, like rectangles, could continue forever. This makes cones more emphatic and directs attention to a focal point. Both are

Large curved forms are regrettably uncommon in homes but are often used in landscape design, as seen in the figures below and opposite.

In his own home in Switzerland, architect Karl Sherrer decided on a semicircular plan to take full advantage of sun and views as well as to achieve an effect of sweeping spaciousness. [*Photograph by Foto Koch. Reprinted from Winkler,* Haus des Architekten, *Verlag für Architektur* (*Artemis*), *Zurich* (*Edition Girsberger*)]

The swimming pool in a garden at Sonoma, California, is fluid and free-form in shape, suggesting the movement of water or of swimmers. Its smooth, flowing curves are quite unlike the irregular, almost angular ones of the trunk and branches of the foreground tree. Thomas Church, landscape architect. (*Photograph by Rondal Partridge*)

compatible to us because they are related to our own arms and legs. They are frequently used for the vertical supports of furniture, lamp bases and shades, candleholders and vases. Furniture legs of wood are often truncated cones, tapering toward the top or bottom for visual lightness and grace. Metal cylinders are also favored for furniture supports, because they are strong in relation to their weight and size, durable and easy to clean, and can be bent into pleasing curves.

Beyond strictly geometric curves are those inspired by nature, and with these the scope of expressiveness is enormous, as suggested by the textiles in Figs. 110A, B, and C. Reminiscent of the luxuriant tracery of plants growing naturally, "River Ferns" is unrestrained and relaxed. When hung in folds, this translucent textile elusively half-reveals the patterns behind it. The silk brocade is a sturdy, opaque cloth appropriately enriched with a vigorous, structural sequence of interlocking forms in tension. More systematic than "River Ferns" in its clear-cut repetition and progression, it is formal but not stiff. Nearly parallel lines that open and then close into dark areas give "Divertissement" a strongly directional, linear movement.

There are, of course, many other materials to which nongeometric curves are appropriate. They seem natural in landscape design (Fig. 109 and Chap. 19), are well suited to ceramics and glass (Chap. 9), and to some kinds of furniture, as illustrated by the chairs in Figures 99A, 101, 103A, and 117.

A   B   C

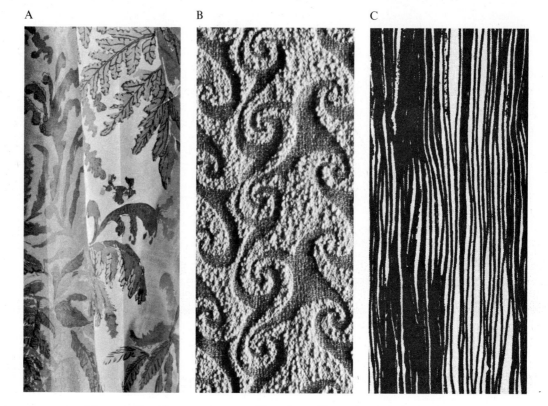

Three textiles illustrate the versatility of curvilinear forms and also the ways in which naturalistic, conventionalized, and abstract ornament differ from one another.

Left. The delicate, naturalistic, informal pattern of "River Ferns" seems to float on a sheer synthetic textile, appearing as unpremeditated as ferns growing beside a stream. (*J. T. Thorp & Company*)

Center. On a heavier silk brocade, the conventionalized curves are more deliberately controlled. They suggest the tentacles of a vigorous vine or of some types of sea life. (*Scalamandré Museum of Textiles*)

Right. Flowing smoothly over the surface of a linen textile, the elongated sinuous curves of "Divertissement" creates an abstract, up-and-down rhythmic pattern. (*Greeff Fabrics, Inc.*)

Size and Direction

Although the character of the form and space in our homes is most obviously established by their basic shapes, the expressiveness of these shapes is also dependent on their **size** and **direction**. In studying the ways in which these affect our feelings and our movements, psychologists and artists have come to such generalizations as the following:

- **Vertical** forms and lines express a stabilized resistance to gravity. If high enough, they evoke feelings of aspiration and ascendancy, as they do in the Millses' living room or the Port Royal parlor (Fig. 99A and Color Fig. 2).

- **Horizontals** tend to be restful and relaxing, especially when long (Fig. 98A). If short and interrupted, they become a series of dashes, as in the brick paving of the Mexican courtyard in Figure 115.
- **Diagonals** are comparatively more active because they suggest movement, as in the Reifs' home (Figs. 118 through 120B).
- **Big upward curves** are uplifting, as can be seen by the trees near the swimming pool in Figure 109.
- **Horizontal curves,** such as those that shape the pool, connote gentleness and relaxed movement.
- **Large downward curves,** seldom seen in homes, express a range of feelings, including seriousness and sadness.
- **Small curves** express playfulness and mirth (Fig. 117).

Verticals should be emphasized—high ceilings, tall doors and windows, or upright furniture—when a feeling of loftiness and cool assurance is desired. Emphasize horizontals—low ceilings, broad openings, and stretched-out furniture—for an impression of informal comfort. Emphasize diagonals—sloping ceilings or oblique walls or furniture—for an environment that suggests activity. Usually several or all of these shapes are brought together at varying levels of dominance and subordination so that the total effect seems varied and complete.

Relationships

The way in which any form or space is developed, and the environment in which it is seen, markedly affect its apparent size and shape, degree of dominance, and character. Although identical in outline, the rectangles in Figures 111A to F do not look the same because of the various patterns into which they have been divided. In Figure 117A the furniture in the alcove at the left looks smaller and less conspicuous because it is linked to the elaborate, predominantly vertical wall treatment. Similar furniture at the right (Fig. 117B), contrasting with its plain white background, stands out sharply and seems larger (even though it is somewhat dwarfed by the sizable painting. This point is also illustrated in Figure 111G and H.

Below left. A form gains importance when placed against a background that accentuates its character. (*Henrose*)

Below right. Combining a form with many similar forms makes it less noticeable as a unit but reinforces the "idea" of the shape. (*Rowen Inc.*)

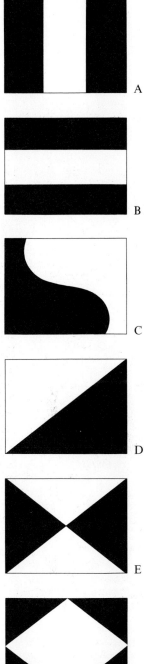

Above. That the character as well as the apparent size and shape of any form is in part determined by what happens within its outlines is demonstrated by six treatments of the same rectangle.

G

H

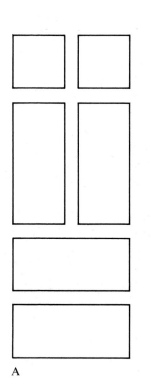

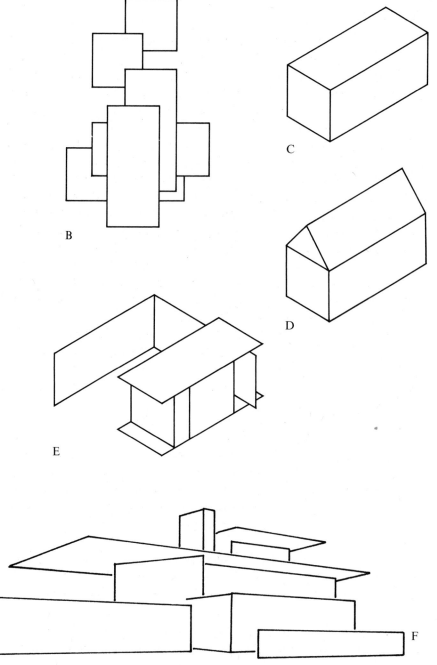

The way in which planes are organized determines their spatial effect. (*Walter Zowajski*)

Above. Six rectangles symmetrically placed with equal space between seem static and two-dimensional.

Top center. If they overlap one another, a suggestion of three-dimensionality results; also, an asymmetrical arrangement gives a greater sense of movement.

Top right. When put together as a box the six rectangles make an enclosed form with little feeling of space.

Middle right. Adding one more rectangular and two triangular planes permits a double-pitched roof, which gives more variety.

Middle above. Pulling the box apart lets space flow in and around the planes.

Above. The Robie house illustrates how planes can be organized in a dynamic complexity of space-form relationships.

Probably the most important changes brought about by different configurations is the organization of planes to shape space. They can be arranged to look like part of a flat surface, an enclosed box, a volume with sloping top and triangular holes in the ends, or a dynamic integration of continuing form and space (Figs. 112A through F).

Examples of these phenomena could be continued indefinitely, but these few should suffice to stress the tremendous consequence of relationships.

TEXTURE

Referring to the surface qualities of materials, texture describes how they feel when we touch them and how they affect the light that strikes them. Essentially, texture is a kind of ornament, but one that deserves special discussion because of its universality. Every surface has a texture that affects us physically and aesthetically, but it is only when it is consciously manipulated to beautify an object that we call it ornament. A distinction is often made between *actual,* or *tactile,* textures, in which the three-dimensional surface qualities can be felt, as in bricks and woolen tweeds or hammered metal, and *visual* textures (also called illusionary or simulated), in which a material reveals a textural pattern under a smooth surface. Sanded wood, polished stone, and many printed fabrics and synthetic floor coverings exemplify the latter. The effectiveness of a texture is again a matter of relationships between forms, colors, and textures themselves. A decided tactile texture will be more obvious against a uniform surface than it will against a rough one (Figs. 113A and B); even the relatively sleek textures of the gardens in the foreground of Figure 97 have more impact than the shaggy trees in the background, because they are contrasted with the smoothness and light color of the outlining paths.

The living room and garden (Figs. 114 and 115) show the vitality injected by surface qualities. In both, a wide range of appropriate textures contributes greatly to the total effect. In the living room the smoothest texture is in the glass of the window (not seen in this view); the roughest is in the rug. Between these extremes is a full scale—smoothly polished tables; walls, floors, and ceiling sanded and finished but not to a glossy sleekness; varied soft-surfaced upholstery; brick and metal-mesh fireplace screen; textured pottery, bronze urns, and books; and the flower arrangement, which although not rough gives a bold textural effect. Predominant in area are the walls and ceiling, with their moderately smooth surface but lively visual texture, against which the very rough and very smooth are accents. In the garden the textures form a series, from the vigorous roof tiles to the elusive smoothness of water in the pool.

Texture affects us in a number of ways, all of which are illustrated in the living room. *First,* it affects us physically in everything we touch. Upholstery fabrics, for example, if coarse and harsh can be actually irritating. If too sleek and shiny, they look and feel slippery and cold. Those most generally liked are neither excessively rough nor smooth. *Second,* texture affects light reflection and thus the appearance of any form. Very smooth materials—polished metal

 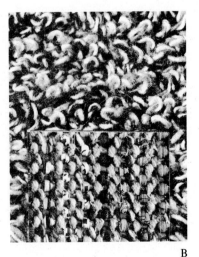

The impact of any texture is greatly affected by its background. (*Waite Carpet Company, Firth Industries, and Bigelow Rugs and Carpets*)

A   B

or satin—reflect light brilliantly, attracting attention and making their colors look clear and strong. Moderately rough surfaces, such as the brick at the fireplace or the pottery on the table, absorb light unevenly; hence their colors look less bright and darker. Very rough surfaces set up vigorous patterns of light and dark, as can be seen in the bands on the rug. *Third,* texture is a factor in household maintenance. The smooth, shiny surfaces of brightly polished metals are easy to clean but show everything foreign; rougher surfaces, such as bricks or rugs with high pile, call less attention to foreign matter but are harder to clean; and smooth surfaces with a visual textural pattern, of which naturally finished wood is an example, combine most of the good qualities of both. *Finally,* texture is a source of both beauty and individuality.

In this living room the natural textures of wood, bricks, textiles, and flowers enrich the simple forms. John Yeon, architect. (*Photograph by Maynard L. Parker Modern Photography*)

In a garden in Cuernavaca, Mexico, the dissimilar textures of brick and tile, water and stone, and of varied plants help define and enhance form and space with their interplay of contrasts. (*Reprinted from Verna Cook Shipway and Warren Shipway,* The Mexican House Old and New. *Copyright © 1960, Architectural Book Publishing Company, Inc.*)

ENRICHMENT OF FORM AND SPACE

Basic structural form (and its counterpart, space) is the taproot of beauty in most modern homes. Man, however, has usually felt a need to enhance basic structural form beyond the demands of use, economy, or structure—an observation to which the illustrations in this chapter are no exception. The living room corner in Figure 105 shows the major means to this end. First, all the *materials* chosen have inherent beauty, as exemplified in the grained wood of the nested tables. Second, the *processing* by which the raw materials were made useful has also endowed them with aesthetic appeal, as in the weave of the upholstery on the sofa. Third, *all shapes are refined* to make them visually attractive. This is evident in the handsome proportions of the sofa and lamp, the sculptural supports of the glass-topped table, and the sensitively scaled nest of tables. Finally, enrichment has been deliberately *applied* to the vase holding the tulips. All of these can be considered as ornament.

Sources and Types of Ornament

There are two major types of ornament: structural and applied. **Structural** ornament comes from the intrinsic character of the materials, the way in which they are fabricated, or the sensitivity with which the object and each of its parts is shaped. It encompasses such sources as:

- The natural beauty of the grain of wood or the qualities of silk or linen
- Textures and patterns originating in the weaving process or in the laying of a brick floor
- The deliberate designing and shaping of objects beyond utilitarian or structural demands so that they provide visual and tactile pleasure

Structural ornament is integral with the object it enriches; it seems natural and fundamental. Usually it is less subject to physical deterioration, such as breakage or fading, and it is less likely to go out of fashion than is applied ornament.

Applied ornament is that which is added to an object after it is structurally complete, such as patterns printed on cloth or wallpaper, carved moldings on walls, or designs etched on glass. Its range is limited only by the nature of the materials and by the imagination and taste of designers. It can be admirably suited to an object's use, basic form, and materials—or it can be distressingly inappropriate.

Ornament, but especially applied ornament, can be divided into three additional categories:

A. Naturalistic   B. Stylized   C. Abstract

Naturalistic ornament is representational. It arouses associations with the subject matter—flowers, fish, landscapes, and so on—and the subject matter becomes a major source of pleasure or displeasure. Also, the subject matter largely determines the ornament's character: it is difficult to make fish formal and impressive but easy to get that effect with irises or roses.

Stylized ornament relies on such devices as simplification and exaggeration, conventionalization and rearrangement to make natural rhythms more pronounced, to emphasize what is most important to the ornament's purpose, and to bring all into equilibrium. Stylized designs usually "wear better" than do the naturalistic type because they have been consciously planned to give lasting satisfaction. At best, stylized ornament penetrates the superficial surface aspects

A   B

French Rococo furnishings and wall paneling (early Louis XV, c. 1725–1759) have handsome basic forms enriched with delicate curvilinear ornament that rates very high on the criteria for ornament stated below. (*The Metropolitan Museum of Art, New York, Gift of J. Pierpont Morgan, 1907.*)

Above left. Seen against richly embellished architectural woodwork typical of the period, the pieces join forces with their setting in a vitally unified composition.

Above right. When placed against a plain white wall, the lighthearted yet ordered contours and carving are emphasized.

of nature to reveal more fundamental qualities; at worst, it merely substitutes smooth curves or meaningless angles for nature's complex richness.

Abstract ornament has been used throughout history whenever people wanted patterns that did not remind them strongly of something else. It is liked by many today because it is frankly what it is: man-made design for man's enjoyment. Also, abstract ornament is an excellent foil for natural forms—people, views into gardens, and live flowers. The three textiles in Figure 110 show each of these treatments developed into an appropriate pattern.

Criteria for Ornament

The most satisfying ornament fits the functions, form, size, and material of which it is a part, and is worthwhile in itself. More specifically:

- Ornament frequently touched should be pleasant to feel. Resting one's arms or back against sharp carving on a chair or handling sharp-cornered silverware can be physically uncomfortable.
- Ornament is usually at its best when it accentuates the form of which it is a part. The textural pattern of the sofa in Figure 105 underscores the basic shape, and the ornamental paneling of the alcove in Figure 117A adroitly fits its allotted space.

- Ornament should be related to the size and scale of the form. Large pieces of heavy pottery are suited to bold ornamentation; after-dinner coffee cups of porcelain are not.
- Ornament should be appropriate to the material. Fine, linear decoration can be effective on smooth, light-reflecting metal or glass (Chap. 9), whereas on wood it might look merely scratchy.
- Ornament should be vital in itself. Spirit and character are as crucial in ornament as they are in the design of form and space.

Attitudes toward ornament, especially toward applied ornament, vary from one period to another, as we shall see in Chapters 21 through 25. In historic homes and furnishings, however, man-made enrichment was an integral component, as is shown in the Rococo wall paneling and furniture in Figure 117. In the nineteenth and twentieth centuries, regard for embellishment has varied markedly. To many Victorians, ornament was synonymous with beauty, and in satisfying their craving for decoration, they reduced form and space to minor roles. Toward the end of the nineteenth century some architects, designers, and craftsmen became interested in unelaborated forms that candidly revealed the materials used and the way in which they were handled. The Craftsman style in architecture, Mission furniture, the Art Nouveau style, and the Arts and Crafts movement are examples. In our century individuals and groups, such as the Bauhaus Institute in Germany, experimented with the precision and simplicity that they, rightly or wrongly, deemed most expressive of machine technology, but they did not ignore the handcrafts. Recently there has been a growing need for something beyond austerity and a realization that both struc-

In the four following figures space, form, and line have been used to open up and expand a small house on a narrow lot, creating long vistas and interesting angles. The chief sources of enrichment are the textures of materials and of plants. Aaron Green, architect. (*Photographs by Maynard L. Parker Modern Photography*)

The entrance loggia, with glass and planting on both sides, leads into the living room and out onto the terrace. Although small and in the center of the house, it seems open and cheerful because space and light have been borrowed from all sides.

The living room has been boldly conceived, from the commanding mass of the fireplace to the delicacy of the mitered window corner that brings unexpected light and color into the space.

tural and applied ornament have their place. This has resulted in a search for enrichment that humanizes our environment without detracting from the primary importance of space and form.

SPACE, FORM, AND ENRICHMENT IN A SMALL HOUSE

The problems put before architect Aaron Green by the Reif family were notably dissimilar from those faced by Willis Mills as discussed at the beginning of this chapter. A long, narrow and almost flat city lot, measuring 50 by 100 feet and hemmed in by neighbors, offered little beyond a convenient location and a few trees. A modest budget added to the challenge of designing a house that seems much larger than its 1650 square feet of enclosed space. Green's ingenious solution (Figs. 118 through 120B) has a richness of interest that belies its basic simplicity.

Access to main and service entrances is afforded by an integrated walk, driveway, and carport. Economically and interestingly planted with ground cover, the front yard is the first step in a sequence of scale from the street into the house. The entrance walk, paralleling driveway and carport but differentiated from both by two planting beds, goes between kitchen and bedroom wings directly to the center of the house. Although straight, it is not dull. A few feet from the public sidewalk several steps introduce the diagonal motif that runs through house and landscape. It also modestly introduces the rhythmic, four-dimensional, organically expanding and contracting treatment of form and space. The unassuming front yard contracts to a small entrance garden as one is passing under an extension of the low carport roof. Briefly, one sees the sky through a trellis that brightens the narrowed space, then the entrance garden widens for a few feet.

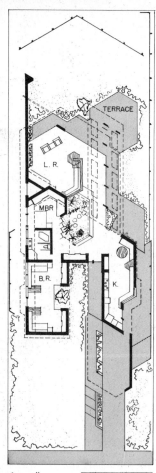

Above. The terrace serves as another room of the house—private, pleasant, and weather-wise. It is roofed partly by sky and trees, partly by the extended roof of the house. It is screened by fencing and a projecting wall of the house, and is paved with concrete.

Left. The plan is an ingeniously unified complex of diagonals and right angles, compact but not restricting, and above all, beautiful.

Once the main door is opened, three vistas appear (but none of these destroys the privacy of any room). Straight ahead one's eyes can travel through the loggia to within a few feet of the back property line. To the right a glass door leads diagonally to a dining terrace. To the left, windows above low bookshelves let one enjoy the tiny garden court, important far beyond its 9-by-17-foot dimensions. The glass-walled, skylighted loggia is more than a hallway, serving as it does for book storage and then widening into a music center as it nears the living room and terrace.

The kitchen, imaginatively planned for convenience and pleasantness, has a laundry and "decontamination" area near carport and service yard; it widens into the food-preparation zone and space for dining adjacent to an outdoor-eating terrace. The compact master bedroom gets light and air from two opposite sides without sacrificing seclusion and has a private door into the compartmentalized bathroom. The second bedroom, illumined and ventilated from four directions, provides two corners for bed-sofas integrated with desks, bookshelves, and storage. Dressing areas for each person are segregated by the indented bay that also added shape interest to the entrance garden.

B ← N   5 0   10   20

The Port Royal parlor (1762) is a formal eighteenth-century American room of the Colonial Georgian period. Furniture made in Philadelphia in the Chippendale style, a brilliantly colored English rug, French silk draperies and upholstery, and English cut-glass chandeliers and wall lights combine to produce hospitable elegance. The warm gray walls are subordinate to the furnishings, but the design of the projecting fireplace creates an important focal point. (*Photograph by Gilbert Ask. Henry Francis du Pont Winterthur Museum*)

5

6

A living room in White Plains, New York, is a striking example of contemporary freedom of taste. The strongly defined architectural background of pure white walls, a lofty natural wood ceiling, and a cork floor do full justice to the inspired furnishings. The red rugs, blue ottomans, and the light yellow-green and deep-violet upholstered seats are all of highly saturated colors and sharply defined form. Contemporary paintings are at home with the spirited furniture as well as with primitive sculpture and accessories from many parts of the world. Milo Baugham, designer. (*Photograph* © *Maris, Ezra Stoller Associates*)

The living room seems spaciously elastic yet intimate and secure, a paradoxical combination of qualities produced by the subtle handling of form, line, space, and texture. First, and most important, is the room's shape. The asymmetric, hexagonal plan is less constricting than the typical rectangularity yet gives a sense of trustworthy security. The slope of the ceiling opens the room upward, a movement that is both accentuated and steadied by the heavy beams. Second is the way in which the walls are opened with glass and closed with masonry. The massive fireplace wall, joined with built-in sofas and tables around three sides of the space, is a solid haven that contrasts with the four views of different magnitude and character that the room offers. The northeast window wall reveals a small segment of the yard secluded by a fence that is a continuation of the room's north wall. A larger expanse of glass facing southeast is oriented toward the living terrace and a far corner of the property. Over the sofa one can see the garden on the south through the loggia, and around the corner is an intimate glimpse into the garden court. Third, line and texture underscore the organization of form and space. Notice how the grooves in the ceiling and the joints in the mortar emphasize the shape and direction of ceiling and fireplace; how the smooth concrete floor and the concrete band above the fireplace-opening key up the masonry textures.

Throughout the house, enrichment seems natural and unaffected: in the texture and color of concrete and brick, wood and glass, pile rugs, woven upholstery, books, and ceramic objects. Everywhere there are growing things in infinite variety of shape and texture: in vases, pots, or planting pockets, indoors and out, and in almost every direction one would look.

CONCLUSION

How to enclose space inexpensively and well has always been a fundamental problem of architecture, and it has seldom been more acute than today with the current high cost of construction and maintenance. This has focused attention on ways of increasing the apparent size of homes, a matter that has been detailed in relation to specific examples but that deserves a brief summary. A sense of spaciousness is gained if the architect and designer have:

- Established a strongly ordered unity accentuated by purposeful surprises, such as the tall window in the Millses' living room
- Emphasized spatial continuity with many and varied vistas for the eyes to explore, as in the Reifs' home
- Treated form as simple and continuous planes that are carried beyond expected stopping points, and constructed them of contrasting materials to maintain their independence
- Accentuated the major direction of shapes—the vertical siding of the Millses' house, the ceiling beam in the tract house, and the pattern of brick in the Reifs' fireplace
- Limited furnishings to those really needed, selected pieces moderately small in size and scale, and arranged the larger ones against walls
- Kept a dominance of small-scale, unobtrusive textures and patterns with a few marked contrasts
- Employed such illusionistic devices as mirrors, paintings with deep perspective, or appropriate scenic wallpapers

The Reifs' home and the other examples shown in this chapter demonstrate the union of order and imagination that characterizes the best contemporary design. Each has a clearly expressed systematic and structural unity growing out of the specific human needs it serves, the environment in which it stands, and the materials from which it was constructed. Equally significant, each expresses the sensitivity and individuality of its designer and owner more fundamentally through relationships of space and form than through any other aspect.

Benches and boxes of marine plywood, painted with eye-dazzling designs in brilliant colors, combine simplicity of form with intricate ornament. William Bell, designer. (*Bell Designs, Inc.*)

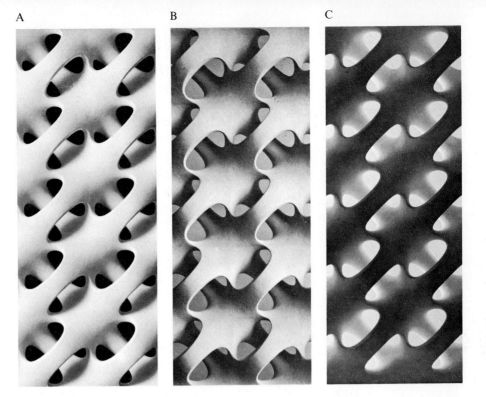

Three views of one of Erwin Hauer's sculptural grilles show how markedly lighting can affect appearances. Direct front lighting (*left*) tends to flatten an object, to minimize shadows. Side lighting (*center*) emphasizes three-dimensionality. Back lighting (*right*) flattens but dramatizes forms.

7 · Light and Color

Light and color are as inseparable as space and form. Without light there is no color, and light is always colored. The world is made visible through light entering our eyes, and from sight we derive more of our understanding than from all other senses combined.

Although color has long been considered a fundamental of home design, only recently have we become fully aware of its potentialities beyond mere pleasantness or unpleasantness, important as these may be. Even more revolutionary are the developments in home lighting—but we are anticipating the discussion of natural lighting in Chapter 12 and of artificial illumination in Chapter 15. Here we simply introduce the subject of light to emphasize its importance as one of the major plastic elements.

LIGHT

Light is a form of energy, a force to which we react immediately, although often subconsciously. Our reactions are a complex of physical and psychological responses as yet imperfectly understood. Physicists, though, know these facts:

123

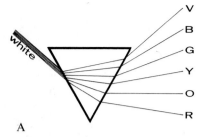

A

When white light is passed through a prism, the component colors are separated into clearly distinguishable bands.

- Light varies amazingly in brightness, the light from strong sunlight being approximately 400,000 times that from the full moon and 1,000,000 times that from a star.
- White, or apparently colorless, light is composed of all the hues of the spectrum (Fig. 124A).

What happens when light hits something varies:

- It may be reflected, absorbed, or allowed to pass through, depending on the degree of transparency or opacity of the material and on its surface qualities.
- Light reflected from such smooth surfaces as metal is bright and sharp, diffuse when reflected from rough surfaces, such as brick.

The appearance of objects is greatly affected by the kind of light that makes them visible:

- Objects illumined by small, sharp light sources show strong contrasts of light and dark, less contrast if the light source is broad and diffuse, and almost no contrast if evenly lighted from all sides.
- Shadows from objects lighted by small, sharp beams are usually hard, sharp, and dark, soft and spread out if the light source is broad and diffuse, and multiple and overlapping if the light comes from more than one direction.
- The shape of objects can be emphasized or subordinated by the direction from which the light comes (Figs. 123A through C).

Perhaps most important is how lighting affects us:

- Contrasts of brightness and darkness are emphatic and dramatic (Fig. 124B); uniform lighting is good for many kinds of work but is also monotonous.
- Bright light is stimulating; low levels of illumination are quieting.
- Warm-colored light is cheerful; light that is cool in color is restful.

B

The low oblique rays of the setting sun create an atmosphere of drama and mystery in the Staehelin residence in Felomeilen, Switzerland. Unexpected aspects assume importance: elongated shadows, sharp silhouettes, and the rough, striated texture of the floor. This is markedly different from the even, front illumination in Figures 129A and B. Marcel Breuer, architect. (*Photograph by Lucien Clergue*)

124

■ Efficient light illumines what we see but does not intrude on our vision. Some lighting fixtures, however, may be decorative features.

COLOR

Like design, color is important only as it affects our living. That it can be influential, for better or for worse, has been proved countless times. Such phrases as "functional color" and "color conditioning" describe its use in business for increased pleasantness and efficiency. In the theater the emotional effects of color have long been exploited. Color can work similar magic in homes. With receding colors or appropriate contrasts, the apparent size of a room can be markedly increased. Ceilings can be made to seem higher or lower with a coat of paint. Where there is no sunlight, its effects can be simulated with yellow walls, and excessive brightness or glare can be reduced with cool, darkish surfaces (Color Fig. 19). Some or all furnishings can be brought into prominence (Color Fig. 2) or allied with their background by the use of color (Color Fig. 1). In short, color can markedly alter the appearance of form and space.

The color of an object that we see results from two factors: the way in which the object absorbs and reflects light and the kind of light that makes the object visible. When light strikes an opaque object, some of its hues are absorbed and others reflected. Those that are reflected give the object its color quality. Lemons and yellow paint, for instance, absorb almost all hues except yellow. White objects reflect almost all the hues in light, while black objects absorb most of them. We say *almost* because pure colors are very seldom found. The true color quality of anything is revealed when it is seen in white light. Usually, however, light is not completely colorless.

The color of light depends on its source and whatever it passes through before coming to our eyes. White, or apparently colorless, light, such as that from the noon sun, contains all the spectrum's hues—violet, blue, green, yellow, orange, and red—balanced and blended so that the effect is colorless. Light from the moon is bluish, while that from open fires, candles, and the typical incandescent light bulb is yellowish. Incandescent and fluorescent lighting, however, come in many colors, and we can choose those that are most effective. We can also alter the color of artificial light with translucent shades that are not white; and daylight can be changed with thin, colored curtains. In general, warm light intensifies red, yellow, and orange and neutralizes blue and violet. Light that is cool and bluish does the opposite.

Color Theory: The Brewster System

Organizing facts and observations on color into a systematic theory is the first step in understanding color relationships and effects. Three different kinds of theories have been developed: physicists base theirs on light, psychologists on sensation, and artists on pigments and dyes. Our interest is chiefly with the last, but even here a choice must be made among the accepted pigment theories. We will follow that developed by Sir David Brewster, whose concept is often called the *three primary*—or *red, blue,* and *yellow*—pigment theory, because it is the simplest and most familiar and leads to effects indistinguishable from those growing out of more complex systems. Two other well-known systems, those of Munsell and Ostwald, are briefly described on pages 135–137.

The Three Dimensions of Color

To describe any color accurately you need to tell something about each of its three major characteristics, which can be diagrammatically visualized and which should be memorized.

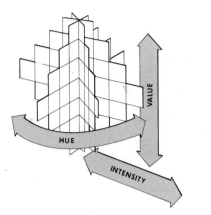

The three dimensions of color can be illustrated by a "color solid," which is often represented as a series of planes. Pure hues are shown on the outer edges. Value is represented on the vertical axis, going from the lightest at the top to the darkest at the bottom. Maximum intensities occur on the periphery and become increasingly neutralized approaching the main axis.

HUE indicates the **color's position in the spectrum** and in the **color wheel** (Fig. 124A and Color Fig. 7). It also indicates a color's **warmth** or **coolness**—red seems warm, blue seems cool, and green looks intermediate. It is typically thought of as the **name** of a color, such as orange, blue-violet, or yellow-green.

VALUE describes the **lightness** or **darkness** of a color, the **quantity of light reflected or transmitted.** White is the lightest value, black the darkest; between these extremes are many value steps. Red can be as dark (as it is in maroon), as light (as in pink), or as any value step between.

INTENSITY refers to the **degree of purity, strength, or saturation** of a color. This is determined by the **quantity of the predominant hue.** Pure red, such as scarlet, is saturated with red. Old rose is noticeably grayed, and pink is much diluted, so that both give the sensation of only a little redness.

We can see how hue, value, and intensity work together when we list brief descriptions of four reds, yellows, and greens.

Color Name*	Hue	Value	Intensity
Artillery	red	middle	full
Peach blossom	red	high light	one-third intensity
Harvard crimson	red	dark	two-thirds intensity
African brown	red	low dark	two-thirds neutral
Chrome lemon	yellow	high light	full
Cream	yellow	high light	two-thirds intensity
Buff	yellow	low light	two-thirds intensity
Olive green	yellow	dark	two-thirds neutral
Peppermint	green	middle	full
Seafoam	green	low light	full
Apple green	green	low light	two-thirds intensity
Evergreen	green	low dark	two-thirds neutral

*Color names that do not refer specifically to hue, value, and intensity are subjective and will change with the times.

In this chart we can see that artillery is full-intensity red. Peach blossom is diluted red, which makes it lighter and less saturated; Harvard crimson has been darkened and somewhat neutralized by the addition of black. African brown is still darker and less pure. Chrome lemon is fully saturated and light in value; cream is also light in value but slightly grayed, and olive green is still basically yellow but very dark and neutral.

HUE: THE POSITION OF A COLOR IN THE SPECTRUM

Notice that the color wheel has the same progression of hues as in the spectrum, but that they are bent into a circle, and the two end colors are combined to make red-violet, a color not in the spectrum. The twelve hues on the color wheel can be divided into three categories:

- **Primary hues,** labeled **1,** are red, blue, and yellow. They are called primary because they cannot be produced by mixing other hues. Mixtures of them will produce nearly every other hue, but with today's pigments, which are not 100 percent pure, these mixtures will be more or less neutralized.
- **Secondary, or binary, hues,** labeled **2,** are green, violet, and orange. Each stands midway between the two primary hues: green is equidistant from blue and yellow; violet from red and blue; and orange from red and yellow.
- **Tertiary, or intermediary, hues** are yellow-green, blue-green, blue-violet, red-violet, orange-red, and yellow-orange. Labeled **3,** these stand midway between a primary and a secondary hue. Yellow-green is between the primary hue yellow and the secondary hue green.

Hues are *actually* changed, or new ones produced, by combining neighboring hues as indicated above. Red, for example, becomes red-violet when combined with violet. If more violet were added, the hue would be changed again. The twelve hues on the color wheel are only a beginning, because there can be an almost infinite number of hues. Light and background can also lead to *apparent* changes. Cool light will make any hue seem bluer, while warm light does the opposite. Backgrounds are equally important: red placed against cool blue or green seems warmer than when seen against orange or red-violet.

Effect of Hues on One Another

When placed next to one another, hues produce effects ranging from harmony to decisive contrast. Some combinations, such as blue, blue-green, and green, give a harmonious, restful sequence. But if blue is put next to orange, there is excitement and contrast. Looking at the color wheel, we can see that hues adjacent to each other are harmonious, those opposite each other are contrasting. Two adjectives are used to describe these relationships:

- **Analogous hues** are adjacent to each other on the color wheel, as are yellow, yellow-green, and green.
- **Complementary hues** lie directly opposite each other, as do yellow and violet, red and green, and blue and orange.

Hues can be combined to produce any degree of harmony or contrast. If only one hue is used in a room, a marked unity results. If *analogous* hues are placed next to each other, the effect is one of harmonious sequence. When actually mixed together, or when small spots of each are intermingled, they create another hue.

Complementary hues, when placed next to each other, contrast vividly, and each color seems to gain intensity if the area of each hue is large enough to be perceived as a separate color (Color Fig. 8B). But if the areas of two complementary hues are very small, as in Color Figure 8A or in a textile woven of fine red and green yarns, the effect at normal distances is lively but more neutralized. And if opposites are mixed together, a brownish gray is likely to be the result.

Thus, many effects may be created with hues, ranging from strong contrasts to soft harmonies. Place sizable areas of orange against blue, red beside green, or yellow-green adjacent to red-violet and there are lively opposition, vibration and excitement, and also well-rounded balance. A combination of blue, blue-green, and green tends to be more restful, because these hues are both related and cool. Yellow, yellow-orange, and orange introduce no sharp conflict, but their harmony is more active than is true of the cooler hues.

Warmth and Coolness of Hues

Each hue has its own "temperature" that affects us and our homes in several ways. Red, orange, and yellow seem warm and active, and they tend to bring together whatever is seen against them. They are called *advancing* hues because they seem nearer to us than they actually are, which leads to two seemingly paradoxical results. Upholstering furniture in intense red increases its apparent size, but painting the walls of a room red decreases its apparent spaciousness because the walls will seem closer (Color Fig. 10). Blue, green, and violet tend to seem cool and restful. Because they appear to be farther away than they actually are, they are referred to as *receding* hues (Color Fig. 19). They reduce the apparent size of objects, but when used on walls they seem to increase a room's dimensions. Yellow-green and red-violet are intermediate.

A too-cold north room can be cheerfully warmed with yellow walls, brown rugs, and orange upholstery. Blues, greens, and violets, especially if light in value and low in intensity, will make a room seem cooler, quieter, and larger. Typical miscellaneous furnishings are likely to seem more related to one another against warm-colored walls than against cool ones unless the objects are predominantly cool in hue. Shapes, especially outlines of objects, are emphasized when object and background contrast in hue, an observation that can be checked by placing a green dish against a blue or green background and then against one of yellow or orange. These are but a few of the ways in which hues can change our surroundings.

A predominance of light values and low intensities plus an abundance of daylight brought in through large areas of glass on three sides make the space in a Los Angeles living room seem large, open, and airy. The opaque walls are of plaster painted white and off-white, with a few panels painted brown for contrast. Lustrous light-gray vinyl on the floor reflects most of the light that hits it. The high vaulted ceiling, sheathed in light natural wood, resembles a tent canopy rather than a tight-fitting lid. The fireplace, the curtains, and the lampshade are white. The clear pastel tones of yellow and coral upholstery contribute to the festive atmosphere. The black fireplace box, the dark window frames, and the black iron chair legs heighten the buoyant luminosity through opposition. With such large windows the blue of the sky and the varied greens of the evergreen foliage outside become an integral part of the color scheme. Smith and Williams, architects. (*Photograph by Julius Shulman*)

128

VALUE: THE LIGHTNESS OR DARKNESS OF A COLOR

The rooms shown in Figures 128 and 129A and B differ markedly in their value patterns. In the California living room all major areas that we can see—ceiling, walls, curtains, and floor—are very light and reflect the abundant daylight brought in through the large windows. The somewhat darker furniture and the very dark fireplace opening and trim around the windows emphasize through contrast the feeling of airy spaciousness and gaiety. Quite different is the Queen Anne living room, in which floor, walls, and furnishings are moderately dark, the effect warm and enclosing, restful and reposed. Lighter curtains, lighter picture and mirror frames, and the patterned rug and upholstery bring variety. The Mexican room has strong, abrupt contrasts of very dark ceiling beams, window frames, and books against the stark white walls and rug, an effect that is repeated in small scale in the sofa's upholstery. Intermediate values occur in the floor, chairs, and tables. *Animated, energetic,* and *vivid* are some of the adjectives that describe the total effect. These rooms and Color Figures 1, 2, and 3 show that strikingly different effects can be created with value alone.

Below left. The most important factor in this Queen Anne room (1717–1720) is the color of the oak walls and floor: a low-intensity orange of middle to darker values. This makes them seem closer than they actually are, an effect accentuated by the paneling of the walls, the parquet pattern in the floor, and the subtle variations in wood grain and color. The monochromatic scheme is based on the natural colors of oak together with the colors of walnut and mahogany in the furniture, but there are also many contrasting elements. The ceiling is white, and the draperies and the picture and mirror frames are much lighter in value. The boldly patterned Oriental rug introduces pronounced contrasts of light and dark as well as many rich, intense colors. Similar in its effect but less pronounced is the multicolored upholstery on the sofa. Although sparsely furnished, the overall effect is welcoming and homelike. (*The Minneapolis Institute of Arts. Gift of Mrs. John Washburn and Elizabeth Washburn*)

A

B

Right. Mexico is noted for its startling contrasts, a characteristic evident in this home in Cuernavaca. The strong opposition of dark brown structural posts and beams against white walls focuses attention on the room's rugged architectural quality. The smooth white plaster walls accentuate the shapes of the dark wood furniture, provincial versions of eighteenth-century styles, and also permit enjoyment of the intricate forms of the handsome metal-and-glass hanging lantern. Other noticeable areas of white are in the two lampshades and the rug. At smaller scale, these opposites (together with a few intermediates) are combined in the bookshelves, the books, and the colorful ceramics. Bluish flagstones on the floor and pinkish-red tiles between the ceiling beams are the only large middle-value areas. This is a bold room in which everything is a decisive statement. There was no need to follow a standard color scheme. Fendall Gregory, architect. (*Reprinted from Verna Cook Shipway and Warren Shipway,* The Mexican House Old and New. *Copyright © 1960, Architectural Book Publishing Co., Inc.*)

The value steps between black and white can be as numerous as you wish, but the seven intervals shown in Color Figure 7 are a convenient number, and they correspond to the *normal values* (the value at which each hue can reach its greatest saturation or intensity) of the hues in the color wheel. Starting at the top and going down either side we get:

Hue	*Value Step*	*Hue*
Yellow	High light	Yellow
Yellow-orange	Light	Yellow-green
Orange	Low light	Green
Red-orange	Middle	Blue-green
Red	High dark	Blue
Red-violet	Dark	Blue-violet
Violet	Low dark	Violet

A gray value scale shows how greatly the appearance of anything is affected by its background. The gray circles are actually identical.

Although every hue can range in value from high light to low dark, we tend to think of hues at their normal values. Yellow, for example, comes to mind as the color of a lemon or dandelion rather than of an olive-drab uniform. Violet suggests the dark color of violets, grapes, or plums. *Tints* are values lighter than normal; *shades* are values darker than normal. Pink is a tint of red, maroon is a shade of the same hue. Sky blue is a tint, navy blue a shade.

Values are changed by making them reflect more or less light. With paints, *actual* changes are made by adding black, gray, or white; any colors lighter or darker than the original; or hues that are complements of the basic color. *Apparent* changes can be made by reducing or raising the amount of natural or artificial light reaching a surface, or by placing it against backgrounds of differing degrees of light or dark (Fig. 130).

Values affect one another much as hues do—contrasts accentuate differences. We have seen that the same gray looks much darker when seen against a light surface than when seen against black. The same holds true for values of any hue.

INTENSITY: THE DEGREE OF PURITY AND SATURATION

Any hue can vary in its purity or strength or, in other words, in the degree to which it differs from gray. Pink, for example is always red in hue and light in value, but it can be *vivid*, almost *pure* pink or it can be *neutralized*, grayed pink. This is called intensity.

Scales of intensity can have as many or as few steps as one wishes. In the intensity scale (Color Fig. 7), there are four steps: **full intensity, two-thirds intensity, two-thirds neutral,** and **neutral.** Full intensities, which are possible only at the normal value of each hue, are often described as *high* or *strong*, the more neutralized as *low* or *weak*.

Intensities can be *actually heightened* by adding more of the dominant hue. They can also be *apparently raised* by illuminating the object with light of that hue or by throwing it into contrast with its complementary hue, a grayed tone of the hue, or a completely neutral color. A wall of grayed yellow can be intensified by repainting it with a purer yellow, by casting yellowish light on it, or by placing chairs in front of it that are upholstered in either violet, a less intense yellow, or gray.

Actual and *apparent* intensities can be *decreased* in several ways. First is to lessen the amount of the dominant hue by adding varying amounts of its complementary hue, as has been done in the intensity scale: yellow is grayed by adding violet, violet by adding yellow, blue by adding orange, and so on. A similar effect is produced by mixing a color with black, gray, or white. Second is to illuminate any object with light of the complementary hue. A blue wall, for example, would be grayed during the day by sheer, orange-tinted glass curtains and at night by translucent lampshades of the same hue. A third device is introducing something—a painting, a wall hanging, a chair, or a sofa— that is noticeably more intense in color than is the wall. This apparent change is most pronounced if the object and the wall are of the same or similar hues.

A great deal can be learned about the qualities of hue, value, and intensity by analyzing the color organizations that you see in rooms, furniture and textiles, and gardens. Trying a few simple experiments will give you firsthand information. Mixing different hues will show you how they change, and you can experiment with neutralizing them with complementary hues or with black, white, or gray.* They can also be diluted with a suitable colorless thinner. With construction paper or textile samples you can see what happens to the apparent hue, value, and intensity of any color when it is placed against varied backgrounds or is illuminated by different amounts and colors of light.

EFFECTS OF HUE, VALUE, AND INTENSITY

Generalizations about color relationships and their effects are well worth knowing, although we should be aware that none of them always holds true.

How do colors affect our feelings and activity? Warm hues, values lighter than the middle range, and high intensities tend to raise our spirits and stimulate us to be active (Fig. 128 and Color Figs. 5 and 10). Pronounced contrasts of any sort, such as blue-green and red-orange (Color Fig. 8B) or deep brown and white (Fig. 129B) have similar effects. Intermediate hues, values around the middle range, and moderate intensities are relaxing and undemanding (Fig. 129A and Color Fig. 4). Cool hues, values below the middle range, and low intensities usually seem quiet and subdued (Color Fig. 13). There are, of course, innumerable other ways of selecting and organizing varied hues, values, and intensities to achieve the effect that is desired. You could, for example, bring together warm hues, middle values, and low intensities or any other pattern that is appropriate (Color Fig. 3).

What colors and combinations attract our attention? Any degree of dominance or subordination can be produced by skillful handling of color. We are immediately attracted by colors that are striking and bold, and these may be

---

*Changing any one dimension of a color almost inevitably changes the other two, at least slightly. Available pigments are almost never absolutely pure: grays, blacks, and whites tend to be either warm or cool and thus alter the hue with which they are mixed. It is possible to change intensity without altering value *if* you use a gray or complementary hue that absolutely matches the color's value, but this is seldom achieved. One of the dimensions can be modified much more than the other two, but it is extremely difficult to change one and hold the others constant.

indicated where dominance is wanted (Color Fig. 2). Extreme values and strong intensities also tend to attract attention, but no more so than emphatic contrasts or unexpected, out-of-the-ordinary color relationships (Color Fig. 5). Colors that are grayed and moderate in value as well as any familiar color combinations are unemphatic and seldom noticed, which makes them passive backgrounds unless they are interestingly textured or otherwise patterned (Color Fig. 13). Thus with color alone attention can be directed toward that which is important and away from that which is less consequential.

How do colors affect apparent size and distance? The degree to which color can seem to alter the size of any object and its distance from the observer is often dramatic, but this too is a matter of complex relationships. In general, warm hues, values above the middle range, and strong intensities make an object look large. Cool hues, darker values, and lower intensities reduce its apparent size. Decisive contrasts, textures, and ornamentation may or may not increase apparent size, depending on exactly how they are handled.

Apparent distance, or spaciousness, is increased by cool hues, the lighter values, and the lower intensities. Although some contrast is needed as a yardstick, strong contrasts usually make objects seem nearer than they actually are.

Putting all of this to work is fascinating but complex. Rooms with white or very light, cool walls seem more spacious than those with darker, warmer surfaces (Color Figs. 10A and B). Houses painted white seem bigger than those of red brick or natural wood (Color Fig. 21). *But* the value relation between any object and its background is important because strong value contrasts make

Four sofas illustrate how color, values, and especially value relationships affect feelings and attention as well as apparent size and distance and the outlines of furnishings.

A refreshing light-value sofa and chair blend with their light background and look comparatively small and somewhat farther away than they actually are. Their outlines are not emphasized. (*Knoll Associates Inc.*)

A

Placing a light-value sofa, chair, and lamp against a dark background gives a dramatic, vigorous effect. The strong value contrasts call attention to the shape of the furnishings, bring them forward, and increase their apparent size. (*Dunbar Furniture Corporation*)

B

A sofa of middle value is quietly harmonious with the wall of similar value and seems quiet and restful. Its outlines are subordinated, and its size seems moderate. The chair and table, however, stand out when seen against the light curtains and carpet. (*Knoll Associates Inc.*)

The sofa, wall hanging, tables, and lampbase, which are all low dark in value, contrast abruptly with the light wall and floor. One immediately notices the shape and size of each piece, and this tends to bring them forward. The sofa bulks large, especially when compared with the slender, small-scale tables. (*Dunbar Furniture Corporation*)

C

133

objects stand out, which tends to increase their apparent size. Thus against a white background a chair with dark upholstery might look larger than it would if covered with a material of lighter value.

How can colors be used to accentuate or de-emphasize the outlines or contours of objects? It is usually desirable to make noticeable the shape of well-designed furniture or accessories and to play down the contours of less note-worthy furnishings. This can be accomplished with appropriate backgrounds. Differences in hues, intensities, and especially values make us conscious of an object's shape. White against black makes the strongest contrast, and as the values become closer to each other, forms tend to merge with their surroundings (Color Fig. 1). The shape of a white lamp is much more emphatic when seen against dark gray or black than when seen against a light value of any hue. Diametrically opposite hues attract attention to outlines, but if the values of the two hues are similar, the edges seem fuzzy rather than distinct. Related hues also soften contours, and warm hues make the edges of anything seem less sharp than do those that are cool. Color Figures 11, 13, and 15 illustrate many of these concepts.

Summary of Effects of Hue, Value, and Intensity*

	Hue	*Value*	*Intensity*
Feelings	Warm hues are stimulating, cool hues quieting.	Light values are cheering; dark values range from restful to depressing; contrasts are alerting.	High intensities are heartening and strong; low intensities are peaceful.
Attention	Warm hues attract more attention than cool hues.	Extreme values tend to attract the eye; but contrasts or surprises are even more effective.	High intensities attract attention.
Size	Warm hues increase apparent size of objects; used on walls, they decrease apparent size of room.	Light values increase apparent size of objects; but strong contrast with background is equally effective.	High intensities increase apparent size of objects; used on walls, they decrease apparent size of room.
Distance	Warm hues bring objects forward; cool hues make them recede.	Light values recede, dark values advance. Sharp contrasts in values also bring objects forward.	High intensities decrease apparent distances.
Outline, or contour	Warm hues soften outlines slightly more than cool hues; contrasting hues make outlines clearer than related hues.	Value contrasts are a potent way of emphasizing contours.	Intensity contrasts emphasize outlines.

*All generalizations about any one of these three factors assume that the other two dimensions of color, the background, and so on, are held constant. For example, artillery red is normally more stimulating than peppermint green—both are of middle value and full intensity. *But* peppermint green is likely to attract more attention than African brown, a color that is red in hue but low dark in value and two-thirds neutral.

COLOR THEORY: THE MUNSELL AND OSTWALD SYSTEMS

Although similar to the older Brewster system in that the hues are arranged in a circle, which becomes a three-dimensional form when fully developed, the systems formulated by Albert Munsell and Wilhelm Ostwald deviate from it in two basic ways. First, the primary hues are not the same, and second, both have intricate, standardized methods of notation with which innumerable colors can be precisely labeled and identified by referring to the appropriate color charts. These are of inestimable value in science, commerce, and industry where universal specifications of colors are necessary; they are also useful to professional designers and decorators for precise communication.

A   B

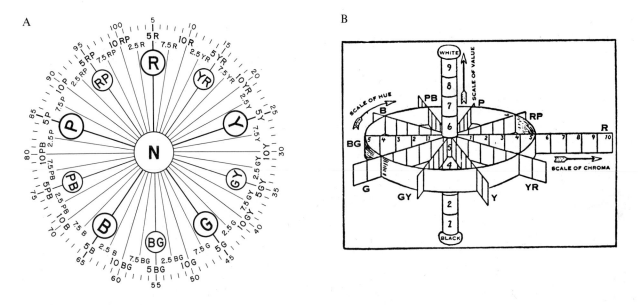

Above left. The Munsell color wheel shows the hues and their relative positions, indicated by letters. Each of these ten hues can be subdivided into ten more hues, making one hundred, as indicated in the outer circle of numbers.

Above right. The relationship of hue, value, and chroma is indicated in a three-dimensional diagram. The circular band indicates the hues. The central, vertical axis has nine neutral value steps from near black to almost white. Chroma, indicated on the radial spokes, goes from neutral in the center to full chroma at the periphery. (*Munsell Color Company*)

The **Munsell system of color notation** has *five principal hues*—red, yellow, green, blue, and purple—and *five intermediate hues*—yellow-red, green-yellow, blue-green, purple-blue, and red-purple (Fig. 135A). Each of these hue families has been subdivided into four parts, indicated by the numerals **2.5, 5, 7.5,** and **10,** which when combined with the initial of a hue designates the exact hue. **5R,** for example, refers to "pure" red, **7.5R** is toward yellow-red, and **2.5R** toward red-purple. Further refinement divides each hue into ten steps, as indicated on the outermost circle of Figure 135A.

Figure 135B shows the nine *value* steps going from **1/,** the darkest, to **9/** as the lightest, with **0/** and **10/** as theoretically pure black and pure white.

The term *chroma* is used instead of intensity. The chroma scale begins with **/0** for complete neutrality at the central axis and extends out to **/10,** or further for very vivid colors (Fig. 135B and Color Fig. 9). The number of chroma steps is determined by the varying saturation strengths of each hue. Notice in the diagram that red, a very strong hue, extends to /**10,** but the weaker blue-green goes only to /**5.**

The complete Munsell notation for any color is written as **hue value/ chroma.** Hue is indicated by the letter and numeral that defines that particular hue on the color wheel (Fig. 135A). This is followed by a fraction in which the numerator designates value and the denominator specifies chroma. Thus **5R 5/10** indicates "pure" red at middle value and maximum chroma. Blue that is light in value and low in chroma is written **5B 9/1.**

The **Ostwald system** is developed from three pairs of complementary color sensations—red and green, blue and yellow, and black and white. The color wheel is begun by placing yellow, red, blue, and green equidistant from one another. Placing five intermediates between each pair of hues makes a circle of twenty-four hues (plus six additional hues that are needed to complete the color range). These are indicated by the numbers around the equator of the color solid (Fig. 136A).

Right. The Ostwald color system is shown in a cutaway diagram of the color solid. As in the Munsell system, the central axis goes from near white down to almost black. The most saturated colors occur at the equator, become increasingly neutralized as they go toward the center, lighter as they go toward the top, and darker as they descend.

Far right. A triangle illustrates the neutral value steps at the far left and 28 variations of one hue, which become more intense as they progress toward the right. (*U.S. Department of Agriculture*)

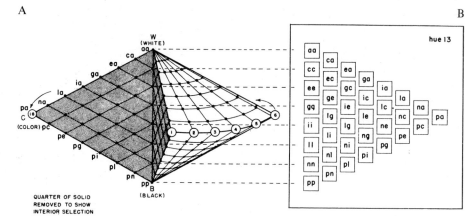

No sharp distinction is made between value and intensity: the hues are lightened or darkened or neutralized by adding appropriate amounts of white and black. This expands the color wheel into a color solid composed of a number of triangular wedges packed together as in Figure 136A. In each wedge there are eight steps from top to bottom and eight from center to periphery.

Colors are designated by a formula, which consists of a number and two letters (**8 pa** for example). The number indicates the hue. The first letter indicates the proportions of white in any color, and the second letter designates the proportion of black. The scale goes from **a,** which is almost pure white, through **c, e, g, i, l, n** to **p,** which is almost pure black. Thus, these two letters tell how light or dark a color is, as well as the degree of saturation. In each triangle there are 28 colors, which multiplied by the 24 hues gives 672 chromatic colors. Adding the 8 neutral steps brings the total to 680, which is about as many as most people need. Study of the diagram and a few examples may possibly make this clear. Pure red has the symbol of **8 pa:** the number indicates "pure" red, and the letters indicate that no black or white has been added.

COLOR WHEEL

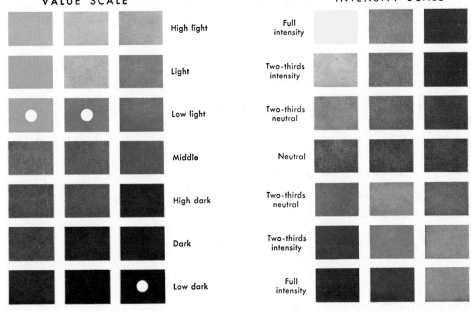

7B
VALUE SCALE

7C
INTENSITY SCALE

Top. The Brewster color wheel shows a sequence of hues in the following order: yellow, yellow-green, green, blue-green, blue, blue-violet, violet, red-violet, red, red-orange, orange, yellow-orange. The numeral *1* indicates primary hues, *2* secondary hues, and *3* tertiary hues.

Left. The value scale shows seven values for each of three hues: green, orange, and violet. Those containing white disks are at normal value.

Right. The intensity scale shows two different degrees between full intensity and neutral for six hues. (*Adapted from* The Art of Enjoying Art *by A. Philip MacMahon as adapted from* Commercial Art *by C. E. Wallace; by permission of McGraw-Hill Book Company, Inc.*)

8A

8B

Two paintings illustrate some of the effects of hue, value, and intensity.

Left. In *All Things Do Live in the Three* (1963), a fairly small painting by Richard J. Anuszkiewicz, dots of blue, green, and yellow are evenly spaced in blocks on a red background, causing it to appear a rosy red or orange, the intensity of which varies according to the color of the dots. (*Oil on canvas, 21⅞″ x 35⅝″. Collection of Mrs. Robert M. Benjamin, New York. Photograph by The Museum of Modern Art, New York.*)

Above. A very large painting by Larry Poons, *Nixe's Mate* (1964), also has spots of blue and green pigment, but here they are more widely spaced on an intense red-orange background, with duller orange spots seeming like afterimages. The overall effect is an optical illusion of violently jumping ovals of contrasting colors. (*Acrylic on canvas, 6′ x 9′4″. Collection of Mr. and Mrs. Robert C. Scull, New York. Photograph by The Museum of Modern Art, New York.*)

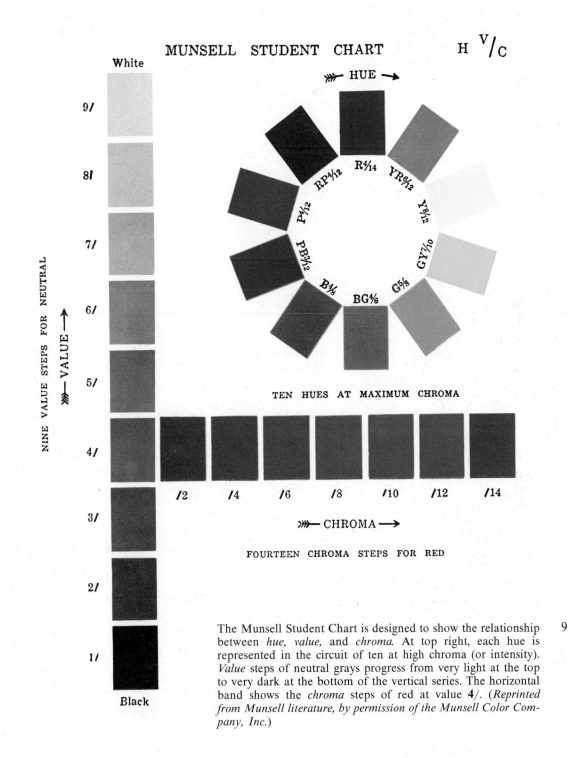

FOURTEEN CHROMA STEPS FOR RED

The Munsell Student Chart is designed to show the relationship between *hue, value,* and *chroma.* At top right, each hue is represented in the circuit of ten at high chroma (or intensity). *Value* steps of neutral grays progress from very light at the top to very dark at the bottom of the vertical series. The horizontal band shows the *chroma* steps of red at value **4/**. (*Reprinted from Munsell literature, by permission of the Munsell Color Company, Inc.*)

9

10A

In remodeling a city apartment, Paul Lester Weiner and Ala Damaz, Associates, used large areas of bold colors and decisive geometric forms to create compositions that are formal, urbane, and spirited. (*Photographs by Louis Reens*)

Above. The dining area has a predominance of light yellow on walls, ceiling, and floor; light-blue on the ceiling; and darker blue on the freestanding space divider—a color scheme that is tranquil and space expanding. Accents of white, black, yellow-orange, and brilliant red are effective contrasts. A large abstract painting, varied sculptures, and the indoor garden enrich the total ensemble.

Below. The living room is in the same spirit but with larger areas of saturated colors, and consequently seems warmer, richer, and more enclosing. A brilliant red wall and ottoman, two red-violet sofas, and luxurious yellow silk draperies are centered around a dark, jewel-toned rug and a glass-topped table. The slate-blue ceiling and distant wall, the gray carpet, and the white dropped ceiling define the architectural planes. A few notable paintings and sculptures, plus books and accessories, increase the feeling of vibrancy while adding points of interest.

10B

Intense orange-red has the symbol **5 pa,** grayed orange-red has the symbol **5 lg,** and dark orange-red has the symbol **5 pn.**

A number of ways of developing color schemes that have an easily perceivable order are suggested in the literature on this system.

TYPES OF COLOR SCHEMES

Planning a color scheme ranks high among the exhilarating aspects of home planning. You can assert your individuality and enjoy the freedom that comes from knowing that satisfying color costs no more than color that lacks character or appeal.

In theory, countless color schemes are suited to homes. In practice, however, only a few can be classified, probably because these types just about exhaust the possibilities of orderly selection from the color wheel. In color, as in design, an underlying sense of order is satisfying; but stereotyped, commonplace organization of anything is tedious. The standard color schemes are nothing more than time-tested basic recipes, but rarely do actual color schemes fit perfectly into any of the categories. They can be varied and individualized, be simply points of departure, or be disregarded, as one wishes.

Typical color schemes fall into two major categories, and each has subtypes:

Related	*Contrasting*
Monochromatic	Complementary
Analogous	Double complementary
	Split complementary
	Triad
	Tetrad

Related color schemes, which are composed of one or several closely neighboring hues, lead toward an unmistakable harmony and unity. Contrasting schemes, based on hues that are far apart on the color wheel, offer greater variety as well as a balance of warm and cool hues. The two types are basically different, but neither is inherently better than the other. Depending on the hues chosen and the dominant pattern of intensities, any of them can be vividly brilliant or comparatively quiet. Thus a monochromatic scheme that features mandarin red is stronger and more lively than one that emphasizes Indian red. A complementary scheme of scarlet and emerald green is striking in comparison with one developed from rose gray and sage green.

Monochromatic Color Schemes

Monochromatic (literally, "one hue") color schemes evolve from a single hue, which can be varied from high light to low dark and from full saturation to almost neutral. White, grays, black, and small amounts of other hues add variety, as do man-made and natural textures and decorative patterns. Thus, even with only one basic hue, the possibilities are legion.

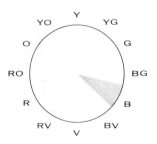

If orange, for example, were chosen, we have the full range of what we usually think of as orange plus the host of browns that are low intensities of that hue. In a room developed from orange, the floors and walls could be of natural wood or cork. Rugs of a terra-cotta color or resilient synthetic floor materials might be put on the floor, and beige grass cloth and matting, hardboard, vinyl-coated fabrics, or wallpaper might surface the walls. Off-white plaster or acoustical panels or wood are possibilities for the ceiling. Floors, walls, ceiling, and furniture could also be painted in any tint or shade of orange as well as in white or gray. Tan or brown bricks, concrete blocks, or stone are appropriate for the fireplace, as is copper. The fabrics used for rugs, upholstery and pillow covers, curtains and draperies are available in myriad variety, ranging in color from peach, buff, tan, and French beige through cadmium and mandarin orange to russet and cocoa brown. They can also be thick or thin, smooth or rough, lustrous or mat, stiff or pliable, or have woven, knit, felt, or vinyl surfaces. For accents blue, violet, and green come to mind, but red, yellow, and saturated orange are also appropriate. It would take an electronic computer to explore all the possible permutations.

The advantages of monochromatic color schemes are that some degree of success is almost assured because unity and harmony are firmly established. Usually, spaciousness and continuity are emphasized, and the effect is quiet and peaceful except in those rare cases in which saturated colors predominate. A major danger—monotony—can be avoided by diversified values and intensities, and by difference in form, texture, and spatial relationships. Color Figure 1 shows the serenity and variety that can be achieved in a room in which white is predominant, but enlivened and defined by the vigor of the textures, the sharpness of the contrasting dark posts and rafters, a glow from light, earth-colored tiles, and the quickening hues of pillows and fruit.

Analogous Color Schemes

Strictly speaking, analogous color schemes are based on three or more hues each of which contains some degree of one hue. In other words, the hues fall within any segment of the color wheel that is less than halfway around it. Thus, if the common hue is blue, the colors could be as closely related as blue-green, blue, and blue-violet, or as separated as blue-green, blue-violet, and red-violet. Often, however, the range of hues is extended.

Analogous color schemes, although basically harmonious, have more variety and interest than do monochromatic color schemes. In a living room on Cape Cod (Color Fig. 2) a color scheme based on red-orange is given depth and diversity by spreading the range into the analogous hues of red and orange. Although warm, it is made cool and refreshing by being placed in a predominantly white room, with the cool green of foliage showing beyond the window wall.

Complementary Color Schemes

Built on any two hues directly opposite each other on the color wheel, complementary schemes are exemplified by orange and blue, yellow and violet, or yellow-orange and blue-violet. They offer a great range of possibilities. Yellow and violet, for example, can be as startling as golden glow and fuchsia, as moderate as ivory and amethyst, or as somber as olive drab and gunmetal. In Color Figure 14 light orange-yellow in draperies and rug, middle value blue-violet in the chair seats, and a dark blue wall are teamed in a modified complementary color scheme that is set off by the dazzling white of the furniture and by touches of red and green in accessories.

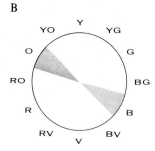

A

B

Double-Complementary Color Schemes

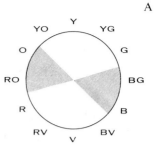

A

A development of the complementary scheme, double complementaries are simply two sets of complements. Orange and red-orange with their respective complements, blue and blue-green, are an example. Worth noticing in this example is the fact that orange and red-orange, as well as their complements, are near each other on the color wheel. This is usually the case, because if the hues are widely separated, it is difficult to see the order on which this scheme is based. However, in Color Figure 6, a bold scheme that unites the range of hues from red-violet to orange with their complements from yellow-green to blue combines the harmonious aspects of analogous color with the contrast found in complementary combinations.

Split-Complementary Color Schemes

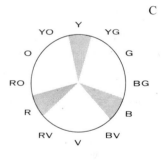

B

Another variation on the complementary theme is that composed of any hue and the two hues *at each side of* its complement, as in yellow with blue-violet and red-violet. Violet, the complement of yellow, is split into red-violet and blue-violet. This makes the contrast less violent than in the simple complementary type and adds interest and variety. A subdued yet rich split-complementary color scheme of red-orange, blue, and green warms the room in Color Figure 30.

Triad Color Schemes

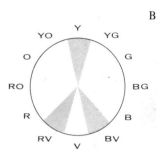

C

Red, blue, and yellow; green, orange, and violet; blue-green, red-violet, and yellow-orange—any three hues equidistant from one another on the color wheel—are known as triad color schemes. In case such combinations sound shocking, remember that full-intensity hues are seldom used in homes. Red, blue, and yellow might be translated as mahogany, French gray, and beige. Green, orange, and violet could be sage green, cocoa brown, and dove gray. Thus, although triad schemes can be vigorous, they can also be subdued. In any case, the effect is one of well-rounded balance with variety held in check by a readily apparent, systematic unity. In Color Figure 10B, a triad color scheme of brilliant red, pure yellow, and subdued blue uses the intermediate violet to pull the red and blue together, and is quieted by a gray-white carpet and some wall and ceiling panels of white.

Tetrad Color Schemes

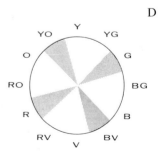

D

Any four hues that are equidistant from one another on the color wheel produce a tetrad color scheme, which is a special type of split complementary color organization. Yellow-orange, green, blue-violet, and red are an example. Such combinations lead to rich, varied yet unified, fully balanced compositions, such as that in Color Figure 15.

DECIDING ON A COLOR SCHEME

Of the many ways of starting to develop a color combination, the following have been found useful:
- Start a scrapbook or clipping file of color combinations that you like. In-

clude advertisements, magazine covers, reproductions of paintings, and so on, as well as illustrations of domestic architecture.

- Collect swatches of cloth, wallpaper samples, paint color cards, and a package of assorted colored paper with which to try out ideas.
- Visit furniture stores, art museums, and model homes and make notes of what you especially like or dislike.
- Study original paintings or reproductions, because painters working freely with pigments to express their ideas are one source of stimulation.
- Study the colors in the nearby landscape and those more distant.
- Look carefully at the colors used in your home and those of your friends, paying attention to first, as well as to the more important lasting, impressions.
- Make a list of your favorite colors.
- Look at a list of color schemes, such as the one on page 142, not as something to copy but as a means to expand your horizons.
- Look at color photographs that have been composed for aesthetic effect rather than as a simple record. Many of the color illustrations in this book are examples.

When you are reasonably certain you know what you want, borrow large samples—a full length of drapery material, a piece of upholstery large enough to cover a good portion of a chair or sofa. It may save money in the long run to get a large piece of wallboard and paint it the color you think is best for your walls. Study these at different times of day or night because their effect will change with the kind of light. Large samples are important because:

- Increasing an area of color often changes its apparent hue, value, and intensity.
- Color combinations at small scale only hint at the full-scale effect.

Factors to Consider in Selecting Colors

Color combinations are generally best when thoughtfully related to you and your family, your possessions, specific rooms and your whole house, and the surrounding environment.

You and your family. The people using a home every day always come first in sensible interior design. For example:

- Active, vigorous families and young people often like strong contrasting colors.
- Quieter or older persons generally prefer somewhat cool, neutralized, harmonious schemes.

Your possessions. The furniture and accessories now owned as well as planned purchases both limit and suggest possible color schemes:

- A collection of antique furniture, good paintings, or individualized accessories might determine colors.
- Miscellaneous furnishings can often be pulled together by a related scheme of warm, middle-value, low-intensity colors.
- If starting from scratch, a favorite color scheme might be the guide in selecting furnishings.

Your rooms. The walls of the rooms, including the windows and their treatment, the doors and fireplaces, are the largest color areas. Floors and ceilings come next in size, then furniture and accessories. *Typical* color relationships are as follows:

- Floors are moderately dark in value and low in intensity to give a firm, unobtrusive base and to simplify upkeep.
- Walls are usually lighter in value than floors in order to provide a transition between them and the ceilings, and typically are quite neutral in intensity to keep them as backgrounds.
- Ceilings are very light in value and very low in intensity for a sense of spaciousness and for efficient reflection of light; frequently they are white but may be tints of either warm or cool hues.

Although this standard approach gives a satisfying up-and-down equilibrium, there are many reasons for deviating from it. Light floors, for example, make a room seem luminous and spacious, and maintenance is no longer such a problem with some of the new materials and textures. Dark walls give comforting enclosure, and they unify miscellaneous dark furnishings (Fig. 129A). Intense colors for floors, walls, draperies, or furniture are a welcome relief from all-too-prevalent drabness. A survey of the color illustrations will disclose many of the devices that can be used successfully to personalize and individualize color schemes.

Room size, shape, and character seem to change with different color treatments, a factor often underestimated. In planning a new house, color should be considered along with the other aspects of design. Older houses are most easily remodeled by an "architectural" use of color. A few examples are:

- Cool hues, light values, and low intensities make small rooms seem larger.
- Rooms too long and narrow can be visually shortened and widened by having one end wall warmer, darker, and more intense than the side walls.
- Rooms that are too square and boxlike seem less awkward if one or two walls are treated differently from the others or if one wall and the ceiling or the floor are similar in color.

Windows and orientation affect the character of rooms and have a bearing on color schemes:

- In rooms well lighted by large windows or good artificial illumination, colors will not be distorted. In rooms with less light, colors seem darker and duller.
- Rooms facing south and west get more heat and more light (of a yellowish hue) than those facing east or north. These differences can be minimized by using cool colors in south and west rooms, warm colors in east and north rooms; they can be maximized by putting warm colors in warm rooms and cool colors in the others; or the differences can be left as they are by using the same colors in all rooms.

Considering color in terms of the **use of rooms** is much less important today than it was when only certain colors were deemed appropriate for specific rooms. Entrance areas can be in any colors that welcome visitors and introduce them to the character of the house. Group-living space is expected to be cheerful and hospitable. Dining space, if it is a separate room used only a few hours

COLOR SCHEMES

Room	Walls	Floors	Ceiling	Furniture and Upholstery	Draperies	Accessories	Comments on Color Schemes
Entrance hall	One of autumn-brown paneled wood; three of sage green; opens into a room paneled in blue-spruce green.	Sage-green shag rug.	Sage green.	Oak: no upholstery.	None.	Oak driftwood, copper bowl, large-leaved plant.	Analogous scheme (green, yellow, and orange); welcoming and natural.
Living room	Blue-spruce green.	Sage-green shag rug.	Sage green.	Oak built-ins, mistletoe-green textured upholstery; two chairs with lacquered-red seats and backs.	Straw-colored, rough-textured.	Brass lamps with bronze shades, brass clock, plants, pewter vases, lacquer-red ashtrays and cigarette box.	Analogous scheme (green, yellow, and orange), as restful as a shady woodland sparked with red berries.
Living room	Fireplace wall white with panel of robin's-egg blue; side walls dark, natural wood.	Carpet of red-orange; area rug of black and white.	Sky blue.	Chairs upholstered in orange, sofa in white, accentuated by dark wood frames.	White.	Paintings with intense colors, sculpture in strong value contrast to walls.	Double-complementary scheme (blue, blue-green, orange, red-orange); striking accents of black and white; decisive, alerting, sparkling.
Family room	One tan wood storage wall, one of pale yellow wallboard, one of red-orange, one glass window wall.	Cobalt blue.	White.	Natural wood frames; vinyl upholstery in sky blue and yellow-orange; Persimmon pillows.	Bamboo shades.	Miscellany of bright travel posters, pennants, and children's paintings, frequently changed.	Split-complementary scheme (blue, yellow-orange, and red-orange); refreshingly active.
Dining room	Lichen green.	Cinnamon, bottle-green, and smoke-brown Oriental rug on oak floor.	White.	Mahogany with chestnut; ivy-green and black needlepoint upholstery.	Castilian-red damask.	Silver chandelier and hollow ware, white porcelain bowl, gold-framed portraits.	Complementary scheme based on green and red; balanced, gracious, cheering.
Kitchen	Three of ash-gray wood; one of salmon-pink plaster.	Reused brick and navy blue vinyl.	White.	Terra-cotta cabinets, stainless steel tops, one black-and-white marble top, stainless steel range units, refrigerator.	Tourmaline-blue, white, and black printed linen.	Stainless steel and copper pans and bowls, white electrical appliances, clear glass jars.	Monochromatic scheme of red-orange, relieved by blue, black, white and gray; varied textures add much interest.
Kitchen	Cabinets and appliances white and royal blue with panels of claret red and lemon yellow.	White vinyl tiles.	Buff corrugated metal.	Black iron supports; tabletop of camelia pink; chair cushions of tangerine.	None.	Copper and stainless steel utensils, brightly colored cannisters.	Triad scheme (blue, red, and yellow); lively and luminous, stimulating.
Bedroom	Laurel pink.	Cardinal red, old rose, and ivory floral carpet.	White.	Headboard and footboard of bed upholstered in ultramarine blue; bedspread champagne yellow.	Ivory.	Framed floral prints, bouquets of varicolored flowers.	Triad scheme (blue, red, and yellow); peaceful but inspiring.
Bedroom	One of emerald green, two of willow green, one of grass green.	Old-ivory and black jaspé asphalt tile; old-ivory shag rug.	Citron (light yellow-green).	Black iron, wicker, and glass; chamois and emerald-green upholstery; deep chrome-yellow and old-ivory bedspread.	Willow-green fishnet.	White pottery breakfast dishes, white picture frames; brass lamps with white shades, brass vases.	Analogous scheme (green, yellow-green, and yellow), sparked with black and white; combines liveliness with restfulness.
Bathroom	Upper walls bisque, lower walls French-gray tile, molding of peach-bloom tile.	Garnet rubber tile; gray plush rug.	Bisque.	Peach-bloom cabinets with dove-gray counter tops, fixtures, chrome fittings.	Garnet drapes and shower curtains.	Garnet and white towels.	Monochromatic scheme (red) with gray; pleasant relief from antiseptic or pallid colors.

a day, can be an appropriate place to experiment with dramatic colors. Kitchens have no limitations other than the constant cleaning required, the need for good illumination, and their tendency to get overly warm. Bathrooms, which are small and used for only short periods, need not have the pallid colors usually seen in them. Bedrooms are the individual's refuge, and it would be out of place to recommend colors for these sanctums.

The **whole house** should be considered when planning a color scheme. Regarding the rooms of a home separately has dangers because a home is a unit, not a collection of rooms, especially with contemporary open plans. Uni-

In a Vassar College Cooperative House, clearly differentiated planes make one immediately aware of articulated openness and enclosure. Blue-gray, middle-value flagstones, laid in large irregular pieces, provide a substantial base that emphasizes the continuity of the space. A painted white brick fireplace stands out from the walls, accentuating its three-dimensional rectangularity and separating living and dining areas. The shape and material of the fireplace, plus the burning fire, the arrangement of dark leaves, and the furniture group, make it a dominant feature. The division between the two areas is further defined by the light and darker natural wood panels, related to the dining furniture in material and color. The far wall, with its timesaving pass-through into the kitchen, is as white as the fireplace but differs from it in its smoothness. The space has clean-cut precision but is not coldly austere. It is an unusually good example of space shaped by color and materials. Marcel Breuer, architect. (*Photograph by Joseph Molitor*)

fied color schemes recognize this and bring harmony and continuity; they increase visual spaciousness and make it possible to shift furnishings from one room to another without disturbing color schemes. This makes sense. But what about monotony? That is a matter of personal opinion—and of the colors used.

If one total color scheme seems too limiting, give thought to having one color carry through all the floors, the walls, the ceilings, *or* the draperies. Or there can be a more complex variation of this: for instance, mellow grays, yellows, and greens of a patterned fabric in the living room are the basic colors and spread out into walls of gray, a ceiling of very pale yellow, and grayed-green carpet. The dining room has the same carpet and ceiling, but one of the greens in the fabric becomes the wall color and the yellow is modified into antique gold for the draperies. The master bedroom has the same carpet, three walls of gray, and the fourth wall and ceiling of yellow; a bedspread and curtains are a vivid print in oranges, yellows, and red. Such devices as these create a sense of wholeness.

Architectural character of a sort positive enough to be a factor in color selection is regrettably uncommon. If, though, your home or even one room in a home has such a quality, regard it as an asset and emphasize it with an appropriate color organization, as has been done in Color Figure 1.

The **geographical environment,** regional and local, is a factor, but how much attention should be given to it is a personal decision. Connecticut, Louisiana, Arizona, and Oregon differ from one another in climate, geography, vegetation, and the architecture these conditions indicate. Specific location is also of consequence. An apartment in San Francisco's fog belt might or might not suggest colors that would be appropriate to a ranch house on the sunny, rolling hills a few miles away (Color Figs. 1 and 3). Sympathetic study of our surroundings helps us find colors that relate to their larger setting.

ECONOMIES WITH COLOR

Color can more than earn its cost; in fact, it can actually save money if wisely used:

- A coat of paint on one or more walls of a room will change the atmosphere more cheaply than any other single device.
- Old, battered, nondescript furniture takes on renewed vitality with new paint.
- Bands of color painted around windows are inexpensive substitutes for draperies; floors painted in suitable colors, possibly textured or patterned, lessen the need for rugs (Fig. 295 and Color Fig. 19).
- A preponderance of light-value colors can cut electric bills and probably improve vision.
- Warm colors in the home make people comfortable at lower, probably more healthful, temperatures.
- Cheering colors lessen the apparent need for vitamins and tonics.
- Colors that do not fade, or that fade gracefully, minimize replacement.
- Nature colors, especially if patterned, not only reduce daily and weekly maintenance but remain passably good-looking longer than do most clear, sharp colors.
- A unified color scheme throughout the house makes for economical interchangeability of furniture, draperies, and rugs.

The distinctive qualities of light and of plastics were exploited by architect Paul Rudolph in his predominantly white, atmospheric living room in New York. Plexiglas seating platforms and a drum table transmit the glow of incandescent lights concealed within them; opaque white Plexiglas is used for sliding doors; and shining white vinyl covers the cushions. Light is broken up by three-dimensional textures introduced in the kid-skin rug, the topographical map on the right wall, and the ridged convolutions of Will Ryman's plastic sculpture. The intricately patterned plaster panels used as backrests were molds designed by the early modern architect Louis Sullivan. The black piano, some bright orange cushions, and feathery greenery are used as accents. (*Photograph by Louis Reens*)

Opposite. Wolfgang Roth's studio is an addition to an old house in Bucks County, Pennsylvania. The rough stone walls, the slate floor, and the beamed ceiling are a congenial background for old and new furniture and accessories of diverse materials. (*Reprinted from* The Personal House *by Betty Alswang and Amber Hiken. Copyright* © *1961, Whitney Library of Design*)

Part III · MATERIALS

A carved wood door set deeply within a plaster recess makes a striking entrance to a house in Cuernavaca, Mexico. Against off-white walls, the Pompeian red of the frame culminating in a conch shell is at once imposing and serene. (*Reprinted from Verna Cook Shipway and Warren Shipway,* The Mexican House Old and New. *Copyright © 1960, Architectural Book Publishing Company, Inc.*)

8 · Wood and Masonry

Our homes are built of materials, each having special potentialities and limitations that indicate appropriate forms and uses. These are fundamental considerations that were given scant attention in the nineteenth century. In this century, Frank Lloyd Wright was a leader in its reaffirmation with his architectural philosophy based on the concept of respect for "the nature of materials" (see Figs. 76, 104A, and 170). Together with planning and design, materials determine the usefulness, economy, beauty, and individuality of our homes.

WOOD

No material but wood could have given so naturally the inviting informal character of the deck terrace shown in Figure 150A or have related it so well to its surroundings. Most immediately noticeable is the floor of redwood boards

149

A

Redwood is handsomely used as the basic exterior and interior material in a hillside house overlooking San Francisco Bay. The Far Eastern character of this home makes it an appropriate setting for the owners' collection of Oriental art. Campbell and Wong, architects. (*Photographs by Morley Baer*)

Above. Geometric yet informal, a spacious sheltered deck projects out over the hill and becomes an extension of the living room. The chairs and the garden fence behind them are made of bamboo.

Below. The meticulously detailed interior is an unobtrusive background for beautiful furnishings and a spectacular view. The table enriched with carving and turning, and the turned lamp base, introduce pleasing variety.

B

laid in a checkerboard design, which introduces a handsome structural pattern of light and dark. Built-in seats and railings echo the clean-cut, simple details of the protecting roof and the structure of the wall. Although all forms are strictly geometrical, with rectangles predominant, the effect is neither hard nor formal. There is, though, a strong sense of man-made order, which contrasts happily with the free-growing trees in the background and in pots.

There were many reasons for selecting wood as the chief building material. One is its remarkable strength in relation to its size and shape. Most notable in this respect is its *tensile* strength: it resists breakage when subjected to bending or pulling forces, as anyone who has handled a bamboo fishpole knows. Tensile strength permits wood to be used for spanning gaps, such as those above the sliding doors, in the railings, and in the built-in seats. Its tensile strength also suits wood to cantilever construction (defined as nonvertical projecting members supported at only one end) as seen in the roof that projects freely beyond the house walls. Wood, further, has considerable strength in *compression* (retains its shape under pressure), which makes it useful for such upright forms as the vertical posts supporting the house wall and the legs holding up the chairs and tables. In addition, wood is slightly resilient, which makes it appropriate for floors and furniture; it does not get as hot or cold as masonry and metal, which is important in outdoor living areas; and it does not readily transmit heat or cold, which makes it a good insulator when used for walls and roofs.

Wood is comparatively inexpensive in original cost, and it can be economically maintained. Such woods as cedar, cypress, and redwood survive exposure to weather with little upkeep. The original cost of wood walls for interiors is greater than for plaster walls, but wood requires less maintenance. At the end of ten years the total cost of wood and plaster is about the same, and from then on wood costs less in time, energy, and money. Hardwood furniture also requires relatively little care.

We would like wood for its beauty and individuality even were it not for its utility and economy. Wood grain and color show a perfect union of variety and unity: no two pieces are identical—even the two ends or sides of one piece are not exactly alike—and yet there is a powerful, organic unity in each piece and among many pieces (Fig. 157). The rhythms are as subtle and inevitable as those in waves or clouds and range from almost parallel linearity to an intricate complexity of curves. Some wood grains are emphatic, others quietly subordinate. Finally, wood is as pleasant to touch as it is to look at.

The major limitations of wood are several: it burns, rots, and decays; it is attacked by insects; and it may swell, shrink, or warp with changes in moisture content. All of these factors, however, can now be minimized, and extensive research is bringing us close to eliminating the less desirable qualities of wood. The first step in overcoming these weaknesses is the consideration of other materials for certain uses: masonry or metal where there is a fire hazard, or masonry where there is excessive dampness. The second step is the selection of the best wood for specific conditions. Redwood and cedar, for example, resist rot and decay; walnut and mahogany have beautiful color and texture and can be intricately carved. The third step is proper drying, which minimizes rotting, shrinking, and warping. The fourth is the designing of wood objects with respect for the nature of the material. The fifth is the application of an appropriate preservative or finish. Finally, comes sympathetic care and maintenance.

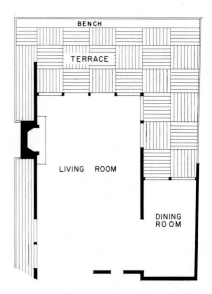

The simple, straightforward plan of the living room, dining room, and terrace is distinguished by a sensitively proportioned regularity, by an adroit disposition of openings, and by opaque and transparent walls.

Both curvilinear and angular forms are appropriate to wood.

A room from a manor house in Suffolk, England (1590–1620), shows how wood was handled in the Late Tudor–Early Jacobean period. Both the frieze above the wood paneling and the ceiling are of intricately shaped plaster; the framing of the grouped windows is of stone. (*The Minneapolis Institute of Arts*)

Selecting Wood

Wood comes from plants ranging from pencil-thin bamboos to Australian eucalyptuses nearly 400 feet in height to California redwoods as large as 100 feet in circumference. Differences in strength, hardness, durability, and beauty are almost as great as is the diversity of appearance of trees. On pages 154–156, the significant characteristics of woods that are often used in homes are tabulated.

Wood is usually classified as *hard* if it comes from broad-leaved trees that in colder climates drop their leaves in winter, such as maple, oak, and walnut; and as *soft* if it comes from those trees with needle-like leaves retained throughout the year, such as pine, cedar, and redwood. In general, the hardwoods are harder, finer in grain, more attractively figured, and more expensive. The less costly softwoods are easier to work using typical tools, but they are less suitable for fine finishes and intricate shapes. There is, however, considerable overlapping between the two types. For example, southern yellow pine is harder than chestnut, gum, basswood, or poplar, although the latter four are classified as hard because they come from broad-leaved, deciduous trees.

In selecting wood, keep in mind that every piece does not have to be top quality in every respect. All wood should be strong enough to do its job; but for some purposes relatively weak wood is adequate. Hardness is advantageous if the wood is subject to wear; it is of less importance otherwise. Capacity to take a high finish is desirable in furniture wood but is not needed for exterior siding or shingles. Beautiful grain and figure are a rewarding type of indoor ornament, but they are pretty much wasted outdoors.

11

Appropriately displayed against natural rock, the work of three California craftsmen displays their interest in the colors and textures of wood. Robert Stocksdale created the large, asymmetrical, mahogany salad bowl and the California almond wood bowl with its yellow and brown markings. Robert Trout carved shallow designs on the outside of the teak bowl at the right and smoothed the interior to a soft gleam. Dovetailed joints and the vigorous grain of English walnut structurally ornament a simply styled small table designed by Espenet. (*Photograph by Richard Gross. California Design/9, Pasadena Art Museum*)

12

Spanning a small stream that flows through a Connecticut woodland, the living room of this inspired house is the connecting link between four private wings placed at each corner (only one can be seen in this view). The low vaults of the living room pavilion, the extended plan, and the generous use of glass fit naturally and romantically into the idyllic landscape; but the regularity of the total composition brings a disciplined restraint. John M. Johansen, architect. (*Photograph by Robert Damora*)

Design in Wood

The oak-paneled Tudor-Jacobean room (Fig. 152) shows many of the basic shapes suited to wood. Flat boards form the wall panels, the floor, the tops of tables and benches, and the seat and back of the chair. Chiefly because of wood's tensile strength, the board or plank is a typical, useful form seen not only in furniture, paneling, and floors, but in ceilings and outdoor siding. A second basic shape is the pole, which is reminiscent of tree trunks and branches. This shape is used in the legs and, slightly squared, in the braces of the table and bench and in the arms of the chair. That wood can go well beyond these simple shapes is evident in the carving that gives the room its special character. From the restrained moldings that frame the small panels of the wall, the carving progresses to the more intricate cornice along the top of the wainscoting, to the pilaster near the window, to the aprons of the table and buffet, and finally to the vigorous, sculptured melon bulbs on the upright supports of the table and the three-tiered buffet. We can sense the delight felt by the artisans who shaped this wood with full respect for its nature and for the spirit of the age in which it was done.

Many persons today hold to the concept that the shapes given to wood, or any other material, should develop out of its special qualities. Wood normally grows in tapering, pole-shaped trunks and branches. Stripped of bark and cut into usable lengths, these poles have been used in most parts of the world as the framework for tents covered with bark or skins, or for huts sheathed with bark or bunches of grass. Refined in shape, such poles are found in homes as posts and pillars, legs of tables, chairs, cabinets (Figs. 152 and 153), and lamp bases. Tree trunks have been used, vertically or horizontally, as house walls in typical log-cabin fashion. Clearly, the pole is a basic wood shape, but further shaping is necessary before it can be used to any great extent.

A

Left. Thick strips of solid wood of different colors and grains form a sculptured tabletop. The three-legged support has been slightly shaped for grace and strength. (*Dunbar Furniture Corporation*)

Above. Three solid walnut stools designed by Charles Eames have the sturdiness of the cylindrical tree trunk from which they were turned. (*Herman Miller Inc.*)

QUALITIES OF WOODS

Name	Source	Color and Grain	Character	Uses
Alder (Red)	One of few native hardwoods in Pacific Northwest.	Pleasant light colors from white to pale pinks, browns; close, uniform grain.	Lightweight, not very strong; resists denting, abrasion; shrinks little. Stains well.	Chairs, other furniture.
Ash (White)	Central and eastern United States; Europe.	Creamy white to light brown. Prominent grain resembling oak; emphatic elliptical figures in plain-sawed or rotary cut.	Hard, strong; wears well; intermediate to difficult to work; intermediate in warping.	Furniture frames requiring strength; exposed parts of moderate-priced furniture; cheaper than most durable hardwoods.
Beech	Central and eastern North America; Europe.	White or slightly reddish. Inconspicuous figure and uniform texture, similar to maple.	Strong, dense, hard; bends well; warps, shrinks, subject to dry rot; relatively hard to work, but good for turning; polishes well.	Middle-quality, country-style furniture; good for curved parts, rocker runners, interior parts requiring strength; also floors, utensil handles, woodenware food containers (no taste or odor).
Birch	Temperate zones. Many species; yellow birch most important.	Sapwood, white; heartwood, light to dark reddish brown. Irregular grain, not obtrusive; uniform surface texture; undulating grain called "curly."	Usually hard, heavy, strong; little shrinking, warping; moderately easy to work; beautiful natural finish; stains, enamels well.	Plywoods; structural, exposed parts of furniture, usually naturally finished (esp. Scandinavian); can be stained to imitate mahogany, walnut.
Cedar	North Pacific coast and mountains of North America.	Reddish brown to white. Close-grained.	Rather soft, weak, lightweight; easily worked; little shrinkage; resists decay; holds paint. Red cedar repels moths.	Shingles, siding, porch and trellis columns, vertical grain plywood, cabinetwork, interior paneling.
Cherry	United States, Europe, Asia.	Light to dark reddish brown. Close-grained.	Strong, durable, moderately hard. Carves and polishes well.	Associated with Early American and Colonial furniture. Now often used as a veneer.
Cypress (Southern)	Southeastern coast of United States; southern Mississippi Valley.	Slightly reddish, yellowish brown, or almost black; weathers silvery gray if exposed.	Moderately strong, light; resists decay; holds paint well.	Doors, sash, siding, shingles, porch materials; occasionally outdoor furniture.
Elm	Europe and United States.	Light grayish brown tinged with red to dark chocolate brown; white sapwood. Porous, open, oaklike grain; delicate wavy figure.	Hard, heavy; difficult to work; shrinks; swells; bends well.	Somewhat sparingly in furniture; curved parts of Provincial types; extensively used now for decorative veneers.
Fir (Douglas)	Pacific coast of United States.	Yellow to red to brownish. Coarse-grained, irregular wavy patterns, especially in rotary-cut plywood; "busy."	Rather soft, quite strong, heavy; tends to check, split; does not sand or paint well.	Plywood for exterior, interior walls, doors; cabinetwork; interior, exterior trim, large timbers, flooring; low-cost furniture, especially interior parts.
Gum (Red or Sweet)	Eastern United States to Guatemala.	Reddish brown; often irregular pigment streaks make striking matched patterns. Figure much like Circassian walnut.	Moderately hard, heavy, strong; tends to shrink, swell, warp; susceptible to decay; easy to work; finishes well.	Most-used wood for structural parts, with or imitating mahogany, walnut; also exposed as gumwood.

Name	Source	Color and Grain	Character	Uses
Mahogany	Central and South America; Africa.	Heartwood pale to deep reddish brown; darkens with exposure to light. Adjacent parts of surface reflect light differently, giving many effects; small-scale, interlocked, or woven grain; distinctive figures.	Medium hard, strong; easy to work, carve; shrinks little; beautiful texture; takes high polish; always expensive.	Most favored wood for fine furniture in eighteenth century; much used in nineteenth century. Used today in expensive furniture finished naturally, bleached, or stained dark.
Maple (Sugar, and Black, both called hard)	Central and eastern United States.	Almost white to light brown; small, fine, dense pores. Straight-grained or figures (bird's-eye, curly, wavy).	Hard, heavy, strong; little shrinking, swelling if well seasoned; hard to work; has luster; takes good polish.	Early American furniture. Now used as solid wood for sturdy, durable, unpretentious, moderate-priced furniture. Good for hardwood floors.
Oak (many varieties; two groups: White and Red)	All temperate zones.	White oaks: pale grayish brown, sometimes tinged red. Red oaks: more reddish. Both have quite large conspicuous open grains; fancy figures rare.	Hard, strong; workable, carves well; adaptable to many kinds of finishes.	Standard wood in Gothic period, Early Renaissance in northern Europe, continuously used in United States. Suitable for floors, wall panels, plywood; furniture, solid and veneer.
Philippine Mahogany (actually Red, White Lauan, and Tanguile)	Philippines.	Straw to deep reddish brown according to species; pales when exposed to light. Pronounced interlocking grain gives conspicuous ribbon figure.	About as strong as mahogany, less easy to work; greater shrinking, swelling, warping; less durable, harder to polish.	Extensively used for furniture in past few decades; also plywood wall panels.
Pine (many varieties similar in character)	All temperate zones.	Almost white to yellow, red, brown. Close-grained.	Usually soft, light, relatively weak; easy to work; shrinks, swells, warps little; decays in contact with earth; takes oil finish especially well, also paint. Knotty pine originally covered with paint.	Used throughout world for provincial, rustic furniture; in Early Georgian furniture for ease of carving, also paneled walls. Often is painted or has decorative patterns. Now used for inexpensive cabinetwork, doors, window-sash frames, structural members, furniture.
Poplar	Eastern United States.	White to yellowish brown. Close-grained, relatively uniform texture.	Moderately soft, weak, lightweight; easy to work; finishes smoothly; stains and paints well.	Siding; interior, exterior trim; inexpensive furniture, cabinetwork, especially when painted or enameled.
Redwood	Pacific coast of United States.	Reddish brown; lightens in strong sun; becomes gray or blackish if allowed to weather. Parallel grain in better cuts, contorted in others; decorative burls.	Moderately strong in large timbers, but soft and splinters easily; resists rot and decay.	Exterior siding, garden walls, outdoor furniture; some use for interior walls, cabinetwork.
Rosewood (several species, grouped because of fragrance)	India, Brazil.	Great variation from light to deep reddish brown. Irregular black, brown streaks in fanciful curves.	Hard, durable; takes high polish.	Extensively used in fine eighteenth-century furniture, chiefly veneers, inlays; nineteenth-century solid wood. Increasing use in furniture today.

Name	Source	Color and Grain	Character	Uses
Teak	Asia (India, Burma, Siam, and so on).	Straw yellow to tobacco brown. Striped or mottled in pattern.	Heavy, durable, oily; works and carves well; takes oil finish beautifully.	Widely used in Far East, both plain and for ornately carved furniture. Now often used by Scandinavians for sculptural qualities.
Tupelo Gum	Southeastern United States.	Pale brownish-gray heartwood merges gradually with white sapwood. Lack of luster makes interlocking grain inconspicuous.	Hard, heavy, strong; good stability; moderately easy to work; tendency to warp.	Same purposes as Red Gum, although it is somewhat weaker, softer.
Walnut (American or Black)	Central and eastern United States.	Light to dark chocolate brown, sometimes dark irregular streaks. Distinctive, unobtrusive figures of stripes, irregular curves; or also intricate, beautiful figures.	Hard, heavy, strong; warps little; moderately easy to work, carve; natural luster; takes good finish.	In America from earliest times for good furniture, but especially in nineteenth century; now in high-grade furniture, paneling.
Walnut (Circassian,) (also called English, Italian, European, Russian, and so on).	Balkans to Asia Minor, Burma, China, Japan. Planted in Europe for wood and nuts.	Fawn-colored. Many conspicuous irregular dark streaks give elaborate figures; butts, burls, crotches add to variety.	Strong, hard, durable; works, carves well; shrinks, warps little; takes fine polish.	A leading furniture wood since ancient times. Used in Italian, French, Spanish Renaissance; in England, during Queen Anne period, 1660–1720, called age of walnut; imported for American furniture.

A

B

The tensile strength of wood makes possible the use of long, slender pieces for many differing purposes.

Left. A screen made from thin strips of bent wood gives an intriguing interplay of solid forms and open spaces. Used as space dividers, such screens can define areas without sealing them off from the rest of the room. The background is of striated plywood. (*Thonet Industries*)

Above. Since early days, wood has been a standard structural material for homes in many parts of the United States. A small-scale model of a stud-wall house shows how a flexible, resilient framework can be constructed of comparatively slender, widely spaced vertical and horizontal members. (*Stanford University*)

Trunks and branches can be squared to make heavy or light beams or can be sawed into planks for siding or into sheets for plywood and veneers (Fig. 157). Rectangularity facilitates fastening them together as shown in Figure 156B. The timber can also be sawed into round blocks suitable for garden paving or can be turned into bowls and plates.

There are three more basic possibilities for handling wood. One is literally "upwrapping" the log by peeling it into very thin continuous sheets for veneers and plywood (Fig. 157F). The second is bending wood into the curved shapes often seen in chairs (Figs. 67A and 159B). The third is grinding or splitting wood into small pieces that are then pressed together for wallboards; grinding, softening, and bleaching it to make paper; or dissolving it and transforming the result into synthetic fibers.

These possibilities demonstrate the great virtuosity of wood, the manifold shapes it will take. Each has advantages that help determine its ultimate use.

Solid wood. Solid wood needs no explanation. Its advantages are:
- Satisfaction comes from knowing all the wood is the same as the surface.
- The edges of tabletops, chair seats, and so on do not expose the layer-cake construction of plywood, although these are usually concealed.
- The wood can be turned or carved.
- The surface can be planed in case of damage, or thoroughly sanded for refinishing, without fear of going through to another wood.
- The surface cannot loosen or peel off (as it may in improperly constructed veneers).

Major disadvantages are high cost and a tendency to warp, shrink, or swell.

Wood structure is a complex organization of fibers and pores. Concentric *annual rings* increase the tree's girth; *vertical fibers* and *pores* run parallel to the trunk; and *medullary rays* radiate from the center at right angles to the vertical fibers and pores. When wood is cut, this structure becomes apparent and is called *grain* and *figure*. The way in which wood is cut produces notably different results.

Quarter-sliced lumber is cut at approximately right angles to the growth rings, producing a series of longitudinal stripes, straight in some woods, varied in others. It shrinks less in width and also twists less than does plain-sliced lumber.

Plain-sliced lumber, cut parallel to a line through the center of the log, is usually cheaper than quarter-sliced lumber. The grain pattern generally is variegated parabolas.

Rotary-cut wood is peeled off the log into thin, continuous sheets by holding a cutter against the log while it is rotating on a lathe —something like taking paper towels off a roll. It often produces complex wavy or ripple patterns. Rotary-cut veneer can be exceptionally wide. (*Fine Hardwoods Association*)

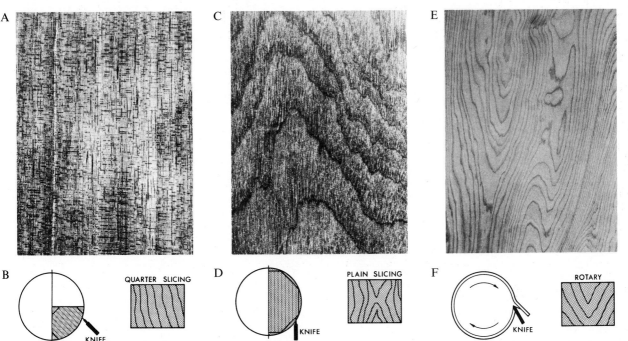

A

B   QUARTER SLICING   KNIFE

C

D   PLAIN SLICING   KNIFE

E

F   ROTARY   KNIFE

Veneers, plywood, and laminated wood. Veneers, plywood, and laminated wood are layer constructions consisting of one or more sheets of thin wood, thicker boards, or paper.

Veneers are thin sheets of wood produced by slicing with a knife, by sawing, or by rotary cutting. They may be glued to the top of thicker lumber to make what is referred to as "veneered wood," glued to paper for wall coverings, or glued to other veneers, as in plywood and laminates. Often, though, the term is used to refer specifically to the exterior surfaces that are usually of wood more expensive than that underneath.

Plywood is composed of an odd number of veneers glued together with the grain of adjacent sheets at right angles to each other. Some plywoods have a center core of lumber or of man-made, pressed-wood board.

Laminated wood is a type of plywood in which the grain of successive layers goes in the same direction. It is frequently used for those parts of furniture—such as the legs of Charles Eames's chair (Fig. 159B)—that are bent and in which the major stresses and strains are in one direction.

The popular notion that veneers and plywoods are cheap substitutes for the real thing is a misconception. To be sure, they are usually less expensive than solid wood, especially in the better grades of hardwood, because the expensive wood goes much further when used as a veneer. But they also have other advantages:

- They are available in much larger pieces (up to 5 feet wide and 16 feet long) than solid wood.
- They are typically stronger than solid wood of the same thickness and weight.
- They are less likely than solid wood to shrink, check, or warp excessively.
- They are less liable to splitting by nails or puncturing by sharp objects.

Plywood can be made in many ways for specific purposes.

A

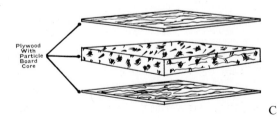

B

C

Above. Veneer-core plywood, used for paneling or curved shapes, has a center core of veneer and all layers of approximately the same thickness.

Above right. Lumber-core plywood, used for tabletops and cabinet doors, has a thick center core of solid wood.

Right. Particle-board plywood, used for table or desk tops, has a thick center core of particle board (hardboard), a composite of small pieces of wood held together with resin binders.

- They give almost identical grain on several pieces that can then be matched to produce symmetrical figures.
- They permit use of fragile, highly figured woods that, if solid, might split apart or shrink irregularly.
- They lend themselves readily to curved and irregular forms.
- They make possible flush surfaces of large size that are dimensionally stable.
- They make possible a more extensive use of rare, costly woods on walls and furniture.

These characteristics open many new design possibilities, some of which are shown in Figures 70A and 160A. Plywood, combining utility, beauty, easy maintenance, and light weight, is ideally suited to the doors, paneling, and drawers in the mobile home. In Charles Eames's home, beautifully matched panels of three rare woods are magnetic accents when seen against many plain but colorful surfaces. Almost all of today's furniture uses some plywood or other laminate because of its superior performance. Interior-type plywood is also used for sheathing walls and ceilings and as a support for resilient flooring. Plywood for exteriors, bonded with waterproof adhesives, is used for outdoor furniture and fences, exterior sheathing or siding, in kitchens and bathrooms, and for the hulls of boats. Both types come with many surface textures—smooth or rough, ribbon stripes, V-grooves, or embossed patterns. They may also have a surface of another material, such as a thin sheet of resin-impregnated fiber or a thicker sheet of hardboard.

Known in ancient Greece and Rome, veneering was revived during the Renaissance, considerably improved in the nineteenth century, and greatly improved during the past few decades. The major drawback—the possibility of the veneers coming apart—has been almost eliminated by new synthetic adhesives.

Hardboard. Also called particle board, wallboard, or pressed wood, hardboard panels are made by transforming wood chips into fibers that are then refined and bonded together with adhesives under pressure. They are dense and hard, and they come in varied surface finishes and patterns (Fig. 159A).

Ornament in Wood: Natural and Man-Made

Wood comes with a great diversity of **built-in,** or **structural, ornament** in its grain and figure. Not only does each species of wood have its own general type of pattern, but different aspects of these patterns can be brought to light by the way in which the woods are cut (Fig. 157). In addition to the beauty of typical grains, some woods show amazingly intricate deviations of figures that have long been cherished by furniture designers. *Stripes* and *broken stripes; mottles* and *blisters* of irregular, wavy shapes; and *fiddleback, raindrop, curly,* and *bird's-eye* figures are but a few, to which must be added all the figures found in *stump* or *butt wood: crotches, burls,* and *knots* (Figs. 160B and C).

Texture. Actual texture of the surface is also a kind of ornament and largely determines the effectiveness of the grain. *Roughly sawn* wood, which has a rough, light-diffusing texture that minimizes the grain, is not pleasant to touch and is usually used for exterior work where a rustic character is wanted; *resawn* wood is considerably smoother, with a soft texture something like a short-pile fabric, and reveals but does not emphasize the grain; *smoothly finished*

A

Hardboard comes in varied smooth surfaces, embossed and perforated patterns. (*Edward Hines Lumber Company*)

B

Plywood and laminated wood extend the uses and appearance of one of man's oldest materials, as seen here and in Figure 160A.

Charles Eames's chair, designed in 1945, has become a contemporary classic. The seat and back are of molded plywood. The laminated wood legs demonstrate that wood can be strong even though thin and lightweight. (*Herman Miller Inc.*)

wood reflects light, emphasizes the figure, and is pleasant to touch. Two new surface treatments, *striated* and *etched* plywood, are illustrated in Chapter 11.

Joints. The way in which different pieces of wood are brought together creates structural patterns of considerable importance. Overlapping shingles and siding have long been appreciated, not only for utilitarian reasons but because of their enlivening patterns of light and dark. A similar effect is produced when boards have beveled edges or when space is left between them, as in the terrace shown in Figure 150A.

Moldings. Long, narrow strips that are not flush with the surface are called moldings. Today they are less favored than in the past because of our desire for simplicity and for easy-to-clean homes. Moldings, though, can be labor-

Below. In his own home built in 1949, Mr. Eames has used splendidly figured veneer plywood on the end wall of a storage unit, more conservative patterns for doors and drawer fronts, very unobtrusive grain for the supports of the coffee table. (*Photograph by Julius Shulman*)

A

Right. Figures in wood bring rich and varied structural ornament into our homes. Both of these examples are mahogany. At the left is a crotch figure and at the right a blister figure. (*U.S. Forest Products Laboratory*)

B

C

savers as in the base moldings and the chair rails that help keep furniture from rubbing against walls. They can also emphasize direction or set up a rhythmic pattern of their own, as they do in board-and-batten construction, in which the narrow battens covering the joints between boards set up a vertical or horizontal movement. In many historic rooms—the Port Royal parlor (Color Fig. 5) for example—they frame such elements as a painting and separate it from its background; they also form transitions between planes, as in elaborate moldings that relate wall to ceiling.

Carving and turning. The nature of wood has suggested carving from earliest days in all parts of the world, and the great periods of furniture are known as much for their carving as for their more basic qualities of design. Gothic carving in oak, Renaissance carving in walnut, and eighteenth-century carving in mahogany effectively enhanced form. "Turning" is also an old art, and ever since man invented the lathe he has enjoyed the diverse ways in which a rapidly rotating piece of wood can be shaped for furniture parts, balusters, and columns. Designers of almost every period produced turnings with distinctive profiles, such as the sixteenth-century melon bulbs (Fig. 152); the seventeenth-century balls or sausages; and the spool, the bead and ball, the knob, the vase, and composite types that were used in many countries at various times.

Elaborate turning and carving of high quality are rare but not unknown in contemporary furniture. Good carving and turning take much time and skill to produce, and they increase household maintenance noticeably—but they can be handsome (Figs. 153B and 161B).

Inlay, intarsia, marquetry, and parquetry. Inlay, intarsia, marquetry, and parquetry are ways of combining different woods, metals, ivory, shell, and other materials so that the contrasting colors and textures make patterns in a plane surface (Fig. 161A). **Inlay** has come to be a somewhat general term covering them all; **intarsia** refers to that type in which the pieces are inlaid in solid wood; **marquetry** is used when the design, usually representational, is inlaid in veneers and then glued to a solid backing; and **parquetry** refers to geometric patterns, especially in floors.

Today there is a marked trend away from the austerity often associated with "modern" design, but there is still very little complex man-made wood

B

A

Carving and inlay are two major types of man-made ornamentation in wood.

Left. Delicate carving and inlay distinguish a classically proportioned English satinwood commode (c. 1770–1780) in the Early Neoclassic style. In contrast to the vigorous door, the scale is small, the ornament stylized, the texture smooth and polished. (*The Metropolitan Museum of Art, New York*)

Above. Deep, sinuous carving on a modern redwood door is appropriate to the rather soft, heavy grain of the wood and to its possible use as an entrance door. Sherrill Broudy, designer (c. 1965). (*Photograph by Richard Gross. California Design/9, Pasadena Art Museum*)

WOOD FINISHES

Name	Composition	Application	Result	Use
Bleach	Various acids, chlorine compounds.	Brushed on (if bleaching agent is strong enough to affect wood, it will also affect skin).	Lightens wood, neutralizes color, usually makes grain less conspicuous; not dependably permanent; wood loses some of its luster.	Used to make furniture and interior wood paneling pale, blond. Also used on outdoor furniture and siding to give a weathered look.
Enamel	Varnish mixed with pigments to give color, opaqueness.	Brushed or sprayed over undercoat since enamel has less body and covering power than most paints.	Generally hard, durable coat, like varnish; usually glossy, may be dull. Wide range of colors.	Used chiefly on furniture, cabinets, walls getting hard use and washing. Also on floors.
Lacquer	Cellulose derivatives, consisting of resins, one or more gums, volatile solvents, a softener, and a pigment (if colored).	Regular lacquer is best applied with spray as it dries rapidly (15 min.); brushing lacquers dry slowly, make brush application feasible.	Hard, tough, durable; resistant to heat, acids; usually not suitable for outdoor wood because of expansion, contraction. Glossy, satiny, or dull.	Transparent lacquers much used on furniture, walls; opaque used on furniture.
Oil	Boiled linseed oil or various other oils; usually thinned with turpentine.	Brushed or wiped on, excess wiped off, allowed to dry, sanded or rubbed; between five and thirty coats—more the better. Hot oil sinks into wood, brings out grain emphatically.	Penetrating, very durable finish with soft luster; darkens and yellows wood somewhat at first, considerably in time. Protective, not conspicuous. Must be renewed.	Oil, often mixed with beeswax, used in Europe from early times to seventeenth century. Now used on indoor and outdoor furniture and on siding.
Paint	Pigments suspended in linseed oil or, more commonly now, in various synthetics. Usually contain a drier to hasten hardening.	Brushed, rolled, or sprayed on.	Opaque coating, varies from hard, durable gloss to softer dull finishes. Hides character of wood. New types dry quickly with little odor, are easy to apply and have good covering power.	Long used to protect, embellish wood indoors, outdoors. Painted furniture was popular in ancient Egypt, the Orient, Europe since Middle Ages. Much Early American furniture was painted. Widely used now on exterior and interior walls and furniture.

ornamentation of good quality. Some people find delight in putting old furniture in contemporary settings (Fig. 163), and some designers are exploring concentrated enrichment suited to our age (Fig. 161B). Many designers are working with sculptural form in furniture that is pleasing when seen from any angle and that combines comfort and convenience with sensuous delight and lyricism. Charles Eames's notable chair, designed some twenty years ago, is an early example; others are the furniture designed by Wendell Castle and DeSanctis and Sterpini (Figs. 38 and 96).

Wood Finishes

Anything done to a freshly sanded piece of wood takes away some of its pristine satiny beauty—but that beauty will soon disappear even if no finish is put on it. All but a few woods used in a few ways need some protective finish to keep the surface from absorbing dirt and stains; to give an easy-to-clean smoothness; to minimize excessive sudden changes in moisture content; to protect the wood from rot, decay, and insects; to keep it from drying out and to replace the lost oils; to minimize fading or darkening of color; to emphasize the grain with oil, change the color with stain, or hide both color and grain with opaque paint—in short, to protect and embellish.

WOOD FINISHES (Cont.)

Name	Composition	Application	Result	Use
Shellac	Resinous secretion of an insect of southern Asia, dissolved in alcohol.	Brushed, rubbed, or sprayed on; dries rapidly; many thin coats, each rubbed, gives best finish.	Changes character and color of wood very little, especially white type. Soft satiny finish to high gloss finish. Fragile; wears poorly; badly affected by heat, moisture. Water spots.	Used today primarily as an easily applied, quick-drying undercoat.
Stain	Dye or pigment dissolved or suspended in oil or water.	Brushed, sprayed, or rubbed on.	Changes color of wood without covering grain (often emphasizes grain or changes surface noticeably); usually darkens wood to make look richer.	Frequently used to alter color of furniture woods thought unattractive, or in imitation of expensive woods. Used outdoors to compensate for weathering.
Synthetics	Wide range of polyester, polyurethane, polyamide, vinyl. Liquid or film. Newest type finish; continuing new developments.	Usually factory-applied. *Liquid* impregnates wood. *Film,* typically colored, is bonded to wood with laminating adhesive.	Very durable, long-lasting finish; resistant to abrasion, mars, chemicals, water, or burns. Clear or colored, mat to glossy surface. Film type is difficult to repair if damaged.	Exterior siding; interior walls, floors, furniture. Very good wherever abrasion, moisture, or weathering is a problem.
Varnish	Various gums, resins dissolved in drying oils (linseed, tung, or synthetic), usually combined with other driers. Dye or pigment makes varnish-stain.	Brushed or sprayed on; many thin coats best. Dries slowly or fast, depending on kind, amount of thinner used.	Thin, durable, brownish skin coating, little penetration; darkens wood, emphasizes grain. Ranges from dull mat to high gloss. Best when not thick, gummy.	Known by ancients; not used again until mid-eighteenth century. Widely used today on furniture, floors, walls, chiefly interior.
Wax	Fatty acids from animal, vegetable, mineral sources combined with alcohols; Usually paste or liquid. Varies greatly in hardness, durability.	Brushed, sprayed, or rubbed on, usually several coats. Often used over oil, shellac, varnish, but may be used alone.	Penetrates raw wood. Darkens, enriches, emphasizes grain. Soft to high luster. Must be renewed often. May show water spots and make floor slippery. Other finishes cannot be used over wax.	Very old way of finishing wood. Generally used today as easily renewed surface over more durable undercoats; some liquid waxes used alone on walls, floors, furniture.

Furnishings from the past enrich many modern homes, as illustrated in a California home. Boldly elaborated, curvilinear Victorian furniture of black walnut contrasts effectively with the crisp rectangularity of smooth wood walls and a carefully laid brick fireplace and seat. Campbell and Wong, architects. (*Photograph by Morley Baer*)

Two freestanding fireplaces designed by architect Marcel Breuer illustrate some of the differences between stone and concrete.

The picturesque irregularity as well as the varied textures and colors of natural fieldstone are emphasized in this robust, rectangular design in the house of the Robinsons in Williamstown, Massachusetts. Setting the fireplace against a window wall permits simultaneous enjoyment of a fire and the view. (*Photograph by Robert Damora*)

Finishes can penetrate or stay on the surface; be transparent and colorless, transparent but colored, semiopaque, or opaque; and they can vary from a dull mat to a high gloss. To say that any one of these finishes is better than the others, except for a specific purpose, would be to fly in the face of facts. Today, however, many people like to see wood changed as little as is compatible with its use and therefore prefer transparent, colorless, dull finishes. Few of us like the finish to be more noticeable than the material underneath, as it often is on heavily varnished, cheap furniture. And we can also say that, *generally speaking:*

- Opaque finishes hide the wood character, give a smooth uniformity, and offer great possibilities for color.
- Transparent finishes reveal the character of the wood and do not emphasize minor damage that comes with use.
- Penetrating finishes produce a soft surface through which stains may penetrate, but they do not chip or crack.
- Glossy finishes reflect more light, are more durable because of their hard dense surface, are easier to clean, but show blemishes more than do dull finishes. Gloss can be reduced by adding more thinner to the paint or by rubbing with sandpaper, steel wool, or pumice. It will also dull with age and use.

The fluid quality of ready-to-be-poured concrete is expressed in the flowing continuity of a sculptural form without joints in the Gagarin house, Connecticut. (*Photograph by Ben Schnall*)

- Many thin coats of any finish, sanded or rubbed between coats, give a more durable, pleasant result than one or two coats applied thickly.
- Synthetic finishes, usually factory-applied, are varied and promising.

That is about as much as can be said on general matters. The more specific ways of protecting and embellishing wood have been summarized in the chart on pages 162–163.

More than other materials, wood ties the typical house together structurally and visually. It remains one of our most useful, beautiful materials and has more than held its own in spite of the great advances in plastics, glass, and metal. In fact, the newer materials, having relieved wood of some uses to which it was not completely suited, have allowed us to see more clearly how wonderful wood is. Much as we admire and respect other materials, few of them arouse the deep responses—love, if you will—that wood generates.

MASONRY

Strictly speaking, masonry is defined as anything constructed of such materials as stone, brick, or tiles that are put together, usually with mortar, by

Each of the basic types of stone masonry has a distinctive character, determined by the way in which the materials are shaped and the patterns in which they are laid.

Rubble masonry, rugged and informal, has untrimmed or only slightly trimmed stones laid irregularly. It is usually the least costly and formal kind of stonework. Eral Leek, architect. (*Photograph by Charles R. Pearson. Reprinted from* Sunset *Magazine*)

A

Random ashlar is more disciplined than rubble masonry but still rustic. The stones are more or less rectangular in shape but varied in size. Usually it gives a decided feeling of horizontality, even though the joints are not continuous. Anshen and Allen, architects.

B

a mason. Nowadays, however, the term also includes plastering and concrete construction. The materials of masonry come from inorganic mineral compounds in the earth's surface. They are of crystalline structure, and typically they are hard, dense, and heavy.

The excellences of masonry materials are numerous. They do not support combustion, rot, or decay, nor do they invite insects or rodents. Most of them are long-lasting, require little maintenance, and retain their shape under great pressure. Their colors and textures range from the smooth whiteness of plaster to the abrasiveness of black lava rock. They can be shaped with rectangular solidity or curved buoyancy, and they can be left plain and simple, laid up in complex patterns, or carved. Above all is a timeless quality—their seeming imperviousness to decay makes us feel secure.

These properties explain why most historic architecture still in existence is of masonry. Best known are the large religious or public buildings, but throughout the world there are thousands of unpretentious houses of stone and brick still in use. The essence of historic masonry construction (with the exception of Roman work in concrete) was the piling of blocks on top of one another and usually joining them with mortar. Because such walls must be very thick and rest on solid foundations, they are expensive. They do not allow large unobstructed openings (unless these are arched), and they offer no space for the pipes and wires now so essential. Thus, solid masonry construction is seldom used today for an entire structure, but it is often used for one or more walls of a home. Varied kinds of masonry also serve well in foundations, fireplaces, and chimneys, and in outdoor paving or interior floors that rest on the ground. In the nineteenth and twentieth centuries, many new methods and materials have been developed. These include masonry reinforced with metal to decrease weight and bulk without lessening strength, hollow blocks of brick or concrete (Fig. 170), and thin-shelled concrete structures (Fig. 175A).

Masonry, though, has limitations other than high original cost. Although comparatively permanent, plaster and stucco crack, concrete blocks chip, and the softer stones disintegrate more rapidly than might be expected. All are difficult to repair. In comparison with wood or metal, masonry is not very strong in tension. Further, most masonry offers fairly poor insulation against cold and dampness, and most of it reflects rather than absorbs noise.

Masonry can be divided into two major categories: the **block materials** —stone, bricks and tiles, concrete or glass blocks—which are delivered to a building site in their finished form and put together on the job with mortar; and the **plastic materials**—concrete and plaster—which may be used at the building in a semiliquid state.

Stone

Stone, a concreted earthy mineral, has so many desirable qualities that it would undoubtedly be used more widely if it were not so costly. Resistant to fire, stone seems naturally associated with walls and fireplaces. Belonging to the earth, it seems at home when used for floors subject to hard use and for outdoor paving. Promising permanence, it gives garden or house walls a uniquely reassuring character. Wherever used, the crystalline structure, varied colors and textures, and differing degrees of opaqueness and translucency add up to a very special visual and tactile appeal.

Ashlar masonry has precisely cut rectangular stones (or bricks) laid with continuous horizontal joints. It is usually the most formal and expensive type. The Palazzo Gondi, a sixteenth-century Renaissance town house in Florence, Italy, is a handsome example. Notice the progression from large, boldly cut stones on the ground floor to smaller, flat-surfaced stones on the top story. Giuliano da Sangallo, architect. (*Italian State Tourist Office*)

Although there are innumerable kinds of stone that could be used in homes, four are most commonly seen today:

- **Limestone,** which includes various sedimentary rocks, is relatively soft and easy to cut. Colors range from almost white to dark grays and tans. Its most common use is in exterior walls.
- **Marble,** a compact crystalline limestone, takes a beautiful polish, is often variegated, and comes in white, grays, pinks and reds, greens, and black. Contemporary designers, searching for structurally ornamented materials, have found it a handsome substance for fireplaces, bathroom walls, and tabletops.
- **Sandstone,** a natural concrete of sand grains, looks and feels sandy. Usually tan, it may also be reddish, greenish, or black. Exterior walls and paving are typical uses.

- **Slate,** a sedimentary rock that splits easily into thin sheets with smooth surfaces, makes good interior floors or outdoor paving. In addition to the typical bluish gray, slate is available in green, red, or black.

The three basic types of masonry composed of blocky materials are **rubble, random ashlar,** and **ashlar.** These are illustrated and described on pages 166, 168, and 169.

Brick and Tile (Clay)

Two of the oldest artificial building materials are bricks and tiles. They are still much in favor because, in addition to having the assets of masonry, they are easily made by hand or machine from clays found almost everywhere. They weigh less than stone, which is important in shipping and laying them. Because of their relatively small size they may be laid up around a hollow core or simply as a facing on one side of a wall, which leaves room for pipes and wiring and still forms a reasonably thin wall. Cavity-wall construction has the additional advantage that the trapped air acts as a nonconductor of heat, cold, and moisture. They come in many sizes and shapes, colors and textures, and they can be laid in varied patterns. Being fireproof, weather-resistant, and easy to maintain, they are frequently used for fireplaces and chimneys as well as for exterior and interior wall surfaces. They make excellent garden paving because their color and texture render them glareless and unslippery.

The precise shape of typical bricks leads naturally to ashlar-type masonry. In contrast to the rough-hewn character of rubble masonry and random ashlar, the rectangular forms in this house are sophisticated and elegant. Thornton Ladd, architect. (*Photograph by Julius Shulman*)

Wherever seen, bricks and tiles introduce an orderly rhythmic pattern of a scale appropriate for homes. They are particularly effective in large, comparatively simple masses (Figs. 163 and 169). Their only drawback is cost.

Typical clay bricks are blocks of clay hardened by heat in a kiln. A standard size is $2\frac{1}{4}$ by 4 by $8\frac{1}{4}$ inches, but their dimensions may vary considerably. Although *brick red* is a common phrase, colors range from almost white, pale yellow, and pink through oranges and reds to browns and purples. On the basis of texture as well as resistance to breakage, moisture, and fire, bricks are conventionally divided into several types:

- **Common,** or **sand-struck, bricks,** made in a mold coated with dry sand, have slightly rounded edges and are used for exposed side walls or as a base for better-quality brick.
- **Face bricks,** usually formed by forcing clay through a rectangular die and cutting it with wire, have sharp edges and corners, are more uniform in color and texture, and more resistant to weather than are common bricks.
- **Paving,** or **flooring, bricks** are those made harder by firing at higher temperatures to withstand abrasion and to lessen absorption of moisture.
- **Fire bricks** are usually yellow, and are used for places subject to great heat, such as the backs of fireplaces.

A second type of brick, known as **adobe,** is made of clay that today is usually combined with a cement or asphalt stabilizer and is dried in the sun. Adobe bricks have been used in warm, dry parts of the world for centuries

As seen on these two pages, prefabricated building blocks have broken out of the shackles that once made them ugly ducklings.

David Wright's home demonstrates the versatility of concrete blocks in a house that coils up from the rocky desert near Phoenix, Arizona. The blocks are visually compatible with this environment and insulate the house against heat and cold. Frank Lloyd Wright, architect. (*Photograph by Maynard L. Parker Modern Photography*)

A

B

Left. Rough in texture and warm in color, thin rectangular concrete blocks make a rugged, informal interior or exterior wall. (*General Concrete Products, Inc.*)

Above. Thick glass blocks with recessed areas of clear patterned glass surrounded by raised areas of opaque, textured, ceramic finish can be joined by mortar to make walls that produce changing patterns of transmitted light. (*Pittsburgh Corning Corporation*)

Below. Design in depth is achieved in pierced wall units that cast unusual shadow patterns. Walls of this material give partial visual privacy while allowing air and some light to come through. Erwin Hauser, designer. (*Arts for Architecture, Inc.*)

Bottom. Short sections of cylinders can be laid in many patterns to produce an ornamental screen wall. (*General Concrete Products, Inc.*)

and have recently come back into favor in the Southwest (Figs. 223 and 224A).

Like bricks, **clay tiles** are composed of heat-hardened clay, but they are usually thin and glazed. They are discussed and illustrated in Chapters 9 and 11.

Concrete Blocks

Once an ugly duckling used apologetically for foundations, concrete blocks are now widely used for their decorative as well as utilitarian qualities. They have many of the characteristics of clay bricks, but they are made with cement, are not fired (although drying may be hastened with low heat), are usually quite a bit larger than bricks so that a single thickness of blocks can be made into a sturdy wall, and are almost always hollow. Most popular today are the *lightweight-aggregate* blocks made with such porous materials as cinders, pumice, or volcanic ash instead of sand and gravel. About half as heavy as the older type, they are less expensive to transport. Being larger than bricks (8 by 8 by 16 inches and 4 by 8 by 16 inches are typical sizes), they can be laid more rapidly. Their porosity and hollow cores provide some insulation against heat and cold and also absorb noise. Finally, their colors are much pleasanter than the older, chilling gray. In mild climates, walls of these blocks need no treatment other than waterproofing, although they can be painted or plastered. If left exposed inside and out, as in Figures 87A and 170, the pleasantly rugged texture appeals to those who like to see that nothing is covered up, that the structure—the interior and exterior walls—is unified and is frankly revealed.

Glass Blocks

Hollow blocks of glass that can be set together in mortar come in many sizes and shapes. They also vary in the amount of light and heat they transmit. Some, for example, reflect the high summer sunlight but allow the winter sun's low rays to warm the interior. Glass blocks are one of the few materials that

C

D

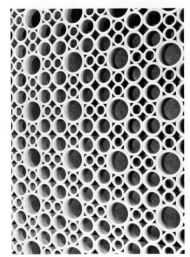

admit light but give varying degrees of privacy, provide reasonable insulation against heat and cold, and make a supporting wall of any strength. Further, the manner in which they diffuse light and create changing abstract patterns out of objects seen through them is highly decorative. They have been used to illumine entrance areas, bathrooms, kitchens, and other rooms where natural light combined with privacy is wanted. They have not, however, been widely used in homes, probably because their glitter seems "commercial" and their cost fairly high, but some of the newer designs in Chapter 11 are promising.

Concrete

Concrete is a kind of stone made by man from cement, sand, and gravel. One volume of cement to two of sand and four of gravel is the usual mix for concrete, which begins its existence as a thick slush, takes the form of any mold into which it is poured, and hardens into artificial stone. The Romans used concrete extensively; hence it is not new. But in the past century the variety of ways in which it has been employed, especially in large structures, makes it seem like something quite different. Its great virtues are its plasticity before it sets and its durability after it hardens. No other material combines these two qualities to the same degree.

Two factors have tended to limit poured concrete to such basic but unemphasized parts of the home as foundations, basement floors and walls, walks, terraces, and driveways. First, the cost of forms used only once on the site is very high for anything other than such simple forms as those for foundations or floors. As yet, this cost has not been completely overcome. Second, ordinary concrete is not attractive in color or texture, and it is associated with basements and sidewalks. Fortunately, there are many ways of getting around this second disadvantage:

- Concrete can be prefabricated in blocks or slabs under efficient mass-production methods, using the same forms over and over.
- Concrete can be made from materials other than sand and gravel to improve its color and texture as well as its insulating qualities.
- The surface can be varied by adding colored pigments, troweling it smoothly, or giving it any number of textures.
- The gravel used in the concrete can be exposed in either of two ways: *terrazzo* is the term used for concrete made with stone chips and polished to reveal an irregular mosaic-like pattern; *broom-finished* describes the pebbly surfaced concrete made with round pebbles from which the surface coating of concrete has been brushed off.
- Paints and dyes (of special types to withstand the strong alkaline reaction of concrete) can be applied to the surface. Paints are usually thick enough to smooth the surface, while dyes are transparent and penetrating.
- Plaster or stucco can be applied as a surface coating.
- Concrete can be carved and enriched with other materials (Fig. 173).

Plaster and Stucco

Plaster and stucco have been widely used for centuries in many parts of the world because of their special qualities. **Plaster** is a thick, pasty mixture of such materials as sand, lime, gypsum, and water. **Stucco** refers to weather-resistant plaster used on exteriors. Both plaster and stucco are usually put

Emile Norman proves that a concrete wall can be of great interest and lasting beauty. (*Photograph by Maynard L. Parker Modern Photography*)

onto a *lath,* a term now used for thin strips of wood spaced like ribs, metal sheets with grillelike perforations, or special types of hardboards. They can also be put on any masonry surface that is rough enough to hold them.

Like concrete, plaster and stucco will hold any shape that is given them before they harden. They can smoothly cover simple or complex surfaces with no visible joints (Fig. 174). Both can be textured, have integral color (Color Fig. 12), or be painted; and interior plaster walls can be covered with paper or fabrics for embellishment and protection. Many historic homes show how well suited these materials are to varied kinds of sculptural enrichment (Fig. 152). A further advantage is their moderate original cost.

Under some conditions both plaster and stucco can raise maintenance problems. Cracks or chips are common unless precautions are taken. On smooth, light-colored walls these are conspicuous, as are fingerprints, soot, and scratches. Although not expensive, the original cost of plaster is higher than for many of the hardboards, which provide better insulation against heat, cold, and noise.

WOOD AND MASONRY · 173

In the tower bedroom of York Castle, which stands on a hill above Tangier, smooth white plaster emphasizes the complex shape of Moorish-inspired windows and acts as foil for a commanding view of the Strait of Gibraltar. Begun in the sixteenth century, the castle has been recently restored. Contemporary furniture is effective in this historic setting. (Interiors for York Castle designed by Planning Unit *Knoll International, France*)

Design in Masonry

With a few exceptions, the design of block masonry in contemporary American homes is limited to selecting stones or blocks that are available in the area and then organizing them into simple, usually rectangular masses. The shapes in which boulders and stratified rock are found can without much effort be adapted to rubble or random-ashlar masonry, which often seems more in the nature of the material than would a precise organization. Concrete blocks and bricks, having been molded to uniform rectangularity, typically are laid in the regularly repeated, clear-cut patterns of ashlar masonry. These treatments are, of course, historic. What is particularly of this century is the way in which the weight and density of stone, brick, and concrete blocks are contrasted with the comparative lightness of wood and with the transparency of large areas of glass (Fig. 169), and the use that is made of these materials to tie the house to its site through extended walls and paving (Fig. 166B).

Another major type of masonry design is that possible with plaster or poured concrete. Holding any shape that they are given by molds or mason's tools, these plastic substances are suitable for myriad shapes that are curved or angular, simple or complex. Although poured concrete has been used in unimaginative ways in the building of apartment and commercial structures for a number of years, its possibilities are also being explored by talented designers (Fig. 173 and Color Fig. 12).

Concrete can be formed into plastic, sculptural shapes that are imaginative and free.

A

John Johansen's project for a thin-shelled house in which concrete is sprayed over a framework of steel rods and steel-and-paper mesh indicates one new way of handling this material.

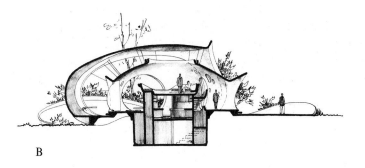

B

A section through the house shows the completeness of Johansen's concept. The convoluted form is used to create new space-form relationships in the interior as well as on the exterior.

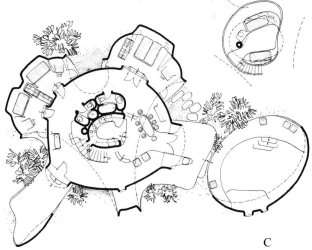

C

The plan is also composed of curved shapes. The small form in the upper right is the second-floor nest, which appears in the center of the section. The larger oval in the lower right is a swimming pool.

Masonry has its very special appeal of long-lasting, substantial security. It comes from the earth, and many of us enjoy seeing its earthy character clearly revealed. That masonry, however, can be treated in many other ways is evinced by the subtle forms created in marble by the ancient Greeks, by the soaring spires and lacelike tracery of the Gothic builders, by the majestic structures of the Renaissance, or by the miraculously thin concrete shells that are reintroducing curved structural forms into contemporary architecture.

For the Gene Bavingers' home, architect Bruce Goff used rough rock and big chunks of glass, metal pipes and steel cables to achieve a dynamic sculptural form rising boldly from its Oklahoma site. Cylindrical masonry walls are built around a tall pole from which cables fan out to support a spiraling roof over the interior space. A hanging bay of concrete, wood, and glass encloses a light-filled seating area. See Figure 18 for an interior view of this house. (*Photograph by Julius Shulman*)

Wonderfully dissimilar materials and shapes have been brought together by Alexander Girard in a high-spirited table setting. (*Georg Jensen Inc.*)

9 · Ceramics, Glass, Metal, and Plastics

Varied materials, imaginatively combined, distinguish the table setting that is reproduced at the top of this page. A thin porcelain bowl enhanced with intricate geometric designs in gold stands on a plate with a vigorously free pattern. To the left, a thicker stoneware plate relies on form and textured glaze alone for its appeal. The tall, slender Venetian glass goblet, whose shape is accented by swirling strands of colored glass, rises gracefully above the small, dark Mexican glass. To the left of the goblet is a short tumbler, whose thin transparency finds support in a richly modeled base, and at the far left is a thick, free-form cigarette holder. Marks of the silversmith's hammer enliven the ashtray's surface, while restrained ornament emphasizes the smooth, reflecting handle of the nearby knife. At each side of the porcelain plate is ornate silverware, sparkling with small-scale detail, that contrasts strikingly with the unornamented spoon of black plastic.

Glass, metal, and plastic are equally eloquent in making the terrace shown in Figure 178 livable and structurally secure. The large sliding panes of glass would not have been feasible without their metal frames and the hidden steel that supports the roof. No material yet discovered, other than metal, could have supported the chairs and tables with such slender forms. Figured glass visually lightens the tabletop, while translucent plastic in the skylight brings light without excessive heat or glare.

In a table setting or in an entire house, ceramics, glass, metal, and plastics are serviceable and beautiful. They have been grouped in one chapter because they have important characteristics in common. Since all are shaped while in a plastic, liquid, or malleable state, the diversity of appropriate shapes is tremendous. All are subjected to heat in processing. With the exception of some plastics, all are inert—which means that they will not burn, rot, decay, or appeal to insects and vermin. Each of these materials, nonetheless, has its own special potentialities and limitations that challenge sensitive designers and bring liveliness to our homes.

CERAMICS

The distinctive qualities of glass and plastic, metal and stone have been resolved in a calm, precise unity for this protected terrace adjoining a living room. Henry Eggers, architect. (*Photograph by Maynard L. Parker Modern Photography*)

Long before early man began to write, he fashioned useful and symbolic objects from clay. From then on, this material has been of continuing and conspicuous importance in homes. All of us are aware of the dishes used for eating, of ashtrays, vases, and lamp bases. But this field also includes many sculptural objects, bricks and tiles, chimney flues, and drain pipes. All these are *ceramics*, which is a short way of saying objects made of clay hardened by heat. Essential steps in the process are:

- Finding a suitable clay or combining several clays
- Moistening the clay sufficiently to make it workable
- Shaping the clay by hand, on the potter's wheel, or in a mold
- Allowing the pieces to dry until they are "leather hard"
- Firing the pieces to harden them permanently

   The process could stop at this point but usually involves:
- Decorating the piece with carving or painting
- Glazing it with a glasslike coating

Ceramics differ in terms of **body** and **glaze, form,** and **ornamentation.**

Body

   The clays used for the body of ceramics affect the characteristics of the finished product. Some are white, others black, and between these extremes are many tans, grays, and reds. Textures range from coarse, irregular, and open to fine, even, and dense. Clays also have different melting points (the temperatures at which they lose their shape). Generally those clays that hold their shape at high temperatures make the stronger objects because the separate particles fuse together, or vitrify, into a dense, homogeneous, glasslike, waterproof mass. Almost always, however, several clays are mixed together in varying proportions to produce the desired combination of qualities. For convenience, ceramic bodies can be grouped into four major types, although each has a wide range of characteristics that may overlap those of other types:

- **Earthenware,** made from coarse clays and fired at comparatively low temperatures, is typically thick, porous, and opaque. It breaks quite easily. The Pennsylvania plate and the hollow tiles used as grilles (Figs. 179A and 182A) illustrate these qualities, as do bricks, flowerpots, and much Mexican pottery. The glazes are usually soft and show scratches. More refined earthenware, however, can be shaped and ornamented as sensitively as the vases in Figure 179B.
- **Stoneware** (Fig. 180) is made from finer clays and fired at higher temperatures. The clay particles are fused together and the body becomes stronger, more waterproof, and more durable than earthenware but, like it, opaque. Stoneware is favored for the better grades of decorative pottery and tableware. Some is used for oven-to-table ware. The medium-soft glazes can be much more varied than can those suited to earthenware.
- **China** is a somewhat general term describing vitrified ware that is translucent if thin. Because its qualities place it between stoneware and porcelain, it might better be called "semiporcelain" but *china,* originally referring to the European ware imitating true Chinese porcelain, has persisted as the most-used name.
  English china or *bone china* has a white, translucent body and a soft but brilliant glaze.
  American vitreous china has unusual resistance to breakage and chipping. Glazes and decorations resist scratching.
- **Porcelain** (Fig. 181) is reserved for high-grade, expensive dishes and ornamental ware. Fired at high temperatures, it is completely vitrified and often translucent. The body resists breakage and the glazes are very hard.

The relationship of ornamentation and glaze to form and material has fascinated potters for centuries, as can be seen in the following four figures.

A

B

Top. On a Pennsylvania earthenware plate made in 1786, a transparent glaze protects a vigorous sgraffito design. (*National Gallery of Art, Index of American Design*)

Above. Katherine Chou, exploring new forms and techniques in the 1950s, has achieved a festive freedom. Glazes and stains actively participate in the total effect. (*Reprinted from* Craft Horizons)

CERAMICS, GLASS, METAL, AND PLASTICS - 179

The purist would say, with some justification, that earthenware suggests simple, vigorous shapes and ornamentation, and that increasing precision and refinement should be expected as one goes from stoneware to china and porcelain. Not always, however, does this happen, for other factors affect ceramic design.

Design in Ceramics

The possibilities and limitations of the shape of any material are determined by its physical properties, the methods by which it is formed, the intended use of the object—and the skill and sensitivity of the designer. These are the physical properties of clay: before firing, it is composed of small powder-like or granular particles that can be mixed with a little water to make a plastic mass or with more water to make a creamy liquid called *slip;* but after firing, clay is hard and brittle, has little tensile strength, and therefore breaks quite easily when hit or dropped. Thin edges or protruding parts are quite vulnerable.

While being shaped, clay is either plastic and therefore responds to any pressure or it is liquid and will take the shape of any mold into which it is poured. Almost any shape is possible, as the history of ceramics proves, but most dishes and vases are round and relatively compact, because round forms come naturally from the potter's wheel and the template and revolving mold (called jigger and jolley) that is used in mass production. They are easy to hold in our rounded hands, and they are a pleasant relief from the basic rectangularity of our homes. Important, too, is the fact that they have a minimum of edges to chip. In short, rounded forms, compact in outline, seem especially appropriate to ceramic dishes and ornamental pieces.

This does not rule out other possibilities. Angular shapes are basic in bricks and tiles; in household ceramics they can occasionally be useful as well as welcome surprises. Some extending forms, such as spouts on teapots or handles on cups, are worth the hazard of breakage. Then, fortunately, there is the creative urge to explore and experiment, to find forms that will reawaken our senses, as do those created by Katherine Chou.

Glazes

Glazes are glassy coatings fused at high temperatures to the body of ceramics. They increase usefulness by making ceramics waterproof and easy to clean. Their textures and colors, an example of structural ornament, are primary sources of beauty. Limitless in variety, they enable each potter to express his convictions in finding a glaze he deems appropriate to the body, shape, and use of each piece.

Figures 179A through 181 illustrate a few of the effects that glazes can produce. On the Pennsylvania plate a transparent glaze, almost as thin and clear as water, protects and intensifies the colors of the applied design. Glazes of earthy colors and varied textures applied in unexpected ways emphasize the sprightly, highly plastic character of Katherine Chou's vases. Thick, treacly, and emphatically textured, the glazes on Maija Grotell's jar intentionally dominate the uneventful, simple shape they encase. Not so with the Chinese porcelain, on which the brilliant, pure-white glaze, as elegantly precise as the vase, is secondary to the form. For each of these pieces, the glazes were sensitively and purposefully chosen.

Maija Grotell, in the 1930s, allowed a heavy brown-and-white glaze to enliven a simple stoneware shape. (*Photograph by Harvey Croze*)

Glazes differ in the degree to which they join with and "fit" the body. A broken piece of glazed earthenware will show that the glassy coating forms a distinct layer on the porous body; but on most porcelains the glazes are so completely integrated with the clay that there is no sharp division between the two. If glaze and body do not have the same coefficient of expansion, the glaze will quickly or with use, develop a series of cracks. In decorative pottery such effects may be planned for their ornamental value. On dishes used for food, these cracks are more likely to be the result of poor workmanship.

Ornament in Ceramics

Often the basic form with the addition of glazes make applied ornamentation unnecessary, a point made clear by Figure 181 and Color Figure 13A. There is, however, an ever-present urge to enrich a plain surface, and ceramics have received their share of decoration. The medium seems to invite modeling, carving, and painting.

Modeling and **carving,** which give a three-dimensional play of light and shade, range from scarcely noticeable incised designs to vigorous shaping and cutting. Figure 179B shows both subtle incised designs and ornament that protrudes from the basic forms. Much more formal is the modeling of the lower portion of the Chinese porcelain vase. *Sgraffito* (literally, "scratched") decoration is done by coating the piece with slip, a thin liquid coating of clay different in color from that of the base, and then scratching through to reveal the color underneath (Fig. 179A).

Colored pigments can be applied with a brush, through a stencil, transferred from decalcomanias, or printed mechanically. This decoration can be underglaze or overglaze, and the design possibilities are endless. *Underglaze* designs are applied before the final glazing, which protects them from scratches and wear. *Overglaze* patterns are applied to the surface of glazed ware and fused with it at a low firing temperature. It is the cheapest and most common type of ceramic enrichment and when well done is moderately durable.

With such possibilities, it is easy for inventiveness and technical skill to exceed taste and common sense. What, then, is suitable enrichment for ceramics? As discussed in Chapter 6, ornament is at its best when it is appropriate to functions, form, size, and material. As an example we can take plates used at the table. Their functions are to hold food and please the eye, but they must also be handled many times. They are shallow, usually circular dishes about 10 inches in diameter, made of fired clay. Suitable enrichment emphasizes these qualities. That is why the decoration, if any, on most plates is circular in movement, rounded rather than angular, flat rather than heavily modeled, conventional or abstract rather than naturalistic. Because clay is either plastic or liquid when shaped, the most natural ornament has something of these qualities. Finally, ornament should be vital in itself.

Architectural Ceramics

Bricks and tiles belong to both ceramics and masonry because they are made of clay and hardened by heat, and are used by setting in mortar. That tiles can be an important component of domestic architecture is shown in the

A seventeenth-century Chinese porcelain vase, disciplined and serene in outline, needs no ornamentation other than the smooth white glaze that emphasizes the sensitive shape. (*The Metropolitan Museum of Art, New York*)

outdoor living room of a Mexican house (Fig. 182A) in which ordinary drain tiles are used to fill the gaps between stone piers. They not only create an ever-changing pattern of light and shade but give protection against rain, sun, and wind. Small mosaic, glazed tiles energize the end walls of a contemporary Connecticut home (Fig. 182B). Durable and maintenance-free, they contrast effectively with the large areas of glass, and with their sparkling juxtaposition of dark and light, relate the structure to the intricate play of sun and shadow on the trees behind the house. Of great importance is the way in which they bring an intimate, human scale to a house that is composed of large, rectangular masses. The revival of interest in tile that is useful and ornamental indicates our need for something more than plain surface.

A

Ordinary tile takes on fresh meaning when used imaginatively in architecture.

Right. Humble earthenware drain tiles create a captivating pattern of light and shade in a contemporary Mexican house. Anshen and Allen, architects. (*Photograph by Maynard L. Parker Modern Photography*)

Below. Mosaic tiles on exterior walls can be at one with the house shape yet add their own active, colorful enrichment. John Johansen, architect. (*Tile Council of America*)

B

Designer Jacob Epstein has intensified the transparent beauty of thick plate glass by floating it on top of an extremely simple, mirror-polished, stainless-steel base, for a coffee table of great purity. In design and materials it has much in common with Figure 187. (*Cumberland Furniture Corporation*)

GLASS

The development of glass from a semiprecious material available only in small pieces to one that can be bought anywhere and installed in large sheets has altered our homes as much as any single factor. Its history is fascinating. Glassmaking appears to have developed from ceramic glazes, some of which were made at least six thousand years ago, but the oldest known glass objects are around four thousand years old. The Romans made glass objects of such beauty that the best were valued higher than vessels of gold. The Romans also had sheets of glass for windows, but window glass was not common in small homes until the end of the eighteenth century. Today glass is an everyday, extraordinarily versatile material.

Glass is made by melting and fusing at very high temperatures the basic ingredients—silicates, alkalis, and lime—plus varied other materials that give special qualities. Crystal, the finest glass, contains lead. Color comes from minerals—red from gold and copper, blue from copper and cobalt, yellow from cadmium and uranium. Special effects, such as opacity, bubbles, or crystallization, and special forms, such as glass fibers and insulation, result from chemicals or the way in which glass is treated.

The general characteristics of glass are as follows:
- Transparency unrivaled until recently by any other common material
- Capacity to refract light in a gemlike way
- Wide range of colors, degrees of transparency, and textures
- Plasticity, malleability, and ductility that permit a great variety of shapes from threadlike fibers to large thin sheets
- Imperviousness to water and most alkalis and acids
- Resistance to burning (but will melt at high temperatures)
- Moderately high resistance to scratching
- Low resistance to breakage through impact, twisting or bending, and sudden temperature changes (except with special types)

Household Glass

Glass tumblers, bottles, and baking dishes are made by *blowing* or *molding*. In blowing glass by hand, the craftsman dips a hollow metal rod into molten glass, blows it into a bubble, and then forms the hot, soft material into the desired shape. Because this is expensive, most household glass is molded. In this process, molten glass is blown or pressed by machinery into cast-iron or wood molds. Molded glass can be shaped with Spartan simplicity or with great intricacy of shape and surface pattern.

Glass is the standard material for the tumblers and goblets from which we drink liquids. It is nonabsorbent, tasteless, and odorless, feels pleasantly cool to hands and lips, is not harmed by anything that we can safely drink, and is inexpensive. Clear, colorless glass allows us to see what we are drinking and to enjoy the crystal clarity of water and the color of lemonade or wine. Colored glassware adds its own special qualities to table settings. Fragility is the major drawback, a small price to pay for its good qualities unless you have small children, eat outdoors or casually in various parts of the house. Then tumblers of anodized aluminum, stainless steel, or durable plastics are worth considering.

Glass is also used for other food receptacles with varying degrees of satisfaction. Glass salad bowls and plates are attractive when filled but become less attractive than opaque wares as the meal nears completion. Glass cups can hold hot tea or coffee but seem less appropriate than ceramics for ordinary use. Glass cooking utensils have their special advantages, but they are harder to clean and less durable than metal.

Along with metal, glass is particularly suitable for candleholders because of the way in which it sparkles. It makes attractive flower containers if you have good-looking flower holders, arrange the stems under water attractively, and keep the water very clear. It is the standard material for mirrors and is also used for tabletops. Glass (especially colorless and transparent glass), though, loses most of its beauty if not kept polished. Finger and water marks or specks of dust are more conspicuous on clear, shiny glass than on most other materials.

The bubble and related shapes are basic forms in hand-blown glass. Transparency is a nearly unique attribute, and flowing plasticity is a cogent design inspiration. Glass can, however, be thick and heavy, richly colored, and translucent or opaque.

Right. Two contemporary Dutch vases of very thin, clear glass look as though they have just been removed from the glassblower's rod. F. Meydam, designer. (*Royal Leerdam Glassworks*)

Far right. A bottle only four inches high, designed by Flavio Poli and made in Venice in 1959, is built up from thick layers of clear and richly colored glass. (*Seguso Vetri d'Arte, Murano*)

A

B

Left. John Burton demonstrates some of the delightfully varied shapes and ornaments that are particularly appropriate for handwrought glass. (*Photograph by Richard Gross. California Design/9, Pasadena Art Museum*)

13A

Right. Lustrous, shimmering, opalescent glazes enhance the basically simple forms of a ceramic bowl and three vases that were created by (*left to right*) Beatrice Wood, Gertrude and Otto Natzler, and Herbert Sanders. Robert Webb's handwoven fabric with irregular stripes and subtle color variations forms an appropriate background. (*Photograph by Richard Gross. California Design/9, Pasadena Art Museum*)

13B

14

A white plastic and cast-aluminum pedestal table and chairs were designed by Eero Saarinen in the flowing shapes that come as naturally in these materials as do the more conventional rectangular forms. They are handsomely set off by the deep-pile carpet and the soft draperies, an unusually mellow, glowing beige. The depth of color of the dark-blue wall is emphasized by its mat surface, by the golden sunburst sculpture, by the greens of the painting, and by the bright blue cushions. Green plants, bright red flowers, and a piece of sculpture on the low cabinet are small-scale, lively enrichment. (*Knoll Associates Inc.*)

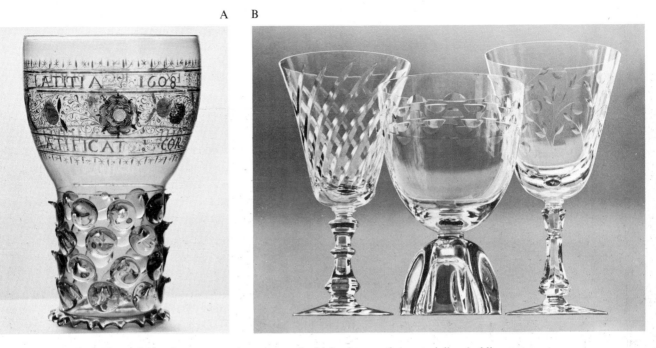

Ornament in and on glass takes many guises, most of which play up the material's sparkling transparency.

Above left. Delicate gilding with touches of red enamel enhances the bowl of a seventeenth-century German goblet of green glass. Defying staid notions of harmony, vigorous "dropped-on" globular ornament strengthens the base. (*The Metropolitan Museum of Art, New York*)

Above right. Clear glass invites complex, diversified shaping, cutting, and engraving to bring out exhilarating patterns of light and dark. The thin, symmetrical bowl of the center goblet contrasts strongly with the heavy, more freely formed base. (*Fostoria Glass Company*)

Form in household glass. What was said about form in ceramics might almost be repeated for glass because, in both, form is given to an amorphous substance while it is plastic or liquid; the final product is hard, brittle, and breakable; and process, material, and use lead naturally, although not exclusively, to rounded forms. As the bowl is a natural shape for ceramics formed on the potter's wheel, the bubble is the natural shape for hand-blown glass (Fig. 184A). *Simple, compact,* and *rounded* are three key words describing what the purists would say are the most basic forms for glass.

Two of the other innumerable and distinctive qualities of glass are significant. The first is that glass, technically speaking, always remains a liquid. Therefore, even when rigid, as it is at ordinary temperatures, it is actually a "supercooled liquid," a characteristic made quite evident in Figures 184A and B. Second, an almost perfect union of form and space can be achieved with glass. We look less *at* a transparent glass bowl or tumbler than *through* it to the space enclosed and the space beyond. Large windows give a similar effect. Contemporary designers and architects interested in the relation of form to space have a special feeling toward this material so closely uniting the two.

Ornament in household glass. It is not easy to draw a sharp line between form and ornament in glass (Color Fig. 13B). Structural ornament can be added before glass is shaped by using substances that give it color, make it translucent or cloudy, or produce such visual textures as bubbles or streaks of opaque materials. Sometimes form becomes so complex that it becomes as highly decorative as the stems of the drinking vessels in Figures 185A and B.

Hand-blown glass. A skilled glassblower can do many things to enrich a piece while it is still hot, and some of these can be reproduced by machine. He can, for example, "drop on" globs of molten glass (Fig. 185A) to produce almost liquid-looking ornament or such useful devices as handles. The whole piece, or parts of it, can be fluted and ribbed, or given swirling patterns, as illustrated in the cigarette holder and goblet in Figure 177.

Molded and pressed glass. The fact that molten glass will take and hold the form of a mold into which it is poured or pressed is put to good advantage in the making of molded and pressed glass. Many complex shapes and patterns are possible with this process.

Cut glass. Although glass was beautifully cut by the Romans, the technique was given new life about A.D. 1600, when a court jeweler in Prague applied gem-cutting techniques to glass. Rich effects come when the design is cut through an outer coating of colored glass to reveal colorless glass underneath. In colorless crystal, cutting gives many surfaces to catch and break up light in a diamond-like manner.

Engraved glass. As with cut glass, engraving is done with wheels and abrasives; but engraving produces a shallow intaglio that by optical illusion often seems to be in relief. Firmness of form, sharpness of edge, and easy-flowing curves distinguish engraved glass from that which is pressed, cut, or etched.

Etched glass. Either hydrofluoric acid or sandblasting is used to etch glass. The frosty etched surface may be left in that state or polished to smooth transparency. Etching is often used to imitate engraving, but the designs are not so sharp nor so subtly modeled. Usually shallow and delicate, etching can be 2 inches deep, as it is in some heavy French pieces.

Enameled and gilded glass. After looking at some of the cheap enameled or gilded glass frequently seen today, we are tempted to call these processes inventions of the devil. But in the past some very beautiful glass was made by burning colored enamels (Fig. 185A) or gold and silver into the surface. This type of ornamentation is at its best when glass, enameling, and gilding are of high quality, the design is precise and refined, and the workmanship skillful.

The most satisfying ornament in glass, no matter how achieved, is that which exploits what the material does with light. It can be as vigorous as that suitable for wood or ceramics; but since the pieces are usually small, heavy ornament is rare. The typically smooth surface and fine, nongranular composition make very delicate, refined, precise decoration highly effective. The transparency of glass makes possible ornament that is embedded in the material, a process that was unique to glass until the development of plastics.

Architectural Glass

Glass for windows is made by two processes. In *drawing,* the way in which inexpensive window glass is made, molten glass is drawn from furnaces in never-ending sheets, flattened between rollers, and cut into usable sizes. Although satisfactory for most purposes, drawn glass is usually not so strong or so thick and free from flaws as is plate glass. In *rolling,* the method by which plate glass is made, molten glass is poured onto an iron casting table, distributed and smoothed by rollers, then ground and polished. Today sheets of plate glass more than 50 feet long can be made.

Although glass for buildings is generally thought of as transparent, colorless, and smooth, it can be frosted or pebbly, ribbed or corrugated, or colored to control light, heat, and vision. Some architectural glass has a core of metal mesh that reduces the hazard of breakage and is also decorative. In the past, one had to choose between opaque walls and transparent windows and then frequently cover the windows with curtains or blinds for protection. Now a single permanent material can provide an entrance area or a bathroom illumined by natural light without sacrifice of privacy, a screen between rooms that divides without separating, or windows that diffuse glareless light. (See Chap. 11.)

Glass Textiles and Insulation

The great versatility of glass is indicated by special types used for draperies and heat-cold insulation. Spun glass was used for centuries in a purely decorative way, but not until about 1893 were its utilitarian values appreciated. Then neckties and dresses of spun glass and silk were exhibited as curiosities: they were heavy, scratchy, and too stiff to fold. As discussed in Chapter 10, glass textiles have come a long way since 1893. Glass fibers today are also widely used for insulation against extreme temperatures and sound. Another development is foam glass, made by introducing a gas-producing agent into molten glass. Filled with so many tiny air bubbles that it will float on water, it has excellent insulating properties.

METALS

Although man learned to reduce metal from ore around 5000 B.C., its use in domestic architecture was unimportant until recently. Today the typical "wood house" uses about four tons of metal, double that used twenty years ago, and the amount is increasing each year. But only a few of these 8000 pounds are visible. Such is not the case with the house illustrated in Figure 187, in which the unique structural qualities of metal, visibly exploited, make possible a new

Architect Jacques C. Brownson's house in Geneva, Illinois, built in the 1950s, brings together audacious frankness and classic poise. It is supported by, or more accurately hung from, four *simple, heavy* steel frames that stand outside the glass walls and above the roof. With this type of structure, interior space can be planned with great freedom. Surrounding woodland gives the needed privacy.

In contrast to the Brownsons' house, Charles Eames's own home, built in 1949 near Los Angeles, has a *light, intricate* steel framework not unlike a boy's Erector set. Walls, windows, doors, and even floors can be flexibly organized, and varied surfacing materials (see Fig. 160A) can be used as desired. That mass-produced, structural metal forms can have their own distinctive beauty is shown in the window walls and in the ceiling. (*Photograph by Julius Shulman*)

approach to house design. Four heavy steel frames, from which a 30-by-85-foot roof is suspended, are the only supports in the Illinois house. Under this sheltering, floating canopy, walls and windows have been placed wherever desired. The result is a boldly confident separation of structure and enclosing surfaces.

Metal, like masonry, ceramics, and glass, is inorganic and therefore does not burn, rot, or decay. But metal differs from these other inorganic substances in some important respects: it rusts or corrodes (with a few exceptions) when exposed to moisture and air, and it has great tensile strength. Metal's capacity to transmit heat, cold, and electricity is unequaled. The surface is usually shiny and nonabsorbent.

With the possible exception of plastics, no other material can be shaped in so many ways. It can be melted and cast in simple or intricate molds. In the solid state, it can be rolled, pressed, or turned on a lathe, as well as hammered, bent, drilled, or cut with saws and torches. Separate pieces can be welded together or joined with bolts and rivets.

This unique complex of qualities—tensile strength, meltability, ductility, malleability, conductivity, resistance to fire and decay, and potential beauty of color and surface—makes a house built today without metals hard to imagine. A partial list would include such inconspicuous but essential uses as structural members and reinforcing in masonry; conductors of water, heat, and electricity; weatherproofing and foil insulation; and nails and screws. Metals are thinly concealed by protective coatings of enamel in stoves, refrigerators, and washing machines. They become noticeable in hinges, handles, and doorknobs; in faucets, radiators, or warm-air vents. They are conspicuous in metal tableware and furniture, cooking utensils and lighting fixtures. More frequent each day is their use for window frames, roofs, and exterior and interior walls.

The following is a brief description of those metals most important in homes.

Aluminum. Not until 1885 was it feasible to extract aluminum economically, even though it occurs in most common clays. It is a whitish metal, light in weight and easily worked. It oxidizes to a soft gray but does not deteriorate indoors or out. Thus it is valuable for cooking utensils, tumblers, pitchers, trays, and easy-to-move outdoor furniture that requires minimum maintenance. It is a carefree material for window frames and screens, siding and roofing, gutters and drainpipes. The surface can be highly polished or brushed to a silvery softness. *Anodizing* gives a satiny surface in a range of bright metallic hues.

Chromium. Chromium, a blue-white metal, takes and keeps a high polish and is widely used as a thin plating where durability, easy maintenance, and brilliant shine are wanted. It is frequently seen on faucets, toasters, kitchen forks and spoons, lighting fixtures, and metal furniture. Because it is hard and resists corrosion it takes little care, except that finger or water marks are conspicuous. Typically, it is cold, hard, and glittery; assertive rather than harmonious. It can be domesticated, though, with a brushed finish.

Copper. Polished copper is a beautiful orange color with a lustrous surface that quickly oxidizes to a dull greenish brown or sometimes to a lively blue-green. Fortunately, oxidation causes no serious deterioration. Copper is soft and easily shaped but durable, which makes it excellent for pipes carrying water. Next to silver, it is the best conductor of electricity. It has a disagreeable taste and odor but conducts heat quickly and evenly, which explains its use on the *bottoms* of pots and pans. It is long-lived, beautiful, but expensive in first cost for eave

The tensile strength of metal is an inspiration to designers in historic and contemporary work, as seen on this and the next page.

The slender "GF 40/4" chair exploits the unique strength and high gloss of chrome-plated steel for the slimmest of supports. The formed metal seat and back will hold up under considerable weight and are vinyl-coated in deep or brilliant colors. The name comes from the fact that forty stacked chairs are only four feet high. David Rowland, designer. (*The General Fireproofing Company*)

troughs and roofs. Inside the house, copper's color and luster have a warm friendliness that is unique.

Iron and steel. A grayish metal known for thousands of years, iron is widely available, strong, and relatively easy to work when cast in liquid form or wrought with tools. Its great disadvantage is the speed with which it rusts. However, it can be *galvanized* with a zinc coating or painted to discourage rust.

Steel is iron that has been made hard with chemically dissolved carbon. Its development has made possible not only skyscrapers and suspension bridges but the houses illustrated in Figures 187 and 188. It is the structural material in kitchen equipment and furnaces and also in many metal window frames. Most so-called iron furniture is made of steel. Because steel rusts like iron, it is invariably painted or enameled. *Stainless steels* are another matter, for they have been made resistant to rust and staining by the addition of chromium. Hard, durable, and a pleasant blue-gray, stainless steels make the most durable and inexpensive (in the long run) of all cooking utensils as well as thoroughly satisfactory, nontarnishable knives, forks, and spoons.

Silver. It is no whim or happenstance that silver has long been cherished as the most desirable of metals for flat and hollow metal tableware: it is the whitest of metals, reflects almost twice as much light as stainless steel and noticeably more than chromium, and takes a genuinely beautiful polish. Furthermore, it is a workable metal, so soft when pure that it must be hardened, usually with copper: sterling silver contains 7.5 percent copper. Its one great drawback is that it tarnishes rapidly and soon becomes blackish if the coating of silver sulfide is not removed; but unlike iron rust, this causes no serious damage. Silver is frequently plated over an alloy base, and if the plating is heavy enough, it will last a long time; but of course solid silver will remain in good condition indefinitely.

A pair of seventeenth-century Italian gates has thin, complex curvilinear forms particularly suitable to metal. (*The Metropolitan Museum of Art, New York, Rogers Fund, 1905*)

Design in Metal

Were it not that metal is heavy and expensive, we might say that almost any form that man can design is suitable for metal. It will take and hold any shape that can be given to wood, masonry, ceramics, or glass. Its most distinctive quality, though, is its great tensile strength, which makes possible, as well as durable, shapes that are slender but strong. Examples of this characteristic are the structural members of the two houses in Figures 187 and 188, the thin grilles of the gate in Figure 190, and the slender legs of the chair in Figure 189. Sharp edges, as on knives, are more durable in metal than in any other material. When used expressively, metal contributes a precise thinness that distinguishes it from the comparatively heavy solidity of wood, masonry, and ceramics.

Ornament in Metal

The surface treatment of metal, which can give varied light-and-dark patterns and reflections, is a basic kind of ornament. Highly polished metal (Fig. 191A) gives mirror-like reflections, interestingly distorted on rounded forms. Softly polished metal produces more mellow and diffuse patterns (Figs. 191B and C). Three-dimensional textures (Fig. 191D) can lead to myriad juxtapositions of highlights and shadows.

As with form, there are almost no physical limitations for ornament; but if we wish to exploit each material's individuality, we will emphasize its most distinctive qualities. This leads to several suggestions. First, the strength of metal is suited to boldly projecting ornamental parts, as in the handle at the top of the mustard pot (Fig. 191C). Second, the very fine grain and smoothness make very delicate embellishment effective, as in the bands that emphasize the meeting point of the pot's top and bowl. Third, the hardness of metal makes linear or angular decoration at ease with the material. Fourth, the long life and cost of most metals may suggest relatively formal, controlled, and precise enrichment but does not prelude other approaches.

A   B   C

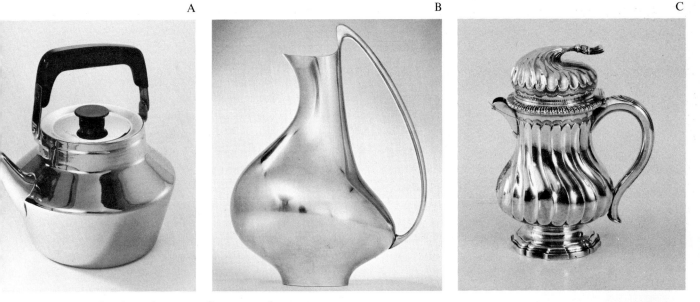

Metal can be given almost any form or surface texture.

Above left. A stainless-steel kettle by Sigvard Bernadotte and Acton Bjørn (1955) has a polished, highly reflecting surface that is emphasized by the black plastic handle and nob. (*Moderna Kök A.B.*)

Above center. A sterling silver water pitcher, designed by Henning Koppel (1951), has a biomorphic shape and two types of satiny surface. (*Georg Jensen Inc.*)

Above right. A French silver mustard pot (c. 1750) only $6\frac{1}{16}$ inches high, demonstrates the plasticity of shape and intricacy of ornament that are distinctively suited to polished metal. (*The Metropolitan Museum of Art, New York, Bequest of Catherine D. Wentworth, 1948*)

Right. Mechanically stamped patterns increase the rigidity of metal sheets and give a lively surface that obscures scratches. They can, as in these examples, be made highly colorful with a porcelain enamel finish. (*National Association of Architectural Metal Manufacturers*)

PLASTICS

The phenomenal development of plastics in the past few decades has affected our homes markedly and will continue to do so. Today's scientists transform wood, coal, milk, and many other substances into new compounds tailor-made for specific purposes, and engineers invent efficient methods of shaping these materials. Thus, we are now able to produce, on an enormous scale, materials in many instances better suited to specific needs than those nature provides. At first, plastics were cheap substitutes for more costly materials and

D

Successful design in plastics takes into consideration the unique combinations of qualities that are possible with man-made substances, as seen below and on the next page.

A

B

Top. "The Invisible Chair" (c. 1960) takes full advantage of a new plastic that is transparent, lightweight, damage-resistant, suitable for indoor or outdoor use, and that can be fashioned into strong molded shapes. (*Laverne, Inc.*)

Above. A chandelier, based on the principle of a two-section, continuous geodesic band, illustrates the sculptural possibilities of translucent vinyl. Ben Gurule, designer (c. 1964). (*Photograph by Richard Gross. California Design/9, Pasadena Art Museum*)

were undistinguished in appearance. Objects were small and seldom durable. Today, plastic dishes are lightweight and durable (Fig. 193B). Chairs and other furniture are molded from transparent (Fig. 192A), translucent, or opaque plastics (Color Fig. 14), and wall and ceiling panels come in great variety (Fig. 193A) of plastic forms. Numerous research projects indicate that homes in which plastics are the major material will be available in the future.

Plastic resins come to forming machines as powders, granules, compressed tablets, or liquids, which under heat and pressure can be shaped as designers wish. Powders and tablets can be compressed in steel molds, liquids can be forced through dies to form continuous sheets, rods, filaments, tubes, or pipes. Some can be drawn into thin sheets or blown into molds. Others can be blown full of gas or air to make light but strong insulation.

Film and sheeting for shower curtains, upholstery, or laminates are made by spreading plastic solutions on wheels up to 25 feet in diameter, by extruding the compound through a wide die, or by calendering, that is, by passing it between several rollers to get the desired thickness and surface texture. Rollers are also used in giving other materials a plastic coating. In laminating such materials as Formica and Micarta, layers of cloth, paper, wood, or glass fibers are impregnated with uncured resin or alternated with uncured plastic film, then pressed into a single sheet.

Families of Plastics

Although there are innumerable plastics, those used most in homes are made from the nine types of resins discussed in the following paragraphs. Each name refers to a family of plastics with basic characteristics in common but with considerable diversity. The terms *plastic* and *synthetic* can be applied to the same material—for example, molded nylon is called a plastic, but nylon threads are referred to as synthetic. In this chapter we will consider only the plastics; the synthetics will be taken up in Chapter 10.

Acrylics. The most glamorous and glasslike of the plastics, acrylics can be made into extremely decorative panels because of their exceptional clarity, brilliant surface, and ability to "pipe" light (Fig. 195). A remarkable combination of qualities—good light transmission, strength and stiffness, ability to withstand outdoor weathering and sudden temperature extremes, and lightness in weight—permits great architectural freedom in flat or domed skylights. For all these uses, acrylics can be colorless or tinted, patterned or plain. Although unaffected by most foods and household chemicals, they are rather easily scratched by grit of any sort. *Lucite* and *Plexiglas* are trade names.*

Cellulosics. Offering designers almost unlimited possibilities, cellulosic plastics come in a wide range of colors, from clear transparent to opaque, including variegations and simulations of marble, wood grain, and mother-of-pearl. They retain a bright, lustrous surface unless scratched by abrasives. Although resistant to most household chemicals, they may be stained by some medicines and foods. They withstand subzero temperatures and water up to 130° F. Their many uses include vacuum-cleaner parts and housings for radios and clocks; piano keys, soap dishes, and cutlery handles; flashlight cases and toys. *Ethocel* (ethyl cellulose), *Lumarith* (acetate), and *Pyralin* (nitrate) are a few of the trade names.

*Many trade names are used for more than one type of plastic.

A

Plain and patterned, translucent acrylic panels make luminous walls, space dividers, and cabinet doors. A plastic skylight brings daylight into the room's center. (*American Cyanamid Company*)

Melamines. The widespread use of melamines for counter tops and table-tops, as well as for dinnerware, is based on their exceptional durability. Hard and not easily scratched or chipped, they resist damage from water, food stains, and heat. When thin, as in the surfaces of such high-pressure laminates as *Formica* or *Micarta*, they transparently reveal whatever pattern or material is underneath. If thicker, as in such dinnerware as *Melmac*, they become translucent or opaque. Colors, extensive in range, do not fade or lose brilliance. Surfaces can be high-gloss, satiny, or mat.

Nylon. Nylon is the generic term applied to this group. Transparent in very thin sections but usually opaque, nylon comes in many colors. Although resistant to abrasion, the hard, glossy surface can be scratched. It has high tensile strength and is relatively rigid and hard. Most common chemicals do it no harm, but coffee, tea, and colored foods leave stains. Neither freezing nor boiling temperatures affect it adversely. It is not, however, recommended for continuous outdoor exposure. These qualities make it useful for some tumblers and dinnerware, bristles and backs of brushes, combs, and soap dishes. It is also made into long-wearing bearings and gears, and into quiet rollers for drawers. *Nylon* and *Zytel* are two trade names.

B

That plastics are amenable to rich ornamentation is demonstrated by new developments in stain-resistant, durable melamine dishes. (*Plastics Manufacturing Company*)

Phenolics. Opaque and tending to darken on exposure to light, phenolics are usually black, brown, or dark-colored. Hard and rigid over a wide range of temperatures, they are resistant to mild acids, alcohol, oils, soaps, and detergents. Because they are a poor conductor of heat and electricity, they are widely used for handles on cooking utensils, electric irons and toasters, as well as for radio and television cases and telephone sets. Newer uses are drawers and other parts of furniture. Roofs made of phenolic-impregnated paper and window frames of phenolics with wood fillers have been successfully produced. Trade names include *Bakelite, Catalin,* and *Plaskon.*

Polyester (reinforced). When reinforced, usually with glass fibers, polyesters can be formed into strong but thin translucent sheets that are widely used as translucent patio roofs, luminous ceilings, and light-transmitting walls and partitions. They can also be molded into lampshades, skylights, rowboats, and the seats and backs of chairs. They range from stiff to flexible and from hard to soft. The color range is good and they show high resistance to chemicals and weather. Among the trade names are *Bakelite, Plaskon,* and *Polylite.*

Polyethylenes. Easily recognizable by their flexible or semirigid character and waxy surface, polyethylenes have gained wide acceptance in squeeze bottles, nesting bowls, refrigerator dishes, pails, and dishpans. Semitransparent to opaque depending on thickness, they come in many colors. They are light in weight and very resistant to breakage and chemicals. Polyethylene objects perform well at subzero temperatures; boiling water can be poured into them, but they should not be boiled. *Alathon, Bakelite,* and *Poly-Eth* are three of the trade names.

Polystyrenes. The lustrous surface of these plastics, ranging from extreme smoothness to satin and many special finishes, is warm and pleasant to touch. Crystal-clear types "pipe" light, as do the acrylics, and there is a limitless range of translucent and opaque colors. They are relatively inexpensive, tasteless, and odorless, and are resistant to household chemicals and foods except cleaning fluids and citrus fruits. Food-freezing temperatures do not affect them. Most types are unharmed by hot foods for short periods but lose their shape if boiled. Hard and rigid, they stand up well under normal household use but not under bending or severe impact. The list of uses is long and varied: kitchenware, refrigerator parts and dishes, measuring spoons and combs; venetian blinds and drawers; wall tiles, and as a core for sandwich-type wall panels. Trade names include *Catalin* (styrene), *Lustrex,* and *Styron.*

Vinyls. The versatile family of vinyls includes rigid and nonrigid types in any transparent, translucent, or opaque color. Varied surface effects are produced by embossing or printing. They are tough, strong, lightweight, and low in cost. Although they withstand foods, chemicals, and normal household use very well, they cut readily and stiffen in cold except for special types. Rigid vinyls are harmed by temperatures above 130° F. Among the diverse uses are shower, bathroom, and kitchen curtains; tablecloths, draperies, upholstery, and wall coverings; lamp shades and luminous ceilings; flooring and counter surfacing; and experimental kitchen sinks. *Bakelite, Dow PVC,* and *Opalon* are some of the trade names.

Despite the variability of plastics, certain qualities taken together differentiate them from other materials. The range of color and texture, actual or simulated, seems limitless, and they come in all degrees of transparency and opacity. They feel warm and pleasant. Truly "plastic," they can be formed into almost any rigid or flexible, seamless shape. Typically, they are tough and durable in relation to weight and thickness. Absorbing little or no moisture, they neither rot nor mildew. Their resistance to chemicals is variable but generally good. Their strength and dimensions are with a few exceptions noticeably affected by extreme temperatures. In price, they vary greatly.

Design in Plastics

Unlike natural materials, the basic qualities of plastics are chemically and physically created by man. Thus, instead of designing to suit a material, man can precisely create the material to meet a specific need. This brings new challenges and problems. It indicates close, continuing cooperation among chemist, manufacturer, and designer. And it gives the designer a characterless powder to mold. There is no age-old craft tradition in which to seek cumulated knowledge or inspiration.

In spite of plastics' potentialities for new forms, comparatively few have been developed. The shapes of plastic dishes and tumblers closely resemble those of clay or glass because these have been found serviceable and pleasant. Handles of knives and forks, even though made of new materials, are fashioned to fit our hands and therefore resemble those made of wood or metal. But in some objects, furniture, wall and flooring materials distinctiveness has been achieved. Floor coverings in which chips of opaque plastic are embedded in translucent plastic, and those that are seamless and have been poured (Fig. 279B), are examples of the way in which the special characteristics of a material have been utilized to produce new forms and effects. A few lighting fixtures take advantage of some plastics' ability to be molded into complex but stable translucent shapes (Fig. 192B). And we have seen the unique "plastic" forms that have been invented for chairs and tables (Color Fig. 14), and the aesthetic effects possible when plastics are treated as art media in the Koblick panel (Fig. 195).

Successful ornament in plastics is still largely the structural type, where the inherent possibilities for varied colors, different degrees of transparency, translucency, or opacity, embedded materials, and molded form and surface texture seem to be in the nature of the materials and in the processes used to form them (Fig. 145). Because the various kinds of applied ornament are so closely

Freda Koblick, interested in the effects of form and light obtained by hardening acrylic plastics at different rates, heightened this impetuous but surely patterned wall panel with embedded slices of semiprecious rocks.

allied with the natural materials they were originally designed to enhance, they are likely to seem weak, imitative, and inappropriate when used on plastics. Perhaps this is so because, as yet, little applied ornament seems to intensify the unique quality of plastics, as, for example, etching or cutting heightens the sparkle of glass or intricate ornament throws into relief the luster of polished silver.

The history of plastics is very short, and the development of any new vocabulary takes a long time. Many consumers and manufacturers conservatively prefer that which is at least partially familiar to that which is completely new. But inevitably, as designers explore the possibilities, they are evolving designs that exploit and enhance these made-to-order materials.

Even though plastics are only beginning to receive distinctive design, they have had enormous impact on homes. Plastic cases for radio, phonograph, and television sets are cheaper than wood or metal. Plastic surfaces and drawers for furniture lighten housekeeping, as do plastic curtains, upholstery, and lamp shades. Floors and counter tops surfaced with plastic reduce noise and breakage, and are easy to keep. Humble objects—dishpans and mop pails—are available in bright, cheerful colors. Plastic furniture of the present and plastic houses of the future may change many of our concepts of home planning and furnishing. Finally, there is the whole realm, as yet hardly explored, of plastics as unexpected sources of visual delight.

Inflatable cushions of clear plastic, supported by an aluminum cradle with an acrylic clear base, form an "Air Chair" remarkable for its lightness, being both visually transparent and light in weight. The Op-art pillows are also of air-filled plastic. Phil Orenstein, designer. (*Mass Art, Inc.*)

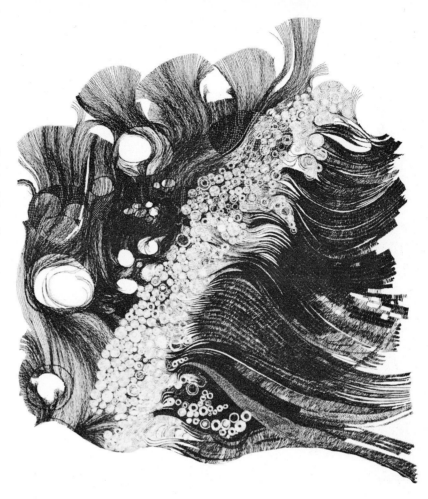

New and old materials and techniques are creatively employed in this detail of Ragnhild Langlet's hand-embroidered "Wave," which combines cotton, linen, and gold Lurex in an exceptionally fluent, intricate pattern. (*Photograph by Richard Gross. California Design/9, Pasadena Art Museum*)

10 · Fabrics

Very early in history, man, finding that animal skins, leaves, and bark were not always available in pieces of suitable size and weight, set about to improve on nature. He wanted something to protect his body, to make his living quarters more comfortable, and to satisfy his need for spiritual stimulation and satisfaction—and he produced fabrics. More than anything in a house except the people, fabrics humanize our homes because of their pliant responsiveness to our needs. They are useful in controlling light coming through windows and in giving privacy without solid walls. They insulate against extreme heat and cold, and they absorb noise. They provide easily removable and cleanable coverings for tables and beds, and pleasant-to-touch upholstery for chairs and sofas. Beyond these service functions, fabrics bring beauty and individuality (Color Fig. 15).

Several distinctive characteristics of fabrics are worth noting:

- No other material comes in such width and breadth and can be readily used in those dimensions.
- Uniquely pliable and manipulatable, they can be folded, draped, pleated, or stretched; and they can be cut, sewn, or glued together with simple home equipment.

A

- They are one of the materials most frequently and easily replaced.
- They are noticed because they are used in quantity throughout the home, look and feel softer than other materials, and are often brightly colored or richly patterned.
- They link together people, furniture, and architecture in a way unequaled by anything else. Carpets and other fabrics fastened to floors and walls adhere strictly to the "architecture" of the house. Upholstery and table linens adapt themselves to the seating or tables on which they are used and at the same time relate those pieces to our clothes. Curtains and draperies can partake of the architectural quality of windows as well as relate openings to the enclosing structure and to the furniture in the room.

Thus, in addition to usefulness, fabrics have two important functions. First, they make their own very special visual and tactile contribution. Second, they can be strong unifying elements within a room and from one room to another. In this chapter, attention will be focused on fibers, the processes by which fibers are transformed into fabrics, and fabric design. In succeeding chapters, consideration will be given to the potential integration of fabrics with walls, windows, floors, and furniture. Thereby, while duly stressing the distinctive qualities of fabrics, we hope we have avoided discussing them as items separate from the whole house.

Fabric is a general term referring to anything manufactured by hand or machine, but it has come to be applied especially to **cloth. Textile** refers only to **woven fabrics.** In addition to weaving, fabrics can be made by knitting, felting, or lacing together natural or man-made fibers and also by fabricating plastics into sheets. Performance and appearance of fabrics are products of several factors: the qualities of the basic material, the process by which it is fabricated, the finish, and the applied ornamentation.

Above. Ruth Asawa's molded vinyl wall covering "Deep Dimension" has a precise, three-dimensional, herringbone pattern that produces a lively play of light, shade, and shadow.

Right. A detail of Marianne Strengell's off-white casement fabric, handwoven of linen, Fiberglas, rayon, and goat hair, shows how each of the fibers is allowed to express its special individuality in seemingly spontaneous freedom. (*Photo by F. Boesch. Research Department of the American Craftsmen's Council*)

Far right. Reflecting a current interest in updated historical motifs, "Venetian Damask" conveys the gay spirit of Venice. It is printed on white cotton in two tones of the same hue that blend together softly. Although the pattern is symmetrical and formal, the effect is neither rigid nor austere. (*Gian Fabrics and Wallcoverings*)

The scope of contemporary fabrics increases each year.

B

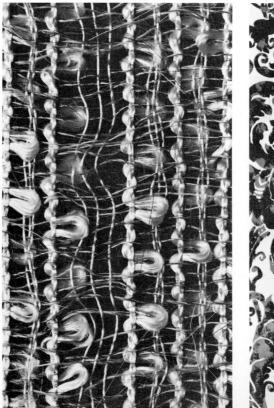

C

A   B

FIBERS

The term *fiber* refers to a threadlike object or filament, but it has also
come to mean that which gives substance or texture. Both meanings apply to
textile fibers. Nature provides an abundance of such fibrous materials as reeds
and grasses, flax and jute, the wool and hair of animals, the fibers enclosing
the seeds of plants, and the filaments some caterpillars spin for cocoons. To
these, scientists have added many of their own invention. The chart on pages
200–201 gives the basic facts about the qualities of the more important fibers.
Fibers differ from one another in many ways: strength and elasticity; resistance
to abrasion, stains, sun, moisture, mildew, and fire; and tactile and visual qualities. Each fiber has its strong and weak points. Although some are more versatile
than others, none is ideally suited to every purpose. Keep in mind, too, that
important developments are occurring all the time—new synthetic fibers are
created, familiar ones are modified, and processing and finishing are being improved.

All man-made fibers share some desirable qualities: they are of unlimited
length in contrast to the comparative shortness of wool and cotton; many of
them repel, rather than absorb, moisture and soil; and they offer little foothold
to insects and fungus. Some synthetics are better suited to specific uses than
are any natural ones. As yet, however, few if any artificial fibers can be used
with full assurance *for as many purposes* as wool or cotton—in part, at least,
because the natural fibers have been used for centuries. Natural fibers, to be
sure, have their limitations, but these are being minimized by new ways of
processing them. For example, they can be made resistant to soil and stains, shrinkage and moths, or crushing and wrinkling.

Textiles can be made entirely of one fiber (Fig. 198C) or of two or more to
increase beauty (Fig. 198B), utility, or both. Different fibers can be spun together into one yarn, or yarns spun from different fibers can be combined in a
single fabric. Nylon, for example, increases the strength of wool and rayon
textiles. Stretch nylon combined with cotton makes form-fitting slipcovers that
are pleasant to the touch.

Fiber and Fiber Substance	Appearance	Uses	Maintenance	Special Characteristics and Processes	Resistances Poor	Resistances Good	Resistances Excellent
Acetates (cellulose diacetate) *Acele Avisco Celanese,* and so on	Drapes well. Good color range.	Bedspreads, curtains, draperies, rugs, upholstery.	Fair soil resistance. Dry-clean or wash; dries quickly. Iron with *cool* iron.	Retains heat-set pleats and creases. Newer processes have color as integral part of fiber, increasing resistances to sunlight, cleaning.	Abrasion, aging, heat, sunlight.	Felting, fire, insects, pilling, shrinking, static electricity, stretching, wrinkling.	
Arnel (cellulose triacetate)	Pleasant luster. Drapes well. Excellent color range.	Draperies.	Slow to soil. Dry-clean or wash; dries quickly. Little ironing, higher setting than diacetates.	Excellent retention of heat-set pleats and creases. Ability to withstand washing, ironing.		Abrasion, insects, pilling, static electricity, stretching.	Aging, felting, fire, mildew, shrinking, wrinkling, sunlight.
Acrylics (acrylonitrile units) *Acrilan Creslan Orlon Zefran,* and so on	Warm, bulky, woollike touch. Good color range in some types.	Blankets, curtains, rugs, upholstery.	Slow to soil. Easy to spot-clean. Dry-clean or wash; dries quickly. Little ironing, under 325°.	Warmth without weight. Retains heat-set pleats and creases.	Pilling, static electricity unless treated.	Abrasion, felting, fire, shrinking, sunlight, wrinkling.	Aging, insects, mildew, sunlight.
Modacrylics (modified acrylics) *Dynel Verel,* and so on	Warm, bulky, heavy, dense.	Rugs, upholstery.	Similar to acrylics, but highly resistant to chemical stains. Iron setting varies.	Self-extinguishing. Special processes result in dense, furlike pile, textured, three-dimensional effects.	Heat, shrinking unless stabilized by heat-setting, sunlight (*Dynel*).	Abrasion, pilling, static electricity, wrinkling.	Aging, felting, fire, insects, mildew, sunlight (*Verel*).
Cotton (cellulose)	Pleasant, soft, dull surface. Fair drape. Excellent color range.	Bed and table linen, bedspreads, draperies, rugs, towels, upholstery.	Soil, stains, wrinkles easily unless treated. Dry-clean or wash; irons easily.	Mercerizing increases luster, softness, strength, dye absorption. Wash-and-wear, spot- and wrinkle-resistant finishes.	Felting, fire, mildew, shrinking, wrinkling.	Abrasion, aging, fading, insects, stretching, sunlight.	Pilling, static electricity. (All resistances greatly improved by special treatments and blends.)
Glass (lime, aluminum, and borosilicate) *Beta Fiberglas J-M Fiber Glass Fiber Glass PPG*	Lustrous, silky; good drape. Fair color range in dyes, printed many hues.	Bedspreads, curtains, draperies, wallpaper.	Slow to soil. Easy spot removal. Hand-wash, hang with no ironing. Dries quickly.	*Beta* yarn one-half size of any other fiber. Can be woven into very sheer fabric. Fireproof, impervious to moisture and salt air. Shed fibers can cause skin rash.	Abrasion, flexing (nonelastic) but new processes increase flexibility.		Aging, chemicals, felting, fire, insects, mildew, shrinking, stretching, sunlight.
Linen (cellulose, from flax)	Clean, fresh, lintless. Fair drape. Good color range.	Curtains, draperies, household linens, rugs, upholstery.	Soils and wrinkles easily. Washes and irons well.	Stronger when wet. *Sanforized* to reduce shrinking. Can be made wrinkle-resistant.	Fire, shrinking, wrinkling unless treated or blended.	Abrasion, mildew, pilling, stretching, sunlight.	Aging, insects, static electricity.
Nylon (polyamide) *6, 66, 501 Antron Caprolan Cumuloft,* and so on	Natural luster. Good drape. Good color range.	Bedspreads, rugs, upholstery.	Slow to soil. Easy spot removal. Dry-clean or wash; dries quickly. Little ironing at low heat.	Outstanding elasticity, strength, and lightness. Can be heat-set to keep permanent shape. Sometimes damaged by acids. May pick up color and soil during washing.	Pilling, static electricity unless treated, sunlight.	Fire.	Abrasion, aging, felting, insects, mildew, shrinking, stretching, wrinkling.

TEXTILE FIBERS (Cont.)

Fiber and Fiber Substance	Appearance	Uses	Maintenance	Special Characteristics and Processes	Resistances Poor	Resistances Good	Resistances Excellent
Olefin (polyethylene, polypropylene, or olefin) *Meraklon Herculon Reevon*	Resembles wool more than any other man-made fiber. Fair color range.	Blankets, rugs, upholstery, webbing.	Slow to soil. Spot-clean or wash. Little ironing, at *very* low heat.	Lightest fiber made. Excellent insulator. Transmits humidity well. Is very cohesive (can be made into nonwoven carpets). Low cost.	Heat, shrinking, static electricity.	Abrasion, aging, felting, fire, stretching, sunlight, wrinkling.	Insects, mildew, pilling.
Polyesters (dihydric alcohol and terephthalic acid) *Dacron Fortrel Kodel Vycron*, and so on	Crisp or soft, pleasant touch. Good drape. Fair color range.	Bedding, curtains, draperies, upholstery.	Soils easily. Dry-clean or wash; dries quickly. Very little ironing, moderate heat.	Lightweight. Ranges from sheer, silklike to bulky, woollike. As strong wet as dry. Retains heat-set pleats and creases. Picks up colors in washing.	Dust, soil, pilling because very electrostatic.	Abrasion, fire, sunlight.	Felting, insects, mildew, shrinking, stretching, wrinkling.
Rayon (regenerated cellulose) *Avril Cupioni Enka Fortisan*, and so on	Bright or dull luster. Drapes well. Excellent color range.	Blankets, curtains, draperies, rugs, table "linens," upholstery.	Fair soil resistance. Dry-clean or wash. Iron like cotton or silk, depending on type, finish.	Most versatile fiber; can resemble cotton, silk, wool. Absorbs moisture and swells when wet unless specially processed. Reduces static electricity in blends. Low cost. Wash-and-wear and spot- and wrinkle-resistant finishes.	Felting, fire, mildew, shrinking, wrinkling.	Abrasion, aging, insects, stretching (poor when wet), sunlight.	Pilling, static electricity. (All resistances greatly improved by blending, finishes.)
Saran (vinylidene chloride) *Rovana Velon*, and so on	High luster. Good drape. Good color range.	Draperies, rugs, upholstery, webbing.	Slow to soil. Spot-clean, sponge, or wash; dries quickly. Little ironing, very *low* heat.	Unusually tough, durable, does not catch, hold dirt. Nonabsorbent, yellows in sun. *Rovana* can be molded into fabrics, not sewn.	Heat, static electricity, wrinkling.	Abrasion, aging, fire, sunlight.	Felting, insects, mildew, moisture, salt air, shrinking, stretching.
Silk (protein from silkworm cocoon)	Lustrous, smooth, unique crunchy softness. Drapes well. Excellent color range.	Draperies, rugs, upholstery.	Good soil resistance. Dry-clean or hand-wash. Irons easily, moderate heat.	Most desirable combination of properties of any fiber: smoothness, luster, resiliency, toughness, adaptability to temperature changes.	Fire (but self-extinguishing), static electricity, sunlight.	Abrasion, aging, felting, insects, mildew, shrinking, stretching, wrinkling.	
Wool (protein from sheep or goat and camel families)	Soft or hard finish. Dry, warm touch. Drapes well. Good color range.	Blankets, draperies, rugs, upholstery.	Good soil resistance. Spot-clean, dry-clean, or wash in cold water. Press over damp cloth at low heat.	Notable for warmth, absorbency (without feeling wet), resiliency, durability. Wool-synthetic blends reduce shrinkage but have tendency to pill.	Insects, felting, shrinking unless treated.	Abrasion, aging, fire, mildew, pilling, stretching, static electricity, sunlight.	Wrinkling. (New processes make it even more resistant to soil, stains, water, wrinkling.)

YARNS

Yarn is the term used to describe fibers that have been twisted together to make them sufficiently strong and long for weaving or knitting. With natural fibers, yarn making includes cleaning the fibers, drawing them out so that they are more or less even and parallel, and spinning or twisting them into yarn. Man-made fibers are clean, continuous, and parallel as soon as they become filaments, so that the process is simply one of twisting them together. Yarns vary in the kinds of fibers used either alone or in combination, the type and tightness of twist, and the size of the finished product.

Long fibers laid parallel to one another and tightly twisted produce smoother and stronger yarns than do short fibers somewhat randomly arranged and loosely twisted. Nature provides only one long continuous fiber—silk—while all synthetics have that characteristic. Any of them, however, can be cut into short pieces for different effects. Length of fiber and tightness of twist lead to the following types of yarns:

- **Cotton.** *Carded* yarns have only the very short fibers removed and the remaining ones somewhat straightened. *Combed* yarns are composed entirely of long fibers laid parallel before spinning, which makes the yarn stronger and smoother. *Lisle* is tightly twisted from combed, mercerized fibers.
- **Silk.** Most high-quality silk is made from long, continuous filaments, but *spun* silk is made from the short fibers that cannot be unreeled from cocoons.
- **Synthetics.** Synthetic fibers originate as continuous, parallel, more or less smooth strands called *filaments,* which are usually twisted into ply yarns. They can, though, be cut into short lengths and blown apart, then brought together in a mass something like cleaned but uncombed cotton or wool, and these *staples* are twisted into soft yarns known as *spun* rayon, nylon, and so on.

Twisting fibers tightly or loosely is only the beginning of possible variations. Fibers can be given a right- or left-hand twist, and these can be put together in two-, three-, or four-ply yarns. There are many special twists, of which crepe and bouclé are only two examples. Elastic cores can be covered with fibers to produce elastic yarns, and fibers can be wrapped with metallic wires.

Size of yarns ranges from spider-web single filaments to silk yarns of two hundred strands or to ropelike cords. Textiles can be made entirely of one size of yarn or may combine several or many sizes (Fig. 199A) depending on need and desire.

FABRIC CONSTRUCTION

There are five basic ways of making fabrics.

Felting, probably the earliest process discovered by man, is simply matting together rough, scaly fibers with moisture, pressure, and sometimes heat, which induces shrinkage and reduces density. The result is a firm, somewhat fuzzy, nonwoven fabric (Fig. 203A). Newer nonwoven fabrics are made from layers of webs of fibers permanently **bonded** or **fused** by applying a binder and then drying and curing. Ultimately, fabrics may be made by spraying fiber-producing materials onto a form, eliminating such steps as spinning, complex fabricating techniques, cutting, sewing, and the final shaping of the fabric.

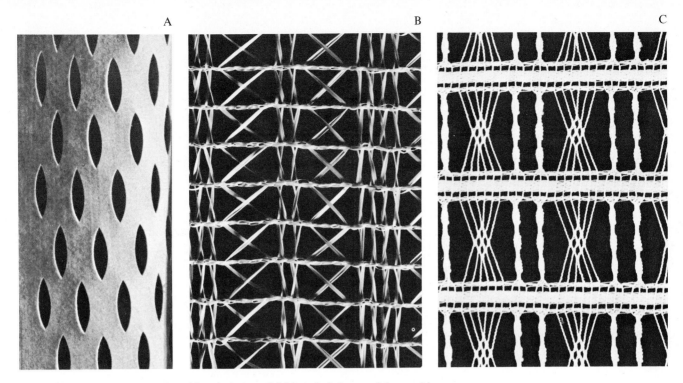

New processes are reviving the old techniques of felting, knitting, and lacemaking.

Above left. "Feutron" is a felt of dacron and Coloray viscose whose open filigree makes it suitable for flame-retarding, durable draperies. (*American Felt Company*)

Above center. "Interplay," a warp knit of 100 percent Rovana, a Saran flat monofilament, has been heat-set to make it resistant to slippage. (*Larsen Design Corporation*)

Above right. Cotton fishnet from Germany is produced on a lacemaking machine 102 inches wide. (*E. C. Carter & Son, Inc., a subsidiary of Greeff Fabrics, Inc.*)

Knitting, an old art, perhaps first used by prehistoric man in making fish-nets, is done by the interlocking of one yarn into a series of connecting loops with a blunt rod or needle. Patterns are produced by combining plain, rib, and purl stitches, plus many variations. Because machine knitting can be two to five times as fast as weaving, its possibilities are being reassessed, and new fibers and techniques have resulted in dimensionally stable knit fabrics (Fig. 203B).

Twisting, the process by which nets and laces are made, is the inter-twining of yarns that run in two or more directions. Although lace has long been out of favor for household use, fresh and imaginative designing and the low cost of manufacture (up to four thousand bobbins can be used) are opening the way to its reintroduction (Fig. 203C). We will probably be seeing more inter-esting uses of this process in the future.

Forming, the method by which plastic sheeting or film is made, is the newest fabric technique and the only one in which fibers are not used. Some of the methods by which synthetic liquids are transformed into fabrics were dis-cussed in Chapter 9 in the section dealing with plastics and are illustrated in Figures 210A through E.

Weaving is the interlacing of warp and filling yarns, usually at right angles, to make textiles. *Warp* yarns run lengthwise on the loom and in the fabric. *Fil-ling* yarns (also called weft or woof) run crosswise to fill and hold together the warp. The apparently enormous complexity of weaves can be reduced to three general categories: **plain, twill,** and **satin** (Figs. 204A through 205B). Three secondary types are **pile, leno,** and **Jacquard** (Figs. 205C through 206D).

Weaves, like fibers, affect durability and maintenance:

- Loose weaves of any kind are subject to shrinkage, and diagonal weaves and those woven of different and inappropriately combined fibers may pull out of shape. Monk's cloth or satin weaves, with long floated yarns on the surface, are likely to catch and break if used on furniture.
- Ribbed or corded weaves often show wear on the raised portions more quickly than do flat or pile weaves.
- Napped textiles show wear and dirt more quickly than pile textiles; both show spot cleaning less than flat weaves. Soft, cut-pile textiles may get mussed-looking by footsteps, for example, on a velvet-weave rug.
- Smooth weaves show spots more readily than rough weaves.

Most of these disadvantages may be overcome, however, by designing and choosing fabrics with use in mind, and by appropriate special finishes.

Each of the three basic weaves can lead to innumerable modifications and innovations.

Plain weave is simply one filling yarn carried over one warp yarn and under the next. In broadcloth, warp and filling are identical in size, which gives a smooth surface; in rep, a definite ribbed texture is produced by having one set of yarns heavier than the other; and in basket weaves, two or more warps are crossed by two or more filling yarns to produce a noticeable pattern, as in monk's cloth.

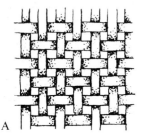

A

B

In plain weaves, the over-and-under pattern can be emphasized by having warp and filling yarns different from each other in size, color, and texture, as in this example by Hilda Dial. (*M. H. de Young Memorial Museum*)

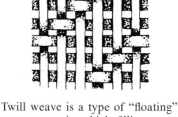

C

D

Twill weave is a type of "floating" yarn weave in which filling yarns float across a number of warp yarns in a regular pattern so that a distinct diagonal line, or wale, shows on the surface, as in serge, gabardine, and denim. They resist soil and wrinkle less than do plain weaves of similar quality.

Yarns of nylon and Saran woven in a twill weave make "Signet" an exceptionally durable textile. The pronounced rib gives a clear-cut, structural pattern that is enlivened by the intentional variations in the thickness of the yarns. (*Virginia Fiber Corporation*)

Satin weaves differ from twill weaves in that filling yarns make long "floats" over several to many warp yarns, or the warp may float over the filling less regularly. This minimizes the over-and-under texture, and if the yarns are fine and lustrous, the surface is smooth and shines with reflected light. Satin, sateen, damask, and chino are examples.

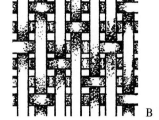

B

Left. In this brocade used for upholstering the back of a chair, a symmetrical pattern has two figures in an intricately designed oval frame and gracefully curved, conventionalized foliage forms. (*The Metropolitan Museum of Art, New York, Anonymous Gift, 1944*)

A

C

D

Pile weaves are distinguished by a set of yarns that stand up from the flat-lying warp and filling. If the loops are not cut, such textiles as terry cloth and frieze are produced. Cutting the loops results in velvet, plush, and the like. Patterns are formed if some loops are cut and some uncut, if some of the pile is higher than the rest, or if different colored yarns are used.

Great richness and unexpected complexity in a geometric pattern called "Ankara" are achieved with yarns of different thickness and texture woven with tufts of varied heights. The "framework" is high and looks irregularly shaggy, while the panels are lower and smoother. The rug is handwoven of pure wool. (*V Soske*)

E

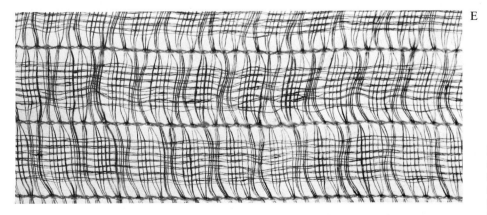

F

Leno weaves give more-or-less open, lacy effects by locking warp and filling in figure eights. Marquisette and many other porous textiles are leno weaves. Usually the weave is at such small scale that the design is hardly noticed, but coarser versions create handsome patterns.

"Lino Sheer," designed by Hugo Dreyfuss, has a linen warp with hemp and rayon filling in a leno-weave curtain material. Its fragile, almost frivolous appearance belies its actual strength. (*Kagan-Dreyfuss*)

Jacquard, or figure, weaves are not types of weave but a mechanized way of producing woven patterns that can be simple or intricate. They include flat *damasks,* raised *brocades,* complex tapestries, and some kinds of carpets.

B

A contemporary brocade named "Mosaique" shows an unusual richness in color variations and in juxtaposition of angular shapes. (*Thaibok Fabrics, Ltd.*)

An open-weave linen Jacquard casement made in Belgium shows another possibility for this process. Series of small "peephole windows" give an intriguing pattern of light and dark that changes with the time of day or night and with the light that shines on or through it. (*E. C. Carter & Son, Inc., a subsidiary of Greeff Fabrics, Inc.*)

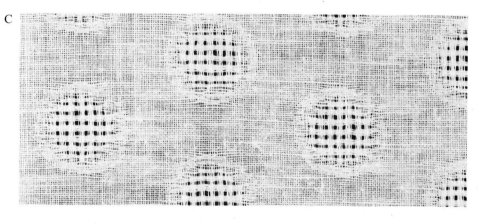

C

"Hellespont" is a Jacquard cotton upholstery fabric that is reversible. The swirling lines have centers of focus in the abruptly reversing curves. The pattern has an ever-changing but overall continuity reminiscent of the rush of the tide through a narrow strait. (*Photograph by Robert L. Beckhard. Jack Lenor Larsen, Inc.*)

D

FINISHING THE FABRIC

Fibers are found or made, spun into yarns, and then made into fabrics. But when most fabrics come from machine looms, they are far from ready to use. Various kinds of finishing give them their final appearance and qualities. *Beetling,* or pounding with steel and wooden hammers, gives luster to linens and linen-like fabrics. Cellulosic fibers can be *mercerized,* that is, treated with sodium hydroxide. If done under tension, the fabric is stronger, more lustrous, and accepts dyes more readily; without tension (slack), the fibers and yarns swell and contract, increasing the crimp of the yarn and its stretchability. In *calendering,* fabrics are pressed between rollers to give smooth finishes and to tighten the weaves, as well as to polish them to a highly glazed sheen or to emboss them with moiré, crepe, or other patterns. *Crabbing* tightens and sets the weave in wool, and *fulling* shrinks and compacts the textile. *Gigging* and *napping* give such textures as are found in flannel and fleece. *Shearing* and *singeing* remove surface fibers, fuzz, and lint, and prevent pilling. *Shrinking* lessens the tendency of most fibers to contract when exposed to moisture. *Starching* makes cotton lustrous and stiffer; *weighting* compensates for gum lost by silk in the cleaning process. By such means, lifeless, sleazy textiles are transformed into usable, attractive materials.

There are also some new, special treatments that notably change the behavior of fiber and fabric. Textiles can be made:

- *Crease-resistant* ("wash and wear," "easy care," "permanent-press") by impregnating the fibers with resins or with agents that cross-link cellulose molecules. This gives textiles more firmness and sometimes better draping qualities; but it may also weaken fibers, reduce abrasion resistance, and wash out. Dyes become more permanent, and shrinkage in spun rayons, light cottons and linens, and velvets is reduced. Bonding to a foam or tricot backing also gives better wrinkle resistance.
- *Fireproof and flameproof* by chemical treatment. A worthwhile safety precaution, this process also makes textiles heavier, stiffer, and longer lasting. It gives additional resistance to weathering and sometimes to insects and mildew.
- *Elastic* by using spandex fiber in the construction or by inserting stretch properties by special construction techniques, such as the twisting or crimping of yarns or the slack mercerization of fabrics.
- *Glazed* with resins that give a more or less permanent smooth, lustrous surface that resists soil and improves draping qualities. Glazing is usually limited to textiles used for curtains, draperies, and slipcovers.
- *Mildew- and moth-resistant* in varying degrees of permanence.
- *Shrink-resistant* chiefly through carefully controlled shrinking. In some processes, chemicals supplement moisture, heat, pressure, and tension.
- *Soil-resistant* by coating or impregnating fibers or fabrics with chemicals that make them less absorbent.
- *Starched* permanently by coating the surface with cellulose chemicals that withstand washing. Starching keeps textiles crisp and firm, gives a smooth, lintless surface and longer life.
- *Water-repellent* by coating or impregnating the fibers with wax, metals, or resins. Such treatment makes fabrics hold their shape better, as well as helping to keep dirt on the surface.
- *Insulating* by applying a thin or foamed coating on the back to keep out the heat rays of the sun and to keep in winter warmth.

Dyeing the Fabric

Textiles can get their dye colors when they are unspun fibers, spun yarns, or woven textiles; and in some synthetics, such as Chromspun and Celaperm acetate, the dye is mixed with the liquid from which the fiber is made. Although generalizations about dyes are risky, the synthetics in which the dye is part of the fiber seem to be the most colorfast. Next come the fibers and yarns dyed before weaving, and last come the textiles dyed after weaving. Today, however, there is less difference between the latter two than in the past.

The kind of dye and its hue affect colorfastness, but almost all will fade in varying degrees if exposed to sun or washed. Unless you want to protect fabrics from sun and use at the possible cost of happy family living, you will do well to get the most nearly fade-proof textiles available. Since all textiles change with time, it seems wise to select those that will mellow gracefully rather than those that will look tired and worn out when they fade. The following characteristics mitigate the results of fading:

- **Color.** The colors most common in nature—grays, greens, browns, soft yellows, and oranges—retain a pleasing appearance longer than do colors of higher intensity. Mixtures, such as in tweeds, do not become as listless as faded solid colors. Dark colors may lose their richness and depth with even a little fading.
- **Texture.** Definite textures with their play of light and shade compensate for loss of color.
- **Pattern.** Intricate or diffused designs lose less of their character than do those whose interest lies chiefly in brilliant contrasts, precision, or clarity.

This is no condemnation of bright, solid, or dark colors or of decisive patterns —but, again, to keep them looking their best they need special processing and upkeep.

Printing the Fabric

The easiest, least expensive way to add applied design to fabrics is by printing, a process known for at least five thousand years. Pigments mixed to the consistency of thick paste are applied to the finished fabric or to the yarns prior to weaving by one of three methods:

- **Roller printing** is by far the most commonly used method. Pigments are applied from copper rollers engraved with the design. One roller is made for each color, but an effect of more colors than rollers can be achieved by engraving different parts of a roller to different depths and by printing one color over another. In warp printing, the yarns are printed before weaving, which gives a soft, diffuse quality, such as in cretonne.
- **Block printing** is done by hand from wood blocks often surfaced with metal or linoleum. Block-printed fabrics have the slight irregularities characteristic of most handcrafts and are expensive.
- **Screen printing,** done either by hand or semimechanically, is a type of stencil printing especially suitable for patterns produced in relatively small quantities.

PLASTIC FABRICS

Barely hinting at their oilcloth ancestry, the new plastic fabrics combine minimum maintenance with a full spectrum of weight, color, and texture possibilities. Vinyl-plastic sheeting comes in varied thicknesses, from the thin films suitable for window and shower curtains to heavier weights for tablecloths and draperies. Upholstery grades are usually fused onto a knit backing. Plastic wall

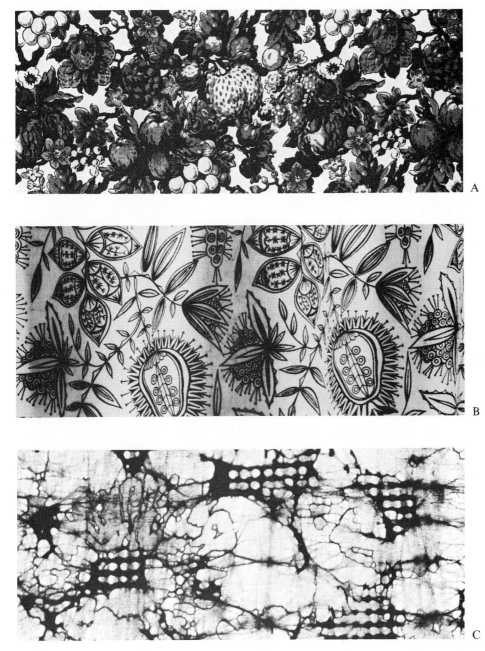

Top. Naturalistic foliage and fruits and flowers interlaced in a manner reminiscent of seventeenth-century English design. The flat textile has been imprinted with three-dimensional forms. (*Arthur H. Lee & Sons, Inc.*)

Center. Conventionalized interpretation in a contemporary print emphasizes inner structure rather than surface appearance. The crisp, informal design is open and spacious without recourse to perspective or light, shade, and shadow. (*D. N. & E. Walter & Co.*)

Bottom. An abstract distillation of natural forms is seen in "Waterlilies," a batik-like design with a fine, filigree tracery that make its own, unpremeditated pattern. Waterlily pads and flowers are suggested by the large, informally arranged areas. It is appropriately printed on velvet for a feeling of softness, depth, and reflected light. (*Photograph by Robert L. Beckhard. Jack Lenor Larsen, Inc.*)

Three printed textile designs inspired by natural forms are markedly different in character.

coverings may or may not have a backing. Strong, flexible, and impervious, the better grades of plastic fabrics are as nearly indestructible as any material suitable for upholstery or easily applied wall covering can be. Resisting stain and soil, their surfaces can be cleaned with a damp cloth. Tough and resilient, they seldom crack, chip, peel, or scratch. Textures range from leather-like smoothness to deeply molded, three-dimensional patterns. They can also be printed, embossed, or flocked with a soft fuzz. The fade-proof colors can be light or dark, brilliant or muted, glossy or dull. Expectedly, many of the designs imitate leather or

A   B   C

Above. "Tigris" is a heavy, deeply textured wall
covering that comes in a range of 16 color variations. (*L. E. Carpenter & Company, Inc.*)

Above center. "Montage" blends irregular rectangles and mottled shadings. (*L. E. Carpenter
& Company, Inc.*)

Above right. "Mozambique" is an upholstery
fabric with stretch-knit back that makes it fit
rounded or rectangular shapes snugly. (*L. E.
Carpenter & Company, Inc.*)

Right. "Fabrilite," a vinyl upholstery designed
by Russel Wright, has a small-scale, nondirectional pattern that is visually altered with each
change of light or angle. (*E. I. duPont de
Nemours & Company*)

Far right. An expanded vinyl upholstery fabric
with a knit back is printed in a multicolor design
of deep intensity. (*General Tire and Rubber
Company*)

Vinyl upholstery and wall coverings in a wide range of textures make
durable, easily cleaned surfaces.

textiles, but a few exploit the unique possibilities of these new products. Although
they seldom have the friendly, tactile qualities of textiles, they are ideal materials
for kitchens, family and children's rooms, and for indoor-outdoor furniture.

FABRIC DESIGN

Nothing used in contemporary homes except wallpaper offers the freedom
of design that comes naturally in fabrics (Color Fig. 15). This is of special significance today, when other materials are likely to be handled with restricted simplicity. The increasing urge for intricate ornamentation and emotional impact
can be most readily and inexpensively satisfied with fabrics.

From the illustrations in this chapter, it should be apparent that fabrics
are available to suit almost every taste and need. There is strict geometry brought
to life by yarns of varied weights, textures, and color in the striped upholstery
textile (Fig. 199A), whose linear rectangularity is obedient to the loom on which
it was woven. The warp-knit Rovana fabric (Fig. 203B) celebrates a sturdy horizontality by opposing it with decided diagonals, but the leno-weave casement

(Fig. 205E) is fluent and carefree in rhythm. The three Jacquard weaves (Figs. 206B, C, and D) are markedly different in character. The first has a compact succession of small figures that coalesce into a dense, overall, quite formal pattern; the second is crisply but unexpectedly punctuated with separated, open-weave circles; and the third has an organic, ever-changing swirl of lines. "Catalano" (Fig. 211B) is delicately small in scale with easy movement in all directions, while "Chiricahua" (Fig. 217A) has large, vigorous motifs that stand completely free of one another. These, and other fabrics throughout the book, exemplify the diversity of feelings and moods that textiles can bring into homes.

All that was said in Chapters 5, 6, and 7 about design concepts is generally applicable to fabric design, which can be structurally part and parcel of fiber and weave, can be applied to the finished cloth, or can be a combination of the two. Yet fabrics have unique characteristics that should be taken into account. Some of the more important qualities—**structure, continuousness, flatness,** and **pliability**—are discussed and illustrated on the following pages.

The **structure** of fabrics is a basic factor in their design. In most textiles the pattern of warp and filling can be seen and felt, and the way yarns are held together in knits and laces is equally apparent. The pattern may be of sufficient interest so that nothing more is needed. If applied ornament is desired, the structure and the fibers merit respect. Delicate patterns lose their effectiveness on coarse fabrics; bold motifs may seem incongruous on fine materials.

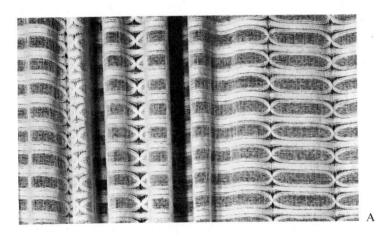

"Horizons," a handwoven fabric of linen, wool, and silk, has a horizontal pattern in which the warp threads are caught up at intervals to create ovoid shapes. Paul Maute, designer. (*Knoll Associates Inc.*)

A

The **continuous,** sheetlike nature of fabrics provides one of the few opportunities in homes for uninterrupted, endless patterns without a definite beginning or conclusion. Designs that lead the eyes easily in all directions seem especially appropriate.

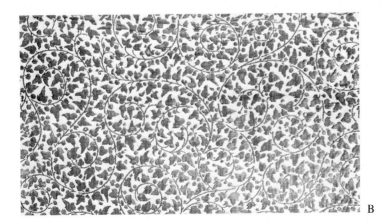

"Catalano" has a mazelike meander of leaves organized on pliant, spiraling stems. Mario Fortuny, designer. (*Fortuny, Inc.*)

FABRICS - 211

B

The two-dimensional **flatness** of most fabrics suggests two-dimensional compositions. There are numerous exceptions to this statement, and many of them are successful. In general, however, an illusion of great depth or of strongly modeled forms is open to doubt.

"Frieze," printed on cotton in two colors, is a refreshing design that does not belie the flatness characteristic of textiles. Kathleen Johnson, designer. (*Isabel Scott Fabrics Corporation*)

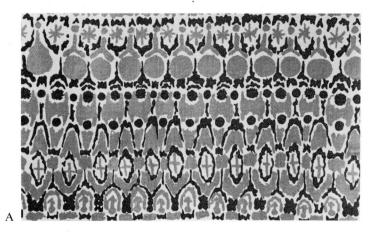

A

Pliability suggests patterns that are supple and pliant, unless the fabric is intended only to be stretched flat on walls or floors. This does not rule out angularity, but it makes its extreme rigidity or hardness questionable.

"Canterbury Bells," a linear conventionalization of flowers and leaves, is a motif that emphasizes the fabric's pliability, especially when draped in soft folds. (*Ben Rose, Designer and Printer*)

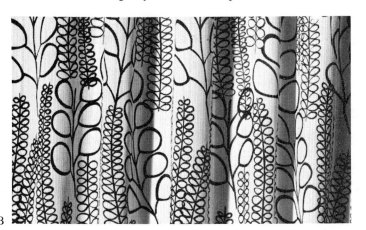

B

LIST OF FABRICS

The following list contains some of the fabrics most frequently used. They have been divided into five categories, based primarily on thickness, which is an important factor in determining their use. There is, however, quite a range within each category and some overlapping between categories. Most of the fabrics can be woven from a number of different fibers, but a few are made from only one. Fabric names are a strange miscellany, being based on the fiber, such as *linen*, which has come to mean a special kind of linen textile; the weave, such as *satin;* the early use, such as *monk's cloth;* or a trade name, such as *Indian Head.*

FABRICS

Very Thin

Almost transparent fabrics suitable for glass curtains; sometimes for summer bedspreads, dressing-table skirts, table coverings. Most can be made of cotton, silk, a synthetic, or even wool.

Bobbinet A fine and sheer to coarse and open plain lace with hexagonal meshes. Soft yet with character; most effective when very full; coarser types best for straight folds; sheer types well suited to tiebacks and ruffles. White, cream, ecru, pale colors.

Cheesecloth Cotton in loose, plain weaves, very low thread count. Very inexpensive; short-lived; informal. Usually off-white.

Dimity Fine, tightly twisted, usually combed cotton; plain weave with thin cord making vertical stripe or plaid. Often mercerized. Fine, sheer, crisp; suited to straight folds or tiebacks. Usually white; occasionally tints or printed patterns.

Filet Square-mesh lace knotted at intersecting corners. Fine to coarse but usually giving a bold, heavy effect. White, cream, ecru, and plain colors.

Marquisette Leno weave in many fibers. Sheer and open; soft or crisp; fine to coarse. Very serviceable; launders well. Usually white, cream, or pale colors; sometimes printed or woven patterns.

Net Any lace with a uniform mesh, such as bobbinet or filet–fine to coarse, sheer to open; made of almost any fiber.

Ninon Plain voilelike or novelty weaves. Very thin; smooth, silky, pleasant sheen; replacing silk gauze. Best in straight folds. Plain colors, self-colored stripes, or shadowy figures.

Organdy Cotton in plain weave; like sheer, crisp muslin, but crispness washes out unless specially treated. Folds keep their place. Often used without draperies; frequently tied back. Many plain colors; also printed or embroidered designs.

Point d'esprit Variation of bobbinet with dots that give it more body. White, cream, and pale colors.

Swiss muslin (dotted swiss) Cotton in plain weaves; usually embroidered or patterned in dots or figures. Fine, sheer, slightly crisp. Can be used alone, usually draped; effect generally informal. White and plain colors, usually light; figures may be colored.

Theatrical gauze Linen or cotton in a loose, open, crisp weave with a shimmering texture. Often used without draperies for colorful, informal effect. Wide range of plain colors, often two-toned.

Voile Open, plain weave, sheer and smooth. Drapes softly; gives more privacy than marquisette. Various textures; many colors, usually pale; sometimes woven patterns.

Dacron ninon with a small embroidered motif. (*E. C. Carter & Son, Inc., a subsidiary of Greeff Fabrics, Inc.*)

Thin

Translucent fabrics suitable for glass curtains or for draperies, and with sufficient body to be used alone and give a measure of privacy, although not at night. May also be used for dressing table skirts, table coverings, and summer bedspreads.

Batiste Delicate and fine, plain weave, usually cotton or dacron, often with printed or embroidered designs. Needs fullness to be effective; when embroidered, has considerable body. Feminine and dainty. White or pastel colors.

Casement cloth Almost every known fiber in plain or figured weaves. Flat and lustrous. Often ecru, but can be other colors. Often used alone as draw curtains.

Fiber glass Glass fibers in varied weaves and weights, from sheer marquisette to heavy drapery fabrics. Translucent to opaque; can be washed and hung immediately without shrinking or stretching. Good range of colors; plain or printed.

Muslin Cotton in a soft, plain weave; light to heavy qualities. Bleached or unbleached; also dyed and printed. Inexpensive, durable, informal; often used alone at windows.

"Mikado," silk gauze with a restrained medallion pattern. Alexander Girard, designer. (*Herman Miller Fabric Collection*)

Osnaburg Cotton yarns, coarse and uneven, in an open, plain weave; similar to crash. Usually medium weight, natural color, but can be light or heavy weight, any color, printed patterns. Strong and long-lasting; rough-textured; informal.

Pongee Wild silk in plain weave with broken crossbar texture caused by irregular yarns; also imitated in cotton and synthetics. Fairly heavy; often used without draperies. Shrinks unless treated. Usually pale or dark ecru, but can be dyed. Similar to tussah, antique taffeta, and doupioné.

Sheeting (*cotton*) Smooth, plain weave, medium to heavy weights. Inexpensive and informal. White, colors, or printed.

Sheeting (*plastic*) Smooth or textured, plain or printed, thin or thick. Used mostly for bath, shower and kitchen curtains, table coverings. Waterproof; wipes clean.

Silk gauze Plain weave with a slight irregularity in threads, making an interesting texture. Hangs well; is never slick. Wide range of colors.

Lightweight

Fabrics suitable for draperies, bedspreads, dressing table skirts, pillows, screens, wall coverings, table coverings, and slipcovers; sometimes for upholstery in the heavier grades. Many can be made of cotton, silk, wool, or a synthetic. They come in a wide color range and can be washed.

Antique satin Variation of smooth satin, with a dull, uneven texture. Variety of weights but usually heavier than satin. Widely used for upholstery and draperies.

Broadcloth Cotton, synthetic, or silk in plain or twill weaves; spun rayon or wool in twill weaves. Varies greatly in terms of fiber and weave. Cotton and synthetic types used for draperies, bedspreads, tablecloths.

Calico Cotton in a plain weave, printed with small-figured pattern. Inexpensive and informal.

Challis Wool, synthetic, or cotton in a soft, plain, firm weave. Usually printed with small floral designs but sometimes a plain color.

Chambray Cotton or linen in a smooth, close, plain weave. White-frosted appearance on wide range of colors.

Chintz Cotton in a close, plain weave, usually with a printed design and often glazed. Washing removes glaze in many types.

Drill Cotton in diagonal twill weave. Firm, heavy, very durable textile. Typical color is gray, but other colors available.

Faille Plain weave with decided flat, crosswise ribs. Difficult to launder, but wears well if handled carefully. Varies from soft yet firm to quite stiff.

Gingham Cotton or synthetic in light to medium weight, plain weave; woven from colored yarns. Strong; launders well. Checked, striped, and plaid patterns.

Homespun Irregular yarns woven in loose, plain weave. Texture somewhat rough and irregular; informal character. Plain colors, dyed, or woven of mixed yarns.

India print Printed cotton cloth from India or Persia with characteristic, intricate design in clear or dull colors. Inexpensive and durable. Fades, but pleasantly.

Indian Head Plain weave, firm and smooth. Trade name for a permanent-finish cotton, vat-dyed, colorfast, shrink-resistant. Inexpensive and durable.

Insulating Fabrics coated on one side with metallic flakes to reflect heat or with foam plastic to trap heat.

Jaspé cloth Plain weave; varied yarns give unobtrusive, irregular, blended stripes. Generally firm, hard, and durable. Can be in any color, but usually fairly neutral, medium dark, and monochromatic.

Linen Flax in a plain, firm weave. Cool to the touch, good body, launders well; wrinkles easily unless specially treated. Often has hand-blocked designs.

Moiré Ribbed, plain weave with a water-marked appearance. Most moiré finishes can be steamed or washed out—more permanent on synthetic fibers.

"Chinoiserie," Belgian linen with a hand-screened print. (*Stroheim & Romann. Courtesy of the Belgian Linen Association*)

A   B   C

Scale and implied activity are critical factors in selecting fabrics that are appropriate
to their setting. The three drapery materials illustrated above have patterns that are
varied in size, rhythm, and contrast.

Left. "Syncron" has little color contrast and is a quiet balance of thin horizontal and wider vertical stripes.
Undemanding but not dull, it would be appropriate where there is no reason for attracting attention to the
window treatment. (*Edwin Raphael Company*)

Center. "Fugitive Stripe" has more dark-and-light contrast, greater variety in the spacing of the horizontal
stripes, and more movement in the long, irregular vertical shapes. (*Schiffer Prints*)

Right. "Suspension" is large in scale, active in rhythm, and stimulating with its rising and falling triangular
motifs. In almost any room it would be an emphatic feature. (*Ruth Adler*)

Oxford cloth   Plain basket or twill weave, light to rather heavy weights. Durable and launders well.

Piqué   Plain weave with narrow raised cords running in one direction or at right angles to each other (waffle piqué). Durable; interesting texture.

Poplin   Plain weave with fine crosswise ribs. Firm and durable.

Rep   Plain weave with prominent rounded ribs running crosswise or lengthwise. Reversible.

Sateen   Cotton, usually mercerized, in a satin weave; flat and glossy, with a dull back. Durable, substantial, but with a tendency to roughen. Often used for lining curtains.

Satin   Satin weave, smooth, delicate fabric with very high sheen. Durable; somewhat slippery.

Seersucker   Plain weave with woven, crinkly stripes. Durable, needs no ironing.

Shantung   Plain weave with elongated irregularities. A heavy grade of pongee, but with wider color range.

Stretch   Knit or woven of cotton, rayon, or nylon with special stretch properties or of spandex. Smooth to rough textures. Valuable for slipcovers and contoured shapes.

Taffeta   Close, plain weave, slightly cross-ribbed. Crisp; sometimes weighted with chemical salts; cracks in strong sunlight. Antique taffeta has unevenly spun threads.

Medium Weight

Fabrics suitable for heavy draperies and upholstery as well as for wall coverings and pillows; some also suitable for slipcovers, bedspreads, screens, and table coverings. Made of heavier fibers of cotton, flax, hemp, jute, linen, silk, synthetics, or wool, they are available in a wide color range, but few are washable.

Bark cloth   Cotton in a firm, plain weave with irregular texture due to uneven yarns. Plain or printed. Durable.

Brocade   Woven on a Jacquard loom, raised designs are produced by floating some of the filling yarns. Usually has a multicolored floral or conventional pattern.

Brocatelle   A Jacquard weave similar to brocade but with a heavier design. Used mostly as upholstery on large sofas and chairs.

Burlap   Loose basket weave. Heavy and coarse; interesting texture. Often fades quickly.

Canvas   Cotton in a plain, diagonal weave. Heavy, firm, and durable. Strong solid colors, as well as stripes or printed designs. Often used for awnings, outdoor curtains, and upholstery.

Crash   Plain weave with a rough texture caused by uneven yarns. Often hand-blocked or printed.

Cretonne   Cotton in a firm, plain, rep, or twill weave. Fairly heavy texture and bold design. Similar to chintz but heavier, never glazed. Patterns are usually more vigorous.

Damask   Any combination of two of the three basic weaves; flat Jacquard patterns. Firm, lustrous, reversible. Similar to brocade but design is not in relief. May be referred to as figured satin. One or two colors used.

Denim   Cotton in a heavy, close twill weave. Warp and filler often in contrasting colors; can have a small woven pattern. Inexpensive; washable; Sanforizing prevents shrinking; reasonably sunfast.

Duck   Cotton in a close, plain, or ribbed weave. Durable; often given protective finishes against fire, water, mildew. Similar to canvas.

Hopsacking   Loose, plain weave. Coarse and heavy. Inexpensive and durable.

Laminated   Any fabric bonded to a lightweight foam backing, or two fabrics bonded together. Wrinkle-resistant; good for upholstery and slipcovers, also as insulating draperies.

Mohair   Hair of Angora goats (now often a mixture of cotton and wool) in a plain, twill, or pile weave or with a woven or printed design. Resilient and durable. Novelty weaves, sheer to very heavy.

"Harmony," a cotton brocade with an overall conventionalized flower design. (*Boris Kroll Fabrics, Inc.*)

15

Intense colors are compatible when adroitly handled. A mass of amethyst, magenta, cerise, rose, orange, and cadmium-yellow flower forms against a green background make an extremely lively hooked rug by Gere Kavanaugh. Allying it with the amethyst upholstery of the simply contoured chair by George Kasparian and with the varied greens shading into bronze of the wood divider by Joyce Aiken and Jean Ray Laury produces a harmonious but vivacious interplay of color and form. (*Photograph by Richard Gross. California Design/ 9, Pasadena Art Museum.*)

16

In the living room of a house designed by George Rockrise, interior designer Frances Mihailoff has used varied fabrics to underscore yet humanize the impact of an imposing fireplace wall. A thick, plush pile rug, designed by V'Soske, complements the off-white, moderately textured upholstery and curtains, and is an effective, comforting contrast to the ruggedness of the stone. The stronger colors in the border of the rug and in the pillows relate to the intense colors in Mark Adams' tapestry. The dominant shapes in the tapestry are as forceful as the heavier but less eloquent bulk of the rock wall. (*Photograph by Bruce Harlow*)

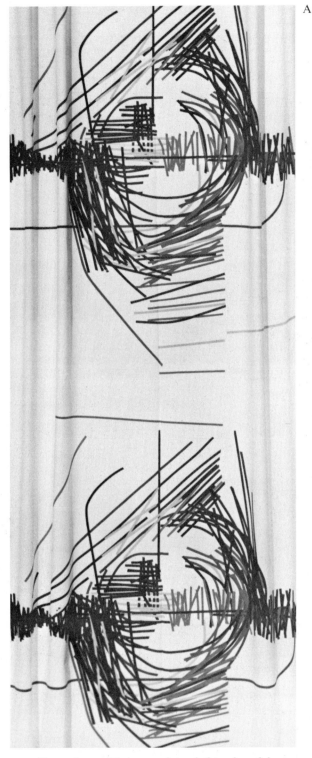

A

Below. Designer Ted Hallman weaves screens whose spontaneity convincingly establishes their own motivation. A detail of one, with varied yarns inset with pieces of plastic in different colors, is reminiscent of the patterns of nature, deviating, separating, curving, and coalescing in response to obstacles and compulsions.

B

C

Above. Some fabrics are intended as forceful, independent statements. "Chiricahua," produced in England, shows a series of unconnected motifs that stand by themselves. Its design breaks through the bonds of expected harmonies, creating a unity of discrepancies held together by their counterforces. (*Arthur H. Lee & Sons, Inc.*)

Above. Fiberglas drapery fabrics come in an array of weaves, prints, and colors. (*Owens-Corning Fiberglas Corporation*)

Monk's cloth Jute, hemp, flax, usually mixed with cotton or all cotton in a loose plain or basket weave. Coarse and heavy; friar's cloth and druid's cloth similar but coarser. Not easy to sew, tendency to sag. Usually comes in natural color.

Sailcloth Plain weave. Heavy and strong. Similar to canvas or duck. Often used on summer funiture.

Serge Twill weave with a pronounced diagonal rib on both face and back.

Heavy

Fabrics suitable for upholstery because of heavy weight and durability; in lighter grades for draperies, pillows, bedspreads, slipcovers, wall coverings, even table coverings. Most available in variety of fibers and in wide color range. Few are washable.

Bouclé Plain or twill weave. Flat, irregular surface, woven or knitted from specially twisted bouclé yarns; small spaced loops on surface.

Corduroy Cotton or a synthetic in a pile weave, raised in cords of various sizes giving pronounced lines. Durable, washable, inexpensive.

Expanded vinyl Plastic upholstery fabric with an elastic knit fabric back. Stretches for contour fit.

Felt Nonwoven fabric of wool, rayon and wool, or synthetics. Nonraveling edges need no hemming. Available in intense colors; used for table coverings, pillows, even for draperies.

Frieze (also called frizé) Heavy-pile weave. Loops uncut or cut to form a pattern; sometimes yarns of different colors or with irregularities used. Usually has a heavy rib. Extremely durable.

Matelassé Double-woven fabric with quilted or puckered surface effect, caused by interweaving to form the pattern. Needs care in cleaning, but otherwise durable.

Needlepoint Originally handmade in variety of patterns, colors, and degrees of fineness. Now imitated on Jacquard loom. At best, has pronounced character, from delicate (*petit point*) to robust (*gros point*); at worst, looks like weak imitation.

Has a clear, hard finish.

Terry cloth Cotton or linen in a loose uncut-pile weave; loops on one or both sides. Very absorbent; not always colorfast; may sag. Not suitable for upholstery, but useful for draperies and bedspreads.

Ticking Cotton or linen in a satin or twill weave. Strong, closely woven, durable. Best known in white with colored stripes, but may have simple designs. Not always colorfast but washable.

Plastic Wide variety of textures from smooth to embossed; used for upholstering and wall-covering. Resists soil, wipes clean. Not for use over deep springs unless fabric-backed, which is more pliable, easier to fit, less likely to split.

Plush Cut-pile weave. Similar to velvet but with a longer pile. Sometimes pressed and brushed to give surface variations; sculptured by having design clipped or burned out of pile, leaving motif in relief. Also made to imitate animal fur.

Tapestry Weaves with two sets of warps and weft; woven on a Jacquard loom. Heavier and rougher than damask or brocade. Patterns usually pictorial and large.

Tweed Soft, irregularly textured, plain weave. Yarns dyed before weaving; often several or many colors combined.

Velour Short, heavy, stiff cut-pile weave. Slight luster and indistinct horizontal lines. Durable.

Velvet Pile weave with loops cut or uncut. Luxurious but often shows wear quickly. Lustrous or dull; light to heavy grades; plain, striped, or patterned.

Velveteen Cotton or a synthetic woven with a short, close, sheared pile. Strong, durable, launders well.

Webbing Cotton, jute, or plastic in narrow strips (1–4 inches) of very firm, plain weave. Plain, striped, or plaid design. Jute used to support springs; cotton or plastic interlaced for webbed seats and backs.

"Coquille," cotton-nylon matelassé with shell forms raised above the surface. (*Boris Kroll Fabrics, Inc.*)

Fabrics used in unexpected ways make designer Mark Hampton's New York living room excitingly different. A black-and-white hexagon-patterned rug, designed by David Hicks, is the most striking component. Walls covered with gray flannel recede into the background behind black sofas. Stark white in the cushions, the wall sculpture, the ceiling, and the chair frames visually brightens the room. The colorless, transparent plastic tables are useful but self-effacing. An old Wells Fargo steel safe and steel foil folding shades at the end of the room add a metallic glitter. (*VOGUE photograph by David Massey; Copyright © 1967 by the Condé Nast Publications Inc.*)

Opposite. A conversation area in the large living room of York Castle, a Moorish-Portuguese fortress built in the sixteenth century and recently restored, combines old and new in a distinctive manner. The generous hooded fireplace, surfaced with white-washed plaster, as are the walls, is a dominant element. The very high, wood-beamed ceiling is visually lowered by its terra-cotta color, and the floor is visually warmed by traditional red tiles. A wood-grilled window echoes the tall, pointed arch openings in the opposite wall. These major elements, forceful as they are, set off the simple, armless chairs designed by Florence Knoll, the long built-in banquette with its many Thai silk cushions in gold, olive, and intense orange, and the traditional English armchair upholstered in a glowing red fabric. All the furniture is arranged in a convivial, U-shaped group around an old Moroccan rug, on which stands a contemporary table of teak and plastic. The round white tables, designed by the late Eero Saarinen, and the raised hearth provide surfaces for ashtrays, flowers, and plants. The pierced wood screen behind the wing chair, as well as the patterned window, brings texture higher up into the room. Figure 379A shows another part of this room. (*Interiors for York Castle designed by Planning Unit, Knoll International, France.*)

Part IV · MAJOR ELEMENTS

Handmade adobe bricks—a building material with a long history—take on new meaning when contrasted with walls of glass. Heat-resistant glass at the back of the fireplace stays clean because the fire pit is large. Cliff May, architect (*Photograph by Maynard L. Parker Modern Photography*)

11 · Walls and Fireplaces

Walls determine our movements and vistas, as well as give protection and privacy, and are perhaps the most strategic elements in our homes. They affect light, heat, and sound. They govern room shape, size, and character to become the enclosure against or with which we live. Walls are becoming increasingly "used" as windows and doors and for built-in storage and for furnishings that are attached to walls rather than freestanding on floors. That walls can be far more than innocuous backdrops can be demonstrated by historic and contemporary examples. Well-proportioned walls are a continuing source of deep satisfaction. Appropriate colors, textures, and materials relate architecture to people and to furniture in a positive manner.

Walls, seen and used in relation to the windows, doors, and fireplaces that are parts of them, to floors and ceilings that complete the enclosure, and to furniture, accessories, and people, should be considered as integral parts of a whole.

WALLS CREATE CHARACTER

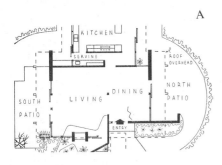

A

The plan of the Cliff May house, Fig. 223, shows how the irregularly shaped hearth extends outdoors to join house and garden. (*Reprinted from* Sunset *Magazine*)

In the remodeled living room on this and the facing page the original dignity has been heightened by a simplified treatment of its lofty spaciousness. Morgan Stedman, architect. (*Photographs by Maynard L. Parker Modern Photography*)

Whether we are conscious of it or not, walls constitute a stage setting, and the mood they establish is important in its influence on everyday living. For the living room in Figures 223 and 224A, the architect has stressed informality and openness rather than protection and dignity. Two walls are largely of sliding glass doors, while a third integrates windows, another sliding door, and a see-through fireplace with a raised hearth that serves as seating, a table, and an outdoor platform for container plants. Visually as well as physically, he has merged the room and its adjoining patios into a sweep of space that is liberating and unaffected.

Quite different in design and character, the walls of a remodeled living room (Figs. 224B–225B) emphasize enclosure and a natural, relaxed dignity, refinement of design and workmanship. The architect established continuity by careful remodeling in sympathy with the original forms, but he transformed this space into an environment congenial to an active, modern family and its collection of fine, old furniture and works of art. For durability and beauty, the walls are covered with natural-finish oak plywood around the fireplace and oak boards elsewhere. Handsomely organized shelves and cupboards make large sections of the walls useful for storage and for display of plaques and vases. But the fireplace and adjacent wall are simply treated to become foils for painting, prints, and furniture.

One end has furniture grouped around a fireplace. The vertical-grain wood and blunt-arrow shape carry upward to the high ceiling, accented but not weighted by beams.

B

The opposite end is a library with comfortable seating, shelves to hold books and accessories, and a broad counter with drawers and cupboards underneath.

A

B

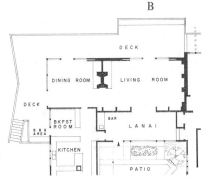

The plan shows how living, dining, lanai, and deck areas open into one another without losing their identity.

The room is a spacious rectangle measuring 18 by 30 feet and is generally symmetrical. Entering the room through an opening in the middle of the west wall, you notice a fireplace centered at one end and balanced by symmetrical bookshelves at the other. Many design factors, though, keep this space from appearing to be just a symmetrical rectangle. The fireplace is flanked on one side by a shallow recess for an antique secretary, but on the left a passageway lined with storage units and unimpeded by doors leads the eye on toward the dining room. Two other broad openings visually extend your attention beyond the confines of the walls. On the entrance side the living room opens into the lanai through a 9-foot "archway," which can be closed with sliding, translucent Japanese panels. Opposite this, but off-center, three sliding glass doors make half the wall a transparent invitation to enjoy the deck and landscape. The only windows as such are panes of fixed glass over bookshelves.

None of these openings—in fact no part of the room—is accentuated as a separate unit by enframing ornament. Continuity and unity of part with whole, quite the opposite effect, has been deliberately sought. Oak on all walls and the ceiling beams brings a consistency of color and texture. The beams carry the rhythms set forth in the walls over and across the room. Built-in light troughs, which send light up or down and almost encircle the room, underscore the horizontal alignment of doorways and shelves in this room and in the dining room beyond. Although the room has overtones of geometric formality and unpretentious elegance, it adroitly avoids stiffness and prescription. Furniture arranged near solid walls brings enclosing security; freedom and openness come with the explicit emphasis on the continuity of this space with that which surrounds it.

A massive, floor-to-ceiling fieldstone wall is a dominant element in the living room shown in Color Figure 16. At first glance it might seem like a clumsy intruder, because its material, scale, and texture differ from anything else in the room. Occupying more than half of one end of the room, the fireplace wall butts up against a projecting, light-colored wood bookcase on the left but stops a few inches short of the window wall on the right, creating a pocket into which the curtains slide when open. It rises through the ceiling without hesitancy, which, together with its clean-cut separation from the bookcase and window, allows it to stand as an independent masonry unit. So far, the fireplace wall seems to have nothing to do with its surroundings except physical proximity. Closer study, however, discloses that the architect and decorator ingeniously made it seem at home. It is firmly related to the dark wood floor by its long, raised hearth of dark, polished concrete. Placed asymmetrically, the fireplace opening is almost square, a shape that might be unduly static and incongruous were it not reiterated by the modern tapestry hung close by, the ceiling grid, and the rectangular tables placed throughout the room. The nongeometric rounded form of most of the stones (except those at the base that are slightly squared to be at ease with the hearth and floor) is consonant with the design of the tapestry and the contours of the upholstered furniture. The thick, textured wool rug in shades of gray, orange, and yellow-orange, the off-white, slightly textured upholstery, and the translucent curtains complete the transition from dark and heavy to bright and light. Strategically placed, Mark Adams' tapestry brings together the light and dark, pure and neutral colors of the room in an intensified statement.

By such devices a rugged, informal wall has been kept in bounds and yet dramatized to give a basic dignity that approaches formality. Contrast this with the way in which the fieldstone fireplace in Figure 246 has been given free rein to extend itself and take over the room.

In contrast to the warm enclosure of the two preceding living rooms, the one in Figure 227 is open and spacious. Cantilevered out over a wooded ravine, it is appropriately light and airy. The geometry of the exposed posts and beams is as pleasant visually as it is structurally efficient. Glass, bookshelves, and panels of plaster painted in light-reflecting colors contrast pleasantly with the naturally finished wood framing. The buoyant feeling is heightened by the light-colored composition floor and the canopy-like plywood ceiling. Set off-center, the fireplace does not compete with the view. The total feeling is lighthearted and gay.

In each of the rooms illustrated so far the walls contributed significantly to the room's personality; but walls perform many other functions. In terms of **use,** they are primarily protective screens separating the house as a whole from its surroundings and partitioning the interior into usable areas. They can insulate against heat, cold, and noise; they reflect or absorb light and sound; and they house the wires, pipes, and ducts for electrical appliances, plumbing, and heating. Increasingly they are used for built-in storage, furnishings, and lighting. Typically, but not necessarily, they support the roof. In terms of **economy,** good walls have low original cost, are long lasting, require minimum maintenance, keep heating and cooling bills low, and take little space. Regrettably, it is almost impossible to find a wall with these five characteristics. This forces us to decide what is most important for *each* wall, because even in one home their functions are not identical. In terms of **beauty,** walls ought to give us the

Panels of clear glass, and white, off-white, and brown plaster form the walls of a treetop living room. Sometimes lightly veiled with sheer curtains or half-obscured by shelves, they alternately reveal and hide the surrounding greenness. Smith and Williams, architects. (*Photograph by Julius Shulman*)

aesthetic pleasure that can heighten all home activities. Exterior walls shape the mass of the house and establish its relationship to its environs. **Individuality** comes when walls genuinely express the family's needs and preferences and are suited to their particular functions.

To get the kind of walls one wants it is essential to consider their design and their materials and construction, as is done in the two following sections.

DESIGN OF WALLS

Contemporary architects and designers enjoy a freedom to use a vocabulary far more extensive than in the past, when walls were almost always fixed, vertical, thick, opaque, and supported the roof. Although many walls today have these characteristics, the following types are becoming common:

- Nonstructural walls that hold up nothing other than themselves, as in Figures 187 and 188
- Thin, transparent, or translucent walls of glass or plastic, as in Figures 223 and 229B

A living-dining area in a contemporary English apartment is distinguished by the decisive organization and treatment of the walls. Strong contrasts between light and dark visually enlarge the space through clear definition of planes, while the intricate wallpaper patterns reinforce the shape and character of the walls. These contrasts and intensifications would have a positive, awakening effect on those who make their home here. Eric Lyons, architect. (*Courtesy of* The Architectural Review)

- Walls that are integrated with ceilings, as in Figure 293
- Movable walls that slide into pockets, fold like accordions, or are storage units on casters, as in Figure 225B
- Storage walls that unite the enclosing functions of walls with many kinds of storage space, as in Figure 224B
- Walls less than ceiling height to give visual privacy without tight, box-like enclosure, as in Figures 34 and 55A
- Spur or freestanding walls (or fireplaces) that stop short of joining the adjacent walls at one or both ends, as in Figures 243A and B

A number of specific qualities can be combined as wished to invest walls with the character thought most appropriate. Some pertain primarily to use; others to economy, beauty, or individuality. Taken together, these qualities determine the expressive and utilitarian properties of walls.

Degree of formality and informality. The Port Royal parlor (Color Fig. 5) is much more formal than the American seventeenth-century hall (Fig. 36B) or the room shown in Figure 227. Formality is achieved when a room gives the feeling of a strict, firmly established, unchanging order. Symmetrical balance and pronounced regularity are the fundamental means to achieve this, but formality is usually increased when the forms seem stable and precise, surfaces are smooth, and proportions make one feel upright. Use almost never indicates symmetrically balanced walls, but they have their own kind of beauty. Today, many rooms are semiformal. The living room in Figures 224B and 225A is not symmetrical, but there is a strong sense of order, the forms are precise and smooth, and the fireplace wall is vertical. In Color Figure 16 informality and formality are brought together in a room that is dignified but not stiff: the formal furnishings are pleasingly related to a rugged stone wall.

Degree of activity or passivity. Walls become active to the degree that their design and materials arouse visual interest, especially if they suggest movement. This is accentuated if they are used for storage or displays of collections and also if they are integrated with built-in furniture (Fig. 225A) or have a fireplace. Typical smoothly plastered, uniformly painted walls are passive except when

A   B

Above left. For a study-bedroom, a softly textured brown cork wall and one with built-in shelves create display space and an appropriate atmosphere of repose and individuality. Welton Becket, architect. (*Photograph by Maynard L. Parker Modern Photography*)

Above right. Patterned glass makes the walls and ceiling of a small entrance inviting. The glass is fitted into simple wood frames that are the structure of the house. The translucency of the glass floods the space with natural or artificial light, creates a changing series of patterns, and affords privacy on a small lot. Gordon Drake, architect. (*Photograph by Julius Shulman. Blue Ridge Glass Company*)

Right. In sculptor-designer Emile Norman's own home in Big Sur, California, walls of tile and wood enclose the skylighted shower. Tile, in general, is easy to clean and is waterproof; but these have the added advantage of being uncommon in design. Made by hand, the multicolored tiles have ingeniously varied, stylized fish motifs that seem appropriate and lead into the shower stall. The wall of small pieces of different woods skillfully selected, arranged, and fitted together displays similar but abstract patterns in the grain of the wood. Taking a shower in a room like this could help get the day off to a good start. (*Photograph by Maynard L. Parker Modern Photography*)

C

their color is vigorous. In Figure 229A, the cork wall is slightly activated by the pattern of joints and the texture of the material, but it is very passive when compared to the adjacent, shelf-lined wall. In Figures 228 and 229C, patterned wallpaper and tiles attract attention with their lively rhythms.

Degree of smoothness or roughness. Here the range is from glassy smoothness to stony roughness with countless intermediate steps provided by plaster and wallboard, tile and brick, wood and plastics. Smoothness is often associated with formality, roughness with informality. A basic pattern of companionable surface textures gives a sense of coherence, but variety and contrast are needed to awaken it.

Largeness or smallness of scale. Of tremendous importance is the scale of the walls in relation to the size of the space, the character of furnishings, and the personalities of the people. The scale of the walls is large in the room with the fieldstone wall, moderate in the remodeled living room, and small in the intimate sitting room in Figure 94A. Large scale is produced by big, bold textures. It reduces visual space but is impressive. Moderate- to small-scale walls make rooms spacious and homelike.

Degree of enclosure or openness. The book-lined corner in Figure 225A is enclosing and protecting, but the wide opening to the lanai extends the space into the patio. Translucent glass, as used in Figure 229B, suggests partial enclosure. Large areas of glass and light color make Figure 227 spaciously open.

Enclosure is brought about by opaque, substantial-looking walls; by warm, dark colors and noticeable textures; by small, separated, framed doors; and by windows with small panes and protective draperies. Openness comes with a maximum of transparent, translucent, or apparently thin, unobtrusive walls and with a minimum of walls that block view or movement. Receding colors and inconspicuous textures are also contributing factors. Of great importance is continuity of materials, forms, and colors, not only within the room, but with the space in adjacent rooms and with the landscape.

Degree of light absorption or reflection. Color value is the most critical factor in light absorption and reflection. White reflects up to 89 percent of the light striking it, and black as little as 2 percent. But surface texture must be considered, because the smoother the surface the more light is reflected. In the past, when windows were small and artificial illumination was poor, very light walls were frequently needed to make rooms bright. Today, with larger windows and improved artificial lighting, many people find that darker, textured walls create a sympathetic enclosure for themselves and their furnishings. Nevertheless, light-colored walls are refreshing, increase apparent size, make rooms easier to illumine, and are an effective background for anything placed against them.

Durability and maintenance. The amount of time and money needed to maintain walls affects the satisfaction they give. Some materials—masonry, tile, and vinyl plastics—are durable and easily maintained anywhere. Some, such as fragile but colorfast wallpapers, last long with little care on walls that do not get hard use. Basic questions are: What kind of use will the wall get? How easily is the material damaged? How easily can it be cleaned or repaired?

Degree of sound absorption or reflection. Smaller houses and open plans, greater freedom for children, laborsaving but noisemaking devices, and the trend away from massive upholstered furniture and heavy draperies make many contemporary homes noisy. Ways of dealing with this problem are discussed in Chapter 15.

Degree of heat-cold insulation. In the interests of economy and comfort, the degree of heat-cold insulation (discussed in Chap. 15) is consequential.

WALL CONSTRUCTION AND MATERIALS

Although we often take walls for granted, the building of efficient, protective enclosures was a notable achievement for early man. Recently there have been tremendous technological advances, especially in factory-made wall units. Although the technology of wall construction is beyond the scope of this book, some knowledge of what walls are and how materials affect their characteristics can help in deciding on the walls most appropriate for homes.

Walls that are fixed, opaque, and of one material are the easiest to understand. Houses built of heavy timbers, such as log cabins and Swiss chalets, and structures of solid stone or brick are examples. These are rare today because they are usually expensive, comparatively poor insulators, leave no concealed space for pipes and ducts, and are not amenable to the broad, unobstructed openings now in favor unless combined with heavy steel or wood beams (Fig.

246). Walls entirely of masonry, however, have great appeal, with their comforting sense of permanence as well as their color and texture. Steel reinforcing increases their stability, and space can be left for insulation and utilities. The enormous possibilities of concrete and metal as distinctive materials have received relatively little attention in residential architecture.

Today most walls are compounded of varied materials or of the same material used in different ways. Wood-frame walls are the most common in homes. They are familiar to builders and not expensive. In addition to resilient stability, they allow space for insulation and utilities. Usually, but not necessarily, they support the roof. Surface treatment, inside and out, can be varied. Although they can have five or more layers, they can be thought of as three-layer sandwiches:

- **Structural frame** of wood studs (closely spaced two-by-fours or more widely spaced heavier posts) from floor to ceiling
- **Exterior layers** of diagonal wood sheathing and insulation or sheets of strong insulating composition board, covered with weather-resistant surfaces of wood, asbestos, or metal siding, shingles or sheets; with lath and stucco; or with a veneer of brick or stone
- **Interior layers** of lath and plaster, of plywood, wallboard, or wood paneling

In 1955 one out of every twelve houses built in the United States was prefabricated. In 1965 over two hundred thousand new factory-made houses ready to be assembled in a few days were carried to their sites on trucks, or more than one out of every five single-family houses built. Prices range from a few thousand dollars for vacation houses to forty thousand dollars and over for luxury models. This may be news, but the principles of prefabrication are old. Prehistoric nomads in southeastern Asia developed portable wooden houses, and our Plains Indians had tepees that could be quickly erected, taken down, and moved. Today there have been great strides made in prefabrication of walls and many striking innovations are promised. Panels of wood, metal, or synthetics, efficiently made in factories, can reduce construction costs without loss of individuality. One company alone produces wall panels that can be used in twelve hundred different designs. Most of these panels are rectangular and are ready to be fitted to wood or metal structural frames. But in experimental models, walls, roof, and even the floor fabricated as one unit points toward completely new concepts of design.

Wall Materials and Surfacings

The chart of wall materials (pp. 234–235) enables us to compare the many differences in wall materials and surfacings. We should also be aware that:

- All exterior materials can be used for inside walls, a possibility highly regarded by contemporary architects and designers because it accentuates indoor-outdoor relationships, and by housewives because it often reduces housework.
- Some materials usually thought of as flooring, such as cork, vinyl flooring, or carpeting, bring to walls the same serviceability they give floors.
- Many new materials expand the range of possibilities.

None of this need concern those who are happy with plaster or wallboard painted white or low-intensity colors, which become passive backgrounds. But it should concern those who want more distinctive walls. Some of the ways in which wallpaper and plaster, patterned glass, and tile can be used on walls are shown on pages 228 and 229, and a sampling of new and old products is illustrated below and on page 233.

Wood and Masonry: Versatile, Time-Tested Materials

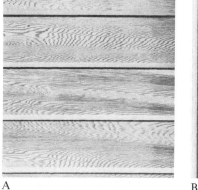 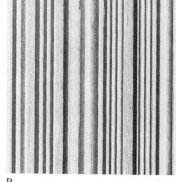 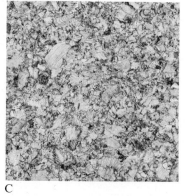

A   B   C

Left. Resembling weathered wood, etched cedar has a conspicuous grain pattern. (*Evans Products Company*) *Center.* In striated plywood, vertical grooves of varied widths minimize the grain and give a pronounced, small-scale directional rhythm. (*United States Plywood Corporation*) *Right.* Pressed cork tiles have infinitely varied, nondirectional patterns. (*Dodge Cork Company*)

D   E   F

Left. Smoothly polished translucent marble is beautiful and costly. *Center.* Roughly cut random-ashlar stonework looks ruggedly substantial. Anshen and Allen, architects (*Photograph by Dean Stone and Hugo Steccati*) *Right.* Cement tiles from Italy are embedded with many materials, such as mother-of-pearl chips, that provide color and textural interest.

G   H   I

Left. Lustrous ceramic tiles ornamented with small rectangular motifs produce scintillating patterns of light. (*International Pipe & Ceramic Corporation*) *Center.* Handmade tiles, muted in color and subtly varied in design and texture, have distinguished individuality. Fausto Melotti, designer. (*Alitalia*) *Right.* Sculptured tiles of unglazed terra-cotta in varied earthen colors give a lively interplay of light and shadow. (*Design-Technics*)

Walls of Glass, Metal, and Plastics: A Comparatively Recent Development

A

Glass building blocks 8 inches square and 4 inches thick have areas of clear molded glass decisively patterned with opaque black bands. They change appearance with each change of light and when viewed from different angles. (*Pittsburgh Corning Corporation*)

B

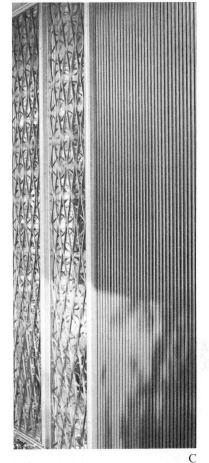

C

Above left. "Spandrelite" patterned glass comes in a wide range of colors and textures. (*Blue Ridge Glass Corporation*) *Above right.* Vibrantly colored aluminum panels and grilles, frankly revealing the material from which they are made, make weather-hardy, carefree walls. (*Aluminum Corporation of America*)

D

E

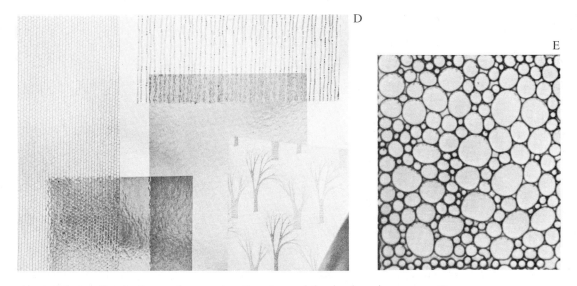

Above left. Acrylic plastic panels come in vibrant or subdued colors, in many patterns and degrees of transparency. (*American Cyanamid Company*) *Above right.* "Circlet Tropical," a plastic sandwich panel reinforced with a core of paper tubing, diffuses light and eliminates glare. (*United States Rubber Company*)

WALL MATERIALS
Exterior and Interior

Material	Character	Use	Finishes	Advantages	Disadvantages
Asbestos (panels, shingles, siding) Cost: moderately low.	New textures and colors make it interesting; may resemble wood from a distance.	Occasionally in interiors where durability and easy upkeep are important. Exterior walls.	None needed, but can be painted.	Rare combination of low cost and upkeep: high resistance to fire, weather, and insects.	None except rather commonplace quality.
Brick (adobe) Cost: varies greatly from one locality to another.	Earthy solidity combined with handcraft informality. Large in scale. Noticeable pattern of blocks and joints unless smoothly plastered.	Interior-exterior walls, chiefly in mild climates.	Stucco, special paints, or transparent waterproofing.	Unique character: resists fire and insects. Newer types made with special binders and stabilizers are stronger and more weather-resistant.	Older types damaged by water. Walls must be very thick or specially reinforced. Sturdy foundations required. Comparatively poor insulation for weight and thickness.
Brick (fired clay) Cost: high but less than stone.	Substantial and solid; small-scale regularity. Many sizes, shapes, and colors. Can be laid in varied patterns.	Interior-exterior walls, exterior surfacing or garden walls. Around fireplaces.	None unless waterproofing necessary; interior walls can be waxed.	Satisfying texture and pattern; durable, easily maintained; fireproof.	None other than heat-cold conduction and noise reflection.
Concrete Cost: moderately high.	Typically smooth and solid-looking, but can be highly decorative.	Interior-exterior walls in mild climates. Exterior walls elsewhere.	Exterior usually painted or stuccoed. Interior painted, plastered, or surfaced with any material.	Permanent, durable, low maintenance. Can be cast in varied shapes and surface-treated in many ways.	Comparatively poor insulator. Requires sturdy foundations and costly forms.
Concrete blocks (lightweight aggregate) Cost: moderate.	Typically regular in shape, moderately textured, and bold in scale, but many variations possible.	Interior-exterior walls in mild climates. Exterior and garden walls anywhere.	Exterior waterproofing necessary; no interior finish needed but can be painted.	Moderately handsome, durable, easily maintained; fireproof; fair insulator.	None of any consequence.
Glass (clear and patterned) Cost: moderately high.	Open and airy. Patterned glass transmits diffused light.	Interior-exterior window walls. Patterned glass for translucent partitions for interiors.	None (except for curtaining for privacy and control of light, heat, and cold).	Clear glass creates indoor-outdoor relationships. Patterned glass combines light and varying degrees of privacy.	Breakable; very poor heat-cold insulation unless thermopane. Needs frequent cleaning.
Metal (panels, siding, shingles, and tiles) Cost: moderate.	Varies greatly depending on size, shape, and finish; often regarded as unhomelike.	Sometimes used in kitchens and bathrooms. Exterior house and garden walls.	Aluminum and steel available with long-lasting factory finishes in many colors.	Lightweight in relation to strength. Resistant to fire, and so on. Enameled and aluminum panels need minimum upkeep.	Although very durable, metal surfaces are difficult to repair if damaged.
Plaster and **stucco** Cost: moderately low.	Typically smooth and precise but can be varied in texture. The only surfacing material that shows no joints, breaks. Excellent, quiet background.	Plaster in any room. Stucco for garden or exterior house walls.	Special weather-resistant paints. Paint, paper, or fabric for interiors.	Moderately durable if properly finished; suited to many easy-to-change treatments; fireproof; special types absorb sound. Transparent.	Often cracks or chips.
Plastic (panels, siding, glazing; often reinforced with glass fibers, Cost: moderate.	Opaque or translucent, often textured and colorful. Thin and flat or corrugated; thicker with cores of varied materials.	Interior walls where durability, upkeep are important; partitions. Interior-exterior walls. Exterior siding. Translucent for garden walls.	None.	Similar to patterned glass except breaks less easily, lighter in weight; can be sawed and nailed. Siding prefinished, durable; low upkeep.	Not thoroughly tested for longevity.
Stone Cost: high.	Substantial, solid; impressive; natural colors and textures.	Around fireplace. Exterior and garden walls.	None unless waterproofing is necessary.	Beauty and individuality; durability, ease of maintenance; fireproof; ages gracefully.	Poor insulator; reflects sound; not amenable to change.

Material	Character	Use	Finishes	Advantages	Disadvantages
Wood Cost: moderate.	Natural beauty and individuality of grain and color.	Interior and exterior walls; garden fences.	Needs protective finish to seal it against water, stains, dirt.	Fairly durable, easily maintained; good insulator; adaptable to many forms; ages well inside.	Few kinds are weather-resistant unless treated; burns; attacked by termites.

Interior Only

Material	Character	Use	Finishes	Advantages	Disadvantages
Cork Cost: moderately high.	Sympathetic natural color and texture.	Any room; only plastic-impregnated types suitable for baths and kitchens.	None needed but can be waxed.	Durable, easily kept; sound-absorbent; good insulator.	Harmed by moisture, stains, and so on, unless specially treated.
Linoleum Cost: moderate.	Smooth, mat surface; great variety of colors and patterns.	Hard-use rooms.	Needs no finish but can be waxed.	Durable, easily maintained; reduces noise somewhat.	None unless you do not like its character.
Plastic (thin, rigid tiles) Cost: relatively low.	Similar to clay tile except variety is sharply limited.	Kitchen and bathroom walls.	No finish needed.	Easy to keep and apparently durable; simple to install; lightweight.	Similar to clay tile.
Plastic (vinyl tiles or sheets) Cost: moderately high.	Great variety of colors, patterns, textures.	Where durable, resilient walls are wanted, such as in play space or above kitchen counters.	None needed but can be waxed.	Very durable and resistant to cuts and stains. Easy maintenance. Can extend into counter tops.	Cost.
Rubber (tiles) Cost: moderately high.	Much like linoleum.	Where durable, resilient walls are indicated.	None needed.	Similar to linoleum, but colors are brighter and clearer.	May be harmed by grease and stains.
Tile (clay) Cost: moderately high.	Repeated regularity sets up pattern; great variety in size, shape, ornamentation.	Kitchens, bathrooms, and around fireplace. Occasionally used for exterior ornament.	No finish needed.	Can have great beauty and individuality; very durable, easily maintained; resistant to water, stains, fire.	Hard and cold to touch; reflects noise; can crack or break.
Wallboard (cane and fiber) Cost: low.	Soft, porous surface; no pronounced character in typical tan or gray, but available in harder, textured surfaces.	Any room.	If not factory-finished, needs paint or wallpaper.	Moderately durable, good heat-cold and sound insulator.	Absorbs moisture and dirt; shows wear.
Wallboard (gypsum or plaster) Cost: moderately low.	Noncommittal. Joints show unless very well taped and painted.	Any room.	Paint, wallpaper, or fabric.	Not easily cracked; fire-resistant; can be finished in many ways.	Visually uninteresting in itself. Needs protective surface.
Wallboard (plastic laminates) Cost: high.	Shiny, mat, or textured surface; varied colors and patterns.	Kitchens, bathrooms, or any hard-use wall.	None needed.	Very durable, unusually resistant to moisture, stains, dirt; cleaned with damp cloth.	Although wear-resistant, it can be irremediably scratched or chipped. Reflects noise.
Wallboard (pressed wood) Cost: moderate.	Smooth, mat surface with slight visual texture; also great variety of patterns.	Hard-wear rooms.	Needs no finish but can be stained, waxed, painted.	Tough surface is hard to damage.	None of any importance.
Wall covering (plastic) Cost: moderately high.	Many patterns; pleasing textures; mat or glossy surfaces.	Walls.	None needed.	Very durable; resists moisture, dirt, stains; cleans with damp cloth.	None of importance.
Wallpaper and fabrics Cost: moderately low.	Tremendous variety of color and pattern.	Any wall.	Usually none but can be protected with lacquer.	Inexpensive; can give decided character; some kinds very durable and easy to keep.	Must be chosen and used carefully.

APPLIED WALL FINISHES AND SURFACING

When a wall surface is not completely satisfactory, it can be quickly and inexpensively changed with paint, wallpaper, or wall fabrics.

Paint

Paints today are made from a broad variety of natural and man-made materials selected for their special attributes, and new types and combinations appear with frequency. Their properties are impressive. Some can be useful on wood, masonry, stucco, metal, asbestos, or composition board; many resist sun, fading, and blistering; and most dry in a short time. Others are fire-resistant or rust-inhibiting. Many of them are easier to apply than the older paints, usually with a roller, and have little paint odor. When dry, they have mat, semigloss, or high-gloss surfaces. Those that are water-based are extremely easy to handle, because paint spots can be wiped up with a damp cloth and brushes cleaned with soap and water. After a short period of curing, they are not affected by water. Solvent-based paints may be more durable, but the application and clean-up is somewhat more tedious. The number of different colors available has been greatly increased by the automatic mixing machines that most paint dealers have.

Being the easiest of all finishes to apply, paint leads many people into doing their own wall finishing. Nothing so quickly and inexpensively changes the character of a room. Paint finds its place in the smallest apartment and the most elaborate mansion in good part because it is an excellent, unobtrusive background for furnishings, art objects, and people. In itself paint has little distinctive beauty or individuality, but these goals can be attained by choosing exactly the right color or a distinctive combination of colors that seem eminently suited to the walls they cover and to the people who live with them.

Next to color in importance is paint's ability to give a uniform surface to whatever it covers. Sometimes smooth paint will not cover all blemishes, and sometimes smoothness is not wanted. Then it can be **stippled** with a stiff brush to obliterate brush marks and to give a soft, mat finish, or it can be **spattered** with one or more colors to give some vibrancy and minimize spots or scratches. More pronounced textures are produced with special paints, by applying the paint with special rollers, or by going over the wet paint with a sponge or a whiskbroom. These are easy and inexpensive ways to cover plaster cracks or wallboard joints, and they give walls varied surfaces.

Wallpaper

Long known in the Orient, wallpaper has been used in Europe for about five centuries and in this country since early days. "Poor man's tapestry" was a good name for it, because wallpaper came into use in humble homes as an imitation of the expensive textiles used by the wealthy. Wallpaper's advantages are many and varied:

- It can be used in any room in the home.
- It can be tested for its effect in advance by borrowing large samples.
- It is available in many colors, patterns, and textures, and in varying degrees of durability.

Natural forms, the discipline of geometry, and the controlled fluidity of ink are among the inspirations for wallpaper design.

Above left. "Malta," printed with white flocking on a deep brown background, transforms clear-cut, interlocking forms into an intricate pattern that leads the eyes in many directions. (*Timbertone Decorative Company*)

Above center. In "Persian Tree" rows of ingeniously stylized trees appear to be enveloped in a misty spaciousness. New printing techniques give the paper a silken effect. (*The Jack Denst Designs*)

Above right. There are no repeats in the handmade papers that exploit the free shapes of printing ink splattered on metallic-coated parchment paper. Reminiscent of tide pools, skies, or aerial photographs of the landscape, the designs encourage each person to see what he wishes. Sarolta Bartha, designer. (*Bartex Novelty Company, Inc.*)

Designs that remind us of the past and those that keep attention on the present stand side by side in today's stores.

Above left. "Antoinette" was inspired by eighteenth-century French taste. Strictly symmetrical and intricately composed, the design is so active and merry that it does not seem forbiddingly formal. (*The Warner Company*)

Above center. "Joseph's Coat" dramatizes vertical stripes of differing widths with strong color contrasts. (*The Jack Denst Designs*)

Above right. "Carioca" boldly prints floating teardrop shapes over wide vertical stripes in a vivacious, dancing rhythm. Larsen Design Corporation, designer. (*Karl Mann Associates, New York*)

- It has the most positive character of any wall surfacing in its price class.
- It makes a room seem to shrink or swell, gain height or intimacy, become more active or subdued, more formal or less formal.
- It minimizes architectural awkwardnesses by illusion or camouflage.
- It hides disfigured walls.
- It makes rooms with little furniture seem furnished.
- It distracts attention from miscellaneous or commonplace furniture.

Wallpaper has a few inherent disadvantages. Some persons may not like its "papery" look and many patterns are dull or ugly; but these are not faults of the material.

It is possible to find papers appropriate to almost any way of living, any kind of furnishings, any exposure or special factor. Wallpapers range from solid colors through textured effects, small and large patterns, to mural or scenic designs. Most have a dull, mat finish that may or may not be washable; but some are glossy. Then there are the less usual types. Flock papers with their raised, fuzzy nap look like textiles. Marbleized papers hint at the gloss and depth of marble, and metallic papers bring luster and can help a little in insulating rooms against heat and cold.

Selecting a pattern and color is not easy. Wall-length samples of several patterns can be brought home, fastened up, and observed at different times of day and night. Wallpaper is a kind of applied ornament that may noticeably affect the apparent size, shape, and character of rooms. Consider it in the light of the criteria for ornament discussed in Chapter 6, making these more specific by keeping in mind that the wall and paper are flat and continuous, like fabrics, and that in most instances the pattern will cover very large areas. In addition:
- Plain colors look much like paint but come in varied textures.

A

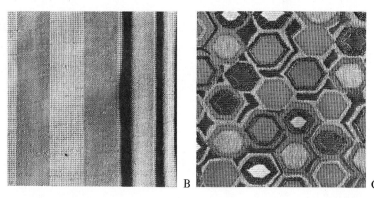

B

C

D

Plastic wall coverings minimize the old distinction between the useful and the ornamental.

Above left. "Quadro" is *embossed* with ½-inch squares of varied textures and comes in fifteen colors. (*United States Rubber Company*)

Above center. "Vana Weve," *woven* from Rovana and Verel synthetic fibers, resists dirt and damage and is available both as a wall covering and as drapery materials. (*C. W. Stockwell Company*)

Above right. "Alhambra" is a vinyl fabric *printed* with a lively pattern of irregular hexagons. (*General Tire & Rubber Company*)

Left. "Tempo" has a minute pattern of leaves and stems *embroidered* in gold nylon thread on an expanded vinyl fabric. (*Masland Duraleather Company*)

Wall fabrics woven of natural fibers bring subtle textures and colors to walls. From left to right: *Grass cloth,* with its inimitable lustrous surface, combines elegance with informality. *Raffia grass cloth* is coarser and usually has a less regular pattern. *Burlap,* as durable on walls as in gunny sacks, is available in many colors. *Hemp paper* is comparatively smooth and small in scale. *Abaca* is stiff and boldly textured. (*Photograph by Clyde Childress. Reprinted from* Sunset *Magazine*)

- Textural patterns are more active, more pronounced in character, and more effective in concealing minor damage than are plain colors.
- Abstract patterns do not go out of fashion quickly and seem especially suitable to walls.
- Stylized designs almost always seem more appropriate than do naturalistic representations.
- Scenic wallpapers are something like mural paintings.
- Bold conspicuous patterns reduce the visual importance of the space, furniture, and people.
- Conspicuous isolated motifs often make walls look spotty.

Wall Fabrics

Just about every fabric known to man has at one time or another been draped over, stretched on, or pasted to, walls. Today—if we think of fabrics untouched by plastics—we are likely to think of such durable standbys as canvas, burlap, or denim. Or we might consider grass cloth, as appropriate today as it was years ago, with its subtly textured woven grass glued to a tough paper backing of soft colors or dull, metallic luster.

More likely, though, we will think of the host of new plastic-coated, plastic-impregnated, or just plastic, fabrics. Most are embossed with textures or have printed designs. They are likely to be far more durable than typical wallpapers, resist stain and dirt, withstand repeated cleanings, and hide serious wall defects—even to holding cracked plaster in place. A number of them perform well as upholstery, thus allowing for harmony between two parts of the interior.

Paint, wallpaper, and wall fabrics are wondrous means of enlivening and protecting walls. Their relatively low cost makes frequent change possible, and their general lack of permanence makes new applications probable. They do not have the substantial character of wood or masonry, but they compensate with their challenging variety.

FIREPLACES

Fireplaces and fires are *costly:* a fireplace may cost as much as a bathroom, and in many places a good log fire is about as expensive as a home-cooked meal for two. Further, storing fuel takes dry space; getting it into the firebox takes labor; and the later cleanup is a chore. Most fireplaces are *used* for fires less than 1 percent of the time. When in use, they provide heat for people or for cooking, and some light and ventilation, all of a hard-to-control sort.

But open fires are *beautiful,* and fireplaces even without fires can be substantial centers of interest. A fire's warm, constantly changing, beautifully shaped and colored flames and embers produce a kind of lighting equaled only by sunrises and sunsets. Open fires are also associated with pleasurable outings and probably deeply buried feelings about the importance of fire to man. There is nothing that lifts the spirits on a cold, cheerless day or night like a fire, warming hands and hearts. Then, too, every fire has its own *individuality;* in fact every moment of a fire differs from every other, and fireplace design need follow no stereotypes. Thus, even though the most perfectly designed fireplace is hopelessly out of date in terms of use and economy, open fires are not outdated in terms of human satisfaction. And they do serve some useful purposes, which are discussed below.

Light is a major contribution of fireplaces today, because the illumination they provide is unique. It is restfully soft and warm enough in color to make even pallid persons look suntanned. The concentrated, flickering light is almost hypnotically relaxing and draws people together like a magnet.

Heat from a fireplace on a cold day seems well worth its cost, even though it creates drafts on the floor and may throw thermostatically controlled furnaces off balance. Heat output can be increased and controlled by designing the firebox to throw heat into the room, having a damper to control the draft and a projecting or suspended hood to radiate heat (Fig. 242). Prefabricated fireboxes and vents, like small warm-air furnaces, circulate heated air effectively.

Cooking over an open fire is a pleasant way to make fun out of much work. It is informal and divides labor among host, hostess, children, and friends. If done often indoors or outside, some or much equipment is needed. Essentials are adjustable grilles, long-handled forks and pans, and a floor not harmed by sparks or grease. Work is lightened if a fireplace is in or near the kitchen, if there is a special cupboard where equipment is permanently stored, or if a wheeled cart is at hand. It sounds complicated but it is enjoyable, especially for those often-difficult occasions when adults and children are at the same party.

Ventilation is hardly a major function of fireplaces, but they do air rooms, violently with a good fire, moderately when they are cold and the damper is open.

Symbolism of "hearth and home" continues to be important. Gathering around a fire for stories, popcorn, or whatever unites persons of all ages and interests, makes them feel relaxed and secure.

Distinctively regional in character, a fireplace in a Seattle home has an unassuming naturalness. Its location near a corner, together with the comfortable furniture group, the shaggy rug, and the built-in bookcases, suggests a sheltering haven. Roland Terry and Philip Monroe, architects. (*Photograph by Dearborn-Massar. Reprinted from* Sunset *Magazine*)

Finally, fireplaces provide busy householders with a somewhat dangerous place to burn trash and the hyperactive host or hostess with a harmless outlet for nervous energy.

Fireplace Design

Certainly the most important technical aspect of a fireplace is how well it draws, because one that does not draw well enough to start a fire or keep it going, or one that sends smoke into the room is worse than useless. This, however, is a matter best left to experts. Safety is equally important. The several hazards can be reduced by fireproof roofs and chimney tops that retard sparks; by screens to keep sparks out of the room; by andirons or baskets to keep fuel in place; and by hearths high enough to keep babies at a safe distance. Then comes fireplace work, which can be lessened if indoor-outdoor fuel storage is nearby, if an ash pit permits outside ash removal, and if the fire pit is lowered a few inches below the hearth to restrain the ashes.

Location. When fireplaces were used for heating, nearly every room had one. Today most houses have but one, and this is in the living, dining, or family space. Sometimes the same chimney serves as a social fireplace in the living room and as a barbecue in the kitchen or family area. Occasionally, one or more additional fireplaces are put in seclusion rooms or master bedrooms. Outdoor fireplaces are usually near the group-living terrace, although they may be at some distance for short, inexpensive vacations away from the house.

There are no rules as to where fireplaces should be put in a room. Several factors should be kept in mind, however. Fireplaces are usually large, more-or-less dominant elements. They demand considerable maintenance when a fire is burning and therefore should be accessible. They are natural centers for furniture arrangement and usually attract as many persons as space around them permits. They are frequently on outside walls, where the chimney can be an exterior design factor.

A pebble wall and raised hearth contrasts strikingly with the smooth steel hood and the white plaster above. Here, as in the rest of the room, the breadth of treatment suggests spaciousness. Dorman and Morganelly, architects. (*Photograph by George de Gennaro*)

Fireplaces in spur walls or in the center of a room can divide space into areas for different activities.

Left. A rough stone hood jutting out from built-in furniture units partitions a living room from a family room. The fire can be enjoyed from three sides. Richard Neutra, architect. (*Photograph by Julius Shulman*)

The typical location is the center of a long wall, a safe, sane, and perhaps too-familiar practice. This leads toward a static symmetry with emphasis in the middle of a long wall, but it tends to shorten the room visually, as in the Port Royal parlor (Color Fig. 5). It allows maximum visibility for large groups and suggests a symmetrical furniture arrangement. The center of one of the short walls is also safe and sane but somewhat less common. Again it is stable, but it makes the room seem longer and may suggest one furniture group near the fireplace with another at the other end (Figs. 224B–225B).

A fireplace may also be in the end of a spur wall that acts as a room divider (Fig. 243A); it can be a freestanding structure that delineates continuous space into areas for different activities (Figs. 104B and 243B); or it can be in

Above. In a house in Midland, Michigan, a rectangular island of brick and plaster articulates areas for group living. The crisp geometry of the fireplace block is repeated at small scale in the shelves and the brick floor and wall. Alden Dow, architect. (*Photograph by Bill Hedrich, Hedrich-Blessing*)

An outdoor feeling penetrates a living room in which a fire pit covered with sand is edged with carefully selected natural boulders. Suspended from the ceiling, the metal hood and flue effectively radiate heat. Harry J. Williams, architect. (*Photograph by Julius Shulman*)

a room corner, a location that emphasizes the room's longest dimension and limits furniture grouping to a quarter circle. Prefabricated fireplaces sometimes deliberately assert their independence of their surroundings (Fig. 244).

Appearance. Although consistency with the whole house is a major consideration, fireplaces can have their own special beauty and individuality. The questions to be answered are much like those about walls:

- What degree of formality is wanted?
- Should horizontal or vertical lines predominate?
- How active and dominant should the fireplace be?
- What degree of roughness or smoothness seems best?
- Which materials are most appropriate?
- Should the fireplace be large, small, or intermediate in actual size and in scale?

Almost any combination of these qualities is feasible, as can be seen in the illustrations in this chapter. For example, the fireplace in Figure 241 is informal and has a vigorous, balanced contrast of horizontals and verticals. Large in size, its dominance is augmented by the varying texture of used bricks, by the sculptured plaques, and by its studied relationship to the flanking shelves. Quite different is the see-through adobe fireplace in Figures 223 and 224A, which is boldly placed in the center of a window wall. It is, however, anchored to a large hearth that extends through the glass into the garden.

Size. Fireplaces can be of any size. Determining factors are size and scale of the room and its furnishings, the effect the fireplace is intended to produce, the materials from which it is made, and the kind of fires wanted. Of all elements in the home, fireplaces lend themselves best to overscaling without seeming unpleasantly obtrusive. But very small fireplaces can have a certain refreshing charm. It is easy to increase the importance and apparent size of fireplaces by enriching them with bands of contrasting materials (Fig. 245), by integrating them with bookshelves or built-in furniture (Fig. 241), or by making them an integral part of large areas of masonry (Figs. 242 and 243B). Also, fireplaces seem larger on small walls than on big ones.

An Early Georgian (1740) fireplace from New Place, Upminster, England, is impressively formal: symmetrical, vertical, smooth, and precise. The columns, the intricate cornices, and the festoon of carved drapery are emphasized by their plain background. (*Philadelphia Museum of Art*)

Relationship to walls, floors, and ceilings. The way in which a fireplace is related to the planes enclosing the room profoundly affects its character. Fireplaces can be simply holes, perhaps framed unobtrusively, in an unbroken wall, and this is the least noticeable treatment of them (Fig 94A). They can project from the wall a few inches or several feet, and this increases their impact. When they leave the wall entirely, as a freestanding block of masonry or as an independent unit in metal (Figs. 243B and 244), they become still more conspicuous. Going in the other direction, fireplaces can be recessed slightly or in a sheltering alcove deep enough for furniture (Fig. 289).

The fireplace unit may extend to the ceiling, which accentuates its verticality. If it terminates a little or well below the room's top, as in Figure 242, it can lead to a horizontal or blocky effect. The bottom of the fire pit may be at the floor level, or it can be at seat height, in which case the hearth is usually extended to give sitting space (Figs. 223, 242, and 246). Raised fires are more comfortably seen and enjoyed, become more a part of the room, than those at floor level. The fire pit can also be lower than the floor. If the depressed space is large enough for furniture (Fig. 28A), it tends to draw people into a convivial huddle and subdivides a room without partitions.

A rugged stone fireplace is part and parcel of the architecture of this house in Berkeley, California, and harmoniously related to the landscape beyond. Roger Lee, architect. (*Photograph by Roger Sturtevant*)

In contrast to the sleekly simple, prefabricated metal fireplace on page 244, those of the Victorian period were delightfully intricate in design. (*Photograph by Ernest Braun*)

Materials. Materials turn our thoughts at once to masonry and metal, since neither is damaged by fire. Brick and stone look substantial and permanent, tile can be plain or decorated, and metal can be shaped in many ways and transmits heat into the room. These materials come in numberless textures: smooth tile and polished marble, shining copper and dull iron, brick and stone in all gradations of roughness. And there is no end to the color possibilities.

The fireplace in Figure 246 is a virile, substantial statement. Walls, fireplace, windows, floor, and ceiling are as handsomely unified as they were in the Port Royal parlor (Color Fig. 5) or the remodeled living room (Fig. 224B)—but here the similarity ends. Stone, wood, and glass are the materials, each used in large areas and each fully revealing its own inherent individuality. The massive stones are rough on the vertical planes but smooth on the ledge and floor. Heavy wood beams support the plank ceiling, lighter beams form the indoor-outdoor trellis, and foot-wide boards and narrow battens sheath the wall at the right. Large sheets of glass unite the room with the landscape.

These materials are organized in a powerful angular, continuing design. A seat-high ledge encircles two sides of the room, forms a planting box inside and out, and then becomes the hearth. The firebox, a simple cavity open on two sides, is part of a wall as decisively vertical as the ledge is horizontal. At one side of the fireplace, glass opens the room over the planting box and through the trellis to the wooded hillside. Then the glass continues across the adjacent wall to open the room to a dramatic view of San Francisco Bay. The inner part of the room is as sheltering as a cave, the outer as open as protection from weather permits.

In conclusion, fireplaces are delightful elements that are natural focal points and bring cheer into a home. Possibilities range from those that are strongly integrated with the architectural enclosure (Fig. 248) to those that are portable and can carry the warm, flickering light of fire wherever it is wanted.

A powerful rough stone pier enclosing a fireplace and chimney is the pivotal center of the "Round House" in Hollywood, California. (See the plan in Fig. 408A) The weightiness of stone and concrete is visually lightened by changing patterns of light that come through the areas of glass. George Frank Ligar, architect. (*Photograph by Julius Shulman*)

In a house with a cross-shaped plan, bands of light-diffusing plastic skylights and large adroitly placed windows give all major rooms high-level natural illumination without glare or gloom. (*Photograph by Ernest Braun*)

12 · Windows, Curtains, and Doors

Windows and doors visually and physically relate one space to another. The "wind's eye" of old was a narrow opening to let out some of the fire's smoke and let in a little fresh air, to help light the room, and to permit peephole glimpses of what was going on outside. These are the three functions of windows—*ventilation, light,* and *view*—but only the last is unique. Ventilation can often be handled better through louvered and shuttered openings, air-conditioning, exhaust fans, and the like. Light can be produced and precisely controlled electrically at lower total cost than natural light can be brought through windows, which, all factors considered, are expensive. But only through transparent windows, doors, and walls can we enjoy the outdoors from protected enclosures. The way in which these elements can open up or shut in space is dramatically shown in Figures 250A and B.

A

Opening the end of an old apartment transformed a dreary room into enjoyable living space. (*Photographs by Morley Baer*)

Above. A window wall with sliding glass doors to the terrace floods the room with light and gives a spectacular view of the city. Ceiling-hung sheer glass curtains diffuse the light when necessary, and draperies provide privacy and insulation against heat and cold. Campbell and Wong, architects.

Right. Before remodeling, the small window and mismatched door did little to enhance the space.

B

TYPES OF WINDOWS

The major types of movable windows used today are illustrated below. They can *slide,* as in the double-hung or horizontally sliding designs, or *swing,* as in casement or awning types.

Double-hung windows usually have two sashes (the frame, usually movable, in which panes of glass are set) that slide up and down. Weights, springs, or friction holds them in place when open. Usually they are higher than wide, and the sashes in each window are of the same size and shape. Their advantages are numerous. They are easy and inexpensive to install and seldom warp or sag. Hardware is simple; weatherproofing is effective. They can be opened top or bottom, and they do not project to get in the way of people and curtains inside or people and plants outside. The major drawbacks are these. Not more than half the area can be opened, and when open, there is no protection from rain. They are difficult to clean from inside unless the sash can be removed or pivoted and inconvenient to operate when furniture is under them. In addition, some persons find the horizontal crossbar that cuts the window in half visually annoying.

Horizontally sliding windows are like double-hung windows placed on their sides, and their advantages and disadvantages are similar. Usually, though, they have the horizontal proportions popular today and are often combined with fixed glass, which gets rid of the bar in the middle.

Casement windows, hinged at one side and swinging in or out, were in common use long before sliding types. Their major assets are that the whole area can be opened, and they can be adjusted to direct breezes into the room or to reduce cold drafts. Equipped with crank-operated hardware, they are easy to operate even when over furniture. In the better types, both sides of the glass can be washed from inside. Casement windows also have drawbacks. In-swinging casements are seldom used because they interfere with furnishings, and those that swing out over terraces or walks are serious hazards. They offer no protection from rain and are not easy to weatherproof tightly. Typically they are tall and narrow.

Awning and **projected windows** are like casements but hinged at the top or occasionally the bottom. Disadvantages are similar to those of casements: small panes of glass, sashes that take space when open, difficulty in sealing them tightly. In addition, they collect dust when open. But they have the notable advantage of giving precise, draft-free control of ventilation while admitting little if any rain or snow.

Prefabricated window units allow great freedom of choice. (*Aluminum Window Manufacturers Association*)

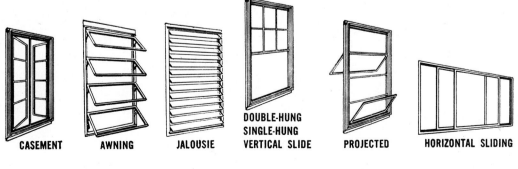

CASEMENT   AWNING   JALOUSIE   DOUBLE-HUNG SINGLE-HUNG VERTICAL SLIDE   PROJECTED   HORIZONTAL SLIDING

Jalousie windows are of the awning type but with very narrow strips of glass. With all of the advantages of the awning type, they are also favored because they take little space and odd shapes are not costly. Difficult to clean and to weatherproof, the many small panes of glass also interfere with views. But for precise control of ventilation, they excel all other types.

In addition to these window types, transparent or translucent materials can be used in other ways. **Fixed glass** or **plastic** can be used in very large single pieces and is inexpensive to install because no hardware or screens are needed. Fixed glass is often combined with doors or windows that open or with louvered ventilators to provide fresh air (Figs. 249, 254, and 257).

Skylights and **clerestories**, windows in the ceiling or high in a wall between two roof levels (Figs. 249 and 253A and B), illumine and ventilate a house with no loss of privacy or interference with furniture arrangement. Perhaps more significant, they can bring daylight or moonlight into the center of the house and make it unnecessary to stretch the plan out for light in all rooms. Economically compact plans can have kitchen, laundry, and bathrooms grouped far from the "windows" yet be well lighted and well ventilated. Light coming from above also reveals hitherto unnoticed qualities in furniture, sculpture, and plants, and can give new dimensions to form and space.

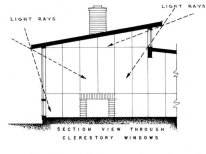

Abundant light coming through glass wall at left is balanced by light from high clerestory windows at right that are also efficient ventilators. (*Victor Thompson*)

Wood and metal are the materials typically used to hold the panes of glass in windows and walls. Metal is stronger (which makes thinner strips possible), does not shrink or swell noticeably, and has a uniform texture harmonious with glass. With the exception of aluminum and stainless steel, metals used in windows must be protected by paint; and because all metals conduct heat and cold readily, moisture may condense on the inside of metal sashes in cold weather. Wood shrinks, swells, and has to be given a protective finish, but it does not encourage condensation.

DESIGN AND LOCATION OF WINDOWS

Views and privacy, light and ventilation, heat and cold, and furniture arrangement are among the major factors determining window design and location. Cleaning and curtaining follow closely. Interwoven with these is the larger matter of architectural composition, the relationship of windows to the mass and space of the whole house and landscape.

Views and privacy. Normally, the larger windows face the best outlook, whether it be a view of a city, a lake, or one's own private patio (Figs. 250A, 254, and 258A). Those necessarily facing the street or nearby neighbors are smaller, higher in the wall, or of translucent material. Most of us nowadays like windows that encourage those inside to look out but not neighbors or passersby to look in. This is achieved by placing large windows toward the rear of the property, by building fences or by planting hedges, and much less well by resorting to view-blocking curtains.

Light. Natural light is cheerful, and for eyes and spirit it is almost impossible to have rooms with too much daylight. But it is unfortunately easy to design rooms that seem unpleasantly bright because strong contrasts of light and dark lead to glare. This comes from *too little light* and in the *wrong places. More light means less glare if the windows are well planned.* Until recently most windows

Skylights and clerestory windows bring natural illumination deep into rooms.

Left. A vigorously patterned, peaked skylight brings sunlight into a "windowless" indoor-garden room in Midland, Michigan. Alden Dow, architect. (*Photograph by Bill Hedrich, Hedrich-Blessing*)

Below. In Libertyville, Illinois, soft light from a clerestory window illumines the ceiling and accents wall textures. Frank Lloyd Wright, architect. (*Photograph by Maynard L. Parker Modern Photography*)

A

B

were holes cut out of the wall, and the first thoughts were of getting curtains to "soften" the light. Large areas of glass in the best contemporary design, however, seldom seem too bright. Here are some of the factors:

- Light coming from more than one direction minimizes heavy shadows and makes one feel enveloped by light rather than being shot by it.
- Light entering the top of a room illumines the ceiling and spreads through the room more than does light entering at lower levels.
- No part of a room ought to be more than about $1\frac{1}{2}$ times the ceiling height from a wall with adequate windows or from skylights.
- Overhangs projecting beyond windows reduce the glare of the sky and mellow the light entering the room (Fig. 258B).
- Windows to the floor are best when the surfacing material outside does not reflect a glaringly bright light. Light-absorbing materials or the shade from trees or trellises is indicated.

No thinking about the light from windows is complete without remembering that windows, the lightest elements in a room by day, are very dark at night unless they are lighted or curtained inside or unless the immediate view outside is illumined.

The full delight of a Vermont lake is enjoyed through a window wall that combines fixed glass with sliding glass doors and awning-type windows for controlled ventilation. Carl Koch and Associates, architects. (*Photograph* © *Ezra Stoller*)

254

Ventilation. The most comfortable ventilation unnoticeably lets stale air out from near the room's top and draftless fresh air in from the floor. High windows or louvered openings above windows (Fig. 253B), skylights, and exhaust fans accomplish the first, while low windows or ventilators (Fig. 257) do the second. There are times, though, when one wants to feel a breeze sweeping through the house from wide-open doors and windows. Rooms are most quickly aired if the openings are on opposite sides, one of which faces the prevailing winds.

Heat and cold. To date, most colorless, transparent materials are poor insulators. Hence extreme temperatures are important factors in window design and placement. By reducing costs for heating and air-conditioning, special types of glass, such as double insulating glass and glass that reflects excess solar heat, usually pay for themselves in about three years. Orientation of windows, however, is more important in achieving equable temperatures indoors at the least cost. Glass facing south brings welcome winter sun, but with a properly designed overhang it excludes summer sun because then the sun is high in the sky (Fig. 255A). Glass facing east brings the morning sun, cheering in winter and seldom

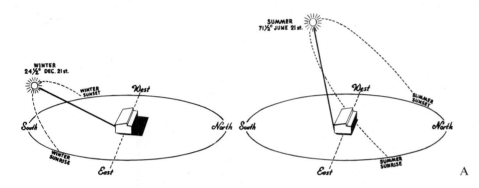

The winter and summer positions of the sun at noon in Chicago. In winter the sun is low and stays well south of due east and west. In summer it is high, and its arc is well to the north. (*Libbey-Owens-Ford Glass Company*)

A

too hot in summer. Glass on the west side of a house, however, brings hot afternoon heat deep into the house, and on the north it brings in winter cold. For comfort, it is then necessary to rely on insulating curtains or something outside, such as nearby shade trees, vine-covered arbors, very wide overhanging roofs or awnings. Thus in terms of heat and cold in most parts of our country, glass on the south is best, followed by that on the east.

Furniture arrangement. The location and design of windows and doors determine in large part how furniture can be arranged. In general, the more openings

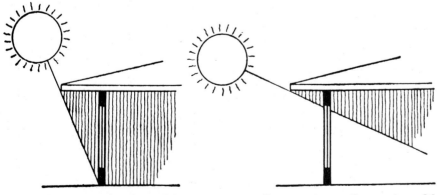

Sun angle on June 21.   Sun angle on December 21.   B

Properly designed overhanging roofs let desirable winter sun in through south windows but keep hot summer sun off the glass. (*Libbey-Owens-Ford Glass Company*)

Practical windowsill heights vary with room use and furniture arrangement. Three heights meet most needs, help unify interior and exterior design. (*Reprinted by special permission from the June 1955 issue of* House & Home. *Copyrighted © 1955 by McGraw-Hill, Inc.*)

A

Separated windows with small panes of glass framed by draperies give an effect quite different from that produced by a band of glass with pulled-back draw curtains and a minimum of bars. (*Matt Kahn*)

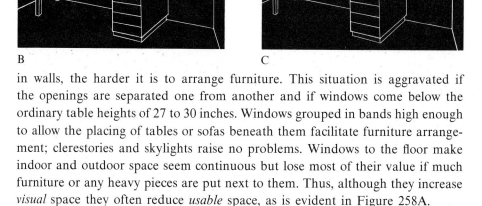

B   C

in walls, the harder it is to arrange furniture. This situation is aggravated if the openings are separated one from another and if windows come below the ordinary table heights of 27 to 30 inches. Windows grouped in bands high enough to allow the placing of tables or sofas beneath them facilitate furniture arrangement; clerestories and skylights raise no problems. Windows to the floor make indoor and outdoor space seem continuous but lose most of their value if much furniture or any heavy pieces are put next to them. Thus, although they increase *visual* space they often reduce *usable* space, as is evident in Figure 258A.

Cleaning. All glass benefits from frequent cleaning, especially in dusty or sooty locations or when it can be reached by small children. It is easiest to clean when the panes are large, when they can be reached without excessive stooping or climbing, and when they are easy to get at, outside as well as inside. Clerestories and skylights bring special cleaning problems, often lessened with translucent glass or plastics.

Curtaining. Although curtains and draperies have much in their favor, they are not without cost. An economical first step is to plan so that as few windows as possible absolutely demand curtaining. High windows or window walls facing screened gardens or protected views are examples. Curtaining problems are simplest when windows are grouped, and when they vary little in size, shape, and distance from floor and ceiling.

Architectural Composition

So far windows have been discussed in terms of what they can do to make home life more comfortable; but stopping at this point might lead to a hodgepodge design. Openings today, as in the past, are a vital factor in architectural design, but no single aspect of home planning shows greater change. The same aims and principles of design operate as general guides, but the specific patterns are notably different from anything known heretofore. Contemporary trends can be summarized as follows:

- Windows and doors are designed as integral parts of the architectural shell rather than as isolated, ornamented, cutout holes.
- Windows are typically grouped in bands, usually horizontal; and when feasible, windows and doors are combined in harmonious units.
- Large areas of glass are placed where they serve best; small windows are strategically located for balanced lighting and ventilation plus privacy.
- Unity and simplicity of effect is emphasized by using as few shapes, sizes, and types as possible and by aligning tops of windows and doors.
- A less formalized attitude toward the design and placement of windows, however, is also becoming evident, with odd-shaped windows sometimes being placed in unusual locations for a forceful design impact.

The design of openings is at least as important, from an architectural point of view, as the design of opaque portions of the home. Windows are conspicuous day and night, inside and outside. Their thin, smooth, light-transmitting material contrasts strikingly with what is around it. Beyond these physical characteristics the fact that enclosed and unenclosed spaces interpenetrate one another through windows and doors endows them with a unique psychological importance.

Window Walls

Audaciously opening the house to its surroundings is in some respects as significant as man's long struggle to secure his dwelling against the environment. Box-tight enclosure has never been completely satisfying to man, and the urge

An informal house of timeless appeal graces a wooded site in the Pacific Northwest. Grouped windows of fixed glass fit into the pattern of structural framing and plywood panels. Ventilating louvers above and below provide ventilation, conceal insect screens, and keep out the rain. John Yeon, architect. (*Photograph by Maynard L. Parker Modern Photography. Douglas Fir Plywood Association*)

A

Above. In architect Eliot Noyes's own home (1954), the interior shows how light is balanced by the two window walls and how closely the living room, covered passage, and the simply landscaped inner court are united, with only a glass screen between.

Below. Deep roof overhangs and projecting fieldstone walls protect the recessed glass walls and sliding doors. The parklike Connecticut setting is easily maintained. (*Photographs* © *Ezra Stoller*)

B

toward the paradoxical union of security and openness has a long, varied history. Walled gardens allowed the early Egyptians, Greeks, and Romans to open part of their homes to the outdoors. In the medieval period, areas of glass large enough to be called "window walls" were introduced. Many houses built fifty or more years ago had sizable "picture windows." Thus seemingly revolutionary, contemporary window walls are an evolutionary step.

Although window walls are now standard features even in many tract houses, they are not unmixed blessings, chiefly because they are incompletely understood. They should not be thought of as merely bigger windows but as a different way of planning the house and garden. They flood rooms with light, and when poorly designed, with glare, heat, or cold. By visually uniting house and yard, they affect furniture arrangements and color schemes as well as the design of the landscape. Some of the major problems they raise, and ways of avoiding or solving them, are listed below:

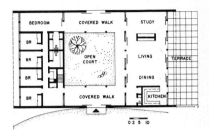

The plan of the Noyes house illustrates the use of a central court to separate the group-living wing from the private-living wing.

Problems	Solutions
Loss of privacy	Face window wall toward private part of property. Build fences or plant hedges. Use curtains and draperies.
Glare of light	Balance light with windows in other walls or with skylights. Have overhanging roof or trellis. Plant suitable shade trees nearby.
Excessive heat or cold	Orient toward south or southeast. Use insulating glass. Provide overhead protection or trees. Have insulating draperies that can be drawn when necessary.
More glass to clean	No easy solution. Use professional window-washer's techniques.
Greater quantity of curtaining	Place window wall so that curtains are not essential.
Furniture arrangement	Plan room so that major furniture group is related both to window wall and other dominant units, such as fireplaces.
Color schemes	Take account of relationship between colors inside and those seen through the glass.
Danger of being mistaken for an open door	Use proper design, such as a raised sill or obvious supports, to indicate physical presence of a window wall. Arrange furniture indoors and out to steer traffic to a door, not a window.
Fading of colors	Choose colors that do not fade or that fade pleasantly. Exclude sun with projecting roof, planting, or curtains.
Black and cold at night	Illumine window with lighting trough above it. Light terrace or garden outside. Use draperies.
Design and maintenance of landscape	Plan at least the immediate landscape architecturally to harmonize with interior; use paving, fixed outdoor furniture, sculpture, and plants that will remain attractive all year with little care.

There are innumerable ways of designing window walls. When they fill an entire wall from floor to ceiling (Fig. 258A), there is a minimum break between indoors and outdoors. If they begin above the floor, there is room for furniture. They can follow a gable to its peak (Figs. 11C and 37A). There may be a minimum of divisions as in the Noyeses' house, or a strong pattern of verticals or horizontals (Fig. 250A). They can, as we have seen, join a room with an extensive view or focus attention on a small enclosed court. Although typically associated with living or dining areas, window walls can make kitchens or halls expansive (Figs. 63A and B and 118). If well planned, they are quite feasible in bedrooms, or even bathrooms, in almost any part of the United States.

Windows are costly. Glass is expensive to buy and replace, difficult to make weathertight around the edges, must be cleaned often, and is likely to run up heating and cooling bills. If the glass is movable, screens and window hardware are needed. Almost all windows bring the added expense of curtains, draperies, or blinds. But sensibly large, well-placed windows are worth their cost.

WINDOW TREATMENT

It is a temptation to say that perfectly planned windows need no "treatment," but we would then ignore the great changes in outdoor light and heat and the varying needs of the people inside. Thus, in terms of *use,* we ordinarily have curtains or draperies, blinds or shades inside to control the privacy of the home, the amount and kind of light that enters it, and heat and cold. From the point of view of *economy,* the less accessories used at windows the more money will be available for other purposes, although efficient window treatment can reduce heating and cooling bills. Furthermore, whatever is put there ought to be durable, ought to resist the ravages of sun, moisture, and moths, and ought to be easily maintained. *Beauty* comes from the inherent attractiveness of the fabrics chosen and from the way in which they relate the windows to the whole room. *Individuality,* here as elsewhere, is less a matter of being "different" than of solving problems well.

Exterior window treatments. Often overlooked, exterior window treatments are out of the way of furniture and take no wall space inside the room.

- **Awnings** of duck can be adjusted as the weather varies to protect windows from sun, rain, and dirt. Available in many designs and colors, they give a soft pleasant light inside and outside. They are, however, short-lived, subject to fading and soiling, as well as to flapping in the wind. Metal awnings, usually aluminum, can be stationary or can roll up. Higher in initial cost, they pay for themselves over the years. Although they can be designed as part of the structure, they often look like afterthoughts.
- **Shutters** are seldom used today except for the dummy ones employed to make small windows look larger on pseudo-Colonial houses, and for securing vacation houses against marauders or windows against violent storms. True shutters can effectively temper light, heat, and cold.
- **Grilles** and **fences** of masonry, wood, plastic, or aluminum placed close to windows or some feet away control privacy, sun, and wind in any degree desired depending on their design and location.
- **Overhanging roofs** and **trellises** are the most permanent exterior shading devices but bring no privacy. They can be solid and opaque, of translu-

cent plastic or glass, or merely a framework for vines. In addition to protecting windows, they can be large enough to shelter outdoor living areas. When well designed, they visually relate the house to its site and contribute greatly to exterior design (Color Figs. 4 and 21).

■ **Trees, tall shrubs,** and **vines** give cool, ventilated shade but not until they are of some size.

Interior window treatments. In addition to curtains and draperies, interior treatments include shades, blinds, and shutters. These can move sideways or up and down, the latter having the definite advantage of being completely out of the way when not wanted.

■ **Fabric roller shades** are inexpensive and can cover part, all, or none of the glass. They reduce light and give privacy in relationship to their thickness and opaqueness. The newer ones are easy to clean and come in many colors, textures, and patterns. A fabric used elsewhere in the room can be laminated onto a plain plastic shade to give unity and individuality. The several drawbacks of roller shades include the fact that when pulled down they cut out the light from the top of the window first—and that is the best light. Also, they block the breeze or whip around noisily, and they have neither the architectural quality of blinds or shutters nor the softness of draperies.

■ **Bamboo** and **split-wood shades** perform much like those made of fabrics. They differ in that they let some light through, give some or much notion of what is outside, and have pleasantly natural textures and colors.

■ **Venetian blinds** made of wood were used in Colonial days, and they now are available in metal and plastic (Fig. 262B). Their special advantages

Imaginatively patterned window shades are welcome surprises that would bring crispness and decisiveness to a room with little character. (*Johanna Western Mills*)

A

"Hard" window treatments are typically architectural in effect.

Right. Vertical metal or plastic blinds come in many colors and can be easily adapted to sloping ceilings or windows of varied heights. (*Stiller, Rouse, Berggren & Hunt*)

Below. A venetian blind with slender, one-inch-wide slats covers just the glass of a window wall and can be adjusted to control the light precisely. (*Levolor Lorentzen Incorporated*)

B

Japanese wood grilles, called shoji panels, backed with rice paper mask unattractive, viewless windows but allow diffused light to enter the room. A similar panel, but without paper backing, makes an airy space divider. Campbell and Wong, architects. (*Photograph by Ernest Braun*)

are almost complete light and air control—straight into the room, down toward the floor, or up toward the ceiling—and complete disappearance behind a valance. They are durable but not expensive, and their horizontal lines are pleasing. They do, however, collect dust and dirt that are not easy to remove.

- **Vertical blinds** of metal, plastic, or fabrics (Fig. 262A) can easily be shaped to fit and unify odd-sized openings. They control light from side to side, rather than from up or down, and emphasize the height rather than the breadth of windows and walls. Of importance to housekeepers, they collect less dust than Venetian blinds.
- **Grilles** or **screens** of wood or other materials deserve consideration, especially when windows are not well designed, when there is no view, and when privacy is requisite. Figure 263 shows how one wall of a small city apartment has been unified with Japanese grilles, called shoji panels, of intricate pattern and how another freestanding panel separates the living room from the entrance.
- **Shutters** of the old-fashioned indoor type have recently staged a comeback. They can become a unified part of the wall (Fig. 46), and for many people they have pleasant associations with the past. Although they last almost indefinitely, their initial cost is rather high.

These interior window treatments can be called "hard" window treatments, since none of them does much toward humanizing windows. For this reason they are often combined with draperies.

CURTAINS AND DRAPERIES

In addition to controlling privacy, light, and heat, curtains and draperies soak up noise in proportion to the area they cover, the thickness of the fabric, and the depth of the folds. They make rooms homelike and effectively cover up the bareness of those not completely furnished—a point worth remembering if you do not get all your furniture at once. With curtains and draperies you can change the apparent size, shape, and character of a room or conceal architectural awkwardnesses. Small rooms look larger if curtains and draperies blend with the walls; low rooms look higher if draperies go from ceiling to floor. Gloomy rooms seem brighter if gay colors or invigorating patterns are used near windows. Walls chopped up with windows or jogs can be unified by generous glass curtains and draperies, and some eyesores can be completely concealed (Figs. 266A and B).

You can direct almost any degree of attention toward windows by the fabrics you select and the way you hang them. Unpatterned materials similar to the wall color, acting as inconspicuous transitions between opaque walls and clear glass, encourage us to look *through windows*. Moderate color contrasts and patterns direct attention *toward windows*. Bold or unusual colors and designs usually cause us *to look at the draperies* rather than the windows.

A few definitions are now in order:

- **Glass curtains** are of thin materials and hung next to the glass.
- **Sash curtains** are a type of glass curtain hung on the window sash. They can be stretched taut between rods on the top and bottom of window sashes or hung in loose folds.
- **Draw curtains,** usually of translucent or opaque fabrics, are mounted on traverse rods. In the past, they came between glass curtains and draperies. Nowadays they are more often used alone.
- **Draperies** are any loosely hung (not stretched) fabric. Thus, the term really includes all curtains. Generally, though, draperies are thought of as heavy fabrics that can be drawn or that stand idly at the sides of windows purely for decoration.
- **Cornices** are horizontal bands several inches wide placed at the window top (or the ceiling) to conceal curtain tops and the rods from which they hang. They can also function more positively in relating the whole window treatment to walls and ceiling.
- **Valances** are simply wide cornices and are often varied in shape. They can be of hard materials or of fabrics.

Glass Curtains

Softening and diffusing light, glass curtains (Figs. 265A and B) also temper the glitter of glass and relate it to the rest of the room, give partial privacy, and decrease the necessity of keeping windows spotless. They make a room seem light and airy, especially when used without draperies. They are needed most when the outlook is unattractive or when there is constant need for some privacy. Glass curtains (along with lamp shades and translucent plastic or glass panels) can make one unique visual contribution: they bring light into the room *through* color and pattern, a little as stained glass does in Gothic cathedrals and in Victorian homes.

A

"Soft" window treatments relate windows to upholstered furniture, rugs and carpets, and clothing.

Above. Loosely woven net, hung from the ceiling, completely covers windows and walls in a New York City apartment, diffusing the light and unifying these elements. Edward Wormley, designer. (*Dunbar Furniture Corporation*)

Left. Sheer glass curtains temper the harsh concentrated light coming in on one side of a room. Figured draperies extending onto an adjoining wall relieve the hardness of the furniture and add color, pattern, and pliancy. (*Owens-Corning Fiberglas Fabric Center*)

B

A   B

Two of the many ways of handling separated windows that are nothing but holes cut in the wall.

Left. Printed draperies, held back with ties, and thinner curtains, cover the whole wall dramatically.

Right. Built-in storage units and a desk cover almost all of the wall. Semisheer café curtains hung in three tiers make the windows look tall and related to the room. (*Celanese Corporation of America*)

Materials. A great variety of simple materials have taken the place of our great-grandmother's beautifully rich curtains. Some of these are listed as "Very Thin" fabrics on page 213. Any fabric that hangs well and withstands sun, washing, or cleaning is suitable.

Color and pattern. Color is especially important because the light filtering through glass curtains takes on their color, giving the whole room that color cast, and also because glass curtains are conspicuous from the outside. Therefore, they are usually a neutral light color and, for exterior harmony, identical or very similar in all rooms. They can, however, be pink or yellow to warm a cool room or pale green, blue, or lavender to cool a hot one. Although customarily plain, suitable fabrics are available with woven or printed patterns, which are useful in rooms that need interest at the windows without adding draw curtains or draperies.

Tailoring and hanging. Simplicity is the best guide to tailoring and hanging curtains: a neat heading that fits its space and is shirred or pinch-pleated on a simple rod, a double hem at the bottom for weight, and a minimum width of at least twice that of the window for ample fullness.

If combined with draperies, glass curtains usually hang inside the window frame, close to it and the glass, and are long enough to clear the sill without leaving a noticeable gap. Used alone, they can be hung outside the frame and cover two or more grouped windows with a unifying film. Sometimes two or more sets of glass curtains are hung in the *café* or *tier* manner (Figs. 266B and 267) to emphasize horizontality or give privacy without always reducing light from the window tops.

Draw Curtains

Flexible control of light, heat and cold, and privacy is the primary useful purpose of draperies that slide on rods. Often, though, they are used alone, and then they take over all the aesthetic functions of window treatment.

Materials. Fabrics used for draw curtains need sufficient strength, durability, and flexibility to withstand being pulled back and forth and to hang gracefully when stretched or pulled together. Thus, many thin glass-curtain materials and some heavy upholstery fabrics are suitable. Between these two extremes is a challenging array in the drapery, bedding, dress, and suiting sections of almost any store. Coarse or fine nets soften without obscuring windows. Organdy, pongee, and silk gauze are relatively smooth and rich looking. Such textiles as monk's cloth, Osnaburg, and tweed are thicker, rougher, and more casual. Denim is sturdy and durable; Indian Head is clean and crisp; chambray has a smooth, slightly silky texture; gingham is informal. Glazed chintz has a crisp shiny surface that intensifies its colors and patterns. Satin hangs in soft folds, is dressy when woven of smooth silk, informal when made of heavier, loosely twisted threads. Damasks, brocades, and brocatelles have woven, often formal, patterns. To this list can be added bamboo and wood textiles, substantial and informal, plus many plastic fabrics.

Color and pattern. Appropriateness to the home and its occupants is the only defensible generalization. Draw curtains are least noticeable when related to the walls. They become more conspicuous if they repeat or echo the color and character of such large units as furniture or floor. They become emphatic when they contrast strongly with the rest of the room.

Three more solutions to the problem of a wall with two separated windows. *Left.* Curtains aligned with the windows cover the wall space and produce a horizontal band. *Center.* Café or tier curtains hung from two rods can give a checkerboard effect, but they also could be slid along the rods to cover either the windows or the walls. *Right.* Curtains from the top of the windows to the floor make the wall and windows seem tall and narrow. (*Matt Kahn*)

Color, chiefly color value, is typically the most noticeable quality of curtains—very dark curtains against a light wall, or vice versa, stand out sharply. Scale and character come next—large-scale patterns with vivid contrasts or those that differ from other large areas in the room become dominant. It is a matter of deciding what degree of dominance or subordination, harmony or contrast, is most appropriate. A sampling of the myriad possibilities will be found in Chapter 10.

Tailoring and hanging. Draw curtains are almost invariably most effective and useful when they hang in straight folds that at least cover all the window frame and begin and stop at sensible points. They fit their setting best when they begin either slightly above the top of the frame or at the ceiling and when they end slightly below the bottom of the frame or near the floor. Usually the longer the better unless there is good reason for stopping them short. Also the fuller the better (from $1\frac{1}{2}$ to $2\frac{1}{2}$ times the width of the space they cover). When pulled back, it seems more sensible to have them cover frame and wall rather than window. French, box, or pinch pleats take care of fullness at the top and a generous bottom hem helps them hang well.

Draperies

Draperies began their life in the textiles that physically and visually warmed the cold walls of early homes and then migrated from the walls to beds and windows. Today they are most often found at windows, sometimes at large door-ways or separating parts of a room. Occasionally they are used as wall hangings. They differ from draw curtains only in that they are sometimes heavier and that they do not necessarily pull across the opening they guard.

Windows are an expensive, valuable asset. Their primary functions of out-look, light, and air should not be unnecessarily interfered with by window "treat-ment." The thoughtful design—location, size, shape, and type—of windows is a distinguishing trait of better contemporary architecture. This is supplemented by due regard for overhanging roofs, trellises, and planting as necessary. Although interior curtains and blinds are still important, they are becoming increasingly less critical. This is another instance of the trend toward thinking about all factors in advance of building and of solving as many problems as possible architecturally. Exterior, interior, and landscape architecture are approaching a functional integration.

DOORS

Doorways allow us and our vision, as well as light, sounds, smells, breezes, warmth, and cold to travel in and out of the house and from one room to another. Doors control this travel in varying degrees depending on their location, design, and material. Contemporary doors run the gamut from stout, opaque doors of wood or metal, which shut everything in or out, through doors of translucent glass or plastics to doors of sheets of glass. Folding doors of wood or bamboo slats or covered with fabrics are additional possibilities. Further, doors can be designed so that only part of them opens, such as Dutch or barn doors, in which the top can be open but the bottom closed.

In rented quarters or in a home already built you can do less about the doors than about the windows, but the following are possibilities:
- Remove unneeded doors to create greater openness.
- Seal up or cover with a wall hanging doors that are unnecessary for traffic.
- Refinish doors and their frames so that they blend with the walls.
- Paint some or all doors in contrasting colors or decorate them so that they become dominant features.

If you plan to buy a house, it pays to look carefully at the location and design of doors. And if you are planning to build your own home, it pays to consider very carefully how doors, and openings without doors, can serve best.

A   Folding and sliding doors are sometimes more convenient than those that swing.   B

Above left. Oak folding doors that match the walls open almost completely to give access to as much of a buffet counter and storage area as desired. When pushed back, they take very little space. Lawrence Schwall, architect. (*Pella Wood Folding Doors*)

Above right. Sliding doors made of reinforced sandwich panels with a core of wood shavings arranged in an irregular pattern are highly decorative. (*United States Rubber Company*)

Types of Doors

As with windows, doors can swing or slide and they can also fold.

Swinging doors, by far the most common type, are hinged at one side, like casement windows. They are widely used because they are easy to operate, have simple hardware, can be made to close automatically with closing devices, and can be effectively weatherproofed and soundproofed. Their major disadvantage is that the arc through which they swing must be left free of furniture.

Sliding doors need not take otherwise usable room or wall space when opened and can disappear completely to give a great sense of openness. They do, of course, have to go someplace and can vanish into a wall. Or they can slide in front of a wall, which is often done when door and wall are of glass (Fig. 258B). Although sliding doors can be suspended entirely from overhead tracks, they usually perform better if they also slide along tracks or grooves in the floor (which are hard-to-clean dirt-catchers). On the debit side, the movements required to open and close them are not so easy to make as for swinging doors, and there is no inexpensive way to make a sliding door, especially a screen door, close itself. Often they do not glide so quietly and smoothly as one would wish; and the backs of sliding doors cannot have narrow shelves or hooks, which are especially convenient on closet doors. The fact that they can be very much wider than swinging doors emphasizes horizontality and spaciousness.

Folding doors slide along tracks, usually at the top, and fold like an accordion. They take little space when collapsed and come in diverse colors and textures. In general, they are not so soundproof as other types and sometimes tend to stick, but they are excellent for those situations in which one wants to be able to open or close a large opening inexpensively (Fig. 269A).

Location of Doors

Because doors and windows have so many points in common, almost everything said about locating windows applies to doors, but there are two important differences. Doors govern traffic paths and they are often opaque.

Traffic paths, like highways, are usually best when short and direct and when they disturb areas for work or quiet relaxation as little as possible.

Furniture arrangement is in part determined by the location of doors, because a traffic path should be left between each pair of doors, and space must be allowed for those that swing. From this point of view a room should have as few doors as is feasible, and the necessary ones should be kept close together if other factors permit.

Views and privacy are controlled by door location and material. In a bedroom, for example, a well-placed door, even when open, does not bring bed or dressing area into full view. Doors between cooking and dining areas are best when they do not direct attention toward the major kitchen work areas. Opaque materials are typically used where there is no view and where privacy is always needed. Translucent materials function well where there is neither view nor the need for absolute privacy. Transparent materials allow two-way vision.

Light can come through doors as well as windows, and transparent doors are frequently combined with windows (Figs. 258A and 272) as a means to architectural unity. Glass doors give a special pleasure in that they permit one both to look out and to go out.

Ventilation can be quickly accomplished by opening doors, especially in opposite walls. There is nothing like opening doors to "air out the house"; but ordinary doors are not suited to gentle, controlled venting.

Heat and cold coming through light-transmitting doors has the same characteristics as that coming through windows and thus the same comments apply. Opaque doors stand somewhere between windows and walls: they do an adequate job if well weatherproofed and concentrated on the side away from winter winds.

Cleaning a glass door is like cleaning a window, except that finger marks are more frequent, and it is easier to get at both sides. Opaque doors, too, get their full share of finger marks particularly around the knobs. Metal or plastic plates help a little and offer a logical place for ornament.

Curtaining is usually accomplished with draw curtains that can cover or expose the entire area of glass (Fig. 250A). The best solution is to locate glass doors where they need never be curtained, but this is not always easy. In older houses, "sash" curtains are sometimes used on glass doors.

Design of Doors

Although paneled doors that are watered-down versions of Colonial design are still in favor, the doors most distinctively characteristic of major contemporary trends are made as visually simple as possible. These include the plain wood doors in which plywood sheathes a strong but light core as well as doors of glass or plastic framed unobtrusively with metal or wood (Figs. 250A, 253B, 258A, and 269A and B). Many doors that are little more than sheets of glass function as both windows and doors and call attention not to themselves but to what they reveal. These are popular today because they are inexpensive, are easily cleaned, and blend in with the shell of the house to give a strong feeling of continuity. They should, however, be of some kind of safety glass and designed so that a closed door is obvious. Folding doors of wood or of bamboo slats (Fig. 269A) or those that are covered with fabrics can provide some visual interest with their textures and patterns of light and shade. Door frames and hardware usually are as simple as possible. Occasionally a door—most often an entrance door—is carved (Figs. 149 and 161B), can display ornamental hardware (Fig. 78B), or has architecturally elaborated detail surrounding it. These satisfy the increasing urge toward positive, eventful design.

Location and design of windows and doors are fundamentals in home planning, and they deserve far more thought than they often get. In many historic houses their design gave architects, designers, and craftsmen opportunity to use their inventiveness in enriching interiors and exteriors. In the re-creation of a Georgian room (Fig. 271) the fireplace, door, wall niches, and windows are set into a unifying pattern of wall panels and given progressive

In a small model of an English drawing room typical of the Early Georgian period (c. 1735), the ornamented doors and windows are handsomely related to the walls, the fireplace, and the ceiling. (*Thorne European Rooms in Miniature, The Art Institute of Chicago*)

A simple but audacious two-story structural grid framing windows and a door projects a hillside living room into a breathtaking panorama of trees, water, and mountains. Joseph Esherick, architect. (*Photograph by Rondal Partridge*)

degrees of emphasis. The centrally located and elaborately ornamented fireplace and overmantle is the dominant element, and its importance is strengthened by the dignity and restraint of the tall windows framing it. The doorway, with its boldly carved projecting pediment, is less emphatic but still assertive on its comparatively simple wall. Less vigorously treated, the niches for the display of Far Eastern ceramics take their place in the wall panels and balance the enrichment of the other walls. All of these units are framed with carved moldings more richly developed than those of the wall panels. In this room the designer's aim was to create beauty and interest *within* the room.

The architect of the room shown in Figure 272 wanted to take full advantage of the impressive beauty *outside* the room. He drew attention to the landscape by the dramatic scale of the windows, which distract as little as possible. The glass is set in a wood grid that is notable for its simplicity and proportions. The door at the right is one of the glass panels, but with a wood frame around it for strength and to signify that it is a door that has work to do. These two rooms show that the openings in our homes can be beautiful and practical. They attain these goals when they are appropriate to their environment and their purpose.

The sliding panel walls of traditional Japanese houses have for centuries doubled as windows and doors. They keep out the weather, let in light, open to provide ventilation and free passage, and slide to make separate rooms or open spaces. [*Photograph © Ezra Stoller* (ESTO)]

A floor that extends beyond a glass wall to become a terrace, and a ceiling that projects as overhead protection, firmly establish continuity of indoor and outdoor space. Frederick Liebhardt and Eugene Weston, architects. (*Photograph by Julius Shulman*)

13 · Floors, Floor Coverings, and Ceilings

Frank Lloyd Wright once said, "A house is more a home for being a work of art," a philosophy he applied as creatively to floors and ceilings as to other aspects of home design. In the Prices' home (Figs. 275A and B), floors and ceilings are integrated with walls and windows to shape space and give it character. The wide passageway, rhythmically divided into bays, has a plain, light, horizontal ceiling that unobtrusively broadens this space, that quietly directs attention on and out. A dark, polished concrete floor is a handsome foil for the rug, designed by Wright, in which squares, rectangles, and lines are inventively diversified. It accents the length of the hall while acknowledging its varying widths. Its strict geometry is consonant with the architecture of the house.

Both floor and ceiling are appropriately different in the living room. This is primarily a space for sitting and relaxing, not for walking through. The large, plain rug has no leading lines or directional patterns, but the ceiling is worth looking at. Following the lines of the hip roof (having sloping ends and sides), the central section rises in proportion to the size of the room, and this ascendancy is underlined by wood battens. The lower horizontal portion establishes a plane that continues throughout the house. It binds together the horizontal floor and the sloping ceiling, gives a sheltering effect, and also provides a place for direct and indirect lighting.

Floors and ceilings in the Harold C. Price, Jr., residence in Bartlesville, Oklahoma, are positive design
elements appropriate to their specific functions and to the size and shape of different rooms. Frank Lloyd
Wright, architect. (*Photographs by Maynard L. Parker Modern Photography*)

A

Above. In the broad passageway, a dominant rug calls attention to the floor. Definite and directional, the
design suggests the movement for which this space was planned. The subordinate ceiling has rhythmically
placed lighting fixtures.

Below. In the living room, a large, plain rug is a passive unifying base for furniture, walls, and ceiling. The
lively shape of the ceiling, accented with wood battens that emphasize the direction of each plane, makes
a special contribution to the room's spaciousness.

B

Floors and ceilings, together with walls and windows, are the big enclosing surfaces that keep us warm, dry, and safe. Depending on their design and material, they can raise, depress, or do nothing for our spirits. They can be commonplace or individualized, costly or inexpensive, easy or difficult to maintain. Appropriateness and relationships are of uppermost importance in these big, permanent architectural elements. One can play around with flower arrangements and table settings, pictures on the wall, or different furniture arrangements, which cost only one's time. Not so with the major architectural elements, where changes are usually troublesome and expensive. New concepts of space, new materials and colors have lifted the design of floors and ceilings well out of the category of a routine necessity into the realm of positive, contributing elements.

FLOORS

Floors are flat, horizontal surfaces meant to be walked on, less often to be run, jumped, or danced on. They take a limited amount of wheel traffic, such as vacuum cleaners, service carts, and children's toys. They support us and our furniture and provide insulation against the earth's cold dampness. As we all know but sometimes forget, floors get the greatest wear and the most dirt of any part of the house. But floor design and materials are not so completely mundane as these factors imply. In fully developed architecture, they contribute to the expressive character of the whole house. They can define and separate areas without benefit of walls, can suggest traffic patterns, and can be as dominant or subordinate as one wishes.

In houses with basements, floors are typically of two sorts. Basement floors are concrete slabs poured directly on the earthen subgrade or on a foundation of crushed rock. Those above grade usually consist of supporting floor joists, a layer of inexpensive wood or plywood for strength, insulating membrane to retard the passage of air and moisture, and a finish flooring of hardwood. Or sheets of plywood or composition board can be used instead of the finish flooring, and these can be covered with such smooth floorings as asphalt tiles or sheet vinyl, or with carpets.

The growing popularity of one-story, ground-hugging, basementless houses has changed these procedures. In such houses, floors are often concrete slabs basically like those in basements but with important differences. They are reinforced with metal to minimize cracking, and the surface is hardened, integrally colored, and carefully smoothed. Heating masonry floors has greatly lessened one former disadvantage—cold, tired feet—for it appears that combined coldness and hardness rather than hardness alone brings foot fatigue. In summer, however, with the heat turned off, the coolness of such floors is welcome. Concrete slab floors reduce construction and maintenance costs. They also make practicable a low house intimately related to outdoor areas, as in Figure 275A.

The matter of suitable floors and floor coverings deserves early and careful planning, especially in view of possibilities hardly dreamed of a generation ago. Some of the important factors are these:

- **Durability** usually comes first because floors take severe punishment, chiefly from the abrasion of feet but also from the weight of furniture, especially when moved. Durable floors have a surface sufficiently tough to prevent wearing through to another material. They do not crack, splinter, or disintegrate, nor do they get permanently indented or otherwise make noticeable the hard use they get.

- **Economy of upkeep** is of great importance, and the generalizations in Chapter 4 about easily maintained surfaces pertain to floors. Upkeep is lessened when floor materials resist stains and bleaches, do not absorb liquids or dirt. Camouflage patterns and neutralized colors near middle in value reduce labor, regardless of material or surface texture. Floor areas without jogs or crevices are easier to sweep, vacuum, or mop than those of complicated shape. And somewhat surprisingly, tests indicate that carpeted floors take less labor to maintain than do those with hard surfaces.
- **Resilience** cushions impact, thereby reducing foot fatigue, breakage, and the noise produced when we move around.
- **Warmth,** actual and apparent, is welcome in all but excessively hot climates. There are three ways to make floors actually warm: to put the heating elements in the floor, to have the heat in the ceiling so that the floor will be warmed by radiation, and to insulate the floor. There are also three ways of making floors look warm: to use warm hues, middle to dark values, or soft textures.
- **Light reflection** is usually associated with ceilings and walls, but much light hits floors day and night. The more light that floors reflect the brighter the home will be and the lower the utility bills. Notice how much more light is reflected by the rug in the Prices' hall than is reflected by the dark concrete floor.
- **Sound absorption** is not the same as the noise reduction resulting from resilience. Rough, porous materials lessen noise already made, an observation that is as true of floors as of ceilings, walls, and furnishings. Pile rugs rate high on this quality.
- **Appearance** brings us again to that everyman's land of likes and dislikes and to appropriateness to specific situations. Few question the importance of use and cost. Many overlook the strategic potential of floors as sources of personalized aesthetic expression and satisfaction. We have seen that they can be keyed up, as in the Prices' hall, or subordinated, as in their living room. They can alter the apparent size, shape, and character of a room (Figs. 138A and B) or suggest division of space without walls. Many illustrations in previous chapters are worth looking at again specifically for the design and treatment of floors.

Obviously these are broad generalizations to which there are many exceptions. For example, durability and economy of upkeep are vastly more critical in a kitchen or a family room than in a study, where appearance might be more significant. These factors also set up conflicts, for there is as yet no one flooring material that is perfect in every respect. Thus, once again, it is sensible to decide what is most important and to make such compromises as are necessary. In part, at least, this explains the practice of covering the permanent floor, partly or completely, with removable fabrics. It is logical to distinguish between the *flooring materials,* either hard or resilient, that are more or less permanent and either part of the structure or securely fastened to it and the soft *rugs* or *carpets* that are relatively easy to remove.

A

B

The beauty of flagstone lies in its subtle variations of color and texture. When sizable pieces are laid in irregular patterns, the effect is ruggedly informal and bold in scale. (*Libbey-Owens-Ford Glass Company*)

Eight-inch squares of dark-red unglazed tile are orderly yet not formal, and are moderately large in scale. They are a handsome background for Oriental rugs. Leslie I. Nichols, architect. (*Photograph by John H. Lohman*)

Large squares of vigorously grained wood make a nonrepetitive, checkerboard pattern. (*Photograph by Hedrich-Blessing. E. L. Bruce Company*)

Small rectangular pieces of many kinds of wood are composed in an intricate, small-scale parquet design. (*Wood-Mosaic Corporation*)

C

D

Hard flooring materials are diversified. Stone and ceramic tile are durable indoors and outdoors and are easily maintained. Wood has visual warmth, infinitely varied grain, and some resilience.

Hard and Resilient Flooring Materials

The rock floors of caves or earth beaten down by use were probably the first hard-surface floors used by man. These were followed by stone smoothed and set in place, and by brick, tile, and wood. Until a century or so ago these were the sum total of possibilities. Today many new materials supplement the older materials. The chart on pages 280–281 briefly summarizes the characteristics of those flooring materials frequently used now. In comparison with rugs, almost all are durable, cool, either hard or moderately resilient, more or less stain-resistant, and easy to clean with a mop. But these general similarities should not obscure the equally important differences among them. Brick, stone, and ceramic tile have high original cost but last for generations, indoors or outdoors, while cheap plastic-surfaced floor coverings may wear through in a few years. Cork and rubber are much more resilient than asphalt or concrete, and some of the newer types of vinyl flooring have an inner core of foam to increase resilience and warmth. Sheet vinyl that comes in rolls 6 to 15 feet wide and up to 100 feet long will have fewer dirt-catching seams than will tiles of the same material; but tiles can be installed with less waste if the floor is irregular in outline, and they can be more easily replaced. Wood, the most popular of the hard flooring materials, varies in cost with the type of wood used. It takes a good deal of day-to-day maintenance but is fairly easy to repair and refinish, and it has a homelike, enduring appeal. Superior quality vinyl is moderately expensive, is highly diversified in color and design, and is probably the nearest approach to an attractive, easily maintained, smooth-surfaced flooring material now available.

Resilient composition flooring is available in literally hundreds of colors and textures and in many sizes and shapes.

A

B

Rectangular tiles can be laid in any pattern that one wishes, an example of mass-produced materials that can be given individuality. (*Kentile*)

Seamless resilient flooring, a new development, is poured directly onto the floor, conforms to rooms of any size or shape. Solid chips and flakes of diverse colors are joined with a clear urethane resin. (*Torginol Seamless Duresque Flooring*)

Sheet vinyl can be embossed with all kinds of patterns to extend its range of visual interest. Luran "Airtred" has a layer of vinyl over a core of vinyl foam and an asbestos backing for resilience, quietness, and insulation. (*Sandura Company*)

Very small, opaque vinyl chips slightly varied in color are bound together with translucent vinyl to become a continuous sheet. The irregular mosaic pattern is pleasing and appropriate for a floor. It also camouflages wear and tear. (*Armstrong Cork Company*)

C

D

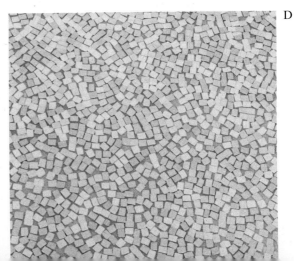

FLOORING MATERIALS

Hard

Material	Source or Composition	Use	Size and Shape	Patterns
Concrete Cost: least expensive flooring; can be both base and finish flooring.	Cement, sand, aggregates, and water; can be integrally colored.	Can be left uncovered indoors or outdoors. The standard base for clay tile, brick, and stone. Can be covered with wood, resilient flooring, or rugs.	Usually poured in slabs but tiles are available. Sometimes marked off in rectangles by wooden or metal screeds.	Can be given surface interest by exposing aggregates. Terrazzo has mosaic-like patterns from marble chips.
Stone Cost: very expensive.	Slate, flagstone, marble, and so on.	Chiefly entrances, outdoor paving, and near fireplaces, but can be used in any room except kitchen.	Usually not more than 2' square; rectangular or irregular.	Natural veining, shapes of stones, and patterns in which they are laid.
Tile and Brick (clay) Cost: expensive.	Heat-hardened clay. Tile is usually glazed; brick used only occasionally.	Areas getting hard wear, moisture, and dirt: entrances, hallways, bathrooms, activity space, or any place except kitchen where effect is wanted.	Tiles are $\frac{1}{2}''$ to 12'' square or rectangular, hexagonal, and so on. Standard bricks are approximately 2'' x 4'' x 8''.	Tile has varied designs. Typical brick patterns come from the way in which it is laid.
Wood (hard) Cost: moderately expensive.	Oak, birch, beech, maple, pecan.	Any room in house except kitchen and bathroom; usually most of it is covered by rugs.	Strips $1\frac{1}{2}''$ to $3\frac{1}{2}''$ wide; planks 2'' to 8''; parquet blocks 9'' x 9'' and so on.	Color and grain of wood. Usually laid in parallel strips; also comes in blocks of varied parquetry patterns.

Resilient

Material	Source or Composition	Use	Size and Shape	Patterns
Asphalt tiles Cost: least expensive composition flooring	Asbestos or cotton fibers, plasticizers, pigments, and resin binders.	Recommended for laying over concrete directly on ground. Especially suitable in much-used areas.	Standard is 9'' x 9'' but others available.	Tiles are plain or marbleized; laying creates typical tile patterns.
Cork tiles Cost: moderately expensive.	Cork shavings, granules compressed and baked to liquefy natural resins.	Floors not subject to hard wear, water, grease, stains, or tracked-in dirt.	Squares 9'' x 9'' or 12'' x 12''; also rectangles 6'' x 12'', 12'' x 24'', and so on.	Chunks of cork of different color give fine to coarse textural patterns.
Linoleum Cost: inexpensive.	Wood flour, ground cork, gums, linseed oil, and pigments pressed onto burlap or felt.	Floor and counter tops for kitchens, bathrooms, children's rooms, activity spaces; also desk tops.	Standard tiles are 9'' x 9''; in rolls 6' to 15' wide.	Practically unlimited; ease of inlaying permits individual designs.
Rubber tiles Cost: moderately expensive.	Pure or synthetic rubber and pigments vulcanized under pressure.	Similar to linoleum except that it can be laid directly over on-grade concrete floors.	9'' x 9'' to 18'' x 36''.	Usually plain or marbleized.
Vinyl-asbestos tiles Cost: inexpensive.	Similar to asphalt but with vinyl plastic resins.	Any indoor floor including on-grade and below-grade concrete floors.	9'' x 9'' tiles are typical.	Mottled, spattered, striated, and corklike are most frequently seen.
Vinyl-cork tiles Cost: moderately expensive.	Same as cork but with vinyl added as a protective sealer.	Any floor where heavy-duty durability is not important.	Same as cork.	Same as cork.
Vinyl sheets and tiles Cost: moderately expensive.	Vinyl resins, plasticizers, pigments, sometimes fillers in cheaper grades, formed under pressure while hot. Sheet vinyl usually laid on backing of alkali-resistant materials.	Any indoor floor. Special types available for basement floors. Also counter tops, wall covering.	Usually 9'' x 9'' tiles. Also by the roll, 6' to 15' wide. New type poured on floor for completely seamless installation.	Great variety, new designs frequent. Marbled, flecked, mosaic, sculptured, embossed, veined, and striated.

Colors	Durability	Maintenance	Comments
Limited range of low-intensity colors, but can be painted, waxed with colored wax, and so on.	Very high except that it often cracks and can be chipped. Serious damage difficult to repair.	Markedly easy if sealed against stains and grease. Waxing deepens color and gives lustrous surface but is not necessary.	Hard and noisy. Cold (welcome in summer) unless radiantly heated.
Usually grays and tans; variation in each piece and from one piece to another. Marble in wide range of colors.	Very high but chipping and cracking difficult to repair.	Easy—minimum sweeping and mopping.	Solid, permanent, earthy in appearance. Usually bold in scale. Hard and noisy. Cold if floor is not heated.
Glazed tiles in all colors. Bricks usually red.	Generally high but depends on hardness of body, glaze. May chip or crack, fairly easy to replace. Appearance of brick, unglazed tile, improves with wear.	Easy—dusting and washing. Unglazed types can be waxed. Porous types absorb grease and stains.	Satisfyingly permanent and architectural in appearance. Can relate indoor to outdoor areas. Noisy and cold.
Light red, yellow, tan, or brown.	High but shows wear.	Medium high—must be sealed, then usually waxed and polished.	Natural beauty, warmth; moderately permanent; easy to refinish; but fairly hard, noisy, not easy to keep looking well, especially in traffic areas.
Full range of hues but colors are neutralized; becoming available in lighter, clearer colors.	Excellent but can be cracked by impact and dented by furniture. Some types not grease-proof.	Moderately easy—mopping and waxing with water-emulsion wax.	Eight times as hard as rubber tile; noisy; slippery when waxed.
Light to dark brown.	Moderately high. Dented by furniture, and so on.	Not easy. Porous surface absorbs dirt, which is hard to dislodge. Sweep, wash, and wax.	Luxurious in appearance; resilient and quiet.
Practically unlimited. New types come in light, clear colors as well as dark and neutral.	Moderately high in better grades. Resists denting better than asphalt, not so well as vinyl.	Moderately easy—wash and wax, do not use varnish or shellac.	Attractive, flexible, quiet. No real disadvantages, except need for frequent waxing.
Unlimited range; often brighter and clearer than in linoleum or asphalt.	Similar to linoleum but more resistant to denting. Some types damaged by grease.	Average—washing with soap and water; wax or rubber polish.	Very similar to linoleum, but twice as resilient.
Fairly wide range but usually muted.	High general durability, resistant to grease, alkali, and moisture. Can be dented by furniture, and so on.	Among the easiest. Resilient underlay retards imbedding of dirt.	As hard and noisy as asphalt and not so durable but more easily kept in good condition.
Same as cork.	Same as cork, but more resistant to denting, dirt, grease.	Very easy—sweep, wash, and wax as needed.	Vinyl makes colors richer; less resilient and quieter than cork.
Wide range including refreshing light, bright colors. In some, translucency gives depth of color rivaling marble.	Promises to give very long surface. Cuts tend to be self-sealing. Resists almost everything including household acids, alkalies, or grease; denting, chipping, and so on.	Very easy. Built-in luster lasts long; imperviousness keeps foreign matter on surface. Can be waxed but not always necessary, especially for poured type.	Pleasant satiny surface. Quiet and resilient, some types have cushioned inner core. Patterns developed from material itself seem better than those imitating other materials.

A

B

An entrance hall with an undemanding floor seems spacious and airy. The large tiles laid parallel to the walls are of cheerful yellow vinyl chips and golden flakes suspended in clear vinyl.

The same entrance with a floor of dark-brown vinyl cork tile has a warm and friendly spirit. White, star-shaped vinyl inserts brighten the cork tones and call attention to the fact that the tiles are laid on the diagonal, which lengthens the sightlines.

Almost-white striated vinyl tiles laid in large squares banded by darker strips seem formal but sprightly. The emphatic strips lead the eye to explore the width and breadth of the space.

A centered, ruglike oblong of white and light-gray bands tends to reduce the room's apparent size but emphasizes its shape. The darker tiles have a tightly interwoven, paisley pattern.

C

D

Floor treatment holds manifold possibilities for diversified character in visual design, as shown in four versions of the same room, all of which use vinyl tiles. (*Armstrong Cork Company*)

A

Plush or "velvet" pile has single-level, cut or uncut loops that are uniformly smooth and soft and quietly harmonious with almost everything. "Consolation" is an uncut plush in pure wool. (*Philadelphia Carpet Company*)

B

A loop pile, densely packed, for durability, comes in nine monochromatic colors and makes an undemanding background. "Jewel Tones" is of 100 percent Acrilan. (*Firth Industries, Inc.*)

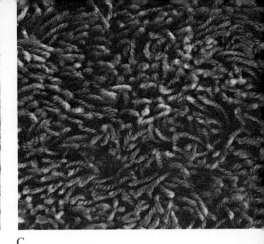

C

Twist piles have long or short loops, cut or uncut to give a nubby or shaggy texture. "Camineau," of 100 percent wool, has long, cut loops that give an informal appearance and conceal dirt and wear well. (*Karastan Rug Mills*)

Sheared textures result from the random or controlled "shearing" of loops left higher than the background loops. "Gala Affair" of Acrilan acrylic has sheared highlights and looks casual because the forms are shadowy and irregular. (*Philadelphia Carpet Company*)

High and low loops can be combined to give three-dimensional patterns as well as texture. This hand-tufted, all-wool example has densely packed islands of high loops separated by meandering, linear areas of low, uncut loops. It suggests easy, graceful movement. (*Don Frazier*)

"Turkish Delight" is a handwoven, all-wool rug that has precise, geometic patterns markedly different in color and texture from their background. The design is vigorous, sculptural, and full of surprises, which would make it a dominant element in a room. (*V'Soske, Inc., U.S.A.*)

D

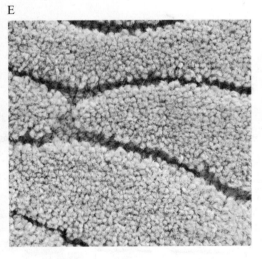

E

F

Except for very light or very dark solid colors, pile rugs mask dust and minor damage. Wool and cotton are the most widely used natural fibers; synthetics include rayon, nylon, and acrylics. All come in countless colors, textures, and patterns.

Rugs and Carpets

Soft floor coverings add warmth, visual softness, texture, resilience, quietness, and a friendly intimacy to floors. As with wallpaper, soft floor coverings give rooms a "furnished" look, even with little furniture. They explicitly relate the floor to upholstered furniture, curtained windows, and clothed occupants. With their color, texture, and pattern, they contribute markedly to the character of homes, and like hard materials, they can alter the apparent size and shape

A

B

A detail of a seventeenth-century Caucasian rug is reminiscent of the lasting beauty and practicality of "Oriental" rugs, as handsome in modern as in traditional homes. (*Philadelphia Museum of Art*)

A detail of a nineteenth-century American hooked rug in wool and cotton on canvas backing uses semiconventionalized flower and leaf forms banded by a border pattern derived from a metal chain. (*The Metropolitan Museum of Art, New York*)

"Flying Carpet" (7′ 1″ x 10′ 10″), designed by the American painter Stuart Davis in 1942 and manufactured by V'Soske, Inc., U.S.A., shows an inspired handling of abstract shapes. (*Collection, The Museum of Modern Art, New York; Edgar Kaufmann, Jr., Fund*)

A Danish high-pile, Rya rug of wool, designed by Richard Winther, boldly contrasts light and dark, definite and amorphous shapes. (*Unika-Vaev Corporation*)

C

D

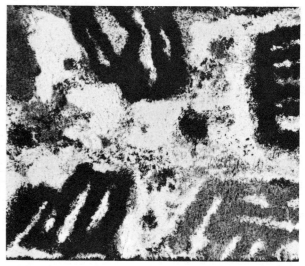

Decorative motifs for rugs have been inspired by natural and man-made forms. The results are typically eventful accents, especially when they are one of a kind and made by hand.

of rooms. Technical advances, together with new concepts of taste and housekeeping, have added countless new possibilities for individual expression.

A few definitions are in order. **Rugs** are made in or cut to standard sizes and are usually not fastened to the floor. **Carpeting** comes by the yard in widths from 27 inches to 18 feet or more, is cut and pieced (if necessary) to cover all the floor, and is fastened down. **Broadloom** refers to floor textiles woven on looms more than 36 inches wide. The term does not describe the weave, fiber, color, pattern, or any quality other than width. The word *rug* will be used here for soft-surfaced floor coverings because it seems to be a more inclusive term.

Many changes have taken place in the manufacture of rugs during the past decade—in the fibers used and in production techniques. There has been great increase in the use of synthetic fibers for the reasons cited in Chapter 10, but the natural fibers are still important. Fibers affect the cost, the cleaning time, and the appearance of rugs. Recall that wool is wiry, resilient, and long-lasting, while cotton is soft and crushable, and harder to keep clean, but the cost is lower. Carpet rayon is fairly strong and dirt-resistant; the colors can be fresh and clear. More resilient than cotton, it is still crushable. Both fibers perform best when the tufts are densely packed together (as, of course, is true of any fiber) and in cotton, uncut pile is more serviceable than cut pile. Acrilan and nylon are durable and dirt-resistant, and come in almost any color and in an increasing diversity of textures. Acrilan has exceptional resilience, softness, and warmth; nylon is amazingly long-wearing; and both scorn spills and stains.

Almost all of the rugs made in this country today have a pile surface, and they can be produced by tufting, weaving, or knitting. **Tufting,** which now accounts for three-fourths of the production of rugs, is a process in which pile yarns are attached to a preconstructed backing by multineedled machines. In **weaving** and **knitting** the surface yarns and backings are interlocked simultaneously. In all three processes the carpet backing is usually coated with latex to hold the surface yarns securely, and most good tufted rugs have an extra layer of backing for greater strength. Woven rugs are sometimes further subdivided into Wilton, Axminster, and velvet, according to the types of looms on which they are made (Fig. 285A). There are, however, a few types of rugs without pile (Figs. 285B, C, and D): braided rugs, flat-woven rugs such as those made

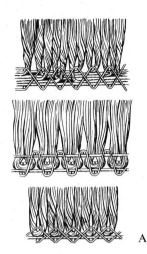

A

Woven pile rugs are made on looms that produce pile and backing in one operation. The three most widely used types are illustrated above.

Top. Wilton comes in many patterns, in solid or combined colors, and in varied textures. The pile can be cut or left as loops.

Middle. Axminster permits great diversity of pattern, because each tuft of pile is individually set by machine. The pile is usually cut.

Bottom. Velvet is often monochromatic, with all pile cut at the same length; but patterns and textures can be created with high and low, cut or uncut pile.

Flat-surface rugs combine some resilience with a cool, clean-cut, informal appearance. They are easy to clean, many can be washed, and nearly all can be turned over when the top surface shows wear. Kraft (strong paper) fibers, linen, rayon, hemp, rush, and sisal are some of the fibers used, but rugs can be woven or braided from almost any fiber. Flat-surface rugs are especially welcome where pile might interfere with such activities as moving furniture. Although not so diversified as pile weaves, they come in varied patterns and textures.

Far left. Hemp (*upper*) and sisal (*lower*) are available in squares that can be sewn together in rugs of any size or shape. (*Photograph by Ernest Braun. Reprinted from* Sunset *Magazine*)

Above near left. Tightly woven kraft yarns in a tweed pattern make a reversible rug that looks crisp and cool. Vinyl coating protects it from wear, soil, and weather. (*Waite Carpet Company*)

Left. Rugs handwoven by Indians of the American Southwest are worth what they cost in terms of individuality, beauty, and durability. The soft, natural colors are delightful to live with. The abstract designs, although regular and geometric, seem informal. (*Photograph by Milton Snow. Courtesy of the Navajo Service*)

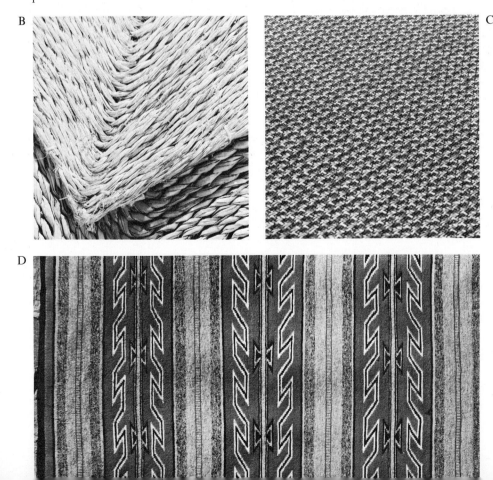

B

C

D

by native handcraft in various parts of the world, and the bonded matting made of one of our newest synthetic fibers, polypropylene. Perhaps of greater interest than rug construction, however, is the variety of textures and patterns now available (pp. 283–285).

Durability of rugs. The durability of rugs is the product of several factors:
- Fibers vary conspicuously in the wear they will take, as noted earlier in this chapter and detailed on pages 200–201.
- In pile rugs, density of pile is of first importance: the more tufts per square inch, the greater the durability. Length of pile is also important, because rugs with high pile last longer than those with short pile. The backing should be strong and flexible, tightly woven, and with the tufts held securely. In rugs without pile, the fibers and thickness plus tightness of yarn and weave prolong usefulness.
- Cushions can add years to a rug's life as well as make it more pleasant to walk on. Under small rugs, they should be skid-proof.
- Rugs that can be turned to equalize wear or that can be reversed save money. Covering heavily used portions with small, replaceable rugs can be an economy, especially with wall-to-wall carpeting.
- Good care is essential. Embedded dirt is harmful, as are many stains and spots. Moths and mildew destroy or weaken many fibers.

Not a few rugs are replaced before completely worn out because they have faded, become permanently stained, or grown tiresome. With today's large windows it pays to get permanent colors or those that fade pleasantly. Stain-resistant fibers or soil-retarding treatments are good investments but no more so than floor coverings that will please as long as they last.

Size of rugs. Personal preferences, the way of living and the character of the home, and cost largely determine the amount of soft floor covering in a home. Rugs, carpeting, or a combination of both can be appropriate.

Wall-to-wall carpeting makes rooms look luxurious and comfortable. If the pattern is quiet and the color muted, it makes rooms seem spacious. It is one of the best means of unifying a room or of relating several adjacent spaces. Because it fits the room exactly and is fastened to the floor, carpeting gives a sense of security and permanence. Covering a larger area than a typical rug, it is more expensive, but it can serve as a finished floor covering, eliminating the need for an expensive flooring material such as polished hardwood. Maintenance costs are less than those of resilient floorings that need constant washing and waxing, but it cannot easily be sent to the cleaners, moved to another room or house, or turned to equalize wear. Once thought appropriate only for the more formal areas of the house, carpeting is now found in all rooms, even the kitchen and bathroom, because of the variety of materials and qualities available.

Rugs are adaptable. They can be had in *many sizes or shapes*. If they cover the entire floor or almost all of it, as in the Prices' living room, the effect is similar to that of carpeting. They can also be small accents calling attention to a special part of the home or, when larger, can hold together a group of furniture. In homes with open plans, they can define areas without enclosing walls. With rugs, it is possible to economize on size rather than on quality and to select those that make a specific impact on one part of a home.

Design of Floors

In the living room shown in Figure 287 the floor was thoughtfully planned as an integral element appropriate to the whole design. Light-colored cork tile visually balances the slightly textured off-white ceiling, emphasizes the horizontality of the space to make it seem larger, and is a sound-absorbing, dirt-concealing cushion underfoot. The main conversation group is centered and coordinated by the area rug placed before the fireplace. The Chinese rug, with its very light figured pattern placed asymmetrically on a plain dark background, reinforces, without reiterating, the design of the fireplace. This leads to a positive, lively harmony quite different in character from the harmony resulting merely from repetition.

Applying the aims and principles of design to floors brings to mind both general and specific points. The expressive character and beauty of the material itself, its effect in the specific space for which it is being considered, and the relation of all the floors in a home to one another and to the whole house deserve careful thought.

Form follows function suggests that color, texture, and pattern look as though they belonged on floors and were meant to be walked on. This makes questionable designs that give the illusion of pronounced three-dimensionality or that employ naturalistic representations of anything on which we would not like to walk.

Crisp rectangularity, contrasting handsomely with the luxuriant foliage seen through the windows and beyond the terrace, is the keynote of a semiformal living room. An acoustical ceiling and a cork floor with an eventful rug reduce noise. Buff, Straub, and Hensman, architects. (*Photograph by Julius Shulman*)

287

Variety in unity applies to the material itself as well as to its relation to the room and to the whole home. Except for rugs definitely planned as accents, it is usually desirable to pay special heed to singleness of effect.

Balance, according to many, dictates that the floor should be darker than the walls, the furnishings, or the ceiling. Exceptions, as numerous as they are delightful, prove that here as elsewhere there are no laws. It is, however, gratifying to have rooms in equilibrium, and the relation of floors, especially in color value, to other parts of the home is consequential.

Rhythm of a type suggesting easy walking seems generally logical. Although only children as a rule dare express in their physical movements the rhythms indicated by strong lines, checkerboards, and sweeping curves (Figs. 275A and 282C), such marked rhythmic patterns unquestionably affect the feelings of adults.

Emphasis is a matter of giving each part of the home the degree of importance deemed most appropriate. Plain floorings and neutral colors emphasize spaciousness and free our eyes for other things. Patterns range from those that almost escape notice to those that are compelling climaxes.

Selection of Flooring Materials

Getting suitable floors takes time, but the dividends from wise planning are large. Money can be saved and long-term enjoyment increased if you give more than a passing glance to every floor you see, not only in homes but in shops, restaurants, and public buildings. Mail-order catalogs and stores that sell floor coverings show what is generally available. Periodicals on interior design —especially those written for professional architects and decorators—report new developments. When this information is related to an analysis of a specific situation, such questions as the following can be answered:

How much and what kind of use will the floor get?
- How heavy will the traffic be?
- Will it bring mud and grit?
- Will traffic be concentrated in spots or paths or be evenly distributed?

How much will the floor cost?
- How much money should be spent on the initial cost of floors?
- How much time or upkeep money is available?

What kind of beauty is indicated?
- Informal or formal, delicate or rugged, passive or active?
- What kind of visual relation between floor and walls, floor and ceiling, one room and others, between indoors and outdoors, is wanted?

How individualized ought the floors to be?
- How can the floors best contribute to the character of the home?
- What degree and what kind of personalization is wanted?

Whatever the answers to such questions, it is best to study large samples of materials in the rooms for which they are being considered. Floors are too big, too expensive, and too heavily used to be taken lightly.

The floor and ceiling in a room designed for a movie set complement each other and are forceful elements in establishing the room's character. A light-colored, plain, and thick pile carpet covers the floor of the main area, emphasizing its large scale, the drama of the high beamed ceiling, and the more intimate fireplace recess, floored with dark, burnished ceramic tile. The bold, high, and spacious ceiling, however, is dominant. Its heavy beams point dramatically to the inviting alcove, where the ceiling is lower and horizontal, and is made to seem even more so by the proportions of the fireplace, with its mantel nearer the ceiling than the floor. The wood paneling on walls and ceiling, and the bulky, deeply cushioned sofas and chairs, contribute to the congenial, expansive atmosphere of the main area, the warm intimacy of the alcove. Shirley Ritts, designer. (*Photograph by Maynard L. Parker Modern Photography. National Lumber Manufacturers' Association*)

CEILINGS

Although not *used* as are the other parts of the house, ceilings protect us, and they affect illumination, acoustics, heating, and cooling. Typical ceilings are the same size and shape as the floors they parallel, are surfaced with plaster or composition board, and are painted white or some very pale hue. There are several reasons for this stereotype: it literally designs itself and is inexpensive to build and maintain; it gives unobtrusive spaciousness; and it reflects light well. In most cases, we notice ceilings little and do correspondingly little about them. Perhaps it is just as well in a busy world to have one large undecorated surface in every room. But ceilings can be otherwise, as we shall see in discussing their height, shape or direction, material, color and texture, and ornamentation.

Height

Ceiling heights are determined by resolving our needs for head room, air, and economy with our desires for space pleasantly proportioned and in character with our living. Minimum human heights are 7 feet for basements, $8\frac{1}{2}$ feet for the first floor, and 8 feet for the second floor. Heights beyond these may well be justified, and lesser heights, especially in a part of a room, may seem cosy and sheltering (Fig. 289).

There are notable and varied differences between the consequences of low and high ceilings. Low ceilings are enclosing, intimate, and typically informal. They reduce winter heating costs but make rooms warmer in summer. High ceilings often seem formal and dignified, as in Figures 274 and 290, but without losing dignity they can express informality, as in Figures 289 and 293. Unless seriously out of scale with a room's length and breadth, high ceilings are likely to make rooms seem airy and expansive.

Ceilings of different heights can also energize space and differentiate one area from another. Dining rooms can be set apart by lowering the floor as well as the ceiling (Fig. 30). Hallways can be distinguished from living and dining rooms by low trellises, and quiet conversation areas can be demarcated by ceilings appropriately lower than those in the rest of the group-living space (Figs. 34, 289, and 293). A desk corner in the living room can be anchored by a supplementary ceiling, low and horizontal (Fig. 51B). Much more than flat lids on the tops of boxes, ceilings can join with floors, walls, and furniture in an exciting complex of interpenetrating planes, as illustrated in Figures 275B, 287, and 291 through 294A.

A miniature salon, evocative of French Baroque design (c. 1660–1700) of the Louis XIV period, is floridly ornamented yet formal and dignified. Although the walls are impressive, the ceiling—high and deeply coved, carved and gilded, with painted center panels and a crystal chandelier—is dominant. The floor of dark polished wood, and the intricately figured rug that suggests the pile "Savonnerie" floor coverings of this period, complement and balance the splendor of the ceiling above. Instead of expressing warmth and hospitality, the room impresses those who see it with the brilliance and opulence of the court of the "Sun King." (*Thorne European Rooms in Miniature, The Art Institute of Chicago*)

Shape and Direction

Although it is easy and commonplace to have ceilings that are nothing more than an uninterrupted horizontal plane, some of the other possibilities hold more interest.

Dropped ceilings can enliven the overhead plane even on the first floor of a two-story house, where horizontal ceilings are almost mandatory. In Figure 291, a dropped band around the perimeter of the living-dining area emphasizes the sweeping expanse of space and provides a recess for indirect lighting that softly illumines the room. Aligned with the tops of the windows and doors, the band is a strong unifying factor. The wood floor and the area rug echo the ceiling treatment. Figures 275B and 289 also show dropped ceilings.

Coved ceilings, in which walls and ceiling are joined with curved surfaces (Fig. 290) rather than right angles, make the space seem more plastic and flexible. If carried to their logical conclusion, ceilings become symmetrical domes, as in the geodesic dome house in Chapter 18, or less formal curved surfaces, as in Figures 294A and 175.

Shed, lean-to, or **single-slope, ceilings** typically seem informal, are good acoustically, and call attention to the highest part of the room (Figs. 22 and 25).

Gabled, or **double-pitched, ceilings** encourage one to look up, and they activate and increase the apparent volume of the space. If the beams are exposed, the eye tends to follow their direction. They can be gently sloping and have

The two houses with horizontal ceilings on this and the next page show how visual interest can be attained.

The ceiling of a ground-floor room in a two-story house can do more than hold up the floor above it. In this Connecticut home the ceiling has been given considerable visual interest through the use of narrow wood decking running across a room framed with a lower, plaster-surfaced lighting trough. John Black Lee and Harrison DeSilver, architects. (*Photograph by Lisanti Inc. Reprinted from* Better Homes & Gardens)

beams going from one end of the room to the other (Fig. 289), which accentuates the room's length. When large beams follow the direction of steeply pitched ceilings (Fig. 293), the room's height is dramatically emphasized. The ceiling planes can also slope in four directions (Fig. 275B), which gives a spreading effect.

Folded-plate roofs and **ceilings** have an accordion-like series of parallel gables (Fig. 274) and are visually active, dominant elements.

Materials

Plaster is a common ceiling material because it provides an uninterrupted surface that can join plastered walls without joints, thereby passively unifying the sides and the top of a room. It can be smooth or textured, plain, painted, or papered. Wallboard is much like plaster except that it leaves joints that can be concealed with tape and paint or emphasized with wood battens. Wood in strips, planks, or plywood is both handsome and homelike. Acoustical tiles in many sizes and patterns bring texture and reduce noise. To date, metal has been used sparingly in homes, but its possibilities are illustrated in Figure 292.

Not all ceilings are opaque. There are skylights of clear or translucent glass or plastic, and there are luminous ceilings that fill rooms with diffused artificial light (Color Fig. 1 and Figs. 22, 229B, and 253A).

Rippling metal roof decking supported by heavy beams and accentuated with louvered skylights, both indoors and outdoors, helps integrate an all-steel house with its site. Notice that the interior floor is continuous with the outdoor paving. A. Quincy Jones, architect. (*Photograph by Julius Shulman*)

Ceilings take precedence over walls in a home in Midland, Michigan. Heavy timbers, supporting the ceiling of matched cedar boards, rise from ground to ridge pole to give dramatic triangularity. The hanging balcony vigorously articulates the space and brings the ceiling down to human scale over the fireplace. In the group-living space, areas for different uses are indicated by brick or concrete floors and a decorative Oriental rug. Alden Dow, architect. (*Photograph by Bill Hedrich, Hedrich-Blessing*)

Structural advances and inventive design concepts are leading to new form-space concepts about floors, ceilings, and roofs.

Above. In North Carolina, a roof and ceiling of laminated wood, measuring 62 feet on each side, project daringly over an enclosed space 38 feet square. Defined as a hyperbolic paraboloid, the shape has a continuously changing double curvature. Eduardo F. Catalano, architect. (*Photograph © Ezra Stoller*)

Right. In a California house built on sloping ground, the floors are a series of terraces connected by cantilevered steps. The ceiling is a subordinate plane over the three-dimensional expression of the site. Boyd E. Georgi, architect. (*Photograph by Julius Shulman*)

Color and Texture

Heaviness overhead is usually not pleasant unless the weight is clearly supported. This fact, together with the advantages of having ceilings that reflect light, explains the frequency of light colors and fine textures. Special effects of considerable impact, however, can be achieved with ceilings painted or papered in strong colors or made of some of the darker woods. It is well to remember that ceilings, especially at night if much light is directed toward them, bathe everything below with their reflected color. A yellow ceiling, for example, would enliven yellows, oranges, or yellow-greens below it but would dull any blues or violets. The ceiling textures in most contemporary homes are comparatively smooth, but acoustical plaster or tiles, unpainted wood, and corrugated metal or plastic can contribute their own distinctive surface qualities.

In conclusion, ceilings are the easiest part of the house to forget. If next to nothing is done with them, hardly one person in a hundred will notice. Moreover, a large, plain foil for the rest of the room has its merits whether people are conscious of it or not. On the other hand, the aesthetic potentialities of ceilings—and floors—ought to be jealously husbanded, not neglected. Two houses that explore these potentialities are shown in Figures 294A and B. In the first, the roof is a dominant, urgent force suspended over a walled court, part of which has been enclosed with glass to form the house proper. Floors and walls have purposely been kept simple to intensify the excitement of the roof form. In the second, the floor is the compelling element, following as it does the stepped-down terracing of a hillside. Plant beds and floating steps mark and divide the levels. A redwood-scored concrete-aggregate patio becomes the dining room floor. And the rough texture of the living room rug repeats the pebbled concrete but with a softened touch. Conversely, the ceiling is smooth and undemanding, a gentle foil for the activity underfoot. In both houses, the architects have looked at floors and roofs creatively, not as mere protection but as motivating forces in their designs.

Designer Jack Lenor Larsen's circular studio on Long Island, New York, contrasts a conical ceiling of bamboo matting above fir rafters with a cement floor painted in involuted patterns by Masahiko Yamamoto, and the natural color of rough cedar siding on the exterior with white plywood interior walls. Fabric sculptures hanging from the rafters are Amazon dance masks. (*Photograph by Kal Weyner. United States Plywood Corporation*)

295

Put on the market in the 1870s, this bentwood rocker with seat and back of cane is once again available. The frolicsome curves exploit the flexibility of wood and suggest a rocking movement. (*Thonet Industries, Inc.*)

14 · Furniture Selection and Arrangement

Furniture is the major transition between architecture and people. It enables us to impress our personal tastes on our living quarters, even when they are architecturally the same as those of our neighbors and when most furniture is mass-produced. Proof of this can be found in Figures 297A and 298A. Although dissimilar in total effect, these two rooms have several general points in common. The unfurnished spaces were identical, and the furnishings for each were selected with a desired character and an arrangement in mind. In both, the furniture is organized into three groups, traffic paths are left open, and separation of living from dining space is suggested. Beyond these basic similarities are many specific differences.

The Merrys' room has a somewhat formal effect, with emphasis on broad continuing forms unified by their similarity. Strict rectangularity of furniture and its arrangement leads to an architectural, almost built-in effect. This is particularly evident in the major conversation group. Two sofas butting against a corner table fit one corner of the room compactly. A convenient L-shaped coffee table stresses the relation of this furniture group to the whole L-shaped space. Diagonally opposite is a secondary group consisting of an easy chair, a small table, and a radio-phonograph, all aligned with the walls. Living and dining areas are differentiated by a substantial storage cabinet projecting into the room. Dining chairs and table fit their space as precisely as do the storage units against the long wall. Unpatterned draperies and carpeting contribute to the overall integration of architecture and furnishings.

A

The living-dining rooms in Minneapolis on this page and the next were exactly the same until they were furnished by families with differing ideas. Both are equally "good." (*Photographs by Warren Reynolds, Infinity Inc. Reprinted by permission from* Better Homes & Gardens)

The O. M. Merry family sought regularity. In design and placement, the furniture corresponds with the lines and character of the room.

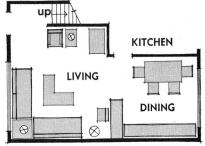

B

A

Less uniform in design and less regular in arrangement, the furniture in the W. W. Dunn home is a counterpoint of lively curves against rectangularity. Both in selection and position the furniture suggests easy rearrangement for varying activities.

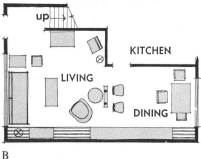

B

Most immediately noticeable in the Dunns' room is variety and spontaneity, a feeling of openness and freedom to move pieces of furniture easily. The major conversation center, in the same logical corner as the Merrys', is a lively combination of straight-lined and curved pieces. A simple rectangular sofa, right-angled to a wall-length bench, acts as an anchor. The reed chair supported by thin metal legs has slightly curved arms. The rectangular plywood coffee table has turned-up edges and curved legs. The capacious, encompassing lounge chair of molded plywood is made resilient with foam rubber and soft upholstery fabric. The lounge chair, placed diagonally near a three-legged round table, leads up to a sprightly room divider—two wood poles holding a painting in mid-air. Casually but not carelessly arranged, the other corner has a cabinet against the stairway wall, a chair at a congenial angle, and a floor lamp. Dining furniture faces the window. The entire long wall, given some prominence by its dark color, is unified with continuous benches flexibly used for seating, table space, and the base for interchangeable cabinets. A group of six family photographs is a focus of interest subtly related but subordinate to the larger portrait. This is a visually active room in which our eyes jump in staccato fashion from one intrinsically interesting object to another. Some pieces, the sculptural plywood chairs for example, assert their independence of the rectilinear space; others, such as the benches and the storage units, obediently follow the lines of the room. Without rigid correspondence, there is agreeable relationship of forms to one another.

Equally practical and pleasing, these two rooms show how families with differing needs and attitudes can individualize their homes with the vast array of furniture available today.

Furniture has been discussed and illustrated on many of the preceding pages. In Chapters 2, 3, and 4 it was considered as a factor in group and private living and in keeping house. In Chapters 5, 6, and 7 attention was focused on design quality, and in Chapters 8, 9, and 10 materials were considered. Keeping these previous discussions in mind, it is now appropriate to think specifically about choosing furniture that has lasting values.

SELECTING FURNITURE

Developing critical ability in the choosing of furniture depends not only on knowledge but on consciously sharpening your native aptitude for seeing and evaluating differences. "Practice buying" rather than random window-shopping is a profitable investment of time. In stores, catalogs, magazines, and books you can see many kinds of chairs, tables, and cabinets. Compare and contrast one with the others, noting carefully the excellences and weaknesses of each piece. Very few are totally good or totally bad. Some chairs and sofas look neat and trim, nicely scaled for typical rooms, but they may not be as comfortable as they look and the price may be high. Others may be very comfortable, durably constructed and upholstered, moderately priced, but big and bulbous. As you continue to look, think, and compare, you become able to size up *all aspects* of a piece of furniture and evaluate it as a whole. So that no factor will be overlooked, it pays to take along a written or a mental checklist.

In this way you will build a sensible but personal scale of values. For some persons, comfort or beauty may transcend all other considerations, although most of us seek a balance. Good as a general scale of values is, none can be applied rigidly to every specific situation.

Use and Economy

Whether furniture is for sitting, sleeping, eating, working, or playing, use and economy are not to be minimized. Convenience, comfort, flexibility, space required, length of service, and cost of maintenance are major factors:

- **Convenience** applies chiefly to efficient storage facilities and to the ease with which often-moved furniture, such as dining and pull-up chairs, can be handled (Fig. 305C). All furniture, however, is moved from time to time and should be no heavier than necessary for use, strength, and appearance. Large pieces should be on gliders or casters.
- **Comfort** applies chiefly to pieces on which we sit or sleep but also to the height of tables and desks and to leg room under them.
- **Flexibility** pertains to furniture that can be used in more than one room or for more than one purpose, such as the storage units behind the lounge

chair in Figure 298A. Until recently most furniture was designed for one room and one use. Typical dining room sets had a table, a china cabinet, and a buffet, appropriate only in an ample, separate dining room. Only the chairs could be used elsewhere; but no matter where they were placed they had a "dining room" character. Now many pieces are multipurpose. There are unit cabinets and chests suitable for any room and in many combinations, and there are chairs usable anywhere. Tables are easily expanded or contracted, and chairs and sofas convert to beds (Figs. 306, 307A, and 50). This saves money and space, unifies homes with open plans.

■ **Space required** becomes increasingly important as homes become smaller. Accordingly, some contemporary designers have eliminated protruding moldings and curved legs on cabinets so that they can be fitted tightly together; brought storage units to the floor or hung them on walls; designed cupboards and drawers to fit their contents; used materials—metal, plywood, foam rubber—that reduce size; developed folding, stacking, and nesting tables and chairs; and reduced both size and scale to a minimum.

■ **Length of service** depends on physical and psychological durability. Physical durability is determined by materials, construction, and finish. Psychological longevity is equally critical but harder to appraise. For continued satisfaction choose well-proportioned furniture that is flexible and seems right for you, and in which the materials are honestly and suitably used.

■ **Cost of maintenance** includes cleaning, repairing, refinishing, and reupholstering. Cleaning burdens can be lightened in the ways discussed in Chapter 4. Strong materials and firm construction lessen repairing. Durability of finish and ease of refinishing are important: painted furniture, whether wood or metal, may need new paint every few years; transparent finish on wood, supplemented by wax or polish, lasts a long time; and such materials as aluminum and chromium may last indefinitely without being refinished. Upholstery fabrics may serve from two to twenty years or more depending on the material and the use it gets. The cost of reupholstering is determined by the price of the fabric, the amount needed, and the labor involved. It would be low for the chairs shown in Figures 305A and B but substantial for the lounge chair in Figure 304C.

Beauty and Individuality

The qualities of beauty and individuality, quite as important as use and economy, have been dealt with in all of the preceding chapters, especially Chapters 1, 5, 6, and 7. In selecting furniture, search for forms that express their functions and that have the kind of unified diversity, balance, rhythm, and emphasis that pleases you.

Italian designers Fabio De Sanctis and Ugo Sterpini dreamed up a fanciful headboard of wrought iron and copper. (*Photograph by Ferdinand Boesch. The Museum of Contemporary Crafts*)

300

FURNITURE TYPES

Furniture can be classified in terms of its primary use: beds, sofas, and chairs; tables and desks; and storage units.

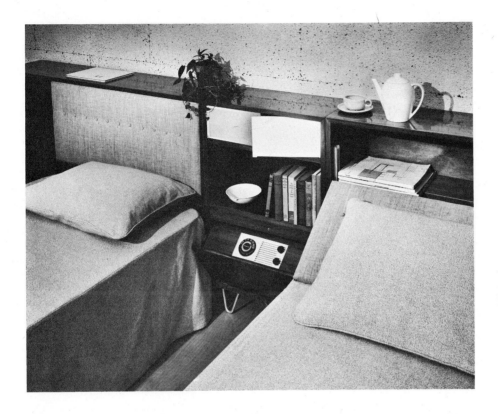

A thoughtfully designed headboard greatly increases the pleasure of reading or listening to music in bed. George Nelson, designer. (*Herman Miller Inc.*)

Beds

Reducing physical strain to a minimum is the purpose of beds. Individuals vary in their specific ideas about sleeping comfort, and about the only way to find out whether a bed is right for you is to try it. Most beds now have a springy foundation and a resilient mattress. The typical foundation consists of either inexpensive, lightweight, moderately comfortable flat springs or more bulky, expensive, and comfortable coil springs. Mattresses have been filled with just about everything from straw to hair—and just air. Today the least expensive are filled with cotton. The better grades have inner springs covered with padding or are of foam rubber. Foam rubber has several advantages: it is lightweight, easy to keep clean, and harbors no insects or allergy producers. It seldom needs to be turned, lasts long, and has about one half-million air cells in each cubic inch for resilience.

Even if funds are low, buy good mattresses and springs, and support them on simple wood legs or the more convenient metal frames on casters. Add the useful but not essential headboards (Fig. 301), footboards, and night tables later. In small quarters or for occasional guest use, a studio couch or a davenport that becomes a bed is a sensible economy.

Bedspreads are usually the most conspicuous part of a bed. Serviceable bedspreads do not wrinkle excessively when taken off the bed or when you nap on them. They are heavy enough to stay in place or they are carefully

A

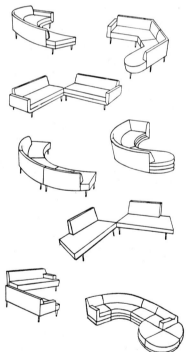

B

C

The design of sofas offers much greater opportunity for individuality than those usually seen might lead one to think.

Top. Luxuriously deep and long, a built-in sofa is shaped in friendly angles, as is the custom-made coffee table. Welton Beckett, architect. (*Photograph by Maynard L. Parker Modern Photography*)

Above left. Sofas in one piece or in separate units come in diverse sizes and shapes, which affect their usability and expressive character. Notice the difference between angular and curvilinear shapes. Those that are supported on legs do not produce the same visual effect as do those that sit directly on the floor. Separate units facilitate change, enable their owners to fit furniture into the available space. Those that come in one piece are usually less expensive and easier to keep in the position wanted. (*Modern Designs*)

Above right. A lightweight, sculptural frame of beech and teak with cane panels and foam-rubber cushions are used in a sofa that takes a minimum of visual space. (*John Stuart Inc.*)

fitted, and they can be laundered or cleaned easily. Strong colors or vigorous patterns on bedspreads make the bed loom large; unobtrusive colors or designs make the room seem larger. Bedspreads, curtains and draperies, and rugs with a family resemblance bring unity: spread and draperies can be obviously matched or can be more subtly related with harmonious or contrasting color, texture, or pattern.

Sofas

Chesterfield, couch, settee, settle, davenport, divan, lounge, or sofa—which do you call the seat for two or more people?

Chesterfield refers to an overstuffed sofa with upholstered ends.

Couch refers to a sofa with a low back and one raised end.

Davenport is used in the United States to describe an upholstered sofa often convertible into a bed, but originally the word meant a small writing desk, and was named after its maker.

Divan is a Turkish term for large, low couches without arms or backs that developed from piles of rugs for reclining.

Lounge refers to a type of couch, often with one high end for reclining.

Love seat refers to a small sofa or "double chair" for two persons.

Settee refers to a long, light seat with a back and sometimes with arms; it is often upholstered.

Settle refers to an all-wood settee.

Sofa comes from an Arabic term and, in America, is used to describe any long upholstered seat for more than one person.

The variety of sofas is legion: straight, curved, or angled to fit a room; with or without arms; in one piece or sectional; long enough for a six-footer to stretch out on or not quite; heavy and massive, delicate and graceful, or light and simple. Here are some suggestions of points to look for when you go to choose a sofa:

- Long enough to stretch out on
- Low and deep enough for relaxation but high and firm enough so that a person can get up under his own power
- Arms for comfort
- Convertible into a bed if extra sleeping space is needed
- Sectional if rearranging furniture is a hobby
- Upholstery that combines beauty and durability

Chairs

Gordon Logie, in *Furniture from Machines* (London, 1947), writes that sitting has become the most universal occupation of man because we work, study, relax, eat, and travel while seated. Leading such a sedentary life, we should be expert sitters; but we are not because until very recently no serious studies of sitting were made. We now know that comfort results when weight and pressure are spread and tension is eased by having:

- The height of the seat somewhat less than the length of the sitter's lower legs, so that the feet rest on the floor and the legs can be relaxed
- The depth of the seat somewhat less than the length of the upper leg so that there is no pressure point under the knee

- The width of the seat ample enough to permit some movement
- The seat shaped or resilient, as in a Windsor chair or as in those shown in Figures 305A, B, and C, so that pressure is not concentrated on the small weight-bearing edge of the pelvis.
- Both seat and back tilted backward slightly to buttress the weight
- The angle between seat and back 95 degrees or more
- The chair back support the small of the sitter's back
- The position of the seat and back adjustable for different persons (as in typists' chairs) or for different ways of relaxing (as in the old-fashioned Morris chairs and some of the new reclining chairs)

Three wing chairs demonstrate the variety possible in one type of furniture. In selecting any piece it is wise to consider all its aspects.

Right. A contemporary design by Charles Eames was the result of an exploration of new and old materials and techniques and of a detailed study of sitting comfort that showed flexibility was essential. A vigorously sculptural shell of molded rosewood, supported by a black and polished aluminum base, promises and provides relaxation. The chair swivels to any position; the ottoman supports the legs and feet for semireclining ease. (*Herman Miller Inc.*)

Bottom near right. Much less restrained than most Queen Anne furniture (c. 1702–1714), this walnut-framed wing chair is notable for its exuberant needlework upholstery. Designed in a robust age that was becoming interested in comfort allied with elegance, the chair is boldly exaggerated in the Baroque manner and is only slightly tempered by Dutch and English propriety. Its vitality and basic sturdiness would make it impressive in one of the large "halls" or "galleries" of the great English homes. (*The Metropolitan Museum of Art, New York, Gift of Irwin Untermeyer, 1955*)

Bottom far right. A simplified version of Georgian wing chairs is much more sedate in contours and upholstery than is the Queen Anne example. Wider, deeper, shorter, and more rectangular, it has been covered with a heavy cotton damask whose small-scale, curvilinear pattern softens the squared outline of the chair and echoes the arcs of the wings and arms. Far less dominating than the Queen Anne wing chair, it is for those neither adventurous nor meek who want a quietly assured environment. (*Baker Furniture Company*)

A

B

C

A   B   C

Easily moved pull-up and side chairs permit flexibility in furniture arrangement. Three Danish designs are notable for their inviting shapes and beautifully crafted natural materials.

Left. An ingenious construction makes it possible to ship this laminated wood chair knocked down and to assemble it quickly. The reversible leather and fabric seat and back slide into specially fitted grooves in the frame. (*Herman Miller Inc.*)

Center. A fresh interpretation of the Windsor chair is convincingly sturdy, easy to grasp, and takes little visual space. The fabric-covered seat can be removed for cleaning or reupholstering. Sonna Rosen, designer. (*Pacific Overseas Inc.*)

Right. A frame of teak or oak finished naturally with oil or wax supports a form-fitting seat of woven sea rush in this "classic" side chair. Hovmand-Olsen, designer. (*Photograph by Fran Stewart. Selig Manufacturing Company, Inc.*)

Comfort is further increased if the chair offers a place to rest the head and relax the neck and has supports for our arms.

Chairs are used for several purposes, and their form should follow their function. The typical family needs chairs for each of the following activities.

Relaxation and reading. In the group-living space, in studies, and in bedrooms, seating that allows each member of the family to relax is desirable. Upholstered chairs and sofas are about the only kinds that adjust themselves to varying individuals and are comfortable over long periods of time. New types of springs and foam rubber have greatly decreased bulkiness and enable us to get pieces as trim, neat, and comfortable as those shown in Figures 302B and C and 304A. Even so, such pieces are relatively heavy and ought to have a permanent position in the room.

Conversation and television viewing. The activities of conversing and of watching television are quite comfortable in the seating mentioned above, but pull-up chairs that give good support are helpful adjuncts. These can have shaped seats of wood, metal, or plastic, or they can be lightly upholstered, webbed, canvas-covered, or they can be Chinese split-cane chairs, which are unbeatable for the price. Whatever the material, pull-up chairs should be easy to get hold of, light to lift, and strong enough to stand frequent moving (Figs. 305A and B and 318A and B).

Eating, working, and games. For eating, working, and games you need sturdy, easily moved chairs with a relatively upright back to keep the sitter alert, a seat and back shaped or lightly padded to lessen pressure, and upholstery that resists abrasion and dirt. The most frequently used family eating place should have enough chairs or built-in seats always ready to seat the family, but it is sensible to have more of the same kind of chairs elsewhere to bring out for large groups. Chairs of this sort can be seen in many illustrations throughout the book.

Tables

The essence of table design is the supporting of a flat slab off the floor; this is reduced to its lowest common denominator when a home craftsman supports a piece of plywood or a flush door on prefabricated, easy-to-attach metal or wood legs—which, by the way, is an inexpensive way to get a good table. There are problems, however, in all table design and these include getting:

- Necessary strength and stability
- Supports out of the way of feet and legs
- Right height, size, and shape for its use
- Durable materials

The typical family needs a variety of tables that differ in use and therefore in size, shape, height, and materials.

Dining tables. Sit-down meals require a table that is stable enough not to be jarred by the unpredictable movements of children or of a man carving meat; that has a top large enough to give each person two feet of elbow room and high enough to give leg room between chair and the lower surface; that

Expandable or stationary, sturdiness and placement of supports are primary considerations in choosing dining tables, as seen on these two pages.

A naturally finished teak table can be folded into an 18-inch-wide rectangle or fully extended into a 64-inch circle. The placement of the supporting legs can be varied to suit the number of place settings. Nvidt and Nielson, designers (*John Stuart Inc.*)

Utterly simple metal supports slide apart to accommodate an extra leaf of a plastic-topped table designed by Florence Knoll. The metal side chairs are designed by Harry Bertoia (*Knoll Associates Inc.*)

A table designed by D. Lee DuSell has slender, elegantly sculptural cast-aluminum supports.

B

has supports out of the way of sitters' feet and knees; and that can be extended in size. Since tablecloths and underpads have become more rare in daily living, it pays to look closely at the durability, ease of maintenance, and beauty of the top surface. Most dining tables are rectangular, because they are harmonious with rectangular rooms, can be pushed snugly against a wall or into a corner, and are slightly less costly to make. In the right place, however, a round or an oval table will give an inimitable friendly group feeling (Fig. 306). Check dining chairs and tables together because often their legs interfere with each other, the heights of the two are not coordinated, or the space between chair and table is insufficient for the sitters' comfort.

Drop-leaf tables (Fig. 306), in use since Elizabethan days, can be quickly and easily expanded or contracted. Add-a-leaf dining tables can be expanded to large size, but they cannot be changed quickly or easily and the leaves require storage space. Some contemporary folding tables can be compacted to 9 inches or stretched to 110 inches (which provides space for 14 people).

Coffee tables. We have come to think that no sofa is complete unless faced with a long, low table on which ashtrays, books, magazines, newspapers, accessories, plants, flowers, and snacks abound. Most coffee tables, though, seem to have been designed only for the long, low, open look—they have no storage space for the little things needed in that part of the room; they are too low to be reached comfortably from the sofa and to give foot room; and if in scale with the sofa, they usually block traffic. The most useful coffee tables are about 20 inches high and have some storage space. Their tops are durable and their supports strong but slender.

End tables. It might be said that the old living room table disintegrated into many little tables, because convenience now seems to demand a table, however small, within easy reach of every chair. Thus you usually find a table at each end of the davenport and probably for each group of chairs. Unlike coffee tables, these end tables seldom interfere with feet and often provide shelves or drawers for supplementary storage. They look better if of the same height as the arms of upholstered davenports and chairs but are more convenient and less a spill hazard if somewhat lower or higher. Often these tables are used for lamps, although a lamp table, strictly speaking, is a little higher. Nests of tables, the top one acting as an end or coffee table, greatly simplify entertaining.

Card and game tables. Seldom handsome, the folding card table is a wonderful invention. Cards and other games are best at tables several inches lower than those for eating, and collapsible card tables are ideal for occasional games, bridge luncheons, buffet suppers, and supplementary serving at festive dinners. Space permitting, a permanent card table with at least two chairs always there is handy equipment for any family liking games, doing homework, or eating away from the dining room.

Kitchen tables. Once banished in the drive for compact efficiency, tables in kitchens or adjacent alcoves are again found to be as useful as our grandmothers knew them to be. Since they often serve for eating and for food preparation, they differ from dining tables only in having greater strength and durability. Not all of them are glaring white and chrome; in fact some have become so friendly that few mind seeing them from the living room.

Desks. The essentials of desks are a suitable surface for writing and convenient and accessible storage for writing materials and papers. That every household needs at least one good writing place is obvious. How large and complex the unit should be and where it is placed depend on the family's habits. A desk can be a table with only one drawer, a compartment in an arrangement of components (Color Fig. 18), or a piece of furniture designed for serious desk work. Spacesaving devices include writing surfaces that fold down and out or slide in and out. A vertical file drawer or two are the most sensible places to store

Small tables are important in contemporary living. They can be simply flat surfaces adequately supported, or they can also provide storage space at point of first use, as seen on these two pages.

A long, low wood and chromium-plated table has a spacesaving lower shelf and drawer. Ico Parisi, designer. (*Singer Cabinet Shops Inc.*)

308

A

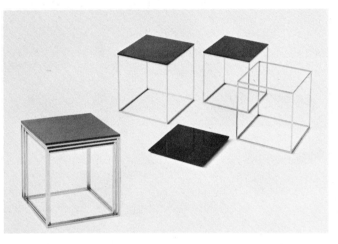

B

C

Above left. A substantial, carved wood base supports a circular marble top to make a notably decorative piece of furniture. (*Weiman Heirloom Quality Furniture*)

Above right. Sewing tables are dual purpose when they have functionally planned drawers and drop leaves. Raising the leaves doubles the length of the top surface. Hans J. Wegner, designer. (*Pacific Overseas Inc.*)

Left. Completely different in every respect from Figure 309A is a nest of three very small cubical tables with slender chromium-plated steel frames and detachable black or white plastic tops. They fit compactly together and are easily moved to where they are needed. Poul Kjaerholm, designer. (*Lunning Design Unit, Georg Jensen Inc.*)

all the pieces of paper related to household operation compactly, conveniently, and accessibly. The file can be part of a desk or purchased separately in units of one to four drawers.

Storage

Storage is a major problem today. Living quarters are smaller and attics, "spare" rooms, basements, barns, and sheds have all but disappeared. More people have more things to put away and apparently have less time in which to do it. Yet we favor the uncluttered look in our homes. An intelligent program is needed:

- Discard things neither used nor enjoyed.
- Cut down on purchases of unnecessary articles, especially bulky ones.
- Plan active storage in terms of criteria listed on page 59.
- Provide as much dead-storage space as needed for seasonal objects of all sizes and shapes. Typical families can use space equivalent to a one-car garage (10 by 20 feet), but it is more convenient if distributed where needed rather than concentrated in one spot.

Functionally planned storage facilities and desks save time and energy.

A

Above. A breakfront secretary was inspired by eighteenth-century forerunners of modern, multipurpose furniture. A leather-lined writing surface folds up when not in use, adjustable shelves adapt the cabinet units to objects of varied sizes and shapes that should be kept dust-free, and drawers hold fabrics and small miscellaneous items. Of beautifully grained mahogany, it is impressive and architectural in size and scale. (*Baker Furniture Company*)

Above right. A simple desk and modified Windsor chair, a flexible lighting fixture, ample built-in storage units, and a couch on casters make the study in the Danish home of architect Eric Stengade efficient and unpretentiously charming. (*Photograph by Andresen*)

Right. Shelves and drawers, racks on the back of closet doors, and a pegboard wall encourage a young lady to keep her possessions conveniently accessible. Another view of this room is shown in Figure 43A. Morgan Stedman, architect. (*Photograph by Maynard L. Parker Modern Photography*)

B

C

Making these dreams come to life means giving at least as much thought to storage in all parts of homes as is typically given to kitchens. Convenience, visibility, accessibility, flexibility, and maintenance are quite pertinent in living rooms and bedrooms. Phonograph records near the player, books convenient to reading chairs, toys where children are supposed to play are but a few examples.

This goes beyond what most of us call furniture and that is precisely what was intended because efficient storage is part of total home design. The least that one should expect is *empty space* for cupboards and chests, and for trunks, baby carriages, bicycles, outdoor furniture, and the like. It is far better if these facilities are *built into* the house (Figs. 310B and C and 314). We store things by standing them on floors or shelves, by hanging them on walls or the backs of doors, or from ceilings, or by putting them in drawers or chests. Which is best depends on the use, size, shape, fragility, and value of the object, but it is provident to take advantage of every inch of available space.

Bookcases. The simplest pieces of furniture are bookcases. Despite the fact that books are manufactured in many different sizes and shapes, easily adjustable shelves can store them conveniently. Books on open shelves are handsome and also absorb noise; but without protection they are not easy to keep clean. Bookcases today usually double as display space, as convenient, safe, and often attractive shelves on which to place objects that have some aesthetic value or interest for us.

Some book and magazine storage can well be used in every room. In kitchens, a single shelf may hold all the household's cookbooks. A few shelves on living room walls or under tables will conveniently hold currently used volumes, but more space is often necessary. Low bookcases double as tables, and if sufficiently long and well planned, unify a wall. They also can reach to the ceiling to become forceful architectural elements (Fig. 310B and Color Fig. 18). They can frame and relate doors and windows or they can be freestanding, partial, or complete dividers between two rooms or parts of one room.

Chests of drawers. Although we take sliding drawers for granted, they were not widely used until the seventeenth century. Chests are best when they have strongly joined, dustproof drawers that slide easily and handles that can be grasped without difficulty. Shallow drawers at the top are a great convenience. Relatively small units that fit together increase flexibility of placement. Drawers either in chests or combined with cupboards are typically used for table linens and silver: shallow drawers with flexible dividers are worth their cost.

Cabinets. Although found infrequently outside kitchens, dining space, and bathrooms, cabinets with doors and adjustable shelves or vertical dividers are welcome in every room. Doors on cabinets beget the same problems as do doors between rooms. Swinging doors work easily and allow narrow storage racks on the back, but they get in the way when open. Sliding doors open only part of the cabinet at a time and give no door-back shelves. Where space in front of cabinets is at a premium or where people move around when doors are open, sliding doors are a good solution, but in other places swinging doors have distinct advantages.

Radio, phonograph, and television cabinets are furniture for which there are no historical precedents. The early ones were overly conspicuous. Nowadays, they are often integrated with other cabinets and bookshelves or are built into the wall (Fig. 324B).

Screens

With a venerable history as ornamental space dividers, screens are especially welcome in open-plan houses or in multipurpose rooms (Fig. 330). They can be moved or adjusted to divide areas into comfortable units without completely shutting out what is beyond. And they can be folded inconspicuously against walls. There are no limits to materials: sheer silk and rice paper, clear or translucent glass and plastics (Fig. 195), tapestry, brocades, and leather, shutters and bamboo poles, curved or flat plywood (Fig. 156A), humble wallboard that can be painted or covered with wallpaper or fabrics. The latter are wonderfully useful for such seasonal or topical displays as Christmas cards, maps, or children's paintings. With these possibilities, screens can be almost as heavy and substantial as walls, actually sliding or folding walls, or they can be light and freestanding. They can be plain or ornamented, the same or different on both sides, harmonious or contrasting with their surroundings.

Outdoor Furniture

Interest in outdoor living has led to many kinds of weather-resistant furniture. There are many good structural materials. Redwood (Fig. 312), cedar, and cypress last long. Aluminum never rusts, stays cool in the sun, and is light in weight. Copper weathers handsomely, and chromium-plated steel is durable.

Outdoor living becomes a pleasure with appropriate furniture, as seen on these two pages.

Chairs, benches, and a table of weather-resistant redwood require little maintenance. A fence and screen define the area. Henry Hill, architect. (*Photograph by Morley Baer*)

A calm and peaceful living room is enlivened by color and by exceptionally handsome furniture. Large areas of light colors in the pale blond carpet, in the round white coffee table, and in the white sofa and draperies increase the apparent spaciousness of the room. The golden-orange draperies, the tan leather cushions, and the radiant metal sculpture introduce sunny colors. The unexpectedly informal terra-cotta sculpture is an earth color. The intense red sofa cushion stands alone. Although basically formal in design and arrangement, the furniture is neither heavy nor rigid in character. (*Knoll Associates Inc.*)

17

18

An architecturally uninteresting room is given a strong focal point by interior designer Albert Herbert, A.I.D., through the use of wall-hung component units designed by Poul Cadovius. Richly-grained teakwood paneling serves as a background and provides the devices that attach a variety of cabinets, hi-fi speakers, a drop-leaf desk, and numerous shelves. The mellow tones of the teak are complemented by the bitter-green painted walls and upholstery on the chairs, the burnished charcoal-brown sofa, and the black fur area rugs. Accents of black and white, red, blue, and yellow sparkle against the dark background colors. The black iron sculpture is starkly silhouetted, and its complex configuration is amplified by the shadows it casts on the green wall. (*System Cado*)

A   B   C

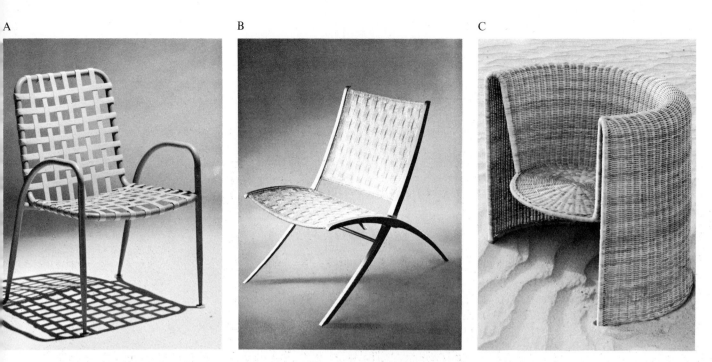

Left. Lightweight, tubular aluminum chairs with resilient synthetic webbing for seats and backs are inexpensive, and are easy to move and maintain. (*The Troy Sunshade Company*)

Center. A modern "gondola" chair from Italy is unusually graceful and refined. Seat and back are of woven cellophane. The anodized aluminum frame comes in satin black or gleaming gold. The chair folds compactly for convenient storage. (*Interiors' Import Company, Inc.*)

Right. Woven rattan molded into a distinctive, humanized shape would bring the warmth of natural materials to an outdoor-living area. Danny Ho Fong, designer. (*Photograph by Richard Gross. California Design/9, Pasadena Art Museum*)

Tables present no special problems; nor do the frames of chairs and chaises. But making upholstery both weatherproof and resilient is not easy. Few if any springs, cushions, and pads remain unharmed by water. The seating most nearly approaching carefree comfort has metal frames with synthetic-webbing seats and backs (Fig. 313A). Then come the wood or metal chairs and lounges with cushions that should not be left out in the rain. With these, it is advisable to have a roofed outdoor-living area (Fig. 24 and Color Fig. 4) or weathertight storage nearby.

BUILT-IN AND UNIT FURNITURE

The first **built-in furniture** may have been a natural rock ledge found in a protected spot and used for sitting or sleeping. It was not, however, until a few centuries ago that furniture integrated with the architectural shell was much used. Even clothes closets were unknown, clothes being stored in bulky wardrobes or chests. In the nineteenth century, home designers began to use walls more intensively. We may no longer care for the elaborate Victorian fireplace mantels loaded with bric-a-brac, but we cannot help admiring the dish cupboards with doors opening into both kitchen and dining room. Early in his career Frank Lloyd Wright began thinking of the house as one unified whole and built storage, seating, and tables as an integral part of the architecture (Fig. 76).

Surprisingly, built-in furniture more often than not promotes flexible living, because such furniture takes less space than movable pieces, thereby leaving

A built-in storage cabinet in a Colonial Georgian dining room at Mount Pleasant, Philadelphia, 1761, is adroitly fitted into the geometrically paneled wall and balances the door at the left of the fireplace. (*Philadelphia Museum of Art*)

the maximum amount of free space in the centers of rooms, as illustrated in Figures 22, 34, 43B, 45A, 46, 70A, 108, 302A, and 314. It also can minimize dust-catching crevices, give a feeling of permanence and security, and break up the boxiness of rooms. At the same time it reduces the visual clutter brought by many isolated pieces of furniture, which have an irritating tendency to get out of their best position.

Like built-in furniture, **unit,** or **component, furniture** answers our desires for coherence and spaciousness. Organizing a variety of storage components into a unified article of furniture is not a new concept, although the flexibility and versatility with which this is now accomplished is. The breakfront secretary (Fig. 310A) meets many kinds of storage needs, but it is a solution designed for a stable, dignified society; it is symmetrical and virtually unchangeable except for adjustable shelves. To answer similar storage needs but for a different kind of living, designer Poul Cadovius evolved a system of components—shelves, cupboards, and drawers—that can be used as ready-made and movable built-in furniture (Color Fig. 18). As shown, the units are hung on individual wall panels and the whole assemblage is attached to a horizontal wall space. But if the owner wishes to use the same storage units in another room or another house, the wall panels can be separated, the units rearranged, new ones added to meet differing needs and other wall shapes.

MATERIALS AND CONSTRUCTION

Grandfather used to say that he could quickly estimate the quality of a man's suit by the way the buttons were sewed on, but there is no quick and easy way to size up furniture materials and construction. Much time and disappointment would be saved if clear and specific labels appeared on each piece or if the manufacturer's specifications were available for each line. Lacking such, you will do well to look at every piece literally from every angle, to get all possible information from the salesman, and to try to purchase from stores that stand behind their merchandise. Furniture is no better than the materials from which it is made, the methods by which it is joined, and the ways in which it is finished. Here are some preliminary tests:

- Does the piece stand firmly on the floor and staunchly resist your efforts to make it wobble? This is particularly important in tables, especially if they are expandable, and in desks and chairs.
- Do all movable parts—drawers, drop leaves—operate easily and steadily?
- Are all joints tightly and smoothly fitted together with some type of interlocking construction?
- Is the finish durable, smooth, and evenly applied? Is it composed of many coats properly dried and rubbed, or of one or two coats that look thick and gummy in any crevice or indentation?

Then look at the places of greatest wear:

Tops of tables, desks, counters, bookcases, cabinets, and chests. Ideally, the tops of pieces of furniture should resist scratching, denting, breaking, staining, and wetting. Properly finished hardwoods are satisfactory if kept reasonably free from liquids. Plastics and plastic finishes on wood are durable, but refinishing is problematical. Linoleum is quiet, but the lighter colors show stains. Vinyl tiles or sheets have all the advantages of linoleum (except low price) plus greater resistance to stains and cuts. Vinyl cork is good to look at and touch, resilient and stain-resistant. Glass is light and airy, a breakage hazard, and needs constant cleaning. And marble is rich, heavy, noisy, and can break and stain.

Edges of tables, doors, and drawers. Edges of pieces of furniture are the surfaces most easily nicked and marred, and all but the most durable materials show wear. Hardwood or replaceable metal or plastic strips help.

Runners of drawers. Hardwood or noncorrosive metals are needed for runners of drawers. Often-used large and heavy drawers should be suspended on rollers and tracks.

Handles, knobs, and hinges. The soil that collects on and around handles and knobs is ample evidence of the use they get. Hardwoods and dull metals are still the most serviceable, but plastics are entering the field. Hinges ought to be of the best possible quality and securely fastened into wood hard enough to hold screws under strain.

Lower part of legs and bases. To be kicked by feet, caressed by mops and brooms, and nuzzled by vacuum cleaners is the preordained fate of the lower part of legs and bases. Reduce to a minimum the parts that touch the floor and then have the necessary ones simple, of medium-dark wood or of metal, with finishes that do not scratch or chip readily.

Seating surfaces, stuffing, and springs are discussed later in the chapter. We now look closer at wood, metal, plastic, and upholstered furniture.

Wood

Wood, the standard furniture material, should be thoroughly dry and of a variety that is stable in size and shape to minimize shrinking, swelling, and warping. Each wood has its own qualities, and the knowing craftsman may combine several kinds in one piece. Structural parts are best when of strong wood, such as ash or birch, but need not take a good finish or be beautiful unless visible. Exposed surfaces ought to wear well, be hard enough to resist scratching and denting, have a pleasant finish, and be beautiful in themselves. Mahogany, walnut, oak, maple, and birch have these qualities. Redwood, on the other hand, has a pleasant color and stands weather, but it is soft and splintery. The advantages of plywood have been stated, and some hard-pressed composition boards have proved their value for tabletops, backs of chests, and parts of drawers.

The way in which wood is joined critically affects the durability and appearance of furniture. Typical joints include, from left to right, *rebated, dovetailed, mortise-and-tenon, tongue-and-groove,* and *butt* joints. (*Matt Kahn*)

Wood in furniture can be joined in a number of ways (Fig. 316):
- **Rebated** or rabbeted joints have a groove cut from the edge of one piece to receive the other member.
- **Dovetailed** joints have flaring tenons (or tongues) on one piece and mortises (or grooves) on the other. They are used in most good drawers.
- **Mortise-and-tenon** joints have a mortise (a hole or cavity) in one piece of wood into which a tenon (projecting piece) cut in the end of the other fits securely. They are usually stronger than doweled joints.
- **Tongue-and-groove** joints are much like mortise-and-tenon joints except that the tongue and groove extend the width of the boards.
- **Doweled** joints have wooden pegs (or dowels) inserted into holes in the two pieces of wood to be joined.
- **Butt** joints are the simplest and the weakest and have no place in furniture unless reinforced with corner blocks.

All joints need glue, and synthetic resins are very much stronger than vegetable or casein glues. Frames of chairs, sofas, and case goods also need triangular wood or metal corner blocks tightly screwed and glued in place for reinforcing. Screws strengthen joints much more than do nails.

Metal

Used since antiquity, metal for furniture is enjoying a new popularity. Mass production has greatly lowered the cost, and designers have found metal uniquely suitable for furniture that is strong and durable but not bulky. Steel with a baked

Thermal assembly is one of the ways that metal furniture may be put together in the future. Predrilled metal bars are heated; then rods of equal section are refrigerated, and then the rods are put into the holes, which contract as the rods expand. The result is a clean, secure joint. George Nelson, designer. (*Chemstrand Company*)

enamel finish is well known in kitchens and bathroom cabinets and, more recently, in indoor-outdoor chairs and tables. It comes in many colors, is easy to wash, and maintains its good appearance if not kicked or banged. Steel is also widely used for legs and frames of chairs, tables, and storage units. The typical rods and tubes or right-angle strips can be handsomely efficient, or they can be merely "blacksmith modern." Rusting quickly, they need a protective surface treatment, and the usual black paint gives many pieces a spidery look. They can, though, be coated with any color, and some metallic enamels have a soft but rich glow. Chromium-plating gives lasting protection and surfaces that range, visually, from glittering hardness to pewter-like mellowness.

Notably different from the "pipe and angle-iron" designs are those based on the sculptural potentialities of metal (Color Fig. 17). In the hands of a sensitive designer steel wire (Fig. 318C) becomes an inspirational, responsive medium for chairs that are both graceful and comfortable. Aluminum, which is lightweight and nonrusting, has also led designers to explore forms that have no association with plumbing shops or forges. Some of the tapering, sculptured pieces (Fig. 313B) are elegant far beyond their cost. Aluminum's natural color is pleasantly sympathetic, but it can be permanently treated with wondrously varied hues.

Metal can be joined by welding, riveting, or bolting. Welding gives smooth, strong joints, but bolts and rivets are satisfactory if you do not mind seeing what holds the pieces together. Most metal furniture is so much stronger than normal household use demands that construction is generally less a problem for the consumer than it is in furniture made of wood. *But* repairs are much more difficult.

Plastics

Man-made materials have affected furniture design and maintenance in two markedly different ways. Most common is the use of durable surfaces—vinyl and laminated melamine sheets for tabletops and counter tops, vinyl upholstery for chairs and sofas—that have greatly extended the range of easily kept colors. More striking is the use of molded plastics for chairs and tables (Fig. 318B and Color Fig. 14). Thin and lightweight, amazingly strong yet slightly resilient, polyester reinforced with Fiberglas can be molded so that the seat, back, and arms of a chair are one continuous piece. The plastic shell, much warmer and pleasanter to touch than metal, can be left as it is, coated with vinyl, or upholstered with foam rubber and fabric. Transparent or translucent plastics, such as Plexiglas, offer designers opportunities for a totally new vocabulary in furniture design (Figs. 145, 196, 219, and 358).

Exciting as these developments are, they are still to be regarded with some caution. There is the possibility of eventual dulling or discoloring, of pitting or scratching, or of breakage. As yet, repair or refinishing runs the short gamut from difficult to impossible.

A

B

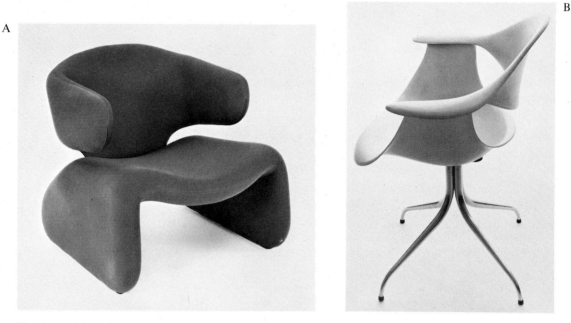

New materials and techniques lead to new forms when approached imaginatively and inventively.

Above left. Designer Olivier Morgue has made use of the tensile strength of tubular steel, the pliancy of rubber webbing and foam rubber, and the stretch properties of one of the new fabrics in designing a chair that is a uniquely personal statement of what a chair might look like. (*George Tanier Inc.*)

Above right. An outspreading Fiberglas shell takes advantage of the infinite shape possibilities of molded plastic in a chair poised airily on four very slender chromium-plated steel legs. George Nelson, designer. (*George Nelson and Company, Inc.*)

C

Right. Resilient steel wire forms the supports and the frame of a lounge chair; molded foam-rubber cushions it; polyester fiber covers it. Shifting optical illusions develop from the spacing of the wires in the base, giving the chair an unexpected buoyancy and visual interest. Warren Platner, architect-designer. (*Knoll Associates Inc.*)

318

A   B

Left. Resilient webbing attached to a wood frame supports contoured foam rubber covered with a textile. (*Fabry Associates, Inc.*)

Right. A strong wood frame of comfortable size and angles plus removable foam-rubber cushions and zippered fabric covers makes an easy-to-maintain chair. (*Jens Risom Design, Inc.*)

Upholstered Furniture

The springs, stuffing, and covering put on chairs and sofas to make them conform to our contours can be of several degrees of comfort.

Fabric stretched over frame. Until the Renaissance, upholstery was chiefly textiles, rushes, or leather stretched over frames and often supplemented by loose cushions. It is still used for lightweight, inexpensive resilience (Figs. 305A and 313A). The frame ought to be attractive as well as strong, the upholstery durable and securely fastened to the frame but easily removable.

Simple padding. Figure 305B illustrates the next step, which consists of thin layers of resilient materials covered with a fabric and secured to the frame. Since the seventeenth century, this has been the standard way of making frequently moved chairs comfortable. Until recently, long, curled hair was the best and the most costly padding, but today rubberized hair and foam rubber are also excellent. Down, kapok, moss, and cotton are moderately satisfactory.

Stuffing and springs Although springs were placed under the stuffing during the eighteenth century, it was not until around 1914 that massively overstuffed pieces came into prominence to raise comfort to a new high and drop beauty to a new low. The materials and steps of this complicated process include:

- *Frame* of strong wood well joined or of metal or plastic
- *Webbing* woven in a simple basket weave and tacked to the frame
- *Springs,* if coiled, tied to the webbing and frame and close enough to prevent sagging but not so close that they rub against one another

- *Burlap* covering the springs, protecting the padding
- *Padding* or *stuffing,* similar to *simple padding,* giving smooth, soft contours
- *Muslin* covering the padding on the better chairs and sofas
- *Final fabric* hiding all

Much simpler is foam rubber on a plywood base or, more comfortably, on webbing (Figs. 319A and B) or firm but thin springs. The last word in complexity—and presumably in comfort—is provided by some "contour chairs," shaped to relax all muscles and equipped with built-in heating, cooling, and vibrating mechanisms.

Upholstery Fabrics

Because fabrics become an integral part, usually the most conspicuous, of the furniture to which they are fastened, and because they are what we most often touch, they deserve attention as *furniture* as well as *fabrics.* The least we might expect is that they look comfortable to sit on, feel good to hands and arms, and resist abrasion and soil. Visual relationship to the shape they cover and the setting in which they are placed lifts them above mere usefulness. Beyond this are fabrics with their own distinctiveness or those used with originality.

Seeing identical pieces of furniture covered with varied fabrics alerts us to the forcefulness of color and design in altering the apparent shape, size, and character of any form (Figs. 320A and B). In rooms with several or many

Upholstery affects the appearance and economy of two almost identical wing chairs, 33 inches wide, 28 inches deep, 50½ inches high. (*Heritage Furniture Company*)

Left. Covered with leather, the chair seems strong and upright. It would need 4 yards, 54 inches wide, of this expensive but very durable, low-maintenance material.

Right. With damask upholstery emphasizing the curves of arms and legs, the chair is slender and delicate and would need at least another 1¼ yds. of material to cover the separate seat cushion—probably quite a bit more in order to center the pattern of this similarly expensive but more fragile textile.

A
B

pieces of upholstered furniture, the whole effect can be changed with different furniture covers. All that we know about the psychological effects of hue and value, emphasis and scale, can be put to use in selecting upholstery. Also our knowledge of fibers, yarns, and weaves is strategic. For upholstery, how does wool compare with cotton, silk, or nylon? In textiles, it pays to look for long fibers and tightly twisted yarns, and for weaves that are tight, because loosely woven textiles snag easily. How do pile weaves compare with flat weaves? Which textiles and patterns contribute to serviceability? Do not overlook materials that are not textiles. Leather has long since earned its place because of its durability and ease of maintenance, its surface pleasant to the touch and to the eye. Today it is challenged by plastic fabrics that are markedly serviceable in hard-wear situations and available in a vast array of colors and textures.

PLANNED BUYING

Without a plan (and by *plan* we mean something that grows and develops, not a static blueprint), acquiring furniture can become as frantic and disordered as Christmas shopping often is. It can be even worse than Christmas shopping because much more money will be spent and we have to live with our purchases. Buying the large essential pieces first, then filling in with the smaller, less costly items is a sensible approach. Over the first two years, it might work out in this way:

First Year	Second Year
Living Room	
Sofa or studio couch	One or two chairs
One easy chair and one pull-up chair	End tables
or two of either type	Desk
Coffee table	Draperies if needed
Rug and curtains	Accessories
Two lamps	
Dining Space	
Table	Two more chairs
Four chairs	Additional storage units
Chest and cabinet for dishes,	if needed
linen, and silver, if not built in	Draperies if needed
Rug and curtains	Accessories
Bedroom(s)	
Springs and mattresses on	Dressing table or bedside tables
legs or frames	Room-sized rug
Chest of drawers for each	Accessories
person	Draperies if needed
Mirror	
One chair	
Lamps	
Area rugs	
Curtains	

Depending on budgets and personalities, it may or may not be wise in the first year to purchase a few really good pieces to have and enjoy, even if that means going without some of the furnishings your friends have. By the third year, things start accumulating, as they will continue to do for many years. It is often wise to put most of the furnishings money away in the third year and perhaps in the fourth so that by the fifth year some of the more temporary pieces can be replaced or relegated to less important areas, and furniture of permanent value purchased.

When buying furniture, keep these points in mind:
- Take your time and watch your budget.
- Buy only what you know you need.
- Keep in mind the total pattern of your furnishings, but also buy only furniture that is good in its own right.
- Express yourself rather than try to impress your friends.

ARRANGING FURNITURE

Furniture arrangement is a matter of coordinating furnishings with both people and architecture, and to do this well we need to consider the alternative ways in which furniture can be placed and the amount of space needed for these placements.

Group-Living Space

The major conversation center is typically the dominant furniture group in the home. (In those homes without family rooms, it may also have to be used for music and television, reading and buffet suppers, although segregating the noisier activities is a boon.) This furniture grouping is best when people can face one another and when the furniture is stabilized in a corner, around a window wall or fireplace, or is built up with eventful furniture and wall treatments. Possibilities for seating arrangements, some of which are illustrated in Figures 322, 323B, and 325A and B, include:
- Chairs and sofa arranged in a circle around a table
- Sofa with a chair or two at each side, all facing a coffee table
- Two sofas facing or one sofa facing two chairs, often at right angles to a fireplace in large rooms
- Two sofas at right angles to each other or one sofa at right angles to two chairs, often in a corner although one unit may project into the room

Major conversation groups are most satisfactory when they are more or less circular in shape and when the maximum distance between people is 8 to 10 feet. Large upholstered chairs are comfortable but space-consuming. Pull-up chairs and sofas takes less space. (*Reprinted from* Architectural Forum. *Copyright* © *1937, Time, Inc.*)

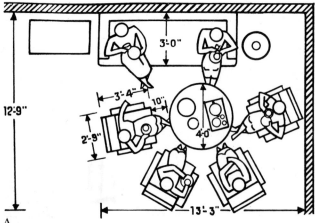

A

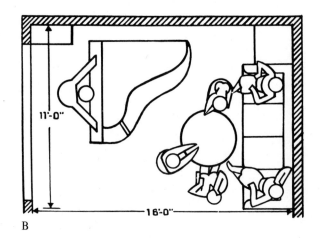

B

A

Above. A room without any architectural center of interest has been furnished in an appropriately flexible, asymmetric fashion. Two easily-moved armless chairs face a large solid sofa that visually balances the painting placed off-center on the wall. Two small benches can be moved for seating or for extra table space where needed. (*Portland Cement Association*)

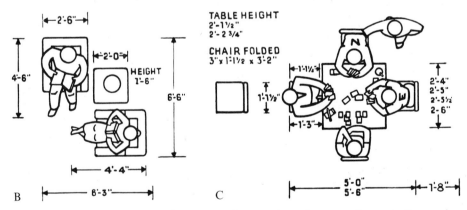

B

C

Left. Secondary conversation or reading groups and a table for games or snacks are useful additions. (*Reprinted from* Architectural Forum, *Copyright* © *1937, Time, Inc.*)

A secondary conversation or reading center often supplements the major group in larger rooms (Figs. 323B and C). It is usually planned for two to four persons and is placed in a minor position. The possibilities include:

- Two chairs, and the necessary table, at right angles to each other
- Two, three, or four chairs (or a love seat or two) facing each other over a table and usually near a window
- Three chairs near a small round table
- Four chairs at the sides of a game or card table

A

Above. A round dining table and four chairs at one end of a large living room would be convenient for reading, conversation, and games as well as for dining. Edward Wormley, designer. (*Dunbar Furniture Corporation*)

Below. Building a television set into a wall arrangement of fireplace, drawers, and cabinets minimizes its bulk, and places it in the right position for viewing from the beds. Richard Neutra, architect. (*Photograph by Julius Shulman*)

B

Television cabinets are conspicuous and often not very attractive, but they have to be placed so as to be easily seen by a number of people:

- Relating a television set to the total design of a fireplace wall often gives an unobstructed view from the major seating group while minimizing the set's bulkiness. It can also be integrated into a storage wall (Fig. 325B).
- A set on casters can be moved into position for viewing, out of sight when not in use.
- Sets on swivel mounts can be placed in walls or cabinets between two rooms where they will serve both.

Radio and phonograph equipment vary tremendously in their importance to different families:

- Small radios and record players can be put almost anywhere but are more satisfactory if integrated with other cabinets.
- Records require convenient storage space, and if the collection is large, a corner of the room or part of one wall can be given over to them.
- Combining equipment and record cabinets with other unit or built-in furniture makes sense.

Pianos are visually large and impressive, and need free space around them for acoustics and people:

- Upright models can be flat against the wall or at right angles to partition a room (Fig. 332).
- Grand pianos are physically large and should not be crowded (Figs. 325A and B). The curved side should face into the room for proper sound dispersion.
- Pianos should be subjected to as little change in temperature as possible, suggesting placement away from windows or heating outlets.

Below. A long, narrow, symmetrical room with two doors presents problems and potentialities. The most serious problem is that of arranging a major conversation group that is relatively free from traffic. Potentialities include zoning the ends for different activities, in this case a music center and an area for quiet reading or desk work. (*Victor Thompson*)

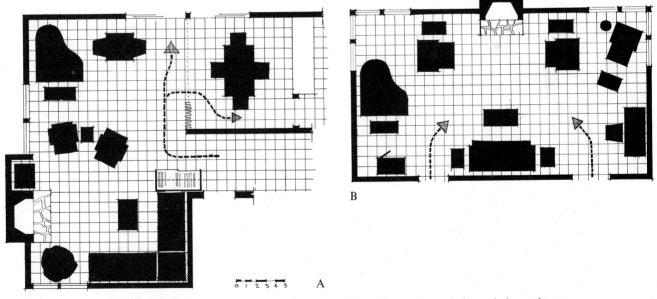

B

0 1 2 3 4 5   A

Above. An L-shaped living-dining space well planned for group living. Two sofas and three chairs make a congenial conversation group around the fireplace and the radio or television at its right. The piano and the card table are appropriately located. The dining space can be opened or closed with a curtain. The excellent circulation pattern enables people to come into the room from the entrance area and proceed to the conversation center, the piano, the card table, the dining space, or the terrace without going through any furniture group. Each square represents 1 foot. (*Victor Thompson*)

Dining Space

Dining tables and chairs or benches, whatever room they are placed in, can be arranged in the ways illustrated in Figure 326:

- A rectangular or round table in the center of a dining room or large kitchen or at one end of the living room increases the importance of meals and simplifies serving.
- A table with one end against a wall takes less floor space and fits into the room architecturally.
- A table and seating, especially built-in, in a corner take minimum space and stay in place, but somewhat complicate getting in and out and also serving the meal.

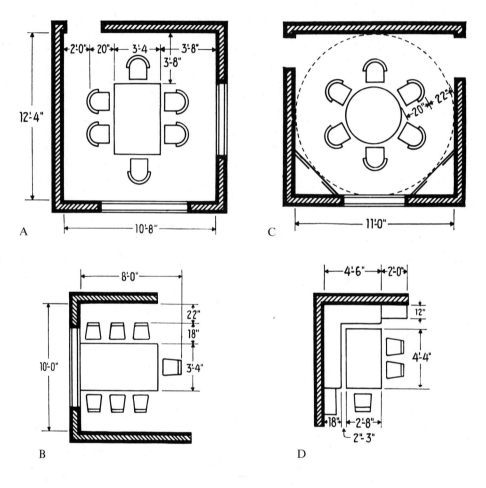

Dining tables can be in the center of the room, in alcoves or corners, or at one end. Space is saved when they are against the wall and seating is built-in; but this complicates getting in and out as well as serving meals. (*Reprinted from* Architectural Forum. *Copyright* © *1937, Time, Inc.*)

Bedrooms

The two major factors in arranging bedroom furniture are that the most-used traffic paths are from the entrance door to the closet and chest of drawers and should be as short and direct as possible, and that beds are large and can be put in only a few places (Figs. 327A, B, and C):

- Beds are usually placed with the heads against a solid wall and with adequate space on three sides.
- Single beds placed broadside against the wall or in a corner give more free space and can double as seating units.

- Double-decker beds really conserve space but are hard to make.
- Chests of drawers are best next to or in closets, near windows if they have mirrors above, or both. Two chests side by side or one double chest save space as well as visually balance the bulk of the bed.
- Drawers combined with cabinets, a dressing table, and possibly a desk will also conserve space (Fig. 324B).
- A dressing table is best placed at right angles to or in front of a window so that adequate light will fall on the face. A dressing table will often fit into the space between two closets (Fig. 46), or it can be combined with one or two washbasins and placed in an alcove.
- A chair placed adjacent to the closet and chest of drawers will complete the dressing center.

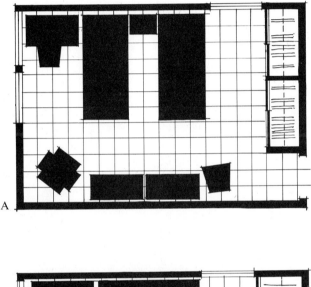

A

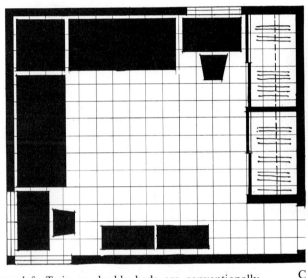

C

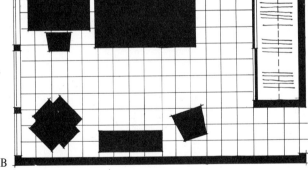

B

Above left. Twin or double beds are conventionally placed with heads against a solid wall. In this plan, the beds do not interfere with the frequent trips from the bedroom door to closets or chests, but they wisely segregate the desk and lounge chair. (*Victor Thompson*)

Above right. Twin beds placed broadside against the walls and in a corner make a bedroom seem larger and offer nicely sequestered space for two desks. This arrangement, however, complicates making the beds. (*Victor Thompson*)

Left. A small bedroom planned and furnished so that it also functions as an individual's retreat. (*Victor Thompson*)

- An easy chair, a lamp, and a small table placed near a window form a pleasant reading spot in a bedroom (Fig. 52A).

Sizes and Shapes of Furniture

Little progress can be made in arranging furniture without knowledge of the size and shape of specific pieces and also of the all-important clearances between pieces of furniture or between furniture and walls for foot room, circulation, and the like. Figure 329 shows typical furniture pieces drawn at a scale of $\frac{1}{4}$ inch equaling 1 foot. The range of sizes and shapes is indicated in the following table.

Furniture Sizes and Clearance Spaces

Living Room

	Small			Large	
	DEPTH	WIDTH		DEPTH	WIDTH
Sofa	2'6"	x 6'	to	3'	x 9'
Love seat	2'6"	x 4'	to	3'	x 5'
Easy chair	2'6"	x 2'4"	to	3'4"	x 3'3"
Pull-up chair	1'6"	x 1'6"	to	2'	x 2'
Coffee table, oblong	1'6"	x 3'	to	3'	x 5'
Coffee table, round	2' diam.		to	4' diam.	
Coffee table, square	2'	x 2'	to	4'	x 4'
End table	1'6"	x 10"	to	3'	x 1'8"
Bridge table	2'6"	x 2'6"	to	3'	x 3'
Flattop desk	1'6"	x 2'8"	to	3'	x 6'
Secretary	1'6"	x 2'8"	to	2'	x 3'6"
Upright piano	2'	x 4'9"	to	2'2"	x 5'10"
Grand piano	5'10"	x 4'10"	to	9'	x 5'2"
Bookcase	10"	x 2'6"	to	1'	x —

Clearances

Traffic path, major	4' to 6'
Traffic path, minor	1'4" to 4'
Foot room between sofa or chair and edge of top of coffee table	1'
Floor space in front of chair or sofa for feet and legs	1'6" to 2'6"
Chair or bench space in front of desk or piano	3'

Dining Room

	Small			Large	
	DEPTH	WIDTH		DEPTH	WIDTH
Table, square	2'6"	x 2'6"	to	5'	x 5'
Table, rectangle	3'	x 5'	to	4'	x 8'
Table, round	2'7" diam.		to	6'4" diam.	
Straight chairs	1'4"	x 1'4"	to	1'8"	x 1'8"
Arm chairs	1'10"	x 1'10"	to	2'	x 2'
Buffet	1'8"	x 4'	to	2'	x 6'
Serving table	1'6"	x 3'	to	2'	x 4'
China cabinet	1'6"	x 3'	to	1'8"	x 4'

Clearances

Space for occupied chairs	1'6" to 1'10"
Space to get into chairs	1'10" to 3'
Traffic path around table and occupied chairs for serving	1'6" to 2'

Bedroom

	Small			Large	
	DEPTH	WIDTH		DEPTH	WIDTH
Twin bed, without head or footboard	6'2"	x 3'3"	to	6'8"	x 3'8"
Full bed, without head or footboard	6'2"	x 4'6"	to	7'	x 6'
Twin bed, head and footboard	6'6"	x 3'3"	to	7'6"	x 3'8"
Full bed, head and footboard	6'6"	x 4'6"	to	7'6"	x 6'
Youth bed	5'9"	x 3'			
Crib	2'	x 4'	to	2'6"	x 4'6"
Night table	1'0"	x 1'3"	to	2'	x 2'
Dresser	1'6"	x 2'6"	to	1'9"	x 5'

Chest	1'4" x 2'6"	to	1'7" x 3'2"
Dressing table	1'6" x 3'4"	to	1'8" x 4'
Bench	1'3" x 1'10"	to	1'6" x 2'
Wardrobe	1'6" x 3'2"	to	1'9" x 4'
Easy chair	2'4" x 2'4"	to	2'8" x 2'8"
Pull-up chair	1'3" x 1'6"	to	1'6" x 1'9"
Chaise longue	2' x 4'	to	2'4" x 5'6"

Clearances

Space for making bed	1'6" to 2'
Space between twin beds	1'6" to 2'4"
Space in front of chest of drawers	3'
Space for dressing	3' to 4' (in both directions)

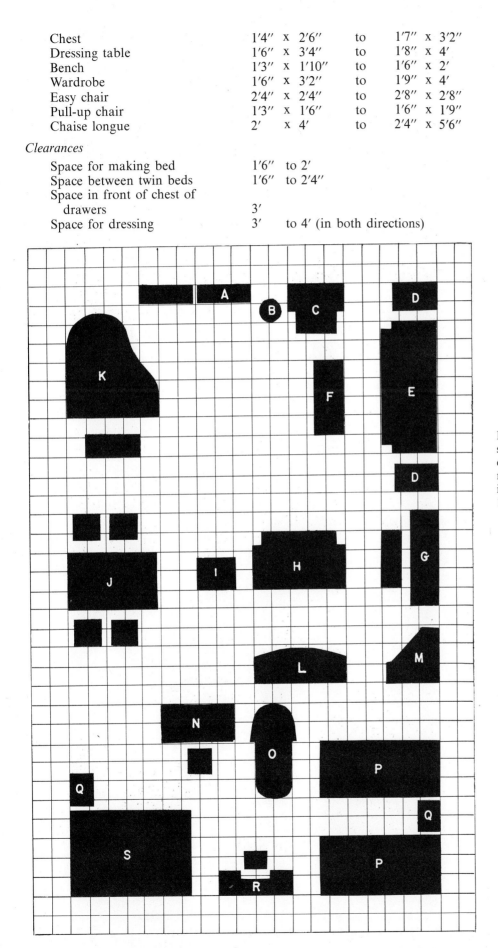

Becoming familiar with furniture sizes and shapes is an important early step in planning arrangements. Each square on this drawing represents 1 foot. (*Victor Thompson*)

329

Arranging Furniture on Paper

To save time and money as well as to avoid disappointments, it is wise to know what you want and how it will fit into your space before buying or attempting to place furniture in the rooms. Planning on paper is worth many times the small effort it takes.

- List all activities you want to provide for, the furnishings and equipment each requires.
- Make accurate drawings of the plan of each room so that $\frac{1}{2}$ or $\frac{1}{4}$ inch represents 1 foot. Cross-section paper helps greatly. First measure total length and breadth of the rooms and draw the major outlines on paper. Then locate doors, windows, fireplaces, radiators or heating vents, jogs, and any built-in features.
- Make cardboard cutouts of your furniture, similar to those in Figure 329 but at the same scale as the drawings of your room. Label each one.
- Put the cutouts on the plan, placing large pieces first and working down in size to accessories. Move them until the arrangement seems best to you. Then check circulation paths by drawing them on the plan.
- Review the arrangement a day or so later and revise if necessary.

Arranging Furniture in a Living-Dining Space

In a New York City brownstone house remodeled for his family, interior architect Joseph Aronson brilliantly demonstrates originality without affectation. The space available for living and dining is long and narrow, lighted only at one end by two windows, and with a fireplace almost centered on one wall. In Figure 330 we can see seventeen pieces of furniture and many accessories

In furnishing the living-dining space of his own house, interior architect Joseph Aronson skillfully solved every problem, including the placement of paintings and decorative objects. (*Photograph by F. S. Lincoln*)

330

ingeniously organized. Immediately apparent is the clear division of this space, by furniture and floor covering alone, into three distinct yet coherent areas. Each was planned in terms of use and beauty with all needed furniture and equipment conveniently and pleasantly placed.

The room is entered (lower left in photograph) from a foyer, which also gives access to the kitchen. A simple dining table, set against the wall to save space, and with four chairs ready for use, is located in the corner. Diagonally opposite is a fifth chair. A triple-purpose cabinet that provides storage space for dining paraphernalia and a table surface for the sofa unobtrusively separates the entrance-dining area from the conversation center. In the room's center is the dominant conversation group, composed of a sofa firmly placed against a solid wall facing the fireplace, an easily moved ottoman, a coffee table, and a lounge chair at a sociable angle. Tables and lamps are convenient to each place where people sit. Beyond is the third group, a subordinate area for conversation or games.

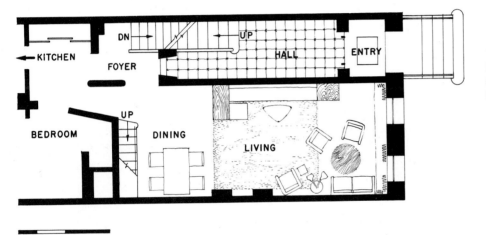

The plan of Joseph Aronson's living-dining space shows how sensibly it has been zoned by furnishings.

Studying this room as a whole, we notice three fundamentals. Space and energy are conserved by placing major pieces in strict relationship to the walls and fitting them as compactly together as their shape and use permits: they are so rightly placed that moving them is seldom if ever necessary. Everything needed for each activity is available and conveniently placed, but there are no unnecessary items. Ample circulation paths are clearly suggested. In short, use and economy were not overlooked.

Nor were beauty and individuality. Singleness of effect amid variety, but no devitalized harmony, is evident. The major pieces of furniture are consonant but not blandly matched, and the arrangement corresponds to their semiformal character. Rectangularity of room and most of the furniture is frankly recognized. Moreover, arrangement carries beyond furniture: the rug aligns with both the sofa and the projecting wall near the fireplace; furniture near the window is appropriately light in character; and within each group the size and scale of furniture, lamps, and accessories are consistent. Variety, needed to keep even the best of ideas from becoming stale, strengthens the unity. Although the large pieces are similar in character, notice that the four small tables and the three lamps are decidedly unlike. Dining table and chest, related in use and shape, are at right angles to the wall while the two sofas are parallel. Sofa and ottoman are covered in glowing red, the lounge chair in copper orange. Paintings, sculpture, and accessories show the family's wide range of interests.

Without being static, the whole room is firmly composed. Parallelism and rectangular shapes, restated many times but with differences, establish the dominant continuity, but when dullness threatens, circles and diagonals come to the rescue with an interplay of contrasts; everywhere, asymmetrical balance implies motion. The conversation group dominates. It is centrally located and defined by the contrasting floor covering. Here are the largest piece of furniture, the sofa, and the most entertaining, the coffee table, with its free-curve glass top showing the sculptural wood supports. Here also is the fireplace, which is the most richly ornamented spot, and the lounge chair, which is the most conspicuous diagonal. As further reinforcement, color intensity and contrast reach their height in this area. But the rest of the room is no monotonous background, for every part has varying degrees of assertion and reticence, minor climaxes and releases, movements and halts.

The living-dining room in Eric Stengade's home has the same delight of consistent freedom shown in his study (Fig. 310B). An upright piano at a right angle to the wall, and a lowered ceiling, differentiate the dining, game, or study space from the living area. The lighting fixture over the table is efficient and attractive. The large wall map is decorative and instructive. (*Photograph by Andresen*)

This is a room in which furnishings have been chosen and arranged to promote the kind of living this family enjoys. It neither overwhelms with an aggressive effort to be different nor follows worn-out formulas. It does not flaunt an "application" of any aims or principles of design, yet it shows a deep personalized understanding of forms expressing their purposes, the coherence of tamed differences, stability teamed with motion, concentration with relaxation of interest. Above all, it conciliates freedom and order.

A "Rabbit-Bird" chair by Thomas Simpson is another example of the fresh approach to furniture design that shows more interest in individualized interpretations than in mass production. Of wood, finished with acrylic paint, it is a whismy that just might be sat upon. (*Photograph by Ferdinand Boesch. The Museum of Contemporary Crafts*)

Crystal and sparkling light are classic partners, as inspiring today as in the past. (*Haasbrock-Sonderburg*)

15 · Lighting, Heating, Ventilation, and Acoustics

Control of illumination, temperature, air movements, and sounds within an architectural shell makes that space comfortably habitable. Only recently have these aspects of the home been given the thought they deserve.

LIGHTING

Light was discussed as a plastic element in Chapter 7 and as a factor in window design in Chapter 12. Now we consider illuminating our homes when daylight is inadequate. Good artificial illumination can:

- Enable us to see quickly and easily
- Prevent accidents, especially at such hazards as stairways
- Protect our health by minimizing eyestrain and by disclosing potentially harmful dirt
- Contribute to the attractiveness of our homes

At night, much of a room's character is determined by its illumination. With light, perhaps even more than with color, we can make rooms seem to shrink or swell, become intimate or formal. Important objects can be spotlighted, those of lesser interest de-emphasized. And with the equipment available today all this can be instantly changed by flicking switches or by turning dimmers.

The architect of the house shown in Figure 335 planned the artificial illumination as an integral part of the building. In the family room and dining room three types of built-in fixtures enable the owners to light the areas as they wish. Over the dining table, a *luminous ceiling* provides even lighting that can be controlled in brightness by a rheostatic dimmer. For a candle-lit dinner the light can be lowered to the merest glow, but if the room is used for a craft or school project, the bright, shadowless light needed for such activities can be obtained by turning a knob. In the area set apart for reading, conversation, or television, the requirements are different. *Floodlights* in the ceiling can be dimmed or brightened as desired. The *eyeball fixtures* that can be swiveled to illumine just the shelves give a lively light-and-shadow pattern. Thus, attention can be focused where desired with precisely controlled emphasis. Although this dominant downward light is excellent as it stands, many persons might want to supplement it with a few portable lamps.

Light-reflecting surfaces contribute to the effectiveness of the illumination. Ceilings are off-white, walls are of light-value plywood or concrete block, and the floor is beige terrazzo. Against this neutral background colorful accents in furnishings range from subtle to vibrant. Mirrors above the built-in cabinets in the dining area reflect the ceiling lights and visually stretch the space. A barbecue on the right wall gives light as soft as glowing charcoal or flames as bright as resinous woods produce. And anticipating the discussion of acoustics, the ceiling is of the sprayed type that absorbs noise.

Lighting fixtures can be integral components of the architectural shell or they can be thoughtfully planned, enriching accents, as seen in the next two figures. (*Photographs by Julius Shulman*)

A luminous ceiling over the dining and food-preparation areas can flood the space with bright light or can be dimmed as much as desired. Fixed and adjustable floodlights and spotlights provide general illumination for the lounge area. Richard J. Neutra, architect.

Hanging opalescent fixtures provide general lighting for both a glass-walled living room and the open terrace beyond it. Another view of this home is shown in Figure 274. Frederick Liebhardt and Eugene Weston, architects.

A different approach is followed in the living room and terrace shown in Figure 336. One part of this high-ceilinged room is open and airy, and extends through a two-story window wall onto a large outdoor terrace. Appropriate to the lighthearted spirit of this space, artificial illumination comes from two regularly spaced lines of floating shell bubbles that give multidirectional opalescent light indoors and outdoors. The other portion is an intimate, lowered conversation area facing the stalwart fireplace. Here the light comes from lamps on tables for reading and the inspiriting light and warmth from the fireplace. The furniture strengthens the mood of each area: low, compact, and built-in for the fireplace areas; generally space-making, lightweight, and movable in the other. Planned in relation to architecture, furnishings, and people, lighting can do far more than merely enable us to see. It is one of the most versatile aspects of home planning and powerfully affects our feelings.

In lighting our homes, we have much to learn from theaters, aquariums, museums, stores, factories, and restaurants. Theaters have long exploited lighting as a vital part of dramatic production. Houselights lower, footlights come on as curtains part, and from then on lights of all colors, brightnesses, degrees of sharpness and diffusion focus attention where wanted and underscore the mood of the play. In aquariums, light is concentrated on the fish, while the spectators have just enough light to let them see around, a practice sometimes followed in museums to rivet attention on a few things. At the opposite extreme are the factories, laboratories, and offices flooded with bright illumination everywhere to step up production. Restaurants range from floodlighted and spotlighted lunchrooms to dark caverns with a candle on each table and gypsy music to reassure or unnerve you, according to your mood.

Types of Lighting

For untold ages man depended on the flames of fireplaces, candles, or lamps to illumine homes at night. Nowadays we seldom depend on flame light except occasionally from candles and fireplaces indoors, barbecues and torches outdoors. Although inefficient, all give a warm, flickering, flattering light that seems hospitable, even festive. Electricity, though, is our major concern, and it produces light in two ways:

- **Incandescent** light is produced by heating any material, but usually metal, to a temperature at which it glows. Typical incandescent bulbs have a tungsten filament in a sealed glass container. A visit to an electric store will show that these bulbs come in many, many types.
- **Luminescence,** or "cold" light, is not produced by heat. *Fluorescence* is the only luminescent light source commonly used in homes. A glass tube with an inside coating of fluorescent powder is filled with vaporized mercury and argon; then the ends are sealed with two cathodes. When electric current activates the gases, invisible ultraviolet rays cause the fluorescent coating to produce visible light. Although fluorescent tubes vary less in size and shape than incandescent, they have a considerable diversity.

Incandescent and fluorescent lighting have these desirable qualities:

Incandescent

Fixtures and bulbs cost less.

There is no flicker or hum and less likelihood of radio or television interference.

Textures and forms are emphasized because the light comes from a relatively small source.

Light is sympathetically warm and "full" because of its orange cast.

Fluorescent

Tubes last about ten times as long, produce three to four times as much light for the current used.

Almost no heat is produced.

Light source is considerably larger, which spreads the light more and produces less glare.

Available in a number of "white" colors, from the blue cast of "Daylight" to the pink of "Natural White."

In terms of purpose and effect, there are two major types of lighting.

General lighting illumines the room more or less uniformly, as the sun illumines the earth. It lets us see all the room in a reassuring way and brings to equal attention the design and color of the whole space. At best, it minimizes

A

A room designed to demonstrate the effects of different kinds of lighting shows how drastically artificial illumination can change appearances. (*General Electric Company*)

Top. Indirect general lighting, when used alone, is often monotonously flat. The white ceiling, which efficiently reflects the light from troughs on two walls, becomes an obtrusive element. Contrasts and accents are needed to avoid the commercial look.

Center. Direct general lighting beamed directly down from ceiling spotlights gives dramatically sharp but harsh contrasts, quite unlike the encompassing illumination in Figure 338A. Shadows are black and heavy, and would not compliment people. The highly questionable design of the lampshades is unfortunately emphasized.

Bottom. Direct and indirect general lighting give a congenial, balanced atmosphere and a satisfying variety in unity. The illumination of the garden visually extends the room and dispels the blackness of uncurtained windows.

B

C

the bulkiness of furniture, the darkness of shadows, and the often harsh contrasts of local lighting. It is most often produced with ceiling fixtures or with lamps having reflector bowls and translucent shades (Figs. 336, 338C, and 347B). It is more truly general when lights concealed in coves evenly illuminate the ceiling or when lighting troughs "wash" large wall areas or curtained windows with light (Fig. 338A). Finally, the entire ceiling or large sections of it can bring light through translucent plastics or glass (335 and 349A).

General lighting can be either *direct* (the light shines directly on objects you want illuminated) or *indirect* (the light is thrown against a surface, usually the ceiling, from which some of it is reflected). Indirect light is usually more pleasantly soft for general illumination than is direct light, but it costs more to operate and may make the reflecting ceilings or walls too dominant. General lighting is monotonously even in effect and seldom bright enough for reading or work. Therefore, it is usually combined with local lighting.

Local lighting provides the kind and amount of illumination needed at specific places for such activities as reading, cooking, sewing, or enjoying paintings (Figs. 335, 346C, and 349B). The light source can be high or low, but eye comfort suggests that it be shielded. Except in kitchens and bathrooms, local-lighting fixtures are most often movable floor or table lamps, but fixtures attached to the wall, ceiling, or major pieces of furniture are far less of a nuisance. A major design factor, local lighting can create moods, emphasize important objects, and bring the visual delights of variety and rhythm.

The **play of brilliants,** seen in recent years only on Christmas trees or in fireworks now that crystal chandeliers (Fig. 334) and candelabra are uncommon, is again being appreciated and in a sense can be considered a third type of lighting. It is produced by fixtures that break the light into many small, bright spots. It can be produced by candles (Fig. 349A), by fixtures with many small bulbs (Fig. 339), or by those in which light comes through many small openings (Figs. 344C, 345C and D, 349A, and 359). A similiar effect is created by focusing a moderately bright light on accessories, wall surfaces, or lamp bases of reflecting materials, especially if they are intricately ornamented. Of high value to the spirit, its contribution is immediately experienced when one enters a room with much sparkling light.

Specific Factors in Lighting

Planned lighting demands attention to brightness, location and size of light sources, direction of light, the color of light and its effect on colors, and the amount of light reflected by colors on ceilings, walls, and floors.

Brightness of light. Our eyes are like fantastic miniature cameras that automatically adjust to different brightnesses. Perhaps their greatest defect is that they do not warn us quickly when they are being strained by ineffective light. Experiments have shown that most people will select as the best the middle of almost any range of brightness they see. If the range is from 10 to 30 footcandles, 20 is most likely to be chosen. When without the observer's knowledge the range is stepped up to from 30 to 100 footcandles, the middle will again be chosen. There is a great difference between 20 and 65 footcandles, but over short periods of time our eyes do not tell us which is better. Many experts, however, agree that the following footcandles are the minimum needed for the activities listed and for general illumination of rooms:

General Lighting	Footcandles
Most rooms	5–10
Kitchen, laundry	10–20

Local Lighting for Activities	
Card playing	10–20
Casual reading, easy sewing, make-up, easy musical scores	20–30
Kitchen, laundry	30–50
Prolonged reading, study, average and machine sewing, difficult musical scores, shaving, benchwork	40–70
Fine sewing, any small detail work	100–200

Note that these are footcandles, the unit of measurement equal to the direct illumination on a surface one foot from one international candle. The wattages necessary to obtain the desired footcandles of light will vary with the distance between light source and surface, the design of the lighting equipment, the amount of reflection from ceiling, floors, and furnishings, and whether incandescent or fluorescent light (which gives three to four times as much light per watt as incandescent) is used. Light meters that measure illumination are widely available.

Although the figures given above are useful for planning the amount of lighting needed for any specific task, the following broad considerations should be kept in mind:

- Bright light is stimulating, calls forth energy, and makes us feel as though we should be up and about.
- Low levels of brightness may seem relaxing and restful, romantic, dingy and depressing, or even frightening, depending on the context.
- Moderately bright light brings no pronounced feeling other than general well-being.
- Balance, rhythm, and emphasis come from appropriate distribution of quantities of light.

Taking these variables into consideration, lighting engineers have made some general recommendations about the placement of light fixtures and the wattage that will provide an adequate amount of light for both general illumination and concentrated light for reading, sewing, and other close work (based on recipes in *See Your Home in a New Light,* Pacific Gas and Electric Company).

Type	*Placement*	*Range of Wattage*
Wall fixtures (incandescent)	At least 66″ above floor.	60–100w every 8′ for general lighting.
Wall fixtures (fluorescent)	Faceboards should be at least 6″ out from wall, and as high in inches as they are in feet from floor, to shield fluorescent tubes.	General lighting—approximately 1′ of channel (10w) for each 15 sq ft of floor area.
Cornice	At edge of ceiling, sheds light down.	Special lighting—approximate width of area to be lighted.
Valance	At least 10″ down from ceiling, sheds light up, down, or both.	
Wall Bracket	50–65″ above floor, sheds light up, down, or both.	
Ceiling fixtures		
Shallow	Centered, symmetrically placed, or placed to illumine special areas.	120–200w in multiple bulbs; 60–80w in multiple tubes.
Recessed	As above.	30–150w bulbs.
Pendant	As above. See "Lamps" when used for reading.	120–180w in multiple bulbs.
Floor lamps (for reading)	Stem of lamp 10″ behind shoulder, **near** rear corner of chair. Bottom of shade 45–48″ above floor.	50/150w–100/300w bulb; 180w in multiple bulbs.
Table lamps (for reading)	Base in line with shoulder, 20″ to left or right of book center. Bottom of shade at eye level when seated, about 40″ above floor.	As above.
Wall lamps (for reading)	42–48″ above floor, 15″ to left or right of book center.	As above.

Glare is to be avoided. It comes from exposed, bright sources of light, incorrectly designed fixtures, too much light, especially from one direction, and excessive contrasts. The contrasting glare and gloom, frequently encountered in night driving and too often in homes, are an eye-fatiguing combination. For close work, the working area should not be more than five times as bright as the darkest part of the room, and a ratio greater than 1 : 10 is undesirable anyplace. But it is also fatiguing—both to the muscles of the eyes and the spirits of the occupants—to have every part of a room equally bright. Moderation in quantity and contrast of light is a sensible solution.

With rheostatic dimmers, brightness of light from almost any fixture can be instantly and smoothly adjusted from a candle-like glow to full brightness. The small cost of these dimmers could, in many instances, be more than made up for by reducing the number of separate fixtures needed without rheostats for varied levels of brightness.

Location and direction. Lighting from above seems normal, accustomed as we are to the sun more or less overhead, while lighting from other places is less expected. Here are some observations:

- Location of both the light source and the surface from which the light is reflected are important in the total effect.
- Light high in the room seems formal, makes us think of standing up and staying on our best behavior.
- Light below eye level seems friendly and draws people together. It is also useful while watching television.
- Light from near the floor flatters people, as do theater footlights. It is also a good safety device near steps and in halls, and is a refreshing surprise.
- Light from a number of sources, or well-diffused light, makes a room seem luminous rather than merely lighted, tends to spread interest throughout the room, and is comfortably undemanding (Figs. 342 and 349A).
- Strongly directed light, such as comes from one or two spotlights, is dramatic, emphatic, and often harsh. Our attention tends to follow its path—up, down, sideways, or diagonally—much as it does a solid form (Fig. 342).
- Light for working should illumine the task without distracting shadows and should not shine in the worker's eyes.

A small pool of light creates an intimate, isolated, or lonely mood, separating one area from darker parts of the room. Many pools of light plus illumination on walls and ceilings make a room seem social and festive. (*Reprinted from An Investigation of the Small House. Copyright © 1957, School of Architecture, Pratt Institute*)

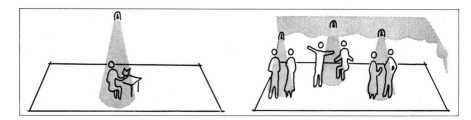

Size of light source. Much depends on the size of the light source. Compare the luminous vault of the sky by day with its myriad play of brilliants at night.

- Broad sources of light—the sky, a skylight or an illuminated ceiling, and a window wall—give flat, glareless, uneventful light excellent for seeing, health, and safety because they minimize contrasts and shadows. Decoratively, though, they can be monotonous.
- Smaller light sources that diffuse light broadly through lenses, translucent shades, or reflectors approximate this effect.
- Very small light sources, especially if bright, have high accent value, emphasize parts of rooms, and make silver and glass sparkle, but they can be visually fatiguing and unless carefully used cause spottiness.

Color of light. We have always been timid about using colored illumination in our homes, perhaps quite rightly because it is difficult and expensive. The color of light is determined by three factors: the light source, the diffusing or reflecting shade, and the room surfaces.

- White light shows colors as they are and has no pronounced emotional effect other than the important sense of normal well-being.
- Warm light flatters people, dispels the chill associated with darkness, and brightens warm colors but deadens blues and purples.
- Cool light makes rooms more spacious, separates objects one from another —and may make people look cadaverous.
- Warm and cool light add variety but should be thoughtfully combined.

Effect of colors on amount of light reflected. No surface in the home reflects or absorbs all the light that hits it; but high-value colors reflect a high percentage, and low-value colors reflect little. Listed below are the percentages of light reflected by some of the common colors. Clearly, white gives the most light for the money paid to the electric company, and black gives the least.

Color	Percentage of Light Reflected	Color	Percentage of Light Reflected
White	89	Buff	63
Ivory	87	Pale green	59
Canary yellow	77	Shell pink	55
Cream	77	Olive tan	43
Orchid	67	Forest green	22
Cream gray	66	Coconut brown	16
Sky blue	65	Black	2

LIGHTING FIXTURES

Ideal fixtures give us the kind and amount of light wanted and where it is wanted (use). They balance original cost with the electricity they use, the ease with which they are cleaned and bulbs are replaced, and the space they take (economy). They contribute to the aesthetic qualities of our homes (beauty). And they underline or create the distinctive character that we seek (individuality). Almost inevitably they contrast with other furnishings because they are quite different in purpose. This suggests that *some of them* be purposefully chosen as accents. In general, though, it is sensible to have most fixtures appropriate in size, scale, and character to the rooms and other furnishings. As with fabrics, lighting fixtures can set up their own pattern of design running through the entire home.

Fixtures today come in bewildering diversity, but the light sources fall into three basic shapes. They can be **lines,** as in fluorescent tubes or in long lighting valances and cornices that lead the eyes in a strongly directional movement and that wash the ceiling, wall, or draperies with light (Fig. 338A). They can also be **spots.** If large, these are like little suns, radiating light in many directions (Fig. 336); if small, as in candles, they are like sparks or stars. Whatever the size, they tend to become more or less static centers of attention. There are also broad **planes** that light large areas evenly (Fig. 335).

Architectural and Built-in Lighting

A

As with built-in furniture, built-in lighting assures us that lighting was not an afterthought. It contributes to the home's total unity and can produce unique effects. The large ceiling panels in Figure 335 illustrate a trend toward illumination from large surfaces of low brightness. These, together with the valances mentioned in the preceding paragraph, can be important parts of the whole architectural concept of a house. A few of the many other possibilities are shown in Figures 349A and B. Closely allied to truly architectural lighting are the many mass-produced fixtures that are set into or attached to ceilings and walls.

Ceiling fixtures, once banished from consideration, have staged a healthy comeback through vastly improved design (Figs. 344A, B, and C). Their possible relation to the ceiling plane is similar to that of fireplaces to walls. Some are inconspicuously recessed in the ceiling or are flush with it (Fig. 335), and the light can be softened with louvers or diffused with lenses. Shallow glass or plastic bowls, dropped a few inches, reflect light from the ceiling and diffuse light through the bowl. They can also direct a pool of light downward, making them an inexpensive, three-in-one way to light space for eating, hobbies, or homework. Others are dropped well below the ceiling, as illustrated in Figures 336 and 344A. Those adjustable in height (Fig. 349B) and also in position give welcome flexibility and facilitate maintenance. Adjustable spotlights and floodlights, now available with shades in many sizes, shapes, and materials, can be turned on work areas or visual centers of interest for direct light or on walls or ceilings for reflected light.

Ceiling fixtures can send light directly downward or upward as well as diffuse it. They are available in a multiplicity of shapes, sizes, colors, and materials.

Below left. "Plexima" is a refreshingly inventive hanging lamp that was inspired by the ways in which some contemporary sculptors manipulate new materials. The fins of notched acrylite strung with nylon cord refract the light in intriguing patterns and subdue the glare of the bulb. (*Paul Secon, Inc.*)

Below right. "Metalites" create dramatic patterns of light, diffused by a polyethylene cylinder and filtered through intricately arranged metal plates in satin brass, chromium, or white finish. Two-circuit wiring makes it possible to have individual control of indirect light from the cylinder and downward flood lighting. George Nelson, designer. (*Howard Miller Clock Company*)

Above. The top and center fixtures have opaque shades that reflect and diffuse light downward and outward from bulbs placed directly below them. The other three have translucent shades to diffuse the light in many directions, but they also direct some light upward or downward through openings in the shade. (*Ledlin Lighting Company*)

344

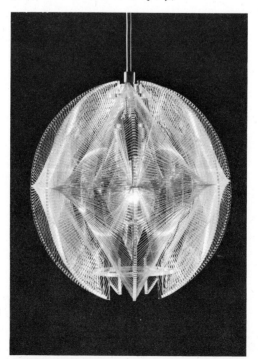

B

C

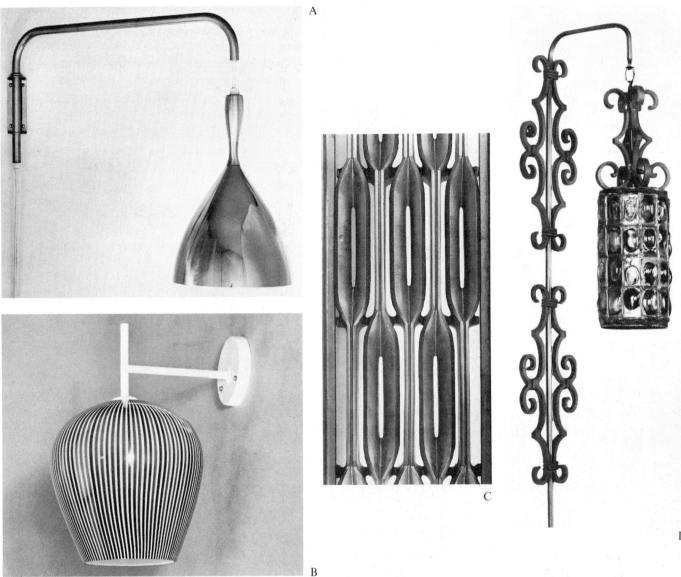

A

C

B

D

Wall fixtures of many types are accessible yet out of the way. They can be primarily utilitarian or decorative, or they can combine these functions. Some are pinups; others are mounted on, or set into, the wall.

Top left. A swing-arm lamp of polished brass can be attached to the wall where needed and raised or lowered to the desired height. All parts—especially the shade—are simple but beautifully shaped. (*Georg Jensen Inc.*)

Above left. Handmade Venetian glass shades in brilliant colors make lamps eventful exclamation points. Paolo Venini, designer. (*Photograph by Kalman J. Chany. Altamira*)

Above center. A cast-aluminum and frosted-glass fixture, designed by Malcolm Leland, stands a few inches away from the wall, allowing the light to "wash" the wall on all sides and to come through the grille. It can also be mounted on the ceiling. (*Photograph by Richard Gross. California Design/9, Pasadena Art Museum*)

Above right. Inspired by Spanish metalwork, a wrought-iron fixture has a shade with many colored blown-glass bubbles that glow and sparkle when the lamp is lighted. (*Beth Weissman Company*)

Wall fixtures (Figs. 345A through D), like ceiling fixtures, were once popular, fell from favor, and are now back in style. It is true that once in a while they interfere with hanging pictures or with changes in furniture arrangement, unless they are of the pinup kind, but they are out of the way and free the table and desk surfaces for other things.

Portable Lamps

Floor and table lamps can be moved when and where needed, and they can be lively decorative accessories. In some instances, those that are unornamented and inconspicuous seem best—but genuinely handsome, decorative lamps can greatly enrich a room at the same time that they provide light. A beautiful piece of ceramic or glass, or a richly modeled work of metal, profits from light above it. So does some sculpture, such as the table lamp in Figure 20B, provided the sculpture is worth lighting and is appropriate to its setting. Unfortunately, good lamps of these kinds are expensive and hard to find. The plethora of "cute" little lamps and large "decorative" concoctions (see Fig. 338) seen in many stores and, even worse, in front of large windows are typically as ugly as they are inefficient.

Floor lamps are portable and versatile, and add a vertical element to a room.

Below. An arm that swings from a horizontal to a vertical position and a shade that swivels to direct the light in any direction add up to unusual flexibility. (*Hosmer Lamps*)

Below left. Two floor lamps designed to diffuse light through plastic shades have a sculptural quality that makes them interesting whether lighted or not. *Left.* Sesto Chiarello's design has a truncated ovoid shade and a slender aluminum base. *Right.* Ben Gurule's freestanding column of light has a strong architectural quality. The center hanging fixture, also by Ben Gurule, was created by joining together a multiplity of rectangles by applying diagonal stress. (*Photograph by Richard Gross. California Design/9, Pasadena Art Museum*)

Below right. Pole lamps, wedged tightly between floor and ceiling wherever one wishes them, are versatile. The top reflector floods the ceiling; the second illumines the paintings; the third diffuses light for reading; and the bottom one washes the wall with light. (*Reprinted from* Better Homes & Gardens)

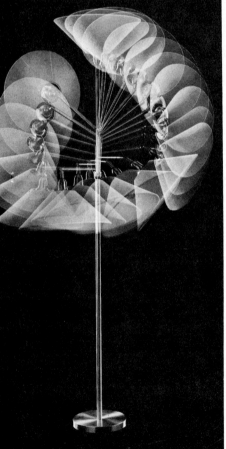

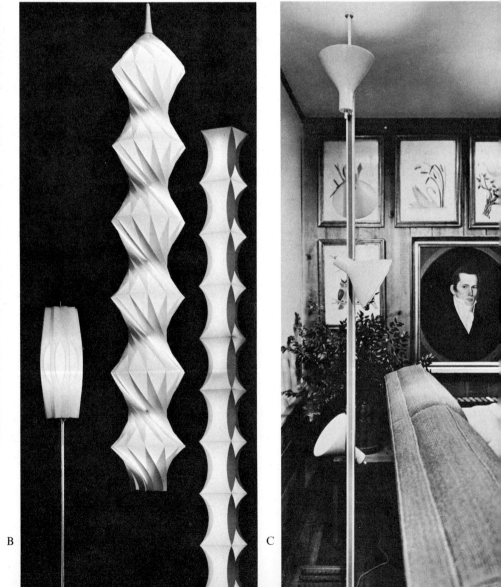

346

A

B

C

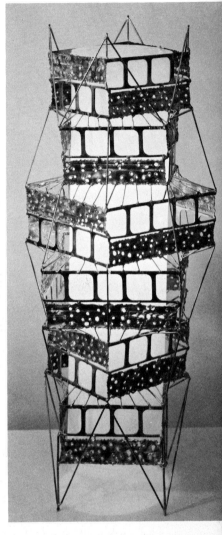

Table lamps come in great variety, each of which has its own special character.

Above. "Stemlights," designed by Bill Curry, have opal-glass shades ranging from the sensuous flattened sphere to the upright cylinder. Bases are of baked enamel in many colors, of Swedish brass, of brushed aluminum, of polished chrome, or of iron. They provide a soft glow rather than the more intense light needed for reading. (*Photograph by Richard Gross. California Design/9, Pasadena Art Museum*)

Left. A seemingly simple table lamp is distinguished by the sensitive shaping and proportioning of the wood base. The textured fabric shade complements the base. Torben Strandgaard, designer. (*Hagen and Strandgaard, Inc.*)

B

Above. A custom-designed lamp by Leo Jensen has a column of light suspended within a cage of pierced and sculptured plates of welded bronze. (*Virginia Frankel Gallery*)

Base and shade, although different in function and usually in material, are parts of one visual unit. This suggests a fundamental agreement between the two, some qualities in common but seldom exact repetition. Pages 346 and 347 illustrate a few of the ways in which variety in unity can be achieved. **Shapes** of lamps ought to grow from their functions: the base supports the bulbs and shade; the shade shields our eyes from glare, directs and diffuses the light. But materials also play a determining role. The simplest base is a cylinder with a foot large enough for stability—breadth is more important than weight in keeping a lamp upright. If the support is of metal or wood, it can be more slender than if of clay or glass. All can be plain for simplicity of effect and maintenance, ornamented for concentrated interest.

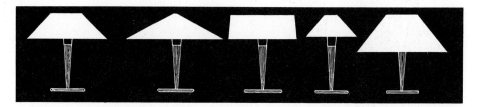

At the far left is a lamp whose shade and base are pleasantly compatible. A slightly broader, pointed cone gives a more energetic effect. A rectangular shade results in a blocky appearance, satisfactory if this character is wanted. A shade that is too small makes the lamp look pinheaded, while one that is too large produces a droopy, top-heavy feeling. (*Matt Kahn*)

Shades are usually drums or truncated cones to spread the light downward and often upward, too, and these can be tall and steep for concentration or low and wide for dispersion. Shades, of course, can be rectangular or triangular; but rounded forms seem more congenial to light, and we welcome the few curves we can sensibly get in our homes.

Size is determined by illumination requirements together with the size of the room and its furnishings. High lamps with large spreading shades illumine large areas and are in scale with large furniture; "overscaled" lamps can be dramatic focal points, but unless sensitively used seem to crowd small space. The more lamps in a room, the smaller each can be; but too many small lamps are cluttering.

Color is important, especially in translucent shades but also in the whole ensemble, because lamps when lighted are very conspicuous. Liking warm artificial light, most of us rule out blue, green, or violet shades of translucent materials, but in some rooms these colors may be desirable in opaque materials. Bases can be in any color needed in the room.

Lighting for Activities

Effective lighting has these characteristics:
- Sufficient, glareless light where needed for close work
- Adequate, pleasant general illumination to reduce fatiguing contrasts
- Good illumination at danger points
- An overall pattern that is rhythmic and balanced, and that shows to advantage what is considered important

In designing a home or revising the furnishings of a room, it pays to draw a plan with furniture arrangements. Next indicate where local illumination is needed. Then think about what kinds of general and accent lighting are wanted in relation to the character of the room, the colors, and the textures of all surfaces.

Entrance areas benefit from friendly, welcoming illumination as a transition from the dark outside to the brightness of the living room, to let guests and hosts see one another in a pleasant light as an introduction to the home. Diffused light from ceiling or wall fixtures, perhaps supplemented by more concentrated, sparkling light on some object of interest, makes a balanced effect.

Living rooms and **family rooms** need general illumination, preferably both direct and indirect, to bring walls and furniture, floors and ceilings into soft visibility. Flexibly controlled, direct light is requisite where people read or sew, play games, or do homework. And some scintillating light adds animation.

Dining spaces deserve primary emphasis on what is most important—the table and the people around it. If some light is directed downward, silver and glass, dishes and food sparkle. Indirectly diffused light lessens glare and unbecoming shadows. That there are no rigid rules is shown in Figures 349A and B.

A

B

Illuminating space and tables is a challenge that can be met with many alternatives.

Above. In an open-plan house emphasizing large simple planes of varied materials, a wood grille is appropriate in scale and character. Faceted into many small spots, the light would make silver and glass scintillate. Alden Dow, architect. (*Photograph by Bill Hedrich, Hedrich-Blessing*)

Left. In an old remodeled farmhouse, illumination from an adjustable ceiling fixture is supplemented and balanced by concealed lighting in the cabinet and at the window. Eugene and Olive Stephenson, designers. (*Photograph by Lisanti Inc. Reprinted from* Better Homes & Gardens)

349

Kitchens need good light directed onto work centers and eating table plus a fairly high level of general illumination. Ceiling lights are almost indispensable, plus bands of light at strategic points (Fig. 61). Kitchens are usually the best-illuminated rooms in the house: much thought has been given to them, and we are likely to think in straightforward terms about this room.

Bathrooms need lights near the mirror to give shadowless illumination to a person's face. This is best achieved by bands of light on all sides of the mirror, next by lights on two sides or above and below. General illumination from a ceiling fixture or two is needed to light the rest of the room.

Bedrooms merit light for dressing, reading in bed, and such activities as desk work, reading, or sewing. Direct-indirect lights over the bed, reading chairs, desks and chests of drawers, and direct lights near mirrors may be all that is needed, but some general lighting is usually advisable.

Halls require some overall lighting, which can come from ceiling (Fig. 275A) or wall fixtures that send glare-free light downward. The fixtures can also be near the floor, as in theaters—the floor is what one needs to see, and it is fun for a change to have light low in the room. Ornamental, colorful fixtures dispel the dullness of most halls.

Stairways are hazardous. Accidents are lessened if the light clearly differentiates the treads from the risers. Ceiling or wall fixtures that send even, glare-free light downward do this well. Spotty or distracting lighting is dangerous.

Exterior lighting is typically slighted. The minimum—seldom met—is illuminating the entrance of the house so that it can be recognized and the house number so that it can be read from the street. It is better when both visitor and host can see each other in a good light at the entrance.

Terraces, patios, and gardens can be enjoyed at night if they are lighted. This has become especially important with window walls and with landscape design that is integrated with the house (Figs. 292 and 336). Seen from inside, lighted outdoor areas greatly increase the apparent size of the interior, lighten the windows, and bring a little illumination into the house. Typical solutions are weatherproof fixtures mounted on exterior walls or overhanging roofs. More elaborate installations have spotlights and floodlights that are concealed in the landscape.

Switches and Outlets

Every room in the house needs a light switch beside any door by which you enter or leave it. Stairs need switches at top and bottom, halls at both ends. Moreover, the switches ought to turn on the lights usually needed in that room. Outlets for lamps and appliances should be in every wall space 3 or more feet wide that is separated from other walls by doors or floor-length windows. On long walls, two or more outlets are often needed to lessen the hazards of long cords.

- Switches controlling bed lamps should be within *easy* reach of a person lying on the bed.
- Switches for outdoor lighting are most convenient if inside the house.
- Some outlets are more convenient if they are at about table height: near ironing boards for electric irons; near dining tables for toasters, coffee pots, and so on; along the back of kitchen counter space for appliances used there; near sewing centers for sewing machines; and in back of electric

dryers and washers. Men appreciate outlets conveniently placed for electric shavers and, in workshops, for electric tools.

Many people find outdoor outlets desirable for electrically operated barbecues, portable lighting, or Christmas decorations.

It is relatively easy to get sufficient light on work surfaces to avoid eyestrain and to get some kind of general illumination. To achieve completely satisfying illumination in the whole house takes thoughtful planning, but our eyes and spirits deserve artificial illumination that is efficient and delightful.

Comfortable temperatures are the result of house orientation and design as well as of mechanical equipment. *Left.* This is the ideal orientation for typical sites in the northeastern United States. *Center.* In summer, all surfaces possible should be shaded by trees. *Right.* Shielding glass by overhanging roofs and sunshades reduces heat gain 70 percent. (*Reprinted from* An Investigation of the Small House. *Copyright © 1957, School of Architecture, Pratt Institute*)

HEATING AND COOLING

Our great-grandparents would be astonished at our assumption that central heating should be built into most homes, for they typically depended on stoves and fireplaces for warmth. Our grandchildren may, in turn, wonder why we paid so little heed to the proved fact that all-year comfort is a matter of house orientation and design, of materials and construction as well as of mechanical equipment.

Artificial Heating

Heating and cooling systems are complicated mechanically. Even more complex is getting the best system for a specific house. Only experts should be trusted with its planning, but a householder benefits from knowing a few basic facts and principles:
- Artificial heat for homes is produced by
    Heating air in a warm-air furnace
    Heating water in a boiler
    Sending electricity through a resistant conductor, as in toasters
- Heat is brought to our living space through
    Registers emitting warmed air
    Radiators that are comparatively small, high-temperature units or long units along baseboard or ceiling
    Radiant panels that are large, low-temperature surfaces
- Heat, then, affects us and our homes by
    Conduction through solid matter, either continuous or in close contact, as when our feet are warmed by a warm floor
    Convection, or moving currents of air, as when the warm air blown from a register decreases the heat loss of our bodies
    Radiation, when heat jumps from one solid to another without making the air uncomfortably hot and stuffy, as in infrared heating lamps.

Only a few years ago we could have written that there were two types of central heating: warm air and hot water or steam, produced in a basement furnace and kept in circulation by gravity. A major improvement came with fans and blowers to force warm air into rooms and cold air out, and pumps to push steam or hot water through radiators. With these mechanical substitutes for gravity, furnaces no longer had to be in basements—and the centrally heated, basementless house became practical. Such a house also gave better circulation of heat. At about the same time, oil, gas, and electricity began to take the place of wood and coal, and thermostats were introduced to keep the temperature about where we wanted it. Then an old concept of heating large surfaces of rooms to relatively low temperatures, used by the Romans, was revived in the reintroduction of radiant-panel heating. The general characteristics of different systems can best be understood if they are grouped in terms of the way heat is brought into our rooms.

Registers. Those systems that convect air warmed in a furnace into rooms through registers, give quick heat, and are moderately low in initial cost are called registers. The moving air, which can be cleaned and humidified or dehumidified, dispels stuffiness and tempers moisture content. Since the same ducts and registers can be used for cooling, the cost of air-conditioning is lowered.

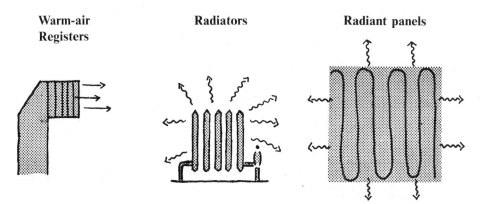

| Warm-air Registers | Radiators | Radiant panels |

Warm-air registers, hot-water or steam radiators, and radiant panels heat our homes artificially. (*Reprinted from* An Investigation of the Small House. *Copyright © 1957, School of Architecture, Pratt Institute*)

The registers, though, may interfere with furniture arrangement and, except in the best installations, temperatures may fluctuate noticeably and the air may seem uncomfortably hot at times. Registers can be of the conventional type set in floors or walls, or they can be long, low baseboard units. The latter, usually along exterior walls, keep temperatures quite uniform.

Radiators. Hot water or steam circulated through radiators gives relatively uniform temperatures, although rooms cannot be so quickly heated or cooled as with registers. Usually more expensive to install, they give no control of the air other than temperature. Radiators unobtrusively fitted into baseboards have gained favor over the old, unsightly, space-consuming type.

Radiant panels. Water or air heated in a furnace or wires that transform electricity into heat can bring floors, ceilings, or walls to warm temperatures, which in turn radiate heat to us and our furniture. They keep us, the architectural shell, and our furnishings pleasantly and uniformly warm while the air stays relatively cool. The complete absence of registers or radiators is a blessing. Radiant panels are rather expensive to install but not to operate, and they require good insulation. Some types, notably hot-water pipes in concrete floors, do not respond so quickly to temperature changes outside as do those using warm air or electricity.

The preceding are the typical "single" systems, but there is a definite trend toward combinations. For example, warm air circulated under the floor and then into the room through registers gives quick responsiveness and uniformity. Hot water can also heat the floor, as well as radiators located at normally cold spots. Then there are the small units, individually heated by gas or electricity and usually placed in walls, which may be all that is needed in mild climates and can effectively supplement central systems in any geographical location.

Artificial Cooling

Home air-conditioning has come to be regarded in many parts of the country as almost a necessity, because excessively high temperatures and humidity are enervating. Operating on the same principle as mechanical refrigerators, air-conditioners take heat and moisture from the air, keep clean air in motion, reduce housecleaning, and tend to keep families happily at home. Central cooling systems (often combined with heating) have many points of superiority over room-size units. It is reported that average homes can have cooling systems installed for about half the cost of a new car, and that the cost of operating them for an hour is equivalent to that of driving an automobile one and one-half miles. As with heating, this is a field in which amateurs can make costly mistakes.

Natural Heating and Cooling

Egyptians and Romans, Eskimos and South Sea Islanders adapted their homes to their climates with an efficiency that should make many of us blush with shame. Even the best-engineered heating and cooling systems cannot give economical comfort in houses designed *against* their physical environment. Windows come to mind first, and as mentioned in Chapter 12, well-oriented glass areas reduce fuel bills. In a Minneapolis house with glass concentrated toward the south, these facts were observed one sunny winter Sunday. Outside temperature hovered around zero; directly inside the south window wall it was nearly 100°, while the rest of the house stayed at 70° with no help from the furnace until the sun set. Heat loss at night and gain during the day were minimized with double-glazing and with insulated walls and roof. Precisely designed overhangs kept summer sun off the glass.

Climate designing varies from one section of the country to another; it can even vary on sites only a few hundred feet apart because of differences in elevation, the presence of trees or bodies of water. In some areas, summer cooling is the big problem, in others it is winter heating. Sometimes it is both, while in a few areas neither heat nor cold is extreme. Although there are a few fairly safe rules of thumb—keep large areas of glass on the south is one—the wise architect studies the general and local climate as carefully as he does the family who will live in the house. Perhaps he should give the climate more thought, for the house is less likely to move than the family.

Putting the sun to work, scientifically, has led to quite new concepts of overall house design and goes far beyond orientation of windows and solid walls. Some of the results are quite startling, not because the designers sought to be "different," but because this aspect of architecture concentrates on different design factors (Fig. 354).

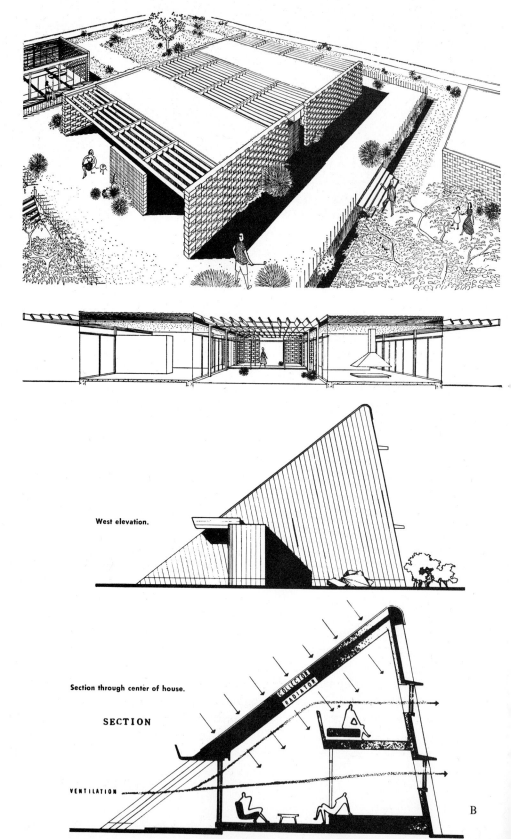

Peter Lee's prize-winning design of a solar house for an Arizona site separates group living from private living with a breezeway. Exterior walls are decorative insulating masonry. The three terraces are roofed with plate-type, water-circulating heat collectors in the form of louvers that provide shade in the summer and collect heat in the winter. (*Reprinted from* Sun at Work)

In a house designed for central Japan, a flat-surfaced heat-collecting roof facing south at a 52-degree angle warms water stored in a reservoir and used as needed to keep the house warm. The drawing at the right is an exterior side elevation; the one below it is a section through the house. (*Reprinted from* Sun at Work)

West elevation.

Section through center of house.

SECTION

COLLECTOR

RADIATOR

VENTILATION

354

B

Double-glazed windows pay big dividends in extreme climates. Moisture condensation on the window at the right comes from warm air hitting cold glass. Two panes of glass in the other window keep cold out, warmth in, and the window free from moisture. (*Pittsburgh Plate Glass Company*)

Insulation

The materials in the house shell, and the way they are put together, are basic factors in insulation. Generally speaking, dense and uniform materials, such as metal and glass, conduct heat and cold readily, while such porous substances as wood or lightweight-aggregate concrete blocks are poor conductors —that is, good insulators. Most houses, regardless of material, need additional insulation. Many heat-cold insulating materials, from sawdust to spun glass, are porous, and it is the air imprisoned in small spaces that makes them effective. Another type is a thin coating of shiny, heat-reflecting metal mounted on heavy paper.

The economies of thermal insulation are startling, and the increased comfort is remarkable:

- Roofs get up to twice as much radiant heat in summer as do walls, and uninsulated flat roofs transmit 25 to 50 percent more heat than pitched roofs. Proper insulation can reduce heat gain in summer and heat loss in winter up to 90 percent. Shade from trees can lower roof temperatures as much as 60 degrees.
- Wall insulation can lessen heat loss by about 60 percent. Protection from cold winter winds and hot summer sun are also significant factors.
- Windows with single glass transmit up to 35 times as much radiant heat in summer, and 10 times as much in winter, as insulated walls. Double-glazing is reported to reduce heat gain and loss from 45 to 60 percent, and weather-stripping eliminates about 70 percent of the heat loss through leakage. One hundred feet of unshaded east or west glass requires an additional ton of air-conditioning at a cost of from $300 to $800.

In planning for year-round thermal comfort, attention should be centered on three interrelated phases of house design: orientation of the house, especially major rooms and large areas of glass; materials and construction plus insulation; and mechanical equipment. Because the whole matter is full of pitfalls for the layman, get acquainted with the fundamentals but leave the technicalities to trustworthy experts.

Some factors we can deal with, however, are those related to color, texture, and form. Recollect that color can, by looking warm or cool, noticeably affect our sensation of physical temperature. The amount of furniture and the textures of materials influence us in much the same way. A crowded room looks warm, a sparsely furnished one cool. Smooth materials seem cold, fuzzy ones hot. Compare the effects of some of the furniture and rooms illustrated. A lounge chair upholstered in wool (Fig. 304B) looks warmer, and actually is warmer, than an open chair of rattan and stretched fabric or one of metal and plastic (Fig. 318B). Draperies and blinds insulate against night coldness and daytime heat transmitted through window glass. Rugs warm a cold floor and screens deflect drafts.

VENTILATION

Good ventilation gets the hot, stale air out of the tops of rooms, brings fresh air in, keeps the air in gentle motion, and accomplishes all this without uncomfortable drafts. Major devices are doors and windows that can be opened, ventilating grilles, exhaust fans, warm-air furnaces with blowers, air-conditioning units, and portable fans.

The hot high air can be removed with windows, grilles, or exhaust fans placed high in the room or with ventilating skylights. Forced-draft warm-air furnaces, with the heat on or off, circulate the air, as does most cooling equipment. Without one or more of these, a layer of practically motionless air is likely to stay near the ceiling. If stale air is taken out, fresher air is bound to come in. Usually it comes through windows or doors, but ventilators strategically placed in the walls are sometimes preferable (Fig. 257). These usually have horizontal louvers on the outside to ward off rain or snow, fixed insect screens, and hinged or sliding panels on the inside to control the flow of air. Their good points are numerous: being unobtrusive they can be more varied in size, shape, and location than can windows; affording privacy, they can be placed where windows are unsuitable; and having permanently fixed and inconspicuous screens, they lessen the need for visually distracting insect barriers at windows.

Of all rooms, kitchens need the best ventilation and usually get it with exhaust fans supplementing windows and doors. Bathrooms come next but seldom fare as well. Windows or grilles high in the wall (Fig. 47A) can be opened much or little; controllable ceiling ventilators combine privacy with fresh air. Living and dining space also needs good air circulation, but this is ordinarily fairly well handled. The rooms are typically large and have windows on two or more sides. In contemporary planning, air flows through this space and to the outside as easily as people do. Doors plus windows and grilles, some high and others low and on different walls, is a good typical solution. Bedrooms benefit from fresh air without drafts. Again high windows or ventilators on two walls, supplemented by windows at normal height and by doors, allow flexible control.

Form and color have a psychological effect on ventilation needs just as they do on every other aspect of our behavior. Warm, dark colors and heavy forms make it seem a little harder to find fresh air than do cool, light colors and small-scale, airy furnishings. Thus, the problem is not only to get adequate ventilation but to furnish homes so that they seem appropriately ventilated.

ACOUSTICS

Noise, noise, noise! Television and hi-fi radio-phonographs, vacuum cleaners and electric washers, automobiles and aircraft—and children—all bring noises unknown in the house a generation or two ago. Yes, there were always children, but now they are seen *and* heard. A high level of noise produces tension and is a causative factor in emotional and physical breakdown, and the kitchen, where the homemaker spends so much time, is the noisiest room in the house. Coupled with an actual increase of noise are four factors that make it more noticeable: Houses have fewer and smaller rooms. Typical contemporary walls are not so soundproof as those thick, expensive walls of many older houses. Open planning has reduced the number of floor-to-ceiling partitions. Furnishings are not so bulky and noise-absorbing as they used to be.

Sound travels through air and through solids. It is readily transmitted through even small cracks around doors or windows. When airborne sound strikes a solid, some sound is absorbed, part is reflected, and the remainder is transmitted to other parts of the house (Fig. 357). Dense, smooth-surfaced materials tend to reflect sound back into the room. Porous materials, such as acoustical ceiling tiles or soft wallboards, absorb most sound if thick but transmit noticeable amounts if thin. New sound-barrier panels only one-half inch thick but engineered to lessen noise promise quieter homes.

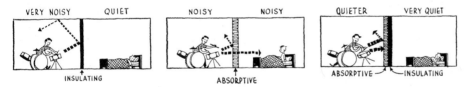

Wall materials can absorb, transmit, or reflect sound. *Left.* A dense insulating wall, such as masonry, lessens sound transmission from one room to another but causes sound to reverberate in the room where it originates. *Center.* Absorptive materials, such as porous wallboard, soak up some reverberation but, if thin, allow sound to travel through the wall. *Right.* Absorptive materials lessen sound reflection in the noisy room; insulating materials reduce sound transmission to the next room. (*Reprinted from* Sunset *Magazine*)

The first principle for a quiet home is, **Find a quiet location** away from factories and stores, heavily traveled roads, and major aircraft lanes. Trees and tall shrubbery absorb unwanted sound originating outside the house.

The second principle is, **Keep noisy spots together and segregate them from quiet zones,** as in Figure 6B. This applies to the location of the rooms in relation to the site as well as to one another. Fortunately, this usually dovetails with other desirable outcomes. Thus, for reasons of acoustics as well as use, it is logical to have the garage near the street, where it can help shield the house from traffic noise and yet be convenient to the kitchen, the laundry, and the home workshop. These, together with indoor and outdoor play space, make a logical unit. Then there can be a progression through the seminoisy dining and living space to the quiet bedrooms and the study or seclusion room. The spot where this principle applies least well is the bathroom, which is noisy but should be near the bedrooms. To take care of this and other situations there are three more principles.

The third principle is, **Reduce unwanted sounds at their sources.** In the kitchen, this indicates the use of resilient materials on as many as possible of the surfaces on which pans, dishes, and leather-heeled shoes are likely to clatter or bang. Counters covered with vinyl cause less noise than do those surfaced with stainless steel, clay tile, or laminated plastics. Resilient floors are quieter than nonresilient floors. Important, too, is the selection of appliances that operate quietly. The kitchen has been singled out, but this principle applies to every part of the house.

Absorb sounds already made is the fourth principle. This can be accomplished by sound-absorbing materials and sound-diffusing forms. Think of the poorest materials and shapes—a precisely rectangular empty room with walls, floor, and ceiling of smooth metal or glass. Every noise would bounce back and forth until all energy was spent. The acoustics would not be improved much if a few pieces of rectangular, smooth metal or plastic furniture were placed parallel to the walls. At the opposite extreme would be a room in which at least two of the walls are not parallel to each other and the ceiling is not parallel to the floor. The walls are broken with a projecting or recessed fireplace and storage cabinets, and the ceiling plane is interrupted by beams. Walls are surfaced with cork, the floor with carpet, and the ceiling with acoustical tile or plaster. The room is furnished with upholstered chairs and sofa, many books on open shelves, large plants on the floor or tables, and thick draperies at the windows. In brief, sound-absorbing materials are soft and porous; sound-diffusing shapes are almost anything other than uninterrupted, smooth, parallel planes.

The fifth principle is, **Use sound barriers to keep noise out of the quiet areas.** Closets with tight-fitting doors and a sound-retarding back wall muffle sound between bedrooms and bathrooms, halls and living rooms. Bookcases, storage walls, and thick fireplace walls help keep group-living sounds from invading private areas.

Lighting, heating, ventilating, and acoustics make our homes physically comfortable. With the notable exception of lighting, they have little to do with beauty or individuality, but they have much to do with human happiness. Planning for them should begin with the selection of the site and should be considered in every facet of home planning and furnishing.

Artificial illumination can be integrated with a piece of furniture in contrast to the general practice of allying it with the structure of a house or treating it as a separate, single-purpose unit. In an 18-inch high "Light Table," an electric bulb in a translucent sphere is suspended within an almost-closed transparent Plexiglas cylinder. Clear, heavy glass, less subject to scratching than plastics, is used for the circular top, which is held in place by the force of gravity. (*Neal Small Designs*)

A lighting fixture suspended from the ceiling is made of pierced bronze medallions attached to a molded wire "cage." It is an eventful piece of sculptural enrichment as well as a source of low-level illumination. Leo Jensen, designer. (*Virginia Frankel Gallery*)

16 · Enrichment

The verb *to enrich* means "to adorn," "to increase the endowments of," "to give richer quality to." It is often thought of only as supplementary, added-on ornament, and in this chapter, this will be emphasized. There are, however, equally or more important sources of enrichment, which include:

- People in the home with their different personalities, changing moods, activities, and clothes
- Materials and structure of the house and its furnishings
- Form and space, color and texture enjoyed by themselves and in relation to one another
- Patterns in draperies and upholstery, floor coverings and wall treatments, ornament on furniture and lighting fixtures
- Books and magazines and personal collections
- Views through windows no matter how limited they are

The logical first step in planning the enrichment of a home is to take inventory of the assets at hand and then to make certain that they are used to full advantage. The next step is to add whatever is needed for greater intensity or deeper impact. For a change of pace, an accent or emphasis through size or shape, color or texture, or intricacy can be added. A few cherished accessories, pictures, or plants can quickly transform bleak, impersonal rooms into space that looks like home.

More than in almost any other phase of home planning, the concept of individuality, freedom of taste, is appropriate in selecting the enrichment for a home. Embellishment without personal significance to those who live with it has little validity. There are, however, other considerations. One of these is intrinsic beauty or character. Appropriateness to the setting is another. And usefulness in the many objects that serve us physically as well as psychologically is not to be ignored.

Freedom of taste allows us to choose and combine what we like most, an approach refreshingly shown in Figures 360 and 361 and in Color Figures 19 and 20. Family heirlooms or simply the things we grew up with, gifts from a friend, or those things made by yourself or by someone close to you can bring warmth and happiness each time they are seen. Too many such objects aes-

The relationship of enrichment to furniture and to the architectural background can be one of cool detachment or warm alliance. (*Photograph by Gene Maggio, New York Times Studio*)

In an architecturally prosaic New York apartment with a spectacular view of the Hudson River, a young Finnish interior designer, Aivi Gallen-Kallela, and her architect husband, David K. Specter, have created their own airy, spacious environment. The simple furniture is augmented by decisively shaped accessories from many parts of the world, arranged so that each one can be individually appreciated. An antique Finnish cupboard, Danish wicker stools, a hanging lamp shaded by thin pine cylinders, and another of white paper forms reminiscent of Japanese lanterns, all have strong, self-contained shapes. A shaggy, dark rug emphasizes the plywood table designed and made by Mr. Specter. The woven Mexican mat on the wall, the pillow covers of complex appliqué made by the San Blas Indians of Mexico, and the one handcrafted by Miss Gallen-Kallela of felt triangles are all of intense, hot colors. Plants soften the composition; but the window has been left curtainless to permit full enjoyment of the river view. Not everyone has access to such diverse, handsome accessories, nor does everyone enjoy such catholicity of taste; but everyone can have a few strong accents with his preference or hobbies.

In the living room of a house in San Miguel de Allende, Mexico, the owner, an architect and designer, has intermixed materials and styles with an exuberance characteristic of Mexican design. Against a background of chinked rubble masonry, stone floor, and heavily beamed ceiling, he has arranged simple, forceful furniture of his own design and has built up the group with an old carved wooden saint, a Mexican religious painting, vivaciously carved wooden scrolls, and urn lamp bases that have richly mottled shades. The crystal chandelier is a surprising note of lightness and elegance. The colors are as stimulating as the forms. The variegated gray stone wall and floor, the rich brown furniture and ceiling, and a black laquered coffee table are sparked by white upholstery on the stools, Empire green on the armchairs, and red and gold pillows on the dark-biege sofa. Norman MacGregor, Jr., architect and designer. (*Reprinted from Verna Cook Shipway and Warren Shipway,* Mexican Homes of Today. *Copyright © 1964, Architectural Book Publishing Co., Inc.*)

thetically unrelated can make a room visually cluttered or disquietingly intimate to others, but if used with discretion, they are a prime source of individuality.

Lasting appeal, however, depends on more than sentimental associations. It is only reasonable to expect that most accessories, prints, or paintings will be of interest to others. Excellence of design, beauty of material and workmanship are of special consequence if objects are to increase the endowments of a home. They need not be rare or expensive, but they add little if they are both commonplace and arranged unimaginatively.

Ideas on "appropriateness to the setting" have changed considerably since the days when "good taste" demanded that everything match. Harmony and unity are still important, but so are surprise and variety. Noncommittal quarters and nondescript furniture, unfortunate conditions which most of us have to put up with at one time or another, cry out for enrichment with impact and individuality. They suggest a few important accessories with strong personalities, such as the owners of the living room in Figure 360 have gathered, or perhaps a large Oriental tray, colorful Italian glass, an India print covering a studio couch, a sizable ceramic bowl made by a local potter, grandmother's soup tureen or her patchwork quilt—almost anything that adds a few strong notes consonant with the occupant's preferences. Reproductions of paintings, original but inexpensive prints, even bright travel posters and a plant or two can compensate for the mechanized, impersonal character of far too many rooms.

In quarters of decisive character—a fine old Colonial house or a profusely decorated Victorian one or a house that suggests English or Spanish parentage —the problem is different. A first impulse might be to search for objects from the period (Color Fig. 5); but good ones are hard to find. A logical alternative is to think carefully about the size and shape, character and environment of the rooms and to get appropriate enrichment regardless of period (Fig. 361). Many apartments and houses, with or without distinctive personalities, provide a congenial setting for contemporary or historic, mass-produced or handcrafted objects (Figs. 362 and 386 and Color Figs. 3 and 19).

Complete freedom of taste in furniture, prints, and accessories, all of which hold personal significance to their owner, make this modern San Francisco bedroom unique. Henry Hill, architect. (*Photograph by Roger Sturtevant*)

Supplementary enrichment falls into four major categories: **accessories,** which are a wondrous group of strange bedfellows, **flowers and plants, table settings,** and the fine arts—**paintings, prints, and sculpture.**

Accessories

The old saying, "One man's trash is another man's treasure," applies aptly to accessories. Some accessories work for us, others are like the lilies of the field. Some are trivial and temporary, others significant and permanent. They can be made at home or in school, found on the beach, in the fields and woods. They are frequently purchased in gift and curio shops, often on trips, or are discovered in secondhand stores and at rummage sales. Although we are seldom conscious of buying many accessories, they tend to accumulate rather rapidly.

Some of the most common types of accessories deserve mention, either because their use suggests limitations or because their character demands special consideration:

- **Bowls and vases** of ceramic, glass, metal, plastics, or wood may work full time, part time, or not at all. If they are workers, check their efficiency as well as their appearance. Make certain that a bowl meant to be used for snacks is easy to pass around and that a vase for flowers is stable and holds enough water.
- **Candleholders** ought to hold candles firmly upright and catch the inevitable drip. If they are to be used for dining tables, they are best when either high or low, to keep the light away from eye level. If they are to be kept on display but seldom used, they should be worth constant appraisal.
- **Natural objects,** such as driftwood or branches of unusual structure, rocks, or shells are in line with the trend toward naturalism. They have much in their favor: little or no expense, long life, natural beauty, and individuality because no two pieces are identical.
- **Mirrors** can be primarily decorative or useful or both, small accents or wall size. They have the paradoxical qualities of allying themselves with what is opposite them, by reflection, and of dissociating themselves from the immediate background because of their striking dissimilarity to most wall surfaces. Their brightness adds sparkle to a room; their reflections increase apparent spaciousness. In entrances they provide a first or last opportunity to check one's appearance. In living rooms and dining rooms they are primarily ornamental and can be hung much like paintings, can fill the space between windows to simulate a window wall, or can cover an entire wall. In halls they can add apparent width or lighten a dark end.
- **Wall hangings and stitchery** fall someplace between accessories and paintings, depending on the degree of creative excellence they display. Tapestries and embroidered or stitched panels can be treated as paintings and hung where they can be admired as works of art, or they can be used as pillow, table, or bed covers, or perhaps hung to brighten a blank wall when they seem more a craft than an art form. However they are used, they add the soft enrichment that is their particular gift.

These are only a few of the many objects that can have decorative value no matter what their major function is. Table mats and magazines, books and bookends, ashtrays and bowls of nuts, sofa pillows and lamps are others in this

Accessories can markedly change the character of a coffee table, as demonstrated in these two arrangements in the Julius Shulmans' home. (*Photographs by Julius Shulman*)

Above. A few circular objects varied in size and rhythmically spaced allow appreciation of each object and of the wood of the table top.

most numerous, if not most important, phase of enrichment (Figs. 364–365). The diversity of size and shape, color and material is tremendous. This calls for special attention to selecting and arranging those objects that are to be seen together.

Variety in unity is of first-rank importance. Groups of accessories are usually most enjoyable when something is preeminent. This "something" can be one large, intricate, or unusual piece, either standing alone or reinforced with smaller objects. Or it can be a dominance of rounded or angular forms, a sensitive study of related textures or colors. Then, a few calculated tensions will heighten the unity. Balance, from all angles, stabilizes the composition; repetition or progression brings rhythmic movement. When well done, the whole effect is many times greater than the sum of the parts.

PLANTS

Figures 360 and 386 handsomely exemplify ways in which plants can humanize interiors. Relatively inexpensive, plants last much longer than cut flowers and with reasonable care become larger. They provide interiors with needed diversity of form and color and give the gardener an indoor hobby.

Each type of plant has its own requirements of light, heat, soil, water, and humidity for best growth. Almost none like dark, hot, poorly ventilated rooms any more than do most of us; but a few will survive even under such unfavorable conditions. For hot, sunny windows, *cactus* and other *succulents* are logical choices. For moderately cool east or north windows, there are many to select from: *begonias,* which range from a few inches to several feet tall; *African violets; coleus* with gay foliage in reds, yellows, greens, and white; *ivy,* either plain or variegated, which can be trained around a window or up a wall; all the *philodendrons;* and even some varieties of *orchids.* For parts of rooms not near windows, such foliage plants as *philodendrons, rubber trees,* and *ferns* are indicated.

The containers in which plants are kept have much to do with their health (drainage is important here), and ornamental value. A little scouting will turn up pots that are unexpected—sensitive and subtle pieces from Japan, bold wares from Mexico and Italy, Victorian jardinieres of brass, and an inspiring diversity from contemporary potters. Usually the container is subordinate to the plant it holds, but no lasting harm results from the opposite. Plants are at their best when treated as any other type of enrichment—selected and placed where they will be true ornaments. Big, bold plants are good for major effects or to fill a space where furniture does not fit (Fig. 386). At the opposite extreme are the small ones whose interesting foliage merits close study. The size varies in terms of the space and purpose. On a coffee or end table, or on a narrow window ledge, a few or many small plants bring a pleasant feeling of small scale. Plants a foot or two high may be needed on a large table or cabinet. On the floor or on a low stand, those from 3 to 6 feet high make their presence felt (Fig. 28A). Within the limits of whatever degree of unity is wanted, the kinds can be varied. Plants, like other decorative appointments, usually seem most at home when several of one type are grouped or distributed in an enjoyable pattern, but a few contrasts enliven the effect.

What could have been an unorganized miscellany is brought together by a dominant floral arrangement and sensitive placement of a low, rectangular cigarette box and books near the corners, and higher rounded pieces near the flowers.

A crystal bowl and a handful of flowers from the garden complement each other in a seemingly artless arrangement. Three white tulips and two clusters of white freezias are grouped securely in the low bowl. A curve of three deep-pastel ranunculuses support the slight verticality of the tallest tulip and in turn are asymmetrically balanced by the single ranunculus on the right. Two sprays of small-leaved English ivy continue the spread of the bowl and its two overhanging lips; the left spray is accented by the small downward-pointing flower on the left, while the three tulips on the right follow the curve of the ivy and lighten their visual weight by the lift of the upper one. Although the arrangement can be analyzed in terms of the principles of design, its effect is largely dependent on the sparkle of the bowl and the bright whiteness of tulips and freezias, the accent of dark-green ivy leaves and colorful swirls of ranunculuses. Tosh Matsumoto, designer. (*Steuben Glass Company*)

FLOWER ARRANGEMENTS

Raised to the level of an eloquent art by the nature-loving Japanese, and assiduously practiced by many in this country, flower arrangement runs the gamut from stuffing some blossoms into a vase to a fascinating hobby. In general, it can be solved just like any other home design problem:

- Decide what general effect and character are wanted.
- Obtain suitable flowers, foliage, containers, and ornaments.
- Arrange these, giving due regard to the nature of the floral materials, the place in which they will be put, and to variety in unity, balance, rhythm, and emphasis.

The **effects** that can be produced are limitless. There are countless steps between symmetrical and strict formality and spontaneous, asymmetrical informality. The number of flowers can range from one exquisitely formed iris, rose, or orchid to branches from flowering trees that have hundreds of blossoms. The dominant movement can be vertical, outward spreading, horizontal, or downward.

The **setting in which an arrangement is to be placed** often suggests possible effects. A none-too-ample dining table with a large lighting fixture hanging low overhead (Fig. 383) does not need a large centerpiece. As flowers, gladioli are fairly formal and balanced, and here they have been symmetrically arranged in a low bowl so that the centerpiece does not interfere with conversation but emphasizes the flat plane of the table and allows the oversize crystal goblets to rise above it and tie in with the glass on the shelf behind. On the dining table in Figure 384, a low centerpiece allows the persons at the table to see one another, but it might seem meager and frittery were it not visually extended into the large asymmetrical spray arrangement that climbs the rough rock wall.

The relation of a flower arrangement to its setting will vary from harmony to contrast. The precise symmetry of very formal rooms suggests formal arrangements, just as informal homes suggest those that are less strict. Often, however, variety and contrast are needed. The solid stability of symmetrically arranged flowers at some point in an unassuming house has an impact similar to that of spirited freedom in formal interiors.

The **flowers, branches, and leaves obtainable** play a decisive role in determining the kind of arrangement that is possible, because each plant has its own character and habit of growth. Some flowers, such as irises, grow tall and upright and lend themselves to vertical arrangements. Poppies and tulips have flexible stems and tend to curve into spreading designs that can be basically either horizontal or vertical. Short-stemmed blossoms and sinuous vines give naturally horizontal compositions (Fig. 366), although many materials may be deliberately modified to give a low-spreading effect when this is indicated. Flowers, however, will cooperate up to a point, but little is gained by pushing them beyond it. Arrangements that emphasize the distinctive personalities of the materials used are likely to be most successful (Fig. 367A).

The **relation of flowers to their containers** is important also but not dictated by rules. In Figure 366, the brilliance of the crystal bowl is matched by the sparkling whiteness of tulips and freesias, and its spreading form leads naturally to a low, horizontal arrangement. Palm leaves, which need no water and no support other than the holder, can be placed in a flat shallow dish whose width gives visual balance to the tall spikes. Carnations, on the other hand, keep best in plenty of water, and in the arrangement in Figure 371A they have been casually organized in an ample ceramic pot whose dark color is a decisive accent for the white flowers and walls.

Any degree of similarity or dissimilarity between flowers and containers can be effective. Usually the container is subordinate to its contents, and simple glass, ceramic, or metal bowls or vases will happily hold varied flowers. Sometimes, though, a distinctive urn, cornucopia, or vase is almost as important as what it holds—there is no law saying that it cannot be more important—but common sense and the principle of dominance suggest that they should not be exactly equal. Those who enjoy arranging flowers appreciate having varied containers because it is stimulating to have a vase or bowl just right in size, shape, color, and texture for its contents and for its position in the home.

Dry Arrangements

Dry arrangements can be divided into the "semidry" compositions of fruits and vegetables that last from a few days to several months and the "bone dry" compositions of everlasting flowers and seedpods, leaves and bare branches, driftwood and rocks (Figs. 367A and B). They cost little or nothing and require no care other than the somewhat tedious job of removing dust. The principles are the same as those from which pleasing arrangements of fresh flowers develop.

Leaves, fruits, wood, and rocks do not need water, and last for a long time.

Below. A few dry palm leaves, a shallow bowl, pebbles, plus imagination and skill add up to a striking dry arrangement that would be practically everlasting. Jack Daniels, designer. (*Photograph by Camera Center Studio*)

A

B

Left. A weathered piece of driftwood can be handsome by itself as "found" sculpture, or it can be the base for changing arrangements of fruits and leaves or whatever the seasons bring. (*Photograph by Maynard L. Parker Modern Photography*)

In summary, these points are worth keeping in mind:

- Start with an idea or develop one as you go along. In most instances, avoid treating the materials as a disorganized blur of form and color.
- Accentuate character and habit of growth.
- Select an appropriate container—one that will hold sufficient water and give any necessary support without tipping over.
- Begin with the largest element and work down to the smallest.
- Keep in mind that the concept of variety in unity, balance, rhythm, and emphasis are important.
- Build the arrangement for the space it will occupy.
- Give it adequate light and pleasant background.
- Rejoice in the fact that these arrangements are one of the best, least costly means of experiment with individualized designs.

PAINTINGS, DRAWINGS, AND PRINTS

Creative artists aim to arouse, sharpen, and deepen our ways of seeing and to enlarge our spiritual experience and understanding. Designers, too, hold these goals but not to the same degree of intensity. Their basic intent is simply to heighten the aesthetic quality of utilitarian objects. In comparison with the design of tableware and furniture, the fine arts are more richly complex and more deeply emotional. They encompass greater diversity and more compelling unity, more intricate and evocative organization of form, space, and color, and, most important, a more profound penetration of significant human concerns. Thus, although paintings, drawings, and prints are often regarded merely as pleasant spots of color or reminders of enjoyable things, they can be the stimuli for vivid experiences that liberate and elevate our spirits. The artist achieves this through his choice and handling of subject matter and content, medium and style.

Subject matter is the material that the artist presents for consideration, the objects that the work of art represents. Typical categories include landscapes, cityscapes, and seascapes, still lifes, and flowers, people, and animals. Much invigorating contemporary painting that is categorized as abstract or nonobjective does not depict any easily identifiable objects (Fig. 369C). It is comparable to music that does not have a "story." But though it has no subject matter in the conventional sense, it can have rewarding emotional content.

Content is the idea or message, feeling or mood that is expressed. Art can convey joy or sadness, delicacy or vigor, restraint or exuberance, or any other human reaction. It is what the artist emphasizes in his subject matter, if any, and what he draws out of himself. The same basic subject matter can have markedly different content—seascapes can be peaceful and serene, exhilarating, or ominous.

Medium refers to the material used in a work of art. Pigments and pencils, paper and canvas (and stone and wood in sculpture) are all media in the general sense.

Style is the distinctive or characteristic manner in which works of art are conceived and executed. The word *style* is used to describe the characteristics of a period, such as the Renaissance or the Victorian age, and also the individuality that a painter, such as Michelangelo, El Greco, or Van Gogh, brings to his work.

Paintings. Oil and watercolor are the typical media of paintings used in homes. Oils, usually on canvas, are done with pigments mixed with oil to produce any effect from thin transparent washes to thick impasto. Watercolors, almost always on paper, tend to be smaller, more thinly painted, more spontaneous, and less expensive than oils. The recent introduction of new synthetic paints that dry rapidly, do not change in color, adhere to many kinds of surfaces, and promise great permanence presents artists with new fields for exploration unhampered by traditional approaches. For special effects several different media may be combined, and these are referred to as mixed media.

Drawings. A delightful but often overlooked form of art, drawings are comparatively inexpensive. Many kinds of pencil, crayon, charcoal, and ink applied with a pen or brush may be used, typically on paper, to produce surprisingly diverse effects from delicate lines to heavily modeled forms, from black and white to a single color or many. Because drawings are often preliminary sketches for other works, they are likely to be more relaxed than paintings, a more direct revelation of the artist's concept; but they can also be precise delineations or full-bodied statements, as completely developed as a painting.

Graphic prints. The graphic processes can be defined as the making of plates and the printing of pictures or designs from these plates. Prints fall into the rare category of quantity-produced originals because a number of "originals" can be printed from each plate and sold at moderate cost. All the typical kinds of prints can be in black and white or in color (Fig. 369A).

Woodcuts and *linoleum cuts* are made by cutting into blocks of wood or pieces of linoleum to make the plate used in printing. Often they are in color, an art raised high by the Japanese.

Etchings typically resemble small, delicate pen-and-ink drawings, but contemporary printmakers have experimented with many effects of texture and mass

Paintings and reproductions, drawings, and graphic prints are a prime source of beauty and individuality in the home, and they are available in profusion and in all price ranges.

Below. Original graphic prints are often moderately priced and readily available. "Hill and Mountain," a lithograph by Adolph Dehn, conveys some of the monumental grandeur of our mountainous areas. (*Print Council of America,* "*American Prints Today—1959*")

A

B

Left. Pablo Picasso's "Woman in White" is an example of paintings that are often reproduced, sometimes with considerable fidelity. Although reproductions do not have the strong impact of original works, they make it possible for all to enjoy masterpieces of art. (*The Metropolitan Museum of Art, New York, Rogers Fund, 1951; from the Museum of Modern Art, New York, Lizzie P. Bliss Collection*)

Below. "Deep Folds," an original work by Ivan Majdrakoff, appears to move in many directions as one looks at it. Because it is an ink drawing by a young artist it might fall within the budget of someone genuinely interested in and sympathetic to his work.

C

369

far beyond the potentialities of an ink-dipped pen. Etchings are made by scratching through a waxy coating on a metal printing plate, then eating out (or "etching") the exposed metal with acid.

Drypoints are made by scratching directly into the surface of a metal printing plate with a sharp point, and except to the expert, are almost indistinguishable from etchings.

Lithographs are produced by drawing with a greasy crayon or ink on a block of stone or a sheet of metal to make the printing plate. They are noted for their rich blacks and silvery grays (Fig. 369A).

Silk-screen prints (or *serigraphs*) are made from a textile stencil through which thick ink is forced onto paper or fabric. This medium is particularly well suited to broad, simple masses of color, as well as to textures and details.

Many prints are quiet, restrained statements and gain emphasis from being hung in groups, especially if they are small. Some modern prints, however, are large, boldly designed and strongly colored. These can stand by themselves as centers of attention.

Selecting Paintings, Drawings, and Prints

There are a few valid guides for selecting pictures for a home. Select those that will give lasting pleasure, that contribute to the character of a home, and that have some measure of aesthetic value.

On **subject matter,** it is nonsense to say that landscapes and flower pieces are best for the living room, still lifes with fruits and vegetables for the dining space, and soporific subjects for the bedroom. Works of art of any merit are too important in themselves to be put into categories of subjects suitable for certain rooms. If a family has special interest in boating and swimming, they can have a predominance of pictures that arouse such associations. If they are bird lovers, they can collect pictures of birds and hang them wherever they are effective. If they do not want to be tied down to specific associations, they can stretch their imaginations on abstractions.

On **content,** the same guides apply. Few persons want to wake up each morning face to face with a deeply tragic work of art, but it does not follow that all works have to be lighthearted. Most persons enjoy art that is varied in content, so that they look at what they want at different times. It is perhaps in the area of emotional and intellectual content that the viewer comes nearest to experiencing the creativity of the artist. No matter what feeling or message the artist intended to convey, it is only in the emotions of the beholder that it can have life. This is true whether or not we are conscious of the way a work of art affects us. Although immediate appeal is a factor, lasting pleasure is more important in anything other than inexpensive reproductions.

On **medium,** it is worth getting to know even a little about the many ways in which materials can be handled. You may develop specific likes and dislikes or come to enjoy diversity.

Style is no longer a matter of regulations. To be sure, there is a deep consistency among works of art from one period, and in an eighteenth-century home with furniture from that period, eighteenth-century paintings would be most strictly appropriate, just as contemporary paintings fit into modern interiors. Today, however, we assume that all art history is our heritage and that there should be no insistence on art that *matches* furniture or walls. If your tastes are conventional, choose a conventional painting by someone living or a reproduction of something everyone has accepted. If your tastes are not stereotyped, find a lively modern, a primitive, or a work by a less-known historic painter.

Color is near the heart of paintings and many prints, yet choosing a painting primarily because the colors are pleasant in the room is about on the level of buying books because of the color of the binding. Regard color, along with all the other attributes, as one important factor in the enjoyment of paintings in their setting. Feel as free to explore passive harmonies with the backgrounds against which the paintings are to be hung as to indulge in exhilarating contrasts.

Size is important because there is a tendency to hang pictures that are too small for the wall space and furniture with which they ought to be in scale. This is especially true of paintings over fireplaces or sofas, for even in the average living room the space above furniture profits from paintings that hold their own (Fig. 371A). The character of pictures, almost as much as their physical dimensions, determines apparent size and visual weight. Thus, a misty painting in pale colors seems "lighter" than one with solid forms clearly defined in intense colors. Grouping a number of small pictures gives an effect somewhat like one large picture (Fig. 371B).

Two rooms in which there is concentrated enrichment of floors and walls in contrast to the furniture, which is simple in shape and color.

In another part of the York Castle living room (see Fig. 221), a tile-patterned rug in blue, ochre, and white is the dominant, eye-catching feature. A large, dark nineteenth-century Persian painting hangs low over a contemporary beige sofa. A mirror in a black antique frame, an ebony-framed cabinet with grass-covered doors, Siamese brass candleholders, and bowls form a composition on the alcove wall and brighten the end of the room far from any windows. The stark whiteness of the walls is picked up again by the pedestals of the low tables. Two yellow ottomans, Eero Saarinen's voluptuous lounge chair, which has become a modern classic, a dark carved wood screen, a lamp, plant, and flowers complete the welcoming design. (*Interiors for York Castle designed by Planning Unit, Knoll International, France*)

A

B

Massed, small pictures of diverse sizes, shapes, frames, and subject matter create a compelling center of attention and have sufficient visual weight to balance the dark studio couches, a small-patterned Oriental rug, and a heavy oak, antique table. Of interest is the way in which the single picture on the side wall gives depth to the alcove and brings the wooden sconce and metal lamp into the composition. (*Reprinted from* Living for Young Homemakers)

371

Frames, Mats, and Glass

Frames visually enclose pictures and contribute to their importance and effectiveness. Also, they form a boundary or transition between the free, intense expressiveness of pictures and the typically more quiet architectural backgrounds. Lastly, they safeguard the edges, may hold protective glass, and facilitate moving and hanging. Their first duty is to enhance the pictures; their second is to establish some kind of relationship with the setting. Generally, this means that frames should either supplement the size, scale, character, and color of what they enclose or simply be unobtrusive bands. Occasionally, marked contrast can accentuate the qualities of a painting. Only exceptionally should the frame dominate the picture. The wide, heavily carved and gilded frames of the past or any that project at the outer edges "set off" pictures from their backgrounds. Those of moderate width and simple design, harmonious in color with the walls and either flat or stepped back, relate pictures to walls.

Mats and **glass** are typical accompaniments of watercolors and graphic prints. Mats enlarge these usually small pictures and surround them with rest space as a foil, especially important if the picture is delicate or if the background is competitive. In *color,* mats are usually of white or pale-hued paper because these concentrate attention on the picture. For special effects, mats can be of pronounced color and of textiles or patterned paper, cork, or metal. Effective if well done, the result may seem affected rather than appropriate after the novelty has worn thin. But they are not to be dismissed because of this risk.

In *size,* mats vary with the size and character of the picture as well as with the frame and the location. Heavy frames lessen the need for generous mats, while large or important locations increase it. To correct optical illusions and give satisfying up-and-down equilibrium, the width of the top, sides, and bottom of mats may be different. In matting a picture, as in creating one, the elusive interaction of form, line, and space—not a set formula—should determine the result. The discerning eye of the owner or framer will be the best judge of the correct mat for any particular picture in its intended location.

Glass is a necessary evil for pictures that cannot be protected from surface dirt, moisture, and abrasion by a durable coating such as varnish. It also seems to intensify the colors; but it produces annoying reflections. A new unreflecting glass solves this problem, but unfortunately it grays and softens what is underneath, especially if used with a mat. Mats and glass usually go together on watercolors, graphic prints, pastels, and sometimes photographs. Oil paintings seldom have either.

Hanging Pictures

Locating paintings, drawings, and prints so that they interact happily with their setting is an art. Since pictures help relate furniture to walls, they are often placed over something—a sofa or group of chairs, a desk, a table, or a bookcase. Centering a picture in a wall space or over a piece of furniture gives stable symmetry (Fig. 371A), while placing one off-center creates more movement (Fig. 362). Keeping pictures at about eye level lets them be seen comfortably, relates them to furnishings, and emphasizes the room's horizontality. From time to time, though, it is refreshing to have a painting stand for what it is worth on an otherwise blank wall. Useful guides to hanging are:

- Choose locations where enrichment of this special kind will be appreciated and where the illumination is appropriate.
- Select works of appropriate size and strength for each location.
- Relate each to nearby furniture or its wall space.
- Group small pictures to avoid spottiness.
- Think about alignment of the major pictures in each room, for aligning the bottoms, tops, or centers brings order.
- Hang pictures flat against the wall with no wires or hooks showing.

Sculpture

Bringing into three dimensions the intensity and expressiveness found in painting, sculpture can have consequential impact in homes. Small sculptures of people and animals abound in gift and variety stores, but, unfortunately, the typical ones are syrupy sweet or cute, pastel-colored, and of very limited interest. But from time to time those with real character are available, and these make good accents in flower arrangements or in groups of accessories.

Sculpture of larger size is worth the time it takes to find, for it can make a unique contribution (Fig. 373C). Working in clay, metal, wood, stone, and plastics, contemporary sculptors are creating many lively pieces suited to homes. Auctions, secondhand or antique stores, and those featuring folk arts are good sources of inexpensive items. In addition, there is wall sculpture that relieves the dull flatness of most walls without taking otherwise usable space, and there are mobiles that hang from the ceiling and create constantly changing patterns.

All that was said earlier about selecting paintings and prints applies with slight adaptation to sculpture.

Sculpture, original or reproduced, deserves more consideration as home enrichment than it customarily receives.

Below. Replicas of Chinese bronze horses of the Han dynasty (206 B.C.–A.D. 220), only a few inches high, are typical of many pieces that are available in museums and gift shops for comparatively little money. (*Museum Pieces*)

A

Below left. Robert C. Fritz's free-form, hand-blown, clear glass vase with floating trails of green glass is completely effective for its sculptural beauty alone, but it could hold a few flowers. (*Photograph by Robert Halbrook*)

Below right. Ibram Lassaw's "Procession" (1955–1956), welded from silver, copper, and various bronzes, is a labyrinth of structural intricacy from which forms appear to be continuously emerging and going forward, as they do in the living world. It is a unique piece with a moderately high price tag, but it could be a lifetime investment. (*Whitney Museum of American Art, New York*)

B

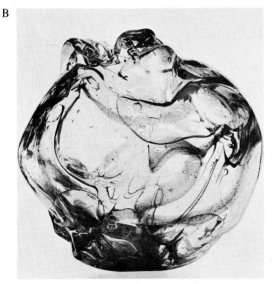

C

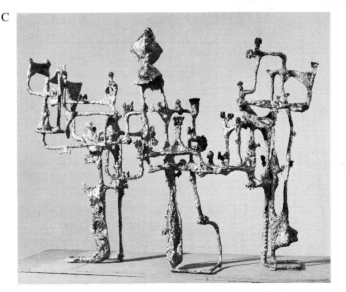

Reproductions and Originals

In concluding our discussion of fine arts in the home, a few words on originals versus reproductions are indicated. It is deeply satisfying to have original works of art in one's home. One of the all-too-few, one-of-a-kind objects, they have qualities that cannot be reproduced. Selecting an original is somewhat akin to creating one, and when purchased, it is uniquely yours. Original paintings, drawings, graphic prints, and sculpture range in price from a few dollars to the very steep prices for recognized work that is in demand. Many galleries and museums now rent original works of art for low fees that can be applied to the purchase price. This is a good way to see how much pleasure different works of art give a family. Drawings and graphic prints are ideal choices with which to start collecting. Works by young artists can be seen in art galleries and municipal art shows, while graphic prints by mature artists with established reputations are often surprisingly inexpensive at art dealers and even from mail-order houses. They are easy to hang and to store, easy to move and to enjoy.

Reproductions do not give the full impact of the original works, for they lack the full range and brilliance of color, the special interests of textures and materials. It begins to sound as though reproductions should be avoided, but this is true only of those of poor quality. Some reproductions of watercolors and drawings are very close to the originals, and some of oil paintings are surprisingly good. The cost is closely related to the faithfulness of the print, but a reproduction of a significant work costs no more than one of something inconsequential. Because reproductions are inexpensive, you can afford to experiment to discover what you enjoy most; frames with removable backs are other inducements to change pictures as often as you wish.

TABLE SETTINGS

Several times a day homemakers provide food for their families. Numerous experiments, as well as our own personal experiences, indicate that the environment in which we eat can affect our health and happiness. We "set" tables, therefore, in order to eat together with comfort and pleasure. Comfort means good chairs and tables well arranged in sufficient space, with suitable light and ventilation, minimum noise, and appropriate tableware and table coverings. Pleasure comes not only from our companions and the food but from the spirit, beauty, and distinctiveness with which the table and the dining space are planned. Because meals are significant in family life, family meals as well as "company" meals deserve more than routine treatment. The kinds of meals enjoyed most often and most thoroughly can well be the chief guide in selecting dishes and glassware, silverware, table coverings, and accessories. Books on etiquette usually divide table settings into formal and informal categories. With the first we need have no concern because it is needed by, and appropriate to, very few people. But within the bounds of today's informal living, there is no dearth of imaginative possibilities.

Two Table Settings

The setting shown in Figure 375A is about as close as most families come to formality, but it is correctly described as informal. The tablecloth and napkins of rich but soft red linen unify and show to full advantage the dishes, silver, and glass. A strong feeling of order permeates this basically simple arrangement in which varied shapes and patterns are harmoniously combined. The many pieces of silver handsomely exemplify variety in unity, and form follows function. The cigarette holder is plain, as befits its subordinate role. Bread-and-butter plates and the efficient, covered vegetable dishes have gadroon borders similar to, but not identical with, those on the ashtrays and candleholders. Knives, forks, and spoons have rich ornamentation of a kind highly appropriate to silver and to the eyes and hands of those who use them. This progression from simple to complex reaches its climax in the candleholders. China and glassware are companionable with the silver. The intricate small-scale decoration on the plates emphasizes their shape and relates them to the knives and forks. The stemware is as sturdily shaped as the vegetable dishes, but the deeply cut pattern brings sparkle and makes it easier to hold. Chrysanthemums in a centered silver bowl bring the color harmony to its fullest intensity and are low enough to allow easy conversation across the table.

This is a setting that would seem at home in a traditional house, or it would be a pleasant but not a clashing contrast in a modern one. One would expect the room and its furnishings to be somewhat dignified, the guests to wear semiformal clothes, and the dinner to live up to its setting.

Markedly different in character, the second table setting (Fig. 375B) is distinguished by its sturdy boldness and by its use of structural ornament as a unifying element. Gordon Keeler's dark "zebra-wood" dishes stand out against the wool cloth handwoven by Catherine Walsh, but their linear grain pattern is picked up by the darker yarns and long fringe of the cloth and also by the feathery leaves of the centerpiece. Thick handblown tumblers, placed on round wood coasters, are amber-colored and dimpled with finger-fitting depressions. The dandelion heads in Gerald Foley's handmade brazed and welded

Dinner tables can be conservatively correct or freely conceived.

Left. A handsome dinner table on which the pieces are correlated in design and spirit, although they do not match. (*Reed and Barton*)

Right. An informal luncheon table, arranged by Betty Alswang, is a study in contrasts of color and texture, held together by unexpected linear patterns. (*America House*)

A

B

Color, accessories, and the structural and applied ornament of the tableware determine the expressive character of a table setting.

Related neutral colors and simple shapes emphasize the structural ornament and textures of different materials. The dinnerware is durable stoneware with an unobtrusively speckled glaze; the silverware is distinctively shaped. The ribbed place mat and wood tabletop are pleasant contrasts, and a centerpiece of fruit reinforces the sturdy, informal character. (*Heath Ceramics*)

A harmony of smooth textures and refined shapes is vitalized by decisive value contrasts in the dinnerware and in the silverware with its black nylon handles. The smoothness and refinement of the setting is more formal than the stoneware setting, but the floral centerpiece and the tablecloth embroidered with sprays of leaves establish a secondary, less formal theme. (*Lunt Silversmiths*)

Set on a bare, polished mahogany table, a traditional practice in the eighteenth century, cream-colored china dinnerware with an ingenuous rhythmic design in soft mulberry has a relaxed but balanced order. Sturdy, gracefully shaped, unornamented silver, pewter, and heavy glass—reproductions of American Colonial pieces—fit their users' hands unusually well. (*Colonial Williamsburg*)

376

19

In his living room overlooking San Francisco Bay, architect John Davis has countered the brilliance of the water- and sky-filled view with soft, muted colors. The enrichment has been chiefly concentrated in the paneled, rough-sawn redwood walls treated with an oil stain to darken and cool them, and in the hand-woven rugs from Pakistan. A projecting section of wall with French doors is painted a soft, grayed blue. The wood furniture repeats the dark tones of the random-width oak plank floor; but the textured white upholstery on the matching sofas and the soft chartreuse velvet chair cushions relieve the somberness of the background hues. (*Photograph by Lyman Emerson*)

20

Designed by architect Hugh Stubbins for his own family, this dwelling is congenial with its historic neighbors in Cambridge, Massachusetts. Dark, earthy colors in the wide oak boards of the floor, the Douglas fir beams and stairway, and the red brick and gray granite of the fireplace contrast decisively with white walls, ceiling, and upholstered furniture, and are related to those in the intricate geometric pattern of the Oriental rug. The disposition of colors emphasizes and articulates the dynamic, complex architectural forms that define an exhilarating spatial composition. The furniture, centered around the rug, is as clear-cut and direct as the architectural shell. (*Photograph © Ezra Stoller*)

metal centerpiece, are also rounded and golden. Contrasting with this fullness is the slenderness of the highly polished, simple silverware designed by John Pripp and the elongation of the metal figures on the place-card holders, both of which relate to the lines in the zebra wood. Individual and untrammeled, this setting promises out-of-the-ordinary food and lively conversation. It is assertive enough to be noticed in a room, but it would not be unduly dominant.

Selecting Tableware

In the table settings just described, it is apparent that success comes as much from the appropriateness of dishes, silver, glass, linens, and accessories as from their arrangement. This is especially evident in the conventional expectedness of the first table and in the independence of taste in the second. But before tables can be set, the equipment must be in hand—chosen with its probable uses in mind.

Selecting tableware differs from most other aspects of home planning and furnishing in several important respects because of the ways in which it is typically accumulated and used. The pieces are acquired not only through planned (and occasional impulse) buying but by unpredictable gifts and inheritances. They can be variously combined and arranged with no cost other than imagination and a little time. The several kinds of tableware usually arrive in sets, and quick replacements may be indicated because of breakage, damage, or loss. Nothing else except cooking utensils is handled, moved from place to place, and washed as frequently. Also, tableware requires easily accessible and specially planned storage to make the constant flow from cupboard to table to sink and back to cupboard as convenient as possible. Finally, many families have everyday and company tableware and linens, a distinction seldom made elsewhere in the home. Putting these factors together raises unique problems and, more significantly, great possibilities for personalizing the home.

The kind of food and the manner of serving it most enjoyed by the family, the present or planned dining and storage space as well as furniture, and the preferred way of living—all of these have direct bearing on the selection of tableware. Use and economy are important, as always, but in this instance beauty and individuality may be more heavily weighted. Because tableware is seen only a few hours a day, there is much greater freedom to have patterns and colors that might be too demanding if always in view. Because each piece may be used in different contexts, it should have its own intrinsic beauty that is versatile yet affirmative. In few other phases of home life is change so easily and economically possible, and each change is a new design challenge. Thus, it is an individual problem satisfactorily solved only in a personal way.

Selecting Dishes

Dinnerware is usually the most conspicuous part of the permanent table equipment and often tends to set the character of table settings. The following points pertaining to **use** and **economy** should be kept in mind in selecting dishware:

- Size and shape are significant. Each dish should be large and deep enough to hold an adequate amount of food without spilling. Plates with rims permit easy grasping and provide a resting place for silverware but do not hold so much food as rimless ones. Cups should have finger-fitting handles, rims that fit the lips. Dishes that can be stored easily save time and storage space.

■ Replacement as well as original costs merit consideration. "Open stock" patterns permit adding to a set as needed but are no longer a guarantee of permanent availability for a long time. Read guarantees and suggestions for maintenance carefully. Vitreous ceramics and the better plastics resist chipping and breakage. Hard glazes reduce unsightly and unsanitary scratches; underglaze decorations are more durable than overglaze. Compact shapes lessen breakage. Raised ornament increases cleaning time, is more subject to chipping and scratching.

■ Dishes that double as cooking and serving containers save time and assure hot food.

The following points pertaining to **beauty** and **individuality** should also be kept in mind:

■ Dinnerware comes in great variety, opening the path to many colors and patterns that should have lasting appeal. Relation to other table appointments, furniture, and quality of life is at least as important as the beauty of pieces seen by themselves.

■ Originality, in a mass-production age, is less likely to come from finding one-of-a-kind pieces than from choosing those that seem compatible with individual preferences and are adaptable to varied settings. Personalization comes with the ways in which they are combined and arranged.

White plates boldly ornamented with asymmetric motifs in Chinese red and green, and silverware also intricately patterned, are semi-formal in feeling. The smooth linen mat, ample in size, acts as a foil, but its lace border echoes the small-scale design on the silver. The unornamented bubble-shaped stemware and candleholders rely on basic form for aesthetic interest. (*Reed and Barton*)

A   B

Selecting Flatware

Flatware may be used by several generations since it is seldom broken or seriously damaged. Therefore, potential permanence of appeal is more important than in other kinds of tableware. The following points pertaining to **use** and **economy** should be kept in mind when selecting flatware:

- Flatware, like dinnerware, is much handled and it ought to handle pleasantly—be easy to pick up and hold firmly, balance well in the hand or on the plate, and have no irritatingly sharp edges.
- Use does not harm sterling silver and stainless steel but, with ordinary care, improves them by mellowing the surface.

Sterling silver and stainless steel lend themselves to varied ornamentation.

Left below. Abstract baroque modeling held within a restrained, contemporary shape characterizes a silverware pattern named "Tapestry." (Compare Fig. 378, in which similar but naturalistic ornament determines the form of the silverware handles.) John Prip, designer. (*Reed and Barton*)

Right below. Closely spaced parallel grooves enrich the handles of an easy-to-hold stainless-steel pattern. (*Dansk Designs*)

Understated elegance characterizes two place settings that lean toward formality.

Left above. Coordinated tableware combines stark black porcelain and white porcelain with a muted stylized border, sterling silver with porcelain handles, and stemware with a heavy base rising to an exquisitely thin rim. Placed on a richly textured handwoven mat, it seems informal; on a different table covering, it would look more formal. Tapio Wirkkala, designer. (*Rosenthal China Corporation*)

Right above. A smooth linen tablecloth, relatively simple silverware, and unornamented glassware allow china with a densely figured Renaissance pattern to dominate. The cool, detached simplicity and symmetry of shape, sharpened by the elaborate design of the salt and pepper set, expresses formality. (*Franciscan Fine China*)

C
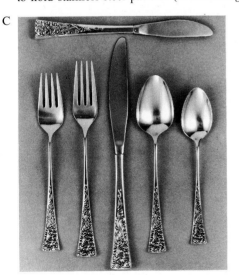

D

- Pieces that cannot be put in a dishwasher raise problems.
- Place settings, the units in which silverware is often but not necessarily acquired, may vary in the number and kind of pieces they include; customarily they consist of knife, fork, teaspoon, salad fork, and dessert or soup spoon, and sometimes butter spreader. Choose the pieces you need.
- **Sterling silver** flatware is originally expensive but does not wear out. **Silverplated** flatware costs less, but the plating wears off rather quickly unless it is double- or triple-plated and reinforced at points of greatest wear. **Stainless steel** is durable, nontarnishable, and seldom discolors. The price of flatware varies by weight and design.
- The extra cleaning time that heavily ornamented patterns take may or may not be compensated for by their rich beauty and the way in which they obscure scratches.

The following points pertaining to **beauty** and **individuality** should also be kept in mind:

- Flatware adds elongated forms and soft sparkle to table settings, but its real beauty is quite as much a matter of how it feels in the hands as of how it looks.
- Plain ware has a simple dignity and can be used in any context. But silver is an ideal material for intricate ornament.
- Flatware, because of its small size and distinctive qualities, offers unusual opportunities to bring contrast and variety peaceably into the home.
- Its cost and long life place flatware (and hollow ware, too) at the bottom of the list of objects with which to experiment with faddish, possibly transitory tastes.

Selecting Glassware

Since almost everything said about dinnerware applies to glassware, only a few specific points are worth emphasizing.

- "Glassware" for everyday use can also be of unbreakable aluminum or stainless steel or of durable plastic.
- Colored glassware enlivens a table—but the color cannot be changed for different occasions and it alters, sometimes unattractively, the color of the liquid.
- Stemware has a buoyant, bubble-like quality that gives a "lift" to the table; but it is hard to wash, is easily broken, and takes much storage space.

Selecting Table Coverings

Comparatively inexpensive and easily stored, table coverings permit variety and change. New fibers and weaves, easily cleaned plastics, strong or subtle colors are a challenge to those with self-reliant discrimination. The following points pertaining to **use** and **economy** should be kept in mind when selecting table coverings:

- Protecting table surfaces and lessening noise are major functions.
- Original cost is typically low to moderate. More important is maintenance time and energy.
- Tablecloths are harder to wash, iron, and store than are table mats.
- Resistance to stains and wrinkles is a significant factor.

The following points pertaining to **beauty** and **individuality** should also be kept in mind:

- Typically regarded as backgrounds to dinnerware and food, table coverings are often plain or subtly patterned, but conspicuous patterns can be refreshing.
- Tablecloths can be decisive unifying factors.
- The soft textures of most table coverings supplement the typically hard smoothness of dishes, silver, and glass.
- A change of table covering can revitalize long-familiar dinnerware and alter its character from one meal to the next.

Selecting Table Accessories

Table accessories are one small but vital part of the home's total enrichment. Those used on the table are similar to, and often the same pieces as, those used elsewhere at other times. Sometimes they are solely decorative; sometimes, as shown in Figures 381A and B, they are handsome ornaments in addition to being utilitarian. Often it is the accessories, the most variable element of the setting, that most strongly underscore the table's theme.

A

Handmade serving dishes personalize table settings.

Sgraffito and painted decorations enhance the shapes of a stoneware casserole and a soup tureen by Ernie Kim.

B

The soft luster of silver is allowed to speak for itself in the work of the modern French craftsman Tuiforcat. (*Photograph by Christof Studio*)

Thinking about accessories naturally turns attention to centerpieces, for they usually are the table's dominant enrichment. We have come to expect that centerpieces be interesting but not conspicuously distracting. Flowers and leaves, fruits and vegetables are the standard components and come in almost inexhaustible diversity; but they must be changed frequently to keep them looking their best. Rocks (Fig. 387A) and shells, a piece or two of sculpture (Figs. 373A and B), or a cluster of candles have the advantage of durability and can often be freshened by the addition of one or two transient items, such as flowers. The relation of centerpieces to the rest of the setting as well as to the size of the table and the room is important. If people sit or walk around the table, centerpieces should be attractive from all angles. It is almost always desirable that centerpieces be low enough to permit those at the table to hold a conversation without interference.

Planning Table Settings

The settings illustrated in this chaper touch but a few of the possibilities for setting attractive tables. Only one characteristic is common to all pleasant settings, *an appropriate idea imaginatively and personally developed.* The idea can be inspired by many things: a unique occasion or a traditional one, seasonal food or flowers, some particular pieces of dinnerware or enrichment, the dining space and its furnishings, the people who will eat the meal, or simply the desire for personal expression. But appropriateness, consistency, and sensitivity are fundamental in fulfilling the idea; surprise and the unexpected enliven the effect. This does not imply stereotyped conformity or obedience to rules, but a feeling for what is effective and most important for any given meal. Thus, even in an informal modern house, a Christmas dinner table set with a white damask tablecloth, elaborate inherited china, and silver candelabra would be appropriate in its connotations of tradition, security, and continuity; consistent in its formal appointments pleasingly combined. We would not expect many meals of this character in such a setting, but the fact that they are exceptional makes them a lively event. Equally effective could be a table set with some of the bright colors and imaginative forms of a Mexican Christmas, which would remind us of the happiness and universality of the occasion and would at the same time be in keeping with the informality of the house.

Although table settings can be in strong contrast to the furniture and architecture of which they are a part, they have a special sense of rightness when they are at one with their surroundings. Two examples are illustrated in Figures 383 and 384.

A city apartment is suggested by the first table: it is urbane, reserved, and seems a part of the storage wall. The porcelain plates, slender stemware, and stainless-steel flatware have precisely refined shapes. Almost the same color value as the tabletop, slightly textured linen mats bring restrained contrast with their grayed-blue hue. The seemingly artless centerpiece performs its job exceptionally well. In their texture and crisply defined form, the gladioli relate themselves to the plates; but whereas the plates are geometrically identical, each of the blossoms is organically different from the others. Laying them flat, a refreshing departure from the usual vertical arrangement, allows full enjoyment of the flowers without interference with conversation.

Handsome materials in uncluttered rectangular and circular shapes bring tableware, lighting fixture, and furniture into complete unison. The effect is one of informal order. George Nelson, designer. (*Photograph © Ezra Stoller, Herman Miller Inc.*)

A table set for dinner at Taliesin North, the Frank Lloyd Wright home, achieves genuine dignity without a trace of pretentious formality. (*Photograph by Maynard L. Parker Modern Photography*)

Frank Lloyd Wright considered that setting the table was a great artistic opportunity. The dining table in his own Wisconsin home (Fig. 384) demonstrates this viewpoint. Table and chairs take their place at one end of a large living space where they are part of a total design (see Fig. 76 for a view of another section of the room). The furniture and tableware recapitulate in a small scale the room's interplay of horizontals and verticals. Gradually ascending verticals draw attention upward from the planes of the floor and table: the low-backed chairs begin the ascent, the tall goblets and the higher chairs continue it. On the dining table the low flower arrangement curves diagonally into the dramatic upright spray that rises up the stone pier. The table setting is fairly simple but an admirable example of harmony and diversity. The rich brown tablecloth ties in with the color of the wood chairs and cupboards, and provides a unifying background. White Oriental plates are ornamented with asymmetrically placed figures in blue, brown, and green. Midway between the plain cloth and the intricacy of the white flowers and green leaves, they echo the Oriental screen on the wall behind the table. Gold-colored Dirilyte flatware and slender goblets, simple but graceful in outline, bring a lightness and sparkle in keeping with the star-shaped blossoms of the casual flower arrangement. Although ingratiatingly unaffected, this setting is an assured exercise in design—in itself and in relation to the surrounding space.

Setting tables and selecting the many things used on them can be daily experiments in three-dimensional design, miniature versions of planning a house or selecting and arranging furniture, differing from these chiefly in their specific purpose and temporary nature. While enjoying great freedom to express personal urges, the facts and principles cited earlier in this book still apply. The six steps listed in Chapter 1 may help in getting started and may lessen mistakes. The larger aspects of dining and food preparation, discussed in Chapters 2 and 4, are closely related to the ways in which tables are set. Design with light and color, form and space, and texture is one fundamental; another is the nature of materials. These are among the many situations in which we are faced with the challenge of responsible choices, perhaps of making the common seem uncommon, certainly of bringing together the serviceable and the beautiful.

LOCATION AND BACKGROUND OF ENRICHMENT

There are two logical types of locations for enrichment: first, those places where persons normally look; and second, those places where we want them to look with interest and pleasure.

People normally tend to look more or less straight ahead; through doors, windows, or wherever distance invites exploration; and at anything that is large, different, or well illumined. Thus, it is reasonable to think about putting some enrichment opposite the entrance door, somewhere in the first view of the living room, more or less opposite seating for conversation and dining, on the wall opposite a bed, in the space above a desk, and at the end of a hall. Outdoors, the major views from inside the house or from the terrace, as well as the ends or turning points of garden paths are logical places on which to concentrate interest. In each of these locations, the size and character of any enrichment deserve serious thought.

Entrance areas are introductions to the home. Usually they are small, which suggests something best seen at close range in a short period of time (Fig. 229B). A good table or chest with flowers, plants, or small sculpture below a mirror is one possibility if space permits. Or the enrichment can be on the wall —a distinctive lighting fixture or mirror, an uncomplicated painting or print, or a pleasing textile.

The first view into the living room is another matter, for the opposite wall or window is some distance away. In many modern homes this first view carries attention through the room out into the garden, which then becomes the place for interesting planting or fences, decorative urns or sculpture. In other houses, the fireplace wall is the first thing seen, and it may or may not need more than the architect has given in its design and materials (Fig. 20A). If the fireplace is small and simple, the wall above may have a painting or textile large enough and strong enough to balance the opening below and to make itself understood from across the room—and also with sufficient interest to be worth looking at over long periods of time (Color Fig. 16). In still other quarters the initial view may end in a blank wall that, typically, has a group of furniture and acces-

Chosen and placed with discerning taste, a profusion of plants and accessories makes designer Alexander Girard's Detroit living room a collector's paradise and a delightful place to enjoy group living. The old Moroccan brass tabletop is a dominant element; the plain wall is a quiet foil. (*Photograph by Charles Eames*)

sories. Whatever the specific situation, remember that it is gratifying to have something of interest greet the eyes. There are, however, instances in which the major point of interest is on a wall seen only after coming into the room. Or it could be the floor enhanced with distinctively beautiful rugs (Fig. 275A).

Then there are the spots in most homes where we have to entice attention, such as uninteresting corners or small wall spaces that must be used. The writers have found in their efforts to arrange furniture in group-living space for both large and small gatherings that it is helpful to suggest, not vocally but visually, that a few guests might be happier in a small, separate furniture group than all overcrowding the major seating arrangement. Often this can be accomplished by reinforcing comfortable furniture with congenial illumination; by having prints, paintings, or textiles on the wall; and by placing interesting objects on the table. Then, what was an unused corner becomes inhabited space, chiefly through appropriate furniture but also to a surprising degree through distinctive enrichment (Fig. 324A).

The effectiveness of any enrichment can be increased or decreased markedly by its setting. Should contrast or harmony be emphasized? Simple white china would hardly be noticed against a white tablecloth, moderately so against gray, but would stand out sharply from dark green. This raises two more questions. How much attention should be attracted to a particular vase? How beautiful is it? Contrasting backgrounds are often recommended to "show up" accessories or paintings, but this is not the only way. Large, significant objects can proclaim their presence by being put in important positions, by being given backgrounds against which they can be readily seen, and by being built up with smaller objects. At the other extreme, some enrichment can take its place unobtrusively, a little murmur in a harmonious setting. Thus varying degrees of emphasis and subordination are achieved.

In summary:
- Select enrichment that is meaningful, contributes to the home, and has intrinsic interest.
- Think first in terms of a few large and important objects in scale with rooms and furniture. Supplement these with others of varied sizes.
- Concentrate enrichment at important points related to the architecture and other furnishings.
- Study the design of arrangements as an artist studies the composition of a painting.
- Change accessories for variety, for the seasons and holidays, and for other special occasions.
- Plan convenient storage for those objects not always used.
- Consider breakage hazards if mobility or small children indicate this.
- Weed out and upgrade the collection from time to time.
- Have courage to try something different, to express individuality.

Many rock and mineral formations have a distinction quite unlike living materials or man-made objects. Quartz crystals from Arkansas range from transparent to opaque, and their diverse shapes and sizes are a remarkable example of variety in unity. (*The American Museum of Natural History, New York*)

A

B

Thomas Simpson's "Dong with the Aluminous Nose" is a unique piece of enrichment that is as much sculpture as it is a clock. (*Photograph by Charles Uht. The Museum of Contemporary Crafts, New York*)

Opposite. One of the most audacious and beautiful houses of this century is "Falling-water" (1937), designed by Frank Lloyd Wright and built at Bear Run, Pennsylvania. Its cantilevered terraces and native stone walls intensify and dramatize the rocky site so effectively that architecture and nature become an organic entity. (*Photograph by Hedrich-Blessing*)

Part V · THE WHOLE HOUSE

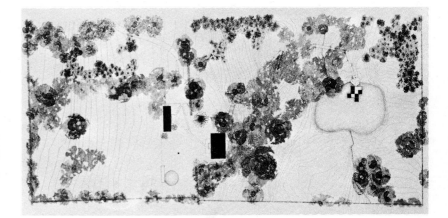

Architect Philip Johnson planned his glass-walled house and the surrounding landscape as two complementary units of one composition. (See also Color Fig. 23.)

17 · Plan

Of all aspects of home planning and furnishings, the plan is probably the most important. It indicates the position of walls and openings, the location, size, and shape of space for living, and the ways in which furnishings can be arranged. In large part, the plan determines the family's living patterns and establishes the basic character of the structure. Many specific aspects of planning have been considered in preceding chapters. Planning is a summation and integration of the varied components into a unified whole. In this chapter we will concentrate on plan, but, especially in the discussion of the first house, we will notice the relationship of plan to interior design and furnishings and to exterior design and landscaping, because all these belong together.

TWO PRIZE-WINNING SMALL HOUSES

The houses illustrated in Figures 392 and 398 deserve more than ordinary study because they were judged the best of 2727 designs submitted in a national competition. The program stated that the enclosed area should not exceed 1000 square feet because this is about as much as many families can afford, *not* because it is all the space even a small family needs. There were to be three bedrooms, and the houses were to fit on lots 60 by 100 feet. The success of these houses is indicated by the fact that within four weeks after the winners had been announced, twenty-two builders from coast to coast were negotiating with the designers for the privilege of building from their plans.

The First-Prize Winner

Let us look at Bruce Walker's design in the light of what was said in earlier chapters about the requirements for group, private, and work activities, about design and color, about materials, and about the major elements of a house.

Living with others. Four integrated areas give space for group living in Walker's plan: indoors, the all-purpose space and conversation alcove; outdoors, the terrace and screened porch. Moderately quiet, small-group **conversation** or **reading** is provided for in the living space by an alcove about 8 by 10 feet, a good size and shape for from two to five persons, with a sofa and end tables against a solid wall, storage built in under the windows, two movable chairs, and

A

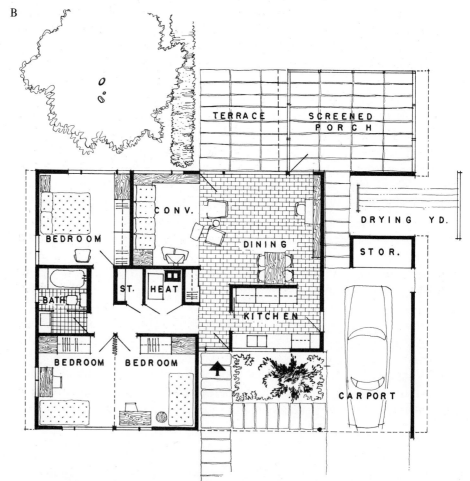

B

An efficient, beautiful plan based on a genuine understanding of a family's needs. The exterior is a logical outgrowth of the plan and of the interior design. Bruce Walker, architect. (*Reprinted from* The Magazine of Building)

392

a fireplace (backed up against the heater room so that only one chimney is needed). South light comes from a row of windows high enough above the floor to give usable wall space underneath and a feeling of enclosure, but low enough so that a seated person can see outdoors. Although no walls separate the conversation area from the all-purpose space, it is differentiated by being a dead-end alcove narrower than the rest of the room, by windows that are higher than those overlooking the terrace, by the different floor treatment, and by the ceiling, which changes direction along the line demarking the two areas. It is a retreat that gives a feeling of permanence and enclosure without becoming boxy, and it can also become the stabilizing element of a much larger furniture group.

Although the conversation area is only a few steps from the front door, the kitchen, and the terrace, it maintains its identity in plan alone, but its separateness could be underscored by furnishings. This is the logical place for the "best" furniture: a comfortable, handsome sofa and chair; a soft rug; and paintings or prints, wall sculpture or fabrics of special interest to the family. Especially in a small house, it would be wise to use colors that carry through from one space to the others, but these need not be monotonously repetitious. Warmer hues, stronger intensities, and lower values enlivened with sparkling contrasts would emphasize the enclosure and importance of this alcove.

Music could be centered in either or both of two locations. The cabinets under the windows in the conversation area could house a radio-phonograph, and the long wall in the all-purpose space could accommodate a radio, phonograph, television, or a piano. The sloping ceiling and the complex shape of this whole space would give good acoustics. **Games** of a quiet sort could be played at the dining table or on a card table placed where wanted.

Eating would normally and most conveniently take place at the table near the kitchen, where there is adequate space for service and also for extending the table for celebrations. For variety, it would be easy to move the table over to the windows; television suppers might be enjoyed in the conversation area in chairs grouped around the receiver. The screened porch, the terrace, and the lawn, all easily accessible, provide more comfortable and varied outdoor eating spots than in many houses twice this size but less well planned.

Small children's activities could be centered in the two bedrooms that can be joined by pushing back the folding wall, but they would also be easily supervised in the all-purpose space, terrace, porch, and yard.

At this point, a few thoughts about the materials and furnishings of the all-purpose area are in order, because they, along with the room's size and shape, affect its pleasantness and maintenance. Notice that the architect has indicated a tile floor that could be of such durable, easily kept materials as vinyl, linoleum, or asphalt. Using the same flooring in the entrance and kitchen unifies the three areas, makes them seem larger. Walls, too, should withstand use. Wood comes to mind, although hard-surfaced wallboards or tough and washable wallpaper or fabric would be suitable. The two fixed units of furniture, built-in or assembled from interchangeable units put tight against the wall, could include cupboard, drawer and shelf space, desk and television, or whatever the family wanted. Furniture that is durable, easy to move, and light in design and color would preserve the room's openness and usability.

In summary, varied kinds of indoor and outdoor group-living spaces have been integrated to give usable and visual space far beyond that found in most houses this small. Large groups could spread from the all-purpose space to the terrace, porch, or lawn because all are interconnected and uncluttered. Terrace and porch more than double the living space in good weather. Moreover, these areas have been handsomely related to space for work and for private living.

Private living. Bedrooms and bath are well segregated in a unit away from the noisy group areas with a sound barrier of coat closet, heater room, linen storage, and bedroom closets. Although not large, each bedroom has a good place for the bed, adequate space for dressing, and sufficient closet space. Notice that chests of drawers are beside each closet, which in turn is near a door. Each bedroom gets light and air from two directions through windows that are high enough above the floor to allow furniture beneath them and afford some privacy yet low enough to give an outlook. Draperies or blinds would give flexible control. The bathroom is exceptionally well located and planned. While not much larger than the minimum, it is subdivided into two units, one with the basin and the other with tub and toilet, which greatly increases its efficiency. This plan solves well the problem of getting space adequate in size, suitable in shape, and efficiently zoned. But this is only the beginning.

Housework and maintenance. With one exception, housework and maintenance have been very well handled. *Getting meals* and *laundering* have been simplified in a kitchen measuring $7\frac{1}{2}$ by 11 feet, which is small enough to save steps without being cramped. It is strategically located near the dining table, the carport, and the front door, and it is not far from the screened porch and terrace and the bedrooms. It is in direct line of vision with the bathroom, where small children often need supervision. The plan is of the "opposite walls" type, putting work centers close together and not in this case inviting much through traffic because of easy alternative routes. *Straightening-up* and *cleaning* are lightened by having some basic furniture built into each room: storage and table units in the conversation alcove; storage, desk, and music in the multipurpose space; and chests of drawers in each bedroom. There is at least one good, permanent place for such big furniture as sofa, dining table, beds, and desks. A walk-in linen cupboard is convenient to bedrooms and bath. Its size and central location make it a logical place to store household and cleaning equipment. Housework would be expedited by having bedroom and bathroom walls and floors smooth, durable, and slightly patterned.

The one moderately serious weakness is insufficient general storage space, a matter that could be taken care of by trebling the carport storage space and designing it as well as the storage space in Figure 394.

Well-designed storage in garage or carport is inexpensive in terms of its contribution to a well-ordered household. J. and C. Roberto, architects. (*Douglas Fir Plywood Association*)

Circulation. This plan is a model of short, straight, desirable routes. The carport is beside the kitchen door and only a few steps from the front door, an ideal arrangement. Its nearness to the service yard and porch saves many trips through the house. From the front door, paths spread like the fingers of a hand to give direct routes to kitchen, coat closet, multipurpose space and conversation area, heater room and linen storage, any of the bedrooms, and the bath—without going through any other room. Yet the area devoted only to halls is small. The paths from front door to terrace and porch are also direct and cause minimum interference with furniture arrangement.

Orientation. Putting the sun, wind, and outlook in the right place has been simplified by designing this house for the ideally oriented lot with the street to the north. Then the important rooms can get winter sun and be related to private outdoor-living areas. The kitchen faces north, good for the house's hottest room. Each bedroom has cross ventilation and light. Planned for a typical flat city lot, the house is as near the street as most city ordinances allow. This shortens the driveway and gives maximum space in the private backyard.

Beauty. The preceding analysis has shown how this house has been designed for use, but function, as we use the term, includes more than the utilitarian. Inside and outside, this house promises happy living. The carefully studied but unpretentious plan sets the stage for informal home life, while the handsome, friendly exterior gives a feeling of shelter and relationship to the site. It would not jostle its neighbors. Although the design takes advantage of new developments, notably in the windows, it is domestic in character and would never be mistaken for other than it is—a small house for a small American family living in the latter half of the twentieth century. In brief, *its form follows its function.*

Can a house plan be beautiful? It not only can but it should be! Bruce Walker's plan is strictly rectangular in whole and in part with a number of interlocking L-shapes that establish a pervasive *unity.* There are three major L's—the whole enclosed area, the group-living and work space, and the zone of private living. Notice that private and group portions interlock with the conversation area, a nice refinement because it is the quietest part of the group-living zone. The L-shaped motif can also be seen in the layout of the functionally related multipurpose space, the terrace, and the porch; in the furniture against two walls of the conversation center; and in the walk from carport to front door. *Variety* comes because no two of the rectangles or L's are identical: each varies from thd others in size and shape, but all grow from the central idea.

The plan has a pleasant asymmetrical *balance,* for the visual weight of the slightly narrower but more solid-looking projecting bedroom wing is compensated for by the greater spread and visual interest of the wing on the right. The front entrance is almost exactly in the center, although it appears to be much less formally placed. The major *emphasis* is found in the amount of space given to group living, logical in terms of use and effect. *Rhythm* is achieved by the consistent rectangles and L-shapes, and especially by the way major lines continue through the house. A strong central axis begins at the right corner of the bedroom wing, is carried through the plan by the floor treatment, and emerges at the rear in the edge of the terrace.

Here is an important point in integrated architecture: not only is this line dominant in plan but it parallels the high point of the roof seen from outside and of the ceiling seen from the inside. Many other lines add their share to continuity: the front line of the bedroom wing is carried through by roof and paving to the carport's far edge; the carport kitchen door is in a straight line with the opposite kitchen door and the bedroom hall; the south wall of the house continues in the wall shielding the screened porch from the drying yard; the south edge of terrace and porch is one line, as is the east edge of porch and carport. You might ask if this "T square and triangle" design is rigidly and coldly geometrical. We think not. Many lines do not carry through; but the major lines, continuing decisively through the house, give satisfying order, clarity, and discipline, too seldom found in house plans.

Interior and exterior design. A house plan not only shows the size, shape, and location of the rooms but also indicates where windows, doors, and opaque walls are. Thus, it is the basis from which the exterior and interior are developed. Now let us start erecting the enclosing walls and roof, as the builder would after laying the foundations, and see what happens. Do they give privacy, light, air, and views where wanted? What is the effect of the whole and of the parts?

From the street, the house is a low, informal composition, thoroughly satisfying at first glance and quite remarkable as its subtleties are investigated. The predominantly horizontal lines of the whole mass, the bands of windows, and the gently sloping roof relate it to the ground. But the absence of overhanging eaves (little needed on the north), the narrow vertical siding, and the opening in the roof near the entrance give an upward movement to balance the dominant horizontality. Had it not been for such devices, the house might have looked squat and pushed into the ground rather than standing on, and rising from, it. The street side is not flat, like the side of a barn, but invites you into a recessed entrance court. This movement is repeated by the carport, the back of which recedes another 10 feet or so. These setbacks give a play of light and shade, a three-dimensional quality of space, time, and movement. They also divide the composition into three units varied in size and treatment to express the interior divisions but bound together by the simple roof line.

A beautifully organized sequence of form-space relationships is experienced as one starts into the house. Walking toward the protectingly opaque door, the visitor comes into the hospitable shelter of the semienclosed entrance court as the first transitional step between outdoor and indoor scale. The width is the same as that of the multipurpose space, and the roof introduces him to the height and slope of the ceiling inside; but an opening above the planting bed gives a last glimpse of the sky as well as bringing light and air into kitchen, entrance hall, and bedroom windows. Small but not cramped, the entrance hall is the second transitional step, and while in it the visitor would notice that the lines of the floor and the ceiling ridge, carried through from outside, lead naturally into the living areas. Pausing while being relieved of coat and hat, he would almost automatically look toward the largest expanse of glass in the house. This is the most emphatic part of the interior, and it is not a confining center of interest, such as the typical fireplace, but an invitation to explore beyond. Fortunately, this is made physically possible by two doors leading to the outside. This all-purpose space is not large, but it is given a big feeling by the knowledge that it is a section of a continuing pattern, by the glass reaching to the sloping ceiling, by the potential of outdoor living, and then by the contrast of the small, secure conversation alcove.

Why was a sloping roof chosen in preference to a flat one? The designer did submit an alternate version with a flat roof and, consequently, horizontal ceilings of uniform height. They would not, however, appear as lively or satisfying as do the buoyant sloping roof and ceiling. The sloping roof introduces the only diagonals in the house, and the rhythmic building up and down gives variety, emphasis, and movement. From outside it fits commonly held ideas of what a roof should look like and from inside gives a refreshing change from parallel surfaces.

Furnishing the house. What kind of furniture and what colors does this house suggest? To us, the house calls for simple, unpretentious but sensitively designed furniture. In a house of this size, usefulness and beauty would be increased if most pieces were small in size and scale and harmonious in color, and if they were not individually "eye-catching" pieces.

Because the house is designed to harmonize with nature, natural colors and textures are indicated. Grays, tans, and browns or combinations of earthy colors for the large floor areas might be sparked with a few rugs in brighter colors. The same colors plus muted blues, greens, yellows, and oranges could be used for upholstery or draperies or on some of the walls. A few accents of jewel-toned scarlet, cerise, magenta, violet, or strong acid green would complete the scheme. The exterior might well be naturally finished or stained lightly with gray or brown. You could, of course, paint the exterior white, yellow, or some other bright color, and the interior could be dazzling with clear strong hues or Spartan-pure with black and white. Certainly, though, neither of these would be a logical outgrowth of the idea from which the house grew.

The Second-Prize Winner

The design illustrated in Figure 398 differs from the first-prize winner in several significant ways. But before discussing them, let us read part of what the architect, Ralph Rapson, had to say (*Architectural Forum,* March 1951, pp. 115–117):

> The design of this small house for a warm climate was predicated on three basic concepts: (1) that "close" living, necessitated by a house of this size, makes it mandatory that the active living be separated from the passive, with the "heart" of the living—the kitchen—in direct control-contact with each; (2) that all major plan elements have through-ventilation; and (3) that these elements be enclosed in a basically simple shape for ease and economy of construction.
>
> The plan evolved from these basic factors provides two distinct though closely interlocking areas. One is a multipurpose area for active living; for children and adult rumpus and play; for sewing, ironing and clothes drying on bad days; where the family might take most of their meals and which the mother would not need to worry about keeping spick and span, since guests would normally be entertained in the second area—the space for the more conventional type of living. The utility core, of which the food center is part, is placed between these elements for ease of access and direct control of both.

This had led to a plan divided into four front-to-back zones: going from right to left, we find a quiet living-dining zone $12\frac{1}{4}$ feet wide, an entrance and utility zone $10\frac{2}{3}$ feet wide, a multipurpose space of the same width, and then a line of bedrooms exactly as wide as the living-dining space.

Let us study this plan by concentrating on the ways in which it differs from Walker's design.

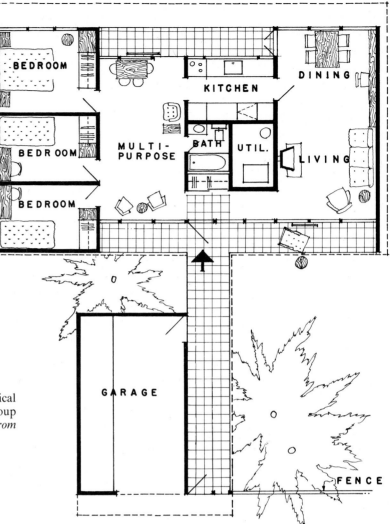

A plan distinguished by a compact, economical utility core that separates two areas for group living. Ralph Rapson, architect. (*Reprinted from The Magazine of Building*)

Group-living space is sharply divided into two separate units. As Rapson points out, dividing the group-living space into two separate sections has notable advantages. It also raises problems. Both are long, narrow rectangles and these proportions are accentuated by window walls at each end. The two cannot be combined for large groups, and the division of group-living space in a house this small cramps everything.

Kitchen, bath, and utilities form a compact central "utility core." The compact utility core puts the kitchen in direct contact-control of both living spaces and of the rear yard; and bringing the expensive, noisy utilities together reduces installation costs. Sensible as this sounds, it is offset in this plan by three serious disadvantages. First, this opaque central block closes the center of the house and robs it of its potential spaciousness. Second, the theoretically private, quiet, and related bedrooms and bath all open publicly off the noisy multipurpose space, and the only paths from bedrooms to bath are diagonally across this highly active space with glass walls at both ends. Third, noise control would be extraordinarily difficult to achieve.

The house is set well back from the street. The lot for which this house was designed is on the north side of the street; and, as is common practice with lots of this orientation, setting the house back gives space for a sunny outdoor-living area. Unfortunately in this case, the only entrance from street to house goes through the fenced front yard, which is thus forced to act as guest and family entrance, service entrance, and questionably private outdoor-living space.

The garage is a separate unit placed in front of the house. Placing the garage forward shields both house and front yard while shortening the driveway. Designing the garage as an independent, loosely connected appendage extends the house pleasantly. *But* this separation increases building costs, because the garage requires four independent walls and a separate roof. More critical over the years, there is no possibility of a service yard adjacent to kitchen and garage, and there is no short, direct path for the many package-laden trips between these units.

Convenient storage for bulky items lines one wall of the garage. Storage space is always a pressing need, and placing it in easily accessible closets on the same level as the living areas of the house adds to its convenience.

Circulation paths are chiefly through rooms. Only about 30 square feet in the entry are allotted solely to traffic, whereas Walker's plan has around 75 square feet in the entry and bedroom hall. At first glance, this appears to be a worthwhile saving of 45 square feet; but it makes for many paths that interfere with furniture arrangement in rooms and, as mentioned above, precludes a private bedroom-bathroom zone.

Orientation is well handled for a mild-climate house to be built on many sites. The window walls at both ends of both group-living areas permit facing the house north or south, and with protection from afternoon sun, it could face east or west.

The design is clean-cut, rational, and possibly a trifle rigid with its four front-to-back zones. Related in widths, these give an easily appreciated order, a systematic rhythm with some variety, but do not produce a satisfying emphasis and forceful unity.

Our analysis has purposely emphasized the weaknesses of this plan to stimulate your critical ability, to get you to look at the parts by themselves and in relation to the whole. In case we have gone too far, let us remind you that this house is superior to most built today and that it has these good points:

- Two separated living and eating spaces
- Economical concentration of utilities
- Abundant light and ventilation in the group areas (but not in the bedrooms)
- Use of the typically wasted front yard
- Basic logic and adaptability of the plan

What furnishings and color does this plan suggest? The plan's clean-cut, precise order might well be underlined so that the house would affirm its man-made character and assert its independence of nature, as houses around the Mediterranean always have and as our Colonial houses certainly did. Lightweight, "functional" metal furniture with plastic upholstery would harmonize with the spirit of the plan. Pronounced contrasting colors could emphasize the planes and space. Thus, as the writers see it, this house would differ as strikingly from the first-prize winner in colors and furnishings as it differs in plan.

The two plans that have been analyzed are economically small and compact, but good as they are for low-cost, single-family dwellings, they would have been more comfortable if they were 200 to 600 square feet larger to ease the tightness of small rooms. Both are one-story plans and deviate little, if at all, from simple rectangles. There are, however, many other kinds of plans.

BASIC TYPES OF HOUSE PLANS

There are two basic determinants in shaping a plan—the family and the lot—and these can be interrelated in countless ways. Family size, resources, age of members, and way of life indicates the amount of square footage desirable and economically feasible, and its disposition for satisfactory living on one level or two, compacted or spread out. The size, shape, contour, and environment of the lot, in turn, indicate whether a given amount of square footage can be contained in one story or will need more than one, whether the plan should be a square or rectangle or can be expanded into a T-shape or a pinwheel shape, and perhaps whether an inward-turning court plan would be better than one that opens outward to a nonexistent view, to a street, or to nearby neighbors and thereby loses privacy.

Merely listing a few effects of the shape of a house plan—initial and long-term costs, space planned and arranged for diverse activities, circulation paths, natural light and ventilation as well as control of heat and cold, interior and exterior design, relation to the site and to outdoor living—indicates its critical significance. Each basic form has its inherent characteristics, as discussed in Chapter 6, and these qualities are more fundamental in the layout of a house than they are in the design of textiles or in the composition of a painting. And each basic shape can be imaginatively varied. We will consider first some of the results of the number of levels in the plan and then concentrate attention on the different shapes that can be used.

One-Story and Multiple-Story Plans

One-story plans are well suited to small houses and to larger ones for which the cost of greater land area and of an extended perimeter will not be an excluding factor. They avoid stairways, permit easy supervision of children, give easy access to the out-of-doors, and generally lead to a horizontal silhouette that fits comfortably on level land.

Multiple-story plans also have impressive advantages. They are cheaper to build (less foundation and roof), to heat, and sometimes to cool (less exterior surface). Zoning is simplified because rooms vertically segregated automatically have more privacy. As the cost of land goes up, they become more necessary and more favored. They can fit onto awkward hillsides, tight city lots, or small suburban sites, where they free more land for outdoor enterprises. Sometimes they rise to catch desirable breezes or an otherwise hidden view. *But,* the necessary stairs can be fatiguing and hazardous. Designing exteriors that avoid high, clumsy boxiness is difficult, but it is feasible as is shown by Figure 402B and C and Color Figure 21. **Split-level plans** usually have three levels, although there may be more, approximately one-half level apart. They have the advantage of shorter stairs between some of the rooms and the possibility of a lively three-dimensional experience. The exterior design is hard to handle aesthetically because of the difficulty of aligning windows, but again, a good architect can turn this difficulty into a design challenge. They usually look best on rolling terrain that makes the change in level appropriate, but with sensitive planning and grading they can be adapted to hillsides or flat land.

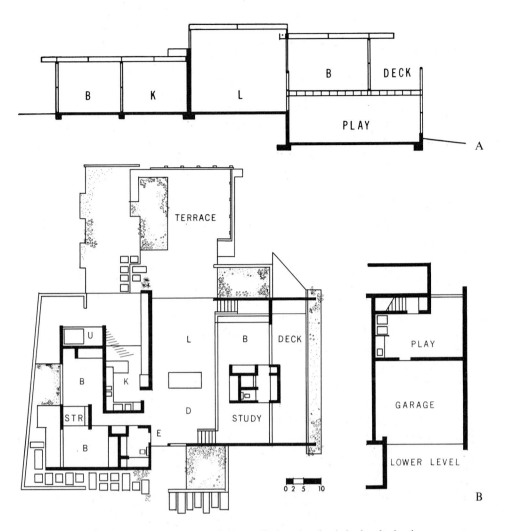

B K L B DECK

PLAY

A

TERRACE

U L B DECK

B K

STR D STUDY

E B

PLAY

GARAGE

LOWER LEVEL

0 2 5 10

B

Architect Robert Skinner used the split-level principle in designing a tract house (Figs. 401A and B) for a small sloping site, but avoided some of its more obvious pitfalls by having the front walls blank except for the dramatic entrance with windows going up to the high roof. This lofty roof extends out over a sizable entrance terrace and part way over a large rear terrace, providing shelter and an exciting definition of the group-living space. The plan is imaginative and at the same time quite workable, except perhaps for the placement of the stairs to the playroom. Ternstrom and Skinner, architects. (*Reprinted from Architectural Record, Record Houses of 1965, copyright © 1965 by McGraw-Hill, Inc., with all rights reserved*)

Square Plans

Of all typical plan shapes, the square encloses the most space with the least foundation, exterior walls, and roof. Construction, exterior maintenance, and heating costs are low. In two-story houses, the square can lead to efficient room layout; in one-story designs, zoning and circulation are usually problems. If large, the center of the house may be dark and poorly ventilated unless skylights, clerestories, or central courts (Fig. 410B) are features of the design. Exteriors are likely to be boxy, especially if of two stories, and hard to integrate with most sites.

A

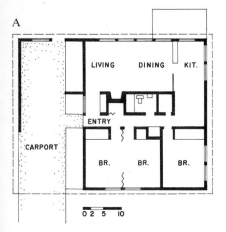

LIVING   DINING   KIT.

ENTRY

CARPORT

BR.   BR.   BR.

0 2 5 10

A carport extends the one-story Michigan house (Fig. 402A) designed by Richard Pollman and thereby greatly improves the exterior. Bedrooms are private and utilities are concentrated. Zoning and circulation are better than average for houses of this size and shape, even though the kitchen is on the side of the house away from the carport.

A two-story house in New Canaan, Connecticut (Figs. 402B and C), has excellent zoning and circulation. The study on the first floor could double as a bedroom when someone in the house is ill, saving many trips upstairs and downstairs. The balconies off the bedrooms give the second story access to the out-of-doors; the split entry is convenient to both levels. Possible boxiness in the exterior design is alleviated by extending the roof to provide shade for the windows and some protection of outdoor terraces, and by the bridge from the driveway to the entrance. The flatness of the roof plane is countered by the vertical posts standing tall and straight, like the trees that surround the house, and by the dark trim around the banks of windows. John Black Lee and Harrison DeSilver, architects. (*Photograph by Lisanti, Inc. Plan reprinted by special permission from the July 1964 issue of* House & Home *copyright* © *1964 by McGraw-Hill, Inc.*)

B

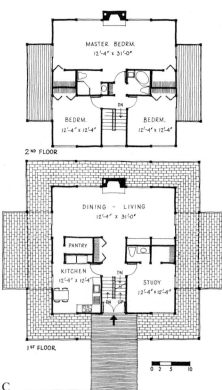

MASTER BEDRM.
12'-4" x 31'-0"

BEDRM.
12'-4" x 12'-4"

BEDRM.
12'-4" x 12'-4"

DN

2ND FLOOR

DINING - LIVING
12'-4" x 31'-0"

PANTRY

KITCHEN
12'-4" x 12'-4"

STUDY
12'-4" x 12'-4"

DN   UP

1ST FLOOR

0 2 5   10

C

Rectangular Plans

Almost as economical to build as squares, rectangular plans can be flexibly varied. If the long dimension faces the street, houses look large and give privacy to the rear yard. Turned the other way they fit deep narrow lots. Longer exterior walls give more area for windows and outside doors, sometimes an advantage in solar heating and summer cooling. Zoning and circulation are easy to handle; exteriors can be pleasantly proportioned.

Special conditions, such as a hillside with access from the top of the site, sometimes make it advisable to have the group-living areas and kitchen on the upper floor. In the plan of Figure 403A they are surrounded by a broad deck for outdoor living. The bedrooms open directly onto the surrounding grounds. John Pekruhn, architect.

William Nathan's plan for a one-story house (Fig. 403B) is well designed. Sensible zoning keeps related areas together, and the efficient circulation takes minimum square footage yet interferes little with other activities. Separating one bedroom from the living room with sliding doors gives desirable flexibility in use of space. Some provisions for screening the work area of the kitchen would also be desirable.

UPPER FLOOR

LOWER FLOOR

A

0 2 5 10

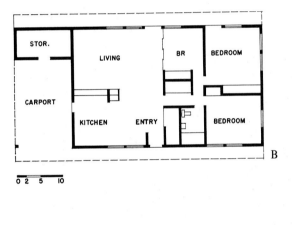

B

0 2 5 10

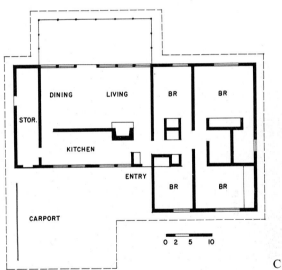

C

0 2 5 10

L-shaped Plans

Spreading out the plan means more foundation, roof, and exterior wall—and usually more land. A large-scale builder has said that every time a plan turns a corner it costs $500. L-shaped plans have six corners, square and rectangular plans have only four. Heating and plumbing costs are also a little higher. But L-shaped plans have these good points: the shape can naturally separate group and private areas and permit excellent circulation, can lead to pleasing exterior design, and can provide an outdoor area sheltered on two sides. There can be more well-placed windows and better advantage can be taken of cooling breezes.

An ample carport makes a sheltered, convenient entrance to Ernest Kump's single-level house (Fig. 403C). Kitchen, dining, and living space are in one wing, bedrooms in the other. Circulation is excellent.

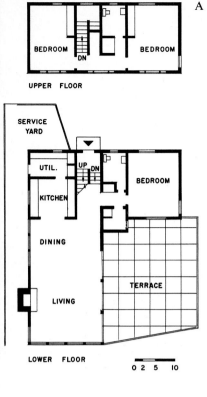

UPPER FLOOR

SERVICE YARD

UTIL.

KITCHEN

DINING

LIVING

UP DN

BEDROOM

TERRACE

LOWER FLOOR

0 2 5 10

No law states that the stories of multilevel houses must be the same size and shape. The plan of the vacation house in Figure 404A could be adapted to many situations. The gently sloping site suggested an entrance between two floors. On the lower floor, a kitchen and utility room have access to the service yard; a living-dining room with windows on three sides and a secluded bedroom and bath for the owners open onto a protected terrace. Upstairs, two bedrooms and a bath align with the kitchen and bedroom below. Wurster, Bernardi, and Emmons, architects.

T-shaped Plans

With no more exterior wall but with two more corners than L-shaped plans, T-shaped plans have somewhat similar advantages and disadvantages. Construction costs are higher, but quiet and noisy areas can be separated. This shape also permits good orientation for all rooms. Two semienclosed, easily roofed areas on opposite sides of the house give a choice of sun or shade for outdoor activities. These terraces are a starting point for landscape design and usually make the exterior more ingratiating.

Anshen and Allen's plan for a one-story tract house (Fig. 404C), designed for a narrow lot, faces the garage toward the street. House and terraces are sheltered and unified by a simple roof. A fence extending the front garage wall would shield the living terrace.

The T-shaped plan at the left (Fig. 404B) is designed for a deep narrow lot that falls abruptly away from the road. The entrance is on the upper level beside a mezzanine master bedroom that overlooks the two-story living room. On the lower floor, a centrally located kitchen easily serves dining room, living room, and playroom, as well as the poolside terrace. A bedroom and bath for a teen-age son opens off the playroom. The house was planned to relate to the spectacular views on three sides and to provide sun and shelter for the pool and terrace. Frederick Liebhardt and Eugene Weston, architects. (*Reprinted from* Architectural Record, Record Houses of 1965, *copyright* © *1965 by McGraw-Hill, Inc., with all rights reserved*)

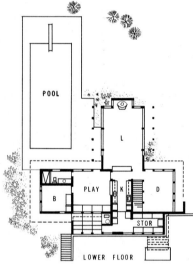

POOL

L

B

PLAY K D

STOR

LOWER FLOOR

0 2 5 10

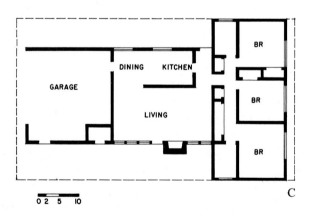

GARAGE

DINING KITCHEN

LIVING

BR

BR

BR

0 2 5 10

C

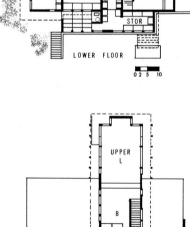

UPPER L

B

E

B

U- and H-shaped Plans

Seldom used in modest two-story houses or in very small ones with a single story, U- and H-shaped plans can really separate several zones from one another. Abundant natural light and ventilation can easily be had because exterior walls may be half again as long as on simple squares, which, of course, increases construction and heating costs. Cooling expense may or may not be reduced depending on the local climate. Plans in these extended shapes tend to relate the house strongly to its site and to landscape development, chiefly through the one or two patios they create. Sizable lots are usually required unless the house is close to property lines. A U-shaped plan with wings on three sides of an open court is traditional, dating as early as the fourth century B.C. A wall on the street side can complete the enclosure and assure privacy as well as protection from bad weather.

A 0 2 5 10

An expandable plan by Samuel Paul (Fig. 405) begins as a compact square enclosing 400 square feet. When living room and carport are added, the shape becomes a T-shape of 706 square feet. A three-bedroom wing adds another 670 square feet to complete the H-shaped house.

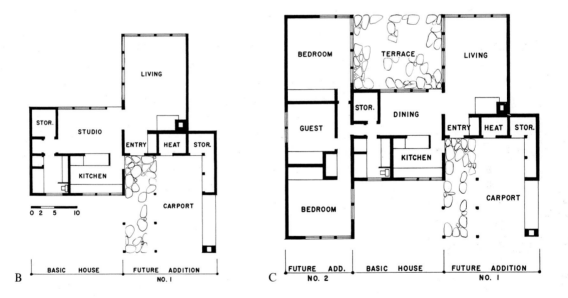

Cruciform and Cluster Plans

Plans of either the cruciform or the cluster type permit clear-cut zoning of different areas, a high degree of privacy, abundant opportunities for natural light and ventilation, and semienclosed outdoor living space. Usually, they require a sizable piece of land, but they can be adapted to difficult terrain. They are obviously expensive to build and maintain because of the lengthy perimeter and many corners. In cruciform plans, rooms are set off in four wings at right angles to each other from a central pivotal area that may be used for group living or merely as a circulation zone. In cluster plans, the rooms are placed in separate pavilions around one or more courts.

This strongly three-dimensional cruciform plan was designed by an architect for his own family, and he placed the rooms with great freedom on three levels to implement the kind of living his family wanted. They wished space for privacy and also space in which they could be together. They enjoy the delights of romanticism yet are very practical. The site is in a wooded area in Iowa, and the family wanted to live with its moods and seasons. Ray Crites organized the rooms around a central core for group living and went in and out, up and down, emphasizing verticality rather than horizontality, because it was less expensive and took many of the rooms up among the tree tops. The plan expands out into the site with decks and terraces, and in places the demarcation of house and setting almost disappears. The result is a home robustly individual, liberating, and poetic (Color Fig. 21). Crites and McConnell, architects. (*Reprinted by special permission from the June 1965 issue of* House & Home *copyright © 1965 by McGraw-Hill, Inc.*)

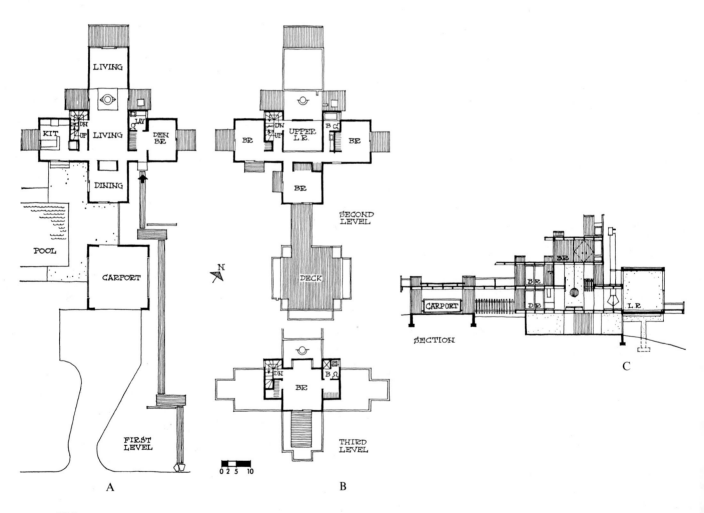

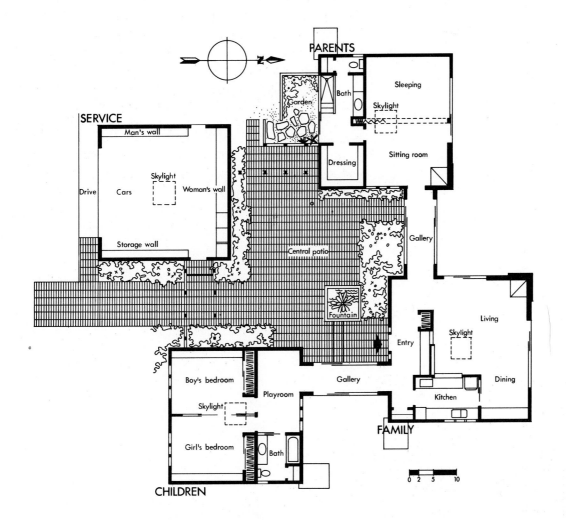

PARENTS

SERVICE

Sleeping

Bath

Garden

Skylight

Man's wall

Skylight

Drive   Cars   Woman's wall

Dressing

Sitting room

Storage wall

Central patio

Gallery

Fountain

Gallery

Entry

Living

Skylight

Boy's bedroom

Playroom

Dining

Skylight

Kitchen

Gallery

Girl's bedroom   Bath

FAMILY

0 2 5   10

CHILDREN

An experimental, built-for-sale house in California is a cluster of four separated pavilions, each for a different aspect of family life: group living, children's space, master bedroom, and service. It would, however, function equally well for a family with grandparents, or for a family that enjoys frequent house guests or that treasures privacy. The pavilions are skillfully placed around a central patio and joined by galleries that adjust to slightly different levels of the site. These could be replaced with steps on a more precipitous site. Each unit has possibilities for windows facing in four directions, can be heated or cooled separately, and can be closed off or used as a rental unit. Henrik Bull, architect. (*Reprinted from* Sunset *Magazine, November 1962*)

Diagonal and Curved Plans

Diagonals and curves, refreshing alternatives to boxy shapes, make lively and distinctive plans. Diagonals shape space dynamically, open unexpected vistas, and visually stretch rooms beyond their actual dimensions. Curves, whether geometric or free form, typically lead to an effect of evolving expansiveness. Each of these variations often increases building costs and makes it more difficult to find appropriate furniture that can be arranged so that it seems to belong to the shape of the house. But many persons find that the spatial advantages outweigh practical matters.

George Frank Ligar's Round House (Fig. 408A) pivots around a free-standing fireplace. Cantilevered concrete benches and a table penetrate the glass wall of the living room in a radial pattern, and ten glass doors open out onto the encircling terrace. In contrast, the bedrooms are built snugly into the hillside. The circularity of the design is emphasized by a steep conical roof that creates a voluminous interior space and reaches a climax in a skylight around the central chimney, where bands of glass and lightweight concrete (see Fig. 248) bring tempered sunlight into the house at all times of day. The extension of the kitchen and the carport to the left is an important factor in tying the house to its site.

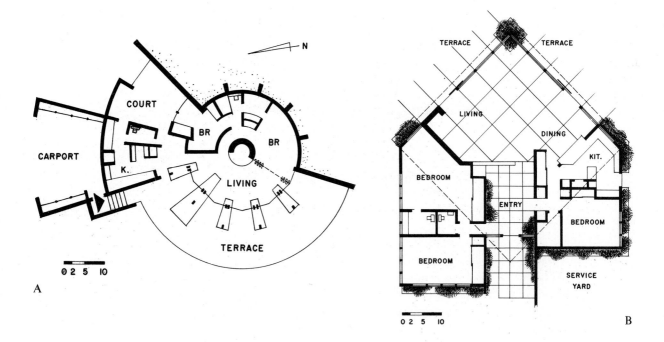

Motivated by a promontory-like site overlooking Los Angeles, Rodney Walker's plan (Fig. 408B) projects the living and dining space into the view by turning them at a 45-degree angle. The unconventional shape is echoed by redwood strips in the polished concrete floor and by the beams of the ceiling, which rises to a high point over the room's center.

Court and Patio Plans

As builders around the Mediterranean, in the Far East, and in Mexico have long known, turning houses outside in gives maximum seclusion and climate control for outdoor living. This approach to house design is adaptable to all climates and to city, suburb, or open country. There are no limits to the ways in which houses and courts can be shaped (even though most are rectangular), and there can be one or several private-living spaces open to the sky. This might seem like an extravagant way to build, which it can be, for such spread-out houses increase perimeter walls. Yet it can give more *usable* private space on costly land while reducing heating or cooling bills.

Architect Eliot Noyes designed the house in Connecticut (Figs. 258A and B) for his family with two concepts in mind: a central court and decisively separated zones for group and private life. The result has been described as a "square doughnut" (Fig. 409). It is a sizable house—the living room wing encloses about 1100 square feet of space, the bedroom wing about 1500—but it seems much larger because the two wings are separated by a partially roofed court, measuring about 40 by 54 feet and surrounded by the house. The wings are joined on the north and south by 90-foot-long, rugged stone walls, unbroken except for wide sliding doors in the center of each. Circulation between wings is handled by two covered passages open to the court; aurally, they are connected by an intercommunication system. The Noyeses have found this satisfactory even in New England winters (heat from the house and sun melt the snow), but the passageways could be enclosed with glass.

Daring as the plan is, it would hardly be worth reporting had it not been carried out with many subtleties. The plan is strictly rectangular, urbane, and formal with strong overtones of symmetry, yet handsomely integrated with the rolling, wooded site. The stone walls harmonize with the natural landscape while solidly defining the house. Fifty-foot-wide walls of glass boldly open the living wing to a sweeping view on one side, to the secluded court on the other. This is not a house for everyone on any site, but it demonstrates how one family solved its problems of shelter with real ingenuity.

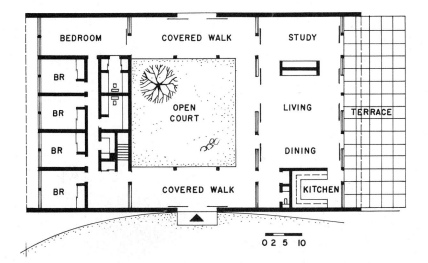

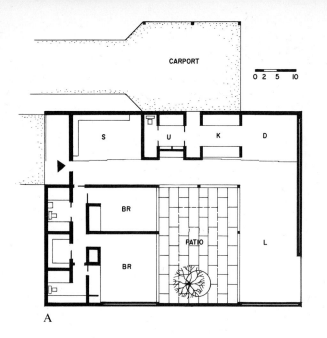

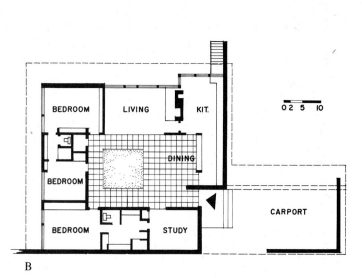

CARPORT

0 2 5 10

S   U   K   D

BR

BR

PATIO   L

0 2 5 10

BEDROOM   LIVING   KIT.

BEDROOM   DINING

BEDROOM   STUDY

CARPORT

A   B

On a small but desirably located site in New Orleans, closely hemmed in by neighbors, a house practically without windows was deemed the best solution (Fig. 410A). Two bedrooms, a kitchen, and dining and living space are compactly organized around a court. Exterior walls are unbroken except for entrance and kitchen doors and sliding glass panels at the end of the living room. Supplementing the light and air from the court are twelve skylights near the periphery of the house. The courtyard, paved and planted, gives a surprising feeling of light and space. Laurence, Saunders, and Calongne, architects.

In some climates, courts covered with skylights function better than those open to the sky. An indoor garden, enjoyable night and day, is the center of a house in Dallas, Texas (Fig. 410B). Although windows and window walls give views outward from bedrooms, living room, and kitchen, all are of fixed glass permanently sealed against dust and weather. Aluminum blinds in the skylight control the sun's heat and light. A cooling system keeps the house comfortable in summer, a radiantly heated ceiling warms it in winter. All do their work economically, because the house was planned for its climate. Enslie O. Oglesby, Jr., architect.

Apartments and Town Houses

When suburbs within an hour's commuting distance of a city become filled and lots everywhere more expensive, a boom in apartment-house building starts, and town (or row) houses become almost a necessity. It is better if the interest in these kinds of dwellings starts *before* all the land is covered, because only in this way can needed open breathing space in crowded urban centers be saved. But this is an area of study so vast that we can only touch upon it here. A full discussion of different types of apartments and town houses would fill many books, because of all the research and technical problems involved. As far as plans of individual apartments and houses are concerned, the criteria for judging them are much the same as for detached houses, but with more emphasis on the needs for privacy. This is primarily a technical matter of sound insulation in floors, ceilings, and party walls, and of orientation of windows and outside areas such as balconies and patios; but the placement of rooms also affects privacy and the livability of the plan.

The plan (Fig. 411A) of the two-bedroom house in a retirement village is excellent. Being semidetached, it shares only one common wall with its neighbor, the living room wall, ensuring quiet bedrooms, and a stout garden wall shields the patio and living room windows. For a house this small, it has a good deal of closet space arranged as a sound-deadening barrier between sleeping and living areas. The bathroom door is not in the line of vision from the living room, and the kitchen could easily be screened if desired. A concern for privacy pervades the whole design. Skidmore, Owings, and Merrill, architects. (*Reprinted by special permission from the November 1964 issue of* House & Home *copyright © 1964 by McGraw-Hill, Inc.*)

The apartments in a twenty-four-story high-rise building in Indianapolis (Fig. 411B) were also laid out with privacy in mind. Bedrooms are placed only next to other bedrooms in adjacent apartments, the corner balconies are a good distance apart and have recessed alcoves, and bathrooms are a sound barrier between bedrooms and the service core of elevators and stairs. Although the apartments are air-conditioned, cross ventilation is possible and views in two directions are provided by placing most apartments on the corners. The Perkins and Will Partnership, architects. (*Reprinted from* Architectural Record, *January 1964, copyright © 1964 by McGraw-Hill, Inc., with all rights reserved*)

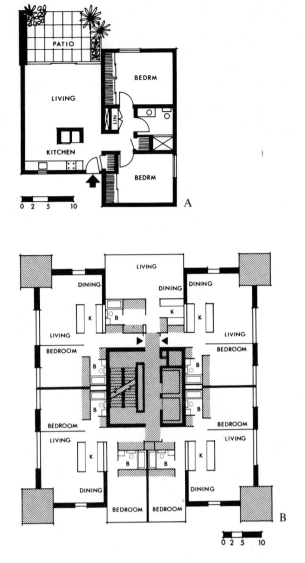

SELECTING A HOUSE PLAN

How to achieve the house with the plan best for you takes careful thinking about many specific factors. In the following section we will concentrate attention on plans while remembering that, except for purposes of analytical study, the house plan should never be thought of as separated from interior, exterior, and landscape design. These are the factors to consider:

Is the total amount of enclosed space, plus the usable outdoor space, suited to your needs? Many of us think that we want as much space as possible until we see a large old house for sale or rent. Then we begin wondering about cleaning, maintaining, and heating it, and how we and our furnishings would fit into rooms planned for another way of life. This leads to the conclusion that amount of space is not the only consideration, even though there is no complete substitute for adequate square footage. Living cramped by too many persons in too few square feet is probably worse than living in an inconvenient, hard-to-maintain, but big house—but not so bad as living in a house bigger than you can afford. Major factors are family size and ages, personalities and way of living, and finances:

- The house as a whole should give each person at least 200 square feet; 250 are better; 300 or more give comfortable living. Bruce Walker's plan would give four persons 250 square feet each. Eliot Noyes's plan allows more than 500 square feet for each of five persons.

- The larger the family the less square footage each person needs (or, at least, is likely to get).
- Families heterogeneous in ages and interests as well as those that are gregarious and extroverted need more space per person than those that are homogeneous and quieter.
- Finances—annual income and accumulated reserves to pay for original and continuing costs—are a major determinant of house size.
- Usable space is increased by good zoning, convenient relationships among rooms, minimum traffic through rooms, rooms that permit good furniture arrangements, and livable outdoor areas.

Is the space appropriately allocated for your needs? All the factors noted in the preceding paragraph affect the general divisions of indoor (and outdoor) space:

- The proportion of space allotted to group, private, and work activities can vary markedly even in houses of the same size. In the two prize-winning houses (Figs. 392 and 398), the square footages (which can be translated into percentages by dropping the last zero) are approximately as follows:

	Group	Private	Work	Total
First	370	530	100	1000
Second	550	350	100	1000

The kitchen and utility areas show little variation, because equipment is standardized and in small houses few people want to use more of their precious space here than is necessary. But notice the great differences in group- and private-living areas. In one plan, bedrooms and bath are larger, and they open off their completely private hall that therefore is regarded as part of that zone. In the other, these rooms are of minimal size, and circulation among them is through group space. The first seems suited to individuals who like privacy, the second to families who will accept cubicle bedrooms in order to have two social areas.

- Divisions within the *group space* are the next consideration. The first plan has minimum separation; the second has two rigidly divided areas. Which would meet your needs best?
- Within the *work space* of small houses, divisions are usually minimal, consisting of nothing more than separating the furnace from the combined kitchen-laundry. In larger houses, segregation of cooking and laundry may be desirable.
- Divisions in *private areas* vary greatly, even in houses of the same size, chiefly in the number of bedrooms and baths but also in the privacy given these rooms by a bedroom hall, by movable partitions between bedrooms or between bedrooms and activity space, and by the inclusion or exclusion of a room for individual hobbies or solitude.

Is the enclosed space well zoned and adjacent to related outdoor areas? Cities are zoned by designating certain areas for specific uses arranged so that related activities are together and those that might interfere with each other are separated. Homes benefit from similar planning:

- The minimum essential is segregating the quiet areas from the noisy areas. Plans can be quickly checked by coloring noisy areas red, quiet areas green, and then studying the pattern made.
- It is desirable to have well-defined zones for group activities, private living, and work, and to have these zones extend into the landscape, as illustrated and discussed in Chapter 19.

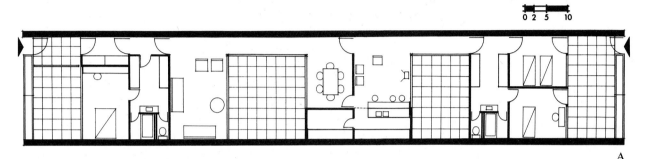

A

Architects Serge Chermayeff and Robert Reynolds, who feel that the problem of integrating community and privacy should have top priority in the design of homes, prove that even on very narrow lots, the zones for adults, for family life, and for children can be distinctly separated. (*Reprinted from* Community and Privacy *by Serge Chermayeff and Christopher Alexander. Copyright © 1963 by Serge Chermayeff. Reproduced by permission of Doubleday & Company, Inc.*)

- Two-story houses with bedrooms on one floor are, almost automatically, at least fairly well zoned.
- Typical zoning errors in one-story houses are often in indoor-outdoor relationships: separating the kitchen from the garage, thereby precluding a single convenient service yard; facing the living room toward the street, which makes it difficult to unite it with a protected terrace or lawn.
- Circulation paths logically come between zones, not through them.

Is the pattern of circulation satisfactory? Short, desirable routes from here to there simplify housekeeping and make home life pleasant, but they are hard to achieve. Little serious thought was given to good circulation, even in palaces, until the eighteenth century. Remember that traffic through rooms greatly reduces their usable space:

- Routes from garage to main and service doors should be short and offer protection in bad weather. Locating these doors near each other helps in this respect (Fig. 405A).
- Ideally, it should be possible to get from outdoors to any room in the house, and inside from each room to any other, without going through another room, except perhaps a multipurpose space.
- Keeping doors close together and near the corners of rooms shortens traffic paths and promotes good furniture arrangement. This applies to entrance doors and to doors into rooms and closets.
- Living rooms should not invite through traffic, as they do in many houses where the living room is the only link between the kitchen and the bedrooms.

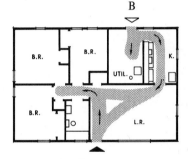

B

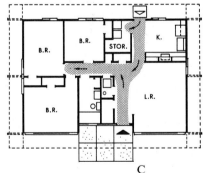

C

Time, energy, space, and maintenance of floors can be saved with an efficient pattern of circulation. Plan B has been used for some years by a manufacturer of prefabricated houses. Plan C is the improvement made by architect Henry Hill. (*Reprinted by special permission from the November 1952 issue of* House & Home. *Copyright © 1952 by McGraw-Hill, Inc.*)

- Important differences between new and old planning include incorporating the garage as part of the house (Fig. 401); more outside doors, especially from group living space, but also from bedrooms to terraces (Fig. 404A); having the "back" door open into a utility or multipurpose area instead of directly into the kitchen (Fig. 6B); having a guest entrance area even in small houses (Fig. 392); widening what would formerly have been a narrow hall into a usable activity space or lining it with cupboards (Fig. 7B).

Are the rooms of suitable size? What was said about the total size of the house applies to room size because, in general, house size is the chief determinant of room size. Room size, however, is somewhat dependent on furniture arrangement (Chap. 14). Below are typical square footages:

	Entrance Area	Living Space	Dining Space	Dining Space in Kitchen	Kitchen	Bedrooms	Bathrooms	Heater Room
Small	25–30	150–200	100–130	25–40	75–90	80–130	33–35	12–15
Medium	35–40	220–280	150–180	50–70	100–140	140–190	40–45	18–25
Large	45+	300+	200+	80+	160+	200+	50+	30+

In thinking about these sizes, keep the following in mind:
- Actual square footages are the basic factor, but usable and apparent size is affected by shape, location, and the size of openings; relation to other rooms and the landscape; treatment of walls, floors, and ceiling.
- Some families prefer or need many rooms, even though each is small. Others prefer fewer and larger separated areas.

Will the rooms take needed furniture gracefully and efficiently? Are the shapes useful and pleasant? Furniture arrangement is a primary concern in planning, buying, or renting a home:
- First consideration is sufficient floor area for furniture and traffic.
- Second is suitable wall space, especially for such large items as beds and sofas.
- Third is the problem of getting the furniture into satisfactory groups, sequestered from and not hampering necessary circulation.

Generalizing about room shapes is hazardous, because their use, size, and character qualify everything said below:
- Square rooms are hard to furnish. An exception is the separate dining room with a round table.
- Rectangles are the normal shapes. They usually work best when their proportions range from around 1 : 1.2 (approximately 10 by 12 feet, 12 by 15 feet, or 16 by 20 feet) up to 1 : 1.7 (approximately 5 by 8 feet, 10 by 16 or 17 feet, or 12 by 18 feet). If more nearly square than the first proportions, rooms lose their rectangularity without gaining the stability of the square. If their proportions closely approach 1 : 2, as they do in the living and activity rooms in Figure 398, rooms become corridor-like unless clearly differentiated by furniture into two or more areas (see Fig. 330).
- L-shapes are happy solutions for dual-purpose rooms, such as living rooms with alcoves for conversation, music, or dining, and kitchens with a semi-

separated laundry. Bedrooms in which either the beds, a desk and chair, or closets and chests are put in their own alcoves are remarkably pleasant.

- All the other wonderful shapes—circles, ellipses, and free curves, hexagons and octagons, nonrigid combinations of straight lines—bring variety and excitement, as illustrated in Figures 408A and B.

Is there adequate storage space? *Abundant* might be a better word because *adequate* all too soon turns out to be *inadequate*. Closets and cupboards protect such things as clothes and china, and if they are well placed and well planned they reduce the amount of furniture needed and result in more living space. Each area in the house has some storage needs; specialized activities add to them. *Minimum* needs are:

- *Bedroom closet space* for each person, 4 feet wide, 24 inches inside depth, 6 or more feet high, with or without drawers.
- *Bathroom cabinets* for medicines and hygiene needs; towels if desired.
- *Linen cupboards* for current and seasonal bedding and bath linens, 20 inches deep, 32 inches wide, 8 feet high.
- *Kitchen wall and base cabinets* of 10 linear feet for kitchenware, tableware, and food supplies (Chap. 4).
- *Cleaning cupboards* for household cleaning equipment and supplies, 16 inches deep, 36 inches wide, 6 feet high, in kitchen, laundry, or bedroom wing.
- *Laundry area cupboards* for washing and ironing supplies and equipment, perhaps for soiled and clean clothing.
- *Dining area cabinets* for dinnerware; sliding shelves or drawers for linens. A complete dinner service for twelve takes 18 linear feet of 12-inch-deep shelving.
- *Garage* or *carport storage* for garden supplies and seasonal and occasional-use items such as garden furniture and trunks. Both closets and open space are needed, although open space in a carport needs a door for security and neatness.

Does the house lend itself to desirable or necessary change? It is impossible to predict specifically what the future will bring, but knowing that life and change go together suggests planning for flexibility:

- Family patterns change as children are born, develop, and leave home. The newborn sleeps near his parents and for several years needs supervision; the child in elementary school begins to assert the independence that marks adolescence; and after high school a child usually lives at home only during vacations. Figures 435A through D illustrate a house planned specifically with these changes in mind.
- Family needs also vary from the unimpeded open spaces needed for large-scale entertaining to separation of areas for different activities.
- The usual limited finances of a young couple often necessitate beginning with a minimum house; but as financial stability increases, the question of upgrading or enlarging the present house or of moving to a new one arises.
- An increase in family size brings similar problems.
- Business opportunities, health, or the desire for change can make it necessary to sell or rent a home. (One in five families moves yearly.)

All these factors indicate the advisability of:

- Selecting a plan that fits or can easily be adapted to the needs of others, possibly with the loss of some highly individualized features
- Making certain that additional space can be economically finished or added
- Keeping to a minimum hard-to-move interior partitions by substituting movable storage walls and sliding or folding doors for maximum flexibility

This may sound as though families should plan for others or for a way of living other than their own present pattern. That is not intended. But the future is well worth thinking about when spending the amount of money a home costs.

Is—or can—the plan be effectively oriented on the site? *Orientation* is best defined as relationship to the environment. This includes the sun, wind, and outlook; the size, shape, and slope of the lot and its relation to the street; and existing trees, rocks, water, and so forth. Orientation affects the directions in which different rooms face, the location of windows and ventilators, and the placement of the house on the lot.

An unusual site can lead to an unusual plan. The upper level is placed on top of a projecting knoll, with the living room extending even further out on three sets of Y-shaped struts; the rooms on the lower level are built into both sides of the knoll. George T. Rockrise, architect. (*Reprinted by special permission from the October 1964 issue of* House & Home. *Copyright © 1964 by McGraw-Hill, Inc.*)

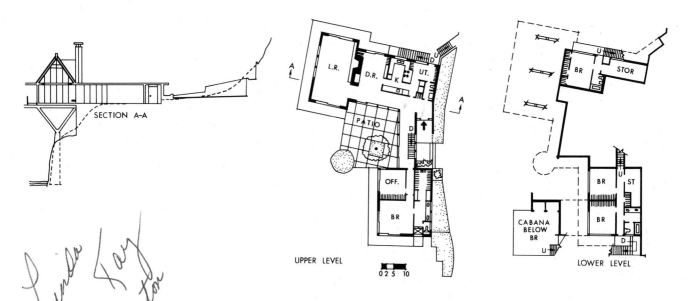

Here are some points to remember:

- The sun brings heat, light, and cheer chiefly from the south.
- Summer breezes usually come from the west and winter winds from the north, but they vary greatly from region to region, even from lot to nearby lot.
- Views follow no pattern—except that on many city lots the best outlook is into one's own private yard.

There is general agreement *for typical situations* on the following:

- Group-living space deserves the best view, the privacy needed for living behind the house's largest windows, and the winter sun. South to southeast is preferred.
- Kitchens also deserve a pleasant vista outdoors and ample daylight, preferably with morning sun. Northeast is desirable.

- Bedrooms need privacy. Southern exposures are most agreeable—but usually there is little choice.
- Bathrooms should be located where most convenient. Privacy can be assured by high windows, and there is no great need for outlook or sun, although these can be most agreeable.
- Utility rooms can be anywhere because they need few if any windows.
- Garages and carports need only be convenient to street and house entrances.

Placement of a house on a lot depends on the size and shape of each, the location of the street, any natural features, and community restrictions. In general, though, the following is good practice:
- Maximum usable private yard and minimum driveway generally are achieved when the long dimension of the house parallels the street and when the house is as near the street as feasible.
- One usable side yard can often be obtained by placing the house nearer one side of the lot than the other.
- On lots facing south, the house is often pushed back and some of the front yard made private, as in Figure 6B.

It is clear that no single house plan will fit every lot, nor is a standardized location on all lots sensible. While there is no excuse for thoughtless orientation, many devices can alleviate difficult situations, as noted in Chapters 12 and 19.

Is the plan beautiful? Once a house is built, the plan is not seen as a whole —but it is strongly experienced in daily living. A plan without beauty and distinctiveness is no more defensible than a fireplace or chair lacking these qualities. The plans in Figures 392B and 402C are unpretentious and informal yet carefully ordered. Eliot Noyes's home (Figs. 258A and B and 409) is based on a self-contained plan of crystalline precision. Ray Crites' home (Color Fig. 21 and Fig. 406) has a dynamic integration of volumes that reach out into the landscape site. Frank Lloyd Wright's plans (Figs. 104B and 417) liberate man's spirit.

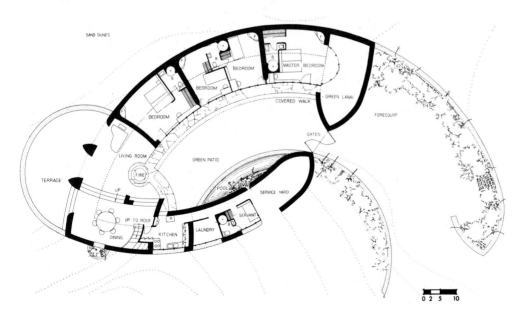

A thirteenth-century castle at Coucy, France, looks romantic to us now, but its form followed its major function—that of a fortress, with very small observation openings on the outer walls and protective parapets around the tops of the watch-towers and walls. Living quarters were on one side, with large windows facing the security of the court. (*Viollet-le-Duc*)

18 · Exterior Design

When homes are designed from "the inside out," exterior design becomes the outer expression of an inner plan for living. Relationship to the geographical and cultural environment and to the specific site may indicate some forms as more appropriate than others. Materials and ways of construction always affect appearance and cost. Individualized concepts of beauty are vital considerations. Bringing these factors into happy balance, giving each its appropriate emphasis in terms of specific conditions leads to designs that are honest and varied.

WAY OF LIVING AND ENVIRONMENT

In the few centuries of American history, New England has produced more than its share of good houses. We will look at two, each of which grew out of a family's needs conditioned by the time and place of living, and then at two houses specially designed for the rigorous winter climate of California's Sierra Nevada Mountains and for a subtropical site in Florida.

418

An Eighteenth-Century House in Salem, Massachusetts

When built in the 1720s, the house shown in Figure 419 represented the newest trend in New England architecture. For some years Salem had been a prosperous seaport in close cultural contact with the mother country, England. And Colonial architecture, as Talbot Hamlin has written, was compounded of memories and of the need for reassurance, of homesickness for the old and of desire for new national pride. The first houses in the New England colonies were adaptations of the medieval structures the pioneers had known. During the seventeenth century, however, leaders in English architecture developed a renewed interest in classical forms. Travelers brought not only this news but architectural handbooks with explicit drawings of the latest style.

This posed problems for Colonial builders who wanted to keep up with the times. Their climate was harsher, and they had neither the skills nor the money for the precise masonry of English Georgian architecture. But Yankee ingenuity was available. In the seventeenth century, New Englanders had developed overlapping wood siding to weather-proof the half-timber structures built from old memories. In the eighteenth century, they used their woodworking skills to adapt the new English designs so completely that a distinctive style was born unintentionally.

The Ropes Memorial has the well-proportioned formality and sensitive detailing admired then—and now. The dominant, slightly recessed doorway leads into a central hall that gives access to the four rectangular rooms on the first

The Ropes Memorial in Salem, Massachusetts, illustrates the impressive formality of eighteenth-century New England exterior design. (*Ropes Memorial, Inc.*)

and second floors. Identical windows with small rectangular panes in double-hung sashes, each at rest in its own allotted space, march regularly across the façade in two ranks. The once-utilitarian shutters stretch out the windows to suggest two horizontal bands. A cornice tight above the second-floor windows conciliates the vertical wall with the sloping roof. Three dormer windows, each under a small roof, help light what was once the "children's dormitory." A simple balustrade obscures the roof's peak. The two symmetrical chimneys mark the location of fireplaces on each of the three floors.

In some respects, designing such houses was easy, because they were based on patterns that permitted only minor liberties. Few questions were raised about formality versus informality, choice of materials or type of construction, location of entrance door and windows, or orientation. Sensitivity to scale and proportion, though, was important, and some inventiveness could be applied to details. Although no two houses were identical, marked similarities led to harmonious towns. There is much to learn from such homes, especially about refinement of proportion and judicious use of ornament.

The Ropes Memorial has responded to the impact of changing conditions. In 1807 Ionic columns were added to the entrance, and large archways were cut through the walls to open the parlor into the dining room. In 1894, when the house was moved back from the street and put on higher foundations, the handsome fence, based on late eighteenth-century design, was erected to carry the spirit of the house out to the sidewalk and to separate the front lawn from the street. In the same year a wing for kitchen, servants' quarters, and bathrooms was added at the rear. The basic character of the house, however, was not altered.

A Contemporary City House in Cambridge, Massachusetts

The house architect Carleton R. Richmond, Jr., built for his family is not many miles from the Ropes Memorial, but more than two centuries of drastic changes in American life separate the two. The site is a well-located city lot, narrow but with a deep backyard facing south—and a six-story apartment building. The family wanted a flexible interior warmed by winter sun and functionally related to livable outdoor space.

For his own home in Cambridge, Massachusetts, architect Carleton R. Richmond, Jr., designed a house the rear of which is extended by a trellis that protects outdoor-living space and large windows from summer sun and neighbors' views. (*Photograph by Joseph W. Molitor*)

A

Above. The façade of the Richmond home is geometrically precise yet asymmetrical. (*Photograph by Joseph W. Molitor*)

Left. Like the façade, the compact plan has a disciplined geometric order.

Below. A section through the house shows how summer sun and observation from without were excluded while permitting the occupants to enjoy an all-year view of the garden and the warmth of winter sun. (*Reprinted from* Architectural Record, Record Houses of 1954. *Copyright © 1954 by McGraw-Hill Inc., with all rights reserved*)

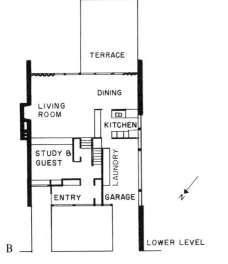

LOWER LEVEL

B

UPPER LEVEL

0 5 10

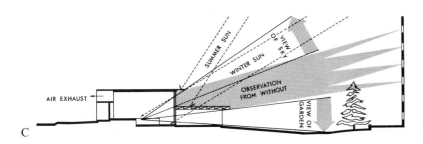

C

Superficially, the street side of the house bears little relationship to the Ropes Memorial. Both house and lot are much smaller. The roof is flat, the glass is concentrated in two large areas, and there is no applied ornament. The balance is asymmetrical, the rhythm is dynamic, and there is no center of interest. Yet it too has a strict, geometric order. Opaque and transparent areas are aligned, horizontally and vertically, and strong lines lead our eyes quickly from side to side, from top to bottom. A detailed analysis would reveal such interesting relationships as the progression of unequal vertical divisions and the diagonal relationships of wood and glass areas. These panels carry to the exterior important subdivisions of the interior space. Moreover, they convey the feeling of dynamic rectangularity found inside.

The façade is penetrated on the right by the garage, which gives quick access to all rooms. On the left, a short, straight walk takes us into a sheltered recess and then into the entry flooded with light yet made private by translucent glass. Passing the study and the stairs to the upper floor, we descend five steps, reflecting a slight ground slope, into a two-story living zone. Sliding and folding doors unite or separate the living room from dining and study areas. A glass wall, floor to roof, dramatically extends this space.

What about views and privacy, sun and ventilation? The front of the house is close to the street, which made figured glass advisable on the ground floor. Directly above the entry is a ventilating grille lined up with the bedroom windows. An unbroken brick wall gives privacy and thermal insulation toward the northeast. The opposite side has windows that light and ventilate the garage, the kitchen, and the master bedroom. It is the garden side, though, that is most noteworthy. By extending the side walls and roof and by designing a trellis, partly open and partly roofed, the architect made it possible to enjoy views of the garden and sky, the warmth of winter sun, and the pleasures of outdoor living without being looked at by neighbors. These practical devices, indicated by the site, also provide delight for the eyes.

The Richmonds had many choices to make—materials, character, and shape of house and roof; size and shape and location of windows. They had no rules but neither did they start in a vacuum, since they were familiar with and influenced by other modern houses. They decided to have a home that is distinctly urban, appropriate to a setting in which man-made streets, sidewalks, and buildings dominate, not evasive about belonging to a machine age. Although concerned with beauty of form, they wanted a design intimately related to their informal living and to their site. Several ways in which contemporary planning affects exterior design are evident. Asymmetric plans, efficient and informal, lead to asymmetric interiors. Private outdoor living suggests locating living rooms away from the street and extending the house with terraces, fences, overhanging roofs, and trellises. Relating windows to room size and use, to sun and wind, leads to shaping, sizing, and placing them as desired rather than by arbitrary rule.

Houses for Extreme Climates

By comparison with New England's climate and topography, California's Sierra Nevada Mountains and the beaches of Florida are extreme. Each of the houses shown on pages 423 and 424 unmistakably reflects the lay of the land and the weather. Two practical factors, heavy snowfall and economy of con-

A

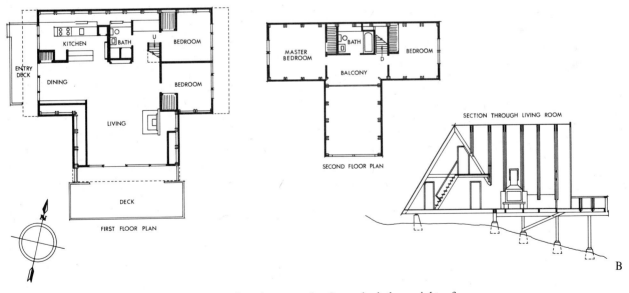

FIRST FLOOR PLAN

SECOND FLOOR PLAN

SECTION THROUGH LIVING ROOM

B

Top. Sharply pitched roofs with eaves coming down to the floor shed the weight of heavy snow, visually relate exterior and interior to a mountainous setting. George Rockrise, architect. (*Photograph by Ernest Braun. Reprinted from* Sunset *Magazine*)

Above. In 1425 square feet of floor space, there are four bedrooms and two baths, kitchen and dining space, and a large living room with walls sloping up to the roof's peak.

A

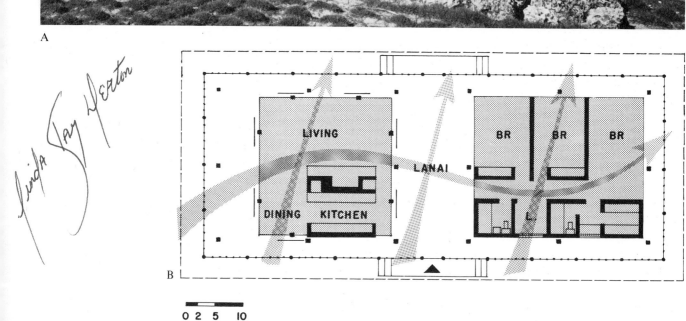

B

0 2 5 10

Top. A house designed by Robert B. Browne is stretched out over, and elevated above, its flat Miami site in deference to tropical winds, rains, and temperatures. (*Photograph © Ezra Stoller*)

Above. Cooling breezes flow through and between the two enclosed units of the house.

struction, led architect George Rockrise to use a triangular, A-shaped timber frame. Perhaps of equal consequence, this shape has a strong visual affinity for mountains and pine trees. Primitive man long ago found that houses in which roof meets floor on two or more sides were simple to build. Now it is feasible to enclose the gable ends partially or completely with glass. This aspiring shape, encouraging us to look up and then out, has profound spiritual impact.

Humidity and hot sun, hurricane winds and high tides, and insects can make most semitropical areas less than paradisaical unless dwellings take these facts of nature into account. Lifting houses off the ground is an old way of letting cooling breezes or surging water go under the house. Doing this with concrete, the material used in the house in Figure 424A, discourages insects. Extending the house over its site allows moderate winds to go through the rooms, especially as in this example when the center is a genuine breezeway. Sliding doors control storm winds, which go harmlessly over and under this low house. Overhanging roofs and insect screens give protected outdoor areas on four sides. Covering the roof with heat-reflecting coral chips is another device to make this an architecturally, rather than mechanically, air-conditioned house. Starting with these factors, the architect ended with a design aesthetically and practically integrated with its environment.

These four houses were all influenced by their surroundings. Where the climate is extreme, as in Florida and the western mountains, recognition of this influence seems particularly important. But how significant is it generally? In certain respects, many "primitive" people have built homes better suited to their environments than have we. Indian pueblos and the raised breezy grass huts of the South Pacific are just about perfect examples of meeting the climate and landscape on its own terms with local materials. But each of these was built by people of a homogeneous culture, similar in their living patterns and restricted in their materials and building techniques. Such people almost inevitably built in a certain style because they had little choice, and over the centuries an efficient, consummate model was produced. Our culture is different. Within the same community are many dissimilar modes of life, and two families living on opposite sides of the continent may be more alike than near neighbors. Local materials are often more expensive than those efficiently processed elsewhere, while local craft traditions have just about died out. It is true that those houses with distinctly local or regional flavor are often deeply satisfying, as is the work of Frank Lloyd Wright. His house for the Arizona desert belongs to that colorful, arid scene as much as his Wisconsin home belongs to its lushly green hilltop (Figs. 170 and 446A). But an overwhelming proportion of building sites have no character other than that given by street layout and nearby houses; moreover, modern heating and cooling methods can combat almost any weather. Then the more subtle hints of specific site orientation and individual domestic patterns can be used to give form to a house, aided by the character of its building materials.

EFFECT OF MATERIALS AND CONSTRUCTION TECHNIQUES ON HOUSE DESIGN

The cost and character of a house, the maintenance it requires, and the kind of living it suggests are in part determined by the materials from which it was built and how they are put together. This applies quite as much to structure,

A

Structure can be as vital a main force in modern house design as it is in Gothic cathedrals, a point ably demonstrated on these two pages by Anshen and Allen's wood house in San Rafael, California.

Above. The pervasive rhythm of posts and beams energizes the whole house with implicit motion. (*Photograph by Rondal Partridge*)

Below. Space flowing in many directions is articulated by the ordered structural frame. (*Photograph by Roger Sturtevant*)

B

which can be visible or hidden, as to the surfaces. The character of materials, their beauty, strengths, and weaknesses, are as important to architects as to potters or weavers—more so, perhaps, because architects work with many more kinds of materials.

A House Built of Wood

In itself, a house built of wood is hardly worth comment since so many houses in this country are built of that material. But the house illustrated in Figures 226 and 227 is exceptional. It was designed for a rocky, mountainous site by the same architects who did the masonry house illustrated on pages 94 and 182. This house stands on an acre of land in rolling, semiwooded hills a few miles north of San Francisco. Although commissioned by a merchant builder with a preset cost, it has marked individuality and was sold before finished. The architects took full advantage of a lot with the street to the north. The pleasant U-shaped plan, three times as large as the two prize-winning houses in Chapter 17, links secluded rooms with a spacious loggia and terrace.

The essence of the design is an age-old system of wood construction—widely spaced *posts* support *beams* that hold up ceilings of *planks.* Not much of this is seen from the street, where the need for privacy indicated a simple façade of redwood siding, but the posts show as structural divisions in a band of windows. A brick chimney directs attention toward a recessed entrance court. On entering the house, however, you experience the sturdy architectural rhythm and unity of the revealed structure. From the south side, you can enjoy the way in which the structure visually binds interior and exterior to each other. The plan, as well as the photographs, shows that this orderly framework permits great flexibility, because the spaces between posts and beams can be treated as desired.

The colonnade of posts demarcating loggia from living room stands free from the floor to the 13-foot ridge, except for the coat closet enclosed only to the necessary height. The spaces between the posts that separate the loggia from the terrace are filled with glass, but there is nothing but air and space between those on the terrace. Plank-and-beam ceilings allow similar flexibility in the ceiling and roof. Over the entrance court, an open panel brings daylight to this area. On the south, where sunlight control is important, a solid roof covers the recessed terrace and shades the window wall except for the space between seven posts where a skylight brightens the interior.

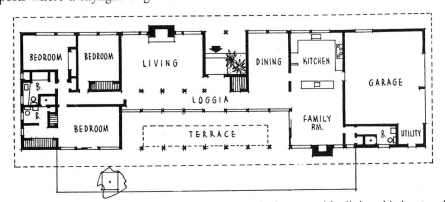

A spacious loggia allied with a terrace connects bedrooms with dining, kitchen, and family space.

Houses with structures of metal permit great freedom of planning, as seen here and on the next two pages.

A steel frame of slender, widely spaced posts and corrugated steel roofing gives sheltered openness and lightness of form. Glass, wood, and plastic, and brick and asphalt tile contribute to the bold counterpoint of lines and planes. Pierre Koenig, designer. (*Photograph by Julius Shulman*)

All structure and surfaces, except for some of the floors, are of handsomely detailed wood. Redwood siding with closely spaced vertical grooves, which produce a small-scale rhythmic play of light and shadow, was used for all exterior walls and many interior ones. Thick cedar shingles make a vigorously textured roof. The slender redwood pillars are refined out of the fence-post category by vertical grooves in the corners. The planks and the beams of the gabled ceiling are of tough fir. For contrast, some interior walls are surfaced with smooth, straight-grain Philippine mahogany plywood.

The regularity of the structural system gives coherence to the plan, the interior, and the exterior. The freestanding colonnades, inside and outside, are the most easily appreciated aspect of this order and at the same time give the house its special character.

A House Built of Steel

Developed centuries ago, steel has been a hard material to domesticate. Unlike wood, it seldom seems homelike. We acknowledge its usefulness in washing machines, automobiles, and skyscrapers, but have been reluctant to accept it for home construction. This, however, has not daunted experimenters.

Designer Pierre Koenig believes that metal houses need not look cold, and one of his essays in this material is shown in Figure 428. This small house is held up by a light steel frame, somewhat like that used in Charles Eames's house (Fig. 188). Roof and ceilings as well as some wall panels are of steel, corrugated for more strength but incidentally giving a vibrating play of light and shade. They were prefabricated in a factory, a process which could affect economies if carried on at a large scale. Because no single material is equally functional for every part of a home, plastics and wood and masonry are used here where they perform better. Even so, it is a steel house.

Remember that steel is very strong, even when posts and beams are slender or when panels are thin. With it architects can span wide gaps with a rigid structure. Open plans and window walls come naturally with steel, as do lightweight, opaque panels. Another attribute of steel is its amenability to precise machining, a quality of great importance when the components of a house are factory-made but assembled on the site. Although metals in themselves give minimum clues to appropriate forms, we have come to accept *structural* metal as being distinctly geometric, usually rectilinear. (That metal can be shaped otherwise is a potentiality for the future.) Accepting present trends in steel fabrication, Koenig has created a home with gratifying variations on a theme of rectangularity. Space is opened and closed, interrupted and continued with controlled vitality. It is delicate, light, livable geometry. But *light steel* construction is not the only way in which metal can affect exterior and interior design. For proof, look at the *heavy steel* frame in Figure 187 from which a glass-walled house in Illinois is suspended, and at the *aluminum* house now to be discussed.

A House of Aluminum and Plastic

What structure covers the greatest amount of space at minimum cost? To Bernard Judge the answer lay in the geodesic domes that Buckminster Fuller had developed for industry. Judge designed and built his house of lightweight

Below and next page. An experimental house of aluminum rods and a plastic skin rests high in the hills above Hollywood, California. Bernard Judge, designer. (*Photographs* by *Julius Shulman*)

The living room on the upper level of the geodesic dome house, shielded overhead by an opaque plastic cap, has a panoramic view.

aluminum rods that were manufactured in Canada, shipped to Los Angeles, and then erected on a hillside in one day. He had to convince the building authorities that a dome with a rigid triangulated frame was structurally safe before he could apply the transparent Mylar skin on the inside. By using this unconventional method of building a house, he freed his imagination to design an unconventional interior as well. The core of the house is composed of a prefabricated fiber-glass and plastic bathroom, banks of closets, and a spiral staircase. The two levels of living platforms are carried on bundles of light steel pipes. Electrical radiating panels heat the house and act as dividers between areas. Ventilation is obtained by leaving open a narrow strip screened with nylon gauze around the perimeter of the dome. An opening 12 feet in diameter at the top of the dome is protected from the sun and rain by a hovering cover of white glass-reinforced neoprene. The dome covers not only the living decks but the grasses, trees, and shrubs growing on the slope, enabling man and nature to live together in a unique way. This is, of course, a highly experimental house. The Mylar skin, which cost $300, will probably have to be renewed in about three years to keep it tight and clear in sun and storm. To some people the lack of privacy would be objectionable; and how well the heating and ventilation systems would work in a climate like Los Angeles', which is subjected to high winds and much rain at times, is a matter to be determined. But as an example of the freedom that our technical and industrial knowledge makes possible, it is inspiring and welcome. Whereas Koenig's house was strictly rectangular, this house is a soaring hemisphere. The emotional effect of the two houses is indeed different, but both illustrate the latitude in planning that the great tensile strength of metal makes possible.

Two Houses of Masonry

As discussed in Chapters 8 and 9, masonry has its own range of individuality. Usually thought of as heavy, massive, and earthbound (Figs. 166B and 168), masonry can also be light, airy, and spirited, as demonstrated by Figure 175B. Especially in the case of concrete in its various forms, it can be the basic structural material for homes (Fig. 170), or it can be a vigorous accent in a fireplace (Figs. 165 and 336) or a wall (Figs. 171 and 173).

In the two houses illustrated in Figures 431A and B, the architects have chosen and handled masonry materials to realize distinctly different effects. On

Masonry can seem cool and detached or ruggedly rooted in its surroundings. (*Photographs by Julius Shulman*)

Below. A house of brick and concrete is a clear-cut, urbane composition that makes no effort to recede into the site. Two wings of the house protect the ample terrace and pool, and a vaulted portico provides a shaded outdoor area. Rick Farber, architect.

A

Below. Resembling a natural outcropping of rock refined by man, a house of concrete and huge boulders stretches out over, and seems almost a part of, its desert site. Windows are deeply recessed under the overhanging roof or protected by a series of projecting fins. Schweikher and Elting, architects.

B

a site in a temperate climate sheltered by large trees, architect Rick Farber did not try to make the house seem part of the land. Instead he used small-scale, man-made masonry to create a light, decisive, almost sprightly contrast to the forms and colors of nature. Precisely cut white bricks are laid up into columns that support a series of very thin, rounded arches, forming at one time ceiling and roof. Glass window walls face onto a broad concrete terrace and swimming pool that seem part of the house rather than of the garden. The materials have been shaped by man, and the design of the house acknowledges this in its sharp contrast with the amorphous mass of the surrounding trees.

For a rugged desert setting, architects Schweikher and Elting used walls of large, rough-surfaced boulders embedded in concrete that promise and provide protection from desert heat and wind. Appropriately horizontal and solid, the structure is as stalwart as the setting demands. The weightiness of the walls is relieved and yet somehow intensified by the cool, dark recesses between the stone piers. Vertical wood fins that support one section of the roof echo the dark verticals in the walls. The long lines of the wooden fascia (horizontal band with a vertical face) pick up the shallow horizontal scoring of the rock walls and the flatness of the earth plane. Using natural materials, the architects designed a house that is not an intrusion on the landscape but is at peace with it.

A Notable Prefabricated House

One of the most important developments in house construction is the prefabrication of houses, which now accounts for approximately one out of every five single-family houses that are started each year. Although many of these have nothing but lower costs and speedy construction to recommend them, the general improvement in overall design during the past decade proves that the concept is sound. The Techbuilt houses designed by Carl Koch and Associates, illustrated on pages 432, 433, 434, and 435, are a remarkable example. Under-

That houses efficiently mass-produced need not look mechanistic is proved here and on the next two pages by the Techbuilt houses developed by Carl Koch and Associates.

Without sentimental or costly compromise, age-old traditions of exterior design in wood are carried into contemporary terms. (*Photograph by Ben Schnall*)

Translating the same concept into all-steel construction results in a lighter but still domestic character. (*Reprinted from* House & Garden, *Copyright* © *by the Condé Nast Publications, Inc.*)

lying every aspect of a Techbuilt house is the desire to give ample, flexible space at moderate cost. Possessing an inner, purposeful strength, the exterior grew out of a way of planning, a method of construction, and an unusual sensitivity to visual design. The shape is simple, the profile low. Broad overhangs contribute to a strong sense of shelter. Windows and exterior doors are organized in four units, one in the center of each wall. The symmetrical balance is assured but far removed from passivity by the dynamic ground-to-roof areas of glass and wood. A compelling rhythmic beat is set in motion by the 4-foot module on which the house was developed, but monotony is dispelled by unifying the four center spaces with glass. This also produces an unmistakable dominance and subordination.

The structure is of the type known as post and beam, the enclosing surfaces are panels. Four heavy wood beams, supported by steel posts, continue through the entire length of the house. Factory-built panels make the walls, the second floor, and the roof. All on a 4-foot module, the opaque panels are plywood sheets bonded to wood frames. Those containing doors and windows can be fitted in as desired. Making these panels in factories saves little money, but putting them in place saves much. Brought to the site in a single truck, they can be bolted to the frame by four men with no special tools or training in two days. Not a few handyman owners, with a little help, have done it themselves. From then on, electricians, plumbers, and so forth can work regardless of weather.

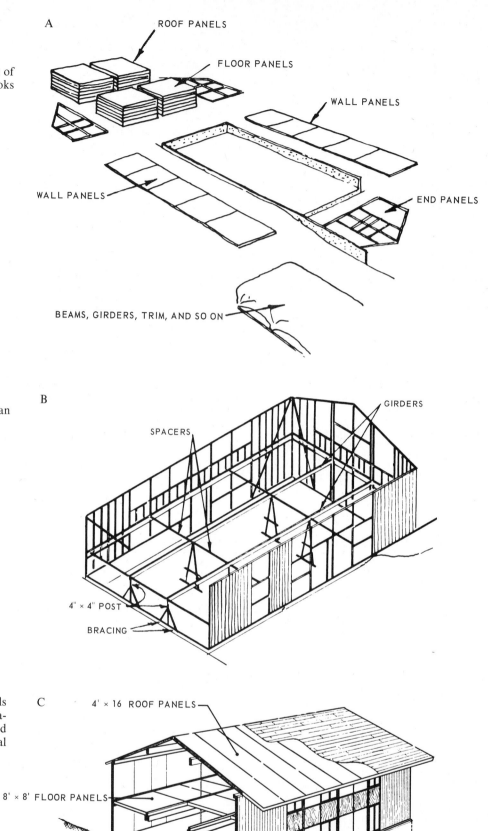

A

ROOF PANELS

FLOOR PANELS

WALL PANELS

WALL PANELS

END PANELS

BEAMS, GIRDERS, TRIM, AND SO ON

The shell of the Techbuilt house of wood, delivered by one truck, looks like this when unloaded.

B

GIRDERS

SPACERS

4" × 4" POST

BRACING

Four men working two days can set up the shell.

C

4' × 16 ROOF PANELS

8' × 8' FLOOR PANELS

4' × 10' WINDOW SECTIONS

10' × 12' SOLID WALL PANEL

Roof, floor, and solid wall panels can be surfaced with varied materials, window sections placed where wanted to meet individual needs.

The planning took into account our needs for change. Simply *enclosing* space is not expensive. "Finishing" it, up to our standards of living, is. *Adding* more space can be nightmarishly costly. Koch's solution was this: weatherproof as much space in the original as will be eventually needed, finish it when necessary, and make it easy to rearrange. Observe that all hard-to-move units—entrance and stairway, fireplace, kitchen, laundry, and baths—are concentrated in the middle third of the plan. Passageways through this core connect the ends—two thirds of the house—which can be partitioned as desired, easily changed with movable storage walls, folding doors, and the like. Thus, the central utility-circulation core produces four other zones, segregated yet interconnecting, suitable in size and shape for many activities.

The space enclosed by a Techbuilt house can be inexpensively modified as family patterns change. (*All plans copyrighted 1953 by Techbuilt, Inc.*)

Top left. A young couple can leave part of the first floor of the 24-by-44-foot house unfinished and enjoy a two-story living-dining space.

Top right. The arrival of children brings a need for more bedrooms and another bath on the upper floor, play space and clean-up facilities on the lower floor.

Below left. When the children have grown up and left home, a house may be converted into two apartments.

Below right. A similar but somewhat larger plan, 24 by 48 feet, is zoned for children and family activities on the lower floor, adults and quiet activities above.

Koch faced the dilemma of two-story houses being economical but unpopular at the time, attics and basements being cheap but seldom comfortable. In essence what he did was to make a whole house out of an attic directly above a basement. By dropping the lower floor only $3\frac{1}{2}$ feet into the ground, most of which is needed for foundations anyway, he took advantage of the earth's costless temperature control for a pleasant ground floor. By raising the eaves just a little, he gained a useful "attic." And he avoided the high boxiness of most two-story exteriors. Obviously, the typical plans fit sloping lots best: there are a good many hillside lots, and they have often led to awkward designs. On flat lots, the earth excavated for foundations must be carted away or used: if houses are designed with this in mind, the excess earth can be economically used to sculpture the land around a house.

What about the relationship to occupants and to specific site? Without sinking into the tar pit of trying to design a house that would please everybody anywhere, Koch has produced one that, quite unbelievably, appeals to "advanced" architects and to people who just want a good home. Perhaps he has devised something that approaches, in its own modest way, the "universal." We are writing, however, as though all Techbuilt houses were identical. As Koch has said, this is not a "package" but a system of converging components whose flexibility facilitates adaptation to varied sites and needs.

Thus individuality is not only possible but nourished. First, the basic plan shown here (many others have been developed) offers sixteen different room arrangements. Second, the plan can be flipped side for side or end for end or the two halves offset or at right angles. Finally, exterior and interior surface materials are chosen by the person who builds or buys the house. The potential permutations lead well up into higher statistics. In an age comforted by conformity yet striving for individuality, this approach to economical mass-produced homes, to the writers' knowledge, has no equal.

BEAUTY AND INDIVIDUALITY

If the preceding sections seem to indicate that exterior design is slavishly bound to efficient living, environment, and construction techniques and materials, rest assured that this was not intended. These materialistic factors are basic, but they are not constricting. All the houses illustrated so far have beauty, and their significant differences show that individualism is perhaps more alive today than in any earlier period.

To reinforce this point, we turn our attention to two houses (Fig. 437 and Color Fig. 21), each designed by an architect for his own family. They are approximately the same size, on similar wooded, sloping sites in not very different climates. Each house grew from an idea evolved by the architect to enable his family to live as they wanted to, and this idea was a unified concept of the two-dimensional plan and the three-dimensional interior and exterior form-space relationships. The most striking features of Ulrich Franzen's design—the floating roof and the substantial masonry base—are emphasized so strongly that the house walls seem almost nonexistent. The platform on which the house rests is defined by brick walls that are low around the living room and decks, higher for privacy around the sleeping areas but still stop short of the roof. The visually exciting diamond-shaped forms of the roof, which seem to float above the plat-

form, were determined by the shape of the lightweight structural steel trusses that constitute the framework of the roof. Because none of the walls bear any significant weight, unobtrusive walls of glass are sufficient to enclose the large living room, to form two walls of the bedrooms, and to fill in the space between the high brick walls and the roof. Ordered geometry has been transformed into architecture that is eminently open, airy, and habitable.

Architect Ray Crites evolved a home (Color Fig. 21) built of wood that frankly expresses the complex, dynamic patterns of an active family with wide-ranging interests. Considerations of cost made a multistory plan desirable because of the amount of space and privacy the family needed and wanted, and Crites used this practical fact as inspiration for the total house. A variety of indoor and outdoor spaces at different levels permits the family to get together and also gives each individual his own special retreat, as can be seen in the plans and section on page 406. Unlike many houses that cover inner complexity with a simplified exterior, this one makes each interior volume explicit on the exterior. The result is an energetic interpenetration of vertical plans that advance and recede and that are balanced by a series of decks and balconies extending the rooms into the landscape. The upper balconies provide shelter for the ones beneath; their forward thrust is tempered by protective fencing of thin wood strips that lighten the structure's blockiness and relate to the vertical lines of the rough-sawn cedar shiplap siding as well as to the tall trees around the house.

Each of these houses achieves individuality in its revelation of the character of the family it shelters and in the nature of the materials that were used. Each attains a coherent beauty because a talented architect concentrated on a strong design concept imaginatively implemented and carried through to a unique conclusion.

On the following pages other ways of capturing those qualities that can make exterior design more than a slipcover are illustrated.

Individual concepts of beauty give architecture its excitement.

Diamond-shaped and cantilevered roof units float on eight slender steel columns above a right-angled masonry base shelter but do not confine the inhabitants of a house in Rye, New York. Ulrich Franzen, architect. (*Photograph* © *Ezra Stoller*)

A

Right. Shingles and siding, architectural materials with a long history, attain new significance when they sheathe the unusual sculptural forms of a wood frame house in Norman, Oklahoma. In wide open country, the structure gives a reassuring sense of enclosure and protection from strong winds. Herb Greene, architect. (*Photograph by Julius Shulman*)

Below. Inspired by African houses, a cluster of three circular buildings with domed roofs comprises designer Jack Lenor Larsen's summer home on Long Island, New York. Two of the structures are of poured concrete; the third is of wood, with cedar siding. Not only is this home a delight in form and materials, but it shows interesting use of color and design in the conical roofs of cedar shingles, in the geometric designs in black, brown, and white painted on the storm shutters, and in the enclosing decorated concrete walls. (See also Fig. 295.) Robert Hays Rosenburg, architect. (*Photograph by Kal Weyner. United States Plywood Corporation*)

B

CONTEMPORARY EXTERIOR DESIGN

Growing out of a new way of living, a new technology of building and new materials, and a tremendous increase in construction costs, exterior design today, expectedly, is not like that of the past. Except for large sheets of glass and slender steel supports, no single aspect differentiates it sharply from all past work. Flat roofs, for example, have a very long history. Continuous bands of windows (with very small panes of glass) occurred in England as early as the fifteenth century. Starkly simple exteriors were common in the American Southwest. The Greeks and Romans integrated indoor and outdoor living handsomely. Nevertheless, contemporary houses differ notably from anything in history. Even though individualism leads to differences and exceptions, the majority of exteriors have some or many of these characteristics:

- The character tends toward the unpretentious and informal, and aims to *express* the way its occupants live rather than to *impress* others (Fig. 426).
- The house is designed for its climate, emphasizing the good aspects and ameliorating the disadvantages (Figs. 423A, 424A, and Color Fig. 22).
- The character of the site—flat or hilly, wooded or open—is often a major design inspiration.
- Increasingly, the house and its environment are thought of as a unit. Interior courts open to the sky or covered with transparent materials, terraces at ground level or raised balconies and decks, projecting roofs and overhead trellises, and extended walls and fences integrate architecture and landscape (Fig. 98B and Color Fig. 21).
- Exterior and interior are harmoniously related through large openings, repetition of shapes and materials, and forms that carry the eyes strongly from one to the other (Fig. 428).
- All sides of a house are "designed," and the exterior facing outdoor-living areas may be more architecturally interesting than that seen from the street (Fig. 431A).
- The shapes made possible by technological developments and new concepts of what is pleasing can free the exterior from conventional right-angled, boxlike forms. The three-dimensionality inherent in architecture is emphasized by advancing and receding masses or by sculptural forms (Figs. 438A and B and 441).
- Although horizontal forms are still widely used because they are well suited to flat sites, suggest comfort and ease, and make structures seem expansive (Fig. 431B), there is an awakening interest in the drama and usefulness of vertical form and space. Two-story interior volumes, emphatic vertical planes, and steeply sloping roofs are appearing more frequently than in the recent past (Fig. 423A and Color Fig. 21).
- Interest and variety are achieved with sensitive design of basic form and space, frank revelation of structural systems, and sympathetic respect for the special qualities of materials (Figs. 426A and 428). Applied ornamentation is rare.
- Balance is usually asymmetric because it more flexibly coincides with utilitarian requirements, seems natural for today's concept of family living, and increases apparent spaciousness (Fig. 166B).
- Rhythms tend to be simple and clear, and carry continuously around and through the compositions, inviting us to explore the space (Fig. 170).

- Emphasis is on the whole composition or on sizable elements rather than being densely concentrated in spots (Fig. 437).
- Livable simplicity, but not austerity, is a goal (Fig. 432).

JUDGING EXTERIOR DESIGN

Exteriors have the basic utilitarian function of sheltering the occupants and their possessions, but few persons are willing to stop at this point. Along with simple statements of fact, expressions of aspirations are needed. In ways appropriate to each specific situation, usefulness and economy ought to be considered in relation to beauty and individuality. A series of questions are listed as one way of stimulating you to think through the various aspects of exterior design for yourself, hoping that you will become clearer on what you want for your own home.

What kind of living does the character of the exterior express? In this and earlier chapters we have seen some houses marked by dignified formality, others by a natural freedom and ease. A few are boldly adventurous with exciting new forms and materials, and there are those more closely related to the past. Compare the roofs. Steep and gently sloping, inconspicuously flat, interlocking diagonals, and repeated arcs—each of these has its own character that affects, variously, those seeing it or living under it.

Which of the exteriors suits you best? Perhaps none. Then you can enjoy the excitement of searching for one that does.

Is the exterior appropriate to its environment? Environment is physical and cultural, general and specific. It is economical to design a house suited to its climate, satisfying to shape it in the spirit of the landscape, sensible to adapt it to its specific site. Culture, traditions, and nearby neighbors ought not be ignored.

Falling complacently in line with what others have done is paralyzing, but undisciplined individuality can shatter community feeling. There is no single, easy, and sure solution. It is rather a sensitive recognition of, and response to, what was there first, while remembering that architecture is always changing, you have your own preferences, and it is the second half of the twentieth century.

Is the exterior consonant with the plan? This is another puzzler. The plan, presumably reflecting the family's space needs, determines wall location and width of openings. Should it do more? We think it should, but how much latitude is there? It hardly seems fair to formalize externally an informal plan. The economies of building many tract houses from one or a few plans is fact. Having the exteriors identical is monotonous, but "treating" exteriors differently with slipcover devices convinces almost no one. If the two-dimensional plan has no life of its own, then it matters little how it becomes three-dimensional space and form.

Are the materials and construction suitable? Suitable for climate, appearance, owners' personalities, initial cost in relation to maintenance? Eager for ready-made certainty as we are, it is overly optimistic to expect it. With understanding of materials, we have to analyze our wants in order of importance and according to our bank accounts.

Is the exterior visually satisfying? Comparable to the rules of grammar, the aims and principles of design help us avoid that which is patently awkward

A house developed logically but brilliantly from an unusual plan (see Figs. 406A and B) seems at ease in its wooded setting near Cedar Rapids, Iowa. Unfinished rough cedar siding used vertically repeats the colors and slender lines of the trees and emphasizes the three-story height of the house. Walls receding and projecting in accordance with the placement of the rooms, and cantilevered balconies protected by slat balustrades, contribute to the play of sun and shadow on the exterior and temper the dominant verticality with stabilizing horizontal lines. Crites and McConnell, architects. (*Photograph by Julius Shulman*)

21

22

On a desert site with a mountainous background near Palm Springs, California, architect Richard J. Neutra designed for Edgar J. Kaufman a large, serene house impeccably proportioned in relation to man and nature. The structure integrates space and form by the juxtaposition of vertical and horizontal rectangular shapes. The man-made materials of concrete, steel, and glass are as uncomplicated and tranquil as possible. Natural materials begin in the use of random-ashlar fieldstone for the chimney and a few walls, and continue in smooth planes of grass and water that gradually blend into the rugged landscape through the placement of large boulders and shrubbery. (*Photograph by Julius Shulman*)

but not the commonplace. We can ask questions about form and purpose, communality encompassing divergence, visual stability, constancy and movement, and degrees of primacy. These are time-tested basics that are useful to the creative architect or home-builder as guide posts. But imagination, knowledge, and discerning judgment are paramount in creating beauty.

"Habitat 67" in Montreal, Canada, is a giant pyramid of precast concrete units hoisted into place. It is a notable attempt to develop a high-density urban structure that can house 158 families and still provide privacy, open space, and individuality. Landscaped terraces for each unit, plus parks and playgrounds, add color and grace. Moshe Safdie, architect. (*Photograph by George Carr*)

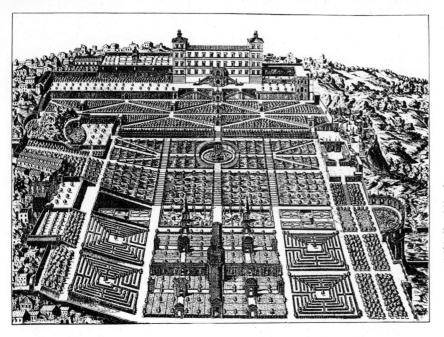

The gardens of the Villa d'Este at Tivoli, near Rome, attributed to Pirro Ligorio and built between 1550 and 1569, show the strong, disciplined geometry that allied gardens and architecture in the High Renaissance.

19 · Landscape

"What shall I do with it?" might well be the question that the man in Figure 443A is asking about his backyard, for it is a common one among homeowners. Most of the conditions are typical—a two-story house of little distinction, a narrow city lot with neighbors nearby, a backyard 40 by 50 feet, and a garage inconveniently far from kitchen and street. Less typical is the living room that overlooks, and is on the same level as, the backyard, with a door giving easy access to the yard. Atypical is the slope of the ground up from the house, which both raises problems and opens up design possibilities. As the yard stands, there is minimum protection from sun and wind, no privacy from neighbors, and no place that suggests comfortable sitting. The miscellaneous tangle of plants, indecisively shaped lawn, inadequate paving, and picayune steppingstones add up to just about nothing—except possibilities. It is easy to understand why this potentially valuable living space was little used or enjoyed. Figures 443A and B and 444A and B show what landscape architects Osmundson and Staley accomplished.

The space was organized into outdoor rooms. Much as architects plan rooms inside the house, landscape architects design the land around the house. In this plan, there are three areas. A *service yard* near the kitchen provides space, courteously screened from the neighbors, for drying clothes and the like. A *patio*

442

A

A unified, imaginative landscape design transforms a backyard into useful and pleasant living space. Osmundson and Staley, landscape architects. (*Photographs by Theodore Osmundson*)

Above. Before it was landscaped, the backyard was an uninviting, almost useless parcel of ground.

Below. Paving, a trellis, walls, plants, and furniture create an outdoor living room that will be enjoyable in good weather throughout the year.

B

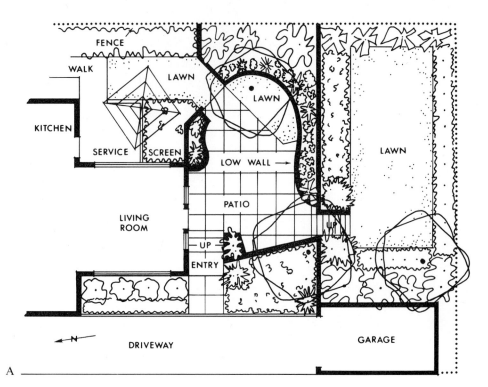

FENCE
WALK
KITCHEN
LAWN
LAWN
SERVICE   SCREEN
LOW WALL →
LAWN
PATIO
LIVING
ROOM
UP
ENTRY
N
DRIVEWAY
GARAGE
A

Right. The plan shows how the area was organized into three outdoor rooms: the patio, a secluded lawn, and a service yard.

B

Above. A free-curve brick wall visually expands the patio, raises plants to a height at which they can be easily enjoyed and maintained.

carries the living room outdoors. A *lawn* at the rear becomes a quiet retreat in this plan, but it could have been a children's play space or a gardener's hobby area. Although each area is differentiated from the others, none is completely separated—"open planning" was developed in landscape design long before architects took it over.

The ground surface was made usable. Sloping ground is attractive in large expanses, but it is not suited to intensive use. With limited outdoor space, the designers wisely made each area level. Further, they paved the most-used parts to provide hard, dry footing for people and furniture. Paving is easily maintained, can be used soon after a rain, warms quickly even in winter if exposed to the sun, and carries the feeling and function of interior floors into the landscape. Its only disadvantages are initial expense and the hard, hot glare that comes when the surface is too smooth and bright and there is insufficient shade. In this patio, raised planting beds, trees, and a pergola cast changing shadows and reduce glare. To give visual interest and minimize cracking, the concrete has been separated into squares with redwood strips.

Protection from the wind, sun, and neighbors was provided. A *fence* of redwood stakes around the rear of the property was the first step in increasing privacy and reducing wind, while serving as another transition between house and garden. The small scale of the narrow stakes increases the apparent size of the whole yard, and the spaces between them permit some circulation of air.

The *trellis* across the end of the living room makes part of the patio shady. In addition, it improves the appearance of the house by reducing its apparent height, and seems to increase the extent of the patio by bringing attention down from the top of the house—or the sky—to a more human level. As the paving was an underfoot link, the trellis is an overhead transition between architecture and landscape.

Several *trees* also control wind, sun, and views from outside while contributing their own unique beauty.

Levels were separated by retaining walls. Economy suggested keeping an existing concrete wall that retained the upper level. Otherwise, a wall of more interesting material would have been placed so that the rear yard would not be divided into two equal strips. The new free-curve brick wall, supporting a flower bed at an intermediate level, brings welcome contrast of shape, texture, and color. In other places, walls are of redwood planks. Low walls such as these have many points of excellence. In comparison with sloping banks, they save space and upkeep time, and they unify house and garden by bringing architectural forms and plants into intimate relationships. All year they state the garden's design clearly and create three-dimensional patterns of materials, light, and shadow. Flowers are raised to a level where they are easily appreciated and maintained. Finally, low walls provide good short-time sitting space for large groups. In this garden, sloping land made walls almost necessary; but even on a flat site, raised beds do much to make outdoor areas useful and interesting.

The garden was given a coherent and sensible design. Rectangles, diagonals, and curves have each been used where their character makes them appropriate. The service yard has a logical rectangularity in keeping with its use. Interest is sensibly concentrated in the patio, for this is the most important area. The free-curve wall and the diagonals invite people to explore its shape. As a quiet foil for the diversity in the patio, the rear lawn is an unembellished rectangle, echoing the right angles of the service area.

Above. Taliesin East, architect Frank Lloyd Wright's home in Wisconsin, appears as a more protected part of the landscape, merging into and enhancing the beauty of the site. (*Photograph by Maynard L. Parker Modern Photography*)

A

Right. A small terrace in a multiple-unit housing complex can encourage enjoyable outdoor living when appropriately furnished with weather-resistant furniture. The lightweight aluminum chairs have polyfoam cushions; the table has a heavy glass top. The sculptural design is agreeable with both the vigorous iron railing and the lighter forms of succulents and shrubbery. Hall Bradley, designer. (*Brown-Jordan Company*)

B

446

PLANNING THE LANDSCAPE

Designing the land that belongs to a house is an integral aspect of the total home design, and ideally indoor and outdoor space are planned at the same time. The well planned house graces its site, and the landscape design complements the structure. To Frank Lloyd Wright a sense of oneness between landscape and architecture was basic, a concept well-illustrated in Taliesin East (Fig. 446A), where he created a consummate union of the house and its environs. Built of native stone from nearby quarries, the structure is spread low and unobtrusively, slightly below the brow of a hill to which it is tied with long retaining walls, steps, paving, and masses of shrubbery and sheltering trees. House and garden seem to have grown from the land, naturally and harmoniously.

In an urban environment, a different kind of integration is called for. In Figures 447A and B the elements and materials of the city, horizontal pavement and vertical walls, concrete and glass, have been discerningly combined in a design that enlarges the group-living space of a small house. Countering the hardness and whiteness of concrete, the still, dark pool brings a sense of peace and a welcome relief from brightness, while the few but well-chosen plants relax the general angularity and provide some color. City-dwellers generally are not avid gardeners, and this landscape design accepts the fact and uses it as a means of fitting the house into the cityscape.

Because landscape design is essentially a matter of strengthening the relation of the site to people and house, the crucial question is: What is wanted from the land not covered by the house? Possibilities include:

Left. An extension of the living room, the terrace of a small town house in Los Angeles is defined by a quiet pool on two sides and softened by a graceful olive tree and wandering vines on the side wall. Killingsworth, Brady, Smith, and Associates, architects. (*Photograph by Marvin Rand*)

Below. The plan shows the total design of the small, 30-by-80-foot lot, with terraces expanding the living area of the house and with high house walls at the front and a fence at the rear of the property giving protection. (*Reprinted by special permission from the June 1960 issue of* House & Home. *Copyright © 1960 by McGraw-Hill, Inc.*)

A

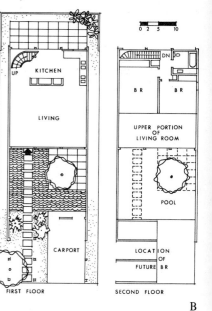

B

LANDSCAPE - 447

Storage facilities are as necessary in the garden as in the house. A utility center of paneled hardboard has many conveniences: perforated hardboard on which tools can be hung, shelves for cans and bottles, slot shelves on the backs of two doors for small items, and an outdoor potting bench. (*American Hardboard Association*)

- A pleasant setting that relates the building to the ground
- Attractive "garden pictures" from windows or terraces
- Space for outdoor relaxation, eating, and entertaining
- Provision for active outdoor games, especially for children
- Room for the garden enthusiast to grow flowers, fruits, or vegetables

On small lots it is not easy to have all these. Then it is necessary to decide on the relative importance of each and to plan the landscape to promote the preferred outdoor activities. Even on a city lot, however, it is surprising how much can be achieved, as demonstrated in Figures 443B through 444B.

Whatever the decision, developing the landscape is so much like other aspects of home planning that almost everything said in the preceding chapters is applicable. Here, too, we are concerned with modifying and controlling the environment for our physical and spiritual welfare. Integration of the practical and the aesthetic stands as the goal; the basic approach outlined in Chapter 1 is valid.

Units of the Home Landscape

As houses are zoned into units for differing activities, so the home landscape is typically organized into *foreground, outdoor living space,* and *service area. Play space* and *gardening areas* may or may not be separate zones.

Foreground, the land between house and street, gives the building a setting and establishes landscape relationships with the community. Appropriateness to the size and character of the lot, the house, and the community is desirable. But this need not mean unthinking duplication of what everyone else has done:

- The foreground can open the house boldly to the street with the typical expanse of shrub-bordered lawn, exposed entrance walk, foundation planting, and trees to frame the house.
- Among the other alternatives are secluding it with fences or hedges (Fig. 447B) or treating it as a garden area (Fig. 451A).
- If not secluded, this area is often of little use to those living in the house and therefore tends to be much smaller than it was some years ago. In urban areas, it may be eliminated.

Living space is the most important unit, unless special interests dictate otherwise, and therefore is usually the largest:
- Privacy from street and neighbors is desirable, suggesting a location at the rear of the property unless such factors as lot orientation or view require another solution.
- Typically, this unit commands the best outlook, even if that is only a controlled view of the garden.
- Close relationships to living, dining, and cooking spaces increase usefulness.
- Livability is furthered by protection from wind, hot sun, rain, and snow.
- Firm pavement and suitable furniture are essentials (Fig. 447A).
- Attractiveness in all seasons deserves thought (Fig. 453).

Service space, suitably designed and located, can relieve the house and yard of needless clutter, for it is here that clothes are hung, trash cans kept, and an untidy miscellany of things accumulates:
- The most efficient location is near kitchen and garage, play space, and gardener's plot (Figs. 444A and 451C).
- Seldom attractive, it is best when screened from view.
- Size depends on specific conditions, but few areas are large enough.
- Firm ground surface is needed, some protection from rain or snow almost a necessity.

Growing space for vegetables, fruits, and cut flowers is ideally in a separated plot where the total visual effect is of minor consequence but where soil and drainage are good. Full sun and protection from wind are recommended, as is convenient garden storage. On small lots or when gardening interests are minor, growing space can be joined with living space—but then everyday appearance is a factor.

Play space for children is most efficient when readily accessible from children's rooms and easily supervised from the kitchen (Figs. 461B and 462A). If play space is visually screened from other areas, adult standards of neatness need not be enforced. Play space merits as much area as can be allowed and some protection from inclement weather.

Maintenance

Maintenance of the landscape, as of the house, is a pervasive and continuing activity throughout all the units and deserves consideration in the basic planning. It includes such work as watering, feeding, pruning, and spraying plant materials; mowing lawns; planting annuals and bulbs; replacing plants that have not fulfilled their promise or have died; and keeping the grounds free of litter and the garden furniture in good shape. The following will generally reduce maintenance time and effort:

- A few major areas of ample size and simple shape rather than many small, complicated ones
- Pavement or gravel in much-used areas and in paths; lawns are much harder to keep in good shape
- Hard-surface paths and ramps at least 3 feet wide to get lawn mowers, wheelbarrows, and other equipment to all areas where they are used
- A conveniently located, well-planned tool-storage-and-garden-work center (Fig. 448)
- Garden furniture that resists weather, staining, and soiling
- Perennials, ground covers, shrubs and trees that are eventful in shape, foliage patterns, flowers, or fruits to provide year-round interest without much labor
- Plants that require frequent or special care kept near the house or garden-work center, those that pretty well take care of themselves near the edges of the property
- Plants with similar cultural requirements in masses rather than scattered in many spots

Making the Plan

Figures 451A, B, and C show how landscape zones can be organized. Placing the house toward the front of the lot gives maximum space for private outdoor living at the rear, and placing it crosswise on the lot opens it broadside to the garden. Economically, the garage is near the street to minimize the driveway area (driveways are expensive and waste land). Also it efficiently opens into the kitchen and is near the service yard, moderately near the front door. This leaves a small foreground that has been secluded with a fence and planting.

An ample terrace leads out into the private outdoor-living area. The terrace is joined with the service area, yet screened from the less sightly parts. What might have been two cramped areas was openly planned to give a sense of expansiveness. Beyond the terrace a lawn performs its usual multiple functions of being useful to walk, sit, or lie on in good weather and of pleasing the eyes. It is a quiet foreground for the bed of flowers that, in turn, is enhanced by a background of fence and planting. Trees are placed to give shade where wanted, adding the high forms gardens need and making a pleasing pattern in themselves. A path invites strolling around and enjoying the landscape from varying angles.

Although this plan provides no specific place for children's play and limited space for hobby gardening, such activities are not ruled out. Service area, terrace, and lawn could accommodate a number of children, and the path encircling the grounds is a potential running track. The upper left portion could become a horticulturist's corner. Not ideal, this overlapping of uses illustrates the compromises most of us have to make.

Curves dominate this design, giving a big, overall unity. Sweeping around from front to back, they suggest pleasant visual and physical movement. They are neither rigidly geometrical nor are they nervous wiggles. They came, as the sketches show, from creative thinking, but this thinking was guided by the size and shape of the lot, the location of the house, and the needs and preferences of the owners. Close study shows that they are adroitly diversified. The fence

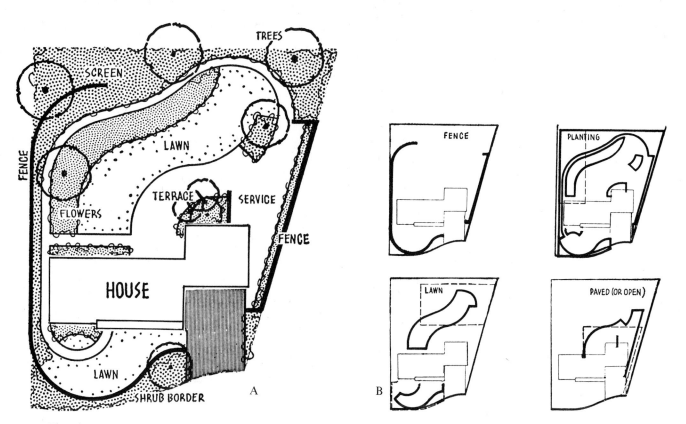

A

B

Planning on paper and by models are excellent ways to visualize designs before investing money and labor. Douglas Baylis, landscape architect. (*Reprinted from* Sunset Ideas for Landscaping Your Home)

Above left. Unifying curves are the basis of this strong and simple plan.

Above right. Sketches show the basic shapes of fence, planting, lawn, and paving. They are noteworthy examples of variety in unity.

Below. The model, adding the third dimension, helps us to envision height relationships that will be so important to the success of the design.

C

across the front starts at the driveway close to the house, swings back to open the front lawn, straightens along the property line, again becomes a curve terminating in the screen planting. It affords privacy without boxed-in confinement. The path echoes without repeating the shapes of both fence and lawn. Beginning as a circular extension of the front porch, it then parallels the fence for a while before going beyond, in a sweep reminiscent of the front lawn, to join the terrace. The flower bed, intentionally simple so as not to compete with its contents, follows without exactly paralleling the path. Then comes the lawn, which is a variation of the flower-bed shape. The terrace carries this progression to its final step. It has the basic character of the lawn and flower bed, but the curve is more pronounced, the small planting beds subdivide it into more intricate shapes than those used elsewhere, and straight lines are introduced. Throughout this plan there is diversity growing out of a single idea, a rhythmic progression of shapes, an intensification of interest near the house, and a gradual simplification as the boundaries are approached.

Undoubtedly the most satisfactory way to achieve good landscape design is to select the land that will be most appropriate and amenable to one's needs, then to have house and landscape designed together by experts. For those who wish to try designing the landscape themselves, the following general procedure is suggested:

- Make a measured plan at a scale of 1 inch to 8 or 10 feet. Indicate property lines, house and garage, driveway and walks, existing trees and shrubs, the slope of the land. A 50-foot tape, cross-section paper, a drawing board, a ruler, and a pencil are the tools.
- List in order of importance the favored outdoor activities. Decide on the general character you want. Read about landscape design and visit every example you can. List ways of achieving your goal while keeping in mind what it will cost.
- Then put the plan on a drawing board, and with plenty of tracing paper and soft pencils begin to design.
- Rough in the major units in a very general way. Try several locations and shapes for each on separate sheets of tracing paper. Review them critically.
- Begin to refine the shapes, thinking of the best size and shape for each part and the unity of the whole design. A basic idea—formality or informality, curves or right angles—brings consistency, and carrying lines through from one unit to the others is a major unifying device.
- Then start thinking about details—kinds of enclosure, types of ground surfacing, location and character of trees and shrubs—that will forcibly carry out the basic idea.
- Check the plan carefully as a whole and in every detail to insure that it provides for all desired outdoor activities and that it has the spirit most congenial to you.
- Set up a five-year development plan if you cannot afford all at once. It is sensible to get the ground surfacing nearest the house and the absolutely necessary enclosure first. Major trees, permanent background planting, and lawn also have high priority. You can wait, though, for highly desirable but expensive plants, fences, and overhead protection that are wanted but are not crucial. You can also delay for a while the development of the land farthest from the center of living.

MATERIALS OF LANDSCAPE DESIGN

A knowledge of materials is as necessary in landscape design as it is in house planning or interior design, for the materials used in landscaping affect the result quite as much as those used in interiors and for constructing the house. Because the living materials grow and change and die, the ability to visualize this knowledge is of added importance (Color Figs. 23 and 24).

Ground Surfacings

As with floor coverings, ground surfacings can be divided into *hard,* such as stone or brick, and *soft,* which includes lawns and ground covers.

Hard ground surfacings, more than any other single factor, make gardens livable. Once installed, they take almost no work, keep the garden's design clear, and relate house to land.

Stone. Usually expensive and nearly always beautiful, stone can be laid in orderly rectangular patterns (Fig. 169) or in informal random shapes (Fig. 178). The choice depends on the character wanted and the funds at hand. It is most effective, though, when the individual slabs are sizable, not too jagged or irregular, and when they are laid in rather large areas of strong, simple shape.

Brick. Effective in old and new gardens, brick is sympathetic in color and texture (Fig. 115). The units, pleasantly small in scale, can be laid in many patterns. They are not slippery when wet, nor do they glare in the sun.

Concrete. Concrete is widely used for its durability, moderate cost, and suitability to straight or curved shapes. New developments in color and texture permit innumerable variations (Figs. 453 and 458B). Radiant heating embedded in concrete can warm outdoor areas in cool weather.

Water in jets, cascades, smooth-flowing channels, and quiet pools is defined by rectangles of concrete in varied textures set against a backdrop of tall eucalyptus trees. No matter what the season the garden has an eventful but peaceful and ordered beauty. Lawrence Halprin, landscape architect. (*Photograph by Morley Baer*)

Tar and gravel. Not a surfacing of great beauty, blacktop or macadam as used for roads is unobtrusively satisfactory and inexpensive. With interest supplied elsewhere, it takes its place as a neutral floor, but it can be enlivened with color or embedded with coarsely crushed rock.

Gravel. Crushed gravel, spread, watered, and rolled, is the least expensive hard surface. It provides dry, quite firm footing and color-texture variations harmonious with plants. As with brick, the cost can be greatly reduced if the owners do the work.

Soft ground surfacings are divided between those that can be walked on and those that can stand little or no trampling. Their purposes are twofold: to cover open ground, preventing it from becoming muddy, dusty, or overgrown with weeds, and to provide an attractive, unifying base for the garden design.

Lawns are about the only natural soft surfacing that can be walked on very much. So common are lawns in many temperate climates that it is a surprise to learn of their rarity in such drier regions as Italy, Spain, or the American southwestern states. And they are uncommon in the Orient, not for climatic reasons but because they have no great appeal for these peoples. Their popularity with us is based on the low cost of getting them started and the moderate cost of upkeep, their usefulness, and their quiet beauty. Physically as well as visually, lawns cool gardens in summer. Often-overlooked limitations include their unusability in wet weather, conspicuous wear with concentrated use, and insistently continuous need for maintenance.

Other soft ground covers, such as *ivy, wild strawberry,* and *trailing junipers,* cover rough earth with little maintenance, but they will not stand traffic. *Tan bark* also gives a somewhat resilient ground surfacing that takes wear and is especially suitable for play yards, and there are now *man-made carpets* reported to withstand weather.

Fences, Walls, and Hedges

Comparable to the walls of a room, fences, walls, and hedges give privacy, lessen wind, and provide a background for plants and people. Architecturally, they delineate the three-dimensional space of the landscape.

Fences and **walls,** unlike hedges or other screen planting, take almost no space or maintenance and give immediate effect. Their variety is legion: they can be high or low; straight, angled, or curved; have open spaces or be solid; emphasize horizontals or verticals, or balance both; and have any degree of ruggedness or refinement. The range of materials, formerly limited to wood, brick, and stone, has been extended by concrete blocks (Fig. 458B), corrugated plastic or metal, plastic-impregnated screen, and clear or colored glass. Although walls and fences are typically similar in character to the house, for economy and to tie in with the planting they are often somewhat more rugged and less precise.

Hedges of one variety of plant, clipped or allowed to grow freely, or of several types of shrubs, provide good green enclosure—if space permits and if one is willing to wait a few years for the full effect and then to work to keep it that way. A high degree of unity is achieved if only one kind is used; variety comes with many. The latter is seldom satisfying unless the selection is limited to about five kinds with at least three or more plants of each type massed together. Deliberately planned exclamation points are, of course, an exception.

Overhead Protection

The sky is a magnificent but undependable ceiling. From it we get light and heat on many days but often too much of both for comfortable outdoor relaxation. On clear, cool nights it takes heat from the earth's surface. The most important function of overhead protection is tempering the climate. Not only does it lessen light, heat, cold, and wind but, if waterproof, protects us, our furniture, and play equipment from rain and snow. A second function is giving the sense of protection and security that comes with having something between us and the sky. The third function is to bring part of the above-eye-level landscape down to human scale. Many persons have found that putting a sunshade over part of a terrace made the terrace look much larger because it was then not judged in relation to the vastness of the sky.

Encompassing almost as many variants as fences, overhead protection can be in the form of completely weatherproof and lightproof roofs of the same material used to cover the house. If of plastic or glass, rain and snow but not light are excluded. Canvas securely fastened to a framework performs much the same way but is relatively short-lived. Sunshades of wood, much like stationary horizontal venetian blinds, reduce heat and glare while allowing air to circulate. Arbors and trellises (Figs. 443B and 462B) with vines bring nature and architecture together happily but offer limited protection. Nature's great overhead shelters, trees, are the primary ones for most of us and will be discussed in the following sections.

A thorough exploration of a weather-conditioned landscape development (Figs. 462A and B) shows how sheltering roofs and terraces, along with paving and walls, can make the outdoors comfortable in many kinds of weather.

Plants

Plants are the materials that most sharply differentiate landscape design from architecture. Varying markedly from one part of the country to another, they exert strong regional influences. It is quite possible to develop a landscape with plants alone, one that can be very beautiful in some seasons and enjoyable on the best of days and nights. With rare exceptions, though, it will fall short of being a "landscape for living."

The variety of plants is endless. Each has its own habit of growth (height, width, shape, and pattern of branching), its own growing needs (kind of soil, amount of water, degree of sun or shade, and temperature range), and its special type of leaves, flowers, and fruits. In no other phase of art can designers select from such diverse materials. Even within one genus and species, there are as many individual differences as in man.

Plants can be categorized in terms of growth and landscape uses.

Ground covers, in addition to the various grasses used for lawns, include an array of low-growing, spreading plants that cover otherwise bare soil and typically take little maintenance. They are useful as low, permanent foreground, under trees or shrubs, and on sloping or rough ground. Because they vary greatly in leaf color, size, and shape, in habit of growth, and in flowers and fruits, they offer opportunities for simple or complex compositions (Fig. 456). All need weeding until they are sufficiently established to discourage unwanted growths;

Plants, water, rocks, and winding paths create a garden full of small-scale interest that can be enjoyed from a brick terrace and that will give the gardener many pleasurable hours pruning and shaping the plants to preserve the composition. (*Photograph by Morley Baer. Reprinted from* Sunset *Magazine.*)

watering, feeding, and pest control according to their specific requirements; and pruning to keep them in bounds and to remove unsightly patches.

Shrubs, low- to moderate-height woody plants with several stems, are used for background or screen plantings and also as decisive accents. Selecting the most appropriate shrubs is a game of deciding what effect is wanted and of then finding the shrubs that will grow well in the specific location. For example, there are junipers with low, spreading branches densely clothed with blue-green needles. Their hardly noticeable flowers and fruits and their retention of leaves make them almost as constant in appearance 365 days a year as a brick wall. Bridal wreath, a member of the *Spiraea* plant family, in contrast, sends up many stems from the ground to arch over in a vase shape. In spring, tender green leaves appear and then for a short period are all but hidden in a burst of white flowers. In summer, they are graceful green mounds, and in winter the branches are bare. Rhododendrons retain their big, leathery leaves the year round and in spring are decorated with massive heads of flowers. These merely hint at the possibilities and limitations of shrubs.

Pruning to keep them within bounds and to emphasize their shapes is the chief maintenance needed for a great many shrubs; others may have to be cut back at specified times to insure desired new growth in the spring. Watering needs may vary, from the native plants that will get along on rainfall to the exotic plants that require special care.

Trees—typically high, single-stemmed, woody plants—are the biggest elements in gardens and deserve the respect that large size demands. Here, too, there is diversity. The difference between a slender, small-leaved birch tree with its delicate white bark and a stately pine with its strong trunk and branches always clothed with dark-green needles is great. Or compare the American elm's graceful vase shape with the rugged vigor of a sturdy oak. The tempering of light, heat, and wind and the controlling of outlooks and inlooks are the important contributions of trees. They are also tall accents, the last step in the progression of heights from lawn or terrace to the sky, and as such are often focal points toward which the landscape builds up. Some of them have showy flowers, edible or decorative fruits, or bright autumn colors.

Most trees require occasional deep watering until they are well established. Some require severe pruning, while others may be left to grow naturally except for the elimination of unsightly, dead, or inconvenient branches.

Flowers, somewhat comparable to the enriching accessories of interiors, bloom on all types of plants. Although we usually think of flowers as low annuals and perennials, the many shrubs and trees that have worthwhile blossoms in addition to giving shade or enclosure are economical of time and space. Flowers show to best advantage against an appropriate background. The sky serves well for flowering trees, but lower plants are best appreciated when given a setting of shrubbery or fences. Although accents and diversity are needed, sizable masses of similar kinds of flowers in related colors make a garden coherent. The purpose should indicate the varieties chosen and the way they are used. Bold displays can be achieved with such herbaceous plants as marigolds, petunias, and geraniums; such shrubs as lilacs, floribunda roses, and azaleas; and the flowering cherries, crab apples, plums, and peaches. At the opposite end of the scale, lilies of the valley and violets never compel attention but are rewarding when looked at closely.

Maintenance depends largely upon whether the flowers are perennials, which come up every year, or annuals, which must be planted each season, and also upon the way in which they wither. When the petals of some blooms fall off, for example, they leave handsome seed pods; some dead flowers are inconspicuous, but many are unsightly and must be removed if the garden is to look well kept.

Fruits, ornamental or edible, are almost as enriching as flowers. Most fruit trees have highly decorative flowers, and those with larger fruits, notably apples, are almost as gay when the fruit is ripe. In warm climates, oranges and lemons have flowers or fruits for many months. Many shrubs—barberry, cotoneaster, and firethorn—add color to the fall and winter landscape with their berries.

Fruit trees may present maintenance problems. They usually need watering and knowledgeable pruning in order to produce fruit; many need frequent spraying if the fruit is to mature and be edible; and the fruit must be picked or it falls to the ground, where it is squashy and unsightly, especially if near terraces, walks, and lawns. For the individual who likes to can or freeze his own fruit, however, they may be well worth their care.

Water

Quiet pools with or without plants (Figs. 447A and 456) are refreshingly cool and reflect the sky or plants above them in ever-changing patterns. Moving water in fountains, cascades, or streams is a joy (Fig. 453). There are, however, practical considerations: water features are expensive to install and require special maintenance. Pools of any depth are also a hazard for small children.

A

Right. A louvered redwood fence is an effective background for shrubs of diverse characters. The pierced ceramic tiles echo the intricacy of the foliage patterns. (*Photograph by Ernest Braun. Reprinted from* Sunset *Magazine*)

Below. Concrete paving blocks that can be made by amateurs or bought commercially individualize paved areas. (*Photograph by Ernest Braun. Reprinted from* Sunset *Magazine*)

B

Man-Made Enrichment

Similar to that used inside homes, but larger in scale and more durable, man-made enrichment is a handsome way of getting permanent interest in the landscape. Sculpture, be it a marble statue, a horse from an old merry-go-round, or an amateur sand casting, is a sturdy note of emphasis. Mobiles provide constantly changing patterns. Some artists have created paintings for outdoor use, others have covered sections of fences with pieces of scrap materials organized much like nonobjective paintings. Ceramic tile and pebble mosaics (Figs. 458A and B), ornamental pots and urns give year-round pleasure. Maintenance care of man-made enrichment is usually limited to an occasional cleaning and cutting back of the surrounding greenery to keep it on display.

ENVIRONMENT FOR LIVING

The phrase *environmental planning* embraces everything to do with the physical and spiritual aspects of living, from land planning on a regional basis down to the design of individual houses and their interiors. Over the larger aspects of regional and city planning we have very little control other than that generated by an intelligent, informed, and willing-to-be-involved citizenry. But most people do have control over their personal environment to some extent. They can choose the community and the kind of housing that will promote the kind of life they want to live, within their financial range. For those who enjoy city life, a hotel, an apartment, or a town house may be the answer. At the other extreme is the farm. In between are intermediate possibilities, each with its complex of advantages and disadvantages.

Selecting the Community

In the long run, the community is perhaps more important than the individual lot, and the first search may well be directed toward finding one that seems congenial and attractive. This usually means an area in which the families have similar socioeconomic status and interests. Community assets include good schools, parks, and recreational facilities, churches, shopping areas, public transportation, and fire and police protection. Nuisances include traffic thoroughfares, railroads, and airports as well as noisy or fume-producing factories. Light industry —quiet, clean, and attractive—can be advantageous because of employment opportunities.

Selecting the Lot

So many, often conflicting, factors crowd together that the perfect lot is seldom found. However, the following factors should be considered:

Convenience. The lot should be near, preferably within walking distance of, schools, parks, library, churches, and shopping—but not adjacent to them because of noise and traffic. Distance from the wage earner's work is important, too.

Streets and Traffic. A basic concern for most of us is finding a lot facing a quiet street. Other factors are the ease and safety of frequently traveled routes and the visual pleasantness of the total street pattern (Fig. 460).

Elevation. Lots that are neither at the bottom of a valley nor on the top of a hill are conservative choices. Hilltops afford fine views, but they may be cold and windy, are often expensive to build on. Low lots may be poorly drained, damp, and cold in winter and hot in summer. To some, they are also depressing.

Size. The right size for the family and house are the only guides. Small-to-moderate lots, from 60 to 75 by 100 feet, bring proximity to neighbors and usually to needed facilities. They are not excessively costly to buy, develop, and maintain. If wisely planned, such lots often give more usable outdoor space than a large one you cannot afford to make livable. Larger lots have the luxury of space and seclusion, and the opportunity for more varied outdoor areas—but they are usually expensive, remote, or both. Lot size is also closely allied to house size and shape. Large houses require more ground than small ones, and sprawling one-story homes take more space than do compact two-story designs.

In some of the new cluster-type developments (Fig. 460), the houses are grouped on quite small lots, but each has direct access to expansive park and recreation areas.

Cluster development of a subdivision offers these advantages: 41 acres in home sites, 51 acres of usable open space, few hazardous thoroughfares, and many pleasant views. A conventional subdivision this size would have 80 acres in home sites but none in parks and playgrounds, almost half as much land devoted to circulation alone. (*Reprinted from William H. Whyte,* Cluster Development. *Copyright © 1964, American Conservation Association*)

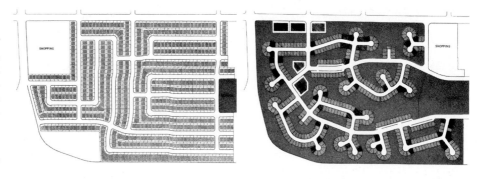

CONVENTIONAL SUBDIVISION   CLUSTER SUBDIVISION

Shape. A rectangle with the narrow side toward the street is the norm, but other shapes may lead to more personalized homes and gardens.

Orientation. With the street toward the north, the house can be opened on the south overlooking the private area. Other orientations take more ingenious planning to enjoy the advantages of privacy and sun.

Slope. Flat land is the easiest to develop—and the least inspiring. Hillside lots bring interest and individuality at a price.

Natural features. Even one tree is an asset, and several expedite landscaping. Streams, lakes, and outcroppings of rocks may or may not be equally valued by lot buyers and lot sellers.

Selecting a location for living is a matter of balancing all factors in order of their desirability. One or more acres of wooded, rolling land in a section where other properties are large gives the spaciousness and inconvenience of country living. A town house or an apartment can be most economical in terms of time.

Unitary House and Landscape Design

As mentioned earlier, there is increasing interest in designing house and landscape together to provide complementary indoor- and outdoor-living spaces.

There are two basic approaches: having the landscape penetrate the house as protected courts and extending the house so that it envelops parts of the landscape with decks or paved terraces, walls or fences, or overhead shelters of various kinds that create protected outdoor-living areas. Architect Marcel Breuer has taken both approaches, designing inner courts and outdoor terraces to provide many degrees of privacy and climate control for a house in Switzerland (Figs. 461A and B).

A

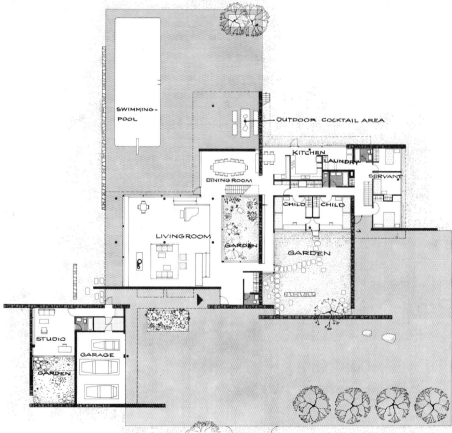

B

When house and landscape are planned together, they fulfill each other.

Above. Inner courts and outdoor terraces interact with interior spaces in the total architectural design of architect Marcel Breuer.

Left. The plan shows the high degree of integration Breuer achieved by staggering and extending the house walls and by enclosing parts of the landscape, some partially, some wholly.

A second example (Figs. 462A and B) that explores the possibilities of a weather-conditioned landscape development shows how sheltering roofs and the walls of the house, together with paving and low walls, can make the outdoors comfortable in many kinds of weather. A roofed terrace at the living room's west end is protected by the house and a solid storage wall along the north side. This shaded terrace leads onto an area for sun lovers that faces south and west and is defined by a low brick wall. The adjoining shade terrace is shielded by a 15-by-30-foot arbor of thin wood slats and plastic panels. Near the kitchen is another small sheltered terrace, and the plans for additional children's rooms include a roofed play terrace with a southern and eastern exposure that is conveniently near, yet secluded from, the adults' zone. Integral with the design of the house, these terraces and walls, roofs and arbor make the house look larger and extend livable space beyond its actual dimensions. No matter what the climate, outdoor living can be made more pleasurable with adroit planning.

Right. Both house and landscape are planned for future expansion.

Below. Usability is greatly increased when the total design offers sun and shade, enjoyment of breezes, and protection from wind. Architect Gordon Drake and landscape architect Douglas Baylis collaborated from outset to finish. (*Photograph by Julius Shulman*)

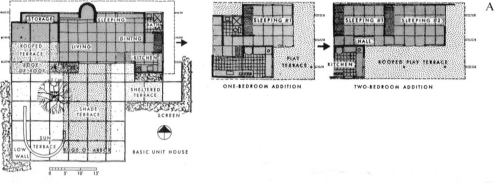

A

B

A rock-bordered pool and some noble pine trees make a relaxing sylvan retreat. (*Photograph by Morley Baer. Reprinted from* Sunset *Magazine*)

Although hard-and-fast lines are no longer drawn between house and garden because, at best, they have much in common, nevertheless they are not identical, and some of the major differences are worth consideration:

Gardens are used less intensively than houses. In part, gardens are used less intensively because of the way in which landscapes are planned. The livability of a garden is closely related to its similarity to architecture and to the amount of climate control provided—a protected patio will be used more frequently than an open lawn.

Landscapes are usually larger than houses and, therefore, are appropriately larger in scale. A single-family suburban dwelling seldom covers more than one-fifth of the lot, leaving four-fifths free for development. Further, the infinitely high sky, not an 8- or 10-foot ceiling, is the top of most landscaped areas. Thus, it is necessary that major landscape features be strong and large in scale or they will seem trivial.

Growing plants are the distinctive landscape materials. Plants are organisms with decisive but changing personalities. They change far more than do the comparatively static materials of houses. This inevitable transformation suggests the need to be familiar with the life cycle of each plant used, to be prepared to modify the growth by pruning or replacing the plant when necessary. Better yet, the landscape should be designed so that the changes become assets.

Landscape design is the modification of the land at our disposal for use and pleasure. For many years it was among the least sensibly handled phases of home design and gave little useful pleasure. Contemporary trends have made us aware of how valuable our land can be in terms of space for living.

Architect Oscar Neimeyer's house in Rio de Janeiro, Brazil. The bold, free-form curves of the roof slab and the pool terrace complement each other and the mountainous landscape. Their stark whiteness stands in dramatic contrast to the natural surroundings. (*Collection of the Museum of Modern Art, New York*)

Two owls, wise and wide-eyed, are gleaming ornaments, handwrought of solid crystal. (*Steuben Glass*)

20 · Costs and Budgets

Discussions of costs and budgets are difficult and hazardous. Costs often vary from one part of the country to another, from one town to its neighbor, and from store to store in the same community. They go up and down with national and regional economic conditions and with new developments in each field. And they vary greatly on objects used for the same purpose, as for example on dining chairs, which can be priced at as little as $6 each and as much as $100 or more.

There is only one way to be certain of the prices of furnishings when you are ready to buy:

- Visit your local stores, read the advertisements in your newspapers and in home magazines, and spend some time with mail-order catalogs.

And there is only one way to get a budget suited to you—

- Study your own situation, needs, and preferences in terms of your income.

HOUSE AND LOT

The average cost of new houses increased more than 50 percent in the last decade, and many experts believe that the upward trend will continue. Generally higher prices account for part of this, but higher incomes have led to larger houses, better materials, more bathrooms, and much more and better mechanical equipment. Surveys show that enclosed-space cost ranges from a very occasional $10 to $20 or more per square foot. As an indication of how building costs vary in different parts of the country, the Dow Building Cost Calculator for 1965 gives this range for a development house in South Pasadena, California (Fig. 401), of 2350 square feet that actually cost $36,000 to build (exclusive of land and landscaping): in Atlanta, $31,250; in the New York area, $43,000.

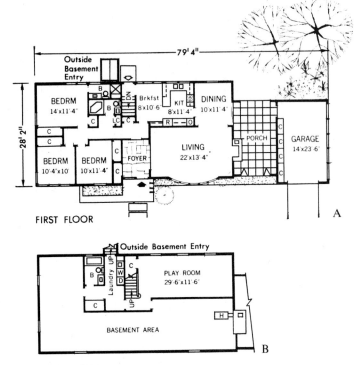

The house plan is one factor affecting total cost, as is shown by four plans in Princeton, New Jersey, and their estimated construction costs. Rudolph A. Mattern, architect; Carl Eldracher, construction estimator. In all of the solutions the main floor, as shown in A, has 1431 square feet of living space. (*Reprinted from* New Homes Guide, *63. Copyright © 1963, Holt, Rinehart and Winston, Inc.*)

Right. A one-story house with a semidetached garage and a full basement with 1404 square feet would cost $24,780.

Above left. Without the basement but with a second floor fitted in under a slightly higher roof, a story-and-a-half house would cost $23,500. Square footage on the second floor, made pleasant by a shed dormer over the bedroom area, is 819.

Above center. Raising the basement halfway out of the ground and incorporating the garage in it results in a split-entry, two-story house also costing $23,500. The lower level has 1373 square feet.

Above right. A split-level house, well suited to sloping ground, would be the least expensive, at $22,700, with 1373 square feet on the lower level.

Among the many factors that account for the variations in cost are the section of the country and the type, quality, and size of the house. The kind and amount of mechanical equipment affect cost, as does the inclusion or exclusion of such items as garages and basements, steel kitchen cabinets and tiled bathrooms, paved terraces and landscaping. In general, the cost per square foot decreases a little as house size increases, and "builders' houses" constructed in large numbers at one time are less costly than custom-designed, individually built homes. To the latter must be added the architect's fee, usually between 10 and 15 percent of the building cost, although some architects work for a flat fee. The services of a sympathetic and sensitive architect are well worth the cost in terms of total satisfaction.

Land costs vary quite as much as do those for buildings. There is a great difference between the value of unimproved farmland and well-situated lots with paved streets and sidewalks, water, electricity, and gas. Lot value is directly proportional to the desirability of the location and the size of the parcel. Because desirable land is getting scarcer, the cost of a lot in many regions now ranges around 18 percent of the total cost of a home, whereas a few years ago it was about 10 percent.

It is encouraging, though, to note that an occasional custom house, skillfully designed, is built for about $13 per square foot (Color Fig. 21), and that typical houses of today tend to compensate for their higher cost with better planning, better materials, and better equipment. Despite costs, houses are being built at about the rate of one million per year.

LANDSCAPING

The cost range of landscape development is even greater than that of house and land. With good soil, a lawn costs only the few dollars spent for seed and fertilizer. Small trees and divisions of shrubs given by friends complete the project. Expenditure of money, but not of time, is negligible. Thus, landscaping costs for small homes often are not even considered in the budget.

If, however, the owner wishes to develop a livable yard with paved terraces and suitable furniture, enclosing fences and overhead protection, and appropriate planting, costs can mount rapidly. Here are a few figures. (In the following sections, and throughout this chapter, costs will be given as a range between probable low and high figures. The middle price between these two figures will usually indicate good quality at moderate cost.)

With a design by landscape architect Lawrence Halprin, the owners did all the labor and spent only $250 for materials. (*Photograph by Ernest Braun*)

467

Ground surfacings. *Costs given are per square foot* and depend chiefly on the amount of work done by the owner.

Lawn	$ .02 to $ .25 (depending also on soil and whether a sprinkler system
Asphalt paving	.25 to .30 is installed)
Concrete paving	.50 to 1.00 (much higher if pebble concrete or if divided by header strips)
Brick on concrete base	1.00 to 2.75 (about the cost of a rug)

Enclosures. Upkeep costs will vary greatly, from almost none for a stone wall to recurrent trimming of hedges. *Costs given are per running foot, 6 feet high,* uninstalled to installed.

Fence (wire)	$2.50 to $10.00
Fence (wood)	3.00 to 10.00
Hedge	.75 to 3.00
Wall (masonry)	8.00 to 20.00

Shrubs and trees. *Costs given are per plant,* depending on size and variety. The costs will be raised considerably if the plants are put in place by professional gardeners.

Shrubs	$ .75 to $ 15.00
Trees	1.50 to 250.00

Outdoor furniture. Ultimate cost will depend greatly on durability.

Redwood table and benches for six	$18.00 to $60.00
Metal or wood chairs	5.00 to 40.00
Suntan cots or chaises with mattresses	12.00 to 60.00

A good landscape architect may save the homeowner money and headaches by eliminating costly mistakes and ensuring a garden as well planned as the house. His fee is typically 15 percent of the cost of landscaping, although he may charge a flat fee or be available for consultation at an hourly or daily fee. His charge may also vary according to whether he oversees the entire project or whether he only draws the plan that the owner then implements when and as funds permit.

FURNISHINGS

As with landscaping, the range of furnishing costs is more impressive and realistic than an average figure. In many instances top prices could be multiplied several times over for the very high in quality or for individualized pieces, and a good sale may put costs below the lower figure.

Price tags on home furnishings are determined by many factors—materials and construction, excellence and individuality of design, supply and demand, and durability. Here are some examples: Silk is usually more expensive than cotton, silver than stainless steel. Handmade objects and those with superior work-manship are usually high in price. Good design quality need not necessarily increase costs, but it frequently does. Unusual or individualized objects are likely to be more expensive than those turned out by the thousands. Durable items are often more costly than those with a shorter life, but price alone is not a certain guide to longevity. For instance, wool upholstery usually wears better than cotton, but an expensive silk damask would probably not withstand as much hard usage as would firm, heavy cotton. When shopping, give thought to what percentage of money is being spent for each of the several factors that affect cost.

Floor coverings (hard). Installation costs more for tiles than for sheet flooring, but there is usually greater waste of sheet material. Installing tile can be a do-it-yourself project. *Costs given are per square yard, uninstalled.*

A 12-by-15-foot floor area can be covered with vinyl-asbestos tile (*below*) for less than $40 if the family does the work (*Azrock Floor Products*). For the same area, pure vinyl sheet flooring (*bottom*) costs between $200 and $300 installed. (*Goodyear Tire and Rubber Company*)

Tiles (9″ x 9″)

Asphalt	$1.00 to $ 2.00
Cork	4.50 to 7.00
Rubber	2.50 to 6.00
Vinyl	2.25 to 10.00
Vinyl asbestos	1.50 to 2.50

Sheet Flooring

Linoleum	$3.00 to $ 4.00
Vinyl	2.50 to 10.00
Vinyl surface	.65 to 4.00

Floor coverings (soft). Wall-to-wall carpeting, because of installation and cleaning costs, is more expensive than an almost wall-to-wall rug. Durability is very important in estimating cost: a cotton carpet costing $10 a yard would last about half as long as a nylon carpet costing $15 a yard.

Flat Surface	Cost per Square Yard	Cost of 9′ x 12′ Rug
Kraft fiber	$2.20 to $ 5.00	$20 to $100
Matting (rush, sisal)	2.50 to 10.00	30 to 150
Braided (wool, nylon, or vinyl)		30 to 200
Polypropylene	4.50 to 8.00	54 to 100
Pile Surface		
Acrilan	7.00 to 15.00	80 to 180
Cotton	3.75 to 10.00	18 to 150
Nylon	4.75 to 30.00	38 to 360
Rayon	3.50 to 15.00	30 to 180
Wool	4.75 to 30.00	55 to 360
Rug Cushions or Pads		
Hair and jute	.95 to 2.00	12 to 20
Sponge rubber	1.50 to 4.00	17 to 50

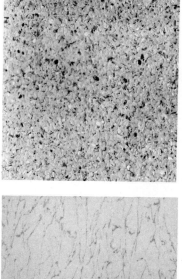
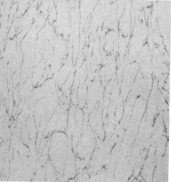

A

B

Wall surfacings. Installation costs vary greatly according to the material and whether it is applied professionally or by the owner. *Costs given are per square yard and are for materials only.*

Grass cloth	$3.50 to $5.00
Paint	.04 to .20
Plastic wall coverings	.75 to 5.00
Wallpaper	.04 to 2.00

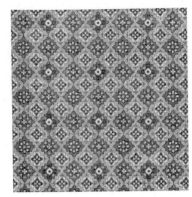

The price per single roll of these wallpapers would be approximately $1 for the embossed pattern (*left*), $10 for "Tulips" (*center*), a gay handprinted paper, and $18 for "Deauville" (*right*), richly flocked in a formal design. (*Montgomery Ward; James Seeman Studios, Inc.*)

Window treatments. The price range of many ready-made or custom-tailored curtains and draperies greatly exceeds the figures given below, depending on the fiber and weave, distinctiveness of design, lining (if any), and quality of tailoring. Cost of material alone ranges from 30 cents per yard for good quality unbleached muslin to $20—or much more—for luxury fabrics. Considerable savings can be effected, however, by making draperies at home. *Costs given are for ready-made window treatments for a window 48 inches wide and 54 inches high.*

Venetian Blinds	$6.00 to $30.00
Roller Window Shades	1.50 to 15.00
Glass Curtains	
Dacron marquisette	2.50 to 7.00
Fiberglas marquisette	3.00 to 8.00
Nylon marquisette	1.50 to 4.00
Draw Curtains and Draperies	
Cotton	3.50 to 20.00
Fiberglas	4.00 to 25.00
Plastic	.90 to 2.00
Rayon and acetate	4.00 to 15.00
Woven bamboo, reed, or wood	1.60 to 20.00

Furniture. In the prices given below, the lowest are for minimum, often unfinished, pieces that may or may not be durable; the highest prices quoted are what one might expect to pay for excellent quality—but not custom-made, handcrafted, or particularly distinctive—furniture. *Costs are per piece.*

Sofas	
Studio couches	$ 40.00 to $200.00
Sofas (6')	100.00 to 400.00
Chairs	
Upholstered, with springs or foam rubber or both	30.00 to 300.00
Split cane or reed	5.00 to 125.00
Webbed	7.50 to 50.00
Padded	13.00 to 100.00
Utility—dining, games, work	6.00 to 75.00

A

B

C

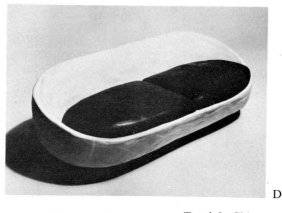

D

Tables	
Dining	$40.00 to $300.00
Coffee and end	8.00 to 150.00
Storage	
Bookcases (small units)	10.00 to 100.00
Chests of drawers	40.00 to 300.00
Cabinets (for dishes, records, general storage)	30.00 to 300.00
Beds	
Foam-rubber mattress and box springs	44.00 to 350.00
Innerspring mattress and box springs	45.00 to 350.00
Six wooden legs	3.50 to 10.00
Metal frame on casters	7.00 to 20.00
Headboard and footboard	9.00 to 200.00
Desks	20.00 to 200.00

Top left. Chinese cane chairs are comfortable, easy to move, and cost about $7 (*Calif-Asia*)

Top right. The superb Barcelona chair, meticulously crafted of chromium-plated steel with leather cushions, is almost a collector's item at over $600. Mies van der Rohe, designer. (*Knoll Associates Inc.*)

Above left. A walnut table, hand-crafted by designer Lawrence Hunter, would be expensive but unique. (*Photograph by Richard Gross. California Design/9, Pasadena Art Museum*)

Above right. A sofa design for the future by Vladimir Kagan. Air-filled, it could just be deflated when moving time arrived, thereby saving on transfer costs. (*Chemstrand Company*)

Upholstery fabrics. Prices go much higher than those given, but the fabrics may or may not be more durable. *Costs are per yard,* usually 36 inches wide for slipcover material, 54 inches wide for upholstery, although these widths may vary.

Slipcover materials (usually cotton and equally suitable for draperies)	$ .75 to $ 4.00
Upholstery materials (heavier rayon-cotton blends, wool, nylon, and so on)	2.00 to 15.00
Plastic upholstery	1.20 to 15.00

Lamps. Custom-made or unusual pieces may be much more expensive, but often double as enrichment as well as fulfilling utilitarian functions. *Costs are per fixture.*

Floor lamps	$10.00 to $150.00
Table lamps	6.00 to 100.00
Pinup wall lamps	6.00 to 100.00

A table lamp designed by Damon Giffard of gilt bronze is expensive, at around $240, but beautifully crafted and distinctive. (*Hansen Lamps*)

A versatile and efficient metal study lamp, costing about $30, has a lean, sculptural quality that is a direct result of its functional design. (*Frederik Lunning*)

A   B

Tableware. In the upper range of prices and beyond, costs are often due to ornateness of pattern, sometimes to whether pieces are handcrafted or whether gold and silver are part of the ornament. *Costs given are for five-piece place settings* for dinnerware and silverware, *per piece for glassware.*

Dinnerware

Bone china	$ 5.00 to $60.00
Earthenware	1.50 to 15.00
Plastic	1.50 to 10.00
Porcelain	13.00 to 75.00
Stoneware	2.00 to 10.00

Glassware

Tumblers, goblets, and so on	.10 to 10.00

23

Architect Philip Johnson's own house in New Canaan, Connecticut, epitomizes the modern trend toward unifying house and landscape. The house has two sets of walls: continuous, transparent glass walls on four sides temper the weather, and a distant, informal hedge of trees and shrubs gives privacy. The extreme simplicity of the architecture is matched by the clean lines of the few pieces of widely spaced furniture and by the quiet expanse of lawn that extends beyond the polished brick floor. The landscaping centers around preserving the pastoral beauty of the site while providing a setting for this house, for a round swimming pool, and for two other architectural units on the property—an almost windowless, brick guest house and an underground art gallery placed beneath a gentle swell of lawn. The glass house, built in 1949, and the furniture, modern classics dating from about 1930, look as startlingly new and refreshing as they did when originally conceived. (*Photograph © Maris, Ezra Stoller Associates*)

24

In landscaping Warren Tremaine's house in Santa Barbara, California, landscape architect Ralph Stevens evolved a succulent garden for a sunny slope that extends between
a paved terrace and a large, sweeping lawn. Although the plants with a few exceptions
came from many other parts of the world, they form a congenial ensemble appropriate
to the dry climate of this area. Smaller plants are grouped in masses of one kind that
blend or contrast with their neighbors, while the larger, more emphatic species are
allowed to stand out as individual accents. Without imitating native landscapes the
effect achieved is of natural informality. (*Photograph by Julius Shulman*)

Silverware

Silver plate (although 24-piece sets may be bought for as little as $5)	$ 3.00 to $20.00
Stainless steel	1.00 to 25.00
Sterling silver	22.50 to 75.00

Table coverings. Specially designed, handmade, or elaborately embroidered cloths may cost far more than the prices given below. *Costs are per mat or for cloths approximately 72 by 90 inches,* large enough for tables seating eight people.

Place mats

Bamboo, grass, rush, and so on	$ .15 to $ 2.00
Cotton	.50 to 2.00
Linen	1.00 to 4.00
Plastic	.25 to 3.00

Tablecloths

Cotton or rayon	4.00 to 15.00
Linen	7.00 to 25.00
Plastic	2.00 to 10.00
Lace	8.00 to 50.00
Linen damask	10.00 to 100.00
Rayon damask	5.00 to 50.00

Enrichment. Although many of the above items can enhance the home in ways beyond their purely functional value, additional enrichment is necessary truly to personalize a home. The fine arts and the accessories that we choose are among the most powerful sources of spiritual and aesthetic satisfaction, and expenditures in these fields can be evaluated only in terms of the individuals concerned.

Paintings

Originals	$25 and up
Reproductions	1 to $15

Graphic prints (originals) — 10 and up

Sculpture

Originals	25 and up
Reproductions	5 to 75

Accessories

Handsome rocks and driftwood cost nothing if you seek them out. Beyond these, the tremendous diversity of kinds of accessories, to say nothing of the range within each type, makes it impossible to state any prices other than that they can be purchased for as little as 10 cents and for as much as hundreds of dollars.

Although many people wish to plan the furnishing of their homes themselves, the services of an interior decorator can be of great value because of his broad knowledge of what is available, where it may be purchased, and how things will look when assembled. The decorating department in a store usually charges no fee if the major purchases are made through that store. Independent decorators may charge in several ways: buying at wholesale or decorator's prices

The Laocoön group (Agesander, Athenodorus, and Polydorus of Rhodes, c. 40 B.C.), long a symbol of the tragedy of those who are trapped in the coils of relentless fate, could also symbolize how some of us feel when struggling with a budget. (*The Vatican Museum, Rome*)

and selling to the client at retail prices, with the difference as profit; or buying and selling at wholesale or decorator's prices, with either a percentage of the total cost as fee or for a fixed fee. Additional charges may be made in each case for expenses, such as preliminary consultations, travel, supervision, and so on. As with landscape design, a decorating plan does not have to be completed all at one time but may be a guide for future planned expenditures.

This survey gives some of the raw data with which to begin the task of planning expenditures in a considered manner. If it has done no more than arouse an awareness of price differences, it will have served a purpose. We hope, though, that it has helped to make clear the *cost relationship* of one item to another. Now we turn to budgets.

BUDGETS

Budgeting is the art and science of planning expenditures so that both ends meet, with some money left for savings. It is probably more a matter of emotions than of intellect, for it is remarkably easy to lay out a budget with a cool head but remarkably difficult to adhere to it when the heart warms toward an extravagance. Our concern is with wise planning for the expenses entailed by shelter and furnishings.

More than in any other part of this book there is need for caution in applying the material in this section. These are the cautions:

- No ready-made budget will fit all families.
- No suggested proportional expenditures can be applied to all situations.
- Each family has to decide, after thorough consideration of all factors, what percentage of its income will be used for the many items in a family budget.

Take them, then, for what they are—generalizations that work in typical cases. Do not assume that everyone should try to follow them if special circumstances indicate other ways of managing money.

Budgeting for Shelter

How much of the monthly or annual income should be spent for renting or buying a home? What are the advantages of renting and of buying?

Proportions of income. The answer to the first question depends on the amount, regularity, and dependability of the income, and on the size, ages, interests, and ideas of the family. If the income is large, regular, and dependable, and there is ample provision for emergencies, more of it *could* be used for shelter than would be advisable on a small, irregular income. Similarly, shelter costs can be increased if the family is small, the children have become financially independent, or the family prefers spending money on its home to other ways of enjoying its income. Typical families, though, spend from 20 to 30 percent of their income on housing.

On purchases, a long-held rule of thumb is that the total cost of the house should not exceed from $1\frac{1}{2}$ to $2\frac{1}{2}$ times the annual income. In general, this is a good rule, but it is safer to limit the cost to not more than twice the income. In addition to all of the factors mentioned above, two others are important. First is the amount of savings the family has accumulated for a down payment, because the larger the down payment, the less the interest on the mortgage, the smaller the monthly payments, the shorter the term the mortgage runs, and the higher the equity in the house. The second factor is the resources that can be called on in case of an emergency, chief of which are insurance and savings not invested in the house.

Another way of determining how much money can be spent on shelter takes into account the individual family's own way of life. It entails totaling:

- The financial obligations to which a family is already committed, such as taxes and life insurance payments, installments on a car or furniture, and other debts
- An estimate of probable costs for food, clothing, medical bills, schooling, entertainment, and anything else that seems vital to the particular family
- An estimate of the probable shelter costs for either owning or renting a home, including not only mortgage or rental payments, but real estate taxes, house insurance, and maintenance, repair, heating, utility, and landscape costs where applicable

When these estimates are compared with a family's assured income, it soon becomes clear how much they can afford to pay for housing. One other factor is somewhat nebulous but very influential. The type and location of the home affect living costs in many ways: in transportation costs and the kind and price of appropriate furnishings, perhaps by increasing clothing or recreation expenditures, or by creating or eliminating the need for a gardener or household help. Although most of us want the best home possible for our families, caution should be exerted to avoid becoming "house poor," no matter whether the poverty comes from payments on a purchase or payments of rent.

Owning versus renting. Both owning a house and renting one have their special advantages, and although today there is a strong national urge toward owning one's own home, it may not be the most advisable plan for everyone.

The financial advantages of owning are:

- Savings of several thousand dollars on a $15,000 house may accrue over a 25-year period.
- Interest paid on the mortgage and taxes paid on the house are deductible from taxable income.
- Owning a home is a reasonably safe investment.
- Monthly payments remain stable with no fluctuation such as may occur with rents. (This is advantageous during times of prosperity, but may well be disadvantageous in depressions.)
- There is great incentive to save for a home.
- Savings can be made by doing some or much of the maintenance, whereas in renting, the landlord is paid (through rent) for doing it. Maintenance costs on new houses usually run about $1\frac{1}{2}$ percent of the cost, 2 percent on old houses, per year.

The monetary advantages of renting are:

- It costs up to $2000 more the first year to buy a low-cost house than it does to rent one, because of down payment, fees for title search and for lawyers, and so on.
- There are no long-term commitments to hinder a move that would otherwise be an advantageous one.

- Renting gives an opportunity to check the desirability of a community.
- There are no unpredictable repair or replacement expenses.
- Real estate taxes, insurance, repairs and general maintenance, and often utility costs are all included in the rent.

Digressing from money matters for a moment, home ownership has such compelling advantages as the satisfaction that comes from a permanent home with its uninterrupted social life for the whole family and schooling for children. It makes a family feel as though it belonged to the community rather than as though it were temporarily roosting there.

Budgeting for Landscape Development

Some part of the total cost of a house ought to be reserved for the development of the yard, but (as explained in the section on landscaping) this is an extremely variable figure. A landscape developed as completely as the typical house would easily come to a total of 10 to 20 percent of the cost of the house, but most families spend only a fraction of this. To cite an example—for a 1200-square-foot house on a 60-by-100-foot lot costing $15,000, an average figure for the thorough development of the 4800 square feet not covered by the house would be around $2250 (15 percent of $15,000). Here, again, it is up to each family to decide for what necessities and pleasures they wish to spend their money. The cost of the landscaping should not be forgotten—but many may, wisely or otherwise, decide to reserve a very small amount for it.

Budgeting for Furnishings

These budget figures are based on the costs of furnishing a home completely with new furniture, but this usually is achieved only after some years. More often than not in the beginning, spending will be concentrated on a few good pieces of furniture for the living room and master bedroom, with the other rooms and the planned-for rugs and draperies coming later. The rest of the necessary furnishings are often a mixture of gifts, hand-me-downs, borrowings, secondhand finds, and our own creations, costing little and being largely expendable. In normal situations, these are general guides:

Furnishing costs usually total about one-half of one year's income or one-fourth of the value of the house. It is desirable to have one-fourth of the total furnishings budget in cash to furnish the first apartment. This both allows buying those few good pieces already mentioned and cuts down on credit costs.

Furniture budgets tend to be divided as follows:

Living room	30 to 40 percent
Dining space	15 to 20 percent
Master bedroom	15 to 20 percent
Child's bedroom	10 to 15 percent
Child's bedroom or guestroom	10 to 15 percent

The amount available for each room is likely to be apportioned as follows:

Furniture	60 to 70 percent
Floor covering	10 to 20 percent
Window treatment	5 to 10 percent
Accessories (including lamps)	2 to 7 percent

Countless factors can alter these proportions:

- The money available for each room is in part determined by the number of rooms to be furnished.
- Good hard-surfaced flooring (asphalt, cork, or vinyl tile) minimizes the need for rugs.
- A separate dining room usually costs more to furnish than does dining space in the living room.
- One or two rooms unusually large or small in relation to the others make a difference.
- Even a few pieces of inherited, cast-off, or bargain furniture affect the expenditures for the rooms in which they are used.

Replacements for furnishings per year average around 3 to 4 percent of the annual income over a period of time but usually show conspicuous fluctuation from year to year. As income increases, this percentage often increases. There is some advantage in concentrating replacement expenditures in certain years, so that a sizable project is carried out at one time with a resulting unity; for example, waiting until it is possible to do a thorough job on the living room or getting rugs for most or all the house.

Many factors determine the percentage of income available or needed for replacing furnishings:

- Family size
- Stage of family cycle—usually there is less money available for this purpose from the time children arrive until they become independent than there is before or after
- Amount and kind of entertaining
- Durability of original furnishings
- The kind of use and care given the furnishings
- Amount of labor undertaken by family—repairing, refinishing, and remodeling furniture; making draperies or slipcovers; and so on

Costs and budgets are of the utmost importance in home planning and furnishing because the way in which a family handles its money is one of the primary sources of security or of frustration and worry. It is inadvisable to give specific advice to others, but we can urge that expenditures be planned at least as wisely as color schemes or furniture arrangements.

Costs and budgets are neither the beginning nor the end of home planning and furnishing, but constant factors in the process. They are seldom exhilarating, but they should not be depressing: they are simply ever-present problems that must be faced and solved. Remember, too, that money is only one factor in the economy of the home, and that economy takes its place along with use, beauty, and individuality as one of the goals of getting and keeping a good home.

Planning your home is an important challenge, because its shell, furnishings, surroundings, and costs shape your living.

(*Drawing by French; Copyright © 1946 The New Yorker Magazine, Inc.*)

Opposite. A room from the Ducal Palace at Gubbio, Italy (c. 1479–1482), is a fascinating tour de force illustrating Italian interiors and furnishings toward the end of the Early Renaissance. The furniture, the cupboards with their contents, the small organ, and the architectural features of the wall were created of wood inlay on completely flat wall surfaces, exploiting outstanding skill in craftsmanship and the exciting new discovery of linear perspective. However, it is also composed in accordance with the reborn classic ideals of clarity and coherence. (*The Metropolitan Museum of Art, New York, Rogers Fund, 1939*)

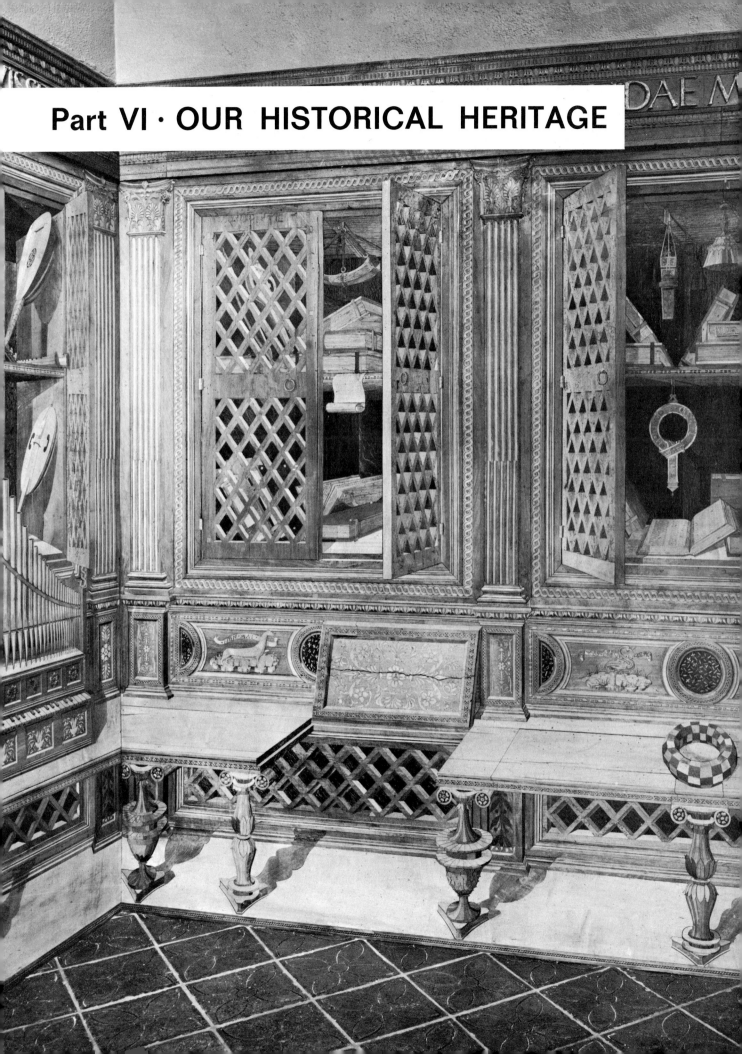

A detail from a commode of lacquered wood, ormolu, and marble shows the fanciful, sinuous, intertwining curves of the mid-eighteenth-century French Rococo style. (*M. H. de Young Memorial Museum, San Francisco, Gift of Roscoe and Margaret Oakes*)

21 · From the Renaissance to the Victorian Period

The very long and extensive history of the home began a million or so years ago when prehistoric man first selected the kind of natural shelter that best met his needs. A giant stride was taken when he began building his own dwelling. We, however, shall limit our discussion to that comparatively short, but important, segment that began in Europe in the fifteenth century A.D. and continued to the beginning of the twentieth century, from which our chief heritage has come.

There are valid reasons for knowing something of what man has done before our times. In the variety that history affords us we can deepen and expand our concepts of design, of form, space, and color, and of the ways in which materials can be used. This feeds our creative and critical energies, for creativity seldom springs from a vacuum, and discerning judgments do not grow from ignorance. Study of history can free our imaginations from the shackles of the too-pressing immediacy of our own problems. Finally, we can derive aesthetic pleasure from historic homes, furniture, and landscapes, much as we do from paintings or music.

Even a brief survey of history will lead us to discover that:

- Homes and furnishings were always changing, sometimes slowly and at other times quite rapidly.
- There was always a "modern" movement that was favored by some and resisted by others.
- Styles are distinguished from one another by varying degrees of emphasis on certain objectives and practices rather than by complete differences.
- Almost every characteristic of contemporary work can be found in historic examples.

There are, however, pitfalls to trap the unwary in studying any phase of art history. It is all too easy to make unwarranted, sweeping generalizations about styles and periods, to mistake ornament for the spirit, to regard a style as a manner of decoration and ignore the concepts and conditions from which it grew. There is also a tendency to assume that styles are born and die suddenly; that their dates coincide exactly with other events, chiefly the reigns of kings or the beginnings and ends of centuries; and that all examples can be put into convenient, named categories. With rare exceptions, styles developed so gradually that many persons living at that time were scarcely aware of a change. Although styles often reached their zenith during the reign of a king, as did French Baroque under Louis XIV, or were a dominant trend during an age, as was the Rococo in the eighteenth century, in almost no instance is the coincidence exact.

As we look back, however, we do find discernible patterns in the history of the house and its furnishings, and we can recognize some clear, strong, influential movements (p. 483). Our study of historic homes begins with the Renaissance, that age when the individuality of man was reaffirmed and when, in consequence, a man's home assumed new importance.

THE RENAISSANCE: THE FIFTEENTH AND SIXTEENTH CENTURIES

The fifteenth and sixteenth centuries were a great age of discovery. Sea routes to new continents were found; the classic heritage of literature, philosophy, and art was rediscovered, and kindled a new and widespread inspiration; the scientific attitude of direct investigation, rather than obedient acceptance of authority, led to new understanding of man and his world; and the dignity of man as an individual was fully appreciated. It was as though man was suddenly freed from restraints that for a millennium had dissuaded him from free inquiry about his own nature and potentialities and from looking squarely at himself in his world. Inevitably, new ways of building, painting, and sculpturing arose because the Renaissance was truly a *rebirth,* not a revival.

A sixteenth-century Italian High Renaissance armchair exemplifies the clear-cut, articulated concept of design that was basic in this period. The pattern on the tooled leather back is held within the rectangular framework of decorative nailheads and fringe and is a varied, much more intricate repetition at small scale of the bowknot and volute forms of the pierced and carved front stretcher. The back supports end in acanthus leaves; the arms roll over into simple scrolls. The total design shows a forthright relation of form to purpose. (*French & Company, Inc.*)

HISTORICAL PERIODS

(Dates are broadly inclusive)

	ITALY	SPAIN	FRANCE	ENGLAND	UNITED STATES
1400	EARLY RENAISSANCE 1420–1500				
	HIGH RENAISSANCE 1490–1580	EARLY RENAISSANCE, OR **Plateresque** 1480–1556			
1500	MANNERISM, OR **Late Renaissance,** or **Early Baroque** 1515–1600		RENAISSANCE **Louis XII** 1498–1515	RENAISSANCE **Tudor-Elizabethan** 1509–1603	
			Francis I 1515–1547		
	BAROQUE 1550–1730	HIGH RENAISSANCE, OR **Desornamentado** 1556–1600	**Henry II, III, IV** 1547–1610		
1600		BAROQUE, OR **Churrigueresque** 1600–1700	**Louis XIII** 1610–1643	**Early Jacobean** 1603–1649	EARLY COLONIAL 1630–1730
		FOREIGN INFLUENCES	BAROQUE **Louis XIV** 1643–1715	BAROQUE **Late Jacobean, Late Stuart,** or **Restoration** 1660–1702	
				William and Mary 1688–1702	
1700	ROCOCO			**Queen Anne** 1702–1714	COLONIAL GEORGIAN 1700–1790
			ROCOCO **Louis XV*** 1715–1774	EARLY GEORGIAN AND ROCOCO 1718–1779	
			NEOCLASSICISM **Early Neoclassicism,** or **Louis XVI*** 1750–1793	NEOCLASSICISM **Early Neoclassicism,** or **Late Georgian** 1760–1800	NEOCLASSICISM **Roman Revival, Federal,** or **Post-Colonial** 1770–1820
	NEOCLASSICISM			**Late Neoclassicism,** or **Regency** 1790–1837	**Greek Revival** 1825–1850
1800			**Directoire** 1793–1804		
			Late Neoclassicism, or **Empire** 1804–1815	MEDIEVAL REVIVALS **Gothic** 1750–1880	MEDIEVAL REVIVALS **Gothic** 1840–1880
			ECLECTICISM 1850——	VICTORIANISM 1837–1901	**Romanesque** 1870–1893
1900			ART NOUVEAU 1896–1910	ECLECTICISM 1850——	VICTORIANISM 1840–1900
				ARTS AND CRAFTS 1861–1910	ECLECTICISM 1880——

*The dates of these periods do not exactly coincide with the reigns of the kings whose names are associated with them.

Renaissance homes, furnishings, and gardens at their best returned to such classic ideals as order, clarity, and moderation; but these were interpreted in individualized ways. All relationships were carefully studied and planned on a coherent, systematic basis, geometrical yet humanized (Figs. 479 and 482). In keeping with classic ideals of clarity, each unit of the composition tended to retain its own identity while at the same time contributing to the whole. The predominant horizontality in architecture, together with the strong, secure equilibrium in which all parts were held, gave Renaissance dwellings a satisfying composure. The major forms were rectangular, with controlled curves employed where needed for variety and grace. The architectural vocabulary of the Romans —columns, cornices, round arches, and barrel vaults—was inventively used and creatively enriched with such classic ornament as acanthus leaves, egg-and-dart moldings, and volutes.

A brief summary can only hint at the character and wealth of contributions made to homes during the Renaissance, but in general they had these characteristics:

- *Aims*—clarity, order, and moderation
- *Character*—formal, full-bodied, reposed; strong design framework with rich embellishment
- *Design*—great variety in compelling unity; symmetrical balance; rhythms strongly architectural, combining strength and grace; each part treated as a unit, emphasized in proportion to its importance in the whole composition
- *Scale*—moderate
- *Shapes*—inspired by the classic search for order, with basic use of rectangles and arcs; predominantly horizontal
- *Ornament*—classical columns, arches, moldings, together with decorative ornament based on that used by the Romans; sensitively related to underlying form
- *Colors*—strong, rich hues; marked contrasts of light and dark

Renaissance homes show a great, conscious coherence of plans, exteriors, interiors, and furnishings; and they demonstrate that forms and ideas from the past can serve as inspiration for creative, original production. The spread of the Renaissance through Europe provides an example of a vital, general concept adapted by different peoples to their own needs and environments.

In the following chapters we will look at the development of Renaissance houses, furnishings, and gardens in Italy, Spain, France, and England. In each country the Renaissance lasted for about 150 years; but it began in Italy almost a century before it reached Spain, France, and England. Although Renaissance ideas reached the New World in the latter part of the seventeenth century, the movement in Europe had lost its force by that time. As the chart on page 483 shows, it overflowed and overlapped in time and space, but for purposes of simplicity the fifteenth and sixteenth centuries are generally called **the Renaissance.**

THE BAROQUE SPIRIT: THE SEVENTEENTH CENTURY

Incongruities of wealth and poverty, national order and international chaos, and increased knowledge and decreased understanding developed in the seventeenth century as an aftermath of the great changes that had taken place in Europe during the fifteenth and sixteenth centuries.

New lands and trade routes were bringing undreamed-of wealth to a few nobles and merchants, while the economic stresses and strains, national rivalries and wars brought poverty and oppression to the many. Rigidly ordered military empires like that of Louis XIV, impossible a century before, were the model. The Renaissance spirit of free inquiry had led to the abandonment of many old standards and to irreconcilable differences of philosophy. Man's physical horizon had been vastly broadened: not only had unknown reaches of the terrestrial world been discovered, but the invention of the telescope opened vast expanses of the universe for study. Man's spiritual horizons had not been able to keep pace, and a great feeling of personal instability and need for personal salvation resulted.

Vivid excitement, dynamic living, horizons so extended that they could not be grasped; abandonment of long-held standards; paradoxes and violent contrasts—these led to a compulsive, searching quality in design that came to be called **Baroque.** The word is probably derived from a Portuguese word, *barroco,* meaning "imperfect pearl," and emphasizes the difference between this style and the regularity of the preceding one. The ordered calm of Renaissance architecture, furniture, gardens, painting, and sculpture was replaced by dynamic movement, space that was both expanding and enveloping, heavily modeled forms, and light and shadows that emphasized change. There was tremendous interest in sensational, sequential effects calculated to awe the spectator. Movement—and time —took hold of the artists' imaginations and found intense expression in expanding S-curves, oblique lines, and radiating vistas. Pediments were broken and columns were twisted. The classical distinction between basic form and ornamentation was obliterated, and in many instances ornament engulfed mass and structure —that is, ornament and form became almost one and the same thing (Fig. 485).

Such concepts are more suited to public and religious buildings than to homes, so that the great palaces were the only dwellings to show the full impact of the movement. In more modest homes the Baroque spirit usually expressed itself only in vigorous ornament around the doorways and fireplaces and rich curves in the furniture.

The Baroque love of ornateness, compulsively contorted curves, and irrepressible energy manifests itself in an English walnut chair with caned seat and back from the period of Charles II (1660–1685). A comparison with Figures 482 and 487 will show how the Renaissance, Baroque, and Rococo styles differ from one another. (*The Metropolitan Museum of Art, New York, Kennedy Fund, 1918*)

In summary, the effects of the Baroque spirit on the arts of the home were in these directions:
- *Aims*—impressive, sensational grandeur
- *Character*—vigorous, aggressive, monumental, ostentatious, extravagant, unloosened
- *Design*—forms dictated by the desire to astonish the beholder rather than by utilitarian function; powerful unity from big, compelling central ideas

and strong geometric order holding together a fantastic degree of variety; symmetrical balance; rhythms of compulsive, sweeping, engulfing strength; emphatic dominance

- *Scale*—large
- *Shapes*—expanding, nongeometric curves—typically S-scrolls—the most distinctive shapes; but all classical forms used in an agitated, exaggerated manner
- *Ornament*—big, bold, and inventive elaboration of almost every interior form and surface; muscular heroes and heroines in strident or contorted poses; bold human and animal masks; semirealistic animals' legs; out-curving scrolls and foliage; Louis XIV's emblem of the sun with radiating rays, and others
- *Colors*—bold, strong colors in vigorous contrast with much gilt

The Baroque movement developed out of, and overlapped, the Renaissance in Italy and France; it attained its height in the seventeenth century, but it began earlier and lost its force later than that hundred-year span.

REASON, THE ROCOCO, AND NEOCLASSICISM: THE EIGHTEENTH CENTURY

The eighteenth century is often called the Age of Reason. It was a period in which the discoveries and explorations of the preceding periods were rationally considered and assimilated. In architecture, the eighteenth century gave birth to two externally different styles: the playful **Rococo** and the sober **Neoclassic** movements.

In this intellectual climate people looked at their homes, and what they saw did not satisfy them. Now men, and more especially women, wanted conveniently planned houses and furnishings that were comfortable as well as beautiful. Weary of ostentatious ritual in palaces that were about as homelike as opera houses or museums, they longed for privacy and personal living, for intimate conversations instead of rhetorical eloquence, for furniture that fitted them as well as the architectural setting. This brought a reaction against the Baroque dramatic monumentality of vast expanding spaces, impressive ornament, and uncomfortable furnishings. Attention was turned toward small objects, delicate relations, and refined discriminations.

Three factors strongly affected the forms in which these new urges were expressed:

- Men recognized natural beauty, as typified by the Englishman who "jumped over the wall and found that all nature was a garden." The most direct result was a new style of informal, naturalistic landscape design in which the pattern of nature rather than formal order was the guide. In the other arts this rediscovery opened men's eyes to a world full of inspiration for ornament.
- Increased trade with the Orient awakened designers to new roads to beauty. The arts of the Orient had been known for centuries but were regarded more or less as beautiful curiosities. Now Oriental ceramics, wallpapers, and furniture were seen as objects to use in homes, and the subtle informality of their designs was translated in many Rococo products that were made in the Western World.

■ Archaeology emerged as a systematic study, and the results were twofold. Most obvious and immediately applied was the discovery of the colorfully decorated, carefully planned, livable houses at Herculaneum and Pompeii, which brought to light an aspect of classical life quite different from the monumental Roman ruins known in the Renaissance. This provided Neo-classic designers with a new vocabulary, first of ornament and spirit, later of actual forms.

The Rococo

The term *Rococo* is generally thought to be derived from the French *rocaille* ("rock-work"), referring to the informal combination of rocks and shells in garden grottoes.

In some respects, Baroque and Rococo art have much in common: they are active rather than passive, have a profusion of ornamentation on a firmly organized framework of design, make conspicuous use of curvilinear forms, and employ many of the same decorative motifs. But one is bold, the other is delicate.

The characteristics of Rococo homes and furnishings are:

■ *Aims*—comfort, luxury, and beauty
■ *Character*—feminine; inviting and intimate; playful and lighthearted; free from restraint
■ *Design*—surpassing but contrived unity achieved by a predominance of curved forms that continue from one form into others; exciting variety in small differences and surprising combinations; fundamentally symmetrical balance, but increased use of asymmetrical parts and motifs, most noticeable in textiles; rhythms resembling rippling water, flickering flames, and vinelike plants; unemphatic dominance and subordination because decoration was spread rather than concentrated
■ *Scale*—small to minute
■ *Shapes*—free-flowing, delicate curves favored; straight lines minimized; angles and geometric curves avoided as much as possible; soft, graceful transitions from one shape to another; small, contracting, introverted C-scroll used as most distinctive shape
■ *Ornament*—all of the Baroque motifs plus many previously considered too small or trivial: cupids, satyrs, dragons, and birds; lace, ribbons, and wreaths; rocks, shells, leaves, flowers, fruits, and many others became more of a surface decoration than was the Baroque three-dimensional modeling
■ *Colors*—delicate and soft; tended to be high in value and low in intensity

But this is only part of the story, for the Rococo developed in the Age of Reason. The exuberance of Rococo ornament was firmly held together by a logical design framework (Fig. 487). Somewhat surprising in view of the lavish ornamentation, house exteriors were simple, plans were convenient, and gardens were often naturalistic.

Although the Italians created some spirited rooms, graceful furniture, gardens decorated with rocks and shells, and a few exteriors with Rococo ornamentation, leadership in interior and exterior design quickly passed to France. From France, the style was transmitted to England, where it had very little influence except in the design of furniture.

Although some Rococo furniture may seem a frenetic profusion of agitated shapes, other pieces, such as this Louis XV armchair, promise comparatively restful comfort. The gilt wood frame is almost exactly symmetrical, composed of gentle, continuing curves; the tapestry upholstery, however, is actively asymmetrical. [*Nelson Gallery—Atkins Museum (Nelson Fund) Kansas City, Missouri*]

A

Left. A predominance of slender vertical forms, basically rectangular contours, strict symmetry and ornament derived from ancient Roman sources are notable characteristics of Early Neoclassic furniture, and are exemplified in a Louis XVI gilded beech armchair upholstered in satin (c. 1780–1790). (*The Metropolitan Museum of Art, New York, Fletcher Fund, 1945*)

Right. A Late Neoclassic chair from the workshop of Duncan Phyfe in New York (c. 1810–1820) has simplified ornament and strong contours. One of the classical forms adapted by Phyfe is the Roman curule, or curved X-shaped base. The reeding on the seat rail and back, also characteristic of his work, is reminiscent of the closely spaced, half-round moldings that were an ancient decorative motif. (*Museum of the City of New York*)

B

Neoclassicism

It was inevitable that a style as sophisticated and highly decorated as the Rococo, closely geared to a decaying French aristocracy, could not survive the main currents of the latter half of the eighteenth century that led to the American Revolution and the French Revolution. The rational impulses of the time caused those with a philosophic turn of mind to reject the frivolity of the French Rococo and the somewhat uncertain unity of English Georgian homes. Once again men returned to the classic fountainhead. Whereas the Baroque and Rococo were clearly outgrowths of the preceding movement—the Renaissance—the **Neoclassic** was a reaction against the Rococo.

The Neoclassic as a whole is distinguished by its relative simplicity. It can be divided into two phases. The first, **Early Neoclassic,** inspired by the small-scale ornamentation of the newly rediscovered Pompeii and Herculaneum, had a refined, reserved delicacy, such as that shown in the **Louis XVI** style (Fig. 488A). The second phase, **Late Neoclassic,** was based on the large public buildings of Greece, Rome, and Egypt, and was marked by greater vigor and stronger convictions. Ordered sensitivity gave way to the imposing solidity of the **Empire** (Fig. 488B) and **Greek Revival** styles. In summary, the two phases are characterized and differentiated in the following manner:

	Early Neoclassic	*Late Neoclassic*
Aims	Refinement and comfort, functional planning.	Bold grandeur for impressiveness.
Character	Delicate elegance.	Commanding strength.
Design	Both phases emphasized continuous straight lines relieved by geometric curves, regulated rhythms, clear-cut centers of attention, and comparatively plain surfaces; but these qualities were differently expressed.	
Scale	Moderately small.	Massive and monumental.
Shapes	Precise, linear, geometric forms.	Architectonic emphasis on three-dimensionality.
Ornament	All of the ancient classical vocabulary was freely and sometimes awkwardly used by both phases.	
Colors	Gay pastels.	Dark, strong, resonant colors.

The Neoclassic styles emerged quite rapidly and decisively in the late eighteenth century in France and England, where they lasted between fifty and seventy-five years, and crossed the ocean to America before 1800.

MEDIEVAL REVIVALS, VICTORIANISM, AND THE INDUSTRIAL REVOLUTION: THE NINETEENTH CENTURY

In an age bent on digging into the past for inspiration, it was inevitable that the **Gothic** and **Romanesque** styles should be reexamined. These revivals broke the stranglehold of classic formulas and encouraged a new freedom of expression (Fig. 489). For many architects and designers, this liberation resulted merely in **eclecticism.** They delighted in borrowing architectural forms and details from a variety of sources, from earlier styles, and from many parts of the world, and attempted to reconcile and fuse them, often with little regard for authenticity. At the same time, the Industrial Revolution challenged other designers to produce original, experimental work using the new techniques that were evolving. In England and later in this country, the trend called **Victorian,** dated by Queen Victoria's reign from 1837 to 1901, was a curious admixture of materialism and romanticism that invented, borrowed, and combined so many styles that more precise classification is not feasible in a short survey.

In the following chapters we will discuss the historic movements as they affected homes in Italy and Spain, France, England, and ultimately the United States.

An armchair designed by John Belter of New York (c. 1840–1860) exhibits the delight in florid ornament that almost completely overwhelms the form in much Victorian furniture. Belter also patented and used laminated panels of from three to sixteen layers of wood that could be molded into curvaceous shapes, a process that had far-reaching implications. (*The Museum of the City of New York*)

Known in ancient Egypt and Rome, X-chairs again found favor in the Middle Ages and the Renaissance. This fifteenth-century Italian variation, often referred to as a "Savonarola" chair, has interlacing curved slats with simply carved back, arms, and base. It is made of beech and can be folded. (*M. H. de Young Memorial Museum, San Francisco*)

22 · Italy and Spain

Although there are significant differences between the homes of Italy and Spain, there are enough similarities to discuss them in one chapter. Both are essentially southern, Mediterranean countries with comparable languages and racial heritages. But the Italians enjoy opera, while the Spaniards passionately love bullfights, a difference in temperament that helps to explain some of the dissimilarities in spirit of Italian and Spanish design.

THE ITALIAN RENAISSANCE: THE FIFTEENTH AND SIXTEENTH CENTURIES

Italy was the home of the Renaissance. The classic spirit had its most persistent roots in that country, and the Italians, unlike the English, did not have to struggle to learn a new philosophy and a foreign vocabulary. The integration of control and freedom, discipline and exuberance, variety and unity came easily to artists who seemed to have a natural sensitivity to formal design (Fig. 479).

490

The Early Renaissance: c. 1420–1500

The Early Renaissance was youthful and exploratory, forthright, yet not naïve. Centering in Florence, the Early Renaissance brought to the homes of the wealthy a new interest in systematic, coherent, and usually symmetrical plans, exteriors, gardens, and interiors. The interiors were humanized in scale and embellished with luxuriant, imaginative, but delicate classical ornamentation that often was not completely integrated with the structure. City palaces, such as the Palazzo Gondi (Fig. 168) and the Palazzo Strozzi (Fig. 491A), were among the chief expressions of the Early Renaissance. (See also Color Fig. 25.)

Plans. The typical palace was organized around an open, central, rectangular court that gave light and air to the rooms and served as the chief way of getting from one room to another. Unlike the Roman atrium or Greek peristyle, the Renaissance court was not used much as a living area. It was entered through a simple vaulted vestibule with broad stairs at one end that led to the *piano nobile*, or main living quarters. Rooms were rectangular and varied in size in terms of their use, but they were not strongly differentiated one from another.

Exteriors and gardens. Simple, solid cubes, the exteriors were frequently divided into three horizontal bands marked by progressively smoother stonework and bands of classic moldings under the windows. Windows on the ground floor were small and heavily guarded; those above were larger and usually organized with an arched frame enclosing the tops of each pair. An impressive cornice, boldly projected around the roof line, brought the composition to a satisfying conclusion (Fig. 168). When space permitted, gardens were designed as extensions of the house, with regularly spaced trees, geometric flower beds, raised benches, fountains, and pools—all quite as orderly as the house to which they belonged.

Interiors and furnishings. Rooms were sparsely furnished, but the ceilings, floors, and walls were richly decorated (Fig. 491B). Early Renaissance furniture,

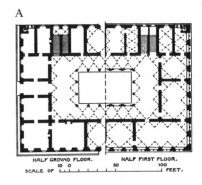

A

The plan of the Palazzo Strozzi (1489), designed by Benedetto da Majano and Il Cronaca, is typical of large Early Renaissance Florentine city dwellings. A series of rectangular rooms are regularly disposed around a central court with arcades, which served as hallways, on three stories. (*Reprinted from F. M. Simpson,* A History of Architectural Development, *Vol. 3. Copyright © 1956, Longmans, Green and Company, Ltd.*)

B

Frescoes, bold in color and intricate in design, visually warm and brighten the cold stone walls in the Palazzo Davanzati, a fifteenth-century Florentine town house. Small, widely spaced, arched windows deeply set into the thick walls are guarded by sturdy wood shutters. The simple, rounded corner fireplace, with a conical hood supported by two colonnettes, is a quiet center of interest. The chair is of a later date. (*Alinari*)

designed to harmonize with architecture rather than to fit people, became increasingly formal and classical. Walnut was a favored wood and was often ornamented with sturdy classical carving or coated with gesso (a kind of plaster) and then painted in strong colors and gilt. Seating consisted of benches, which were sometimes built into the walls (Fig. 479), simple stools, and chairs of two main types: large, rectangular, high-backed "stage seats" and many variations of the ancient X-shaped frame (Fig. 490), in which arms and legs form continuous curves. The large tables were typically of the medieval board-and-trestle type that could be set up in different rooms as needed for eating and then folded up and put away. Low chests, enriched with carving, intarsia, or paint, were the major case goods. Textile designs were strong and vigorous; accessories were rich and varied; and paintings and sculpture became important units in the total effect.

The High Renaissance: c. 1490–1580

An age of great architecture, furniture, and gardens, as well as of painting and sculpture, the High Renaissance was mature and assured. Continuing in the direction of the earlier period, the High Renaissance brought a deepened concern for careful total planning, consistency of purpose and design, good construction, and the relation between ornament and form. The rapid growth of Rome under the popes and the papal court led to its becoming a major center and brought many artists from northern Italy into their first direct contact with Roman ruins. This personal observation turned them away from the externals of antiquity—the ornamentation—and toward the basic principles of classical building. Grandeur of form with appropriate detail was the aim. City palaces, although basically similar to the earlier Florentine dwellings, showed great variety and individualism, and the Italian villa, with its compelling unity of house, furnishings, gardens, and views, was developed to new heights.

Plans. Still rectangular and focused around open courts, High Renaissance palaces showed increasing command of strong axial relationships (in architecture,

The vigorously modeled Palazzo Corner della Ca' Grande (1532) in Venice was designed by Jacopo Sansovino, a sculptor and architect. The heavily rusticated (masonry with roughened surfaces and deep joints) base raises the ground floor comfortably above the water level and with its splayed sides and stairway provides a visual as well as structural foundation. The lower section is dominated by the three tall entrance archways. The two floors above resemble each other closely but are not identical: the windows, much larger than those of the Palazzo Gondi (Fig. 168), are framed by pairs of columns, but the column capitals are different, and the third floor joins itself with the top band of oval windows and crowning cornice. (*Italian State Tourist Office*)

492

The hillside gardens of the Villa d'Este (1550–1569) at Tivoli, near Rome, attributed to Pirro Ligorio, are famous for their spectacular display of water in fountains, cascades, and quiet pools. A strongly ordered plan (Fig. 442), however, unifies the exuberant diversity. (*Italian State Tourist Office*)

an *axis* is an imaginary, central line along which the parts are usually symmetrically organized) and of continuing vistas from room to room and from house to garden (as contemporary houses do in a much smaller, less formal way).

Exteriors. During the High Renaissance, architecture became more vigorously and complexly personalized with increased emphasis on three-dimensionality, as a comparison of the Palazzo Gondi and the Palazzo Corner della Ca' Grande (Figs. 168 and 492) makes evident. The latter, built in Venice forty years after Columbus discovered America, faces the Grand Canal from an imposing site. A luxurious example of the Venetian manner, it shows great sensitivity to proportion and scale, and surpassing ability to integrate a richly varied assemblage of details within the basic cube.

Gardens. In gardens, too, the whole was more important than the parts, and gardens were designed as one phase of the total composition. The architect, who often designed house and garden together, composed the landscape with stone walls, balustrades, seats, and sculpture; with water used with amazing ingenuity in quiet pools, small fountains, and almost overwhelming jets and cascades; with the many greens and textures of foliage; and with the views from the site. A notable example is the Villa d'Este near Rome (Figs. 442 and 493), which, despite four centuries of inadequate maintenance, still retains much of its original monumental grandeur.

A

The great hall in the Palazzo Massimi, built in Rome from 1532–1536, has comparatively plain walls divided into panels by Ionic pilasters, and a coffered ceiling of great visual interest. It is an impressive example of humanized geometry. Baldassare Peruzzi, architect. (*Reprinted from Paul Marie Letarouilly,* Édifices de Rome Moderne)

Interiors. Palace interiors were designed for the elaborate social life of the period (Fig. 494A). Although richer and more fully developed than earlier work, the clear-cut architectural ornament was subordinated to the more fundamental aspects of the design. The walls were enhanced with paneling, pilasters, and frescoes, as well as with tapestries, velvet, and gilded leather. Some of the ceilings were made impressive with coffers (recessed panels), carving, and color. The floors were frequently of inlaid marble.

Furniture. Bold, brilliant carving, using the whole classical vocabulary from acanthus leaves to rosettes, flutings to cartouches—but all within a strong architectural framework—made High Renaissance furniture a positive element in the total ensemble. Benches, stools, and chests were still in common use for seating, but padded chairs became more prevalent as the desire for comfort increased (Fig. 482). Tables, often supported on carved pedestals (Fig. 494C) or turned legs, were varied in size and shape. Chests retained the importance they had held for centuries but now enjoyed considerable diversity in shape and ornament (Fig. 494B) and were often decorated by the great artists. It was during this period that chests of drawers were introduced.

B

C

Top. An early sixteenth-century walnut cassone (chest) made in Rome inventively adapts and combines ancient Roman motifs. The triumphant procession of figures is firmly held in check by vigorous moldings and fanciful figures at the corners shielded by coats of arms. (*French & Company, Inc.*)

Above. A monumental table (c. 1565–1573), designed by the Italian Late Renaissance architect Jacopo Barozzi da Vignola, has three magnificently sculptured supports of marble and an inlaid top. Many tables of similar design were constructed of wood. (*The Metropolitan Museum of Art, New York, Dick Fund, 1958*)

Left. The exterior of the Palazzo Carignano (1680) in Turin has an undulating central portion flanked by rectangular masses, with typical Baroque curves in the window frames on the upper floors. (*Italian State Tourist Office*)

A

Textiles, marked by ornateness in design and color and by great technical skill in weaving, included velvets, brocades, and damasks with formal, conventionalized patterns of foliage, animals, and classical motifs. Accessories—delicate Venetian glass, Cellini metalwork, and ceramics of tremendous richness and vitality—were superbly designed and crafted. Throughout the house, colors were strong, brilliant, and polychromatic.

By 1520, Italy was in a period of transition. Called by some authorities the **Mannerist** period, by others the **Late Renaissance,** it was a time when the classic precedents were more subjectively interpreted. One of the original connotations of Mannerism was "personal style," and the architecture of the epoch reflects the individualism of its creators and the conflicting trends that resulted. Some architects continued High Renaissance forms or strove to refine them, while others sought new directions and led into the Baroque so clearly that their work is sometimes called **Early Baroque.**

THE ITALIAN BAROQUE: c. 1550–1730

The Baroque age was a turbulent search for dynamic contrasts and sequential developments in architecture. Movement through space was valued more than repose and serenity. It is the kind of design ideally suited to being recorded by a motion-picture camera because only by that means, by walking in, through, and around the total composition, can one sense the exhilaration of dramatically organized time, motion, and space.

Plans. Baroque architects produced plans (Fig. 495B) that were thoroughly studied and composed as magnificent, exciting designs, but that showed little concern for privacy or function. Rectangles and cubes, although still used for their stabilizing qualities, lost their primacy, especially in stairway design, to the swelling curves, ellipses, and diagonals that better expressed man's spirit.

Exteriors. The basic mass of many Baroque dwellings remained surprisingly simple, to sustain the impact of the richly plastic ornament at windows and entrances, to make the elaborate interiors a stunning surprise, and to act as a foil for the uninhibited gardens. In some examples, however, the desire for movement led to exteriors with undulating walls (Fig. 495A) that, like the interiors, seem always to be unfolding and promising more beyond.

Below. The Palazzo Barberini, Rome (1626–1629), was designed by three of the greatest Baroque architects: Carlo Maderna, Francesco Borromini, and Gianlorenzo Bernini. The plan shows the Baroque interest in sequentially related interior space. Unlike the plan of the Palazzo Strozzi, curves, rectangles, and squares are directly yet complexly interrelated. (*Reprinted from, F. M. Simpson,* A History of Architectural Development, *vol. 3. Copyright © 1956, Longmans, Green and Company, Ltd.*)

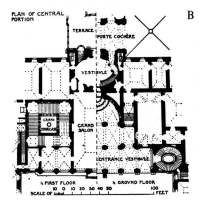

B

Gardens. The Baroque spirit was most unleashed in the gardens of the age. Hillsides were sought as the ideal terrain on which to build monumental cascades, fountains, and lavishly curved stairways, suggesting the effect of a garden in continually flowing motion. Here the designers were freed from any vestige of concern with use and could devote their talents to astounding the observer. Strong contrasts were introduced by such devices as placing very smooth, realistic sculptures of people and animals in the midst of great, rough rocks and splashing water. Surprises were more than visual in many grottoes, where trick mechanisms caused jets of water to douse the unwary.

Interiors. Repose was as carefully avoided in the interiors as it was in the gardens by taking full advantage of the fourth dimension of design—time. A walk through a Baroque palace is still a memorable experience in time and space because of sequential contrasts of room size and shape and the amount and kind of light. So varied and filled with the unexpected were the palatial homes that an impression of spontaneity belied the tremendous study and planning that unified the diverse elements. Baroque architects, no longer interested in expression through plain surfaces and solid structure, turned their energies to compositions in light and shade. Often they deliberately integrated sculpture, painting, and ornament to destroy the visual solidity of walls and ceilings.

Furnishings. The classical standards of rectangular silhouettes that had persisted in Renaissance furniture were relaxed (Figs. 496 and 497A and B). Twisted turnings, broken and reversed curves, bold carving, and inlays and appliqués of brilliant materials made Baroque furniture dramatic compositions of highlights and shadows. Out of context, much Baroque furniture seems overemphatic, but when seen in the monumental settings for which they were designed, the pieces are handsomely appropriate.

Chairs of the period differed from those of the Renaissance in that their outlines were more flowing. They were heavily carved and often gilded, and they were upholstered in large-patterned velvets, silks, and stamped leather, often with nailheads used decoratively. Typical tables were of the console type, with tops of marble or other colorful materials supported on bases carved with cherubim, mermaids, scrolls, shells, foliage, and fruit. Tall cabinets, broken and undulating in outline, were profusely decorated, and the variety of beds ranged from dramatic four-posters to those with large, painted panels. Mirrors were larger than previously and had rich, heavy frames.

The back of a Baroque wood bench (1718) from northern Italy is painted with an opulent composition of human figures and animals engulfed in swirling draperies. The base emphasizes bold S-curves in scrolls, cherubs, and fantastic animals. Only in the central vase and in the shield below are our eyes allowed to rest momentarily. (*M. H. de Young Memorial Museum, San Francisco, Gift of Mrs. Robert A. Magowan*)

A

Above. An Italian Baroque credenza of walnut (first half of the seventeenth century) has a strong, clearly evident, basic design. The contorted figures of children, the scroll at the end, and the busts of three women unexpectedly half-emerging from the panels express the Baroque spirit. (*M. H. de Young Memorial Museum, San Francisco, Gift of William Randolph Hearst*)

Left. An early eighteenth-century Venetian stool is supported by reverse-curved legs and by stretchers that seem to be in continuous motion. Even the urn that marks the point at which the stretchers meet is contorted. The easy grace of some of the smaller curves reflects the emerging Rococo. [*Nelson Gallery—Atkins Museum* (*Nelson Fund*), Kansas City, Missouri]

B

Textiles and accessories also became larger in scale, more florid and free in design. Richer surface finishes and more abundant decoration than had been previously used all but obscured basic materials and structure in the interests of sculptural plasticity. A wide range of colors, with emphasis on the strong and brilliant, were used, but less for their own beauty than as another means to the atmospheric, plastic splendor sought in all Baroque art.

Baroque urges in Italy persisted into the eighteenth century. There were also notable developments in the Rococo and Neoclassic styles, but the achievements in France and England had much more effect on American homes (Chap. 25).

THE SPANISH RENAISSANCE: THE SIXTEENTH CENTURY

Spain is a land of strident, sometimes brutal, contrasts in geography, climate, and temperament. Most of the peoples of the ancient world established settlements on the Iberian peninsula, but the Moors, who dominated it for some seven centuries, made the most pervasive impact. In 1492 two events drastically changed Spanish history, art, and architecture. The Spaniards wrested control of their country from the Moors, and Columbus claimed the richest section of the New World for the Spanish monarchs. In a few decades, undreamed-of wealth and political power made the sixteenth century Spain's greatest age. Although strongly affected by outside influences, an unmistakably distinctive character evolved. Whereas most Italian work was assured and coherent, Spanish work often seemed a tense combination of starkness relieved by densely concentrated embellishment.

The Early Spanish Renaissance, or Plateresque: c. 1480–1556

Long after the Renaissance style reached Spain, Moorish craftsmanship and passion for intricate design, such as starlike shapes and very small, intersecting, geometric patterns, continued (Fig. 500). The classical motifs, derived from Italy, were freely adapted in a drive for more abrupt contrasts and more dynamic intensity of feeling. Named after the *plateros* ("silversmiths"), the **Plateresque** was primarily an application of energetic surface ornamentation that had only minor effect on all but a few domestic interiors and furnishings.

Plans, exteriors, and gardens. With the exception of very small houses, plans continued to follow the Mediterranean practice of arranging rooms around an open patio that served both as a living area and a means of getting from room to room. Bright sun, extremes of temperature, and scant rainfall led to thick masonry walls, rather small, widely spaced windows, and gently sloping tile roofs. Although many houses had comparatively plain exteriors, the more ambitious had ornament at unexpected places that has been described by some as "loose and nonfunctional" and by others as "rich and poetic." A later phase brought a more unified, ordered sense of design, such as that of the Alcazar in Toledo (Fig. 498).

Gardens were a blend of Moorish and Italian concepts, with an emphasis on secluded patios enlivened with water, tiles, sculpture, and ornamental urns. In larger gardens, many geometric units were linked together in a manner somewhat similar to those in the Villa d'Este (Fig. 442).

The north façade of the Alcazar in Toledo, Spain, was completely remodeled in the Plateresque style near the middle of the sixteenth century. The arched doorway is framed by Ionic pilasters topped by statues. The iron-barred windows on the first floor are accentuated by moldings, pediments, and plain stonework. The balconied windows on the second floor are more richly ornamented. And the top story is unexpectedly of heavily rusticated stone. It is a comparatively simple but assured application of classic forms. (*Reprinted by permission of the publisher and the copyright owners from Sir Banister Fletcher, A History of Architecture, 17th ed. Revised by R. A. Cordingley*)

A

B

Above. A long walnut table (c. 1600), supported on columnar turned legs and plain, straight stretchers, has a deep apron with four drawers, and is a typically Spanish design. The geometric carving is in low relief, following the Moorish tradition of surface decoration, and the iron drop handles are simple and functional. (*French & Company, Inc.*)

Right. A Spanish armchair of the sixteenth century, simple and rectangular in shape, has fretted front and back stretchers, hinged in the middle and at the sides so that it can be folded for easy transportation. The tooled leather seat and back are attached with large ornamental nails. (*The Metropolitan Museum of Art, New York, Gift of George Blumenthal, 1941*)

Interiors and furnishings. Rectangular rooms typically had plain or painted plaster walls enlivened with leather, fabric hangings, or polychrome tiles. Sometimes the walls were accented with plaster relief figures or patterns, painted and gilded. Spanish furniture in general followed Italian expression but with overt Moorish overtones. The proportions were more squat, the structure heavier, and ornament fitted the forms more capriciously. In large homes, the public rooms often had a raised platform with two ornamented chairs, a table, and a cabinet to give the owners a sense of importance. Chairs had leather seats and backs (Fig. 499B) or were made softer with velvet cushions. The ornamentation of tables and cabinets ranged from inlays of silver, ivory, ebony, and other rich materials to elaborate or flat carving (Fig. 499A). Wrought iron was used as supports for furniture, and was even used for entire pieces of furniture. Cabinets, especially the *vargueños* (chests with drop fronts and supported on a table or chest) were a distinctive achievement in this and the following century (Fig. 500).

The Spanish High Renaissance, or the Desornamentado: c. 1556–1600

A style followed in some public buildings, the **Desornamentado** was unadorned, austere, and slavishly attempted to be correct. It found little favor with most Spaniards and had almost no effect on domestic architecture and furnishings.

THE SPANISH BAROQUE, OR THE CHURRIGUERESQUE: THE SEVENTEENTH CENTURY

The imaginative, fervid, explosive qualities of **Churrigueresque** exuberance suited the Spanish temperament ideally, and religious and public architecture was released from the straitjacket of the preceding period. It was not, however, suited to any domestic architecture other than palaces, and had little effect on homes except as accents, and in furniture and accessories. Doorways and windows were more lavishly ornamented, and some walls and ceilings were frescoed. In most houses, however, plain, plastered walls, beamed ceilings, and inlaid floors heightened the apparent intensity of the furnishings. Chests covered with leather and with designs outlined in nails were common, and in the seventeenth century the *vargueños* (Fig. 500) were fancifully enhanced with ivory and bone, tortoise shell, and other unusual materials.

In the great houses, architecture, gardens, and furnishings were based on the imported French and Italian Baroque examples. But during the same period, Spain profoundly affected much New World architecture, an influence that is still alive, as can be seen in Figures 15, 25, 115, 129B, 149, 309A, 345D, and 361.

By the end of the seventeenth century, foreign influences had become so powerful that no distinctively Spanish styles were developed, and from then on Spanish architecture and furnishings drew heavily on other European work.

A seventeenth-century Spanish *vargueño* and cabinet, made of carved and partly gilded walnut, painted bone and wrought iron, show the persistence of the Moorish tradition of exceptionally fine geometric design. When the drop front is opened, a series of small, highly ornamented drawers is revealed. The lower cabinet has similar embellishment, but simpler and larger in scale. Baroque influence appears in the many minute spiral colonnettes and in the two S-shaped broken pediments, as well as in the shell-shaped handles on the members that support the writing surface. (*The Metropolitan Museum of Art, New York, Gift of the Duchesse de Richelieu, 1960*)

Completed in the sixteenth-century, the Château de Chenonceaux used the river Cher to provide the traditional protection of the moat. Its gardens (restored) were executed as pure exercises in design with no attempt to blend with the buildings. The union of architecture and water, however, is notable and may profitably be compared with Figures 389 and 513. (*Aéro-Photo Paris*)

23 · France

When Louis XII ascended the throne of France in 1498, the centralization of the national government was well under way, and the French rulers then turned their efforts toward military conquests abroad, chiefly in Italy. These military expeditions introduced the French upper classes to a way of building and living far in advance of what they had known at home. They responded by taking the ideas, and in many instances the artists and artisans, home with them. Nevertheless, the French people as a whole were slow to adopt the new ideas, because France still had a vital and creative Gothic tradition that was especially strong in residential architecture and that was stoutly defended by the conservative guilds.

THE FRENCH RENAISSANCE: c. 1500–1643

Although the transition from medieval to Renaissance ideals began under Louis XII, it was during the reign of Francis I (1515–1547) that the tempo of development quickened and the character of large French residences changed. Francis I liked the new and experimental (and at that time it was the Italian Renaissance that deserved those adjectives), and he loved to build new châteaus. Moreover, he encouraged the nobility to follow suit, and new residences sprang up in many parts of the country. Progress was greatly expedited by the establishment of a center for the new style at Fontainebleau, where Italian artists congregated and worked assiduously with the French.

The Château de Chenonceaux combines three styles of French architecture. The chapel at the left front corner is predominantly Gothic. The front section, built between 1515 and 1523, illustrates the early coalition of Gothic towers, steep roofs, and boldly vertical dormers with Renaissance symmetry and freely adapted classic detail. The rear wing, added in 1556, is comparatively long, low, and quietly reposed in the Late Renaissance manner. The horizontal mass is emphasized by horizontal moldings; the windows, surmounted by arches, are treated separately rather than in groups; and the relatively small dormers with oval windows are ornamented with pediments and curved moldings.

Plans, exteriors, and gardens. Symmetry and regularity of plans displaced the freer, sometimes more functional medieval concepts of how rooms should be arranged and joined together. Many houses continued to be built around four sides of an open court, but others spread their wings into U- or H-shapes. Frequently, the French Renaissance structures were additions to older buildings, and then the French architects displayed typically French ingenuity in bringing new and old together.

In exterior design, regularity and symmetry of the total mass and of the window organization, together with a classical emphasis on horizontality and order, brought a new kind of harmony. But the French did not quickly give up the high, pointed roofs, chimneys, towers, and dormers that made the outlines of their homes picturesquely varied. The Château de Chenonceaux (Figs. 501 and 502) aptly illustrates the changes that took place.

The importation of Italian ideas and artists changed garden design considerably, but the French did not follow the Italian practice of integrating landscape with architecture until late in the period. There was an increased geometric regularity, but in the early phase the gardens were frequently only casually related to the dwelling. In some cases, as in Figure 501, this was dictated by geography, but there are many examples that indicate that this disassociation was preferred.

Interiors. During this period, beamed Gothic ceilings were continued for some time but then gave way to panels; walls were covered with tapestries, leather, damask, painted plaster, or wood paneling decorated with Renaissance ornament. Fireplaces became the dominant features of the rooms and were laden with an assemblage of carving. The Francis I salon, shown in Figure 503, although lacking in coherence and unity, is a strikingly handsome, creative room, fit for a king who wanted to civilize France in a hurry. The furniture now placed in the room, however, comes not from this period but from the Baroque age of Louis XIV.

Furniture. Conservatively rectangular in basic shape, the furniture of this period was highly decorated with fine Renaissance carving and marquetry. Geometric and conventionalized foliate motifs were favorites; but they were freely combined with grotesque figures and, sometimes, elaborate turnings. This profusion was held in bounds by geometric paneling and deep, framelike moldings. Polished walnut gradually replaced the oak and the polychromatic painting of the medieval period, and ebony began to be highly prized.

Although stiff, high-backed chairs were not entirely discarded, typical chairs were smaller in size and made comfortable with flat cushions or, later, with fixed upholstery. Tables were heavy and architectural, supported on carved bases and elaborately turned legs in the later years. Beds often had four posts for the needed curtains or for a regal canopy. Cabinets, which reached one of their highest

The salon of Francis I, built in 1528 at the Château de Fontainebleau, is a truly regal, Early French Renaissance room. The central feature is a monumental fireplace embellished with classical motifs; the walls are divided into panels and decorated with pictorial scenes, elaborate moldings, and carving; and the ceiling has a complex pattern of coffers between the painted beams.

developments, were usually double-bodied with a slightly narrower upper section. They carried the architectural spirit of the rooms in their simple, paneled rectangularity, but often were almost entirely covered with intricate carving (Fig. 504A).

A

In the century between the reigns of Francis I and Louis XIV, the Renaissance gradually moved toward the Baroque.

THE FRENCH BAROQUE, OR THE LOUIS XIV STYLE: c. 1643–1715

Although the Baroque movement, which had originated in Italy several decades earlier, was beginning to impress France at the time of Henry IV, it did not gain full momentum until Louis XIV came to the throne. Government by then had become strongly centralized, and a nationalistic urge for a distinctive French expression reached a new peak with the emergence of the French Academy of Arts as the fountainhead of design. The Academy controlled the training and practice of architects, painters, sculptors, and designers, and thus a great unity of style resulted.

Plans. Larger houses were formal, regular, and rectangular; were often built around courts open on one side; and had typical Baroque sequences of rooms planned, it would seem, primarily for pageants. These progressions were consummated in "glittering barracks," such as the Hall of Mirrors at Versailles.

Exteriors and gardens. The simple, blocky, monumental exteriors were handsomely proportioned, and their enrichment helped bring them into human scale. Their size gave them dignity and power; their proportions and detail gave them elegance. Low roofs obscured by balustrades replaced the earlier high roof lines. The Palace of Versailles (Fig. 504B), built by Louis XIV, epitomizes the design of the period although more grandiose, in keeping with the Sun King's status.

Above. A sixteenth-century walnut cabinet of the period of Henry II shows the architectural monumentality of French Renaissance furniture that provided a restraining framework for the profusely carved surfaces. [*Nelson Gallery—Atkins Museum (Nelson Fund), Kansas City, Missouri*]

Below. The Palais de Versailles (1645–1708), designed by Jules Hardouin Mansart and built by Louis XIV, is a royal Baroque complex of staggering size (1935 feet long). The comparatively simple front has a central block flanked by long set-back wings. Each of the three units is composed in three horizontal bands, and each has three projecting units accented by columns. The columns and the balustrade around the roof are surmounted by vigorously carved figures. The expansive gardens, designed by André Le Nôtre for spectacles, fetes, and promenades, are sequentially organized on radiating axes that converge on the Sun King's living quarters. Broad paved areas enriched with elaborate flower beds and water features are surrounded by densely wooded retreats. (*French Government Tourist Office*)

B

25

The Dream of St. Ursula, painted by Vittore Carpaccio c. 1495, is assumed to depict accurately the character of bedrooms in the larger Venetian Renaissance palaces of the late fifteenth and early sixteenth centuries. The dominant rectangularity, relieved by round arches and a circular window, compose an orderly, quiet background. With the exception of the bed and the fanciful Gothic chair beside it, the sparse furnishings are almost austere and architectural in character. A preponderance of muted greens and dull golds is accentuated by the red-orange bedspread and canopy, and by the painted arches over the windows. Sculpture and two urns with plants, latticework and patterned glass, and delicate moldings and pilasters humanize the architectural enclosure. (*Accademia, Venice. Photograph by SCALA*)

26

A room from the Hôtel de Tessé, Paris, c. 1770, typifies the restrained brilliance of French Early Neoclassic interiors. Comparison with the Adam room (Color Fig. 28), however, shows that the French approach is less governed by archaeological precedents and is more lighthearted than English rooms of the same period. A sparkling color scheme is established by the white walls adroitly enriched with gilt ornamentation and supplemented by mirrors, a crystal chandelier, and the glass of the windows. More positive colors are used in the satin damask and coral velvet upholstery on the chairs. The range of color values is completed by the very dark fireplace and the rich, dark, reddish brown of the parquet floor and the mahogany table in the center of the room. (*The Metropolitan Museum of Art, New York*)

In 1688, Louis XIV built the Grand Trianon as a setting for less ceremonious living than was feasible in the vast Palais de Versailles. Later Napoleon I furnished it according to his taste. The French government's recent restoration combines the two periods with pleasing results. In the Salon des Jardins, the chastened Baroque of the late Louis XIV paneling is dramatized by the long vertical folds of the translucent draperies and repeated in the straight lines and rectangular forms of the Empire furnishings. The predominately white and gold background is brilliantly accented by the richness of the violet cut-velvet upholstery, the red and white figured marble fireplace, a crystal and gold chandelier, the large landscape paintings, and several handsome urns on marble pedestals. The total effect is light, open, and elegant. (*Photograph by Heinz Zinram, Time Magazine. © Time Inc.*)

28

The dining room in Saltram House, Devonshire, England, was designed by Robert Adam, c. 1768, and exemplifies his belief in integrating architecture, furniture, and enrichment. This Neoclassic room is a simple, rectangular volume of exquisite proportions, strengthened and enlived by disciplined, inventive ornament that contrasts straight and curved lines. The pale-green walls are accented by rectilinear white frames around dark doors, by a fireplace, and by paintings of classical ruins. The ceiling is dominated by circular forms that are repeated with some variations in the carpet below, and underscored by round plaques on the walls and in the cornice of swags and horizontal moldings. The chairs, which are of Hepplewhite design, also have slender straight and curved forms that are light and open. (*Photograph by A. F. Kersting. National Trust*)

Furnishings of the late seventeenth century arranged as in a state bedroom illustrate the lavishness of the period of Louis XIV. The great carpet, made for the Louvre at the Savonnerie Manufactory, the wall hangings, and the embroidered hangings on the state bed all incorporate the Baroque period S-scroll in tightly packed, inventive designs. The ivory and ebony cabinet (c. 1640–1650), although rich, is somewhat more restrained, but the chair and candlestand behind it again show the magnificent but disciplined flair of the Grand Siècle. (*The Metropolitan Museum of Art, New York*)

The gardens of Versailles exhibit a grandeur of planning unknown in earlier periods. Strictly symmetrical yet full of the unexpected, the vast gardens are strongly related to the architecture in their plan and in their profusion of formal terraces, balustrades, broad flights of steps, statuary, brocade-like parterres, and meticulously trimmed trees and shrubs. Quiet pools of water are complemented by the movement and excitement engendered by countless fountains.

Interiors. Inside the palaces, there were large public rooms, very formal and somewhat pompous, with large-scale ornament and costly craftsmanship. The major elements, especially the walls and ceilings, were a unified composition of carving and paneling, allegorical paintings, tapestries, and mirrors (Fig. 290). Wood walls were customarily painted to show off the gilded carving, and furniture, pushed back against the walls, was secondary to the enclosing surfaces. Bold accessories of many kinds completed the ensemble.

Furnishings. French Baroque furniture was large in scale, ornate, and full blown (Figs. 503 and 505). Although straight lines were not discarded, there were many big S-curves in the arms and stretchers of chairs and in the supports of tables. The rich, plentiful, often gilded carving represented almost everything, from abstract ornament to animals' legs, water lilies and sphinxes to agricultural tools.

In provisions for seating, the sofa was an important introduction, and chaise longues were much in vogue. Chairs, gorgeously upholstered in cloth or leather, ranged in order of rank from the throne chair to armchairs and chairs with backs, then to joint stools and folding stools, and finally to hassocks. Chair legs were scrolled, flat, or turned, and the well-molded arms usually joined the back in great curves. Tables, rectangular and curvilinear, came in great variety for special purposes. The earlier monumental, all-purpose cabinet declined in favor of smaller, more specialized pieces for storing books, hats, and the like. Commodes (Fig. 506) with drawers for clothes appeared, and flat-topped bureaus for desks. Furniture woods were rich and varied, and elaborate inlays of tortoise shell, horn, ivory, brass, pewter, tin, and mother-of-pearl were popular, as was painting, especially in red and gray-green, gilt and silver. Boldly figured floral designs were typical of French Baroque interiors. Velvet, satin, needlepoint, and Gobelin tapestries, as well as printed linens and cottons, were the major fabrics.

A Louis XIV commode elaborately inlaid with tortoise shell and decorated with ormolu (gilded bronze) is an example of the specialized type of cabinet that was introduced in the Baroque period. [*Nelson Gallery—Atkins Museum (Nelson Fund), Kansas City, Missouri*]

THE FRENCH ROCOCO, OR THE LOUIS XV STYLE: c. 1715–1774

Once again change came first in details. The revolt against Baroque grandeur began while Louis XIV was still on the throne, and during the **Regency** (1715–1723) furniture was softened and feminized. Soon thereafter flowing outlines and delicately curved structural members gave furniture the completely new character of the **Louis XV style** (1723–1774). Much more important, though, were the basic changes that fundamentally transformed homes. Whereas typical French Baroque houses are suitable today for little more than museums, many of the workable, economical, beautiful eighteenth-century homes need only minor alterations to satisfy contemporary needs.

Plans. The French have long been regarded as a rational people, but it was not until the eighteenth century, when French women came into a new dominant role, that this quality was expressed in the planning of homes. New in French plans were compactness and coherence, convenience of room arrangement, segregation of group- and private-living space, rooms designed for special purposes, pleasant variation of room size and shape (often rounded at the corners) in terms of function, and provision for paths of circulation that made rooms private. In larger houses the central courtyard was retained and the major rooms, one delicate stairway above the ground, overlooked the private gardens at the rear. In smaller houses the courtyard was eliminated and plans were simple rectangles.

Exteriors and gardens. House exteriors were restrained and had a minimum of ornament. Frequently only simple moldings around the closely spaced windows, wrought-iron railings, a delicate cornice, and well-mannered ornament around doorways and windows accented the simple masses, subtle proportions, and good workmanship. The exteriors did not exhibit the curvilinear decoration profusely used inside the house because the Rococo was fundamentally an "interior style." Paved terraces and gravel walks, neat but not fancy beds of flowers, and orderly arrangements of shrubs and trees made the small, intimate gardens of this period suitable for outdoor living.

Interiors. French Rococo interiors, it has been said, were never intended to be taken too seriously, although they were brilliantly designed with the most careful attention to the whole and to every detail (Fig. 507). Rooms were com-

An alcove of a Rococo interior (c. 1720–1730) is typically delicate, playful, and feminine. The elaborate low-relief decoration on the walls has asymmetrical features within a symmetrically balanced framework. The chair and stools are humanized in scale and are comfortably padded, curvaceous, and intricately ornamented yet self-contained. (*The Metropolitan Museum of Art, New York, Gift of J. Pierpont Morgan, 1906*)

paratively small in size, extremely delicate in scale, and planned so that the comfortable furniture could be pleasantly arranged for sparkling conversation or intimate tête-à-têtes. Walls were divided into alternately wide and narrow panels, but the corners, and often the tops and bottoms, were softened with curved moldings. Sometimes the ornamentation seemed to break through its boundaries and spread from the wall onto the ceiling. Paintings or stretched textiles often filled the panels, and mirrors were much used for their brilliant reflections. Wallpaper came into popularity in the homes of those who could not afford more expensive wall coverings. Even wihout color these rooms would have been gay, but colors were used with rare understanding of their expressive possibilities. Gay, light colors, such as pale rose, light green, turquoise, and many yellows, emphasized the lighthearted forms.

Furnishings. At first curves and ornament only slightly modified the substantial, architectural character of Baroque furniture; later the structural parts of the furniture began to flow into one another. The cabriole leg was retained, but the curves were changed so that the legs and seats of chairs were more smoothly joined, as illustrated in Figure 487. Fully developed Rococo furniture avoided right angles and geometric curves as avidly as the Renaissance had sought them. Seating was dimensioned, shaped, and softened with loose down cushions to put the occupants luxuriously at ease. Chaise longues, sofas, and ottomans contributed to cordiality and comfort. Tables and all kinds of case goods, invariably supported by graceful cabriole legs, continued in great variety for specialized purposes.

In the trend toward lightness, walnut and ebony were partially superseded by a tremendous variety of domestic and imported woods, including rosewood, mahogany, satinwood, and fruit woods of many kinds. Marquetry was used to decorate many of the surfaces, but painted furniture became common by the middle of the century. Beautifully shaped metal appliqués continued as a favored type of enrichment (Fig. 508).

Textiles were usually asymmetrical in pattern (Fig. 487). They, together with the painted panels, are the most conspicuous expression of the desire for freedom from arbitrary formality. Flowing, interlacing, delicate flowers, foliage, ribbons, and shells wandered with a deceptive air of nonchalance over the smooth,

A commode of lacquered wood, ormolu, and marble from the Louis XV period (c. 1750) is a masterpiece of Rococo design. Flickering flames of ormolu outline the easy, flowing shape and emphasize the center keyholes, while a darker lacquer design in the Chinese manner covers the slightly curved front. Although S-curves are used to some extent, it is the smaller C-curve that comprises the theme and variations. (*M. H. de Young Memorial Museum, San Francisco, Gift of Roscoe and Margaret Oakes*)

508

Endeavoring to recapture the classic spirit, French architects in the Early Neoclassic (Louis XVI) period designed houses as relatively low, horizontal masses with rectangular or arched openings and simply detailed surfaces. Claude Nicolas Ledoux's Hôtel Thélusson in Paris shows many of these characteristic forms. (*Reprinted from J. Karl Krafft and F. Thiollet; Choix des plus jolies maisons de Paris et de ses environs*)

finely woven silks as well as on the heavier needlepoints, tapestries, and velours. Printed cottons known as *toiles de Jouy* portrayed pictorial scenes in monochromatic colors for those who could not afford the more expensive silks.

The Rococo style has been characterized as untrammeled imagination playing over the bedrock of reason. Quickened, elated curves lead one's attention over the surface (Fig. 191C), but basic form is emphasized, not obscured, by these seeming divertissements.

FRENCH NEOCLASSICISM: c. 1750–1815

About the middle of the eighteenth century, a renewed interest in antiquity started a series of Neoclassic styles. **Early Neoclassicism** began in the 1750s, and when **Louis XVI** ascended the throne in 1774, two years before the Declaration of Independence was signed, the reaction to Rococo frivolity was complete, and the new style often is known by his name. The years around the turn of the century were ones of disturbed transition, and the only stable political entity gave its name, **Directoire** (c. 1793–1804), to the austere prevailing style. **Late Neoclassicism** (c. 1804–1815), associated with Napoleon I, is called the **Empire** style.

Early French Neoclassicism, or the Louis XVI Style: c. 1750–1793

Early Neoclassicism, too, affected exteriors, plans, and gardens far less than it did interiors and furnishings. Quite monumental exteriors were marked by continuous, straight lines, simple surfaces, and accurately copied detail (Fig. 509). What had been learned earlier in the century about convenient house plans was not forgotten, but a great interest in one-story houses (how history repeats itself!) came from the excavation of Pompeian dwellings. Rectangular forms had only a few precise curves for accents (Color Fig. 26). Emphasized cornices came back to make clear the distinction between vertical walls and horizontal ceiling, and wall panels were framed with exquisitely detailed, small, thin moldings and often filled with painted or carved arabesques, with textiles, with wallpaper, or with mirrors. Fireplaces, too, shared this emphasis on the right angle with their clear geometric shapes and little columns or bundles of reeds.

Furnishings. Although full-bodied curves were not completely abandoned, the distinctive character of this period was a slender, delicate linearity that emphasized vertical lines (Fig. 510). Chairs and tables typically had thin, straight legs usually emphasized by vertical channels. The backs were squared off or circular. Although unified, the parts of each piece of furniture did not merge but stood out clearly. Mathematically symmetrical ornament recalled that of the Baroque, but very much tamed. To keep the surfaces smooth and yet satisfy needs for enrichment, geometric marquetry, usually in diamond or lozenge pat-

The characteristics of Early Neoclassic (Louis XVI) interiors are evident in a late eighteenth-century room from Bordeaux. The straight line has returned, decoration is relatively unostentatious and refined, and emphasizes the architectural character of the room. In the furniture, too, carving is subordinated to the more geometric, simple contours of the period. The carved oak woodwork is painted greenish gray. The fireplace of white marble is small and restrained. (*The Metropolitan Museum of Art, New York, Gift of Mrs. Herbert N. Strauss, 1943*)

An upright secretary of the Early Neoclassic period has marquetry patterns of various woods in squares and rectangles, disciplined, sedate gilt bronze mountings, and a marble top. It illustrates the return to geometric symmetry that marks the period. (*M. H. de Young Memorial Museum, San Francisco, Roscoe and Margaret Oakes Collection*)

terns, enlivened many cabinets (Fig. 511) made of mahogany or ebony. Other furniture was painted grayish white, gray-green, and other soft tones, or lacquered in black and gold. Upholstery conformed in character—delicately colored brocades, embroidered satins, and stamped velvet in small floral patterns, feather motifs, or stripes.

Late French Neoclassicism, or the Empire Style: c. 1804–1815

Napoleon's wish to give Paris the monumental dignity and large-scale character of Rome was the dominant influence in the Empire period. Old aristocratic forms were hated, and yet inspiration was sought in exactly the same culture from which they had been derived.

Plans, exteriors, and gardens. An increased knowledge of Roman planning was reflected in plans, exteriors, and gardens, and the architects of the period undertook the task of producing comfortable living quarters that embodied both nineteenth-century convenience and Roman ideals. Given this program, they could not simply copy. Wisely they sought workable plans and broad, simple effects enriched with intricate classical details. Exteriors were simple masses bounded by plain stucco or stone walls, penetrated by well-spaced windows and sometimes a graceful loggia. Gardens were similar in character to the houses.

Interiors. Interiors, too, were remarkable for their simplicity, masculinity, and breadth of treatment. Columns and pilasters divided the walls into large panels, often painted in rich Pompeian colors. Painted friezes and panels over doors added interest. Windows were elaborately curtained, and this urge toward drapery extended to textiles hung in sweeps, draped, or stretched over the entire walls. Harsh, militant reds, greens, yellows, and blues were the dominant colors.

Furnishings. Heavy, solid proportions, absolute symmetry (Fig. 512 and Color Fig. 27), and beautifully grained wood surfaces with little carving are basic characteristics, and gilt brass or bronze decorative castings were much in evidence. Many chairs and sofas were stiff and uncomfortable, because designers were more concerned with antique motifs than with the anatomy of those who sat on them. Tables, often round and topped with marble, stood on pedestal or tripod bases. Case goods were designed like miniature architecture, some desks being constructed in Roman temple forms. Beds suggestive of boats, with richly scrolled head and foot rising to the same height, were typical. Textiles were enriched with isolated motifs: rosettes, torches, bundles of reeds, the letter *N* and bees (Napoleon's symbols).

The state bed given to Alexander I of Russia by the city of Paris in 1815 epitomizes the majestic grandeur sought by many furniture designers of the Empire period. The flat surfaces of handsomely grained wood are decorated with gilt bronze castings, the massive posts are crowned by statues. It is a piece of furniture designed to impress those who see it rather than to provide relaxation. (*French & Company, Inc.*)

ECLECTICISM AND EXPERIMENTS: THE NINETEENTH CENTURY

Even before the nineteenth century began, a visionary architect, **Claude Nicolas Ledoux** (1756–1806), who built many structures in the Neoclassic modes (Fig. 509), had been inspired by his study of the ancient precedents to experiment with basic forms (Fig. 513). After the Neoclassic lost its impetus around 1815, other French architects began to study their historic heritage from a structural point of view. **Eugène Emmanuel Viollet-le-Duc** (1814–1879) advocated the idea that structure should be the basis for design and was convinced that iron, glass, and ceramics were appropriate materials for a new architecture. A few engineers and architects put this into practice in markets, libraries, the amazing Eiffel Tower, and a number of exposition buildings. At the same time, the **École des Beaux-Arts,** which dominated architectural education for well over fifty years, rejected these radical notions and clung academically to the forms of other eras, illustrated so beautifully in the many architectural books of the period. **Eclecticism** became the accepted mode, usually in a modified French Baroque, with its emphasis on pure spatial design and without much thought for functional or structural problems.

A partial breakthrough came around 1896 with the **Art Nouveau movement** that soon spread to other countries. It was a reaction against eclecticism and advocated fresh observation and thought as the chief sources of inspiration. The search for new forms led to a study of nature, and the most distinctive motif became a sinuous line ending in a whiplash curve, reminiscent of some growing plants, especially vines. Although it primarily affected furnishings and decoration more than basic architectural design, it was one more step toward twentieth-century developments.

Claude Nicolas Ledoux (1756–1806) based some of his projected designs on pure geometric forms that are symbolic, expressive, and imaginative. This house for a director of waterworks is a powerful composition composed of cubes and a cylinder through which the river flows. (L'Architecture de C. N. Ledoux)

Sometimes called a "turned" or "thrown" chair, this late sixteenth- or early seventeenth-century example follows an ancient pattern. It is stoutly constructed of ash and is robust in scale. (*The Metropolitan Museum of Art, New York, Rogers Fund, 1909*)

24 · England

Although English homes changed in a sequence not unlike that of France and Italy, the several periods are not identical in dates or character. The English temperament, which clung tenaciously to medieval ways of building, and the English climate precluded a full acceptance of homes created for warmer, sunnier countries with deeply rooted, classical traditions.

THE ENGLISH RENAISSANCE: c. 1509–1649

The English Renaissance, a period of almost a century and a half, can be divided into two phases: the **Tudor-Elizabethan** phase and the **Early Jacobean** phase. Henry VIII, whose reign coincided almost exactly with that of Francis I in France, tried to awaken his country to the great movement that had developed in Italy and spread to France, but it did not really take hold until Elizabethan times. During the reigns of James I and Charles I, the Renaissance reached its full maturation, and a true understanding of Italian work was introduced by Inigo Jones.

514

The Tudor-Elizabethan Style: c. 1509–1603

In all phases of home planning the early designers faced the problem of reconciling the new desire for symmetry and regularity with the old love of flexible asymmetry and picturesqueness. Plans, exteriors, and gardens gradually became more regularized, as the medieval Gothic gave way to the Renaissance. Rectangular or round-arched openings superseded pointed arches, horizontality rather than verticality was a goal, and ornament was typically bounded by frames. At first, as is invariably the case in transitional periods, superficial details rather than basic concepts were taken over but not assimilated.

The *great hall* of larger homes remained the center of activities, but the Tudor-Elizabethan examples differed markedly from earlier ones, as a comparison of Figures 19 and 515 demonstrates. Planned only for the family and guests, they had become smaller. The fire retreated from its dominant, dangerous open hearth in the center of a room to a fireplace and chimney in the wall. Windows were greatly increased in size. Wood wainscoting, divided into small rectangular panels, covered all or most of the walls.

A model of a Late Tudor-Elizabethan great hall (c. 1550–1600) shows many Renaissance characteristics, especially in the rectangular paneling of the wainscoting. The Elizabethan table and bench are amply illuminated by a bay with very large windows. Beyond them, the wainscoting becomes a screen to shield a passageway. The fireplace is large but simply treated. Although the elaborate plaster ceiling is typical of this period, the checkered stone floor belongs to the seventeenth century. (*Thorne European Rooms in Miniature, The Art Institute of Chicago*)

A regal but ponderous Elizabethan bed (late sixteenth century) is made of oak inlaid with walnut, ebony, and ash. The columns supporting the canopy awkwardly combine an odd assortment of classical motifs in a manner more Flemish than Italian. At night the hangings were closed for warmth and privacy. (*Metropolitan Museum of Art, New York, Gift of Judge Irwin Untermeyer, 1953*)

Furniture became much more plentiful and somewhat more comfortable, but nothing directly comparable to continental work evolved during Elizabeth's reign. Oak was still the favored wood, although the occasional use of walnut permitted more detailed carving. The structure was clearly evident in boldly scaled, large pieces. Rectangularity was predominant. A distinctive feature was the oversize, melon-bulb swelling on vertical members (Figs. 93A and 516). Medieval board-and-trestle tables, which could be folded up and put away, were gradually replaced by solid pieces, often with drawers in the top, as can be seen in Figure 515. Huge beds were heavily laden with miscellaneous ornamental details. Despite the foreign influences, however, the pieces had a distinctive English character.

The Early Jacobean Style: c. 1603–1649

This phase brought a deeper comprehension of Renaissance principles. Architecture became more formal and ordered, and ornament was brought into more harmonious relationship with form.

Plans. A compromise was achieved with plans that were coherent without being arbitrary. Great halls, retained as symbols of the past, became monumental vestibules, because their former functions were taken over by long galleries lighted by many large windows and often running the full length of the house and by a series of smaller, more private rooms (Fig. 517). Corridors were introduced to channel traffic around, not through, rooms, and orientation was given some thought. Plans ranged in size and shape from small, simple homes to large country houses built around one or more courts.

Exteriors. Except in larger, later houses, the desire for pronounced Renaissance symmetry was limited to a more careful alignment of windows, more simple and horizontal masses, and classical molding and decorations around doors and windows. Glass had become a common material, and along with greater security and slightly improved heating, led to expansive windows (Fig. 517), even to window walls in the long galleries.

Gardens. The English climate, admirably suited to lawns and horticulture in general, and the Englishmen's interest in outdoor exercise and hunting, were powerful determinants in the design of English gardens. Unlike French and Italian gardens, lawns and woods were planned and planted for *use*. The earlier work had fairly small garden units enclosed by walls or hedges. Often these were square and divided into four smaller squares that were planted in interwoven designs worked out in flowers and foliage called "knot gardens." High and low trellises, arbors, and summer houses were in favor. Frequently, these areas were sunken, with broad terraces on the sides, and one or more high mounds provided not only exercise but views. Stonework and water were used sparingly. As the period progressed, gardens increased in size and showed more Italian and French influence.

Interiors. Rooms were spacious, dignified, and comfortable. Walls were typically covered with wood wainscoting, the necessary fireplaces became richly decorated focal points, and the ceilings had vigorous, intricate plaster ornamentation. All kinds of motifs were borrowed from the Italian Renaissance. Pilasters and sometimes columns divided the wainscot into clearly discernible units. In general, all parts of the rooms and their furnishings had a more consistent sense of scale. Ornament was refined and more thoughtfully integrated with the form of which it was part and with the function for which it was intended. A room that is transitional between the Tudor-Elizabethan and Early Jacobean periods is illustrated in Figure 152.

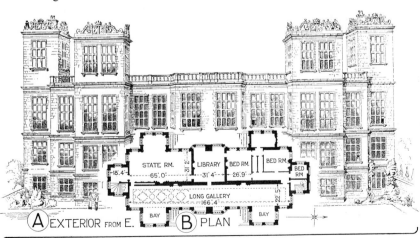

The plan and exterior of Hardwick Hall, Derbyshire (1590–1597), show the orderly rectangularity that is characteristic of the Renaissance. The plan is basically a symmetrical block with six projecting rectangular bays. Most remarkable in a house built more than 350 years ago are the large expanses of glass, which caused people to say, "Hardwick Hall, more glass than wall." (*Reprinted by permission of the publisher and the copyright owner from Sir Banister Fletcher,* A History of Architecture, *17th ed. Revised by R. A. Cordingley*)

Furnishings. In the early part of this period, furniture became smaller, lighter, and less profusely ornamented. Such classical motifs as columns and capitals, acanthus leaves and carved scrolls, while not always "correctly" proportioned, had their own kind of vigor. The carving was flatter and the turning less bold than in Tudor-Elizabethan times. Gateleg and drop-leaf tables came into use, and chairs (Fig. 518) and sofas with upholstery nailed to the frames marked a great step forward. The X-chair (Fig. 490) came by way of Italy, and there were also convenient footstools. Textiles were colorful, and rich embroidery was much admired. Mirrors with intricate frames, gold and silver plateware, and glassware introduced a lively sparkle.

An early seventeenth-century armchair of the Early Jacobean period. Rectangular in outline, low in height, and with the structure explicitly expressed, it is a substantial, comfortable chair. The turned arms, legs, and stretchers, as well as the colorful, decorative upholstery, are typical of this phase of English furniture. [*Nelson Gallery—Atkins Museum* (*Nelson Fund*), *Kansas City, Missouri*]

In the latter half of this period, a newer, more classically correct style of architecture evolved under the leadership of **Inigo Jones** (1573–1652); it was to have lasting effect on English domestic architecture and eventually on Colonial Georgian houses in New England and Virginia. After three years of study in Italy, Jones had returned to England imbued with the ideals of classic propriety, dignified restraint, and strong, lucid compositions. His philosophy was to develop the plan in terms of use and then to compose and adorn the structure in terms of good taste and function. His interiors were carefully proportioned and simple in basic shape; the enrichment was vigorous but thoughtfully placed and harmonious. Coleshill (Figs. 519A and B) is a good example of the style that Inigo Jones introduced.

A

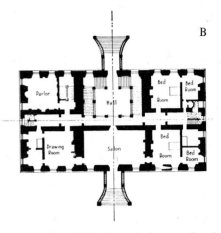

B

Coleshill House (1650–1662) in Berkshire, designed by Sir Roger Pratt, probably with advice from Inigo Jones, is an excellent example of the restrained monumentality of the period. Although built during the Commonwealth, it carried forward design trends of the Early Jacobean period and anticipated Georgian practices. Houses of this sort set a tradition that remained forceful into the 1900s. (*Reprinted from* The Evolving House *by Albert Bemis and John Burchard by permission of The M.I.T. Press, Cambridge, Massachusetts. Copyright 1933 by Albert Farwell Bemis*)

Above left. A vertical, central axis established by the stairway, door, window, and dormer terminates in the cupola. Each floor is delineated by moldings, and a simple cornice relates the block of the building to the roof. Although the house is Italian in inspiration, the steeper roof and emphatic chimneys mark it as English.

Above. The plan shows an orderly disposition of rooms balanced around two intersecting axes. The hall with its double stairway functions as an impressive entrance.

A truly British union of northern spirit and southern Renaissance had been achieved during the Early Jacobean period, and Inigo Jones introduced pure Classical coherence. With the beheading of Charles I in 1649, almost all building in the country ceased; and during the eleven-year Commonwealth regime, puritanical ideas of simple austerity were fostered by Cromwell.

THE ENGLISH BAROQUE AND ROCOCO: c. 1660–1760

In 1660, Charles II came out of exile in Holland and ascended the throne of England as the first Restoration monarch after the Commonwealth. Charles II was in sympathy with the lavish ostentation that his cousin, Louis XIV, carried to such a high point in France—and the Baroque philosophy of design was transplanted to England. He was supported in this by many of the nobility, who also returned from exile with foreign ideas. But the Baroque concept of centralized, autocratic government was not acceptable to many Englishmen, and Baroque architectural grandeur made only a few of the English feel at home. Furniture, however, felt the Baroque influence rather strongly. Gradually in the 1730s the Rococo spirit appeared, but the change was neither so abrupt nor complete as in France. Many Baroque practices, such as the elaboration around doorways, persisted until the end of the period, as did the restrained Classicism that Inigo Jones had introduced around 1650. Because there are no sharp dividing lines separating these three influences, the discussion will be organized on the basis of the English interpretations that evolved.

The Late Jacobean, William and Mary, and Queen Anne Styles: c. 1660–1714

Sir Christopher Wren (1632–1723), the leading architect during these periods, did not commit himself to any one fashion. Although many of his churches are Baroque in concept, he also designed Gothic structures, and his red-brick additions to the royal Palace of Hampton Court are quiet and residential in character. **Sir John Vanbrugh** (1664–1726), another influential architect, was thoroughly imbued with the Baroque and fully expressed it in the great palaces (Fig. 523A) that he designed. But the great majority of architects built houses along the Renaissance lines laid down earlier by Inigo Jones and his followers.

Plans. Logic and convenience distinguish the plans of the many homes that were truly English. Separate rooms for relaxation, dining, and sleeping were sensibly related to one another. A strong continuing axis carried through the house and landscape from front to back to form the backbone of the design. A driveway, forecourt, or walk brought the visitor to the centered front steps, into a spacious entrance hall, through a wide doorway into the major living room, and then through doors and down steps to a formal garden.

Exterior and gardens. Straightforward simplicity, rectangularity, and symmetry characterized the exteriors, which were usually of red brick and had tile roofs pierced by dormers above a projecting cornice. Windows and doors were pleasantly proportioned, well spaced, and quietly ornamented. Although French gardens, especially Versailles (Fig. 504B), in which architecture and landscape developed from a single idea were highly esteemed, the English work was much simpler. Long, straight avenues of trees, often three or five radiating from the same point, shaded wide, convenient paths and helped join the house with its setting. Embroidery-like parterres were popular but were subordinated to large expanses of lawn. Sculpture, balustrades, and so on were cautiously used.

A Late Jacobean–William and Mary room (1670–1700) in the style generated by Sir Christopher Wren. Quiet oak paneling contrasts with vigorous carving in the panels and cornice, above the doors, and around the painting. The plaster ceiling also has quiet and lively areas, quite different from that seen in Figure 515. The furniture is from several related English Baroque periods. The tables at the left are in the William and Mary style, the side chair at the right anticipates the Queen Anne fashion, and the mirrors are also Queen Anne. The cupboard at the left is Late Jacobean, with elaborate marquetry in many colors as practiced by the Dutch. (*Thorne European Rooms in Miniature, The Art Institute of Chicago*)

B

A

Far left. A Late Jacobean chair (1685–1688) in the then newly popular walnut that allowed more elaborate carving than the traditional English oak. Strong Baroque influence is seen in the constantly reversing curves of the back panel; but the frame of the chair still has the structural simplicity of Renaissance form. [*Nelson Gallery— Atkins Museum (Nelson Fund), Kansas City, Missouri*]

Left. A walnut cabinet from the time of William and Mary is a lively example of late seventeenth-century furniture. Most conspicuous at a distance are the jaunty, broken-S-curved supports that rest on curved stretchers and ball feet. On closer examination it is the upper section that holds attention. Rectangular in basic shape, the cabinet has doors and sides embellished with intricate, interlacing marquetry. Less complex inlay enhances the drawer, part of the supports, and the stretchers. (*The Metropolitan Museum of Art, New York, Bequest of Annie C. Kane, 1926*)

Interiors. Walls were usually paneled to the cornice. Oak was finished naturally (Fig. 129A), but pine was painted white or green and accented with gilt. The principal rooms often had ornamental carvings in which foliage, flowers, fruit, and numerous unexpected objects were sensitively composed in interweaving designs. Often the ceilings were of richly decorated plaster. The interiors echoed Baroque tendencies in their monumentality, ornamentation, and furnishings, but with only a hint of turbulence. A typical drawing room is shown in Figure 520.

Furnishings. The late seventeenth and early eighteenth centuries were an era of rapid change and of different ideas being developed simultaneously. It can be divided into three phases especially applicable to furnishings.

The Late Jacobean Style: c. 1660–1688. During these years, Baroque exuberance in walnut supplanted the long-cherished, straightforward, structural designs in oak. Spiral-twist turnings were used on the supports of chairs and tables; carving of a heavy, florid character came into prominence (Figs. 485 and 521A) and C- and S-shaped scrolls were introduced. Important additions to English furniture included chests of drawers on stands, and elongated chairs or daybeds.

The William and Mary Style: c. 1688–1702. William of Orange and his wife, Mary, who came from Holland to rule England, reinforced the basic trends but with modifications and some innovations. Furniture became smaller in scale and was characterized by comfortable domesticity. The result was less a fundamental change than an acceptance of fashionable details, as well as the adaptation of Baroque forms to English ways of living. A new love of high polish, of delicate veneers, and of elaborate marquetry and inlay brought greater delicacy to chests (Fig. 521B) and chairs.

The Queen Anne Style: c. 1702-1714. Furniture showed a continuance of the search for comfort, but during Queen Anne's reign chairs (Fig. 522) and case goods became more graceful, sleek, and sophisticated. (Figure 304B, however, shows an example of quite a different trend, also of this period.) The custom of serving tea called for many small tables, and the vogue of collecting Oriental ceramics brought the introduction of china cabinets. Baroque inspiration resulted in many curved, sculptural ornaments, such as scallop shells, acanthus leaves, and broken curves, and in chair seats and backs unified by curves. That the furnishings were moving toward the Rococo is especially noticeable in the cabriole leg, which, while based on Baroque reverse curves, became increasingly slender and refined.

Typical of the Queen Anne style, a walnut armchair has an easy, fluent rhythm. Simple cabriole legs with scroll decorations at the knees differ markedly from the supports in Figure 521B. The curved seat rails permit easy removal of the padded seat. Dutch influence is seen in the shape of the back and molded arms. (*The Minneapolis Institute of Arts, Gift of Mrs. Sumner T. McKnight*)

The Early Georgian Style: c. 1714–1765

The eighteenth century was a great age of English homes and furniture, both of which were strongly echoed in the United States. Widespread interest in house and furniture design was part of the cultural pattern. Except, however, for a very few, very wealthy people, Englishmen continued to want dignified, moderate, comfortable homes and furniture growing out of an English way of life. During the time of George I and George II, what might be called the **Georgian** compromise kept English architecture on its own course while permitting Rococo decoration to play over its interior surfaces and furnishings. Many people wanted to be fashionable, and that meant following the French; but the English temper was not really suited to frivolity. Chippendale helped solve this dilemma as far as furniture was concerned.

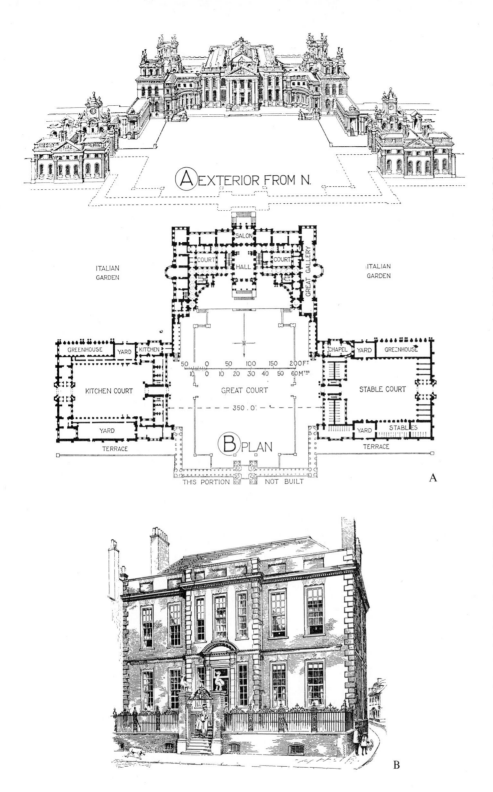

A EXTERIOR FROM N.

ITALIAN GARDEN

ITALIAN GARDEN

SALON

COURT   HALL   COURT

GREAT GALLERY

GREENHOUSE   YARD   KITCHEN

CHAPEL   YARD   GREENHOUSE

KITCHEN COURT

STABLE COURT

YARD

GREAT COURT

YARD   STABLES

TERRACE

— 350.0 —

TERRACE

B PLAN

THIS PORTION   NOT BUILT

A

Blenheim Palace, designed by Sir John Vanbrugh, and built near Oxford between 1705 and 1720, is one of the most grandiose Baroque mansions in England. In plan and exterior, and in interior design, impressiveness was placed above convenience. The entrance court covers three acres, and the great gallery is 180 by 22 feet. (*Reprinted by permission of the publisher and the copyright owner from Sir Banister Fletcher,* A History of Architecture, *17th ed. Revised by R. A. Cordingley*)

B

Swan House, built in Chichester in 1711, represents what is usually thought of as Georgian architecture. Occasionally built entirely of stone, Georgian houses were typically brick—often, as in this instance, with stone quoins at the corners and stone trim around the doors and windows. The large, double-hung windows are customary, as is the simple rectangularity of the basic masses, the low hip roof, and the tall chimneys. Figures 523A and B point up the vast differences between noble palaces and more modest homes in the eighteenth-century. (*Reprinted by permission of the publisher and the copyright owner from Sir Banister Fletcher,* A History of Architecture, *17th ed. Revised by R. A. Cordingley*)

Plans, exteriors, and interiors. Early Georgian dwellings can be separated into two distinctly different types. The first were the great palaces that stood out as extravagant deviations from the main course of English domestic architecture (Fig. 523A). The second type were the smaller, restrained, typically English houses (Fig. 523B), following the manner associated with Inigo Jones and Sir Christopher Wren. These houses had good, livable plans, and the exteriors were unpretentiously genteel.

An early eighteenth-century room with painted wood walls discreetly divided into rectangular panels forms an unobtrusive background for the furnishings and occupants. The fireplace, enhanced with small-scale ornamentation, is obedient to the disciplined rectangularity of the room. The ceiling has two bands of carved plaster but is much plainer than those seen in Figures 515 and 520. The cabinet and the wing chair are early eighteenth century, but the chair near the center table dates from around 1750. The two console tables, supported by reverse-curved dolphins, are Baroque in character. [*Nelson Gallery—Atkins Museum* (*Nelson Fund*), *Kansas City, Missouri*]

The early interiors were simple but less austere than in the preceding period, and their basic geometry was more evident. Wood walls were painted (Fig. 524). Later, plaster (sometimes with curvilinear designs) was widely used (Fig. 525B), and fabrics, French wallpapers (especially *flock* papers with textured surfaces imitating fabrics), and Chinese scenic wallpapers became popular. Doors, windows, and especially fireplaces were focal points for ornamentation.

Gardens. During this period the English developed an informal, naturalistic approach to landscape design. Imitation of nature was the aim. Freely shaped lawns and meadows, clumps of trees and shrubbery, and informal lakes and meandering streams were punctuated with occasional artificial ruins or little pavilions of Oriental inspiration. Although the rusticity of these landscapes seems at the opposite pole from the fastidious, modified Rococo interiors, both originated in the desire for the unrestrained curves found in nature.

Furniture. During the first part of the century, furniture showed a consistent development of the handsome, comfortable, Queen Anne work. It was characterized by a pure, simple beauty of predominantly curved lines subtly enhanced with carving. Chairs conformed to human dimensions and relaxed postures, and their pleasantly curved backs, arms, and legs made them look comfortable. In the 1730s mahogany had largely replaced walnut. Its greater strength made feasible more-slender Rococo forms, and the ease with which it could be carved suggested more ornamentation.

Thomas Chippendale (1718?–1779) is the celebrated furniture maker of the early Georgian period (Figs. 525A and B). In 1754 he published *The Gentleman and Cabinet-Maker's Director,* a compendium that influenced furniture design enormously and connected his name with much that he never saw. Rather than creating wholly original designs, he refined and combined French Baroque and Rococo curves, Gothic linearity and pointed arches, genteel Queen Anne work, and complicated Chinese fretwork. Among his chairs, for example, are those that are rectangular in outline, straight-legged, and with delicately carved ladder backs, as well as ribbon patterns, Gothic arches, or Chinese frets. Others have cabriole legs of great diversity. Later he produced furniture for houses where the Adam brothers had also worked and was strongly influenced by their restrained, unified interpretation of the classic spirit.

A

Right. The details of a mahogany side chair (c. 1750) show the rare union of strength and grace—oneness without repetition—that typically distinguishes pieces done under Chippendale's influence. The carving at the tops of the staunch cabriole legs visually relates the legs to the seat, and the claw-and-ball feet are decisive terminals. The more slender back has gracefully flaring supports and a carved and pierced splat. (*The Metropolitan Museum of Art, New York, Gift of Judge Irwin Untermeyer, 1951*)

Below. The vivacious Rococo stucco decorations on the walls of a room from Kirtlington Park, Oxfordshire (c. 1748), are free and curvilinear, quite in contrast to those of the room opposite. The massive library table, the small table at the end of the room, the Chippendale-type chairs, and the playful chandelier are in the same spirit as the walls and ceiling. (*The Metropolitan Museum of Art, New York, Fletcher Fund, 1932*)

B

The furniture just described fitted well into the smaller homes but was not adequately monumental for the great edifices. Architects, therefore, designed furniture to fit their architecture rather than their clients. It was large in size and scale, opulent and boldly curved, with columns, cornices, and pediments, and foretold some of the tendencies of the Neoclassic period.

The Baroque-Rococo period in England was a prosperous one in which many ideas were tried and assimilated with varying degrees of success. These included the continuing traditions of Jones's and Wren's dignified houses and of the unpretentious Queen Anne furniture, and of more than a flirtation with French and Oriental ornamentation. Somehow or other, some or all of these influences were pleasantly combined in Early Georgian homes. Perhaps it is their variety, their homelike gathering of many things, that still gives them and their American counterparts wide appeal.

ENGLISH NEOCLASSICISM: c. 1760–1837

The basic characteristics of this period as a whole have been discussed in Chaper 21. In England, it can be divided into two phases.

Early English Neoclassicism, or the Late Georgian Style: c. 1760–1800

At about the time the French were losing interest in playful curves, the English, too, were ready for a different approach to design, and they found it in the work of **Robert Adam** (1728–1792), whose name is often used as epitomizing the Early Neoclassic in England. After careful study of the dignity of Roman palaces and the delicacy of Pompeian decoration, Adam integrated these in houses, rooms (Color Fig. 28), and furniture of unparalleled unity. His great concern as an architect and a designer of interiors and of all kinds of furnishings was that every part of the dwelling be perfectly attuned to the whole, and he was happiest when entrusted with the design of the house and everything that was placed in it.

Plans, exteriors, and gardens. Although there was no immediate, drastic change in the plans, exteriors, and gardens of homes, a new line of development began that was influenced, in part, by Robert Adam. In plans, the earlier, eighteenth-century concern with privacy and convenience was intensified, but rooms shaped as ovals, circles, octagons, squares, and rectangles, often with niches, were organized to produce a sequential feeling of spatial unfolding that made even city houses seem large and interesting (Fig. 526).

The exteriors of the typical brick houses retained the simplicity of well-proportioned masses with orderly arrangements of windows and doors. They became, however, smaller in scale, more refined and coherent in detail, and generally with flatter surfaces—variety and interest were brought by slightly projecting pavilions and subtly proportioned pilasters. Garden design continued as a simplified translation of French formalism or in the newer naturalistic manner.

Interiors. Although quite as formal and precise as the exteriors, the interiors did not share their simplicity. First, there was the progressive variation of room volumes. Second, there was the rich but delicate classic ornament that enlivened but did not overwhelm the plain surface or distract from the space these surfaces

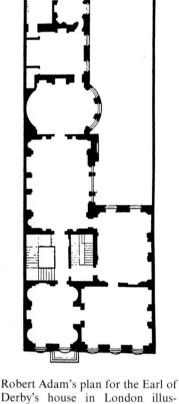

Robert Adam's plan for the Earl of Derby's house in London illustrates how rooms were shaped for use, grace, and sequential variety in unity. (*Reprinted from* The Works in Architecture of Robert and James Adam)

A Hepplewhite-style settee (c. 1785) of satinwood, and upholstered in green taffeta, has slender, straight legs and interlacing heart-shaped back. The painted ornament is obedient to the forms it enhances. (*The Metropolitan Museum of Art, New York, Fletcher Fund, 1929*)

enclosed. Because of its plastic susceptibility to small-scale ornament, plaster replaced wood as the major wall material. When wood was used, it—like the plaster—was usually painted white or a pale color to dematerialize it in the interests of the whole composition. Moldings, friezes, and ceilings had such Greek or Pompeian ornamentation as frets, vase forms, honeysuckle, and a variety of arabesques (Color Fig. 28). Painted panels, too, were fitted into appropriate spots. Fireplace designs were elaborated and slenderized, and became one of the chief inspirations for the later eighteenth-century American mantelpieces. Ornament, though widely used, was always self-contained in its space and was repeated sufficiently to bring continuity to the whole. Pilasters regularized and stabilized wall compositions. A hitherto-undreamed-of unity was sometimes established by rugs that exactly repeated the ceiling patterns above them (Color Fig. 28).

Furniture. The ancient sources of inspiration in addition to some French influence made the furniture of this period the most delicate that England produced. Although Chippendale executed furniture with Neoclassic characteristics, it was first Adam and then Sheraton and Hepplewhite who were the leaders.

Robert Adam's furniture makes evident his preoccupation with architectural concepts in its straight-lined rectangularity combined with geometric curves, clear revelation of structure, and ornament intrinsically in scale and character with the piece and its setting. Sideboards, side tables, and settees, mirrors and commodes were his major contributions to furniture design.

George Hepplewhite, from around 1760 until his death in 1786, designed furniture that showed a strong Adam influence and was of exceptionally graceful and charming elegance (Color Fig. 28). After early experiments with Rococo shapes, he soon turned to straight lines and geometric curves. His continued influence, like Chippendale's, was assured by a book of furniture designs published two years after his death. Hepplewhite-style chairs (and also settees, as illustrated in Fig. 527) had straight, round, or square legs tapered toward spade or thimble feet. Chair backs were of five types—camel, heart, oval, shield, and wheel—but all were rounded in contour and filled with pierced, usually lightly

Six drawings for chair backs are only a small sample of the many designs Sheraton illustrated. Straight lines and segments of circles or ellipses rather than serpentine Rococo curves are basic characteristics of his style. The vertical members are usually linear and delicately carved; the top rails are often straight, but convex and concave curves frequently appear. The shield back (*lower row, center*) was also a favorite shape, and elongated urns, lyres, and garlands were among the motifs employed. (*Reprinted from Thomas Sheraton,* Cabinet Maker and Upholsterer's Drawing-Book)

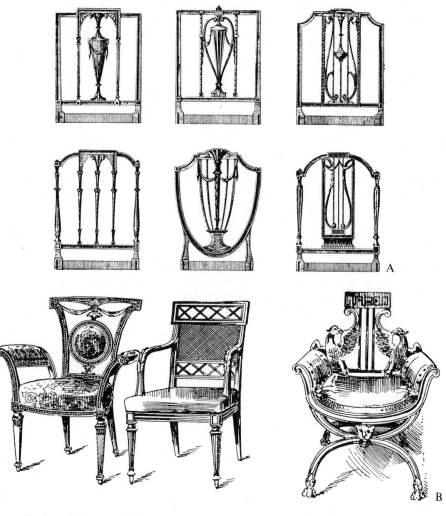

Three of Sheraton's later designs are marked by the heavy handling of classical motifs popular at the time and by a continuing search for new forms that led both to the almost-grotesque (*far right*) and to variations of Neoclassic shapes (*left and center*). (*Reprinted from Thomas A. Strange,* English Furniture, Decoration, Woodwork and Allied Arts)

carved splats. The serpentine curve used on the top of the shield-back chairs was frequently also the dominant contour of sideboards and console tables. The favorite satinwood was frequently inlaid with delicate, architectural motifs, but much of this furniture had painted decorations.

Thomas Sheraton (1751–1806) established his reputation by the book he published in 1791. In many details, his earlier furniture (Fig. 528A) resembled that by Hepplewhite: the scale was small and the forms slender; the woods were the same; inlay and painted medallions were used decoratively; and chair legs were almost identical. Chief among the differences were greater emphasis on straight lines, especially noticeable in chair backs; back legs of chairs continuing into the back braces; arcs of circles combined with straight lines, rather than continuous, serpentine curves; Wedgwood plaques used as decorations; and sturdier construction throughout. His later work (Fig. 528B) became much heavier and developed into the Regency style.

Late English Neoclassicism, or the English Regency Style: c. 1790–1837

As time went on, bold simplicity and large-scale compositions replaced the somewhat delicate Early Neoclassic work. The exteriors of houses became more monumental, geometric forms were emphasized, and ornament was chastened. House plans and gardens had no especially distinctive qualities, but interiors were much plainer. Often the walls were plastered and painted with quite intense, dark shades of brown, green, or red, against which white pilasters, cornices, and window and door frames stood out. Sometimes the walls were painted to imitate draperies or marble. In other homes pale, clear colors were favored, and wallpapers decorated with floral patterns, stripes, or stars were combined with printed chintz and linen.

Late Neoclassic furniture, often referred to as **English Regency,** forms a bridge between the delicate designs of Sheraton and the heavier Victorian work of the nineteenth century. The creativity that led to the great eighteenth-century designs was gone, and in its place came a literal imitation of Roman, Greek, and Egyptian forms and ornament, even by Sheraton himself, as in Figure 528B. Although generally heavy and masculine, as was the French Directoire and Empire work, Regency furniture shows considerable diversity. Some chairs closely resembled the early work of Sheraton, but curving X-shaped supports held up many chairs, and old Roman forms—couches with curved ends for example—were revived. Case goods were invariably heavy and adorned with ornament originally designed for buildings. In isolated instances, handsome pieces were produced, but far more often forms were clumsy in themselves and in their relationships, and ornament was applied to them in a way that anticipated the furniture of the Victorian Age.

REVIVALS, VICTORIANISM, AND THE CRYSTAL PALACE: THE NINETEENTH CENTURY

As in France, nineteenth-century English architecture and design were marked by a series of turbulent crosscurrents. The **Gothic** was the first and most significant of the medieval styles to be reviewed in the search for the romantic and picturesque that marked this period, with results that were more often a transcription of outer forms than a penetration of the essence. Permeating the entire period was the exuberant, capricious **Victorian** design that uncritically combined without integrating a bewildering array of forms and ornament (Fig. 529). Details from such scattered sources as English Elizabethan, Jacobean,

Below. The "Kenilworth Buffet," displayed at England's Great Exposition of 1851 at the Crystal Palace, was carved from a colossal oak tree felled near Kenilworth Castle by Messrs. Cookes and Sons. The ornamentation, an uninhibited mixture of carved forms, was inspired by *Kenilworth,* Sir Walter Scott's novel of the romance of Queen Elizabeth I and the Earl of Leicester. Statuettes of such persons as Shakespeare and Sir Walter Raleigh, heterogeneous monograms, Elizabethan motifs, and other forms for which it is difficult to trace the lineage crowd the surface. Its design could be called "pure Victorian." (*Reprinted from* The Illustrated Exhibitor, *August 16, 1851*)

and Regency; French Baroque and Rococo; and the Orient were all used at one time or another, often by untrained designers. Typically bold and emphatic, Victorian architecture, furniture, and decorative objects ranged from the coarse and clumsy to the vigorous but controlled examples of eclectic design.

While all of this was going on, engineers designed ingenious, daring bridges, railway stations, and the Crystal Palace in London, constructions that advanced the technology of metal and glass architecture (Fig. 530) and gradually established new concepts of design. A renewed respect for craftsmanship and materials, as well as for the individuality of the artisan, formed the basis for the **Arts and Crafts movement** that began after mid-century as a protest against tasteless, uninspiring, mass-produced objects. Some of this furniture, pottery, glass, textiles, and wallpaper had a welcome, fresh, and invigorating simplicity. Although the movement itself was not long-lived, it had some influence on machine-made objects of the time, and it was a forerunner of the contemporary interest in the handcrafts and in creative rather than imitative design.

The Crystal Palace, designed by Joseph Paxton to house the Great Exposition of 1851 in London, was the first large building (1851 feet long and covering an area of 800,000 square feet) constructed of glass, iron, and timber. In this revolutionary structure, with its structural simplicity clearly revealed, the romantic eclecticism of the period was displayed in the form of objects designed in every known style. The wrought-iron gateway, with its clustered, florid curves, and the buffet shown in Figure 529 are examples. (*Etching by Lothar Bucher, 1851*)

A Carver armchair (1650–1700), named after one owned by Governor Carver of Plymouth, has the stalwart, rectangular simplicity of the Early American period. Made of ash, the parts are turned with just enough diversity to prevent monotony. The frame is agreeably proportioned, and the rush seat is resilient. (*The Metropolitan Museum of Art, New York, Gift of Mrs. Russell Sage, 1909*)

25 · The United States

When the earliest settlers landed on these shores, they brought with them the building traditions of their homelands. Adapting to the necessities imposed by the weather and by different construction materials, they built modified developments of the homes they had known in Europe. Along the Atlantic Coast the English rapidly gained leadership, and because their homes and furniture were the most lasting, widespread factors in the American tradition, we will concentrate on that work.

It should not, however, be forgotten what other groups did. The Dutch, chiefly around New York, built city houses with steeply gabled roofs and dormers, and their farmhouses, with roofs sloping generously down and out to cover the long front porches, were quite different from English work. In and around Pennsylvania, the Germans established a tradition of building stalwart, charming houses of stone that had a distinctive character. The French, in Louisiana and in occasional districts in eastern seaboard cities, produced their own style, a blending of French medieval features and of the outdoor, roofed galleries the Spanish developed in the humid atmospheres of the West Indies and Central America, which set the pattern for plantation houses in the South. Especially in the Southwest, but also in Florida, the Spanish built houses much like those in their native land. Built around an open, arcaded courtyard, their thick-walled, masonry houses with small windows and gently pitched tile roofs have lasting appeal.

THE EARLY COLONIAL STYLE: c. 1630–1730

Of special interest is the work done in New England. The Pilgrims arrived two centuries after the Renaissance began in Florence. In the early seventeenth century the Baroque spirit dominated Italy, and in France the Renaissance was nearing its end. But America was just beginning, and the Pilgrims, by nature and socioeconomic position, knew little about what the fashionable wealthy had done. They were stern, hard-working men and women who were struggling for religious freedom and physical survival. There was neither time nor inclination to search for beauty, self-conscious individuality, or architectural style. Immediate need for protection forced these early settlers to live in caves, dugouts, or structures much poorer than they had known at home. As soon as possible they began to build from memories of their homeland, but the outcomes were affected by the climate, the available materials, and the scarcity of craftsmen. Out of these conditions their houses developed the following characteristics:

- *Aims*—use and economy
- *Character*—straightforward, vigorous solutions of problems; strength and directness akin to medieval houses; crude and uncomfortable
- *Design*—highly unified because there was so little variety; symmetrical or asymmetrical balance as indicated by function; rhythms decisive and rectangular; dominance and subordination almost entirely the direct result of function
- *Size*—no larger than necessary for basic needs
- *Scale*—moderately large (no time or tools for refinements)
- *Shapes*—dictated by function and memories of what they had known at home; strong, basic rectangularity; curves limited to a few rounded parts of furniture; minimum of softening, transitional forms
- *Ornament*—fortuitous structural and textural enrichment growing directly out of material or process; minimum of applied ornamentation until later in the period
- *Colors*—natural materials: wood, brick, stone, metal, and wool (dyed in a few strong colors)

Plans. Then, as now, economy was a controlling factor. The typical earliest plans were small, compact, simple rectangles divided into a small entrance area at one side with a tiny stairway to a low attic, and with one multipurpose room for living, cooking, eating, and storing, dominated by a large fireplace that served for heating, lighting, and cooking.

As the family grew and resources increased, a parlor similar in size and shape to the first room was added at the other side of the entrance; then a lean-to was added at the rear for cooking and sleeping, producing the "saltbox" house, which was to persist into the late eighteenth century and reappear in the twentieth century. Soon houses were built with upper stories. Characteristic of all early houses is the large, central chimney into which went the smoke from as many as three fireplaces on each floor (Figs. 537B–E). Equally characteristic was the functional freedom with which the parts of the home were balanced. Asymmetrical balance prevailed when indicated by use, economy, or the nature of the site on which the house was to be built; and additions to the home were often disposed in a picturesque manner. If, however, there was no good reason for asymmetrical balance, the design was symmetrical.

The Whipple house in Ipswich, Massachusetts, is a well-preserved example of a typical Early American exterior. The original one-room structure was built around 1640; the house was expanded to its present size in 1682. It has a central chimney, narrow clapboarding, and asymmetrically placed windows with diamond-shaped leading to hold the small panes of glass. (*Photograph by Frank O. Branzetti. Library of Congress*)

Exteriors. The Whipple house (Fig. 533) is a well-preserved, characteristic example of seventeenth-century exteriors. It is severely simple, strong as a blockhouse, and promises the protection then needed. It is also undeniably handsome. The steeply pitched roof is unbroken by dormers, and the upper stories project over those below, a device reminiscent of many medieval houses. Windows are small, frequently grouped, and asymmetrical but orderly. They are of the casement type and filled with small, diamond-shaped glass set in lead frames (see also Fig. 534). Such houses were built of heavy oak posts and beams, and at first the spaces between were filled with wattle and daub (twigs and clay), later with brick or stone. But the extreme climate quickly led to the innovation of an outer layer of clapboard siding (overlapping, horizontal boards), which changed the exterior from the picturesqueness of a completely exposed structure of varied materials to the quiet simplicity of weathered, silver-gray boards. Later, the clapboards were painted dark brown or red, and still later white or light colors.

Interiors. Rooms were small, rectangular spaces with low ceilings of exposed, heavy beams (Fig. 534) and very large, unornamented fireplaces (Fig. 36B). Plaster, vertical boards, or both sheathed the walls. Floors in the first houses were beaten clay; then wide oak planks were used. The total effect was darkish, low, and enclosing, for protection from the environment and conservation of heat were primary aims.

Furnishings. Made by local craftsmen or imported from England, furniture was a combination of simplified medieval, Elizabethan, and Jacobean influences, as seen in Figures 531 and 534. It was as four-square as the house in outline, but the severity was relieved by turned arms and legs on chairs, by some flat carving, and by paint.

Various woods were used for their special properties: soft, easy-to-work, but durable pine; close-grained maple was favored for turned parts; and tough oak, ash, and hickory for strength, as in the supports of chairs. By 1700 walnut was the preferred wood, and it remained in favor long after the introduction of mahogany. Later in the century the furniture used by the well-to-do seaboard merchants was much influenced by the William and Mary style and by contacts with Holland, Spain, and the Orient. In this walnut furniture can be found the beginnings of the eighteenth-century practices: inverted cup-shaped and spiral turnings, elementary cabriole legs, and somewhat clumsy carved shells and pediments.

Seating consisted chiefly of the simplest possible stools and benches, some with heat-conserving high backs, and a few cane- or wood-seated chairs carefully reserved for the elders.

Tables of the medieval trestle type were used in many houses (Fig. 36B), but small tables gave hint of the variety that was to come in the eighteenth century. Around 1700 a number of variations on the drop-leaf arrangement came into use.

Case goods consisted of chests and boxes. Paneled chests with drawers were

A room from Hart House (c. 1670), also from Ipswich, is arranged as a multipurpose room. A heavy, centered beam supports the lighter ones going across the room. With the exception of the sturdy gateleg table from Pennsylvania, all of the furniture is from New England. The oak court cupboard is a simplified version of Elizabethan furniture. The carved wainscot chair at the left is strongly architectural, and the sturdy stool is typical of the Early American period. (*Henry Francis du Pont Winterthur Museum*)

534

An Early American oak and pine chest on drawers (1704) is a type often found in seventeenth-century Connecticut homes. Its simple, boxy shape is emphasized by horizontal moldings and the carved balusters delineating the upper section; but the curvilinear, low relief carving and the painted decorations show unexpected playfulness. (*The Art Institute of Chicago*)

low and sometimes decorated with simple, flat carving and painted designs in red, black, and yellow (Fig. 535). For greater convenience, the chest was placed at a fairly early time on a stand with drawers, and this became the high chest or highboy. Small, boxlike chests with flat or slanted tops stood on tables to hold spices or the few books and papers and the all-important Bible.

Beds were mere frames with slats or ropes holding mattress bags of straw or feathers. Since they were often in the living room and no part of the home was warm, hangings on the beds were often used to meet the need for warmth and privacy.

Textiles and accessories were limited in number, durable, and strong in character. Window and bed curtains were of red-brown, indigo, and natural home-spun wool and occasionally linen. Checkered weaves, India prints, and knotted "Turkey" work (imitating Oriental rugs) were introduced toward the end of the century, about the time that the natural wood and plaster background changed to paneling painted brown, red, green, or yellow. The first dishes were platters, bowls, and goblets made of wood burls, supplemented by a few pieces of imported glazed earthenware pieces, although the more prosperous people imported pewter or silver dishes. All used iron andirons, cranes, kettles, and candleholders made by blacksmiths.

THE COLONIAL GEORGIAN STYLE: c. 1700–1790

Toward the end of the seventeenth century, increased prosperity and population brought some stratification in American society, and those in the upper levels increasingly desired greater elegance and refinement in their homes. They had a "margin for leisure" and looked to England, especially to the work of Inigo Jones and Sir Christopher Wren, for inspiration. Sometimes referred to as the "Age of Architectural Books," this period was one in which English and Italian handbooks with explicit details became common. Although most houses built in this period followed seventeenth-century precedent, the larger ones, especially in cities or on extensive estates in the South, grew from new ways of thinking and building. The homes were smaller and less elaborate than those of the English, but considerably larger and richer than those of the Early Colonial period. The work of each region had its own special character, although all shared a common set of aims and language of design.

Plans. Houses became larger, with more separate rooms, and circulation was greatly improved by a spacious central hall, which had been precluded in Early Colonial houses by the single central chimney. Often the plans are classified by number and position of chimneys (Figs. 537B, C, D, and E). Strict symmetry is noticeable in all but a very few plans. In the northern states, the climate kept houses compact, but in the milder southern states they spread their wings, with service buildings connected by arcades in miniature versions of the great eighteenth-century English palaces.

Exteriors and gardens. We have already seen in the Ropes Memorial (Fig. 419) a typical eighteenth-century New England exterior, and Figure 536 illustrates one from Virginia. Both were influenced by the English Georgian style. Although they were not quite designed according to formula, most exteriors showed some or all of the following characteristics: simple, symmetrical, rectangular mass with pitched roof; long side facing the street; centered doorway emphasized with simple moldings, pilasters, columns, pediments, or a small porch; vertical windows with two double-hung sashes filled with small rectangular panes, slightly or much emphasized by moldings or pediments and dark shutters; usually two windows at each side of the door and five windows in the story above; and cornices, ranging from simple projecting moldings to complexly ornamented types, forming transitions from wall to roof. As the style developed, roofs became flatter and were often partially or almost completely concealed by balustrades.

Westover, built around 1730 in Charles County, Virginia, is one of the most handsome Georgian homes in the United States. The dark-red brick emphasizes the white ornamentation, especially the impressive entrance. It differs markedly from the Whipple house but bears a decided resemblance to Coleshill (Fig. 519), built in England almost a century earlier. (*Photograph by Thomas T. Waterman. Library of Congress*)

29

Monticello, the country home of Thomas Jefferson, designed and
built in Albemarle County, Virginia, between 1770 and 1808,
marked the beginning of the Federal style in the United States.
The long, low block of the dark-red brick house is capped by two
white balustrades that de-emphasize the low-pitched roof. A series
of setbacks, terminating in bays at each end, contribute to the
vigorous three-dimensionality that pervades the structure. A wide
flight of steps leads up to an impressive portico. Above it rises a
domed octagon that completes the dignified, classically inspired
composition. (*Thomas Jefferson Memorial Foundation, Inc.*)

The parlor from Vauxhall Gardens, a house built in southern New Jersey c. 1700–1725, is appropriately furnished chiefly with American pieces in the Queen Anne style, popular during the Colonial Georgian period. The paneling of the fireplace wall is comparatively simple, and the wood is unpainted. Understated Delft tiles frame the fireplace opening. The wall at the left is covered with green flocked canvas from England, in a design that is similar in character to the cut-velvet upholstery on the chairs. On a large, multicolored, vigorously patterned Oriental rug stand a typical Queen Anne drop-leaf table and three chairs with smoothly flowing lines and restrained ornamentation. Above the table is a Dutch chandelier of metal that is in harmony with the furniture and especially with the accessories on the table. The high walnut chest, made around 1750, is in the English Georgian tradition. (*Henry Francis du Pont Winterthur Museum*)

30

31

A room from the Samuel Powel house, Philadelphia, c. 1768, juxtaposes angular linearity and Rococo curves in a vigorous amalgamation of diverse Colonial Georgian elements. The geometrically paneled wood fireplace wall, painted off-white, contrasts sharply with the Oriental wallpaper, the freely extended, carved plaster ceiling ornamentation, the gay crystal chandelier, and the fluently curved settee and wing chair. The fireplace facing of densely figured gray marble is visually contained by a geometric molding. Ornate, scroll-shaped consoles support a thin, linear mantel. The overmantel is also rectilinear, accented by Rococo carving in the projecting corners, and topped by a broken pediment that repeats at smaller scale the design of the cornice above. The warm analogous color scheme ranges from the vivid red of the upholstery, through the red-orange of the floor and furniture wood, to the soft yellow of the wallpaper and is moderated by the large expanses of white on the paneled walls and the ceiling, and by the physical coolness of the bare floor. (*The Metropolitan Museum of Art, New York*)

32

The Red Room in the White House, Washington, D.C., has recently been restored in the Neoclassic style of 1810–1830, which is appropriate to the architectural style of the building. The walls, hung with cerise silk bordered with gold scrolls, have a white dado at the base, white frames around doors and windows, and a simple cornice with egg-and-dart moldings joining the walls and the white ceiling. Against this clearly ordered background, the furnishings and accessories find their place. The French and American Empire furniture have frames of dark wood and cerise upholstery, both embellished with gold motifs typical of the period. A red and beige Savonnerie carpet unifies the furniture. A large gilt chandelier, smaller lamps and accessories, and historical paintings provide many points of concentrated interest. The predominately red color scheme belongs to the monochromatic category, but a tendency toward monotony is relieved by large and small areas of white, by the dark wood and paintings, and by the many gold accents. (© *White House Historical Association. Photograph by National Geographic Society*)

A

Above. A faithful restoration of the Colonial Georgian garden of the Deane house in Williamsburg, Virginia, is based on eighteenth-century records. The symmetrical, geometric plan has brick walks dividing flower beds accented by clipped boxwood hedges and regularly spaced trees. Higher, conical-shaped boxwood accentuates the corners of the beds. A white wood picket fence encloses the garden on the left side. (*Photograph by Richard Garrison. Colonial Williamsburg, Inc.*)

Right. Colonial Georgian house plans, almost invariably symmetrical, are often classified by their chimney arrangements. (B) Large central chimneys with three fireplaces were used in early types such as the Whipple house (Fig. 533). (C) Two end chimneys permitted the center of the house to become a spacious stair hall. (D) Two interior chimneys, as in the Ropes Memorial (Fig. 419), provided fireplaces for four rooms and allowed a central hall leading through the house. (E) Four end chimneys, as in Westover (Fig. 536), were the final development in Colonial chimney arrangements. (*Reprinted from* The Evolving House *by Albert Bemis and John Burchard by permission of The M.I.T. Press, Cambridge, Massachusetts. Copyright 1933 by Albert Farwell Bemis*)

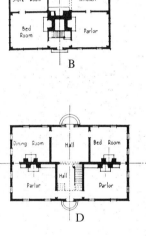

B

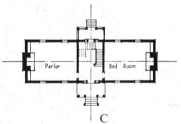

C

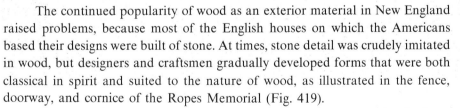

D

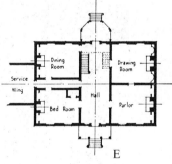

E

The continued popularity of wood as an exterior material in New England raised problems, because most of the English houses on which the Americans based their designs were built of stone. At times, stone detail was crudely imitated in wood, but designers and craftsmen gradually developed forms that were both classical in spirit and suited to the nature of wood, as illustrated in the fence, doorway, and cornice of the Ropes Memorial (Fig. 419).

Gardens, too, followed English precedent but were more modest. On large properties, such as Westover, sweeping expanses of lawn with well-placed trees were dominant features, but at the sides or back of the house smaller gardens, similar to that shown in Figure 537A, were in fashion. On smaller sites, lawns and formal gardens were necessarily reduced in size. Such architectural features as handsome fences, pergolas, and trellises of wood painted white accented the composition.

Interiors. The three rooms from this period shown in Color Figures 5, 30, and 31 suggest the diversity of design, as do Figures 314 and 538. The bedroom from Patuxent Manor and the Vauxhall room are comparatively quiet and restrained, but the living room from the Powel house is a lively combination of elements. All of these rooms, however, share an architectural treatment of walls and sometimes ceilings; fireplaces (if present) are treated as focal points; frames of varying degrees of emphasis outline windows and doors. Renaissance, Baroque, and Rococo decorative motifs are freely combined.

In comparison with the seventeenth century, interiors of this period were more open and spacious: rooms were larger with higher ceilings; windows were much larger and more numerous; and openings between rooms were increased in size. The plain, vertical boarding of the seventeenth century gave way to paneling with clearly demarked units. Sometimes wood paneling was confined to the fireplace wall, with a dado around the other walls (Color Figs. 30 and 31), but in many instances it went from floor to ceiling (Fig. 538). Plaster walls, if not covered by paper or fabric, were painted in light, pastel colors or more positive, intense tones so that the qualities of the basic material did not distract attention from the details of panels, moldings, dados, and so on. Fully developed Colonial Georgian interiors have a rare coalition of logic and fancy, reticence and exclamation, marking a century that saw the decline of the Baroque, the rise and fall of the Rococo, and the light delicacy of Early Neoclassicism lead into the pomposity of the Empire period.

Furnishings. Changes in furniture were as marked as changes in plans, exteriors, and interior design. Lightness, elegance, and curves supplanted the sturdy

A bedroom that is also a sitting room, from Patuxent Manor, Maryland (1744), shows the serene integration of one aspect of the Colonial Georgian interior. The completely but discreetly paneled walls, painted yellow-gray, emphasize the handsome contours of the dark mahogany furniture. The plain wood floor is a foil for the multicolored Oriental rugs. The chairs, chest, and card tables on each side of the bed follow Chippendale designs, and the Philadelphia tea table with a pie-crust top is set with English porcelain. The imposing bed has crewel embroidery curtains. (*Henry Francis du Pont Winterthur Museum*)

538

Substantial in material, construction, and shape, a block-front dressing table (c. 1750–1775) from Rhode Island shows Chippendale influence. Resting on a sturdy base with eight short, S-curved feet, the well-scaled upper portion is simple and clear in contour. The most noticeable ornaments are the four large shell carvings and the outspreading metal plates of the drawer handles. Closer observation reveals that the two shells above the projecting side sections of the drawers are convex; the concavity of the other two shells reflects the receding kneehole section. (*The Metropolitan Museum of Art, New York, Gift of Mrs. Russell Sage, 1909*)

angularity of seventeenth-century designs (compare Fig. 534 with Fig. 538). Reverse curves, as seen in the cabriole legs of chairs, chests, and tables (Color Figs. 30 and 31), were a basic motif. Although American eighteenth-century furniture closely resembled English designs, it relied more on linear rhythm than on rich materials or ornament; and by 1750 distinctive styles of furniture developed in Boston, Newport, New York, and Philadelphia. Walnut and mahogany were the major woods; maple and pine were used for more humble country homes.

Seating pieces were varied but generally were shaped to fit the human form. Queen Anne chairs with cabriole legs, smooth slipper feet, and splat backs were typical in the earlier decades (Color Fig. 30). Upholstered couches and chairs, including the comfortable wing chair, became increasingly popular. By 1760, Chippendale-inspired chairs with bow backs and pierced splats (Fig. 538) came into use, and the straight leg began to compete with the cabriole form. All-wood Windsor chairs, which combined strength, lightness, simplicity of construction, and comfort, came to America around 1725 and were widespread in modest homes by 1760. They were made in many forms: with or without headrests, writing arms, and drawers under the seat.

Tables of the simple gateleg type were succeeded by those with cabriole legs and drop leaves (Color Fig. 30), later enlarged by adding semicircular ends, and were used along with rectangular side or serving tables. Rimmed tea tables, circular stands supported on tripod bases (Color Fig. 31), and card tables (some of them folding) with sturdy legs were widely used (Fig. 538).

Case goods, consisting of lowboys (Figs. 538 and 539), chest-on-chests, and secretaries (an early example of multipurpose, unit furniture produced by putting a bookcase on top of a desk), were handsomely proportioned, enriched with carved panels, shells, fluting, scrolled pediments, finials, and fine imported brass hardware, and were often supported on slender cabriole legs (Fig. 93B).

Beds were large and imposing, and the functional hangings were integral components of the design (Fig. 538). After 1750 more attention was given to the frames, which by then had finely reeded posts, cabriole legs, and claw-and-ball feet; the hangings slowly diminished in size and then disappeared to expose the four tall posts as vestiges with no function other than decoration.

Textiles of great diversity ranged from luxurious silk damask, brocade draperies and upholstery, and Oriental rugs (Fig. 538) to the more serviceable wool, linen, and cotton curtains and upholstery, and to hooked or braided rugs that made the humble dwellings as cheerful, if not as refined, as the larger homes.

Accessories, both made at home and imported, contributed greatly to the sparkle and richness of interiors. "China" was imported from the Orient; but good glassware was made at home. Pewter was widely distributed, and the silversmiths, including Paul Revere, raised their art high. Mirrors became larger, with carved and gilded frames. Lighting was greatly improved with better candles, whale-oil lamps, glittering chandeliers (Color Fig. 30), and ingenious and beautiful glass and metal reflectors and ornaments.

The eighteenth century in the United States was an age of assimilation and achievement. Although houses were designed from handbooks and furnishings derived from European models, the original styles were not slavishly copied. Proportions were seldom "correct," but they were spirited. Ornament was seldom "pure," and the whole ensemble did not follow the rules later laid down for the guidance of the unimaginative. In comparison with eighteenth-century French interiors, many American interiors look provincial, but it is perhaps the minor awkwardnesses, the coalition of native and foreign impulses, and the union of Renaissance, Baroque, and Rococo influences that give Colonial Georgian homes their wide appeal.

The years of the American Revolution and those of the following decade, a period of great social and economic turbulence, were not conducive to notable domestic architecture. By 1790, however, conditions became sufficiently settled for the leaders to look for an architecture expressive of the new republic. But here, as in Europe, a series of revivals that lasted into the twentieth century dominated architecture. Obscured by the fashionable borrowings were the tremendous creativity of engineers who designed structures in more efficient, often beautiful ways and the inventiveness of designers who faced the possibilities of mass-produced furniture that established the basis for twentieth-century work.

AMERICAN NEOCLASSICISM: c. 1790–1850

Turning first to Rome and then to Greece for inspiration, American architects and designers sought dignity and grandeur in simple monumental masses embellished with classical motifs. Baroque and Rococo forms fell from favor. Although there was more attention to authenticity of detail than in the preceding periods, there was also greater freedom and individuality in total planning.

The Federal Style, Roman Revival, or Post-Colonial Style: c. 1790–1820

Although this period had its inception around 1770, with the design of Monticello (Color Fig. 29), it became established some two decades later. Roman architecture somewhat tempered by French and English influence was the fountainhead, but two of the major centers—Virginia and New England—produced quite different results. In New York and other areas, distinctive furniture was produced that was strongly motivated by English designs.

Thomas Jefferson (1743–1826), an accomplished architect as well as statesman, was the leader in Virginia and the surrounding areas. Impatient with Colonial Georgian, which he regarded as crude or frivolous, he created in his own home (Color Fig. 29) and many other structures an architecture that had monumental simplicity, dignified proportions, and detail that visually strengthened the composition. His influence on the architecture of Washington, D.C., was profound.

In Jefferson's architectural philosophy, exteriors, interiors, furnishings, and gardens should be integrated components of one composition. As architectural as the exteriors, his interiors were a perceptively organized series of volumes that varied in size and shape according to their functions. Ample windows and broad openings between rooms made them seem spacious beyond their dimensions, and columns, cornices, and other classical elements looked as though they belonged exactly where they were placed. Bilateral symmetry was followed unless special reasons indicated otherwise. In general character, they were not unlike the Adam room shown in Color Figure 28. The landscaping of Monticello has a breadth and dignity that was new to American work at the time. Toward the river, an expansive semicircular lawn has widely spaced trees around its boundaries to frame views of the river. The gardens on the other side are a little like those shown in Figure 537A, but they are larger in scale, more broadly conceived, and more ingenious in detail. More important, though, is their strict relation to the building.

In New England especially, but also in some other regions (Fig. 541), the **Federal style** was a chastening of the earlier, more vigorous Colonial Georgian work. The influence of Robert Adam's simple masses, slender proportions, and

The Gardner-White-Pingree house, designed by Samuel McIntyre and built in Salem, Massachusetts, in 1810, illustrates the Federal style in New England. Basically a simple, well-proportioned block with nothing but the portico breaking the smoothness of the façade, the house has three floors, which are indicated by thin string courses. A cornice helps protect the walls from rain, and a balustrade hides the low, pitched roof. Generous windows, but of reduced height on the third floor, are remarkably pleasant in shape and arrangement and are emphasized by dark shutters and the flat white architraves above. The focal point is the graceful, projecting portico supported on very slender columns. (*Photograph by Wayne Andrews*)

A fluent, free-hanging staircase dominates the Federal-style entrance hall (c. 1822) of Montmorenci, in Warrenton, North Carolina. Slender balusters and dark handrails and treads call attention to its sinuous form. Plain white walls framed by a dado and cornice and by finely molded plasterwork over the triple windows accentuate the interesting structural design of the Sheraton-type settees and chairs. French influence can be seen in the straight-lined satinwood and mahogany pier table that stands below a mirror with a gilded, foliate frame. The ceramics are from China and the rugs from Turkey. The total effect is open, airy, light, and gay. (*Photograph by Gilbert Ask. Henry Francis du Pont Winterthur Museum*)

small-scale Pompeian detail was assimilated, and by the turn of the century many homes were models of delicate refinement. The Boston houses by Charles Bulfinch, and those in Salem by Samuel McIntyre (Fig. 541), built after 1800, were more original and personal, had greater clarity and more fastidious dignity than earlier work. Wood detail became increasingly refined: moldings were often so thin that they look wiry, and columns were greatly attenuated.

Plans and exteriors. Placement of rooms showed no radical innovations, but more were planned for specific purposes, there was great freedom in room shape and size, and curving stairways that were excitingly free from the walls appeared (Fig. 542). The most typical exteriors were simple to the point of severity. Large, rectangular, three-story masses of red brick (Fig. 541) or painted wood were relieved only by the windows and doorways. Low-pitched roofs were more or less obscured by balustrades. The earlier houses had one-story entrance porches supported by columns, but later slightly recessed entrances framed with delicately detailed side and fan lights were favored. Sometimes whole city blocks were designed so that each house fitted in as a unit.

Interiors and furnishings. Rooms were simply treated. Paneling practically disappeared, and the delicate detail around openings were of wood or plaster.

A

B

Above. A sturdy mahogany armchair (1785–1795) was strongly influenced by Hepplewhite, especially in the shield-shaped back. The horizontal arms rest on vigorously but quietly carved supports. The thick legs are something of a compromise between straight and curvilinear lines. (*The Metropolitan Museum of Art, New York, Kennedy Fund, 1918*)

Left. A cabinet-top desk (c. 1800) resembling Robert Adam's designs is noteworthy for its clear, decisive contours, the delicacy of the linear inlay that accentuates the shape of the parts, and the inserted painted glass panels. Mahogany, satinwood, holly, ivory, glass, and metal are adroitly used in an integrated composition. (*The Metropolitan Museum of Art, New York, Fletcher Fund, 1934*)

White and cream succeeded the earlier positive colors for woodwork and plaster, although walls were sometimes painted in pale colors or were papered. Ceilings became higher, and windows, with thin bars between the panes, were wider and taller.

In furniture design the impact of what Robert Adam had begun in 1760 did not reach America until around 1790, and at first indirectly through the pattern books of George Hepplewhite and Thomas Sheraton. A good example of the Hepplewhite influence is the chair in Figure 543B; and the settees in Figure 542 are in the manner of Sheraton. A definite Adam influence is seen in Figure 543A. Although there were many designers and craftsmen, Duncan Phyfe, who had a shop in New York City from 1795 to 1847, is the best known name. During his half-century of productivity he infused European models with his own distinctive originality. Beginning with Sheraton's ideas, he faithfully followed the changes that were taking place, first turning toward the English Regency,

A

B

Two Duncan Phyfe sofas illustrate the diversity of this designer's production.

Top. An early Sheraton-style sofa (c. 1805) is slender and relatively small in scale. The front legs and arm supports are gently turned. The front rail is accentuated by Phyfe's characteristic reeding; the back rail has a delicate, carved motif. Every aspect of this sofa has the refinement of the Early Neoclassic. (*The Metropolitan Museum of Art, Gift of Mrs. Harry H. Benkard, 1942*)

Bottom. An Empire sofa (c. 1815) is a distinguished example of Late Neoclassic design. The strong, controlled curves and decorative motifs of the painted and gilded cherry frame are admirably emphasized by the unornamented black haircloth upholstery. (*The Metropolitan Museum of Art, New York, Gift of Mrs. Bayard Verplanck, 1940*)

which he handled inventively, and then to the heavier Directoire and Empire work, which gradually became more ponderous and coarse. His early work, however, set high standards of design and craftsmanship (Figs. 544A and B).

The Greek Revival: c. 1820–1850

The United States and much of Europe were greatly stimulated by the Greek War of Independence (1821–1833) and by the appearance of books on Greek architecture, an influence that was widespread, long-lasting, and paradoxical. Inspiration came from Greek temples and was most impressively used on large edifices, but it also reached the homes of the period. Its most basic effect was a sense of controlled inventiveness.

Plans and exteriors. House plans showed great diversity and originality. They were compact or extended, symmetrical or not, as conditions indicated. A distinctive T-shaped plan evolved that was used in city houses as well as in modest farm homes. Rectangular rooms were the norm, but architects felt free to introduce other shapes.

Exteriors, too, were varied. The complete temple type with colonnades on four sides was rare, but numerous homes, especially in the South, had two-story colonnades on three sides (Fig. 545), which fitted their environment admirably. Two-story colonnades across the central portion were common, often with lower wings on each side or a wing projecting from the rear. Simpler dwellings dispensed with columns and used only small pilasters at the entrance and restrained moldings. The Doric order was favored over the Ionic that had been much used in the Federal style, or over the Corinthian. Walls were treated as simple planes of plaster, sometimes marked to imitate stone; they were also of brick, often painted, or of wood. Windows were tall and narrow, and those on the first story reached from the floor almost to the ceiling. Roofs were as nearly flat as they could be made and still take care of rain and snow.

Interiors and furniture. Indoors, houses had a serene, elegant clarity that was, however, often obscured by the heavy furnishings then in vogue. Even so, a sense of spaciousness greater than in most earlier work came from the high ceilings (10 to 14 feet), tall windows, plain walls, and the very large openings between the front and rear living rooms. Concentrated, vigorous ornament gained emphasis against the broad, plain surfaces.

Furniture by 1820 was changing from its earlier lightness toward heavier, more impressive, often clumsy, Empire designs. Moldings were coarser, carving

Andalusia, in Andalusia, Pennsylvania, was remodeled in 1833 in the Greek Revival manner. Patterned after an early Doric temple, the portico has six heavy columns standing on a raised base and supporting a simplified entablature and pediment. Rows of columns extend along two sides of the main block of the building. The lower wings at either side are quietly subordinated to the major section of the house. (*Photograph by Wayne Andrews*)

more naturalistic, and plain surfaces of vigorously figured grain replaced the subtle inlays of the Sheraton style. Bold acanthus leaves and scrolls, cornucopias, lions' paws and sphinxes, and other Roman and Greek motifs came into general use (Color Fig. 32). Typical settees were fashioned with flowing forms, sometimes elegant (Color Fig. 32), sometimes awkward, which were adapted from classical couches. Sideboards and secretaries became heavier and more massive, and wardrobes with gilt-decorated columns held clothes (closets were yet uncommon). Tables were often supported by short classical pedestals from which three or four legs curved outward. The weightiness of the furniture was accentuated by dark stain on the woods and intense reds, greens, and blues in the upholstery.

A New York room (c. 1830–1840) gives a good idea of Greek Revival interiors and Empire furniture. Tall windows are framed with lightly ornamented pilasters, and the curtains are typical of the period. The walls are plain and painted mauve. A mantelpiece of Italian marble is supported by figures reminiscent of Greek caryatids. The tables have columnar bases ending in paw feet and contrast the fortuitous patterns of smooth wood grain with heavy carving, sometimes encased in ormolu. The chairs have simple curves and only a modest amount of carving. The chandelier, although of crystal, is heavy in scale. The total effect is rich, impressive, and rather stolid. (*Henry Francis du Pont Winterthur Museum*)

MEDIEVAL REVIVALS, ECLECTICISM, AND THE BEGINNINGS OF THE MODERN STYLE

Before the middle of the nineteenth century, many persons wanted more excitement, awe, tenderness, and sentiment than Neoclassicism had provided, and they turned to other periods, and especially to the Middle Ages, for stimulation. But they also borrowed from such diverse sources as Italian Renaissance villas, French Baroque chateaux, and Louis XV Rococo interiors.

The Gothic Revival: c. 1840–1880

The **Gothic** now seemed as liberating as the Greek had been controlled. Picturesqueness rather than purity, surprise rather than conformity were the new aims. Irregularity of plan and exterior blossomed in rich variety. Bay windows and recessed porches broke the mass of the building. Tall pointed arches, crenelated towers, and complex, steeply pitched roofs emphasized the vertical. Balconies, windows, and gables were hung with intricately carved openwork. The results at different times seem whimsical and romantic or frenzied and irrational.

Interiors were long, tall, and narrow in proportion and only dimly lighted by small, curtained windows. A predominance of dark colors, patterned walls and carpets, and a profusion of machine-carved, pseudomedieval ornamentation contributed to a heavy-handed informality. In a naïve attempt to design furniture harmonious with the architecture, Gothic structural and decorative elements were awkwardly applied, such as pinnacles on bedposts, buttresses on chairs, and pointed arches wherever they could be forced. But much of the furniture followed the Victorian practice of conglomerate ornamentation derived from many sources. The naturalistic garden was completely at home with these romantic houses.

The Romanesque Revival: c. 1870–1893

Unlike the preceding styles, the **Romanesque Revival,** spearheaded by the American architect Henry Hobson Richardson, led directly into one phase of contemporary architecture through Louis Sullivan and his pupil Frank Lloyd Wright. Plans were orderly but creatively varied; interior spaces flowed from room to room; windows were grouped in continuing bands; and country houses were low, with broad roofs carried out over porches and terraces (Fig. 548). Materials were used with such respect for their distinctive qualities that additional ornament was applied sparingly. Wisely, no attempt was made to design Romanesque gardens, and furnishings still continued to overwhelm interiors with Victorian profusion.

Eclecticism: c. 1880—

The Romanesque Revival was abruptly halted by an immediate, widespread acceptance of eclectic principles, culminating in the Columbia Exposition in 1893, which once again sent architecture off on a round of warmed-over Roman, Greek, or Renaissance forms on public and commercial buildings and on a few large houses. Smaller homes, however, went off on diverse tangents, and during the last decade of the nineteenth century and the early decades of the twentieth century, it was a toss-up whether a family would build an American Colonial, an English, a French, or a Spanish house, or just a carpenter-designed shelter with no special character. Interiors and furnishings were equally unpredictable. The Romanesque Revival, however, had established principles and practices that are much alive today. Because contemporary trends are the substance of the first twenty chapters of this book, they need not be discussed here.

We hope that this brief coverage of the American historical heritage has made it clear that homes and furnishings were, and are, always changing in keeping with the spirit of the time, and that the same general movements affected many countries in Europe as well as in the New World. Each country, and often sections of each country, responded to them in its own time and in its own way, and within each country the response of all persons was far from the same. In spite of dominant trends, most individuals exercised considerable freedom of choice, as we do in our homes today.

The W. Watts Sherman house, designed by Henry Hobson Richardson and built in Newport, Rhode Island, between 1874 and 1876, is a forthright statement of vigorous masses and of materials used naturally. The long, continuing, horizontal lines and grouped windows bear a direct relation to the work of Frank Lloyd Wright (see Fig. 104A). (*Photograph by Wayne Andrews*)

Index

(Pages on which illustrations occur are italicized)